Third edition

APPLETON & LANGE'S REVIEW FOR THE USMLE STEP 3

Samuel L. Jacobs, MD

Appleton & Lange Reviews/McGraw-Hill
Medical Publishing Division

New York Chicago San Francisco Lisbon London Madrid Mexico City
Milan New Delhi San Juan Seoul Singapore Sydney Toronto

McGraw-Hill

A Division of The ***McGraw-Hill*** *Companies*

Appleton & Lange's Review for the USMLE Step 3, Third Edition

1 2 3 4 5 6 7 8 9 0 DOW/DOW 0 9 8 7 6 5 4 3 2 1

ISBN 0-8385-0398-5

This book was set in Palatino by Rainbow Graphics.
The editor was Patricia Casey.
The production supervisor was Lisa Mendez.
Project management was provided by Rainbow Graphics.
The cover designer was Elizabeth Pisacreta.
The index was prepared by Oneida Indexing.
R.R. Donnelley & Sons was printer and binder.

This book is printed on acid-free paper.

Notice

Medicine is an ever-changing science. As new research and clinical experience broaden our knowledge, changes in treatment and drug therapy are required. The authors and the publisher of this work have checked with sources believed to be reliable in their efforts to provide information that is complete and generally in accord with the standards accepted at the time of publication. However, in view of the possibility of human error or changes in medical sciences, neither the authors nor the publisher nor any other party who has been involved in the preparation or publication of this work warrants that the information contained herein is in every respect accurate or complete, and they disclaim all responsibility for any errors or omissions or for the results obtained from use of the information contained in this work. Readers are encouraged to confirm the information contained herein with other sources. For example and in particular, readers are advised to check the product information sheet included in the package of each drug they plan to administer to be certain that the information contained in this work is accurate and that changes have not been made in the recommended dose or in the contraindication for administration. This recommendation is of particular importance in connection with new or infrequently used drugs.

Library of Congress Cataloging-in-Publication Data

Appleton & Lange's review for the USMLE step 3 / [edited by] Samuel L. Jacobs.—3rd ed.
p. ; cm.
Includes bibliographical references and index.
ISBN 0-8385-0398-5
1. Medicine—Examinations, questions, etc. I. Title: Review for the USMLE step 3. II. Title: USMLE step 3. III. Title: USMLE step three. IV. Jacobs, Samuel L.
[DNLM: 1. Medicine—Examination Questions. W 18.2 A6492 2001]
R834.5 .A662 2001
610'.79—dc21

2001030093

ISBN 0-07-118259-4 (international edition)

Contents

Contributors

Ellen F. Brooks, MD
Associate Professor of Psychiatry
Robert Wood Johnson Medical School at Camden
Camden, New Jersey

Andreas Carl, MD, PhD
Resident Associate Professor
Department of Physiology & Cell Biology
University of Nevada School of Medicine
Reno, Nevada

Edison Catalano, MD
Professor and Chief
Department of Pathology
Robert Wood Johnson Medical School at Camden
Camden, New Jersey

Stephan R. Glicken, MD
Associate Professor of Pediatrics
Tufts University School of Medicine
Boston, Massachusetts

Samuel L. Jacobs, MD
Associate Professor
Department of Obstetrics and Gynecology
Director of Undergraduate Medical Education, OBGYN
Robert Wood Johnson Medical School at Camden
Camden, New Jersey

David A. Johnson, PhD
Associate Professor of Pharmacology and Toxicology
Mylan School of Pharmacy
Pittsburgh, Pennsylvania

Frank C. Koniges, MD
Associate Professor of Surgery
Robert Wood Johnson Medical School at Camden
Camden, New Jersey

R. Peter Meyer, PhD
Associate Professor
School of Health Professions
MCP-Hahnemann School of Medicine
Philadelphia, Pennsylvania

Glenn C. Newell, MD
Associate Professor of Internal Medicine
Robert Wood Johnson Medical School at Camden
Camden, New Jersey

Ira Schwartz, PhD
Professor
Department of Biochemistry & Molecular Biology
New York Medical College
Valhalla, New York

Wendy L. Thompson, MD
Professor of Psychiatry
Director of Undergraduate Education, Psychiatry
Robert Wood Johnson Medical School at Camden
Camden, New Jersey

Jocelyn C. White, MD
Associate Professor of Internal Medicine
Oregon Health Sciences University
Portland, Oregon

William W. Yotis, PhD
Professor Emeritus
Department of Microbiology
Loyola University of Chicago
Maywood, Illinois

Preface

Appleton & Lange's Review for the USMLE Step 3, Third Edition is a comprehensive review with cogent explanations and current references, coupled with the self-assessment tool of a practice test. Here the reader can assess strengths and weaknesses as well as review cognitive knowledge, and diagnostic and therapeutic skills. Moreover, all the subjects, question types, techniques, and frameworks encountered on the official examination are presented in this book.

The content has been designed with careful consideration of the appropriate material and is written in a style that is both easy to read and sound in its approach to studying. We enlisted the help of a team of authors and editors of various specialties (involved in both academic and clinical settings) from around the country both to write and review the questions and explanations. All of the contributors hold faculty appointments at various medical schools and most are involved in undergraduate medical education as well. Once this process was completed, another team of editors expert in the health-science question-writing field was employed to edit the questions further for style and content to ensure accuracy and readability.

This volume is part of a three-book series designed exclusively for candidates for the United States Medical Licensing Examination Steps 1, 2, and 3. Combined, the three books consist of more than 3200 exam-type questions, including case studies, with detailed explanations.

Computer-based testing (CBT) began for Step 1 in May 1999, for Step 2 in August 1999, and for Step 3 in November 1999. The conversion of USMLE to CBT marks the end of one era and the beginning of another. Many changes in the test and question format had to be made. Scheduling flexibility was also introduced. We have strived to keep on top of these changes in the 3rd edition of this book as well.

As a result, we believe you will find the questions, their explanations, the clinical-encounter settings, and the general format of the text to be of assistance to you during your review.

Key Features and Use:

- Approximately 332 questions are covered in the basic sciences review: Anatomy, Physiology, Biochemistry, Microbiology, Pathology, Pharmacology, and Behavioral Sciences.
- Approximately 502 questions are covered in the clinical science review: Obstetrics and Gynecology, Pediatrics, Internal Medicine, Surgery, Psychiatry, and Preventive Medicine.
- Questions are followed by a section with answers and detailed explanations referenced to the most current and popular resources available.
- A subspecialty list at the end of each chapter helps assess your strengths and weaknesses, thus pinpointing areas for concentration during exam preparation.
- A practice test also contains questions organized within clinical-encounter frames as presented on the examination. These are helpful in assessing the physician's abilities in initial work-ups, continuing care, and emergency care within each of the settings.
- An index at the end of the text to help find subject matter.

The Editors and the Publisher

Acknowledgments

As always, I would like to thank all the individual contributors for their invaluable effort. In my capacity as OBGYN clerkship director, I would also like to thank my students at Robert Wood Johnson Medical School at Camden, who have taught me a thing or two over the years. I would like to thank Trish Casey from McGraw-Hill for her editorial assistance and her patience, and to my life partner, Bill Steinberg, for putting up with me while trying to meet manuscript deadlines.

Samuel L. Jacobs, MD
Editor

Introduction

This book is designed for those preparing for the United States Medical Licensing Examination (USMLE) Step 3. It provides a comprehensive review source with approximately 1000 "exam-type" multiple choice questions covering both the basic and clinical sciences. All questions are referenced with detailed explanations and the latest up-to-date references for the answers. In addition, the last chapter is an integrated practice test for self-assessment.

THE UNITED STATES MEDICAL LICENSING EXAMINATION, STEP 3

Examination Format

Step 3 consists of multiple-choice items and computer-based case simulations, distributed according to the content blueprint. The examination material is prepared by examination committees broadly representing the medical profession. The committees comprise recognized experts in their fields, including both academic and nonacademic practitioners, as well as members of state medical licensing boards.

Step 3 is a two-day examination. You must complete each day of testing within 8 hours. The first day of testing includes approximately 350 multiple-choice items divided into blocks of 25 to 50 items. There will be from 30 to 60 minutes of time allowed for completion of each block of test items, depending on the number of items in the block. There is a maximum of 7 hours of testing on the first day. There is also a minimum of 45 minutes of break time and a 15-minute optional tutorial. Note that the amount of time available for breaks may be increased by finishing a block of test items or the optional tutorial before the allotted time expires.

The second day of testing includes approximately 150 multiple-choice items, also divided into blocks of 25 to 50 items. These blocks will take from 30 to 60 minutes depending on the number of items. Approximately 3 hours are allowed for these multiple-choice item blocks. The second day also includes a CCS tutorial for which 15 minutes is allowed. This is followed by approximately 9 case simulations, for which approximately 4 hours are allotted. A minimum of 45 minutes is available for break time. There is an optional survey at the end of the second day, which can be completed if time allows.

There is particular emphasis on patient management to include initial work-ups, emergency care and continued care, histories, physical examinations, diagnostic studies, prognosis, management therapies, and the application of mechanisms of basic science.

As in both the Step 1 and the Step 2 examinations, the categorization and content will vary from test to test. However, the framework will be the underlying structure for those changes, emphasizing the unsupervised practice of medicine.

Purpose of the Examination

The purpose of Step 3 is to determine if a physician possesses and can apply the medical knowledge and understanding of clinical science considered essential for the unsupervised practice of medicine, with emphasis on patient management in ambulatory care settings. The inclusion of Step 3 in the USMLE sequence of licensing examinations ensures that attention is devoted to the importance of assessing the knowledge and skills of physicians who are assuming independent responsibility for providing general medical care to patients.

ORGANIZATION OF THIS BOOK

This book is organized to cover each of the basic and clinical science areas you will encounter on the examination. The individual subject sections present the material in isolation, while the case studies use an integrated clinical approach to the application of that material. Each chapter lists questions first, followed by the answers and explanations, a subspecialty list, and a bibliography for further study. Most of the question formats presented here have been chosen to conform with the style you will encounter on the examination and will help to familiarize you with the styles before you sit for the examination.

As is done for the actual examination, the sample test items are arranged in blocks that are organized by one of the four clinical settings described below. The amount of time allotted to complete each block of the sample test is proportional to the amount of time that will be available for each block of questions in the actual examination. During the allotted time to complete the test items in a block, examinees may answer the items in any order, review responses, and change answers. After exiting a block, no further review of items or changing of answers within that block is possible. Policies regarding review of test items may be changed without notice. The most current policies regarding review are provided on the Internet (www.usmle.org). The computer interface includes, among other features, clickable icons for marking questions to be reviewed, automated review of marked and incomplete items, and a clock indicating the time remaining.

Step 3 patients are intended to reflect the diversity of health care populations with respect to age, sex, cultural group, and occupation. The patient population mix is intended to be representative of data collected from various national databases that study health care in the United States.

Clinical Settings

The multiple-choice items are organized into blocks that correspond to the clinical settings in which you will encounter patients. Each setting is described at the beginning of its block; these descriptions are shown here as they would appear during the examination.

Setting I: Community-Based Health Center

This is a community-based health facility where patients seeking both routine and urgent care are encountered. Hospice and home care are included here. Students from a nearby small university use this setting as a student health service. Several industrial parks and local small businesses send employees with on-the-job injuries and illnesses and for employee health screening. Usually the patients are being seen by you for the first time. There is capability for x-ray films, but CT scans, MRIs, and tests such as echocardiography must be arranged at the medical center.

Setting II: Office

Your office is in a primary care, generalist group practice located in a physician office suite adjoining the hospital. Patients are usually seen by appointment. Most of the patients you see are from your own practice and are appearing for regularly scheduled return visits. Occasionally you will encounter a patient whose primary care is managed by one of your associates; reference may be made to the patient's medical records. Known patients may be managed by telephone, and you may have to respond to questions about information appearing in the public media, which will require interpretation of the medical literature. The laboratory and radiology departments have a full range of services available.

Setting III: In-Patient Facilities

You have general admitting privileges to the hospital, including to the children's and women's services. On occasion you see patients in the critical care unit. Postoperative patients are usually seen in their rooms unless the recovery room is specified. You may also be called to see patients in the psychiatric unit. There is a short-stay unit where you may see patients undergoing same-day operations or being held for observation. Also, you may visit patients in the adjacent nursing home/extended care facility and the detoxification unit.

Setting IV: Emergency Department

Most patients in this setting are new to you, but occasionally you arrange to meet there with a known patient who has telephoned you. Generally, patients encountered here are seeking urgent care. Also available to you are a full range of social services, including rape crisis intervention, family support, and security assistance backed up by local police.

Step 3 Test Item Formats

Multiple-Choice Items

Mulitple-choice items are presented in several formats within each test block. Each of the formats requires selection of the one best choice. The general instructions for answering items are as follows:

Read each question carefully and in the order in which it is presented. Then select the one best response option of the choices offered. More than one option may be partially correct. You must select ONE BEST answer by clicking your mouse on the appropriate answer button or pressing the letter on the keyboard.

Single Items

This is the traditional, most frequently used multiple-choice format. It usually consists of a description of a patient in a clinical setting and a reason for the visit. The item vignette is followed by four or five response options lettered A, B, C, D, E. You are required to select the best answer to the question. Other options may be partially correct, but there is only ONE BEST answer.

Process for Single Items, Positively Phrased

- Read the patient description of each item carefully.
- Try to formulate an answer and then look for it in the option list.
- Alternatively, read each option carefully, eliminating those that you think are clearly incorrect.
- Of the remaining options, select the one that you believe to be the most correct.
- If unsure about an answer, it is better to guess since unanswered questions are automatically counted as wrong answers.

Directions for this format and an example item follow.

Example Item I

The following is an example of a single item, positively phrased question.

1. A 45-year-old African-American man comes to the office for the first time because he says, "I had blood in my urine when I went to the bathroom this morning." He reports no other symptoms. On physical examination his kidneys are palpable bilaterally and he has mild hypertension. The information in his history that is most pertinent to his current condition is

(A) chronic use of analgesics
(B) cigarette smoking
(C) a family history of renal disease
(D) occupational exposure to carbon tetrachloride
(E) recent sore throats

(Answer C)

Process for Single Items, Negatively Phrased

This style of item also contains a description of a patient but the focus of the question is negatively phrased, as indicated by a capitalized word such as LEAST, NOT, or EXCEPT.

- Read the patient description of the item carefully.
- Then, identify the options that are true statements or correct for the situation presented.
- Eliminate those options that are true statements or correct for the situation presented.
- Then choose among the remaining options the one that is not true or least likely to be correct in the situation presented.
- If unsure about an answer, it is better to guess since unanswered questions are automatically counted as wrong answers.

Example Item 2

2. A 2-year-old boy is brought to the emergency department by his mother because of a large laceration on his hand. The mother says "He is always playing with knives and is so careless. That's probably how he got hurt this time." On physical examination the patient appears unkempt. There is a 4-cm laceration on the palmar aspect of his left hand. Child abuse is suspected. In addition to referral to the child protective services, management should include each of the following EXCEPT

   (A) careful review of the patient's hospital records
   (B) direct confrontation of the accompanying parent
   (C) a nonjudgmental elicitation of the circumstances of the injury
   (D) thorough physical examination
   (E) x-ray film survey of the long bones

(Answer B)

Multiple Item Sets

A single patient-centered vignette may be associated with two, three, or four consecutive questions about the information presented. Each question is linked to the initial patient-centered vignette, but is testing a different point. Items are designed to be answered independently of each other. You are required to select the one best choice for each question. Other options may be partially correct, but there is only ONE BEST answer.

Process for Multiple Item Sets

The process for answering these items is the same as for single items. Items are usually phrased positively, but occasionally they may be stated in the negative. Sometimes there will be one or more of each phrasing in a set. Pay particular attention when a negatively phrased item is included. It is indicated by a capitalized word such as LEAST, NOT, or EXCEPT.

Example Items 3 to 5

A 38-year-old white woman, who is a part-time teacher and the mother of three children, comes to the office for evaluation of hypertension. You have been her physician since the birth of her first child 8 years ago. One week ago, an elevated blood pressure was detected during a regularly scheduled examination for entrance into graduate school. Vital signs on examination today are:

Temperature	Normal
Pulse	100/min
Respirations	22/min
Blood pressure	164/100 mm Hg (right arm, supine)

3. The most likely finding on physical examination is

   (A) an abdominal bruit
   (B) cardiac enlargement
   (C) decreased femoral pulses
   (D) thyroid enlargement
   (E) normal retinas

(Answer E)

4. The most appropriate next step is to order

   (A) complete blood count
   (B) determination of serum electrolyte and creatinine concentrations
   (C) determination of serum glucose concentration
   (D) determination of serum thyroxine concentration
   (E) urine culture

(Answer B)

5. To assess this patient's risk factors for atherogenesis, the most appropriate test is determination of

   (A) plasma renin activity
   (B) serum cholesterol concentration
   (C) serum triglycerides concentration
   (D) urinary aldosterone excretion
   (E) urinary metanephrine excretion

(Answer B)

Case Clusters

A single-patient or family-centered vignette may ask as few as two and as many as six questions, each related to the initial opening vignette. Information is added as the case unfolds. **It is extremely important to answer the questions in the order presented.** Time often passes within a case and your orientation to an item early in a case may be altered by the additional information presented later in the case. If you do skip items, be sure to answer earlier questions with only the information presented to that point in the case.

Each item is intended to be answered independently. You are required to select the ONE BEST choice to each question.

Process for Case Clusters

The process for answering these items is the same as for single items. Items are usually phrased positively but occasionally they may be stated in the negative. Pay particular attention when a negatively phrased item is included. It is indicated by a capitalized word such as LEAST, NOT, or EXCEPT.

Example Items 6 to 9

A 24-year-old man comes to the office because of intermittent chest pain that began a few weeks ago. You have been his physician for the past 2 years and he has been in otherwise good health. He says he is not having pain currently. A review of his medical record shows that his serum cholesterol concentration was normal at a pre-employment physical examination 1 year ago. You have not seen him since that visit and he says he has had no other complaints or problems in the interim. He reminds you that he smokes 1 pack of cigarettes per day. When you question him further, he says that he does not use any alcohol or illicit drugs. Although the details are vague, he describes the chest pain as a substernal tightness that is definitely not related to exertion.

6. The finding on physical examination that would be most consistent with costochondritis as the cause of his chest pain is

   (A) crepitance over the second and third ribs anteriorly
   (B) deep tenderness to hand pressure on the sternum
   (C) localized point tenderness in the parasternal area
   (D) pain on deep inspiration
   (E) normal physical examination

(Answer C)

On physical examination today his blood pressure is 142/86 mm Hg and his pulse is 90/min. He appears slightly anxious. He denies illicit drug use. Eye, nose, mouth, extremities, lungs, and liver are normal. Blood tests show a normal serum thyroxine concentration and a serum cholesterol concentration of 186 mg/dL.

7. The aspect of the history and physical examination that is LEAST suggestive of possible cocaine use is his

   (A) anxious appearance
   (B) blood pressure of 142/86 mm Hg
   (C) pallor of nasal mucosa
   (D) palpable liver edge
   (E) pulse of 90/min

(Answer C)

8. In light of the patient's original denial of drug use, the most appropriate next step to confirm a diagnosis of cocaine use is to

   (A) ask the laboratory if serum is available for toxicologic screening on a previous blood sample
   (B) call his family to obtain corroborative history
   (C) obtain a plasma catecholamine concentration
   (D) obtain a urine sample for routine analysis but also request toxicologic screening
   (E) present your findings to the patient and confront him with the suspected diagnosis

(Answer E)

Cocaine use is confirmed. The patient admits a possible temporal relationship between his cocaine use and his chest pain and expresses concern about long-term health risks.

9. He should be advised that

(A) cocaine-induced myocardial ischemia can be treated with blocking agents
(B) death can occur from cocaine-induced myocardial infarction or arrhythmia
(C) the presence of neuropsychiatric sequelae from drug use indicates those at risk for sudden death associated with cocaine use
(D) Q wave myocardial infarction occurs only with smoked "crack" or intravenous cocaine use
(E) underlying coronary artery disease is the principal risk for sudden death associated with cocaine use

(Answer B)

Answers, Explanations, and References

In each of the sections of this book, the question sections are followed by a section containing the answers, explanations, and references to the questions. This section (1) tells you the answer to each question; (2) gives you an explanation and review of why the answer is correct, background information on the subject matter, and why the other answers are incorrect; and (3) tells you where you can find more in-depth information on the subject matter in other books or journals. We encourage you to use this section as a basis for further study and understanding.

If you choose the correct answer to a question, you can then read the explanation (1) for reinforcement and (2) to add to your knowledge about the subject matter (remember that the explanations usually tell not only why the answer is correct, but also why the other choices are incorrect). **If you choose the wrong answer** to a question, you can read the explanation for a learning and reviewing discussion of the material in the question. Furthermore, you can note the reference cited (e.g., Last, pp 478–484), look up the full source in the bibliography at the end of the section (e.g., Last JM, Wallace RB, Barrett-Connor E. *Maxcy–Rosenau–Last Public Health and Preventive Medicine,* 13th ed. Norwalk, CT: Appleton & Lange; 1992.), and refer to the pages cited for a more in-depth discussion.

Subspecialty Lists

At the end of each section of this book is a subspecialty list for each subject area. These subspecialty lists will help point out your areas of relative weakness, and thus help you focus your review.

For example, by checking off your incorrect answers on, say, the preventive medicine list, you may find that a pattern develops in that you are incorrect on most or all of the biostatistics questions. In this case, you could note the references (in the explanation section) for your incorrect answers and read those sources. You might also want to purchase a biostatistics text or review book to do a much more in-depth review. We think that you will find these subspecialty lists very helpful, and we urge you to use them.

Practice Test

The last chapter is a 180-question Practice Test consisting of 120 single items and 60 case study questions arranged in the clinical encounter setting categories. It presents the material from each of the subject areas in an integrated fashion, with like question types grouped together. This format attempts to present the material in a format similar to what you will encounter on examination day. In using the test, we suggest you simulate examination conditions to the best of your ability to help you prepare for the actual exam. Once you have taken the Practice Test, you can check your results for strengths and weaknesses using the subspecialty list provided at the end.

HOW TO USE THIS BOOK

There are two logical ways to get the most value from this book. We will call them Plan A and Plan B.

In **Plan A,** you go straight to the practice test and complete it according to the instructions on page 249. After taking the practice test, you check your answers and then tick off the ones you got wrong on the subspecialty list on pages 307 through 309. The *number* of questions you got wrong will be a good indicator of your initial knowledge state, and the *types* of questions you got wrong will help point you in the right direction for further preparation and review. At this point, you can use the first and second chapters of the book, with the lists and discussions, to help you improve your areas of relative weakness.

In **Plan B,** you go through the basic and clinical science sections, checking off your answers, and then compare your choices with the answers and discussions in the book. Once you've completed this process, you can take the practice test, check your answers as described above, and see how well prepared you are at this point. If you still have a major weakness, it should be apparent in time for you to take remedial action.

In Plan A, by taking the practice test first, you get quick feedback regarding your initial areas of strength and weakness. You may find that you know all of the material very well, indicating that perhaps only a cursory review is necessary. This, of course, would be good to know early on in your exam preparation. On the other hand, you may find that you have many areas of weakness (say, for example, in all of pediatrics and psychiatry and in some of the subspecialties of preventive medicine). In this case, you could then focus on these areas in your review—not just with this book, but also with textbooks of pediatrics and psychiatry.

It is, however, unlikely that you will not do some studying prior to taking the USMLE Step 3 (especially since you have this book). Therefore, it may be more realistic to take the practice test *after* you have reviewed the basic and clinical science sections (as in Plan B). This, of course, will probably give you a more realistic test-type situation since very few of us just sit down to a test without studying. In this case, you will have done some reviewing (from superficial to in-depth), and your practice test will reflect this studying time. If, after reviewing the basic and clinical science sections and taking the practice test, your scores still indicate some weaknesses, you can then go back into the subject review sections and supplement your review with your texts.

SPECIFIC INFORMATION ON THE STEP 3 EXAMINATION

The official source of all information with respect to the United States Medical Licensing Examination is the National Board of Medical Examiners (NBME), 3930 Chestnut Street, Philadelphia, PA 19104. Established in 1915, the NBME is a voluntary, nonprofit, independent organization whose sole function is the design, implementation, distribution, and processing of a vast bank of question items, certifying examinations, and evaluative services in the professional medical field.

To sit for the Step 3 examination, you must have obtained the MD degree (or its equivalent) and meet the requirements imposed by the licensing authority that is administering the exam.

You must be familiar with the *2001 USMLE™ Bulletin of Information,* which contains policy and procedural information for all applicants. It is essential that you also be familiar with the contents of the CD-ROM entitled, *2001 USMLE™ Information on Steps 1, 2, and 3,* which contains all of the information as well as a tutorial to acquaint examinees with the software, and sample test materials in computer format, including multiple-choice items and Primum® Computer-based Case Simulations (CCS). *It is essential that examinees practice the case simulation format on the computer prior to taking the examination.* Experience shows that those who do not practice with the format and mechanics of managing the patients in *Primum CCS* are likely to be at a disadvantage when taking the cases under standardized testing conditions.

The CD also contains other information that will be useful for those applying to take computer-based USMLE Step 3 in 2001. Information on the USMLE examinations is also provided on the Internet (www.usmle.org).

Applying for CBT and Scheduling Test Dates

As described in the *2001 USMLE Bulletin of Information,* Prometric®, Inc., a subsidiary of Thomson Learning™, will provide scheduling and test centers for USMLE. The process for obtaining Step 3 application materials from the appropriate registration entity; i.e., the individual state medical licensing authorities or the Federation of State Medical Boards, and for scheduling test dates with Prometric® testing centers is also described in the *Bulletin.*

General instructions for taking the computer-based Step 3 and a description of the standardized testing conditions at the Prometric® test centers are provided in the *2001 USMLE Bulletin of Information.*

Physical Conditions

The NBME is very concerned that all their examinations be administered under uniform conditions in the numerous centers that are used. Except for several No. 2 pencils and an eraser, you are not permitted to bring anything (books, notes, calculators, etc) into the test room. In addition, examinees are moved to different seats at least once during the test. And, of course, each test is policed by at least one proctor. The object of these maneuvers is to frustrate cheating or even the temptation to cheat.

HOW THE COMPUTER-BASED USMLE AFFECTS YOU

Although CBT was implemented over a year ago, test-takers are still likely to be apprehensive about what they will encounter at the test center.

On the day of the exam, don't forget to bring either your Scheduling Permit or an unexpired, government-issued photo ID such as a driver's license or passport. You must have both. Second, there is a mismatch between the name on your Scheduling Permit and the name on your photo ID. Your name must match exactly on both. And last, arriving too late—more than 30 minutes after your scheduled testing time. If you find yourself in any of these predicaments, you'll have to reschedule your exam and pay a fee to Prometric to do so.

Keep in mind that you'll have a minimum of 45 minutes of break time to take at your own pace throughout the day and you are responsible for keeping track of the amount of break time you use. You may add to your overall break time by exiting out of the 15-minute tutorial or by finishing a block of questions early. Further information on use of break time is provided in the news item at the USMLE website entitled "'Guidelines' for Registered Step Applicants."

You may also be wondering about the possibility of technical difficulties with the computer on which you test. If a problem occurs, don't panic! Notify a proctor right away. Your exam can usually be restarted within a few minutes. Your resurrected screen will show the same question you were working on at the time of the crash, with no loss of testing time. But what if your exam can't be restarted or the power goes out in the test center? If Prometric can't get the exam going again or if fixing the problem is out of their control, then your exam will be rescheduled with no additional charge by Prometric.

Of course, USMLE standards for test administration are very important in assuring that your exam experience was fair and in compliance with these standards. As part of the USMLE Quality Assurance Program, you may receive a survey in the mail about the quality of your test-taking experience in areas such as whether or not you experienced distractions or had a problem with your computer, the number and length of your breaks, etc. Please take a few minutes to complete and return this survey—your feedback is important to ongoing enhancements to the test administration process.

If you are registered to take the computer-based USMLE and want more information on topics such as planning ahead, checking in and starting the examination, or receiving your scores, please visit the USMLE website (http://www.usmle.org). Now relax, and good luck!

USMLE STEP 3 LABORATORY VALUES

An astrisk (*) indicates a laboratory value included in the biochemical profile.

BLOOD, PLASMA, SERUM	REFERENCE RANGE	SI REFERENCE INTERVALS
* Alanine aminotransferase (ALT), serum	10–40 U/L	10–40 U/L
* Alkaline phosphatase, serum	Male: 30–100 U/L	Male: 30–100 U/L
	Female: 45–115 U/L	Female: 45–115 U/L
Amylase, serum	25–125 U/L	25–125 U/L
* Aspartate aminotransferase (AST), serum	15–40 U/L	15–40 U/L
* Bilirubin, serum (adult), total // direct	0.1–1.0 mg/dL // 0.0–0.3 mg/dL	2–17 μmol/L // 0–5 μmol/L
Calcium, serum (total)	8.4–10.2 mg/dL	2.1–2.8 mmol/L
* Cholesterol, serum		
Total	150–240 mg/dL	3.9–6.2 mmol/L
HDL	30–70 mg/dL	0.8–1.8 mmol/L
LDL	<160 mg/dL	< 4.2 mmol/L
Cortisol, serum	8:00 AM: 5–23 μg/dL //	138–635 nmol/L //
	4:00 PM: 3–15 μg/dL	82–413 nmol/L
	8:00 PM: # 50% of 8:00 AM	Fraction of 8:00 AM: # 0.50
Creatine kinase, serum	Male: 25–90 U/L	25–90 U/L
	Female: 10–70 U/L	10–70 U/L
* Creatinine, serum	0.6–1.2 mg/dL	53–106 μmol/L
Electrolytes, serum		
* Sodium (Na^+)	135–146 mEq/L	135–146 mmol/L
* Potassium (K^+)	3.5–5.0 mEq/L	3.5–5.0 mmol/L
* Chloride (Cl^-)	95–105 mEq/L	95–105 mmol/L
* Bicarbonate (HCO_3^-)	22–28 mEq/L	22–28 mmol/L
Ferritin, serum	Male: 15–200 ng/mL	15–200 μg/L
	Female: 12–150 ng/mL	12–150 μg/L
Follicle-stimulating hormone, serum/plasma	Male: 4–25 mIU/mL	4–25 U/L
	Female: premenopause 4–30 mIU/mL	4–30 U/L
	midcycle peak 10–90 mIU/mL	10–90 U/L
	postmenopause 40–250 mIU/mL	40–250 U/L

	REFERENCE RANGE	SI REFERENCE INTERVALS
Gases, arterial blood (room air)		
Po_2	75–100 mm Hg	10.0–14.0 kPa
Pco_2	35–45 mm Hg	4.4–5.9 kPa
pH	7.35–7.45	$[H^+]$ 36–44 nmol/L
* Glucose, serum	Fasting: 70–110 mg/dL	3.8–6.1 mmol/L
	2-h postprandial: < 120 mg/dL	< 6.6 mmol/L
Immunoglobulins, serum		
IgA	76–390 mg/dL	0.76–3.90 g/L
IgE	0–380 IU/mL	0–380 kIU/L
IgG	650–1500 mg/dL	6.5–15 g/L
IgM	40–345 mg/dL	0.4–3.45 g/L
Iron	50–170 µg/dL	9–30 µmol/L
Lactate dehydrogenase, serum	45–90 U/L	45–90 U/L
Luteinizing hormone, serum/plasma	Male: 6–23 mIU/mL	6–23 U/L
	Female: follicular phase 5–30 mIU/mL	5–30 U/L
	midcycle 75–150 mIU/mL	75–150 U/L
	postmenopause 30–200 mIU/mL	30–200 U/L
Osmolality, serum	275–295 mOsmol/kg H_2O	275–295 mOsmol/kg H_2O
Phosphorus (inorganic), serum	3.0–4.5 mg/dL	1.0–1.5 mmol/L
Proteins, serum		
Total (recumbent)	6.0–7.8 g/dL	60–78 g/L
Albumin	3.5–5.5 g/dL	35–55 g/L
Globulin	2.3–3.5 g/dL	23–35 g/L
Thyroid-stimulating hormone (TSH), serum	0.5–5.0 µU/mL	0.5–5.0 mU/L
Thyroxine (T_4), serum	5–12 µg/dL	64–155 nmol/L
Triglycerides	35–160 mg/dL	0.4–1.81 mmol/L
Triiodothyronine (T_3) resin uptake	25–35%	0.25–0.35
* Urea nitrogen, serum (BUN)	7–18 mg/dL	1.2–3.0 mmol/L
Uric acid, serum	3.0–8.2 mg/dL	0.18–0.48 mmol/L

CEREBROSPINAL FLUID	REFERENCE RANGE	SI REFERENCE INTERVALS
Cell count	0–5 cells/mm^3	0–5 × 10^6/L
Chloride	118–132 mEq/L	118–132 mmol/L
Gamma globulin	3–12% total proteins	0.03–0.12
Glucose	40–70 mg/dL	2.2–3.9 mmol/L
Pressure	70–180 mm H_2O	70–180 mm H_2O
Proteins, total	< 40 mg/dL	< 0.40 g/L

HEMATOLOGIC	REFERENCE RANGE	SI REFERENCE INTERVALS
Bleeding time (template)	2–7 minutes	2–7 minutes
CD4 cell count	> 500/mm^3	
Erythrocyte count	Male: 4.3–5.9 million/mm^3	4.3–5.9 × 10^{12}/L
	Female: 3.5–5.5 million/mm^3	3.5–5.5 × 10^{12}/L

Erythrocyte sedimentation rate (Westergren)	Male: 0–15 mm/h	0–15 mm/h
	Female: 0–20 mm/h	0–20 mm/h
Hematocrit	Male: 41–53%	0.41–0.53
	Female: 36–46%	0.36–0.46
Hemoglobin blood	Male: 13.5–17.5 g/dL	2.09–2.71 mmol/L
	Female: 12.0–16.0 g/dL	1.86–2.48 mmol/L
Hemoglobin A_{1c}	≤ 6%	≤ 0.06%
Leukocyte count and differential		
Leukocyte count	4500–11,000/mm³	4.5–11.0 × 10⁹/L
Neutrophils, segmented	54–62%	0.54–0.62
Neutrophils, band	3–5%	0.03–0.05
Eosinophils	1–3%	0.01–0.03
Basophils	0–0.75%	0.0–00.75
Lymphocytes	25–33%	0.25–0.33
Monocytes	3–7%	0.03–0.07
Mean corpuscular hemoglobin (MCH)	25–35 pg/cell	0.39–0.54 fmol/cell
Mean corpuscular hemoglobin concentration (MCHC)	31–36% Hb/cell	4.81–5.58 mmol Hb/L
Mean corpuscular volume (MCV)	80–100 μm³	80–100 fl
Partial thromboplastin time (activated)	< 28 seconds	< 28 seconds
Platelet count	150,000–400,000/mm³	150–400 × 10⁹/L
Prothrombin time	< 12 seconds	< 12 seconds
Reticulocyte count	0.5–1.5% of red cells	0.005–0.015
Volume		
Plasma	Male: 25–43 mL/kg	0.025–0.043 L/kg
	Female: 28–45 mL/kg	0.028–0.045 L/kg
Red cell	Male: 20–36 mL/kg	0.020–0.036 L/kg
	Female: 19–31 mL/kg	0.019–0.031 L/kg

URINE	REFERENCE RANGE	SI REFERENCE INTERVALS
Calcium	100–300 mg/24 h	2.5–7.5 mmol/24 h
Creatinine clearance	Male: 97–137 mL/min	
	Female: 88–128 mL/min	
Osmolality	50–1400 mOsmol/kg H_2O	
Oxalate	8–40 μg/mL	90–445 μmol/L
Proteins, total	< 150 mg/24 h	< 0.15 g/24 h

CHAPTER 1

Basic Sciences Review

Anatomy

R. Peter Meyer, PhD

DIRECTIONS (Questions 1 through 23): Each of the numbered items or incomplete statements in this section is followed by answers or completions of the statement. Select the ONE lettered answer or completion that is BEST in each case.

1. Which of the following arteries arise from the mandibular portion of the maxillary artery?

(A) masseteric
(B) buccal
(C) sphenopalatine
(D) descending palatine
(E) deep auricular

2. The pterygoid plexus communicates with the cavernous sinus of the cranial dura mater by an emissary vein that passes through the

(A) foramen rotundum
(B) foramen ovale
(C) foramen lacerum
(D) jugular foramen
(E) foramen spinosum

3. Which of the following statements correctly applies to the tongue?

(A) It is composed of an anterior one third and a posterior two thirds separated by the sulcus terminalis.
(B) The muscles of the tongue are innervated by the vagus nerve.
(C) The vallate papillae lie posterior to the sulcus terminalis.
(D) The apex of the sulcus terminalis is directed anteriorly.
(E) The mobility of the tongue is enhanced by its suspension from three bilateral attachments.

4. The muscles of the palate include all of the following EXCEPT the

(A) palatoglossus
(B) tensor veli palatini
(C) styloglossus
(D) palatopharyngeus
(E) levator veli palatini

5. All of the muscles of the palate are innervated by the vagus nerve EXCEPT the

(A) palatopharyngeus
(B) palatoglossus
(C) musculus uvulae
(D) tensor veli palatini
(E) levator veli palatini

6. The nasolacrimal duct drains into the

(A) sphenoethmoidal recess
(B) inferior meatus
(C) hiatus semilunaris
(D) bulla ethmoidalis
(E) orifice of the auditory tube

7. All of the statements concerning the maxillary sinus are correct EXCEPT

(A) it is the largest of the paranasal sinuses
(B) its floor is formed by the alveolar process of the maxilla
(C) it communicates with the nasal cavity via the hiatus semilunaris

(D) the maxillary division of the trigeminal nerve supplies the lining of the maxillary sinus
(E) the drainage of the maxillary sinus is most efficient in the erect posture

8. All of the following foramina are associated with the maxillary division of the trigeminal nerve and its branches EXCEPT the

(A) incisive
(B) greater palatine
(C) infraorbital
(D) mental
(E) lesser palatine

9. All of the following are diagnostic signs of cervical sympathetic trunk injury EXCEPT

(A) ptosis
(B) dilated pupil
(C) miosis
(D) anhidrosis
(E) enophthalmos

10. All of the following structures refract light entering the eye EXCEPT the

(A) pupil
(B) cornea
(C) aqueous humor
(D) lens
(E) vitreous humor

11. All of the following statements concerning the stapedius muscle are correct EXCEPT

(A) it inserts on the neck of the stapes
(B) it is innervated by the facial nerve
(C) the contraction of this muscle tends to dampen the vibrations of the stapes
(D) it has a protective function
(E) it takes origin from the anterior process of the malleus

12. The smooth, depressed area between the two superciliary arches is the

(A) pterion
(B) supraorbital margin
(C) glabella
(D) zygoma
(E) crista galli

13. All of the following bones were formed from the cartilaginous neurocranium EXCEPT the

(A) occipital
(B) maxilla
(C) sphenoid
(D) ethmoid
(E) petrous portion of the temporal

14. All of the following muscles develop from the mesodermal germ layer EXCEPT the muscles of

(A) the iris
(B) facial expression
(C) mastication
(D) the lower limb
(E) the pharynx

15. The free margin of the falciform ligament contains a remnant of the

(A) bile duct
(B) portal vein
(C) hepatic artery
(D) hepatic vein
(E) umbilical vein

16. All of the following are associated with the tetralogy of Fallot EXCEPT

(A) pulmonary stenosis
(B) right ventricular hypertrophy
(C) interventricular septal defect
(D) overriding aorta
(E) patent ductus arteriosus

17. The fourth aortic arch forms the

(A) maxillary
(B) right common carotid
(C) proximal segment of the right subclavian
(D) proximal segment of the right pulmonary
(E) ductus arteriosus

18. Which of the following is one of the most frequently seen abnormalities of the great vessels?

(A) a patent ductus arteriosus
(B) a double aortic arch
(C) abnormal position of the pulmonary trunk
(D) a right aortic arch
(E) a double superior vena cava

19. The closure of the distal parts of the umbilical arteries after birth forms the

(A) ligamentum venosum
(B) medial umbilical ligaments
(C) ligamentum teres hepatis
(D) ligamentum arteriosus
(E) urachus

20. The main pancreatic duct is formed by the

(A) distal part of the dorsal pancreatic duct and the entire ventral pancreatic duct
(B) prominal part of the dorsal pancreatic duct and the distal portion of the ventral pancreatic duct
(C) entire dorsal pancreatic duct
(D) entire dorsal and ventral pancreatic ducts
(E) proximal parts of both the dorsal and ventral pancreatic ducts

21. Whenever the intestinal midgut loop fails to return from the umbilical cord into the abdominal cavity, the defect is known as

(A) gastroschisis
(B) an omphalocele
(C) Meckel's diverticulum
(D) a vitelline fistula
(E) a left-sided colon

22. The mesonephric duct persists to form the

(A) prostate
(B) testes
(C) seminal vesicle
(D) ovary
(E) uterine tube

23. An undescended testis that remains in the pelvic cavity or somewhere in the inguinal canal is known as

(A) a hydrocele
(B) hypospadias
(C) epispadias
(D) cryptorchidism
(E) hermaphroditism

DIRECTIONS (Questions 24 through 33): Each set of matching questions in this section consists of lettered headings followed by a set of words or phrases. For each numbered word or phrase, select the ONE lettered heading that is most closely associated with it. Each lettered heading may be selected once, more than once, or not at all.

Questions 24 through 33

(A) first pharyngeal arch
(B) head somites
(C) third pharyngeal arch
(D) second pharyngeal arch
(E) first pharyngeal pouch
(F) second pharyngeal pouch
(G) fourth and sixth pharyngeal arches
(H) third pharyngeal pouch
(I) fourth pharyngeal pouch

24. Which of the above structures gives rise to the stapes?

25. Which of the above structures gives rise to the stylopharyngeal muscle?

26. The superior parathyroid gland is formed from which of the above structures?

27. The malleus and incus are formed from which of the above structures?

28. The thyroid, arytenoid, corniculate, and cuneiform cartilages of the larynx are formed from which of the above structures?

29. The auditory tube is formed from which of the above structures?

30. The muscles of facial expression are formed from which of the above structures?

31. The muscles of mastication are formed from which of the above structures?

32. The thymus gland is formed from which of the above structures?

33. The anterior two thirds of the tongue is formed from which of the above structures?

DIRECTIONS (Questions 34 through 43): Each of the numbered items or incomplete statements in this section is followed by answers or completions of the statement. Select the ONE lettered answer or completion that is BEST in each case.

34. All of the following statements apply to a synovial joint EXCEPT the

(A) cartilage is usually the hyaline type
(B) cartilage has nerves and blood vessels
(C) synovial membrane produces synovial fluid
(D) articular capsule envelops the articulation or joint
(E) cartilage is nourished by the synovial fluid

35. All of the following types of joints are classified as synovial EXCEPT

(A) hinge
(B) condyloid
(C) saddle
(D) symphysis
(E) ball and socket

36. All of the following statements concerning ribs are correct EXCEPT the

(A) first seven pairs of ribs are called true ribs
(B) 8th to 12th pairs of ribs are vertebrochondral ribs
(C) third to ninth ribs are typical
(D) second rib has a prominent scalene tubercle
(E) first rib is the broadest and most curved of all ribs

37. Which of the following nerves are parasympathetic?

(A) greater splanchnic
(B) lesser splanchnic
(C) pelvic splanchnic
(D) hypogastric plexuses
(E) trigeminal nerve

38. All of the following statements concerning the coracobrachialis are correct EXCEPT it

(A) arises from the coracoid process
(B) inserts into the humerus
(C) is innervated by the median nerve
(D) arises with the short head of the biceps
(E) both adducts and flexes the arm

39. All of the following statements concerning the cruciate ligaments are correct EXCEPT:

(A) The anterior cruciate attaches to the lateral side of the medial condyle of the femur.
(B) The posterior cruciate arises from the posterior intercondylar area of the tibia.
(C) Both cruciate ligaments are tense during full extension.
(D) Both cruciate ligaments are tense during full flexion.
(E) The anterior cruciate ligament is longer than the posterior cruciate.

40. The bare area of the liver is in contact with all of the following structures EXCEPT the

(A) aorta
(B) diaphragm
(C) inferior vena cava
(D) right suprarenal gland
(E) right kidney

41. The external surface of the tympanic membrane is supplied by the

(A) zygomatic branch of the facial nerve
(B) auriculotemporal nerve
(C) temporal branch of the facial nerve
(D) great auricular nerve
(E) tympanic nerve

42. All of the following statements concerning the otic ganglion are correct EXCEPT it

(A) contains postganglionic parasympathetic cells
(B) is located in the pterygopalatine fossa
(C) is located medial to the mandibular nerve
(D) is posterior to the medial pterygoid muscle
(E) contains cells that are secretory to the parotid gland

43. All of the following statements concerning the thoracic duct are correct EXCEPT it

(A) is the main lymphatic duct
(B) begins in the cisterna chyli
(C) ascends through the aortic hiatus
(D) ascends in the posterior mediastinum
(E) drains into the azygos system of veins

DIRECTIONS (Questions 44 through 50): Each group of items in this section consists of lettered headings followed by a set of numbered words or phrases. For each numbered word or phrase, select the ONE lettered heading that is most closely associated with it. Each lettered heading may be selected once, more than once, or not at all.

Questions 44 through 50

(A) azygos vein
(B) pulmonary veins
(C) coronary sinus
(D) superior vena cava
(E) anterior cardiac veins
(F) anterior intercostal veins
(G) hemiazygos veins
(H) great cardiac vein
(I) internal thoracic veins
(J) posterior intercostal veins

44. The posterior intercostal veins anastomose with which of the above veins?

45. Which of the above veins empty into the left atrium?

46. Which of the above veins is the main vein of the heart?

47. Which of the above veins drain the apex of the heart?

48. Which of the above veins connects the superior and inferior venae cavae?

49. Which of the above veins are located in the superior mediastinum?

50. The coronary sinus drains all of the venous blood from the heart except that carried by which of the above veins?

ANSWERS AND EXPLANATIONS

1. **(E)** The branches of the mandibular portion of the maxillary artery include the deep auricular, the anterior tympanic, the middle meningeal, the accessory meningeal, and the inferior alveolar. The pterygoid portion of the maxillary artery includes the masseteric and the buccal arteries. The pterygopalatine portion of the maxillary artery includes the descending palatine and the sphenopalatine arteries. *(Woodburne and Burckel, pp 268–269)*

2. **(B)** The pterygoid plexus communicates with the cavernous sinus of the cranial dura mater by an emissary vein that passes through the foramen ovale. The foramen rotundum contains the maxillary division of the trigeminal nerve. The foramen lacerum contains cartilage and minor vessels. The jugular foramen contains cranial nerves IX, X, and XI. The foramen spinosum contains the middle meningeal artery. *(Woodburne and Burckel, pp 270, 322)*

3. **(E)** The mobility of the tongue is enhanced by its suspension from three well-separated bilateral attachments: the mandible, the styloid process, and the hyoid bone. The muscles of the tongue are innervated by the seventh, ninth, tenth, and twelfth cranial nerves. The tongue is composed of an anterior two thirds and a posterior one third. The anterior part is separated from the posterior part by a V-shaped sulcus terminalis. The apex of the V is directed posteriorly and ends in a median

pit, the foramen cecum of the tongue. The vallate papillae lie anterior to the sulcus terminalis. *(Woodburne and Burckel, pp 274–275)*

4. **(C)** The styloglossus is a muscle of the tongue. The muscles of the palate include the levator veli palatini, tensor veli palatini, muscular uvulae, palatoglossus, and palatopharyngeus. *(Woodburne and Burckel, pp 275–276)*

5. **(D)** The tensor veli palatini muscle is supplied by the mandibular division of the trigeminal nerve. All other palatal muscles are supplied by the contributions of the vagus nerve to the pharyngeal plexus. *(Woodburne and Burckel, p 278)*

6. **(B)** The inferior meatus receives the slitlike termination of the nasolacrimal duct. The sphenoid sinus empties into the sphenoethmoidal recess. The bulging mass in the middle meatus is known as the bulla ethmoidalis. The hiatus semilunaris is the deep groove anterior and inferior to the bulla. The orifice of the auditory tube is posterior to the opening of the nasolacrimal duct. *(Woodburne and Burckel, pp 282–283)*

7. **(E)** The drainage of the maxillary sinus is very poor in the erect position, and the dependent drainage of the sinuses requires the laying of the head on one side. The communication of the maxillary sinus with the nasal cavity is via the hiatus semilunaris. It is the largest of the paranasal sinuses, and its floor is formed by the alveolar process of the maxilla. *(Woodburne and Burckel, pp 284–285)*

8. **(D)** The mental nerve, a branch of the inferior alveolar nerve, emerges onto the face through the mental foramen. The nasopalatine nerves, branches of the maxillary division of the trigeminal nerve, pass through the incisive canal, where they communicate with terminals of the greater palatine nerves. The greater palatine nerve emerges onto the oral surface of the palate at the greater palatine foramen. The lesser palatine emerges at the lesser palatine foramen. *(Woodburne and Burckel, pp 265–268, 285–288)*

9. **(B)** The superior tarsal muscle is innervated by fibers traveling through the cervical sympathetic trunk and the internal carotid plexus. If the trunk is interrupted, the muscle is paralyzed, causing drooping of the eyelid (ptosis). This is one of the signs of cervical sympathetic trunk injury. The affected pupil is smaller than the pupil of the opposite eye. It does not dilate when the pupil is shaded (miosis). The face is dry (anhidrosis), red, and warm. *(Woodburne and Burckel, p 294)*

10. **(A)** The iris is a thin, contractile membrane having a central aperture, the pupil. Light rays are bent at the interfaces of materials of different densities. The refractive media in the course of light entering the eye are at the cornea, the aqueous humor, the lens, and the vitreous humor. *(Woodburne and Burckel, pp 300–301)*

11. **(E)** The pyramidal eminence is hollow, and its walls give rise to the fibers of the stapedius muscle, whose central tendon emerges at an aperture on the summit of the eminence and inserts in the posterior surface of the neck of the stapes. The facial nerve sends a small branch into the muscle at the base of the pyramidal eminence. The contraction of the stapedius muscle tilts the footplate of the stapes, tending to dampen its vibrations, and thereby serves a protective function. *(Woodburne and Burckel, pp 306–307)*

12. **(C)** The smooth, depressed area between the two superciliary arches is the glabella. The pterion is located at the junction of the sphenoid, frontal, parietal, and temporal bones. The frontal bone of the forehead turns into the orbits below, forming the supraorbital margins. The zygoma forms the prominence of the cheek. The crista galli is part of the ethmoid bone and gives attachment to the falx cerebri. *(Woodburne and Burckel, pp 310, 313–316, 320)*

13. **(B)** The cartilaginous neurocranium is a number of separate cartilages that fuse and ossify to form the base of the skull. The occipital bone is formed by the parachordal cartilage. Rostrally, the hypophyseal cartilages

and the trabeculae cranii fuse to form the sphenoid and ethmoid bones. The periotic capsule gives rise to the petrous and mastoid parts of the temporal bone. The viscerocranium consists of the bones of the face and is formed mainly by the cartilages of the first two arches. The first arch gives rise to a dorsal part, the maxillary process, which gives rise to the maxilla. *(Sadler, pp 164–165)*

14. **(A)** The muscular system develops from the mesodermal germ layer (with the exception of the muscles of the iris, which form from the optic cup ectoderm) and consists of skeletal, smooth, and cardiac muscle. *(Sadler, p 187)*

15. **(E)** The free margin of the falciform ligament contains a remnant of the umbilical vein. The free margin of the lesser omentum contains the bile duct, the portal vein, and the hepatic artery. The hepatic veins empty into the inferior vena cava. *(Sadler, pp 279–280)*

16. **(E)** An unequal division of the conus results in a narrow right ventricular outflow region known as a pulmonary stenosis. A large defect of the interventricular septum places the aorta directly above the septal defect from both ventricular cavities, and the resulting higher pressure on the right side causes hypertrophy of the right ventricular wall. The ductus arteriosus is the distal part of the left sixth arch during intrauterine life. *(Sadler, pp 230–238)*

17. **(C)** The fourth aortic arch, on the right, forms the proximal segment of the right subclavian artery. The first arch largely disappears; however, a small portion persists as the maxillary artery. The third arch forms the common carotid. The sixth arch forms the proximal segment of the right pulmonary artery and the ductus arteriosus. *(Sadler, pp 239–243)*

18. **(A)** A patent ductus arteriosus is one of the most frequently seen abnormalities of the great vessels (8/10,000 births), especially in premature infants, and may occur either as an isolated abnormality or in combination with other heart defects. *(Sadler, p 244)*

19. **(B)** The closure of the distal parts of the umbilical arteries form the medial umbilical ligaments. After obliteration of the umbilical vein and ductus venosus, the umbilical vein forms the ligamentum teres hepatis in the lower margin of the falciform ligament. The ductus venosus is also obliterated to form the ligamentum venosum. The obliterated ductus arteriosus forms the ligamentum arteriosum. The lumen of the allantois is obliterated to form the urachus, to become the median umbilical ligament. *(Sadler, pp 251–254, 283–284, 316–317)*

20. **(A)** The main pancreatic duct (of Wirsung) is formed by the distal part of the dorsal pancreatic duct and the entire ventral pancreatic duct. The proximal part of the dorsal pancreatic duct either is obliterated or persists as a small channel, the accessory pancreatic duct. *(Sadler, pp 286–287)*

21. **(B)** When the midgut loop fails to return from the umbilical cord into the abdominal cavity and is covered only by amnion, the defect is known as an omphalocele. In the most severe cases, there is a defect in the anterior abdominal wall and all the viscera, including the liver, may be found outside the abdominal cavity. This is known as Meckel's diverticulum. The vitelline duct may remain patent over its entire length to form a vitelline fistula. A left-sided colon is related to malrotation. *(Sadler, pp 287–297)*

22. **(E)** The mesonephric duct elongates to form the ductus epididymis, ductus deferens, ejaculatory ducts, and the epididymis. The testes and ovary develop from the genital or gonadal ridges. The uterine tubes develop from the paramesonephric duct. *(Sadler, pp 324–331)*

23. **(D)** One or both testes may remain in the pelvic cavity or somewhere in the inguinal canal and this condition is known as cryptorchidism. Connections between the coelomic cavity and the vaginal process may remain

open with irregular obliteration of this passageway, leaving small cysts known as hydroceles. Hermaphroditism is a condition in which the gonads and external genitalia of both sexes are present. Abnormal openings of the urethra may be found along the inferior aspect or dorsum of the penis, and this is known as either hypospadias or epispadias, according to the aspect on which the opening occurs. *(Sadler, pp 303–304, 309, 331–338, 342)*

24. (D) The cartilage of the second, or hyoid, arch (Reichert's cartilage) gives rise to the stapes, styloid process of the temporal bone, the stylohyoid ligament, lesser horn, and the upper part of the body of the hyoid bone. *(Sadler, pp 348–350)*

25. (C) The cartilage of this arch produces the lower part of the body and greater horn of the hyoid bone. The musculature is limited to the stylopharyngeal muscle. *(Sadler, pp 348–350)*

26. (I) The epithelium of the dorsal wing of the fourth pharyngeal pouch forms the superior parathyroid gland. *(Sadler, p 352)*

27. (A) The first pharyngeal arch forms the maxillary and mandibular processes. Part of the mandibular process persists to form the incus and malleus. *(Sadler, pp 346–348)*

28. (G) The cartilaginous components of the fourth and sixth pharyngeal arches fuse to form the thyroid, cricoid, arytenoid, corniculate, and cuneiform cartilages of the larynx. *(Sadler, p 352)*

29. (E) The first pharyngeal pouch forms a stalklike diverticulum, the tubotympanic recess, which comes in contact with the epithelial lining of the first pharyngeal cleft, the future external auditory meatus. The distal portion of the outpocketing widens to form the middle ear cavity, whereas the proximal part forms the auditory tube. *(Sadler, pp 352–354)*

30. (D) The muscles of the second (hyoid) pharyngeal arch are the stapedius, the stylohyoid, the posterior belly of the digastric, the auricular, and the muscles of facial expression. *(Sadler, pp 348–349)*

31. (A) The musculature of the first pharyngeal arch is formed by the muscles of mastication (temporalis, masseter, pterygoids), the anterior belly of the digastric, the mylohyoid, the tensor tympani, and tensor veli palatini. *(Sadler, pp 346–348)*

32. (H) The ventral part of the third pharyngeal pouch forms the thymus. *(Sadler, pp 350–351)*

33. (A) The tongue appears in the form of two lateral lingual swellings, and one medial swelling, the tuberculum impar. These three swellings originate from the first pharyngeal arch. The swellings merge to form the anterior two thirds. *(Sadler, pp 362–364)*

34. (B) The articular cartilage is usually of the hyaline type. This cartilage has no nerves or blood vessels. It is nourished by the synovial fluid. The articular capsule envelops the articulation or joint. The synovial fluid lubricates the joint. *(Moore and Dalley, pp 23–24)*

35. (D) Both the pubic symphysis and the mandibular symphysis are examples of secondary cartilaginous joints where bone is united by either hyaline cartilage or fibrocartilage. There are six types of synovial joint, all classified according to the shape of the articulating surfaces or the type of movement they permit. They include plane, hinge, condyloid, saddle, ball and socket, and pivot joints. *(Moore and Dalley, pp 23–26)*

36. (D) The first rib is the broadest and most curved of all the ribs. It is flat and has a prominent scalene tubercle on its superior surface. The first seven pairs of ribs are called true or vertebrosternal ribs. The 8th to 12th pairs of ribs are false or vertebrochondral ribs. The 3rd to 9th ribs are typical, and the 1st, 2nd, and 10th to 12th pairs of ribs are atypical. *(Moore and Dalley, pp 62–63)*

37. (C) The pelvic splanchnic nerves represent the sacral portion of the craniosacral (parasympathetic) portion of the autonomic nervous system. The greater and lesser splanchnic nerves are sympathetic. The hypogastric plexuses are formed by the superior mesenteric plexus. *(Woodburne and Burckel, pp 502–507, 562)*

38. (C) The coracobrachialis muscle arises with the short head of the biceps from the coracoid process and passes downward to insert into the medial border of the body of the humerus. It is innervated by the musculocutaneous nerve. The coracobrachialis both adducts and flexes the arm. *(Rosse, p 252)*

39. (A) The longer anterior cruciate ligament arises from the anterior intercondylar area of the tibia, adjacent to the medial condyle, and extends obliquely upward, backward, and laterally to attach to the medial side of the lateral condyle of the femur. The posterior cruciate ligament arises from the posterior intercondylar area of the tibia and attaches the lateral surface of the medial condyle. Both ligaments are most tense during full extension and full flexion. *(Rosse, p 384)*

40. (A) Most of the bare area of the liver is in direct contact with the diaphragm and, in addition, with the inferior vena cava and, just to its right, with the right suprarenal gland and a small area of the right kidney. *(Rosse, pp 571–572)*

41. (B) The external surface of the tympanic membrane is supplied by the auriculotemporal nerve, a branch of the mandibular division of the trigeminal nerve. Some innervation is supplied by a small auricular branch of the vagus nerve. This may contain some glossopharyngeal and facial fibers. The zygomatic and temporal branches of the facial serve only those areas designated by the name. The great auricular is from the cervical plexus. The tympanic nerve is a branch of the glossopharyngeal and is located on the interior of the tympanic membrane. *(Moore and Dalley, pp 962–967)*

42. (B) The otic ganglion is a parasympathetic ganglion located in the infratemporal fossa, just inferior to the foramen ovale, medial to the mandibular nerve, and posterior to the medial pterygoid muscle. Preganglionic parasympathetic fibers travel with the glossopharyngeal nerve and synapse in the otic ganglion. The postganglionic parasympathetic fibers are secretory to the parotid gland. *(Moore and Dalley, pp 922–923)*

43. (E) The thoracic duct opens near or at the angle of union of the internal jugular and subclavian veins. The thoracic duct is the main lymphatic duct. It begins in the cisterna chyli and ascends through the aortic hiatus in the diaphragm to the thorax. *(Moore and Dalley, pp 153–154)*

44. (F) The posterior intercostal veins anastomose with the anterior intercostal veins, which are tributaries of the internal thoracic veins. *(Moore and Dalley, p 91)*

45. (B) Four pulmonary veins (two superior and two inferior) enter the posterior wall of the left atrium. *(Moore and Dalley, p 129)*

46. (C) The coronary sinus is the main vein of the heart. *(Moore and Dalley, pp 136–137)*

47. (H) The great cardiac vein is the main tributary of the coronary sinus. It begins near the apex of the heart and ascends in the anterior interventricular groove with the anterior interventricular artery. *(Moore and Dalley, pp 136–137)*

48. (A) The azygos vein connects the superior and inferior venae cavae, either directly by joining the inferior vena cava or indirectly by the hemiazygos and accessory hemiazygos veins. *(Moore and Dalley, p 155)*

49. (D) The superior vena cava, the great vein draining blood from the head and neck, is located in the superior mediastinum. *(Moore and Dalley, p 143)*

50. (E) The coronary sinus drains all of the venous blood from the heart, except that carried by the anterior cardiac vein and the venae cordis minimae. *(Moore and Dalley, p 136)*

REFERENCES

Moore KL, Dalley AF. *Clinically Oriented Anatomy,* 4th ed. Baltimore: Williams & Wilkins; 1999.

Rosse C, Gaddum-Rosse P. *Hollinshead's Textbook of Anatomy,* 5th ed. Philadelphia: Lippincott-Raven; 1997.

Sadler TW. *Langman's Medical Embryology,* 8th ed. Baltimore: Williams & Wilkins; 2000.

Woodburne RT, Burckel WE. *Essentials of Human Anatomy,* 9th ed. New York: Oxford University Press; 1994.

SUBSPECIALTY LIST: ANATOMY

Question Number and Subspecialty

1. Cardiovascular system
2. Skeletal system
3. Digestive system
4. Muscular system
5. Peripheral nervous system
6. Respiratory system
7. Respiratory system
8. Peripheral nervous system
9. Autonomic nervous system
10. Special sensory—eye
11. Special sensory—ear
12. Skeletal system
13. Embryology
14. Embryology
15. Embryology
16. Cardiovascular system
17. Cardiovascular system
18. Cardiovascular system
19. Embryology
20. Digestive system
21. Embryology
22. Embryology—urogenital system
23. Embryology—urogenital system
24. Special senses
25. Muscular system
26. Embryology—endocrine system
27. Embryology—special senses
28. Embryology—respiratory system
29. Embryology—special sensory
30. Embryology—muscular system
31. Embryology—muscular system
32. Embryology—lymphatic system
33. Embryology—digestive system
34. Cardiovascular system
35. Cardiovascular system
36. Cardiovascular system
37. Autonomic nervous system
38. Muscular system
39. Skeletal system
40. Digestive system
41. Special senses
42. Autonomic nervous system
43. Lymphatic system
44. Cardiovascular system
45. Cardiovascular system
46. Cardiovascular system
47. Cardiovascular system
48. Cardiovascular system
49. Cardiovascular system
50. Cardiovascular system

Biochemistry

Ira Schwartz, PhD

DIRECTIONS (Questions 51 through 75): Each of the numbered items or incomplete statements in this section is followed by answers or by completions of the statement. Select the ONE lettered answer or completion that is BEST in each case.

51. Which of the following interactions are involved in the maintenance of protein secondary structure?

(A) hydrophobic interactions
(B) peptide bonds
(C) hydrogen bonds
(D) polar interactions
(E) disulfide bonds

52. Which of the following clotting factors is present only in the intrinsic pathway of coagulation?

(A) fibrinogen (factor I)
(B) accelerin (factor V)
(C) prothrombin (factor II)
(D) antihemophilic factor (factor VIII)
(E) Stuart factor (factor X)

53. The active sulfhydryl group of coenzyme A (CoA) is derived from

(A) lipoic acid
(B) pantothenate
(C) cysteine
(D) hyaluronic acid
(E) folic acid

54. The free-energy change ($\Delta G^{\circ\prime}$) for the hydrolysis of phosphoenolpyruvate is –14.8 kcal/mol and that of ATP hydrolysis to ADP and orthophosphate (P_i) is –7.3 kcal/mol. Which of the following values represents the standard free-energy change for the production of phosphoenolpyruvate by the reaction shown below?

$$\text{ATP} + \text{pyruvate} \rightleftharpoons \text{phosphoenolpyruvate} + \text{ADP} + P_i$$

(A) + 7.5 kcal/mol
(B) – 7.5 kcal/mol
(C) +22.1 kcal/mol
(D) –22.1 kcal/mol
(E) –14.8 kcal/mol

55. The ATPase activity required for muscle contraction is located in

(A) myosin
(B) troponin
(C) myokinase
(D) sarcoplasmic reticulum
(E) actin

56. Which of the following saccharides enters glycolysis at the level of three-carbon intermediates?

(A) lactose
(B) mannose
(C) galactose
(D) maltose
(E) fructose

57. The effect of aspirin is to inhibit

(A) endorphin synthesis
(B) conversion of essential fatty acids into arachidonic acid
(C) essential fatty acid synthesis
(D) arachidonic acid release
(E) prostaglandin cyclooxygenase

58. Which of the following base pair sequences is palindromic?

(A) TCC
AGG
(B) CCTAGG
GGATCC
(C) CTCT
GAGA
(D) CCAGGG
GGTCCC
(E) ACTGT
TGACA

59. During intense muscular activity the glycolytic end product that increases significantly is

(A) pyruvate
(B) phosphoenolpyruvate
(C) lactate
(D) 3-phosphoglycerate
(E) 2-phosphoglycerate

60. The ingestion of candy immediately before or during marathon running is thought to be deleterious to the efforts of a long-distance runner because it may lead to

(A) stimulation of glucagon secretion
(B) inhibition of glycogen synthesis
(C) stimulation of insulin secretion
(D) inhibition of glycolysis
(E) hypoglycemia

61. The central processing system for intracellular and plasma membranes is the

(A) Golgi apparatus
(B) lysosome
(C) nuclear membrane
(D) rough endoplasmic reticulum
(E) smooth endoplasmic reticulum

62. The action of morphine is mediated through receptors for

(A) histamine
(B) endorphins
(C) alloxan
(D) thyroxine
(E) acetylcholine

63. In the formation of methionine, a methyl group derived from serine is transferred to homocysteine. The coenzyme involved in this reaction is derived from the vitamin

(A) folate
(B) biocytin
(C) pyridoxine
(D) lipoate
(E) cyanocobalamin

64. Up to one third of the amino acid residues of collagen are

(A) serine
(B) hydroxyproline
(C) valine
(D) proline
(E) glycine

65. Which of the following compounds is an essential fatty acid?

(A) oleic acid
(B) stearic acid
(C) linoleic acid
(D) palmitoleic acid
(E) arachidonic acid

66. In the posttranslational modification of collagen, ascorbate (vitamin C) acts as

(A) a carrier of amino acids
(B) a reducing agent
(C) a carrier of hydroxyl groups
(D) an oxidizing agent
(E) an enzyme

67. Medium-chain fatty acids are transported from the cytoplasm of cells into the inner matrix of mitochondria in the form of
    (A) esters of glycerol
    (B) lipoprotein complexes
    (C) acyl CoA thioesters
    (D) free fatty acids
    (E) acyl carnitine esters

68. Which of the following fatty acids has the highest melting point?
    (A) 14:0 (14 carbons, 0 double bonds)
    (B) 16:0
    (C) 18:0
    (D) 18:1
    (E) 18:2

69. The terminal step of protein glycosylation occurs in which of the following structures?
    (A) Golgi apparatus
    (B) plasma membrane
    (C) endoplasmic reticulum
    (D) lysosomes
    (E) endosomes

70. Allopurinol is a drug that is employed in the treatment of gout. This drug
    (A) causes a decrease in hypoxanthine and xanthine excretion
    (B) inhibits hypoxanthine phosphoribosyltransferase
    (C) inhibits xanthine oxidase
    (D) causes an increase in uric acid excretion
    (E) inhibits de novo purine biosynthesis

71. The effects of diisopropylphosphofluoridate (DFP) on chymotrypsin can be characterized as
    (A) competitive inhibition
    (B) feedback inhibition
    (C) reaction with a histidine at the active site
    (D) reaction with a serine at the active site
    (E) reaction with a lysine at the active site

72. The catabolism of amino acids may involve
    (A) amidation
    (B) transamination
    (C) nitrogenation
    (D) phosphorylation
    (E) carboxylation

73. Which of the following will not be a cause of diabetes mellitus?
    (A) stimulation of glycolysis
    (B) secretion of proinsulin instead of insulin
    (C) secretion of structurally abnormal insulin
    (D) defective insulin receptors
    (E) lack of pancreatic beta cells

74. The number of moles of ATP (and/or GTP) produced by complete oxidation of one mole of pyruvate in mitochondria is
    (A) 3
    (B) 4
    (C) 12
    (D) 15
    (E) 24

75. The synthesis of messenger RNA in eukaryotic cells is catalyzed by
    (A) RNA polymerase I
    (B) RNA polymerase II
    (C) RNA polymerase III
    (D) reverse transcriptase
    (E) poly A polymerase

DIRECTIONS (Questions 76 through 84): Each of the numbered items or incomplete statements in this section is followed by answers or by completions of the statement. Select ONE (OR MORE) lettered answer(s) or completion(s) for each case.

76. The following bonding reactions are important in the stabilization of the tertiary structure of proteins. (SELECT 4)
    (A) peptide bonds
    (B) hydrophobic interactions
    (C) ionic bonds
    (D) hydrogen bonds between peptide groups

(E) hydrogen bonds between side chains of amino acids
(F) phosphodiester bonds
(G) glycosiclic bonds

77. The following statements regarding protein synthesis in eukaryotes are true. (SELECT 4)

(A) Most eukaryotic mRNAs may contain a modified "cap" structure at the 5′ end.
(B) A "Shine-Dalgarno" sequence is required upstream of the translation initiation site.
(C) GUG is the main initiation codon.
(D) The mRNA is monocistronic.
(E) Most eukaryotic mRNAs contain a poly A sequence at their 3′ end.
(F) Most eukaryotic mRNA is synthesized as a primary transcript, which includes non-coding sequences.

78. The following statements about enzymes are true. (SELECT 4)

(A) Enzymes alter reaction equilibria.
(B) They are highly specific in choice of substrates.
(C) They increase activation energies of reactions.
(D) They bind substrate in the first step of catalysis.
(E) They may assist in transforming one kind of energy to another.
(F) They may be composed of either protein or RNA.

79. Quaternary structure is important in the function of the following proteins. (SELECT 4)

(A) hemoglobin
(B) collagen
(C) ribonuclease
(D) insulin
(E) lysozyme
(F) carboxypeptidase
(G) immunoglobulin G

80. Concerning the structure of the plasma membranes of mammalian cells, the following statements are correct. (SELECT 4)

(A) Phosphatidyl serine is usually located on the outer leaflet of the membrane.
(B) Cholesterol influences the fluidity of membranes.
(C) Membrane proteins do not undergo transverse diffusion (flip-flop) across bilayers.
(D) Proteins may span the entire width of a membrane.
(E) The portion of the protein that spans the membrane is composed mostly of hydrophilic amino acids.
(F) Membrane lipids undergo lateral diffusion within the plane of the membrane.
(G) Sugar residues of glycoproteins and glycolipids are usually located on the cytoplasmic surface.

81. All of the following cell events are stimulated by epinephrine. (SELECT 4)

(A) glycogenolysis
(B) glycolysis
(C) gluconeogenesis
(D) lipolysis
(E) glucose oxidation
(F) glycogen synthesis
(G) ketogenesis

82. Sickle cell anemia can be characterized by the following features. (SELECT 4)

(A) A deletion of three amino acid residues in the α chain.
(B) Sickling occurs when there is a high concentration of the deoxygenated form of hemoglobin S (HbS).
(C) A single amino acid residue in the β chain is altered.
(D) The inability of the α and β chains to interact.
(E) Sickling is promoted by high oxygen levels.
(F) The solubility of deoxygenated HbS is abnormally low.
(G) HbS has an abnormal electrophoretic mobility.

83. The following reactions may increase in rate during strenuous physical exercise. (SELECT 4)

(A) fatty acid + CoA + ATP $\rightarrow$ acyl CoA + AMP + P_i
(B) ATP + H_2O $\rightarrow$ ADP + P_i
(C) fructose 6-phosphate + ATP $\rightarrow$ fructose 1,6-bisphosphate + ADP
(D) pyruvate + NADH + H^+ $\rightarrow$ lactate + NAD^+
(E) creatine + ATP $\rightarrow$ phosphocreatine + ADP
(F) 2 ADP $\rightarrow$ ATP + AMP

84. Vitamin D is correctly described by the following statements. (SELECT 4)

(A) It is broken down by exposure to ultraviolet light.
(B) It promotes absorption of calcium from the gut.
(C) It is modified into an active form by the kidney.
(D) It participates in carboxylation of glutamate residues.
(E) Deficiency in adults may result in osteomalacia.
(F) Conversion to its active form is stimulated by thyroid hormone.
(G) It is derived from 7-dehydrocholesterol.

DIRECTIONS (Questions 85 through 96): Each group of items in this section consists of lettered headings followed by a set of numbered words or phrases. For each numbered word or phrase, select the ONE lettered heading that is most closely associated with it. Each lettered heading may be selected once, more than once, or not at all.

Questions 85 through 87

For each principle below, select the phenomenon that provides the best proof.

(A) A substitution mutation changes only one specific amino acid of the protein coded.
(B) A codon codes for one specific amino acid.
(C) Deletions or insertions cause frame shifts starting at the codon for the amino acid affected.
(D) The sum of purines in double-stranded DNA is equal to the sum of pyrimidines.
(E) Most of the 64 possible base triplets have been shown to code for 1 of about 20 amino acids.

85. The genetic code is degenerate

86. The genetic code is nonoverlapping

87. The sequence of bases in DNA is read sequentially from a fixed starting point

Questions 88 and 89

For each disease condition, choose the affected enzyme.

(A) thymidylate synthase
(B) xanthine oxidase
(C) hypoxanthine-guanine phosphoribosyltransferase
(D) adenine phosphoribosyltransferase
(E) adenosine deaminase

88. Lesch–Nyhan syndrome

89. Severe combined immunodeficiency

Questions 90 through 92

For each reaction described below, choose the enzyme that catalyzes it.

(A) glucokinase
(B) glucose 6-phosphate dehydrogenase
(C) glycogen phosphorylase
(D) glucose 6-phosphatase
(E) glycogen synthase

90. Inorganic phosphate is a substrate

91. UDP-glucose is a substrate

92. ATP is a substrate

Questions 93 through 96

For each statement below, choose the reaction from the pathway that best applies.

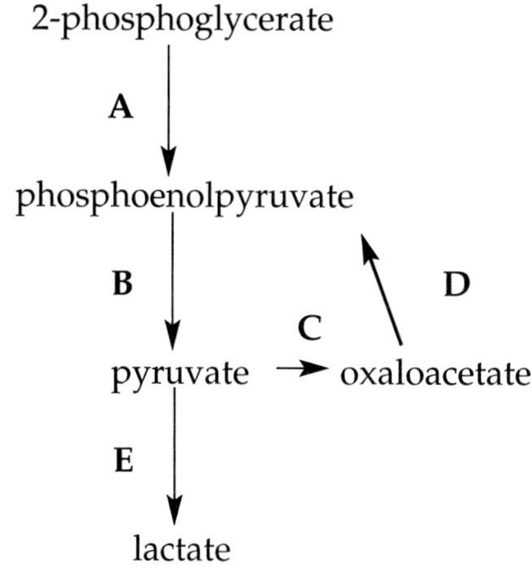

93. ATP is required

94. ATP is formed

95. NADH is required

96. CO_2 is released

ANSWERS AND EXPLANATIONS

51. (C) The secondary structure of a protein is maintained by virtue of hydrogen bonding between the α-amino and α-carboxyl groups of the substituent amino acids. The secondary structure of a protein can assume either an α-helical or a β-pleated sheet conformation. Hydrophobic interactions, polar interactions, and disulfide bonds are involved in the stabilization of the tertiary folding of a protein. The primary structure of a protein is defined by the sequential attachment of amino acids via peptide bonds. *(Stryer, pp 27–37)*

52. (D) The activation of factor X is the final reaction of both the extrinsic and intrinsic pathways of clotting. Activated factor X proteolytically cleaves prothrombin to thrombin, which in turn cleaves fibrinogen to fibrin. Accelerin stimulates the activation of factor X, and fibrin-stabilizing factor (factor XIII) stabilizes the clot by cross-linking fibrin. All of these factors are part of the common pathway. The defect in hemophilia is a deficiency in factor VIII, or antihemophilic factor. This factor acts at the last step of the intrinsic pathway. Factor VIII acts in concert with factor IX, a proteolytic enzyme, to activate factor X. *(Stryer, pp 252–255)*

53. (C) Coenzyme A (CoA) is synthesized from cysteine, AMP, and the vitamin pantothenate. Its major function is the transfer of acyl groups. To attach acyl groups, CoA forms a thioester linkage between the carboxyl of the acyl group and the sulfhydryl of the β-mercaptoethylamine moiety derived from the amino acid cysteine. *(Stryer, pp 451–452, 754–755)*

54. (A) During glycolysis, pyruvate is synthesized from phosphoenolpyruvate with the concomitant production of ATP from ADP. The equilibrium of this reaction lies far to the left for the reaction as written:

$$\text{ATP} + \text{pyruvate} \rightleftharpoons \text{phosphoenolpyruvate} + \text{ADP} + \text{P}_i$$

The standard free-energy change ($\Delta G^{\circ\prime}$) for the hydrolysis of ATP is –7.3 kcal/mol, whereas the $\Delta G^{\circ\prime}$ for the phosphorylation of pyruvate to phosphoenolpyruvate is +14.8 kcal/mol (the opposite of the $\Delta G^{\circ\prime}$ for the hydrolysis of phosphoenolpyruvate). Thus, the calculated $\Delta G^{\circ\prime}$ for the thermodynamically unfavorable production of phosphoenolpyruvate is +7.5 kcal/mol. *(Stryer, pp 444–446, 491)*

55. (A) Myosin contains the ATPase activity that hydrolyzes ATP and allows contraction to proceed. The binding of actin to myosin enhances the ATPase activity of myosin. In fact, actin alternately binds to myosin and is released from myosin as ATP is hydrolyzed. This reaction, which requires magnesium ion, is the driving force of contraction. Although troponin is not directly involved in the ATPase reaction, it binds calcium released by the sarcoplasmic reticulum; this action allows conformational changes in tropomyosin and actin to occur, permitting contraction. Myokinase catalyzes the formation of ATP and AMP from two molecules of ADP. *(Stryer, pp 392–404)*

56. (E) Of the monosaccharides and disaccharides listed in the question, only fructose enters the glycolytic pathway at the level of three-carbon intermediates. Fructokinase catalyzes the phosphorylation of fructose by ATP to fructose 1-phosphate, which is then cleaved to glyceraldehyde and dihydroxyacetone phosphate by aldolase. The glyceraldehyde is phosphorylated to glyceraldehyde 3-phosphate. Thus, two intermediates of glycolysis are formed from one molecule of fructose. In contrast, galactose and mannose enter glycolysis at the level of glucose 1-phosphate and fructose 6-phosphate, respectively. The breakdown products of maltose (i.e., glucose) and lactose (i.e., glucose and galactose) enter glycolysis at the level of six-carbon sugars. *(Stryer, pp 491–493)*

57. (E) Arachidonic acid (eicosatetraenoic acid) derived from the diet or obtained by modification of the essential fatty acid linoleate is stored as a part of cell membrane phospholipids. It serves as the precursor for most of the prostaglandins synthesized in humans. When prostaglandin synthesis is stimulated, arachidonic acid is released for use as a precursor by the action of phospholipase A_2. A cyclopentane ring is formed, and three oxygen atoms are introduced by the action of prostaglandin cyclooxygenase (also called prostaglandin synthetase). Aspirin (acetylsalicylate) inhibits the oxygenase activity of this enzyme by acetylating the terminal group of one of its subunits. The inhibition of prostaglandin biosynthesis is thought to be the main pharmacologic activity of aspirin. *(Stryer, pp 624–625)*

58. (B) Restriction endonucleases recognize specific base pair sequences usually of four to six base pairs when they possess twofold rotational symmetry. Such a symmetrical placement of base pairs leading to an identical reading from 5′ to 3′ on one strand and from 3′ to 5′ on the other strand is called a palindrome. Of the sequences shown in the question, only CCTAGG GGATCC contains a palindrome. The exact center of symmetry lies between the complementary TA–AT base pairs. *(Stryer, pp 120–121)*

59. (C) Under anaerobic conditions, such as intense muscular activity, the rate of formation of pyruvate during glycolysis exceeds its oxidation by the citric acid cycle. As a result, pyruvate is converted to lactate by the action of lactate dehydrogenase. This enzyme employs NADH as a cofactor. Phosphoenolpyruvate, 3-phosphoglycerate, and 2-phosphoglycerate do not accumulate under these conditions. *(Stryer, pp 490–491, 497–498, 577)*

60. (C) The ingestion of candy leads to increased blood glucose levels, which in turn stimulate the α cells of the pancreas to release insulin. Insulin antagonizes the actions of glucagon and epinephrine, which stimulate glycogenolysis and lipolysis. The major energy source in long-distance running is fatty acid metabolism, which spares glucose utilization. Carbohydrate loading—i.e., the ingestion of carbohydrates long before a race—is thought to be the best method for building up glycogen stores. These stores will then be released gradually during the race without a dramatic build-up of insulin, which would interfere with fatty acid release through lipolysis. *(Stryer, pp 773–774)*

61. (A) The Golgi apparatus sorts membranes and proteins that are transported from the endoplasmic reticulum to the cell surface. During this process, glycoproteins are modified. Lysosomal membranes and proteins route through the Golgi apparatus. Endocytotic vesicles and their contents that derive from the cell surface also interact with the Golgi apparatus. The Golgi apparatus is a stack of flattened membrane sacs that receive membrane from the endoplasmic reticulum as vesicles fusing with the concave face. Plasma membrane vesicles interact with the convex face of the Golgi apparatus. *(Stryer, pp 922–924)*

62. (B) Opiate receptors in brain tissue are, in fact, receptors for endorphins. Endorphins are peptide hormones that are released by the anterior pituitary and are natural analgesics. They are thought to regulate perception of pain. Morphine, which is an opiate alkaloid derived from the juice of poppy seeds, interacts with the same receptors, thus mimicking endorphin action. The actions of both endorphins and morphine are blocked in the presence of the antagonist naloxone. *(Stryer, 3rd ed., pp 992–993)*

63. (A) Tetrahydrofolate, which is derived from the vitamin folate, is a major intermediate carrier of hydroxymethyl, formyl, and methyl groups. Folate is widely distributed in plants. Dietary deficiency results in an inhibition of growth and a variety of anemias. The one-carbon transfers with which it is involved include the synthesis of purines and pyrimidines and the intermediary metabolism of amino acids. *(Stryer, pp 719–723)*

64. (E) Collagens are a unique class of proteins in several respects. The amount of glycine in collagen is unusually high, composing as much as 35% of the amino acid residues. In addition, collagen contains two other amino acids that are present in few other proteins found in nature, hydroxyproline and hydroxylysine. These residues are important in the cross-linking of collagen fibers. *(Stryer, pp 31–32)*

65. (C) Mammals lack the ability to synthesize linoleic or linolenic acid. Because these compounds serve as the precursors for the synthesis of other fatty acids they must be provided in the diet. *(Stryer, p 623)*

66. (B) Ascorbate (vitamin C) is a cofactor necessary for the action of the enzymes prolyl hydroxylase and lysyl hydroxylase, which catalyze the posttranslational modification of proline and lysine in collagen to hydroxyproline and hydroxylysine. At their active sites these enzymes contain a ferrous atom, which must be kept in a reduced state. Because ascorbate is used as a reducing agent, it activates the enzymes. A deficiency of vitamin C leads to scurvy, a disease characterized by skin lesions and blood vessel fragility. Citrus fruits, which are rich in vitamin C, supply a sufficient amount of the vitamin when eaten regularly. *(Stryer, pp 454–455)*

67. (D) Approximately 10% of the fatty acids obtained from the diet are short (2 to 4 carbon atoms) or medium (5 to 10 carbon atoms) in chain length. Unlike long-chain fatty acids (> 10 carbon atoms), short-chain and medium-chain fatty acids are freely diffusible across the mitochondrial membranes. Once inside the mitochondrial matrix, these free fatty acids are activated to fatty acyl CoA complexes by mitochondrial matrix fatty acyl CoA synthetases (thiokinases). In contrast, long-chain fatty acids are activated into acyl CoA thioesters by thiokinases located on the outer mitochondrial membranes. These activated long-chain fatty acids are transferred from the sulfur atom of CoA to the hydroxyl group of carnitine to form acyl carnitine, which diffuses across the inner mitochondrial membrane. On the matrix side, the acyl group is transferred from carnitine back to CoA. This carnitine-mediated transfer of activated long-chain fatty acids is catalyzed by the enzyme fatty acyl CoA:carnitine fatty acyl transferase. Activated fatty acyl CoA derivatives present in the mitochondrial matrix are the substrates of β oxidation. Triacylglycerols (fatty acyl esters of glycerol) are storage forms of fatty acids. They are transported in the blood packaged as lipoprotein complexes. *(Stryer, pp 606–608)*

68. (C) The degree of unsaturation and the chain length of fatty acids contribute to their physical properties. The melting point of fatty acids decreases with the degree of unsaturation; each double bond kinks the otherwise saturated hydrocarbon chain of a fatty acid, producing a fixed angle of about 30°. The melting point of fatty acids increases with increasing chain length. Long, saturated fatty acids are hard waxes, whereas shorter, polyunsaturated fatty acids are oils. Of the fatty acids listed in the question, 18:0 is the longest saturated fatty acid. *(Stryer, pp 604–605)*

69. (A) Core glycosylation of proteins occurs on the luminal side of the endoplasmic reticulum membrane. Dolichol phosphate, a lipid carrier of oligosaccharides, transfers oligosaccharides to either asparagine, serine, or threonine residues of proteins. Terminal glycosylation (trimming and remodeling of the attached oligosaccharide units) occurs after transfer of the nascent glycoprotein to the Golgi apparatus. Lysosomes, which contain hydrolytic enzymes, and the plasma membrane are not sites of biosynthesis of glycoproteins. Endosomes are vesicles formed during the process of endocytosis. *(Stryer, pp 920–924)*

70. (C) Gout is characterized by an elevation in the serum levels of uric acid (hyperuricemia). This condition may be caused by a variety of metabolic factors that lead to increased intracellular levels of nucleotides, e.g., increased synthesis of ribonucleoside monophosphates or impairment in salvage pathway function. Because uric acid is the end product of purine degradation, elevation of purine nucleotide levels results in overproduction of uric acid. The enzyme xanthine oxidase catalyzes the last two reactions of purine degradation, i.e., the conversion of hypoxanthine to xanthine to uric acid. Allopurinol is a substrate analogue of hypoxanthine and is a competitive inhibitor of xanthine oxidase. The result of allopurinol administration is an inhibition of xanthine oxidase activity, a decrease in uric acid production, and a concomitant increase in hypoxanthine and xanthine formation, since these latter compounds cannot be metabolized further. Allopurinol has no direct effect on de novo purine biosynthesis. *(Stryer, pp 755–757)*

71. (D) DFP is a reagent that reacts covalently with active site serines. Because the reagent forms a covalent bond with the enzyme, chymotrypsin is irreversibly inhibited. Chymotrypsin is among a group of proteolytic enzymes referred to as serine proteases because they possess an active site serine that is required for enzymatic activity. Other members of this group include trypsin, thrombin, and elastase. Competitive inhibition involves reversible binding of a structural analogue of the substrate to the active site. Feedback inhibition is characterized by inhibition of the first reaction of a metabolic pathway by the end product of that pathway. *(Stryer, pp 196–197, 222–225)*

72. (B) Catabolism of amino acids involves removal of the α-amino group followed by conversion of the resulting carbon skeleton into a major metabolic intermediate. Deamination of most amino acids is accomplished by transfer of the α-amino group to α-ketoglutarate to form glutamate (transamination), followed by oxidative deamination of glutamate to yield ammonium ion and α-ketoglutarate. *(Stryer, pp 629–631)*

73. (A) The complex disease known as diabetes mellitus may be caused by a variety of underlying molecular defects. Any defect that prevents the action of insulin will yield the clinical symptoms of diabetes. These defects include (1) a lack of insulin resulting from destruction of the beta cells of the pancreas, (2) a defective conversion of proinsulin to insulin prior to secretion, (3) structurally abnormal and functionless insulin molecules as a result of mutation, and (4) abnormal insulin receptors. Inhibition of glycolysis, rather than its stimulation, is a hallmark of diabetes. *(Stryer, pp 779–780)*

74. (D) Pyruvate is converted to acetyl-CoA in an oxidative decarboxylation reaction catalyzed by pyruvate dehydrogenase.

$$\text{Pyruvate} + \text{CoA} + \text{NAD}^+ \rightarrow \text{acetyl CoA} + CO_2 + \text{NADH}$$

The acetyl CoA then enters the citric acid cycle. The overall stoichiometry of the cycle can be represented as follows:

$$\text{Acetyl CoA} + 3\ \text{NAD}^+ + \text{FAD} + \text{GDP} + P_i + 2\ H_2O \rightarrow 2\ CO_2 + 3\ \text{NADH} + \text{FADH}_2 + \text{GTP} + 2\ H^+ + \text{CoA}$$

Thus, from one mole of pyruvate a total of 4 moles of NADH and 1 mole each of $FADH_2$ and GTP are produced. Each NADH yields 3 moles of ATP via mitochondrial electron transport and oxidative phosphorylation. The same processes result in the production of 2 moles of ATP per mole of $FADH_2$. In sum, the complete mitochondrial oxidation of 1 mole of pyruvate yields 15 moles of ATP (+GTP). *(Stryer, pp 513–514, 551–552)*

75. (B) Eukaryotic cells contain three different DNA-dependent RNA polymerases that are responsible for the synthesis of different types of RNA. RNA polymerase I catalyzes the synthesis of ribosomal RNA, RNA polymerase II is responsible for synthesis of messenger RNA, and RNA polymerase III mediates the production of transfer and 5S RNA. Most eukaryotic mRNAs contain poly A tails of varying lengths at their 3′ ends. This is synthesized by poly A polymerase. Reverse transcriptase is found in most retroviruses and is responsible for synthesis of DNA from the genomic RNA of these viruses. *(Stryer, pp 91–93, 853–854, 859)*

76. (B) (C) (D) (E) Although peptide bonds define the primary structure (the sequence of amino acids) and, hence, supply the information necessary to specify the three-dimensional structure of a protein, they play no active role in stabilizing the tertiary structure of proteins. Four major types of weak bonds are important in tertiary structure—hydrogen bonds between R groups of the amino acids composing the protein, hydrogen bonds between the peptide groupings of α-helical and β-pleated sheet regions, ionic bonds between positively and negatively charged R groups, and hydrophobic interactions between nonpolar R groups. Study has revealed that hydrophobic interactions are the most important forces involved in maintaining the tertiary structure of proteins. Phosphodiester bonds and glycosiclic bonds are involved in determining the structures of nucleic acids and sugars, respectively. *(Stryer, pp 33–39)*

77. (A) (D) (E) (F) Most eukaryotic mRNAs are modified at both the 5′ and 3′ ends. The modification at the 5′ end involves attachment of a 7-methylguanylate residue by an unusual 5′-5′ phosphodiester bond. This is referred to as the 5′ cap structure. At the 3′ end the mRNA is modified by the sequential addition of up to 250 adenylate residues by the enzyme poly A polymerase. This modification is referred to as the poly A tail. Most eukaryotic mRNA is synthesized as primary transcript, which includes sequences that are subsequently cleaved out (in a process called splicing), and are not found in the mature mRNA. The excised sequences are referred to as introns and those which remain in the final, mature mRNA are called exons. Essentially all eukaryotic mRNAs have a single initiation site for protein synthesis and thus direct the synthesis of a single polypeptide chain; they are monocistronic. The initiation codon is almost always AUG. Protein synthesis is initiated by binding of the 40S ribosomal subunit to mRNA at the 5′ cap. The ribosome then migrates along the mRNA to the first AUG codon and protein synthesis begins. In contrast, mRNA binding to ribosomes during initiation of protein synthesis in prokaryotes is mediated by an rRNA–mRNA interaction. This involves the association of a specific sequence, the so-called Shine–Dalgarno sequence, on the 5′ side of the AUG initiation codon in mRNA and a complementary sequence at the 3′ end of the 16S rRNA. The Shine–Dalgarno interaction occurs only in prokaryotes. *(Stryer, pp 858–859, 895–896, 903–905)*

78. (B) (D) (E) (F) As a catalyst, an enzyme cannot alter the equilibria of chemical reactions. In catalyzing a reaction, enzymes increase the rate at which equilibrium is attained, by decreasing the energy of activation, not increasing it. During the first step of a reaction, enzymes specifically bind to substrate to form a complex. In many reactions, enzymes transform the energy of reactants into a different form of energy. For example, in photosynthesis, light energy is changed to the energy of chemical bonds; in respiration, the free energy of small molecules is stored as ATP; and in contraction, the energy in ATP is converted into mechanical energy. All enzymes were thought to be proteins, however, recently several examples of RNA catalysts, called ribozymes, have been described. These include the self-splicing RNA of some ciliates and ribonuclease P. *(Stryer, pp 115, 181–190, 864–869)*

79. (A) (B) (D) (G) Quaternary structure of a protein refers to the way that the chains in oligomeric proteins interact. Obviously, if a protein is composed of one uninterrupted chain, it has no quaternary structure. Except for ribonuclease, all the proteins listed in the question are composed of two or more subunits. Hemoglobin and immunoglobulin G are tetramers with two pairs of unlike chains. Collagen has three chains, which may be identical or unlike, depending on the type of collagen. Insulin has two unlike chains. Ribonuclease A, lysozyme and carboxypeptidase function as single polypeptide chains. *(Stryer, pp 25, 31–32, 37–39, 154–157, 367–369)*

80. (B) (C) (D) (F) The plasma membranes of all cells are functionally and structurally asymmetrical. Sugars and complex carbohydrates of glycoproteins and glycolipids are usually exposed to the external environment on the outer cell surface. This results in a glycocalyx or carbohydrate coating of most cells. Sphingomyelin and phosphatidyl choline are preferentially localized to the outer leaflet of the lipid bilayer, and phosphatidyl serine and phosphatidyl ethanolamine are primarily in the inner leaflet. Proteins are asymmetrically oriented so that polarized functions may occur. Some proteins, such as those that form channels, span the entire bilayer of the membrane, with different parts of their polypeptide chain exposed to the cytoplasm and the external surface. The portion of the protein that is embedded in the membrane is comprised largely of hydrophobic amino acids. The lipid milieu of the bilayers is fluid. This fluidity is dependent on the length and number of double bonds present in the fatty acyl chains of the phospholipids. The amount of cholesterol present in plasma membranes regulates their fluidity. Increasing amounts of cholesterol decrease membrane fluidity. Both lipids and proteins diffuse laterally in the plane of the membrane, but proteins do not diffuse transversely (flip-flop) across the bilayer. *(Stryer, pp 263–281)*

81. (A) (C) (D) (G) Epinephrine promotes the formation of blood glucose from glycogenolysis in the liver and the release of fatty acids by stimulation of lipolysis in adipose tissue. Epinephrine, which is released when blood glucose levels are low, promotes glucose sparing by encouraging lipolysis and gluconeogenesis. Increased fatty acid levels also lead to increased ketogenesis in the liver. The ketone bodies released into the bloodstream further spare glucose utilization. In contrast, insulin is secreted when blood glucose levels are high. Insulin stimulates the entry of glucose into cells and encourages the utilization and storage of glucose. Thus, increased glucose oxidation and glycogen synthesis would be expected in the presence of insulin but not in the presence of its antagonist, epinephrine. *(Stryer, pp 773–774)*

82. (B) (C) (F) (G) In the genetic disease known as sickle cell anemia, homozygous persons suffer from hemolytic anemia caused by the presence of sickled erythrocytes in the venous circulation. The sickle effect is a result of the change of one amino acid (glutamate to valine) at position 6 of the β chain of hemoglobin. The α and β subunits interact to form Hb S, but this amino acid substitution results in aggregation of deoxygenated Hb S. The solubility of the deoxygenated Hb S is lower than normal, and precipitation of the aggregates causes the observed sickle shape. This occurs when oxygen levels are low. The substitution of the highly polar glutamate with nonpolar valine leads to a change in the electrophoretic mobility of Hb S when compared with normal Hb. *(Stryer, pp 168–172)*

83. (B) (C) (D) (F) The hydrolysis of ATP to ADP and inorganic phosphate by interacting filaments of actin and myosin is the driving force of muscle contraction. As the level of ATP drops in active muscle, a variety of mechanisms come into play to increase cell ATP. Phosphocreatine, the reservoir of high-energy phosphate bonds in muscle, donates its phosphoryl group to ADP to form ATP. Adenylate kinase (myokinase) produces ATP and AMP from ADP. In addition, the lowered energy charge of exercising muscle stimulates the rates of glycolysis, the citric acid cycle, and oxidative phosphorylation. Hence, production of fructose 1,6-bisphosphate and ADP is increased. Lactate production also is increased, because the rate of production of pyruvate by glycolysis exceeds the rate of oxidation of pyruvate by the citric acid cycle. Likewise, the rate of NADH production in glycolysis is greater than the rate of its oxidation by the respiratory chain. Subsequently, lactate is produced by lactate dehydrogenase and NAD^+ is regenerated. Lactate diffuses from muscle into the blood and is carried to the liver, where it is converted to glucose. The glucose may then be transported back to muscle. This manner of interaction between the liver and actively contracting muscle is referred to as the Cori cycle. By contrast, in resting muscle the major energy source is derived from the oxidation of fatty acids. *(Stryer, pp 393–394, 447–448, 497–498, 577–578, 771–772)*

84. (B) (C) (E) (G) Vitamin D can be obtained by ingestion or formed by the action of ultraviolet light on 7-dehydrocholesterol, an intermediate in the pathway of cholesterol synthesis. It is stored in the kidneys as 25-hydroxycholecalciferol. When calcium levels are low, parathyroid hormone stimulates the kidneys to modify 25-hydroxycholecalciferol to 1,25-dihydroxycholecalciferol, the active form of vitamin D. This compound induces the synthesis of specific proteins that participate in the transport of calcium from the gut. Poor exposure to sunlight and absence of fish products in the diet can lead to a deficiency of vitamin D. In growing children vitamin D deficiency causes rickets, a disease of improper calcification of bones. Adults may develop osteomalacia, a condition characterized by bone fragility. The carboxylation of glutamate residues is mediated by vitamin K. *(Stryer, p 707)*

85–87. (85–E, 86–A, 87–C) The genetic code defines the relationship between the sequence of bases in DNA and the corresponding sequence of amino acids in proteins. Three bases form a codon that codes for an amino acid. Since it has been demonstrated that most of the 64 possible arrangements of bases into codons do code for specific amino acids, and since there are only 20 amino acids, the code is degenerate (i.e., the same amino acid may be coded for by more than one codon). If a single base pair is substituted, only one amino acid is changed (provided, of course, that the new codon does not also code for the original amino acid). This phenomenon demonstrates that the code is not overlapping but that codons are read sequentially, one after the other. Finally, deletions or additions of a single base pair cause a shift of the reading frame subsequent to the point of change. Consequently, all amino acids in the coded protein subsequent to that point will be altered. This change demonstrates a sequential reading of bases from a fixed starting point. *(Stryer, pp 103–104)*

88–89. (88–C, 89–E) Lesch–Nyhan syndrome is caused by a decrease or lack of hypoxanthine-guanine phosphoribosyltransferase (HGPRT) activity. HGPRT is a salvage pathway enzyme that catalyzes the synthesis of inosinate (IMP) or guanylate (GMP) from hypoxanthine or guanine. Lesch–Nyhan syndrome is characterized by compulsive, self-destructive behavior. Adenosine deaminase catalyzes the conversion of adenosine to inosine and normally functions in the breakdown of adenine-containing nucleotides to uric acid. Adenosine deaminase deficiency results in severe combined immunodeficiency. This is due to the buildup of dATP, which inhibits cellular DNA synthesis because it blocks the biosynthesis of deoxyribonucleotides. Thymidylate synthase catalyzes the synthesis of thymidine monophosphate, xanthine oxidase catalyzes the conversion of hypoxanthine to xanthine and uric acid, and adenine phosphoribosyltransferase is a salvage pathway enzyme that catalyzes the synthesis of AMP from adenine. *(Stryer, pp 744, 749–750, 755–758)*

90–92. (90–C, 91–E, 92–A) Glycogen phosphorylase catalyzes the sequential removal of glucose residues from glycogen yielding glucose 1-phosphate. The reaction is

$$\text{Glycogen}_{(n)} + P_i \rightarrow \text{glucose 1-phosphate} + \text{glycogen}_{(n-1)}$$

The synthesis of glycogen is mediated by glycogen synthase, which catalyzes the addition of glucose residues to a growing glycogen chain. The glucose must be in the activated form of UDP-glucose.

$$\text{Glycogen}_{(n)} + \text{UDP-glucose} \rightarrow \text{glycogen}_{(n+1)} + \text{UDP}$$

Glucokinase catalyzes the formation of glucose 6-phosphate from glucose and ATP. Glucose 6-phosphate dehydrogenase catalyzes the first step of the pentose phosphate pathway. The reaction is

$$\text{Glucose 6-phosphate} + \text{NADP}^+ \rightarrow \text{6-phosphoglucono-}\delta\text{-lactone} + \text{NADPH} + \text{H}^+$$

Glucose 6-phosphatase catalyzes the hydrolysis of glucose 6-phosphate to glucose and inorganic phosphate. This enzyme occurs in liver and allows for the release of free glucose from the liver. *(Stryer, pp 495, 560, 585–587)*

93–96. (93–C, 94–B, 95–E, 96–D) Reactions A, B, and E are part of the glycolytic pathway, whereas C and D are steps in gluconeogenesis. Pyruvate kinase catalyzes the conversion of phosphoenolpyruvate to pyruvate (reaction B) with the release of ATP. Under anaerobic conditions (e.g., muscle during strenuous exercise), pyruvate is reduced to lactate in a reaction requiring NADH as a cofactor. The first phase of gluconeogenesis is the conversion of pyruvate to phosphoenolpyruvate via oxaloacetate. The reactions are

$$\text{Pyruvate} + CO_2 + \text{ATP} + H_2O \rightarrow \text{oxaloacetate} + \text{ADP} + P_i + 2\,H^+$$

$$\text{Oxaloacetate} + \text{GTP} \rightarrow \text{phosphoenolpyruvate} + \text{GDP} + CO_2$$

The sum of these two reactions permits the conversion of pyruvate to phosphoenolpyruvate in gluconeogenesis. In glycolysis, formation of pyruvate from phosphoenolpyruvate is essentially irreversible. *(Stryer, pp 490, 497–498, 569–572)*

REFERENCE

Stryer L. *Biochemistry,* 4th ed. New York: WH Freeman Co Publishers; 1995.

SUBSPECIALTY LIST: BIOCHEMISTRY

Question Number and Subspecialty

51. Protein
52. Blood
53. Vitamins
54. Thermodynamics
55. Muscle contraction
56. Carbohydrates
57. Lipids

58. Molecular biology
59. Carbohydrate metabolism
60. Integration of metabolism
61. Membranes
62. Hormones
63. Vitamins
64. Proteins
65. Lipids
66. Vitamins
67. Energy metabolism
68. Lipids
69. Proteins
70. Nucleotide metabolism
71. Enzymes
72. Small molecule metabolism
73. Hormones
74. Energy metabolism
75. Molecular biology
76. Protein
77. Molecular biology
78. Enzymes
79. Protein
80. Membranes
81. Hormones
82. Blood
83. Muscle contraction
84. Vitamins
85. Molecular biology
86. Molecular biology
87. Molecular biology
88. Nucleotide metabolism
89. Nucleotide metabolism
90. Carbohydrate metabolism
91. Carbohydrate metabolism
92. Carbohydrate metabolism
93. Carbohydrate metabolism
94. Carbohydrate metabolism
95. Carbohydrate metabolism
96. Carbohydrate metabolism

Microbiology

William W. Yotis, PhD

DIRECTIONS (Questions 97 through 129): Each numbered item or incomplete statement in this section is followed by answers or by completions of the statement. Select the ONE lettered answer or completion that is BEST in each case.

97. A 36-year-old man has duodenal stomach ulcers. The MOST likely etiological agent is

(A) *Streptococcus pyogenes*
(B) *Streptococcus pneumoniae*
(C) *Helicobacter pylori*
(D) *Listeria monocytogenes*
(E) *Vibrio vulnificans*

98. The leukocyte deficiency MOST likely responsible for chronic granulomatous disease in children is

(A) glucose-6-phosphate dehydrogenase
(B) glutamine reductase
(C) myeloperoxidase
(D) reduced nicotinamide–adenine dinucleotide phosphate oxidase
(E) nicotinamide–adenine dinucleotide phosphate-linked lactate dehydrogenase

99. The MOST likely statement about chemotherapy is

(A) peak attainable serum levels can determine whether or not a particular antibiotic will be useful in treating a given disease
(B) administration of two different antibiotics at the same time never leads to treatment failure
(C) none of the antibiotics require host activation to produce the active agent
(D) the location of infection cannot determine the degree to which it will respond to chemotherapy
(E) if an organism is sensitive to a given antibiotic in vitro, it must also be sensitive to that antibiotic in vivo

100. The use of DNA probes for the direct detection of a pathogen from the patient's specimen sometimes lacks sensitivity. A technique to increase the sensitivity MOST likely is to

(A) use duplicate specimens
(B) use a nonradioactive probe
(C) perform more frequent assays
(D) increase the incubation time
(E) use a DNA probe directed at ribosomal RNA

101. A 4-year-old child with X-linked agammaglobulinemia is brought to the emergency room because of a laceration sustained in a traffic accident. This child can BEST be treated with

(A) administration of tetanus toxin
(B) administration of tetanus toxoid
(C) injection of heat-killed *Clostridium tetani*
(D) administration of human immune globulin against tetanus toxin
(E) administration of horse immune globulin against tetanus toxin

102. A positive tuberculin skin test indicates

(A) no immunity to *Mycobacterium tuberculosis*
(B) a parasitic infection
(C) prior exposure to *M. tuberculosis*
(D) active pulmonary tuberculosis
(E) active nontubercular mycobacterial infection

103. Patients with the Chediak–Higashi syndrome have phagocytes that

(A) produce proteins that interfere with chemotaxis
(B) lack C3b receptors, which are needed for attachment to bacteria
(C) show a reduced ability of their lysosomes to fuse with phagosomes to release microbicidal substances
(D) produce limited amounts of myeloperoxidase
(E) show defects for the engulfment of microbes

104. A virus that does not encode a DNA-dependent DNA polymerase is

(A) adenovirus
(B) herpes simplex virus type 1
(C) herpes simplex virus type 2
(D) papovavirus
(E) vaccinia virus

105. A college student has hereditary angioneurotic edema. This individual is MOST likely to have a deficiency in

(A) C1 esterase inhibitor
(B) C3b inactivator
(C) C3 activator
(D) β1H-globulin
(E) carboxypeptidase

106. Immunoglobulin E (IgE), the antibody involved in atopic allergies, can be described by which of the following?

(A) can cross the placenta
(B) has an affinity for basophils and mast cells
(C) can activate complement
(D) contains J chains
(E) contains α heavy chains

107. Activated macrophages

(A) cannot kill facultative intracellular bacteria, such as mycobacteria
(B) are not involved in granuloma formation and type IV hypersensitivity reactions
(C) stain negative for many esterases
(D) have increased C3b receptors
(E) are incapable of killing any type of tumor cell

108. Monoclonal antibody

(A) has antigen-combining sites that are not identical
(B) may belong only to IgM, IgA, or IgG classes
(C) may be present in the serum of patients with multiple myeloma
(D) cannot be obtained by the hybridoma technique
(E) shows a lower level of specificity than the polyclonal antibody

109. Class I major histocompatibility complex determinants are

(A) nucleoproteins
(B) found only on T cells
(C) not involved in the recognition of a virally infected cell by CD4+ cytotoxic T cells
(D) the heterodimers of a heavy IgG chain that is bound to beta-2 microglobulin
(E) not involved in transplant rejection

110. The autoimmune disease with a characteristic antibody response to autologous immunoglobulin G (IgG) is

(A) pernicious anemia
(B) rheumatoid arthritis
(C) Goodpasture's syndrome
(D) myasthenia gravis
(E) Wiskott–Aldrich syndrome

111. A 22-year-old man has gonorrhea, caused by a penicillinase-producing strain of *Neisseria gonorrhoeae.* An antibiotic without a β-lactam ring that can be used for the treatment of gonorrhea is

(A) methicillin
(B) cephalothin
(C) oxacillin
(D) spectinomycin
(E) penicillin

112. Lysogenic conversion is responsible for the

(A) production of β-hemolysin
(B) production of coagulase
(C) production of diphtheria toxin
(D) antigenic conversions in certain strains of *Borrelia burgdorferi*
(E) tetanus toxin

113. The pilus, a bacterial organelle found on the cell surface, can be described as it

(A) is involved in attachment to host cell membranes
(B) is found on all gram-negative bacteria
(C) does not play a role in conjugation
(D) can be an organelle of locomotion
(E) is found in all gram-positive bacteria

114. A single-stranded nucleic acid core is found in

(A) adenovirus
(B) reovirus
(C) herpesvirus
(D) paramyxovirus
(E) papillomavirus

115. A 16-year-old otherwise healthy woman is complaining of frequent and painful urination. A urine specimen is obtained and sent to the laboratory for culture and sensitivity. The laboratory reports back 100,000 *Escherichia coli* and 1000 *Staphylococcus epidermidis* per mL. A suitable course of action will be to

(A) reculture the staphylococci
(B) admit and catheterize the patient
(C) treat for *S. epidermidis*
(D) treat for *E. coli*
(E) treat with penicillin

116. *Staphylococcus aureus* produces

(A) enterotoxin
(B) erythrogenic toxin
(C) excruciating toxin
(D) verotoxin
(E) endotoxin

117. A 27-year-old man infected with the human immunodeficiency virus developed progressive multifocal leukoencephalopathy. The MOST likely etiological agent is

(A) SV 40 virus
(B) polyomavirus
(C) human papillomavirus
(D) BK virus
(E) JC virus

118. A 40-year-old housewife developed aseptic meningitis. The virus MOST frequently associated with aseptic meningitis is

(A) hepatitis A virus
(B) coxsackievirus
(C) hepatitis B virus
(D) coronavirus
(E) rotavirus

119. The human immunodeficiency virus (HIV)

(A) is a double-stranded DNA virus
(B) is a member of the arenaviruses
(C) contains a DNA-dependent RNA polymerase
(D) infects and destroys CD4+ lymphocytes
(E) contains glycoprotein 60 in its envelope

120. A 25-year-old male patient is experiencing inability to swallow and has speech difficulty. The patient was in perfect health prior to the consumption of home-canned green beans. He also stated that the jar lid was swollen prior to being opened. The MOST likely method of treatment is

(A) administration of staphylococcal enterotoxin antiserum
(B) treatment with penicillin
(C) immunization with *Staphylococcus aureus* enterotoxin toxoid
(D) administration of trivalent botulinum antitoxin
(E) placement of the patient in a hyperbaric oxygen chamber

121. The pathogenic antibody in Graves' disease has specificity for the

(A) nucleus
(B) adrenal cell
(C) thyroglobulin
(D) thyroid-stimulating hormone (TSH) receptor
(E) acetylcholine receptor

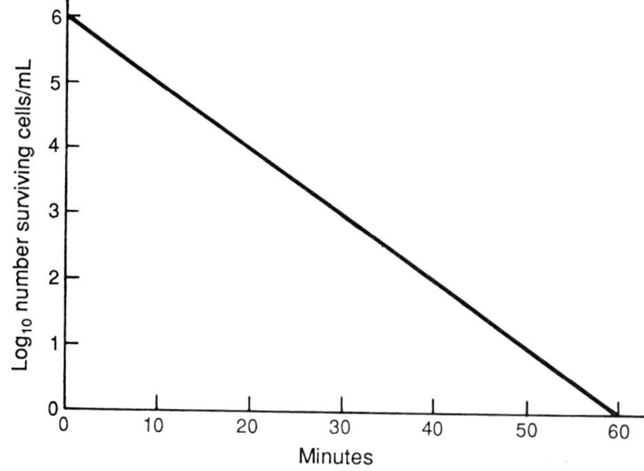

122. The figure above represents the death curve of microorganisms. According to this graph, the percentage of cells dying every 10 minutes is

(A) 100
(B) 0.1
(C) 9
(D) 10
(E) 90

123. The AIDS virus (HIV) differs from the RNA tumor viruses in that it

(A) does not require T4 receptor protein for adsorption to host cells
(B) contains two copies of single-stranded RNA in its virion
(C) contains the *gag* gene
(D) contains the *pol* gene
(E) lyses the host cells

124. A rapid method using molecular biology techniques that may be useful for the specific diagnosis of cytomegalovirus infections in the clinical laboratory is the use of

(A) Gram stain
(B) labeled DNA probe and hybridization
(C) agglutination using latex particles tagged with cytomegalovirus
(D) acid-fast stain
(E) silver stain to detect capsid antigens

125. A 10-month-old baby was vaccinated against varicella. He developed a progressive necrotic lesion of the skin, muscles, and subcutaneous tissue. The growth of the attenuated virus and subsequent reaction resulted from

(A) B-lymphocyte deficiency
(B) reaction to the adjuvant
(C) complement deficiency
(D) immediate hypersensitivity produced by IgE reactivity to the varicella virus
(E) T-lymphocyte deficiency

126. You are examining a 4-year-old boy showing lethargy, fever, painful cervical dorsification and an inflamed throat. The MOST likely approach you will take is

(A) perform a spinal tap and send the specimen to the clinical laboratory for culture, antibiotic sensitivity, and chemical tests
(B) perform a Gram stain on the spinal fluid
(C) after drawing the spinal fluid, begin treatment with penicillin G
(D) obtain several throat swabs and send them to the laboratory for culture and antibiotic sensitivity tests
(E) consult with public health officials to see if there is an outbreak of similar cases in the area

127. The MOST likely component responsible for the production of overwhelming septic shock complicating bacteremia with *Neisseria meningitidis* is the

(A) capsular polysaccharide
(B) pili
(C) lipopolysaccharide in the outer membrane
(D) low-molecular-weight outer membrane proteins
(E) peptidoglycan

128. A high school student has infectious mononucleosis. The infection is MOST likely caused by

(A) Epstein–Barr virus
(B) varicella-zoster virus
(C) variola virus
(D) herpes simplex virus
(E) rubeola virus

129. Q fever is an acute infectious disease of worldwide occurrence that

(A) is caused by *Rickettsia akari*
(B) stimulates the production of proteus agglutinins
(C) involves a rash that spreads from the trunk to extremities
(D) is acquired by inhalation of dust containing infected animal excreta
(E) is usually acquired by tick bites

DIRECTIONS (Questions 130 through 138): Each group of items in this section consists of lettered headings followed by a set of numbered words or phrases. For each numbered word or phrase select the ONE lettered heading that is most closely associated with it.

Question 130

For the description below, select the type of immunoglobulin with which it is MOST likely to be associated.

(A) immunoglobulin A (IgA)
(B) immunoglobulin D (IgD)
(C) immunoglobulin E (IgE)
(D) immunoglobulin G (IgG)
(E) immunoglobulin M (IgM)

130. Immunoglobulin cytotropic for mast cells

Question 131

For the description below, choose ONE of the following:

(A) *Clostridium perfringens*
(B) *Bacteroides melanogenicus*
(C) *Bacillus stearothermophilus*
(D) *Streptococcus pyogenes*
(E) *Neisseria meningitidis*

131. Spore-forming anaerobe

Questions 132 and 133

(A) interferon-γ
(B) interleukin-2
(C) tumor necrosis factor
(D) transfer factor
(E) blastogenic factor

132. Substance responsible for hypotension induced in a 24-year-old patient with septicemia caused by *Salmonella typhi*

133. Stimulates the growth of helper and cytotoxic T cells

Questions 134 and 135

(A) *Leismania donovani*
(B) *Aspergillus fumigatus*
(C) *Entamoeba histolytica*
(D) *Trypanosoma cruzi*
(E) *Histoplasma capsulatum*
(F) *Toxoplasma gondii*
(G) *Cryptococcus neoformans*
(H) *Trichophyton rubrum*
(I) *Trichomonas vaginalis*
(J) *Coccidioides immitis*
(K) *Plasmodium falciparum*
(L) *Sporothrix schenckii*

134. An 11-year-old boy is hospitalized with anemia, pigmentation, hypertrophy of spleen, and prolonged fever of 41°C that fails to remit. Giemsa stain blood smears showed the kidney bean–shaped gametocytes illustrated in the figure below. Treatment with chloroquine resulted in marked improvement of the patient.

135. A middle-aged, male, immunocompromised patient, living in an area infested with pigeons, is admitted to the local hospital. He has fever, headache, stiff neck, and disorientation. His spinal fluid is clear, but it has mononuclear cells. An India ink staining of the spinal fluid and culture on Sabouraud's agar at 37°C following staining showed the encapsulated yeast cells illustrated below.

Questions 136 through 138

(A) variable regions of light and heavy chains
(B) constant regions of light and heavy chains
(C) constant region of heavy chain
(D) J chain
(E) hinge region
(F) HLA-A
(G) HLA-B
(H) HLA-C
(I) C5a
(J) Fc

136. Macrophage and neutrophil attractant

137. Determines isotypes

138. Determines idiotypes

ANSWERS AND EXPLANATIONS

97. (C) Since *Helicobacter pylori* was first isolated from biopsy specimens, derived from patients with acute and chronic gastritis, gastric and duodenal ulcers, and other gastrointestinal disorders, there have been studies of the efficacy of *H. pylori*-associated gastritis that have shown a significantly better response in the antibiotic-treated group. *Streptococcus pyogenes, Streptococcus pneumoniae, Listeria monocytogenes* and *Vibrio vulnificans* have not been associated with stomach ulcers. *(Levinson & Jawetz, pp 110–111)*

98. (D) In chronic granulomatous disease (CGD) of childhood, polymorphonuclear leukocytes fail to kill phagocytosed bacteria even though they can ingest microbes efficiently. Normally, when the membranes of the phagocytic leukocytes are stimulated during phagocytosis, there is a marked stimulation of the reduced form of nicotinamide–adenine dinucleotide phosphate (NADPH) oxidase. NADPH is formed as a result of increased activity of the oxidative portion of the hexose monophosphate pathway. In the absence of NADPH reoxidation to nicotinamide–adenine dinucleotide phosphate by NADPH is suppressed. This leads to concomitant suppression of the production of peroxides and superoxides that destroy microbes. All the other enzymes listed in the question are involved in some phase of bacterial killing after phagocytosis, but only NADPH oxidase is specifically decreased in CGD. *(Roitt et al, pp 291–292)*

99. (A) If a microbe is sensitive to the antibiotic in vitro, it may or may not be sensitive to the antibiotic in vivo. Many problems must be overcome, such as the protein binding of the antibiotic (only the free antibiotic is effective); intracellular location of the microbe; inability of the antibiotic to reach acceptable levels in serum, urine, or serous fluids because of permeability problems or rapid excretion and destruction of antibiotic. *(Levinson and Jawetz, pp 66–67)*

100. **(E)** Currently, molecular biologic techniques are frequently used to detect various pathogens from clinical specimens. Thus, DNA probes directed at ribosomal RNA, which contains highly conserved regions characteristic for a given species, are now used to increase the sensitivity of pathogen detection (ribotyping). Utilization of duplicate specimens, nonradioactive probes, and frequent or prolonged assays are not likely to address adequately the problem of the occasional lack of sensitivity of DNA probes, which may contain common areas of homology in the base sequences of DNA among closely related bacterial species. *(Murray et al, pp 140–141)*

101. **(D)** Although antitoxin from a horse can be used for prophylactic purposes at the time of injury, the risk of anaphylaxis and serum sickness makes it more preferable to use human immune globulin against tetanus toxin in this case. Since the patient is unable to produce immune globulin because of the underlying genetic defect, active immunization with tetanus toxoid is useless. For active immunization against tetanus, toxoid is used for individuals who can produce immunoglobulins, because administration of tetanus toxin can be lethal. Furthermore, since tetanus is an exotoxin-associated disease, immunization with heat-killed *Clostridium tetani* cells will not elicit immunity to tetanus. *(Murray et al, pp 299–302)*

102. **(C)** The tuberculin test constitutes an important diagnostic tool for tuberculosis. It is used to detect recent or past exposure to *Mycobacterium tuberculosis* or other mycobacteria. The infection does not have to be active pulmonary tuberculosis or active nontubercular mycobacterial infection. Since the antigen injected intradermally in the tuberculin test is a purified protein derivative isolated from *M. tuberculosis* or other mycobacteria, a positive test will not indicate parasitic infection. Delayed hypersensitivity does not appear to be responsible for acquired immunity to tuberculosis, because animals rendered tuberculin positive by administration of wax D and the purified protein derivative (PPD) do not show increased resistance to tuberculosis. Therefore, the tuberculin test does not indicate immunity to *M. tuberculosis. (Levinson and Jawetz, p 126)*

103. **(C)** Resistance of microbes to killing by polymorphs and macrophages can be attributed to the production of phagocyte repellents, by blockage of the attachment of phagocytes via the C3b receptor to microbes, or blockage of microbial engulfment. Phagocytosed microbes can defy destruction by preventing fusion of the phagosomes with lysosomes. This fusion results in the release of antimicrobial substances from lysosomes and the killing of microbes. In patients with the rare congenital disease known as Chediak–Higashi syndrome, there is a diminished capacity to lysosomes to fuse with phagosomes. This diminished capacity leads to recurring bacterial infections. *(Levinson and Jawetz, p 383)*

104. **(D)** Papovaviruses are the smallest double-stranded DNA viruses. In these viruses, viral DNA replicates using the host's DNA-dependent DNA polymerase. *(Levinson and Jawetz, pp 156–161)*

105. **(A)** Individuals with an inherited deficiency of C1 esterase inhibitor have the disease known as hereditary angioneurotic edema. These individuals experience acute episodes of local accumulation of edema fluid. The disease is inherited as an autosomal dominant trait. Administration of ε-amino caproate, an inhibitor of plasmin activation of C1, reduces the frequency of the episodes. *(Roitt et al, pp 290–291)*

106. **(B)** IgE has an affinity for basophils and mast cells. The antibodies react with the cell membrane through the Fc portion of the molecule. When specific allergen reacts with the cell-bound molecule, it triggers the release of various pharmacologic mediators from the cell, such as histamine, serotonin, slow-reacting substance of anaphylaxis, heparin, and the eosinophil chemotactic factor. *(Roitt et al, pp 302–304)*

107. (D) The histologic picture of delayed hypersensitivity reaction shows an intense mononuclear cell (granulomatous) inflammatory infiltrate composed of lymphocytes and macrophages. Certain cell surface receptors (C3b) or markers (esterase) are quite prominent in activated macrophages. Only activated macrophages can effectively kill facultative intracellular pathogens, such as mycobacteria and listeria. Activated macrophages may also kill some tumor cells. *(Murray et al, p 98)*

108. (C) Monoclonal antibodies may be present in the serum of patients with multiple myeloma; have antigen-combining sites that are identical; may belong to IgM, IgA, IgE, IgD, or IgG classes; are ordinarily obtained by the hybridoma technique; and show a higher level of specificity than the polyclonal antibodies. *(Levinson and Jawetz, pp 337–338, 349, 357)*

109. (D) Class I major histocompatibility complex (MHC) determinants, intimately involved in transplant rejection, are found on all activated T cells as well as on virtually all cells of the body. The structure of class I MHC determinants consists of an alpha-glycosylated polypeptide heavy chain of 45 kD, which is noncovalently associated with a nonglycosylated beta-microglobulin of 12 kD. *(Levinson and Jawetz, pp 350–354)*

110. (B) One of the autoantibodies commonly found in persons with rheumatoid arthritis is rheumatoid factor. This antibody, usually IgM, is specific for IgG. Affected individuals may also have anti-DNA antibodies, and the levels of complement may be depressed, particularly during an exacerbation of rheumatoid arthritis. Anti-inflammatory therapy is recommended. However, lymphotoxic drugs, such as cortisone are used only when other nonsteroidal drugs have failed. *(Levinson and Jawetz, pp 371–372)*

111. (D) Spectinomycin is commonly used to treat gonorrhea caused by penicillinase-producing gonococci. It does not contain a betalactam ring, and is actually an aminocyclitol antibiotic that acts on the bacterial ribosome to exert its antimicrobial action. Methicillin, oxacillin, and cephalothin are semisynthetic antibiotics, which block the cross-linking reaction in bacterial cell wall synthesis. Like penicillin, these semisynthetic antibiotics contain a beta-lactam ring, however, this ring is resistant to hydrolysis by beta-lactamases. *(Levinson and Jawetz, pp 48–52, 90)*

112. (C) The genetic information needed for the synthesis of any product, be it an exotoxin or a new cell surface antigen, resides in the genome of bacteriophage. If the bacteriophage is able to establish a lysogenic (temperate) relationship, these genes will be expressed in the host bacterium. This phenomenon is called lysogenic conversion. The gene required for the synthesis of diphtheria toxin is part of a temperate bacteriophage. *(Levinson and Jawetz, p 96)*

113. (A) Pili are found on some gram-negative, or a few gram-positive bacteria. They have two known functions: adherence to host cell surfaces and transfer of genetic material. Somatic pili are involved in the adherence of bacteria to host cells, and conjugal pili are involved in gene transfer. *(Levinson and Jawetz, pp 11, 17)*

114. (D) Most DNA viruses, including adenoviruses, herpesviruses, and papilloma viruses are composed of double-stranded DNA. Most RNA viruses are composed of single-stranded RNA. However, the reovirus contains segmented, double-stranded RNA. Paramyxoviruses contain single-stranded RNA. *(Levinson and Jawetz, pp 202–203)*

115. (D) *Escherichia coli* is the most common cause of urinary tract infections. Women are more likely to have urinary tract infections at a young age, because of differences in anatomic structure, sexual maturation, or other reasons. Urinary tract infections are associated with frequent, painful urination, and *E. coli* counts of 100,000 or more organisms per mL of urine. The bacterial concentration is a key diagnostic feature for urinary tract infections, and thus it must be well documented. For this reason a repeat sample of urine must be taken, and the number of *E. coli* be redetermined by viable plate counts. The diagnosis of urinary tract infections is based on the examination of the normally sterile urine for evidence of bacteria and accompanying inflammation. Critical to this examination is the use of appropriate techniques for specimen collection. Voided urine is invariably contaminated with *Staphylococcus epidermidis,* or other urethral normal flora and, in women, vaginal secretions that can confound the laboratory test results. Although contaminants can never be completely eliminated, their quantity may be diminished by carefully cleaning the periurethral area before voiding and allowing the initial part of urine to flush the urethra before collection of a specimen for culture. This clean-voided midstream urine collection procedure is preferred to catheterization for routine purposes because it avoids the risk of introducing bacteria into the bladder. Treatment should be directed against the causative agent of the urinary tract infection, that is, usually *E. coli* and not the contaminants. *(Levinson and Jawetz, pp 102–104)*

116. (A) The majority of *Staphylococcus aureus* strains isolated for clinical specimens produce various types of enterotoxins, known as A, B, C_1, C_2, D, E, F, that are responsible for food poisoning. Staphylococcal food poisoning is the most common form of microbial food intoxication. It is caused by the ingestion of food that contains preformed enterotoxin. The symptoms include abdominal pain, nausea, vomiting, and diarrhea and appear 2 to 6 hours after the ingestion of food containing enterotoxin. Erythrogenic toxin is produced by *Streptococcus pyogenes* and is responsible for the development of scarlet fever. Verotoxin is produced by some strains of *Escherichia coli.* Endotoxins are produced by gram-negative bacteria. *(Levinson and Jawetz, pp 78–80)*

117. (E) Progressive multifocal leukoencephalopathy is an uncommon, generally fatal, disease that occurs in immunocompromised hosts. It is caused by infection of oligodendrocytes by JC virus. There is no known treatment for this disease. *(Levinson and Jawetz, p 249)*

118. (B) Coxsackieviruses can cause aseptic meningitis. These viruses can be isolated from the cerebrospinal fluid of patients with aseptic meningitis. Hepatitis A and B virus, coronavirus and rotavirus are not particularly neurotropic. *(Levinson and Jawetz, p 221)*

119. (C) The human immunodeficiency virus (HIV) is the causative agent of acquired immunodeficiency syndrome (AIDS). This virus is a member of the retrovirus group, which contains single-stranded RNA viruses. Retroviruses contain reverse transcriptase which allows these viruses to synthesize DNA from RNA. Reverse transcriptase is an RNA-dependent DNA polymerase. HIV multiplies in CD4+ lymphocytes, and this multiplication leads to severe leukopenia due to lysis of CD4+ lymphocytes. *(Levinson and Jawetz, pp 251–254)*

120. (D) The patient described in this question is showing the typical symptoms of botulism, which is commonly caused by types A, B, or E *Clostridium botulinum* toxin. Thus, administration of potent botulinum antitoxin against toxins A, B, and E constitutes the most appropriate type of treatment. *(Levinson and Jawetz, pp 93–94)*

121. (D) The pathogenic antibody to thyroid-stimulating hormone (TSH) receptor is seen in Graves' disease. Autoantibodies of nuclei (DNA) are found in patients with systemic lupus erythematosus. In Hashimoto's thyroiditis antithyroglobulin is the pathogenic antibody. In Addison's disease, antiadrenal cell antibody is involved. Antiacetylcholine receptor antibody is the pathogenic antibody in myasthenia gravis. *(Levinson and Jawetz, pp 375–378)*

122. (E) An examination of the death curve of organisms indicates that for every 10 minutes that elapse, there is a drop of one log in the number of surviving cells per mL. That is, at zero time there are 1,000,000 surviving cells per mL ($\log_{10} = 6$); 10 minutes later there are 100,000 surviving cells per mL ($\log_{10} = 5$); at 20 minutes the live cell population drops to 10,000 cells per mL ($\log_{10} = 4$). In each case the percentage of cells dying every 10 minutes is 90%, that is, 90% of 1,000,000 is 900,000 deaths with 10% or 100,000 surviving. *(Levinson and Jawetz, pp 71–72)*

123. (E) An important difference between the AIDS (HIV) virus and the RNA tumor viruses is that HIV lyses the host cells, whereas RNA tumor viruses transform the cells that they invade but do not possess cytolytic activity. The tropism of the AIDS virus for the T4 lymphocytes depends upon the presence of T4 protein on the surface of T4 lymphocytes. This protein serves as the receptor for the adsorption of the AIDS virus to T4 lymphocytes. The AIDS virus is a member of retroviruses. Retroviruses contain two copies of RNA, which harbor the *gag, pol,* and *env* genes. Therefore, the AIDS virus cannot be expected to differ from tumor viruses in these genes. *(Levinson and Jawetz, pp 251–254)*

124. (B) DNA homology (in the case of DNA viruses such as cytomegalovirus) is most accurately determined by the DNA-DNA hybridization technique using labeled DNA probes. DNA from a suspected viral strain is denatured by heating or treatment with alkali, so as to separate the two strands. These are then adsorbed on some supporting matrix. To them we add some small, broken, denatured DNA oligonucleotide strands derived from a known strain of cytomegalovirus, which is radioactively labeled. The mixture is then heated and allowed to anneal by cooling slowly. If the two DNA samples are entirely homologous, radioactively labeled DNA is hybridized and is then converted to the DNAase-resistant form. If they are completely dissimilar, all radioactive DNA remains DNAase sensitive. Retention of radioactivity with the supporting matrix after DNAase treatment and washing becomes a measure of hydridization and DNA homology. The acid-fast stain is used in the initial diagnosis of mycobacteria. The Gram stain is used to distinguish between gram-positive and gram-negative bacteria. Silver stains are used to stain spirochetes. *(Murray et al, pp 140–141)*

125. (E) The development of progressive necrotic lesions in skin, muscles, and subcutaneous tissues following vaccination with vaccinia virus is a good example of T-cell deficiency. In general, establishment of delayed type hypersensitivity and destruction of intracellular parasites, such as viruses, fungi, some protozoa, and certain bacteria, depends on the presence of a complete array of properly functioning T cells. T cells are involved in the production of interferon-γ and cytokinins produced by T lymphocytes that stimulate the macrophages and natural cytotoxic lymphocytes that are active participants in the destruction of virus-infected cells. Furthermore, T cells play a regulatory role in T-cell–dependent antibody production by B cells against viruses and other intracellular parasites. Thus, T-lymphocyte deficiency is revealed by enhanced susceptibility to infection by viruses, or other intracellular parasites, and absence of delayed type hypersensitivity reactions. *(Levinson and Jawetz, pp 329–332)*

126. (A) Given the circumstances of age (38 months), the case history most likely indicates meningitis caused by *Haemophilus influenzae.* Diagnosis of meningitis due to *H. influenzae* requires spinal tap specimen removal and submission to clinical laboratory, which conducts the following assays: Gram stain, culture, antibiotic sensitivity, detection of capsular polysaccharide of *H. influenzae* in the spinal fluid, tests for sugar and protein levels in the spinal fluid. Meningitis caused by *H. influenzae* leads to a decreased concentration of glucose and an elevated protein content in the spinal fluid due to the presence of bacteria in this fluid. Chloramphenicol should be used initially, not penicillin G, which is susceptible to destruction by penicillinase-producing strains of *H. influenzae.* Throat swabs and cultivation are intended for the detection of carriers, and/or initial stages of infection. Consultation with public health officials are advised to determine if an epidemic of meningitis is starting and the infection is not due to *H. influenzae. (Murray et al, pp 276–280)*

127. (C) The lipopolysaccharide, or endotoxin, in the outer membrane is the most likely component of *Neisseria meningitidis,* which is responsible for the production of overwhelming septicemic shock during meningococcemia. It causes intravascular activation of the complement system, the kallikrein kinin system (hypotension), and the clotting cascade (hemorrhage). *(Murray et al, pp 226–229)*

128. (A) The majority of normal individuals living in the United States possess antibodies against Epstein–Barr virus. Conversion from seronegative to the seropositive state occurs during the acute phase of infectious mononucleosis. *(Levinson and Jawetz, pp 198–199)*

129. (D) Q (query) fever is a zoonosis caused by *Coxiella burnetii.* It is a respiratory disease that may be severe enough to develop into interstitial pneumonia. The microorganism is a natural parasite of cattle and sheep, and humans are incidental hosts, being infected by inhalation of infected excreta or contact with contaminated animal tissues. *C. burnetii* is spread from animal to animal by ticks, and remains as an inapparent infection in animals until parturition. The organisms multiply readily in the placenta and other birth tissues. They can also be found in the urine and stool, which contaminate the soil and serve as the source of infection for humans. *(Murray et al, pp 360–361)*

130. (C) Immunoglobulin E (IgE) is cytotropic for mast cell and basophilic leukocytes of peripheral blood. When these cell-bound antibodies react with their specific allergen, the cells degranulate and secrete vasoactive amines. Among the pharmacologically active substances released by these cells are histamine, serotonin, eosinophil chemotactic factor of anaphylaxis, heparin, and several enzymes (e.g., chymase and arylsulfatase). After the interaction of allergen and antibody occurs at the cell membrane, the synthesis of other pharmacologically active compounds called secondary mediators occurs. The most important of these products is SRS-A (slow-reacting substance of anaphylaxis). In addition, various kinins and platelet-activating substances are synthesized by mast cells and basophils after allergen contact.

IgA is the secretory immunoglobulin and is found in highest concentration in the secretions that bathe certain body surfaces. They are the primary line of defense in tears, saliva, bronchial fluids, and intestinal contents. In addition, milk contains high concentrations of IgA. IgM is the antibody first produced in any immune response. It is the only antibody that is present in the serum of neonates, and is of endogenous origin. In contrast, IgG is present in fetal blood, and is of maternal origin. *(Levinson and Jawetz, pp 337–343, 367–369)*

131. (A) *Clostridium perfringens* is a gram-positive, spore-forming anaerobe. It ranks second only to staphylococci as the leading cause of food poisoning in the United States. *C. perfringens* produces an enterotoxin particularly in meat products allowed to sit out at room temperature for a considerable period of time after cooking.

Neisseria meningitidis is a gram-negative coccus that can cause meningitis. During fulminant meningococcemia, adrenal insufficiency associated with bilateral adrenal hemorrhage may occur (Waterhouse–Friderichsen syndrome). Vasomotor collapse and shock often lead to death.

Bacteroides melanogenicus is part of the normal flora throughout the upper portion of the alimentary canal. This gram-negative rod may be found in mixed infections in the mouth or other areas of the body.

Streptococcus pyogenes is a gram-positive coccus that grows aerobically or anaerobically. This organism causes many different infections in humans. It is associated with cellulitis, scarlet fever, sore throat, erysipelas, puerpural sepsis, rheumatic fever, acute glomerulonephritis, meningitis, and other infections.

Bacillus stereothermophilus is a gram-positive, heat-tolerant, aerobic rod found in the hot springs of Yellowstone National Park and other similar hot environments. *(Levinson and Jawetz, p 94)*

132–133. (132-C, 133-B) Tumor necrosis factor is a cytokine produced mostly by macrophages following stimulation by endotoxins of gram-negative bacteria, such as *Salmonella typhi.* Tumor necrosis factor is associated with endotoxin-induced hypotension that can lead to shock and death. Interferon-γ is another cytokine produced by T lymphocytes, and it can influence natural killer T cells, macrophages, or other cells. Interleukin-2 stimulates the growth of T cells. Transfer factor is a lymphocyte-derived cytokine, which is used to transfer specific delayed-type hypersensitivity to a nonreactive individual. Blastogenic factor causes the transformation of some lymphocytes into actively dividing blast cells. *(Levinson and Jawetz, pp 334–336)*

134. (K) *Plasmodium falciparum* is the etiologic agent of malaria. The most outstanding feature of malaria is anemia, which results from the destruction of red blood cells by the parasite. Other features include pigmentation due to deposition of red blood cell pigment, hypertrophy of spleen and liver, and a prolonged fever of 41°C to 42°C. Definitive diagnosis of malaria caused by *P. falciparum* is made by the demonstration of kidney bean–shaped gametocytes in blood smears stained with Giemsa. None of the other microorganisms listed in the question produce kidney bean–shaped gametocytes. *(Murray et al, pp 634–635)*

135. (G) Cryptococcosis is a fungal disease caused by *Cryptococcus neoformans,* which is found in the soil and in pigeon droppings. The incidence of this disease is higher in immunocompromised individuals than in persons whose immune system is intact. Thus, such patients as those with AIDS, lymphoma, or leukemia are particularly susceptible to cryptococcus. Disseminated cryptococcosis features meningitis, fever, headache, stiff neck, and disorientation. Examination of India ink stains of spinal fluid from patients with cryptococcosis, and culture on Sabouraud's agar at 37°C shows yeast cells with large capsules. The other microorganisms listed in this question may produce meningitis, but India ink stains or culture of spinal fluid from these cases of meningitis will not reveal yeast cells with large capsules. *(Murray et al, pp 586–588)*

136. (I) C5a is a component of complement. Chemically, it is a protein found in the normal human and animal serum. Activation of complement by immune complexes or endotoxin produces C5a, which is a macrophage and neutrophil attractant. Intradermal administration of C5a induces vasodilation and local accumulation of macrophages and neutrophils. The variable regions, the constant regions of light and heavy chains, the J chains and the hinge regions represent moieties of the immunoglobulin molecule and do not possess chemotactic properties for macrophages. HLA-A, HLA-B, and HLA-C represent the three genes for the human leukocyte antigens (HLA), and they control the synthesis of class I antigens. The success of tissue and organ transplants depends on the donor's and recipient's HLA complex encoded by the HLA-A, HLA-B, and HLA-C genes. The Fc is the crystallizable fragment of the immunoglobulin molecule, which cannot bind the antigen. It is involved in complement fixation, in placental transfer of IgG, and in attachment to various cells. *(Levinson and Jawetz, pp 350–357)*

137. (C) Based on the structure of their heavy chain constant regions, immunoglobulins are divided into 5 major classes known as IgA,

IgD, IgE, IgG, and IgM. These classes can be distinguished not only by their amino acid sequences of the constant regions of their heavy chains, but also by the antigenic structures of these sequences. For example, by injecting human IgG myeloma protein into a rabbit it is possible to produce an antiserum that can be absorbed by mixtures of myelomas of other classes to remove cross-reacting antibodies, and that will then be able to react only with IgG. Since all the heavy-chain constant region structures produce the immunoglobulin, classes are called isotypes, or isotypic variants. Variability in the variable regions of the light and heavy chains determines immunoglobulin idiotypes; constant regions of light and heavy chains determine immunoglobulin allotypes. *(Levinson and Jawetz, pp 337–343)*

138. (A) It has been stated in the previous answer that it is feasible to produce antibodies that recognize isotypic variants. It is also possible to produce antisera that are specific for individual antibody molecules, and distinguish between one monoclonal antibody from another, independently of isotypic structures. Such antisera delineate the individual determinants unique to each antibody, collectively called idiotype. The idiotypic determinants are located in the variable regions of light and heavy chains of immunoglobulins. Anti-idiotypic sera constitute useful reagents for demonstrating the same variable region on different heavy chains and on different cells. For reasons why the other choices listed are inappropriate, see answer to previous question. *(Levinson and Jawetz, pp 337–343)*

REFERENCES

Levinson WE, Jawetz E. *Medical Microbiology and Immunology,* 5th ed. Stamford, CT: Appleton & Lange; 1998.

Murray PR, Rosenthal KS, Kobayashi Gsm Pfaller MA. *Medical Microbiology,* 3rd ed. St. Louis: Mosby; 1998.

Roitt I, Brostoff J, Male D. *Immunology,* 5th ed. Philadelphia: Mosby; 1998.

SUBSPECIALTY LIST: MICROBIOLOGY

Question Number and Subspecialty

97. Pathogenic bacteriology
98. Immunology
99. Antimicrobial agents
100. Molecular microbiology
101. Immunology
102. Pathogenic bacteriology
103. Immunology
104. Virology
105. Immunology
106. Immunology
107. Immunology
108. Immunology
109. Immunology
110. Immunology
111. Antimicrobial agents
112. Virology
113. Bacterial physiology
114. Virology
115. Pathogenic bacteriology
116. Pathogenic bacteriology
117. Virology
118. Virology
119. Virology
120. Pathogenic bacteriology
121. Immunology
122. Antimicrobial agents
123. Virology
124. Molecular microbiology
125. Immunology
126. Pathogenic bacteriology
127. Pathogenic bacteriology
128. Virology
129. Pathogenic bacteriology
130. Immunology
131. Pathogenic bacteriology
132. Immunology
133. Immunology
134. Parasitology
135. Mycology
136. Immunology
137. Immunology
138. Immunology

Pathology

Edison Catalano, MD

DIRECTIONS (Questions 139 through 164): Each of the numbered items or incomplete statements in this section is followed by answers or by completions of the statement. Select the ONE lettered answer or completion that is BEST in each case.

139. The major pathologic change found in the hearts of persons with hypertensive heart disease is

(A) right ventricular dilation
(B) right ventricular hyperplasia
(C) right ventricular hypertrophy
(D) left ventricular dilation
(E) left ventricular hypertrophy

140. The most common cause of spontaneous subarachnoid hemorrhage is

(A) primary brain tumors
(B) blood dyscrasias
(C) arteriovenous malformations
(D) intracranial congenital aneurysms
(E) tumors metastatic to the brain

141. An elderly patient expires with the diagnosis of adult respiratory distress syndrome. The initial pathological cellular damage occurs in

(A) bronchial cells
(B) upper respiratory tract
(C) diffuse alveolocapillary cells
(D) pneumocytes type II
(E) pulmonary arterioles

142. Niacin deficiency is associated with

(A) night blindness
(B) bleeding diathesis
(C) altered formation of connective tissues
(D) neuromuscular and cardiac problems
(E) dementia

143. Diverticulosis occurs most frequently in the

(A) cecum
(B) ascending colon
(C) transverse colon
(D) descending colon
(E) sigmoid colon

144. The histologic changes seen in the connective tissue from the joint space of the great toe shown in the photomicrograph on page 40 are pathognomonic for

(A) rheumatoid arthritis
(B) suppurative arthritis
(C) gout
(D) osteoarthritis
(E) ankylosing spondylitis

145. The occurrence of malignant mesothelioma has been correlated with industrial exposure to

(A) beryllium
(B) silica
(C) coal dust
(D) asbestos
(E) nitrogen dioxide

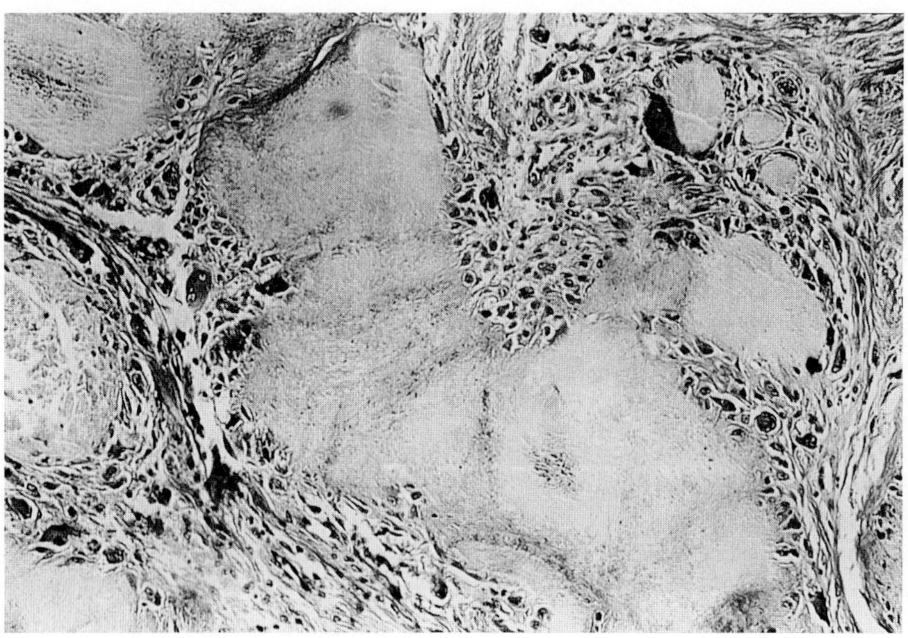

Figure for use with question 144.

146. The changes seen in the kidney shown in the photograph below most likely were produced by

(A) postrenal obstruction
(B) renal infarct
(C) hypertension
(D) renal cell carcinoma
(E) abuse of analgesics

147. Down syndrome is produced by the genotype

(A) trisomy 13
(B) trisomy 18
(C) trisomy 21
(D) XO
(E) XXY

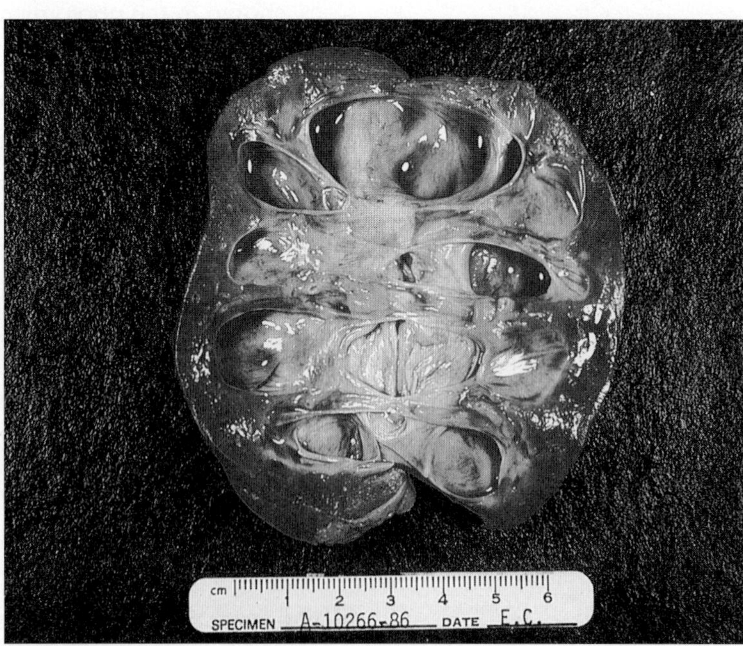

Figure for use with question 146.

148. A red (hemorrhagic) infarct rather than a pale infarct is most likely to occur in the

(A) kidney
(B) brain
(C) lung
(D) heart
(E) spleen

149. Which of the following is true in normal cells that is not present in neoplastic cells?

(A) increased sensitivity to contact inhibition of growth
(B) decreased sensitivity to density-dependent inhibition
(C) loss of anchoring ability for growth
(D) infinite potential for replication and survival
(E) the ability to produce malignant transformations in synergistic hosts

150. Pulmonary tuberculosis is MOST frequently encountered in

(A) U.S. whites
(B) U.S. blacks
(C) Scandinavians
(D) Black Africans
(E) Japanese

151. Which of the following statements describing toxemia of pregnancy is true?

(A) It occurs in 50% of pregnant women.
(B) Deficient placental production of prostaglandins may play a causative role.
(C) Symptoms become manifest in the first trimester.
(D) Hypotension is a prominent feature.
(E) The presence of disseminated intravascular coagulation (DIC) is diagnostic of preeclampsia.

152. Polyarteritis nodosa typically involves

(A) large elastic arteries
(B) small or medium-size muscular arteries
(C) arterioles
(D) capillaries
(E) venules

153. The most likely cause of the pathologic findings in the spleen pictured below is

(A) amyloidosis
(B) metastatic carcinoma
(C) septic infarct
(D) Hodgkin's disease
(E) traumatic rupture

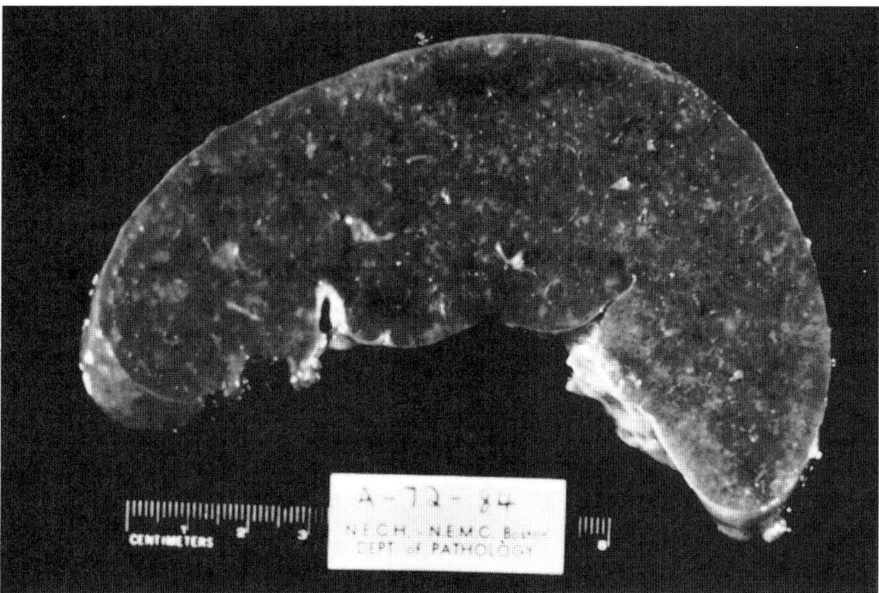

Figure for use with question 153.

154. Which of the following diseases is caused by a protozoan?

(A) aspergillosis
(B) toxoplasmosis
(C) camdodoasos
(D) typus fever
(E) leprosy

155. Mutations of the p53 gene are associated with

(A) carcinogenesis
(B) micrognathia
(C) cystic fibrosis
(D) pulmonary fibrosis
(E) essential hypertension

156. The term used to describe an abnormal toxic yellow pigmentation found in the brains of neonates exposed to excessive unconjugated hyperbilirubinemia is

(A) kernicterus
(B) mucoviscidosis
(C) zellballen
(D) cholestasis
(E) sequestrum

157. Which statement is FALSE concerning breast cancer?

(A) incidence lower in Japan than in the United States
(B) increased incidence with early menarche or late menopause
(C) increased incidence with high fat diet
(D) decreased incidence with atypical ductal or lobular hyperplasia
(E) increased incidence with family history of breast cancer

158. A testicular tumor that exhibits more than one germ layer (combination of ectoderm, endoderm, and mesoderm) is

(A) seminoma
(B) choriocarcinoma
(C) embryonal carcinoma
(D) Leydig's cell tumor
(E) teratoma

159. Which of the following is MOST likely to be associated with systemic effects produced by products of the tumor?

(A) osteogenic sarcoma
(B) follicular adenoma of thyroid
(C) papillary carcinoma of thyroid
(D) pheochromocytoma
(E) anaplastic carcinoma of thyroid

160. The photomicrograph pictured on the facing page is of a bone biopsy. The most likely diagnosis is

(A) benign neoplasm
(B) cellular hyperplasia
(C) osteogenic sarcoma
(D) metastatic lesion
(E) chronic leukemia

161. Which of the following non-Hodgkin's lymphoma are considered high grade in the working formulation classification?

(A) Burkitt's lymphoma
(B) follicular small cell cleaved lymphoma
(C) diffuse small and large cell cleaved lymphoma
(D) small lymphocytic lymphoma
(E) M.A.L.T. (mucosal associated lymphoid tissues) lymphoma

162. Which of the following represents irreversible morphologic changes associated with cell death?

(A) hydropic swelling
(B) fatty metamorphosis
(C) apoptosis
(D) hypertrophy
(E) atrophy

163. One factor that significantly increases the risk of coronary artery disease is

(A) low fat diet
(B) diabetes mellitus
(C) high levels of HDL
(D) post-menopausal estrogen replacement
(E) antioxidant agents

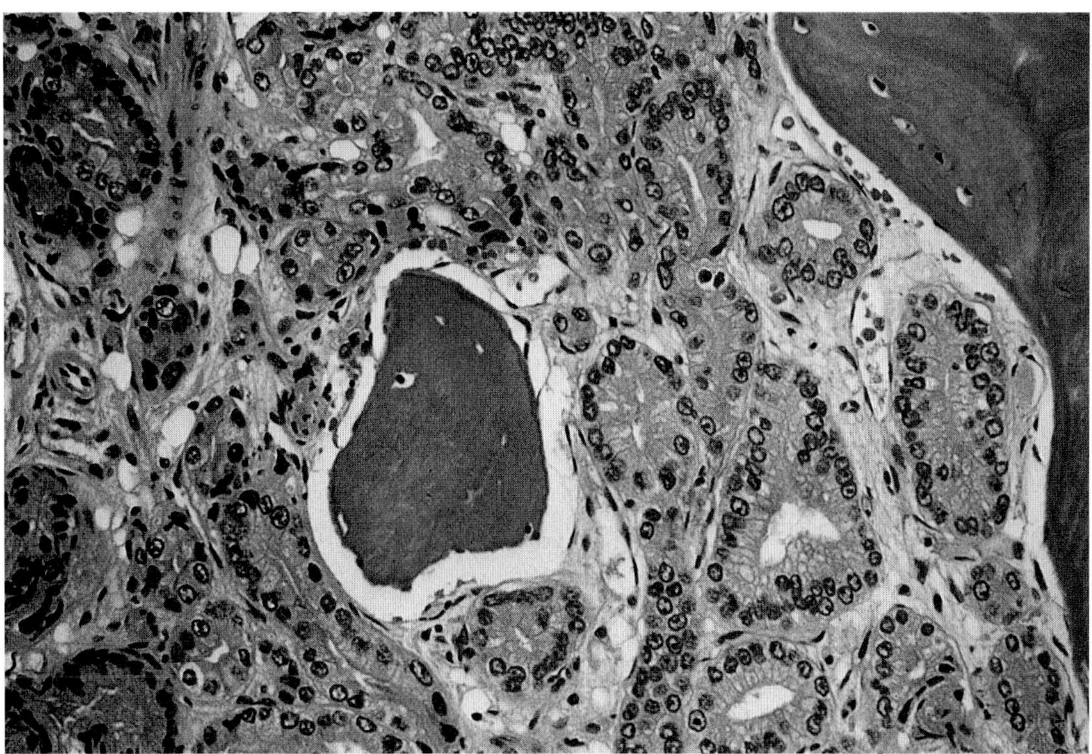

Figure for use with question 160.

164. Fibrocystic change of the breast, apocrine metaplasia, epitheliosis, and cyst formations are some of the histological changes seen in

(A) acute mastitis
(B) fibroadenoma
(C) lobular carcinoma-in-situ
(D) fibrocystic changes
(E) atypical ductal hyperplasia

DIRECTIONS (Questions 165 through 186): Each group of items in this section consists of lettered headings followed by a set of numbered words or phrases. For each numbered word or phrase, select the ONE lettered heading that is most closely associated with it. Each lettered heading may be selected once, more than once, or not at all.

Questions 165 through 168

(A) metaplasia
(B) hypertrophy
(C) hyperplasia
(D) dysplasia
(E) atrophy

165. A nonmitotic increase in cell size

166. An atypical potentially precancerous cellular alteration

167. Shrinkage of cell substance from inactivity, lack of trophic stimuli, or senescence

168. The replacement of one adult cell type by another adult cell type

Questions 169 through 171

(A) coarctation of the aorta
(B) ventricular septal defect
(C) Ebstein's anomaly
(D) patent ductus arteriosus
(E) tetralogy of Fallot

169. Most common congenital cardiac defect

170. Congenital abnormality of tricuspid valve

171. Abnormal persistent communication between pulmonary artery and aorta

Questions 172 through 175

(A) *Yersinia pestis*
(B) *Treponema pallidum*
(C) *Rickettsia typhi*
(D) *Bordetella pertussis*
(E) *Rickettsia rickettsii*

172. Etiologic agent of Rocky Mountain spotted fever

173. Etiologic agent of syphilis

174. Etiologic agent of plague

175. Etiologic agent of whooping cough

Questions 176 through 179

(A) systemic lupus erythematosus
(B) primary biliary cirrhosis
(C) amyloidosis
(D) pemphigus vulgaris
(E) pernicious anemia

176. Autoantibodies against parietal cells or intrinsic factor

177. Autoantibodies against surface antigens in keratinocytes

178. Autoantibodies against mitochondria

179. Autoantibodies against nuclear antigens

Questions 180 through 183

(A) hemophilia A
(B) thalassemia
(C) myeloma
(D) methemoglobinemia
(E) megaloblastic anemia

180. Usually seen with folate deficiency

181. X-linked hereditary disorder with inadequate factor VIII activity

182. Malignant proliferation of plasma cells

183. Hereditary disorder with discordant globin chain synthesis

Questions 184 through 186

(A) sinus histiocytosis
(B) metastatic carcinoma
(C) non-Hodgkin's disease
(D) Hodgkin's disease
(E) tuberculosis
(F) metastatic melanoma
(G) angiosarcoma

184. A 4-cm lymph node is removed from an otherwise healthy 32-year-old dentist. Microscopically the nodal architecture is effaced by a polymorphous infiltrate of neutrophils, plasma cells, eosinophils, and Reed–Sternberg cells.

185. Numerous enlarged inguinal lymph nodes are removed from a 45-year-old female. Microscopically the nodal architecture is effaced by anaplastic noncohesive cells with prominent nucleoli and cytoplasmic melanin. Two years earlier the woman had a "black" lesion removed from the ipsilateral foot.

186. An enlarged axillary lymph node is removed from a 61-year-old female. Microscopically the nodal architecture is effaced by anaplastic gland-forming cells. Special studies on the tissue confirm the presence of estrogen and progesterone receptor proteins.

ANSWERS AND EXPLANATIONS

139. (E) Hypertensive heart disease is a common form of heart disease in the elderly population, affecting men more often than women and blacks more often than whites. The majority of cases are of idiopathic origin, but some cases are secondary to renal, cerebral, endocrine, or cardiovascular disease. Because of the increased resistance to blood flow, the most significant pathologic change is left ventricular hypertrophy with increasing size of the myocardial cells. There is no actual increase in cell number (hyperplasia). There is thickening of the left ventricular muscle wall concentrically, with narrowing of the chamber. Endocardial fibrous thickening may also occur. Left ventricular wall thickness is increased as much as 2 cm, and the heart weight may be doubled. With long-standing hypertrophic heart disease, there is gradual dilatation and hypertrophy of the right ventricle and dilatation of the right and left atria. Enlargement of the myocardial cells, an increased number of nuclei per cell (boxcar nuclei), degenerative changes, and fibrosis may be seen microscopically. *(Cotran, pp 564–565)*

140. **(D)** The most common cause of spontaneous subarachnoid hemorrhage, and the cerebrovascular lesion most often responsible for death in young adults, is a ruptured intracranial aneurysm. Intracranial congenital aneurysms (berry aneurysms) account for 85% of spontaneous subarachnoid hemorrhages. Such aneurysms are seen in 4% of adults at autopsy; in 20% of these cases they are multiple. Aneurysm formation is thought to be related to a combination of congenital and acquired factors. A defect in the media of the artery wall is believed to be the major congenital defect and is particularly significant at arterial bifurcation sites. Atherosclerosis and hypertension appear to be the most significant acquired factors causing fragmentation of the elastic lamina. Other causes of spontaneous subarachnoid hemorrhage include arteriovenous malformations (10% of cases) and tumors, blood dyscrasias, and mycotic aneurysms (5% of cases combined). *(Cotran, pp 1310–1313)*

141. ARDS is a descriptive term for a syndrome caused by diffuse alveolocapillary damage. It is clinically characterized by the rapid onset of severe life-threatening respiratory insufficiency, cyanosis, and severe arteriole hypoxemia that is refractory to oxygen therapy and might progress to extrapulmonary multisystem organ failure. The pathology in the early stages is characterized by congestion, intra-alveolar edema, inflammation, and hyaline membranes. In the latest stages, interstitial fibrosis, chronic inflammation, and focal alveolar damage is present. The pathogenesis is considered diffuse damage to the alveolocapillary walls produced by an interaction of leukocyte mediators, that damage the pneumocytes, as well as endothelial cells. *(Cotran, pp 700–703).*

142. **(E)** A wide variety of afflictions may be caused by vitamin deficiencies. Niacin deficiency, also known as pellagra, is associated with dermatitis, diarrhea, and dementia. Papular dermatitis and night blindness (nyctalopia), with or without keratomalacia, suggest vitamin A deficiency. Vitamin K deficiency may manifest itself as a bleeding diathesis because of the role of vitamin K in the formation of prothrombin and clotting factors VII, IX, and X. Scurvy, or vitamin C deficiency, results in the altered formation of connective tissues such as collagen, osteoid, dentin, and intercellular cement substance. Thiamine deficiency, or beriberi, presents in three ways that generally overlap to some extent in any given patient. Neuromuscular signs and symptoms alone are known as "dry beriberi" but in association with edema are known as "wet beriberi." Heart failure, generally high-output failure, accounts for so-called cardiac beriberi. *(Cotran, pp 448–449)*

143. **(E)** Clinically detectable diverticulosis is seen in about 1 in 8 patients older than 45 years of age; in autopsy series, the incidence estimate is higher. Diverticulosis occurs in the sigmoid colon in 95% of affected individuals. Other segments of the large bowel become involved by diverticulosis as follows: descending colon, 30%; transverse colon, 4%; and entire colon, 16%. The sigmoid is the only region of the colon involved with disease in about 41% of cases. In underdeveloped and tropical countries, as well as in Japan, diverticulosis is rare, apparently partially because of the high-residue diets in these regions of the world. The most consistent abnormality seen in diverticulosis is an abnormality of the muscle wall, which leads to herniation of the colonic mucosa and submucosa through the muscularis and eventually into the pericolic adipose tissue. Fecal material may become trapped in the diverticulum, leading to ulceration, inflammation, and rarely perforation. *(Fenoglio-Preiser, pp 767–776)*

144. (C) The pathognomonic lesion of gout is the tophus—a collection of crystalline or amorphous urates surrounded by an inflammatory response consisting of macrophages, lymphocytes, fibroblasts, and foreign body giant cells. In the photomicrograph that accompanies the question, the darker stellate deposits denote the center of the tophus. These urate deposits would appear golden brown, in contrast to the pink-staining tissue about them on hematoxylin-eosin staining. Gout is a systemic disorder of uric acid metabolism resulting in hyperuricemia. Urates precipitate out of the supersaturated blood and deposit in the joints and soft tissues. Rheumatoid arthritis, which includes ankylosing spondylitis, is characterized by a diffuse proliferative synovitis; suppurative arthritis, by a prominent neutrophilic inflammation; and osteoarthritis, by cartilaginous and subchondral bone changes. *(Cotran, pp 1253–1257)*

145. (D) Mesothelioma is the most common malignant tumor of the pleura. It is a highly invasive lesion and has been linked to inhalation of asbestos fibers, especially by persons in the shipbuilding and insulation industries. A history of smoking dramatically increases the risk of developing a mesothelioma. Histologically, the tumor may be either sarcomatous (composed of mesenchymal stromal cells), carcinomatous (resembling tubular or papillary structures), or a combination of these two types. These tumors are highly malignant, and most patients die within a year of diagnosis. *(Cotran, pp 732–734)*

146. (A) The photograph that accompanies the question demonstrates severe hydronephrosis, which is due to obstruction of the flow of urine. The obstruction may be located at any site along the urinary outflow tract and may be partial or total, unilateral or bilateral. Because glomerular filtration may continue for some time after the development of the obstruction, the renal pelvis and calices become dilated by continued urine production. The resultant back-pressure produces atrophy of the renal parenchyma with obliteration of the pyramids. The degree of hydronephrosis depends on the extent and rapidity of the obstructive process. *(Cotran, p 988)*

147. (C) Down syndrome is the most common chromosome abnormality, occurring in 1 out of 800 live births. It is characterized by a trisomy 21 karyotype with an extra G group chromosome (chromosome 21), making 47 total chromosomes. In the majority of cases, the parents are phenotypically and genetically normal, and Down syndrome is secondary to a meiotic error in the ovum. The risk of having a Down syndrome child is proportional to increasing maternal age. The clinical features of Down syndrome include fat facies, epicanthic folds, oblique palpebral fissures, and mental retardation. The majority of affected individuals die early from cardiac or infectious complications. Thirty percent have a ventricular septal defect.

Trisomy 13 is also called Patau's syndrome, and affected children have microcephaly and severe mental retardation with absence of a portion of the forebrain. These children die soon after birth. Trisomy 18, or Edwards' syndrome, is also a very severe genetic defect, and the average life-span is 10 weeks. Affected children have severe mental retardation and cardiac anomalies, including ventricular septal defect. Persons with an XO karyotype have Turner's syndrome and are phenotypically females. Only 3% of affected fetuses survive to birth; fetuses that do survive have severe edema of the hands, feet, and neck. Affected persons have a webbed neck, short stature, and congenital heart disease. At puberty there is failure to develop normal secondary sex characteristics, so their genitalia remain immature. Klinefelter's syndrome, or testicular dysgenesis, is characterized by an XXY karyotype. It occurs in 1 out of 600 live births. Affected individuals usually are diagnosed after puberty and have eunuchoid habitus, long legs, small atrophic testes and penis, and, often, low IQ. *(Cotran, pp 170–173)*

148. (C) Infarction of any organ is produced by occlusion of the main arterial blood supply. The common feature is ischemic change. The secondary events that take place in the tissue are to some extent determined by the nature of the tissue and whether or not the blood supply is extensive and whether there is more than one blood supply. An organ suffering infarction that has a rich vascular network and in which there is more than one blood supply with a considerable overlapping and anastomotic potential will suffer the consequences of infarction quite differently from one in which the vessels are end arteries.

Particularly, in the kidney and the brain the end arterial system is well developed and, therefore, localized forms of infarction will occur. These infarcts tend to become ischemic and pale in appearance and wedge-shaped. This is also true to some extent in the spleen.

In the heart, there is more possibility of anastomotic overlap, but the tissue is also firm in consistency and rigid, thus also producing more pallor in the infarcted area.

The lung exhibits the difference that allows for a hemorrhagic or red infarct. The lung tissue is spongelike and blood seeps into the ischemic area very easily from the adjacent lung tissue, producing a large amount of hemorrhage into the infarcted or ischemic area. In addition, there is a dual blood supply to the lung that allows the tissues to be still permeated although ischemic by blood from adjacent area. *(Cotran, pp 132–133)*

149. (A) Neoplastic transformation is a phenotypic change in cells that characterizes the malignant state and is passed on to progeny. These transformed cells show anaplasia and transplantability. They also show decreased sensitivity to contact inhibition and to density-dependent inhibition for growth. Thus, these tumor cells are more mobile and do not cease to grow when in contact with other cells or when more than a monolayer of confluent cells is present; instead, they continue to replicate and pile up. Unlike normal cells, these tumor cells also can grow and divide on fluid media and have lost the need for anchorage to grow. Malignant transformed cells have an infinite ability to replicate and survive under appropriate conditions. These transformed cells are capable of tumorigenesis, so they are able to produce a neoplasm when placed within a synergistic host. *(Cotran, pp 298–309)*

150. (D) Although pulmonary tuberculosis is worldwide, changes in public health awareness and treatments have reduced the incidence of the disease in many of the developed Western countries, although sporadic cases still occur, particularly in the poorer areas of these countries. Blacks in the United States have a higher rate of tuberculosis than U.S. whites. The disease is very much reduced in modern times in Scandinavians and in Japanese. However, Black Africa is certainly the area where tuberculosis still remains one of the major causes of morbidity and mortality. It has been said that tuberculosis is the great tropical disease of Africa and still represents a major life-threatening disease to its inhabitants. *(Cotran, p 349)*

151. (B) Toxemia of pregnancy occurs in about 6% of pregnant women, usually in the third trimester. Hypertension, proteinuria, and edema characterize the less severe form of the disease, preeclampsia. Women who also develop convulsions, disseminated intravascular coagulation (DIC), and coma have eclampsia. Anatomic lesions associated with eclampsia include acute atherosis in placental vessels, accentuated aging of the placenta with epithelial atrophy, hepatic hemorrhage, and fibrin thrombi in the small vessels of the liver, kidney, and brain.

The two most important factors in the pathogenesis of toxemia of pregnancy appear to be hypertension and DIC. Hypertension seems to be caused by both a hypersensitivity to angiotensin and a decreased production of prostaglandins by the placenta following an ill-defined immunologic insult to the uterine vasculature. Further organ damage develops as a result of hypertension-induced vascular changes. The pathogenesis of DIC is uncertain. Among the several theories explaining the occurrence of DIC is increased release of thromboplastin substances from an ischemic placenta. *(Cotran, pp 1082–1084)*

152. (B) Polyarteritis nodosa (PAN) typically involves small to medium-sized muscular arteries. In contrast, large arteries and the aorta are involved in Takayasu's arteritis, and small arteries and arterioles are involved in a number of other diseases, including systemic lupus erythematosus. Active lesions in PAN demonstrate a neutrophilic infiltration of the involved vessel wall with thrombosis and segmental, fibrinoid necrosis. Intermittent healing produces fibrosis of the arterial wall and intimal thickening, which may lead to obstruction and infarction. Aneurysmal dilations may arise as a result of asymmetrical involvement. Although the lesions in PAN resemble other immune-mediated vascular lesions, the exact etiology of the disorder has not been elucidated. PAN generally affects middle-aged men and has a poor prognosis, although steroids may be beneficial. *(Cotran, pp 520–521)*

153. (A) Amyloidosis is caused by the deposition of an abnormal proteinaceous material between cells. The majority of the cases are idiopathic, but a small percentage are secondary to chronic infection or inflammation, plasma cell dyscrasias, or immune diseases. One of the characteristic presentations of amyloidosis is splenic infiltration and splenomegaly caused by deposition of amyloid in the follicular regions. Grossly, the spleen has a diffuse, pink, glassy, waxy appearance with obliteration of the white pulp. Amyloid infiltration also can affect the kidneys, liver, and heart. Clinical symptoms are usually due to functional impairment of the diseased organ. The diagnosis of amyloidosis is made by tissue biopsy or, more recently, by fat-pad biopsy looking for amyloid deposits. With Congo red stain, amyloid appears red; with polarization, it shows an apple-green birefringence, which is diagnostic of amyloid. *(Cotran, pp 251–257)*

154. (B) Toxoplasmosis is caused by *Toxoplasma gondii,* which is an obligate intracellular protozoan parasite. It is widely distributed among domestic animals and humans throughout the world. Aspergillosis, as well as candidiasis, are diseases caused by fungus. Leprosy is a slowly progressing infection caused by mycobacterium and typhoid fever (*scrub typhus*) is produced by a *Rickettsia. (Cotran, pp 382–383)*

155. (A) The p53 gene is a well-studied tumor-suppressor gene that is located on chromosome 17p13.1, and the single most common target for genetic alteration in human tumors. It has been frequently found in solid tumors of humans, up to 50%. This includes carcinomas of the lung, colon, and breast. The fact that p53 mutations are common in a variety of human tumors suggests that the p53 protein serves as a critical gatekeeper (the guardian of the genome) against the transformation into cancer. The wild type of p53 responds rapidly to DNA damage and leads to cell cycle arrest, leading to apoptosis, if the reparative mechanisms of the DNA fail. Macrognathia, cystic fibrosis, pulmonary fibrosis, and essential hypertension have not demonstrated a relationship with mutated p53. *(Cotran, pp 290–292)*

156. (A) Kernicterus (bilirubin encephalopathy) is the morphologic term that describes toxic yellow discoloration seen in brains of severely jaundiced neonates. The pigment is especially prominent in the basal ganglia, pontine nuclei, and cerebellar dentate nuclei. Premature infants are more susceptible to developing kernicterus at lower levels of hyperbilirubinemia than are term infants. Surviving infants all experience some degree of neurologic impairment. *(Cotran, pp 474, 849)*

157. (D) About 1 in 11 women in the United States will have breast cancer during her lifetime. The incidence of breast cancer is much higher in the United States than in Japan.

Other factors that have been associated with an increased risk of developing breast cancer include a family history of breast cancer, a high-fat diet, early menarche, late menopause, and atypical ductal or lobular hyperplasia. *(Cotran, pp 1104–1107)*

158. (E) Teratoma refers to a complex group of tumors having various cellular organoid components reminiscent of normal derivatives from more than one germ layer. Pure teratomas are more frequent in children, in adults they are rare; however, they are frequently increased in combination with another histologic type. Grossly, teratomas are usually large and the gross appearance is heterogenous. Histologically, three variants are recognized based on the degree of differentiation, mature teratomas, immature teratomas, and teratoma with malignant transformation. *(Cotran, pp 1021–1023)*

159. (D) Pheochromocytoma. Although many tumors can produce systemic effects by means of products of the tumor cells, the pheochromocytoma is by far the best choice of the ones listed because characteristically, in a high proportion of cases, it produces adrenalin and noradrenalinelike substances and, therefore, dramatic changes in the vasculature and in the blood pressure. It is often the symptoms produced by these substances, the by-products of which can also be measured in the urine, that first bring to light the presence of the tumor. Osteogenic sarcoma does not produce such effects and neither does anaplastic carcinoma of the thyroid. Follicular adenoma of the thyroid may occasionally be associated with increased uptake of radioactive iodine but does not produce the thyrotoxicosis characteristically seen in some cases of follicular thyroid carcinoma. Papillary carcinoma of the thyroid rarely produces such effects. *(Cotran, pp 1164–1166)*

160. (D) The photomicrograph accompanying the question shows bone marrow spaces replaced by a well-differentiated adenocarcinoma. The bone spicules are normal. The glandular structures replacing the interspicular spaces and replacing the marrow elements are diagnostic of metastatic adenocarcinoma. *(Cotran, pp 268–271)*

161. (C) Burkitt's lymphoma is a neoplasm of B-cell lymphocytes that is classified as a high-grade lymphoma of the small, noncleaved cell type, according to the National Cancer Institute's new working formulation classification system for non-Hodgkin's lymphomas. The search for the cause of Burkitt's lymphoma has revealed an association with the Epstein–Barr virus (EBV) in many cases. In endemic African Burkitt's lymphoma, 80 to 90% of tumors contain copies of the EBV DNA genome. However, in the sporadic and less frequent nonendemic cases of Burkitt's lymphoma, there has been an infrequent association with EBV (15 to 20% of cases). The search for a chromosomal abnormality has revealed an 8–14q translocation in many cases. However, this translocation is not apparent in 10 to 20% of cases; nor is it identified in all tumor cells in any given Burkitt's lymphoma. Despite many hypotheses, the cause of Burkitt's lymphoma remains unclear. *(Cotran, 662–663)*

162. (B) Apoptosis occurs when a cell dies through activation of an internally controlled suicide program. It is a subtly orchestrated disassembly of cellular components designed to eliminate unwanted cells during the embryogenesis and various physiologic processes. Apoptosis should be distinguished from coagulative necrosis for several histological, as well as electron microscopy changes. Those are: 1. cell shrinkage; 2. chromatin condensation; 3. formation of cytoplasmic blebs and apoptotic bodies; 4. phagocytosis of apoptotic cells or bodies. Hydropic swelling is a form of reversible cell injury due to accumulation of fluid within the cisternae of the endoplasmic reticulum. Subcellular alterations also occur in the cell in response to sublethal stimulae, such as accumulation of lipid in the cytoplasm (fatty metamorphosis). Hypertrophy, as well as atrophy are adaptive responses to the cells either with an increase or decrease in cell function. *(Cotran, pp 2–4, 18–25)*

163. **(B)** In both forms of diabetes mellitus, type I and II, there is an increased risk of coronary artery disease. Atherosclerotic events such as myocardial infarction, cerebrovascular accidents, gangrene of the legs, and renal insufficiency are the most threatening and most frequent complications. High levels of HDL has been shown to be protective from developing coronary artery disease, as well as replacement of estrogen therapy in postmenopausal women and the ingestion of antioxidant agents. *(Cotran, pp 550–551, 926)*

164. **(D)** Fibrocystic disease is a common benign disease of the breast that usually affects women between the ages of 25 to 45 years. It is thought to be related to hormone levels. The process is usually bilateral, but one breast is often more affected than the other. The microscopic appearance of fibrocystic disease varies; changes may include duct dilatation with cyst formation, apocrine metaplasia, fibrosis, chronic inflammation, duct hyperplasia, papillomatosis and lobular distortion. Acute mastitis is seen most frequently in the earliest week of nursing and is secondary to bacterial infections developing in cracks or fissures of the nipples, most frequently by staphylococcus. Fibroadenoma of the breast is the most common benign tumor of the female breast and as its word implies is composed of both fibrous and glandular tissues. Lobular carcinoma or atypical ductal hyperplasia are not features of fibrocystic disease. *(Cotran, pp 1098–1100)*

165–168. **(165-B, 166-D, 167-E, 168-A)** Hypertrophy is an amitotic increase in size of a cell. Hyperplasia is defined as an increase in the number of cells present without regard to the size of the individual cells. Dysplasia is an atypical potentially precancerous alteration usually characterized by nuclear enlargement and hyperchromatism. Metaplasia is the replacement of one adult cell type by another. Atrophy refers to loss of cell volume due to senescence, lack of trophic stimuli, or inactivity. *(Cotran, pp 32–38, 266)*

169–171. **(169-B, 170-C, 171-D)** The most common congenital cardiac defect is a ventricular septal defect. Defects usually occur near the base of the heart and vary in size from small holes to nearly complete absence of the muscular septum. In the Ebstein's anomaly one or more of the tricuspid valve leaflets are abnormal. Heart failure, right ventricular dilation, arrhythmias, and sudden death may complicate the anomaly. A patent ductus arteriosus is an abnormal persistence of the channel between the aorta and pulmonary artery (ductus arteriosus). This channel usually closes shortly after birth. Persistent patency can result in heart failure, cardiac hypertrophy, and pulmonary vascular sclerosis. *(Cotran, pp 591–598)*

172–175. **(172-E, 173-B, 174-A, 175-D)** Rocky Mountain spotted fever is caused by *Rickettsia rickettsii.* Rash, fever, headache, and myalgia are systemic components of the disease. The organism is particularly well demonstrated in endothelial cells sampled by skin biopsy. Syphilis is a systemic infectious disorder with protean clinical findings. The etiologic agent is *Treponema pallidum.* Bubonic plague is caused by *Yersinia pestis.* Wild rodents and some domesticated animals serve as reservoirs. Fleas transmit the disease to humans. An enlarged, painful lymph node (bubo) arises in the area drained by the flea bite. Massive terminal ecchymoses give rise to the appellation "black death." Whooping cough (pertussis) is caused by *Bordetella pertussis.* Upper respiratory symptoms characterize the disease. Forced inspiratory stridor may produce a "whooping" sound, for which the disease is named. *(Cotran, pp 383–385)*

176–179. **(176-E, 177-D, 178-B, 179-A)** Pernicious anemia is due to a lack of vitamin B_{12}. Autoimmune destruction of gastric parietal cells or immune inactivation of intrinsic factor leads to inadequate absorption of the vitamin. Megaloblastic anemia, leukopenia, thrombocytopenia, and demyelination of the posterolateral spinal cord columns are seen in the fully developed disease. Pemphigus vulgaris is a bullous lesion of the skin caused by autoantibodies to surface antigens on keratinocytes. Primary biliary cirrhosis is an autoimmune disorder characterized by chronic destructive cholangitis in the early stages and micronodular cirrhosis in the late stages of the disease. Antimitochondrial antibodies are seen in more than 90% of affected individuals. Systemic lupus erythematosus is an autoimmune disease with high titers of antinuclear antibodies. Facial rash, renal insufficiency, serositis, and pneumonitis are features of the disorder. *(Cotran, pp 216–220, 791–792, 878–879, 1201–1202)*

180–183. (180-E, 181-A, 182-C, 183-B) Folate deficiency is usually seen with inadequate dietary intake. A megaloblastic anemia may result. Unlike the megaloblastic anemia seen with pernicious anemia, folate deficiency does not produce concomitant neurologic disease. Hemophilia A is a hereditary disorder characterized by spontaneous hemorrhage. The disorder is inherited in an X-linked manner, and abnormally low factor VIII activity is present. Myeloma is a malignant disease caused by an uncontrolled proliferation of plasma cells. The plasmacytes usually produce a monoclonal immunoglobulin molecule that can be detected in the serum, in urine, or in both serum and urine. Thalassemia is a hereditary disorder of discordant globin chain synthesis. Anemia is the most common clinical feature. *(Cotran, pp 615–619, 621–622, 639, 663–667)*

184–186. (184-D, 185-F, 186-B) Hodgkin's disease is a malignancy of lymphoreticular tissue. Adenopathy is a common clinical finding. The diagnostic Reed–Sternberg cell is large and binucleated, with prominent multiple eosinophilic nucleoli. The background has a variegated cellular population, which is composed of lymphocytes, plasma cells, eosinophils, neutrophils, and histiocytes. Areas of fibrosis can be present in some types of Hodgkin's disease and be very prominent as in nodular sclerosing type. The metastasis of a malignant melanoma into a regional lymph node depends mostly on the depth invasion in the skin, or the tumor stage when located in internal organs. It entirely or partially replaces the lymph node and the cells are epithelioid or spindleloid with very prominent nuceoli and occasionally they display cytoplasmic melanin. Metastatic carcinoma may be present in surgically removed lymph nodes. If these are coming particularly from the axilla of a female, and microscopically showed a partial or total replacement of the lymph node by glandular structures, further studies should be undertaken to demonstrate the breast origin of this metastatic lesion. The most important immunoperoxidase stains for these lesions will be estrogen/progesterone receptors. Positive results will be very suggestive of metastatic tumor of mammary origin. *(Cotran, pp 670-674, 1114–1116, 1177–1179)*

REFERENCES

Cotran RS, Kumar V, Robbins SL. *Robbins Pathologic Basis of Disease,* 5th ed. Philadelphia: WB Saunders Company; 1994.

Fenoglio-Preiser CM, Noffsinger AE, Stemmermann GN, Lantz PE, Listrom MB, Rilke FO. *Gastrointestinal Pathology: An Atlas and Text,* 2nd ed. Philadelphia: Lippincott-Raven Publishers; 1999.

SUBSPECIALTY LIST: PATHOLOGY

Question Number and Subspecialty

139. Cardiovascular system
140. Circulatory disorders
141. Respiratory system
142. Nongenetic syndromes
143. Alimentary system
144. Cutaneous, osseous, and muscle systems
145. Respiratory system
146. Kidney and urinary systems
147. Genetic syndromes and metabolic diseases
148. Circulatory system
149. Neoplasia
150. Respiratory system
151 Abnormal growth and development
152. Nongenetic syndromes
153. Genetic and metabolic syndromes
154. Processes of infection
155. Neoplasia

156. Nervous system
157. Breast
158. Genital system
159. Neoplasia
160. Neoplasia
161. Blood and lymphatics
162. Cellular injury and response
163. Circulatory system
164. Breast
165. Cellular injury and response
166. Cellular injury and response
167. Cellular injury and response
168. Cellular injury and response
169. Cardiovascular system
170. Cardiovascular system
171. Cardiovascular system
172. Infectious diseases
173. Infectious diseases
174. Infectious diseases
175. Infectious diseases
176. Immunologic diseases
177. Immunologic diseases
178. Immunologic diseases
179. Immunologic diseases
180. Blood and lymphatics
181. Blood and lymphatics
182. Blood and lymphatics
183. Blood and lymphatics
184. Neoplasia
185. Neoplasia
186. Neoplasia

Pharmacology

David A. Johnson, PhD

DIRECTIONS (Questions 187 through 224): Each of the numbered items or incomplete statements in this section is followed by answers or by completions of the statement. Select the ONE lettered answer or completion that is BEST in each case.

187. The mechanism of action for propylthiouracil in treating hyperthyroidism is

(A) interference with the incorporation of iodine into thyroglobulin
(B) interference with the concentration of iodide by the thyroid gland
(C) inhibition of inositol phosphate signaling pathways within the thyrocyte
(D) destruction of thyroid tissue
(E) antagonism of thyroid hormones at receptor sites

188. Beta-lactam antibiotics are thought to act by

(A) interfering with protein synthesis at the ribosome
(B) attaching to sterols in cell membranes
(C) inhibiting bacterial cell wall synthesis
(D) inhibiting the transport of amino acids into bacteria
(E) inhibiting dehydrofolate reductase

189. In persons suffering from severe anaphylactic shock, the drug of choice for restoring circulation and relaxing bronchial smooth muscle is

(A) epinephrine
(B) norepinephrine
(C) isoproterenol
(D) phenylephrine
(E) dopamine

190. Primidone is metabolized to

(A) phenobarbital
(B) phenytoin
(C) butabarbital
(D) valproate
(E) diazepam

191. Acyclovir-induced nephrotoxicity is caused by

(A) the formation of toxic metabolites
(B) decreased glomerular filtration rate
(C) the precipitation of acyclovir in renal tubules
(D) direct tubular cytotoxic injury
(E) hypersensitivity interstitial nephritis

192. Which of the following is utilized primarily as a supplement to maintain general anesthesia?

(A) halothane
(B) enflurane
(C) nitrous oxide
(D) cyclopropane
(E) *d*-tubocurarine

193. Which of the following statements about the hypnotic effects of the benzodiazepines is true?

(A) Only flurazepam has true sedative-hypnotic properties.
(B) They have no effect on rapid-eye movement (REM) patterns.
(C) They are all absorbed rapidly and thus can be taken at bedtime.
(D) The accumulation of metabolites enhances the hypnotic activity of some drugs.
(E) None of the above.

194. Which of the following antiviral agents has as its primary mechanism of action, inhibition of reverse transcriptase?

(A) ganciclovir
(B) penciclovir
(C) amantadine
(D) zidovudine
(E) alpha-interferon

195. The uricosuric agent probenecid has as its mechanism of action the

(A) inhibition of xanthine oxidase
(B) inhibition of cyclooxygenase
(C) facilitation of urea metabolism
(D) inhibition of renal urate reabsorption
(E) facilitation of hepatic urate reabsorption

196. Which of the following can produce a potentially lethal drug interaction when administered with thiazide diuretics?

(A) uricosuric agents
(B) quinidine
(C) insulin
(D) vitamin D
(E) sulfonylureas

197. A potent inducer of cytochrome P-450 drug-metabolizing enzymes is

(A) chloramphenicol
(B) hydrochlorothiazide
(C) phenobarbital
(D) penicillin G
(E) digoxin

198. During therapy for angina, reflex tachycardia and exacerbation of symptoms are concerns most closely associated with the use of

(A) propranolol
(B) nitroglycerin
(C) verapamil
(D) dobutamine
(E) isoproterenol

199. The most appropriate agent for long-term control of ventricular arrhythmias in a patient with congestive heart failure is

(A) propranolol
(B) lidocaine
(C) quinidine
(D) disopyramide
(E) verapamil

200. The biological half-life of a drug is generally related to

(A) the time for a drug to be absorbed into the blood
(B) the time for a drug to take effect following administration
(C) the time for the body burden of a drug to be reduced by 50%
(D) the serum concentration of a drug that is 50% of the toxic level
(E) a value that is half the duration of action of a drug

201. Antineoplastic drugs that are alkylating agents have as their primary mechanism of action

(A) inhibition of purine and pyrimidine synthesis
(B) binding of tubulin
(C) cross-linking of DNA
(D) intercalation into DNA
(E) inhibition of dihydrofolate reductase

202. The mechanism of heparin requires

(A) blockade of prothrombin synthesis
(B) inhibition of the action of thrombin on fibrinogen
(C) inhibition of the synthesis of factors IX, X, XI, and XII
(D) the presence of synthesis factor II
(E) the antagonism of vitamin K

203. Epinephrine is often administered along with local anesthetics because it

(A) prolongs and increases the depth of local anesthesia
(B) neutralizes the irritant action of the local anesthetic agent
(C) increases the rate of systemic absorption and therefore hastens the onset of action of the anesthetic agent
(D) increases the pH of the anesthetic so that less anesthetic is required to produce nerve block
(E) blocks neurotransmitter release (thus decreasing pain perception) via stimulation of presynaptic β_2 receptors

204. The mechanism of action of theophylline is related to

(A) the stimulation of adenylate cyclase
(B) the stimulation of β_2 receptors
(C) inhibition of histamine H_1 receptors
(D) the stimulation of presynaptic α_2 receptors
(E) the inhibition of presynaptic adenosine receptors

205. Which of the following would not be effective in treating asthma?

(A) terbutaline
(B) beclomethasone dipropionate
(C) cromolyn sodium
(D) methacholine
(E) theophylline

206. Phenylbutazone interacts with

(A) warfarin
(B) penicillin
(C) acyclovir
(D) A and B are correct
(E) A, B, and C are correct

207. Which drug can be used as a treatment for warfarin toxicity?

(A) heparin
(B) allopurinol
(C) coumarin
(D) vitamin E
(E) vitamin K

208. Vitamin D supplementation can be helpful in treating which disease(s)?

(A) hyperparathyroidism
(B) hypoparathyroidism
(C) rickets
(D) B and C are correct
(E) none of the above is correct

209. Overdose with tricyclic antidepressants can result in lethal toxicity associated with

(A) coma
(B) respiratory depression
(C) paralysis
(D) hyperthermia
(E) cardiac arrhythmias

210. Which antidepressant drug has the least anticholinergic side effect?

(A) imipramine
(B) fluoxetine
(C) nortriptyline
(D) amitriptyline
(E) doxepin

211. Which of the following arrhythmias may occur in association with digitalis toxicity?

(A) sinus bradycardia
(B) complete sinoatrial block
(C) atrioventricular junctional tachycardia
(D) ventricular tachycardia
(E) all of the above

212. The immunosuppressive properties of tacrolimus include

(A) myelosuppression
(B) inhibition of activation of helper T-cells
(C) inhibition of B-cell formation
(D) impairment of leukocyte chemotaxis
(E) macrophage destruction

213. The mechanism of action of lithium in manic depression is related to

(A) inhibition of reuptake of norepinephrine
(B) inhibition of reuptake of serotonin
(C) blockade of dopamine receptors
(D) down-regulation of β receptors
(E) none of the above

214. Pharmacologic agents that are useful in treating acute pulmonary edema associated with congestive heart failure include

(A) propranolol
(B) diltiazem
(C) furosemide
(D) mannitol
(E) spironolactone

215. Diuretic agents that reduce potassium loss by an aldosterone-independent mechanism include

(A) chlorothiazide
(B) spironolactone
(C) acetazolamide
(D) ethacrynic acid
(E) triamterene

216. A patient who has experienced a severe hypersensitivity reaction to penicillin in the past should NOT be given

(A) tetracycline
(B) cefotaxime
(C) sulfamethoxazole
(D) erythromycin
(E) trimethoprim

217. Estrogen replacement therapy, without progestin, in postmenopausal women, is most frequently associated with an increased risk in

(A) breast cancer
(B) endometrial cancer
(C) ovarian cancer
(D) hepatic cancer
(E) lung cancer

218. In treating patients for gout, which of the following is effective in reducing the synthesis of uric acid?

(A) indomethacin
(B) colchicine
(C) allopurinol
(D) probenecid
(E) sulfinpyrazone

219. The drug-metabolizing capability of the liver may be inhibited by

(A) cimetidine
(B) phenobarbital
(C) ethyl alcohol
(D) methylcholanthrene
(E) penicillin

220. Rapid reversal of the anticoagulant effect of heparin is produced by administration of

(A) cimetidine
(B) heparinase
(C) clofibrate
(D) protamine sulfate
(E) vitamin K

221. Which antidepressant drug is linked to alterations in plasma membrane phosphatidylinositides as a possible mechanism of action?

(A) fluoxetine
(B) amitriptyline
(C) phenelzine
(D) maprotiline
(E) lithium

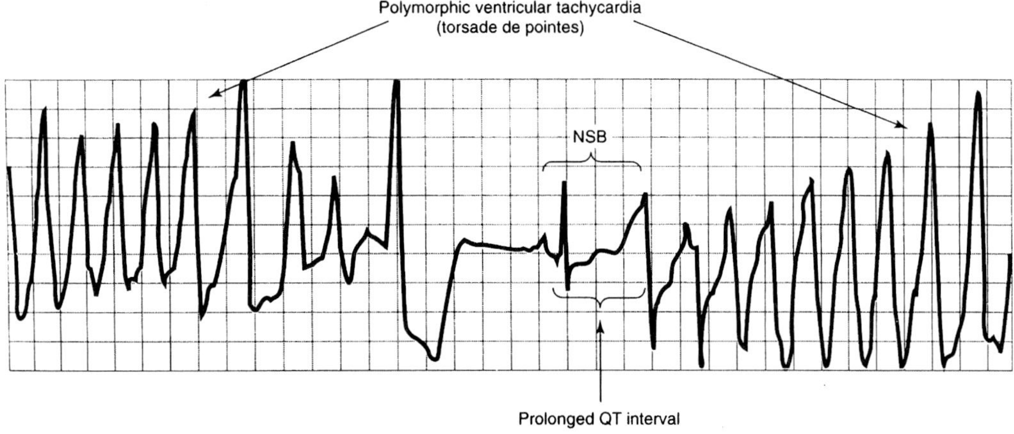

Figure for use with question 224.

222. Cholestyramine adversely affects the absorption of

(A) lipid-soluble vitamins
(B) carbohydrates
(C) amino acids
(D) hydrophilic molecules
(E) ethanol

223. Which of the following would be least likely to increase bleeding time?

(A) aspirin
(B) celcoxib
(C) naproxen
(D) indomethacin
(E) ketorolac

224. Which of the following would most likely induce the cardiac arrhythmia pictured above?

(A) adenosine
(B) lidocaine
(C) phenytoin
(D) flecainide
(E) quinidine

DIRECTIONS (Questions 225 through 232): Each group of items in this section consists of lettered headings followed by a set of numbered words or phrases. For each numbered word or phrase, select the ONE lettered heading that is most closely associated with it. Each lettered heading may be selected once, more than once, or not at all.

Questions 225 through 228

For each side effect listed below, select the antineoplastic agent with which it has been associated.

(A) bleomycin
(B) cisplatin
(C) cytarabine
(D) vincristine
(E) doxorubicin

225. Peripheral neuropathy

226. Cardiotoxicity

227. Renal failure

228. Pulmonary toxicity

Questions 229 and 230

For each insulin preparation below, select the appropriate duration of action.

(A) 2 to 4 hours
(B) 6 to 8 hours
(C) 12 to 24 hours
(D) 20 to 24 hours
(E) 24 to 36 hours

229. Lente

230. Protamine zinc

Questions 231 and 232

For each combination of electrophysiologic effects listed below, select an antiarrhythmic drug most closely associated with it.

(A) quinidine
(B) lidocaine
(C) encainide
(D) phenytoin
(E) amiodarone

231. Marked depression in the rate of rise of membrane action potential and minimal effects on the duration of membrane action potential and effective refractory period of the ventricle.

232. Depressed rate of the rise of membrane action potential and prolonged effective refractory period.

DIRECTIONS (Questions 233 through 236): Each of the numbered items or incomplete statements in this section is followed by answers or by completions of the statement. Select ONE (or MORE) lettered answer(s) or completion(s) for each case.

233. Which of the following concerning digoxin is true? (SELECT 4)

(A) a high margin of safety
(B) a number of effects on cardiac electrophysiology
(C) increases AV-nodal conduction
(D) inhibits the sodium/potassium ATPase pump
(E) blocks calcium channels
(F) has positive inotropic effects
(G) enhances vagal tone
(H) eliminated primarily through hepatic metabolism

234. Aminoglycoside toxicity may be characterized by which of the following untoward effects? (SELECT 4)

(A) ototoxicity
(B) depression
(C) nephrotoxicity
(D) pseudomembranous colitis
(E) neuromuscular blockade
(F) optic nerve damage
(G) pulmonary edema
(H) splenomegaly
(I) bone marrow depression

235. Bupivacaine is a local anesthetic agent that is much more potent and whose duration of action is considerably longer than procaine. Possible reasons for this difference include (SELECT 4)

(A) higher partition coefficient for bupivacaine than for procaine
(B) more rapid distribution to site of action
(C) covalent binding to the receptor site
(D) higher protein binding of bupivacaine than procaine
(E) decreased rate of metabolism of procaine compared to bupivacaine
(F) pKa of bupivacaine is closer to 7.4 pH
(G) bupivacaine constricts blood vessels
(H) bupivacaine inhibits the activity of plasma pseudocholinesterases

236. Which of the following are associated with angiotensin converting enzyme (ACE) inhibitors? (SELECT 4)

(A) cough
(B) inhibition of angiogensin I synthesis
(C) treatment for rheumatoid arthritis
(D) treatment for hypertension
(E) agranulocytosis
(F) vasodilation
(G) treatment for heart failure
(H) blockade of beta-2 receptors

ANSWERS AND EXPLANATIONS

187. (A) Drugs used to treat hyperthyroidism can be divided into 4 categories: (1) antithyroid drugs, which interfere directly with thyroid hormone synthesis, such as propylthiouracil; (2) ionic inhibitors such as thiocyanate, which block iodide transport mechanisms; (3) high dose iodide administration, which decreases the release of thyroid hormones; and (4) radioactive iodide, which destroys thyroid tissue via γ-radiation. In particular, propylthiouracil inhibits the incorporation of iodine into tyrosyl residues of thyroglobulin and also inhibits the coupling of iodotyrosyl residues to form iodothyronines. These effects are the result of inactivation of the enzyme peroxidase, which occurs when the heme moiety is in the oxidized state. *(Hardman et al, pp 1397–1406)*

188. (C) Cephalosporin and penicillin antibiotics act by interfering with the late stages of bacterial cell wall synthesis, although the precise biochemical reactions are not entirely understood. Peptidoglycan provides mechanical stability to the cell wall because of its high degree of cross-linking with alternating amino pyranoside sugar residues (*N*-acetylglucosamine and *N*-acetylmuramic acid). The completion of the cross-linking occurs by the action of the enzyme transpeptidase. This transpeptidase reaction, in which the terminal glycine residue of the pentaglycine bridge is joined to the fourth residue of the pentapeptide (D-alanine) thereby releasing the fifth residue (D-alanine), is inhibited by β-lactams. *(Hardman et al, pp 1074–1075)*

189. (A) Epinephrine is the drug of choice for treating severe anaphylactic shock, because it has both α and β effects. The α and β effects constrict the smaller arterioles and precapillary sphincters, thereby markedly reducing cutaneous blood flow. Veins and large arteries also respond to epinephrine. The β effects of epinephrine cause relaxation of the bronchial smooth muscle and induce a powerful bronchodilation, which is most evident when the bronchial muscle is contracted, as in anaphylactic shock. Neither norepinephrine nor dopamine would be the drug of choice, since neither has action on the β_2 receptors and therefore would not cause the bronchodilation needed for treating anaphylactic shock. Isoproterenol has a powerful action on all β receptors but almost no action on the α receptors, so vasodilation instead of vasoconstriction would be produced. Phenylephrine would be a poor drug of choice for anaphylactic shock because it has little effect on the β receptors and causes no bronchodilation. *(Hardman et al, pp 204–209)*

190. (A) Primidone is an anticonvulsant used to treat epilepsy. It is metabolized to both phenobarbital and phenylethylmalonamide. Both of these compounds contribute to the overall anticonvulsant activity of primidone. *(Katzung, pp 394–395)*

191. (C) Acyclovir is a useful antiviral drug. When used intravenously, acyclovir can precipitate in renal tubules, resulting in nephrotoxicity. This adverse effect especially occurs in dehydrated individuals. *(Hardman et al, p 1197)*

192. (C) Nitrous oxide is primarily used during surgery as an adjuvant to more potent anesthetic gasses. This is because when administered in combination with halogenated anesthetics such as enflurane, lower concentrations of the more potent agents may be administered to achieve surgical anesthesia. Therefore, the incidence of respiratory and circulatory depression is reduced and recovery is more rapid. As a single agent, nitrous oxide is an effective analgesic; however, it cannot reliably induce surgical anesthesia without being administered under hyperbaric pressures. Cyclopropane is no longer utilized because of its flammability. *d*-Tubocurarine is not an anesthetic, but a neuromuscular blocker that has no anesthetic properties. *(Hardman et al, pp 319–321)*

193. (D) All benzodiazepines have hypnotic effects at appropriate doses. Although these agents may decrease the time required for a person to fall asleep, they have been shown to alter REM sleep patterns. The onset and duration of action of these agents depend on their absorption, metabolism to inactive or active products, and extent of accumulation in the body. Some agents (e.g., temazepam) are absorbed slowly from the gastrointestinal tract; peak plasma levels may not be obtained for 2 hours or more after a dose. Therefore, these agents should be administered well before bedtime. Flurazepam is extensively metabolized to active metabolites; one of these metabolites is excreted very slowly from the body. The accumulation of this metabolite appears to enhance the sedative–hypnotic effects of flurazepam by approximately the second or third night of administration. *(Hardman et al, pp 368–371)*

194. (D) Zidovudine (AZT) is the prototype antiviral agent utilized against retroviruses such as human immunodeficiency virus (HIV). AZT is sequentially phosphorylated to the triphosphate, which then can competitively inhibit reverse transcriptase by substituting for thymidine triphosphate. Ultimately, zidovudine is incorporated into DNA and causes inhibition of viral DNA polymerase. Amantadine inhibits viral uncoating and also viral assembly. Alpha-interferon contributes to viral resistance by stimulating the synthesis of a number of proteins which ultimately have antiviral action. *(Hardman et al, pp 1204–1205)*

195. (D) Probenecid is used in the management of hyperuricemia. Its mechanism of action is related to its ability to enhance the excretion of uric acid by inhibiting urate reabsorption from the renal tubule fluid. Small doses of the drug, however, may actually raise blood urate levels. *(Katzung, p 597)*

196. (B) Quinidine can prolong the QT-interval resulting in the development of polymorphic ventricular tachycardia (Torsade de pointes). Hypokalemia, a side-effect of thiazide diuretics increases the risk of Torsade de pointes, which can then degenerate into fatal ventricular fibrillation. Thiazide diuretics may decrease the effectiveness of uricosuric agents, insulin, and sulfonylureas and may increase the effects of vitamin D. However, these effects tend not to be life-threatening. *(Hardman et al, p 704)*

197. (C) The cytochrome P-450 enzyme is an important component of the mixed-function oxidase primarily located in the smooth endoplasmic reticulum of the liver. This enzyme and others are important in catalyzing drug inactivation by oxidation, reduction, and conjugation. Phenobarbital is a potent stimulator of cytochrome P-450 and causes enhanced metabolism of this agent as well as other drugs (e.g., warfarin). Chloramphenicol is capable of inhibiting this enzyme; penicillin, hydrochlorothiazide, and digoxin have no known effects on cytochrome P-450. *(Hardman et al, p 16)*

198. (B) The goal of treatment of angina is to relieve symptoms and prolong exercise capacity by improving the relationship of oxygen demand and supply. Nitroglycerin is a smooth-muscle relaxant that produces both venodilation (reduced preload) and arteriolar dilation (reduced afterload). Although the combined effect is to reduce myocardial oxygen demands, the potential exists for reflex tachycardia and increased contractility. These reflexes tend to increase oxygen demands as well as potentially reduce coronary blood flow and should be avoided. Avoidance can be accomplished by carefully titrating the dose of nitroglycerin or the concurrent use of a beta blocker such as propranolol. Verapamil is a calcium channel blocker that is particularly useful in primary angina. It has minimal ability to reduce afterload and thus is usually not associated with reflex tachycardia. This is in contrast to nifedipine, which has disadvantages similar to those of nitroglycerin. Isoproterenol would be contraindicated in angina because by itself it may increase myocardial oxygen demands. Similarly, dobutamine, an analogue of dopamine, is a β_1 adrenoreceptor agonist and would not be used to treat angina. *(Katzung, pp 179–196)*

199. (C) Both propranolol and disopyramide may cause severe impairment of left ventricular function, particularly in persons with preexisting heart failure. Quinidine has less of an adverse effect on ventricular performance and would be the drug of choice for controlling ventricular arrhythmias in patients with congestive heart failure. Verapamil is not as effective in treating purely ventricular arrhythmias as quinidine. Because it must be given intravenously, lidocaine is inappropriate for long-term use. *(Hardman et al, pp 856–871)*

200. (C) The biological half-life of a drug is the time required for 50% of the dose to be eliminated. This value is useful in determining the duration of a drug's effect and therefore proper drug dose regimes. Half-life can be described mathematically by the formula

$$t_{1/2} = 0.693 \times V/CL$$

where V is the value of the volume of distribution for the drug and CL is the drug clearance. *(Hardman et al, pp 21–22)*

201. (C) The antineoplastic alkylating agents work by covalently binding to DNA strands, linking them together. The result is strand breakage leading to inhibition of cell replication. The drugs of this class tend to be nonspecific and relatively toxic, but there is little cross resistance with other anticancer medications. Thus, alkylating agents are frequently administered in combination therapies with other classes of antineoplastic drugs. *(Hardman et al, pp 1233–1238)*

202. (B) Heparin acts by binding to a cofactor, antithrombin III. Antithrombin III is a normally circulating α_2-globulin that has the potential to bind to enzymes in the coagulation cascade. In combination with antithrombin III, heparin inactivates clotting factors IXa, Xa, XIa, XIIa, kallikrein, and thrombin, therefore inhibiting conversion of fibrinogen to fibrin. The synthesis of prothrombin and the clotting factors is not affected by heparin. Oral anticoagulants such as warfarin, not heparin, antagonize vitamin K. *(Hardman et al, pp 1344–1345)*

203. (A) The duration of action of a local anesthetic is proportional to its contact time with the nerves. Therefore, if the drug can be localized at the nerve, the period of analgesia should be prolonged. Using a vasoconstrictor such as epinephrine decreases the systemic absorption of the local anesthetic. Once the absorption is decreased, the anesthetic remains longer at the desired site and is systemically absorbed at a slower rate, which allows destruction by enzymes and less systemic toxicity. *(Hardman et al, pp 336–337)*

204. (E) Theophylline and other methylxanthines are known to alter intracellular calcium availability and also inhibit cyclic nucleotide phosphodiesterases; however, at therapeutic levels the main effect of these drugs seems to be inhibition of adenosine receptors. The role of adenosine in asthma is not well understood; however, inhalation of adenosine can precipitate bronchoconstriction in asthma patients yet have no effect in normal individuals. *(Hardman et al, pp 673–677)*

205. (D) Methacholine, a cholinergic agonist stimulates bronchoconstriction, and so would exacerbate asthma. In fact, methacholine is used diagnostically to test for bronchial reactivity. Terbutaline is a β_2-agonist that stimulates bronchodilation. Beclomethasone dipropionate is a glucocorticoid anti-inflammatory. Cromolyn inhibits pulmonary mast cell degranulation. Theophylline is a methylxanthine that relaxes bronchial smooth muscle via a mechanism which is not well understood, but may involve adenosine antagonism. *(Hardman et al, pp 145, 660–678)*

206. (A) Phenylbutazone has a well-known interaction with warfarin that results in increased bleeding time. This effect is mediated in part by the displacement of warfarin by phenylbutazone from plasma proteins, thus increasing warfarin's availability for binding with its target. In addition, phenylbutazone potentiates the effects of warfarin by inhibiting the renal elimination of its more active enantiomer. *(Hardman et al, p 643)*

207. (E) Warfarin acts as a vitamin K antagonist by blocking the regeneration of the reduced form of the vitamin. The result is a decrease in clotting factors II, VII, IX, and X, leading to an increase in bleeding time. Warfarin toxicity can be alleviated by increasing the availability of vitamin K. *(Hardman et al, pp 1346–1349)*

208 (D) Vitamin D is actually a hormone that, along with parathyroid hormone and calcitonin, regulates plasma calcium concentration. One action of vitamin D is to increase plasma Ca^{2+}, which can be reduced in hypoparathyroidism. Rickets is a bone disease caused by either a diet deficient in vitamin D or inadequate exposure to sunlight. *(Hardman et al, pp 1529–1532)*

209. (E) Some of the more serious symptoms of toxicity associated with tricyclic antidepressant overdose include anticholinergic symptoms, coma, seizure, and cardiac arrhythmias. Cardiac toxicity characterized by supraventricular tachycardia and/or QRS widening can be especially difficult to manage. Children may be especially vulnerable to overdose resulting in death. *(Hardman et al, pp 442–443)*

210. (B) Fluoxetine is an atypical antidepressant with little anticholinergic activity. Because of its high specificity as a serotonin uptake inhibitor, fluoxetine does not have many of the symptoms linked to muscarinic blockade such as dry mouth, tachycardia, and drowsiness, which are typical of tricyclic antidepressants. *(Hardman et al, pp 258–259)*

211. (E) Although the likelihood of cardiac toxicity from digitalis glycosides is related to the presence of underlying heart disease, almost any arrhythmia may be associated. Sinoatrial block and sinus bradycardia probably result from the combinations of vagal effects and diminished sympathetic influence, as well as direct effects of the drug. Enhanced phase 4 depolarization can result in atrioventricular junctional tachycardia. Ventricular tachycardia occurs as a consequence of increased automaticity of Purkinje fibers. *(Hardman et al, pp 819–820)*

212. (B) Tacrolimus (FK506), inhibits T-cell activation by binding to a specific protein FKBP. The result is inhibition of calcinekurin-dependent activation of lymphokine gene expression, apoptosis, and degranulation. Cyclosporin has a similar mechanism, but binds to a different cytoplasmic protein (cyclophilin). *(Hardman et al, p 1299)*

213. (E) The mechanism of action for lithium effects in bipolar depression is not well understood. It may inhibit the phosphatase responsible for the intracellular release of inositol; however, the connection to manic behavior remains uncertain. Lithium is useful in treating acute manic episodes but is also utilized prophylactically to decrease the occurrences of mania and to decrease the intensity of the depression phase. *(Katzung, pp 475–479)*

214. (C) Furosemide is effective in treating the acute pulmonary edema associated with congestive heart failure by virtue of its potent diuretic action, which rapidly eliminates excess body fluid volume. Both propranolol and verapamil may decrease cardiac output and thus exacerbate congestion. Mannitol tends to increase vascular fluid volume, which can result in increased congestion. Spironolactone is not potent enough as a diuretic to be effective in treating this condition. *(Hardman et al, pp 697–701)*

215. (E) Triamterene interferes with the transport of sodium in the collecting ducts of the nephron, which results in a modest increase in Na^+ excretion. Since Na^+ is normally exchanged for K^+ in this segment of the nephron, decreased sodium transport results in decreased potassium excretion. The actions of this diuretic are similar to those of spironolactone but do not involve aldosterone receptor blockade. *(Hardman et al, pp 704–706)*

216. (B) Cross-sensitivity between penicillin and cephalosporins ranges from 5% to 20%. Cephalosporins all have a β-lactam ring, which is the major determinant of penicillin allergy. All these agents should be avoided by persons with severe previous hypersensitivity reactions. Since none of the other agents are structurally related to penicillin, cross-reactivity would not be a concern with their use. *(Hardman et al, pp 1095–1096)*

217. (B) The administration of estrogens alone is associated with an increase in endometrial cancer of 1.7 to 15 fold. The risk varies with both the dose administered and the duration of treatment. The co-administration of progestins with estrogen reduces the risk of endometrial cancer even below that of nonusers. Most studies report no increase in the risk of breast cancer for women who take estrogen alone or in combination with progestin, although continued use for longer than 10 years may be associated with a slight increase in risk. Oral contraceptive use appears to slightly lessen the risk of ovarian cancer. Hepatocellular carcinoma is a rare complication of oral contraceptives. *(Katzung, p 660)*

218. (C) All of the drug choices in the question are useful in the management of gout, a condition resulting from hyperuricemia. Allopurinol reduces the synthesis of uric acid by blocking the metabolism of xanthine and hypoxanthine to uric acid via xanthine oxidase inhibition. Probenecid and sulfinpyrazone enhance urate excretion by blocking the reabsorption of urate from the proximal tubule. Colchicine is effective in treating acute gout attacks by inhibiting leukocyte migration and phagocytosis. Indomethacin and other NSAIDs can be effective in treating acute gout attacks by inhibiting urate crystal phagocytosis, however, low dose aspirin may actually increase the risk of acute gout. *(Katzung, pp 595–599)*

219. (A) Cimetidine inhibits the metabolism of other drugs by affecting hepatic microsomal enzyme activity. Therefore, serum levels should be monitored when cimetidine is used concomitantly with drugs with a low therapeutic index, such as warfarin, phenytoin, and theophylline. Phenobarbital, ethyl alcohol, and methylcholanthrene induce liver enzymes. *(Katzung, pp 60, 1064)*

220. (D) Protamine sulfate is a strongly basic molecule that is thought to inhibit acidic heparin electrostatically. It may not, however, affect heparin-induced platelet aggregation. Cimetidine is an H_2-antagonist that *increases* the anticoagulant response by an as yet unknown mechanism. Clofibrate is an agent used to reduce plasma lipid levels. Vitamin K is used to reverse the effect of warfarin. Heparinase is not used clinically. *(Katzung, p 551)*

221. (E) The mechanism of action for lithium is somewhat uncertain but may be related to inhibition of the phosphatase that converts inositol monophosphate to inositol. Fluoxetine, amitriptyline, and maprotiline inhibit the reuptake of norepinephrine, serotonin, or both neurotransmitters. Phenelzine is an inhibitor of monoamine oxidase. *(Katzung, pp 475–476)*

222. (E) Cholestyramine, a bile acid sequestrant, reduces plasma cholesterol levels by decreasing concentrations of low-density lipoproteins. Orally administered drugs (especially those that are lipid soluble) may be bound by cholestyramine as well. This problem may be avoided to a large extent by administering other drugs at least 1 hour before or 4 hours after cholestyramine. Steatorrhea may be another side effect, impairing absorption of fat-soluble vitamins. If this condition develops, vitamin supplementation is recommended. *(Hardman et al, p 889)*

223. (B) Celecoxib belongs to a new generation of nonsteroidal anti-inflammatory drugs (NSAIDs), which are selective for the inhibition of mediators of inflammation synthesized via the enzyme cyclooxygenase (COX) II isoform. COX I is expressed constitutively in most tissues including platelets, while COX II is not. In platelets, COX I mediates the synthesis of the eicosanoid thromboxane, which promotes platelet aggregation. Therefore, unlike older NSAIDs, which are nonselective for COX isoforms and increase bleeding time by inhibiting the synthesis of thromboxane via inhibition of COX I, celecoxib does not have this effect. *(Abramowicz et al, pp 11–12)*

224. (E) Quinidine is a class IA cardiac antiarrhythmic drug, which prolongs the duration of the action potential as reflected in a lengthening of the QT interval. This effect is associated with Torsade de pointes in approximately 2 to 8% of patients administered quinidine and can even be induced at plasma levels of the drug, which are subtherapeutic. Lidocaine and phenytoin shorten the duration of the action potential. Adenosine and flecainide do not alter QT interval. *(Katzung, pp 223–229)*

225–228. (225-D, 226-E, 227-B, 228-A) The clinical toxicity of vincristine is mostly neurologic. Paresthesia, loss of deep-tendon reflexes, foot drop, and other adverse effects may occur. Doxorubicin use may result in dose-related cardiotoxicity, which manifests as a cardiomyopathy resulting in intractable congestive heart failure. Dose-related renal failure is associated with cisplatin therapy. The pulmonary toxicity of bleomycin is also dose related. The antimetabolite cytarabine causes severe myelosuppression. *(Hardman et al, pp 1257–1273)*

229–230. (229-B, 230-C) Preparations of insulin are divided into three categories according to their onset and duration of action after subcutaneous administration. The short-acting preparations include crystalline zinc (regular) insulin as well as semilente. The two long-acting insulins, protamine zinc and ultralente, have a duration of action that extends beyond 24 hours. Intermediate-acting insulins (NPH and lente) have an onset and a duration of action intermediate between those of regular and protamine zinc insulins. These preparations are most often used for diabetic persons whose insulin requirements can be met with a single daily injection of insulin. *(Hardman et al, pp 1498–1500)*

231–232. (231-C, 232-A) Although it is difficult to assign categories of antiarrhythmic drugs according to their mechanism of action, certain generalities have proven useful, especially as new drugs are developed. Class I antiarrhythmic drugs are characterized by their ability to affect sodium entry during cardiac membrane depolarization and affect the required membrane potential to be achieved before the membrane becomes excitable and can propagate an action potential. Typical of class IA compounds is quinidine, which decreases V_{max} of phase 0 and prolongs cardiac action potential duration. Lidocaine and phenytoin are typical of type IB agents, which do not affect phase 0 and shorten cardiac action potential duration. Encainide is a newly developed drug that is unique (type IC) in markedly decreasing V_{max} of phase 0 and not significantly affecting cardiac action potential duration. In contrast, amiodarone is a class III-type agent and does not affect phase 0 of depolarization while prolonging the duration of the action potential. Other classes not discussed included class II (propranolol) and class IV (calcium channel blockers such as verapamil). *(Katzung, pp 226–227)*

233. (B, D, F, G) Digoxin has a number of effects on cardiac electrophysiology related to its mechanism of action, inhibition of the sodium/potassium ATPase pump. The result is enhanced intracellular concentrations of calcium, which leads to increased force of contraction (positive inotropic effect), as well as much of its toxicity. Digoxin also has vagotonic effects that result in decreased AV-nodal conduction. Unlike digitoxin, which is both longer acting and primarily eliminated through hepatic metabolism, over 80% of digoxin is eliminated unchanged in the urine. *(Hardman et al, pp 862-864)*

234. (B, C, E, F) Aminoglycosides can induce ototoxicity distinguished by both vestibular and auditory dysfunction. Moreover, aminoglycosides accumulate in the proximal tubular cells of the kidney, resulting in a defect in renal concentrating ability and reduced glomerular filtration after several days. Impairment of renal function is almost always reversible. Aminoglycosides can inhibit prejunctional release of acetylcholine and reduce postsynaptic sensitivity to the transmitter, resulting in neuromuscular blockade when administered intraperitoneally or intrapleurally. Streptomycin, in particular, may damage the optic nerve. *(Hardman et al, pp 1110–1113)*

235. (C) Local anesthetics exist in solution in uncharged base and charged cationic forms. The base diffuses across the nerve sheath and membrane and then reequilibrates within the axoplasm. It is intracellular penetration of the cation into and attachment to a receptor at a site within the sodium channel that leads to inhibition of sodium conductance and ultimate conduction blockade. Bupivacaine is typical of amide-linked local anesthetics with high anesthetic potency and long duration of action (class III). Procaine is typical of class I agents that are ester-linked and have low anesthetic potency and short duration of action. Important features of group III compounds include: (1) high degree of lipid solubility or high partition coefficient that aid in penetration of the drug, (2) high degree of protein binding that aids in attachment of the drug once it has penetrated the cell, and (3) pKa closer to pH = 7.4 so that more of the drug is in the un-ionized form and is free to penetrate the membrane. Ester-linked anesthetics, such as procaine, are rapidly metabolized by pseudocholinesterases, whereas bupivacaine is slowly degraded by hepatic enzymes. *(Hardman et al, pp 331–339)*

236. (A, D, F, G) Angiotensin-converting enzyme (ACE) inhibitors inhibit the metabolism of angiotensin I to angiotensin II. Angiotensin II is one of the most potent endogenous vasoconstrictors. Therefore, ACE inhibitors lower blood pressure and are effective in treating CHF via a decrease in peripheral resistance and by lowering afterload. Moreover, ACE inhibitors lessen salt and water retention by decreasing the release of aldosterone. One of the most common side effects associated with ACE inhibitors is cough, which is thought to result from an increase in autacoids such as bradykinin. *(Katzung, pp 206-207, 293)*

REFERENCES

Abramowicz M. Drugs for rheumatoid arthritis. *Medical Letter.* 2000;42:57–634.

Hardman JG, Limbird LE, Molinoff PB, Ruddon RW, Gilman AG, eds. *Goodman & Gilman's The Pharmacological Basis of Therapeutics,* 9th ed. New York: McGraw-Hill; 1996.

Katzung BG, ed. *Basic & Clinical Pharmacology,* 7th ed. Stamford, CT: Appleton & Lange; 1998.

SUBSPECIALTY LIST: PHARMACOLOGY

Question Number and Subspecialty

187. Endocrine system
188. Chemotherapeutic agents
189. Cardiovascular and respiratory systems
190. Central and peripheral nervous systems
 Anticonvulsants
191. Chemotherapeutic agents (topical and systemic)
 Antiviral drugs
192. Central and peripheral nervous systems
 Anesthetic agents
193. Central nervous system drugs
194. Antibiotics
195. Kidneys, bladder, fluids, and electrolytes
196. Kidneys, bladder, fluids, and electrolytes
 Diuretics
197. General principles
198. Cardiovascular and respiratory systems
199. Kidney, bladder, fluids, and electrolytes
 Diuretics
200. General principles
201. Chemotherapeutic agents
202. Blood and blood-forming organs
203. Central and peripheral nervous systems
204. Endocrine system
205. Cardiovascular and respiratory systems
206. Analgesics, nonnarcotics
207. Anticoagulants
208. Endocrine system
209. Central nervous system drugs
210. Central nervous system drugs
211. Cardiovascular and respiratory systems
212. Immunosuppressive drugs

213. Central and peripheral nervous systems (mood and behavior)
214. Cardiovascular and respiratory systems
215. Kidney, bladder, fluids, and electrolytes
Diuretics
216. Chemotherapeutic agents
Antibacterial drugs
217. Endocrine system
218. Chemotherapeutic agents
219. General principles
220. Blood and blood-forming organs
221. Central nervous system drugs
222. Cardiovascular and respiratory systems
223. Cardiovascular and respiratory systems
224. Cardiovascular and respiratory systems
225. Antineoplastic and immunosuppressive agents
226. Antineoplastic and immunosuppressive agents
227. Antineoplastic and immunosuppressive agents
228. Antineoplastic and immunosuppressive agents
229. Endocrine system
230. Endocrine system
231. Endocrine system
232. Endocrine system
233. Cardiovascular and respiratory systems
234. Chemotherapeutic agents
Antibacterial drugs
235. Central and peripheral nervous system, local anesthetics
236. Cardiovascular and respiratory systems

Physiology

Andreas Carl, MD, PhD

DIRECTIONS (Questions 237 through 262): Each of the numbered items or incomplete statements in this section is followed by answers or by completions of the statement. Select the ONE lettered answer or completion that is BEST in each case.

237. Stimulation of the sympathetic fibers to the heart most likely will

(A) increase myocardial blood flow through an increase in local metabolism
(B) decrease myocardial blood flow by vasoconstriction of endocardial arteries
(C) decrease myocardial blood flow because of increased afterload
(D) not affect myocardial blood flow, since there is little innervation of the blood vessels of the heart
(E) not affect myocardial blood flow because of autoregulatory mechanisms

238. If systolic pressure is 120 mm Hg, diastolic pressure is 90 mm Hg, right atrial pressure is 0 mm Hg, cardiac output is 5 L/min, and stroke volume is 50 mL, then which of the following values is correct?

(A) Mean systemic arterial pressure is 110 mm Hg.
(B) Total peripheral vascular resistance is 20 mm Hg/L per min.
(C) Pulse pressure is 100 mm Hg.
(D) Heart rate is 72/bpm.
(E) Stroke work is 6000 mm Hg/mL.

239. A local anesthetic causes transmission to first become depressed in the nerve's

(A) A α fibers
(B) A β fibers
(C) A δ fibers
(D) B fibers
(E) C fibers

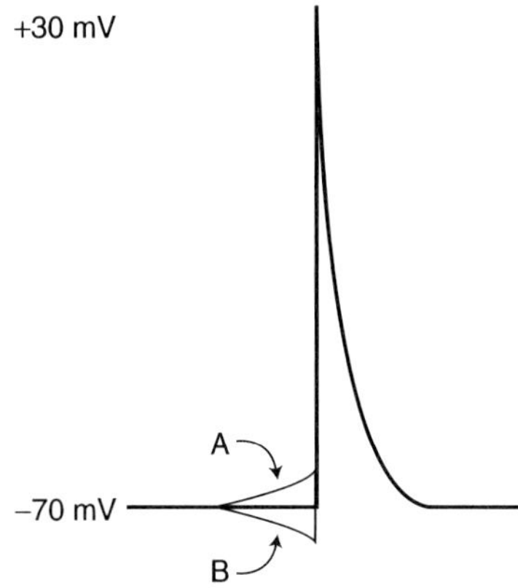

240. The action potential shown above recorded at the soma of a spinal motor neuron after stimulation of a ventral root is

(A) preceded by an excitatory postsynaptic potential (EPSP)
(B) preceded by an inhibiting postsynaptic potential (IPSP)
(C) evoked only after multiple stimuli
(D) unaffected by blockage of synaptic transmission
(E) graded in amplitude

241. Primary adrenal insufficiency (Addison's disease) is frequently associated with hyperpigmentation of the skin. This is most likely due to

(A) increased photosensitivity associated with decreased cortisol
(B) increased melanin deposition secondary to hyperkalemia
(C) pleotropic effects of ACTH
(D) increased levels of serum tyrosine in the low cortisol state
(E) none of the above

242. Patients suffering with Graves' disease have circulating autoimmune antibodies that mimic the effects of TSH. Symptoms of this condition would be expected to include

(A) obesity
(B) cold intolerance
(C) hyporeflexia
(D) tachycardia
(E) constipation

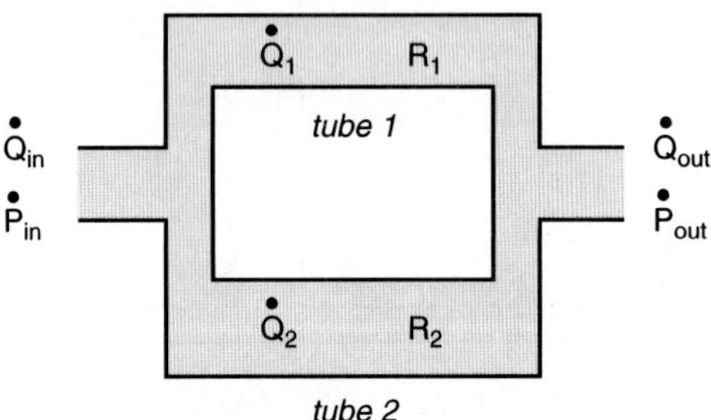

243. In the figure above, two nondistensible tubes (tube 1 and tube 2) are arranged in parallel. Flow in ($\dot{Q}_{in}$) equals flow out ($\dot{Q}_{out}$). The pressure in (P_{in}) is initially higher than the pressure out (P_{out}). The resistance in tube 1 (R_1) is greater than the resistance in tube 2 (R_2). The resistance of the entire system (R_T) is represented as follows:

$$R_T = (P_{in} - P_{out})/\dot{Q}_{in}$$

$\dot{Q}_1$ and $\dot{Q}_2$ are flows in tubes 1 and 2, respectively. Which of the following statements is true?

(A) $\dot{Q}_{in} = (\dot{Q}_1 + \dot{Q}_2)$
(B) $R_T = R_1 + R_2$
(C) P_{in} in tube 1 is greater than P_{in} in tube 2
(D) $\dot{Q}_1 = \dot{Q}_2$
(E) flow will continue through tube 1 only when P_{out} equals P_{in}

244. The figure below is a schematic representation of force developed during isometric contraction of cat papillary muscle. Which pair of drugs would most likely elicit this response?

Drug A **Drug B**

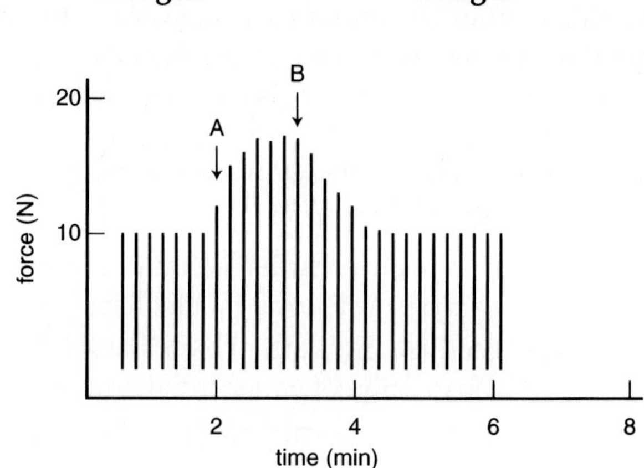

	Drug A	Drug B
(A)	norepinephrine	propranolol
(B)	epinephrine	phenoxybenzamine
(C)	isoproterenol	phenoxybenzamine
(D)	acetylcholine	atropine
(E)	atropine	epinephrine

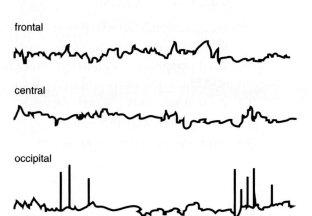

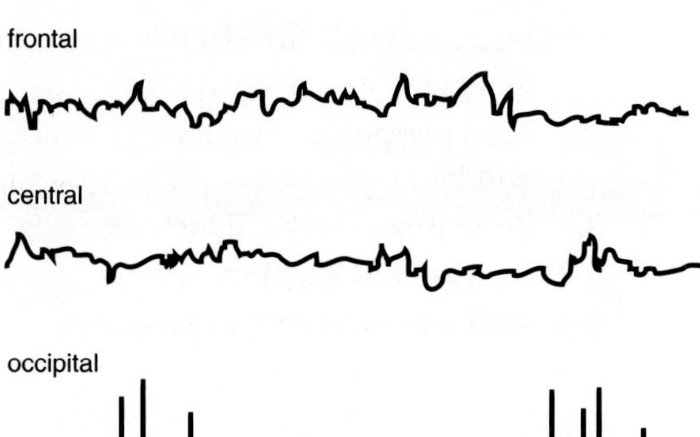

245. Pontogeniculooccipital spikes shown in the EEG at the bottom of the facing page are most closely associated with

(A) arousal
(B) slow-wave sleep
(C) paradoxical sleep
(D) epileptic seizures
(E) painful stimuli

246. In a normal individual, 15 mg of Evans blue (a substance that rapidly binds to plasma proteins) is injected intravenously, and a blood sample is drawn 10 minutes later. The concentration of dye in plasma of this sample is 5 μg/mL, and the hematocrit (corrected for trapped plasma and whole body differences) is 40%. The person's blood volume is

(A) 1.25 L
(B) 3.00 L
(C) 5.00 L
(D) 10.00 L
(E) 12.50 L

247. The structure and effects of which of the following substances most closely resemble those of growth hormone?

(A) somatomedin C
(B) epidermal growth factor
(C) thyroid-stimulating hormone
(D) human chorionic gonadotropin
(E) human chorionic somatomammotropin

248. Temporary occlusion of both common carotid arteries is promptly accompanied by

(A) vasodilation throughout the peripheral circulation
(B) an increase in the number of impulses from the carotid sinus nerve
(C) an increase in venous capacity
(D) an increase in arterial pressure
(E) a decrease in heart rate

H_3C OH H H H HO

249. In normal adult men, the major source of the steroid hormone shown above is provided by

(A) secretion from Leydig's cells in the testes
(B) secretion from Sertoli's cells in the testes
(C) the action of aromatase on circulating androgens
(D) the action of aromatase on circulating estrone
(E) release from the inner layers of the adrenal cortex

250. Tumors of acidophilic cells in the anterior pituitary of adults are most likely to lead to

(A) dwarfism
(B) acromegaly
(C) Cushing's syndrome
(D) gigantism
(E) adrenogenital syndrome

251. The most active form of thyroid hormone in the stimulation of oxygen use is

(A) thyroxine
(B) thyroglobulin
(C) triiodothyronine
(D) reverse triiodothyronine
(E) monoiodotyrosine

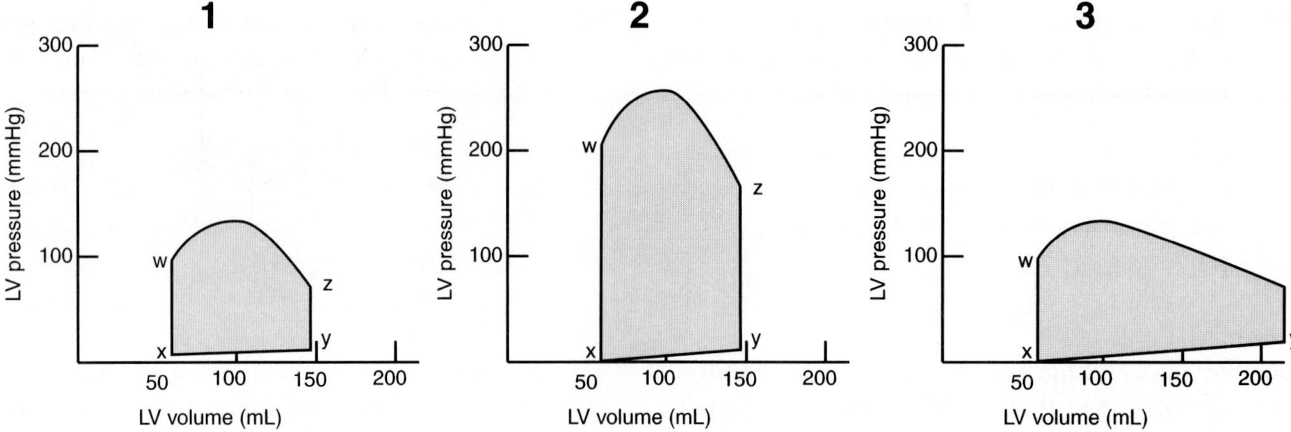

Figure for use with questions 253 and 254.

252. In the normal heart, the major source of energy for oxidative metabolism is

(A) glucose
(B) lactate
(C) fatty acids
(D) pyruvate
(E) amino acids

Above are illustrated three left-ventricular pressure-volume loops. PV loop 1 represents a normal, healthy adult at rest. PV loop 2 develops a mean arterial pressure (MAP) that is twice as high as that in PV loop 1 but with the same stroke volume (SV). PV loop 3 has the same MAP as PV loop 1 but has twice the SV.

253. Which of the following statements about the external work of the left ventricle with each beat (stroke work) is correct?

(A) The stroke work performed in either PV loop 2 or 3 is double that in PV loop 1.
(B) The stroke work performed in PV loop 2 is twice that in PV loop 1 but three times that in PV loop 3.
(C) The stroke work performed in PV loop 2 is twice that in PV loop 3.
(D) The stroke work performed in PV loop 2 is one half that of PV loop 3.
(E) The stroke work performed in all three PV loops is the same.

254. Which of the following statements about the left-ventricular myocardial oxygen consumption ($LVM\dot{V}_{O_2}$) or myocardial efficiency is correct?

(A) The $LVM\dot{V}_{O_2}$ for PV loop 2 is greater than that for PV loop 3.
(B) The $LVM\dot{V}_{O_2}$ for PV loop 1 is greater than that for PV loop 3.
(C) The $LVM\dot{V}_{O_2}$ for PV loops 2 and 3 is the same.
(D) The $LVM\dot{V}_{O_2}$ for all three PV loops is the same.
(E) The myocardial efficiency for all three PV loops is the same.

255. In myelinated nerve fibers, action potentials are not conducted continuously down the axon but "jump" from node to node. This process of saltatory conduction is characterized by which of the following?

(A) Conduction is considerably lower than that in unmyelinated fibers.
(B) The increased capacitance of myelinated fibers results in more rapid repolarization.
(C) Depolarization at nodes only results in a much smaller expenditure of metabolic energy in reestablishing sodium and potassium gradients.
(D) Saltatory conduction is more efficient, as it carries with it no requirement for ion flow through axoplasm or extracellular fluid.

(E) Conduction of the nerve impulse is accomplished almost entirely by sequential changes in voltage-gated potassium channels.

256. Choreiform movements in humans are most likely to be associated with degeneration of the

(A) subthalamic nuclei
(B) nigrostriatal tracts
(C) cerebellum
(D) lateral spinothalamic tracts
(E) caudate nucleus

257. The stimulation of electrodes implanted in the medial forebrain bundle of experimental animals is most likely to lead to

(A) repeated self-stimulation
(B) rage reactions
(C) avoidance reactions
(D) temporary paralysis
(E) repeated turning movements

258. Insulin deficiency leads to

(A) decreased glucose uptake by the brain
(B) inhibition of exercise-mediated increase in glucose uptake by skeletal muscle
(C) decreased catabolism of proteins
(D) increased glucagon secretion
(E) increased entry of potassium into cells

259. Many neurons in the basal ganglia are observed to begin to discharge

(A) in association with somatosensory stimulation
(B) at the onset of acoustic stimulation
(C) before the onset of slow movements
(D) at a low rate that is independent of motor activity
(E) during visual accommodation

260. The introduction of cold water into one ear may cause giddiness and nausea. The primary cause of this effect of temperature is

(A) temporary immobilization of otoliths
(B) decreased movement of ampullar cristae
(C) increased discharge rate in vestibular afferents
(D) decreased discharge rate in vestibular afferents
(E) convection currents in endolymph

261. Reflex sneezing is most likely to be initiated by

(A) inhibition of olfactory receptor neurons
(B) stimulation of olfactory receptor neurons
(C) stimulation of nasal trigeminal nerve endings
(D) stimulation of gustatory receptors
(E) stimulation of efferent fibers from olfactory striae

262. A patient comes to your office stating that he has difficulty hearing, especially with his right ear. You perform the Weber test by placing a vibrating tuning fork on top of the patient's skull. With a surprised look the patient states that he hears the sound more clearly with his right ear. You conclude

(A) the patient has conductive hearing loss on the left side
(B) the patient has conductive hearing loss on the right side
(C) the patient has sensory hearing loss on the left side
(D) the patient has sensory hearing loss on the right side
(E) no conclusion can be drawn unless a Rinne test is performed

DIRECTIONS (Questions 263 through 269): Each group of items in this section consists of lettered headings followed by a set of numbered words or phrases. For each numbered word or phrase, select the ONE lettered heading that is most closely associated with it. Each lettered heading may be selected once, more than once, or not at all.

Questions 263 through 265

For each of the functions listed below, choose the region of the hypothalamus or pituitary gland that animal studies have shown to be involved in its control.

(A) ventromedial nucleus of the hypothalamus
(B) suprachiasmatic nucleus of the hypothalamus
(C) posterior lobe of the pituitary gland
(D) intermediate lobe of the pituitary gland
(E) anterior lobe of the pituitary gland

263. Circadian rhythms

264. Satiety

265. Milk-ejection reflex

Questions 266 through 269

For each of the numbered alterations listed below, identify the determinant of cardiac performance (A–E) on which it exerts its most profound influence.

(A) end-diastolic volume
(B) heart rate
(C) aortic pressure
(D) inotropic state
(E) pulmonary artery diastolic pressure

266. Parasympathetic discharge

267. Peripheral vasoconstriction

268. Ventricular noncompliance

269. Increased venous return

DIRECTIONS (Questions 270 through 278): Different regions of a juxtamedullary nephron are indicated by letter choices (A through G) on the illustration below. Following the illustration are several numbered descriptions or statements. For each numbered description or statement, select the ONE lettered item that is most closely associated with it. For this set of questions, letter choices may be used once, more than once, or not at all.

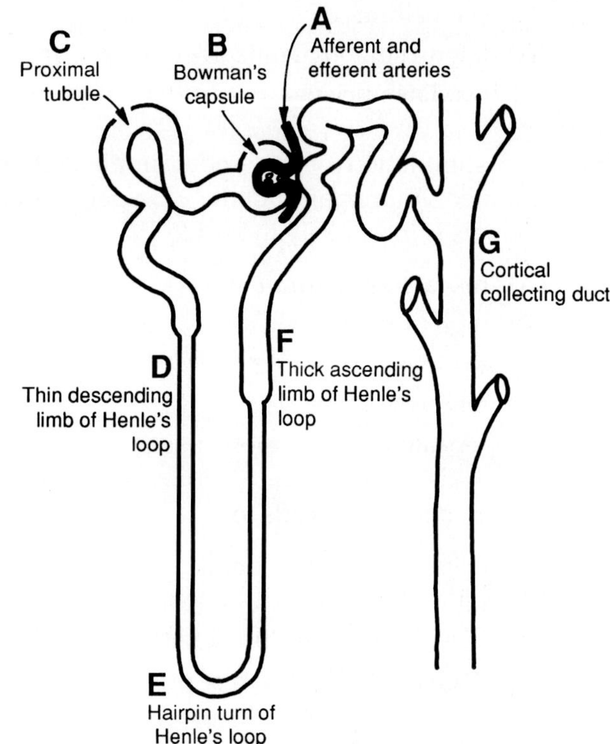

270. Principal site of aldosterone action on sodium reabsorption

271. Site of action at which autoregulation mediates its effect

272. Principal site of potassium secretion

273. Primary location of D-glucose reabsorption

274. Primary site of action of antidiuretic hormone (ADH, vasopressin) on water permeability

275. Location of most intercalated cells with proton-secreting ATPase activity for acidification of the urine

276. Location with maximal osmolality

277. Location with very low permeability to water at all times in a normal, healthy adult

278. Site of reabsorption of 65% of filtered sodium

DIRECTIONS (Questions 279 through 283): Lettered headings (A through I) are followed by a set of five numbered descriptions or conditions. For each numbered condition select the ONE lettered heading that is most closely associated with it. Lettered headings may be used once, more than once, or not at all.

(A) increased exchange vessel hydrostatic pressure ($\uparrow P_c$)
(B) decreased exchange vessel hydrostatic pressure ($\downarrow P_c$)
(C) increased interstitial hydrostatic pressure ($\uparrow P_{isf}$)
(D) decreased interstitial hydrostatic pressure ($\downarrow P_{isf}$)
(E) increased plasma colloidal osmotic pressure ($\uparrow \pi_{pl}$)
(F) decreased plasma colloidal osmotic pressure ($\downarrow \pi_{pl}$)
(G) increased interstitial colloidal osmotic pressure ($\uparrow \pi_{isf}$)
(H) decreased interstitial colloidal osmotic pressure ($\downarrow \pi_{isf}$)
(I) decreased lymphatic flow ($\downarrow J_{lymph}$)

279. Responsible for local edema secondary to venous occlusion or obstruction

280. Responsible for mobilization of some of the interstitial fluid into blood in victims of severe hemorrhage

281. Responsible for edema in individuals on a protein-deficient diet

282. Responsible for edema following prolonged infection with filarial worms *Wuchereria bancrofti* or *Brugia malayi*

283. Responsible for the myxedema of hypothyroidism

DIRECTIONS (Questions 284 and 285): Each of the numbered items or incomplete statements in this section is followed by answers or by completions of the statement. Select ONE (or MORE) lettered answer(s) or completion(s) for each case.

284. Which of the following are important mechanisms for body temperature regulation in persons exposed to extreme cold? (SELECT 3)

(A) vasodilation of the skin
(B) conscious behavioral adjustments
(C) increased heat production resulting from circulating epinephrine and norepinephrine
(D) increased heat production resulting from thyroxine production
(E) due to activation of prefrontal cortical neurons

285. Which of the following are important compensatory mechanisms in hemorrhagic shock? (SELECT 3)

(A) tachycardia
(B) venoconstriction
(C) decreased peripheral vascular resistance
(D) loss of fluid from the interstitial space
(E) formation of angiotensin II

ANSWERS AND EXPLANATIONS

237. (A) Stimulation of the sympathetic nerves to the heart will most likely increase heart rate and contractility and thus increase myocardial metabolism. Through mechanisms as yet unknown, changes in myocardial blood flow appear to parallel closely those changes in local metabolism. Thus, even though sympathetic stimulation may tend to cause direct vasoconstriction as a result of α effects in the myocardial blood vessels, the indirect vasodilation accompanying increased metabolism is dominant. This effect is independent of afterload and overrides any autoregulatory mechanisms. *(Berne and Levy, pp 481–482)*

238. (B) Mean systemic arterial pressure (P_a) is the time-averaged pressure in a cardiac cycle. It is the area under the arterial pressure curve divided by the time of the cardiac cycle and may be estimated as follows: $P_a = P_d + \frac{1}{3}(P_s - P_d)$, where P_d is diastolic and P_s is systolic pressure. Thus, in the example given in the question, $P_a = 90 + \frac{1}{3}(120 - 90) = 100$ mm Hg, not 110 mm Hg. Total peripheral vascular resistance = $(P_a - P_{ra})/\dot{Q}$, where P_{ra} is right atrial pressure and $\dot{Q}$ is cardiac output. Resistance = (100 − 0)/5 = 20 mm Hg/L per minute. The pulse pressure = $(P_s - P_d) = 120 - 90 = 30$ mm Hg. Heart rate equals cardiac output/stroke volume = (5 L/min)/50 mL = 100/min. Stroke work is the product of stroke volume times P_a, or 50 mL × 100 mm Hg = 500 mm Hg mL. *(Berne and Levy, pp 419–422)*

239. (E) Different types of nerve fibers may be classified according to their conduction velocities. This classification is readily accomplished by extracellular recording of compound action potentials from, for example, the dorsal root fibers. The slowest conducting fibers are the C fibers, which have a conduction velocity of about 0.5 to 2.0 m/sec. These fibers are the most sensitive to local anesthetics but are the least sensitive to pressure or hypoxia. *(Ganong, pp 56–57)*

240. (D) Motor neurons in the anterior horn of the spinal cord send their axons into the ventral roots. Stimulation of the ventral roots produces an action potential that is propagated both orthodromically toward the neuromuscular junction and antidromically toward the anterior horn. The earliest response recorded at the soma of the motor neuron is therefore the all-or-none antidromically propagated action potential, which is not affected by a blockage of synaptic transmission. *(Ganong, p 53)*

241. (C) A portion of the sequence of ACTH is homologous to the hormone α-melanocyte stimulating factor (α-MSH). It is hypothesized, therefore, that the extremely high levels of ACTH achieved in primary adrenal insufficiency exert a direct pigmenting effect through the action of this hormone's α-MSH portion on melanocytes. Thus, hyperpigmentation appears to be due to a pleotropic effect of ACTH. *(Guyton, pp 967–968)*

242. (D) Hyperthyroidism (from Graves' disease or any other cause) is associated with an elevated state of metabolic activity. Its symptoms, therefore, include weight loss, sleep loss, heat intolerance, diarrhea, tachycardia, and hyperreflexia, among others. *(Guyton, pp 948, 953)*

243. (A) In the example given in the question, flow through the system occurs when P_{in} exceeds P_{out} and stops when P_{out} is equal to or greater than P_{in}. Since $\dot{Q}_{in}$ equals $\dot{Q}_{out}$, then $\dot{Q}_{in} = \dot{Q}_1 + \dot{Q}_2$. R_T in a parallel system is equal to

$$\frac{1}{R_T} = \frac{1}{R_1} + \frac{1}{R_2}$$

Thus, R_T is always less than the resistance in any individual segment of a parallel array. Although the pressure drop is by definition identical in each tube, if the resistance in one tube is higher than that in another, then $\dot{Q}$ will be lower in that respective tube. Accordingly, since $R_2 < R_1$, then $\dot{Q}_1 < \dot{Q}_2$. *(Berne and Levy, pp 406–408)*

244. (A) Myocardial contractility is under the influence of neural control. This fact can be demonstrated in isolated papillary muscle undergoing isometric contraction, as illustrated in the figure that accompanies the question. The sympathetic nervous system can increase contractility, predominantly by the action of β receptors on the myocardial muscle. Parasympathetic input is minimal and, if anything, may decrease contractility. In the figure, norepinephrine (drug A), by its β-receptor-mediated effects, increases contractility and propranolol (drug B), a β blocker, antagonizes this effect. Epinephrine or isoproterenol would also increase contractility, but phenoxybenzamine, an α blocker, would not be expected to antagonize the β effect of either agent. Cholinergic effects of acetylcholine either would not affect this preparation or would decrease contractility. Atropine, in itself, might increase contractility very slightly; however, epinephrine (drug B), even in the presence of atropine, would increase rather than decrease contractility. *(Berne and Levy, pp 392–394)*

245. (C) Pontogeniculooccipital (PGO) spikes are phasic electrical potentials, usually occurring in groups of three to five, that may be recorded in the brain. The potentials originate in the pons and are propagated to the occipital cortex through the lateral geniculate bodies. Under normal circumstances the onset of PGO spikes is closely associated with the onset of paradoxical rapid-eye-movement sleep. The role of PGO spikes in the various physiologic changes that occur during paradoxical sleep has, however, not been fully elucidated. Although the other choices listed in the question may be associated with specific changes in the electrical activity of the nervous system, they are not closely associated with PGO spikes. *(Ganong, p 188)*

246. (C) The dye generally used for measuring plasma volume is Evans blue. By the dilution principle, blood volume equals the quantity of dye injected divided by the concentration of dye dispersed in the fluid drawn. In the individual described in the question, this would be represented as 15 mg/(5 μg/mL) = 3L. Because the dye binds to plasma proteins and thus defines plasma volume, whole blood volume for the person described is represented as follows:

$$\frac{\text{plasma volume}}{(1-\text{hematocrit})} = \frac{3\text{ L}}{1-0.4} = 5\text{ L}$$

The rate of loss of Evans blue was ignored. *(Guyton, p 302)*

247. (E) The structure of human growth hormone closely resembles that of human chorionic somatomammotropin (hCS). Both have a peptide chain of 191 amino acids, of which only 29 differ in the two proteins. Both proteins also resemble prolactin, and it is generally assumed that these proteins evolved from a single ancestral protein. During pregnancy, hCS is secreted in large amounts, and its effects are generally similar to those of growth hormone. *(Ganong, pp 428–429)*

248. (D) Temporary occlusion of both common carotid arteries will decrease vascular pressure within the carotid sinus area. This important peripheral baroreceptor reflex is significant in maintaining relatively constant arterial pressure on a short-term basis. A decrease in pressure will **depress** the number of impulses that travel from the carotid sinus nerve. Because these impulses normally inhibit the central vasoconstrictor area and excite the vagal center, a decrease in impulses will reflexively cause arterial pressure to rise and heart rate and contractility to increase. Virtually the entire circulation will be stimulated to constrict. Venoconstriction will also occur, thus reducing venous capacitance. *(Guyton, pp 213–215)*

249. (C) Aromatase is the enzyme that controls the conversion of testosterone to estradiol. It also catalyzes the formation of estrone from androstenedione. The major proportion of circulating estradiol in adult men is formed directly by aromatization of these circulating androgens. Lesser amounts may be secreted by Leydig and Sertoli cells in the testes and by the adrenal cortex. *(Ganong, pp 407, 420)*

250. (B) Acidophilic cells of the anterior pituitary are those cells that stain with acidic dyes. The major peptide hormones found in cells of this type are growth hormones and prolactin. Tumors of acidophilic cells may lead to excessive secretion of growth hormone, causing gigantism in children and acromegaly in adults. Acromegaly is associated with changes in facial features and enlargement of the hands and feet. Dwarfism may be the result of deficiencies in growth hormone or of growth factors. Cushing's syndrome is caused by excess secretion of glucocorticoids and may result from tumors of ACTH-containing cells in the pituitary. In contrast to the growth-hormone–containing cells, the cells that synthesize ACTH may be chromophobic or basophilic. Adrenogenital syndrome results from excessive adrenal secretion of androgens. *(Ganong, p 379)*

251. (C) The thyroid gland synthesizes and secretes thyroxine (3,5,3′,5′,-tetraiodothyronine, T_4) and 3,5,3′-triiodothyronine (T_3) as well as lesser amounts of reverse triiodothyronine (3,3′,5′-triiodothyronine, RT_3) and monoiodotyrosine. Of these, T_3 is most active in stimulating oxygen consumption in the body, being three to five times as potent as T_4, although it is secreted in smaller amounts. RT_3 and monoiodotyrosine are not active. Thyroglobulin is a glycoprotein of the thyroid gland that plays a major role in the synthesis of thyroid hormones. It is not, however, believed to play a role in the actions of the thyroid hormones. *(Ganong, pp 304–308)*

252. (C) Although the heart is versatile in its use of substrates, more than 60% of myocardial oxygen consumption is derived from free fatty acids. Glucose and lactate are the major carbohydrate sources but make up only 30 to 35% of the total sources for myocardial energy. In the normal heart, pyruvate uptake is very low and oxidation of amino acids provides little input to myocardial energy expenditure. In general, the heart uses the substrate in greatest supply—for example, ketone bodies may be used during diabetic acidosis. However, under normal conditions free fatty acids are the major substrate. *(Berne and Levy, pp 486–487)*

253. (A) Although external left ventricular work for each beat (stroke work) is doubled in both PV loops 2 and 3 compared to that in PV loop 1, their rates of left-ventricular myocardial oxygen consumption ($LVM\dot{V}_{O_2}$) are not increased equally. The myocardial efficiency of pressure work (PV loop 2) is not as high as that for volume work (PV loop 3), and therefore the $LVM\dot{V}_{O_2}$ is higher for PV loop 2 than it is for PV loop 3. *(Guyton, pp 113–115; West, p 256)*

254. (A) For each beat, the stroke work performed by the left ventricle could be accurately measured from the area within the pressure-volume loop. A more convenient estimate can be made by multiplying the mean arterial pressure (MAP) developed by the stroke volume (SV) ejected (pressure times volume is equivalent to force times distance, the physical definition of work). It should be evident that by this estimate, or by visual inspection of the areas illustrated, that there is a twofold increase in stroke work if MAP is doubled while SV remains the same (PV loop 2) or if MAP is the same but SV is doubled (PV loop 3). *(Guyton, pp 113–115; West, p 256)*

255. (C) Saltatory conduction does have ion movements through axoplasm and extracellular fluid (otherwise no current flow would be possible). Saltatory conduction is 5 to 50 times faster than conduction in unmyelinated fibers. The fact that depolarization occurs only at nodes results in a much smaller net movement of ions for a given transmission distance. Thus, less metabolic energy is required to reestablish ion gradients between action potentials. Myelination provides excellent insulation and greatly diminishes the total membrane capacitance. Fewer ions have to move in order to produce a depolarization. Repolarization occurs as soon as the sodium channels close and before the bulk of the potassium channels have had time to open. Therefore, propagation is accomplished almost entirely by sequential changes in sodium conduction, with little need for contribution by potassium channels. *(Guyton, pp 68–70)*

256. (E) Huntington's disease in humans is characterized by the degeneration of the caudate nuclei. This is associated with the appearance of disorganized, choreiform movements. Damage to other regions of the nervous system involved in the control of movements may produce other forms of movement disorders. For example, damage to the subthalamic nuclei may result in sudden, intense, and involuntary movements, termed ballistic movements. Degeneration of the nigrostriatal dopaminergic system characterizes Parkinson's disease, which is associated with akinesia and tremor. Lesions of the cerebellum may result in the incoordination of voluntary movements, termed ataxia. The spinothalamic tracts convey sensory information to the thalamus, and their loss does not produce choreiform movements. *(Ganong, pp 206–207)*

257. (A) Experiments have been performed in which stimulating electrodes were implanted in certain regions of the nervous system of rats and the animals were allowed to control the stimulus by pressing a bar that triggered the application of the stimulating current. Electrodes implanted in the medial forebrain bundle, as well as in areas of the frontal cortex, caudate nucleus, ventral tegmentum, and the septal nuclei, frequently led to repeated self-stimulation by the animals. The neural circuits that subserve this self-stimulation behavior have been considered to constitute an endogenous reward system within the brain. Rage reactions and avoidance reactions may be induced by stimulation of other parts of the CNS, such as regions of the hypothalamus. Temporary paralysis or repeated turning movements are not normally observed on stimulation of the medial forebrain bundle. *(Ganong, pp 249–250)*

258. (D) One of the effects of insulin is to inhibit the secretion of glucagon from the α cells in pancreatic islets. Thus, a deficiency of insulin, such as occurs in diabetes mellitus, is associated with increased secretion of glucagon, which contributes to the observed hyperglycemia. The increased levels of glucagon are also apparently due to increased glucagon release by cells in the gastrointestinal tract. Although insulin deficiency may cause coma from a variety of causes, insulin does not control glucose uptake in the brain. In insulin deficiency, an increase in the rate of uptake of glucose into skeletal muscle may still be observed with exercise, and the rate of catabolism of proteins is increased. The latter effect contributes to increased gluconeogenesis in the liver. *(Ganong, pp 324–328)*

259. (C) The basal ganglia constitute part of the extrapyramidal system concerned with the control of movement. Many neurobiologists believe that the basal ganglia play an important role in the initiation of voluntary movement. Consistent with such a notion is the experimental observation that unit activity in the basal ganglia is associated with movements and that many units start to fire before the onset of slow, sustained movements. Basal ganglia units are less likely to discharge during rapid movements. The discharge of units in basal ganglia has not been linked to somatosensory stimulation, acoustic stimulation, or visual accommodation. *(Ganong, pp 204–207)*

260. (E) Water that is either higher or lower than body temperature and that is introduced into the external auditory meatus may set up convection currents within the endolymph of the inner ear. These currents may result in the stimulation of the semicircular canals by causing movements of the ampullar cristae. Conflicting, different information from the right and left sides, in turn, may result in vertigo and nausea. Decreased movement or immobilization of the otoliths or of the ampullar cristae are not caused by such changes in temperature. Furthermore, changes in the discharge rate of vestibular afferents, which must occur with caloric stimulation, are most likely to be caused by the changes in the activity of the receptors rather than being a direct response of the afferents to changes in temperature. *(Ganong, pp 175–176)*

261. (C) The olfactory mucous membranes are rich in trigeminal nerve endings, which may respond to nasal irritants and initiate a variety of reflex reactions that include sneezing and lacrimation. Neither olfactory nor gustatory receptors nor the efferent pathways to the olfactory bulb are believed to be involved in the initiation of such reflex responses. The activation of trigeminal nerve endings by certain olfactory stimuli may, however, contribute to the characteristics of certain odors. *(Ganong, pp 177–180)*

262. (B) Conduction deafness and nerve deafness (sensory hearing loss) can be distinguished by simple tests using a tuning fork.

The Weber test is performed by placing a vibrating tuning fork on top of the patient's skull. If conductive hearing loss is present, the sound will be perceived louder on the deaf side due to the masking effect of environmental noise and nerve cell sensitization. If sensory hearing loss is present, the sound will be perceived louder on the healthy side. The Rinne test is performed by placing a vibrating tuning fork on the patient's mastoid process until the sound cannot be heard anymore. Normal subjects and patients with partial sensory hearing loss will hear the sound again if the still vibrating tuning fork is held in the air next to the ear (air conduction is better than bone conduction). However, patients with conductive hearing loss will not be able to hear this sound. *(Ganong, p 172).*

263–265. (263–B, 264–A, 265–C) The suprachiasmatic nuclei in the hypothalamus play a central role in the control of the circadian rhythms. Lesions in these nuclei disrupt the approximately 24-hour cycle that can be measured in the circulating concentrations of hormones and in the activity patterns of animals. Input to cells in the suprachiasmatic nuclei from the retina serves to entrain the endogenous circadian rhythm to the daily light–dark cycle.

Stimulation of ventromedial nuclei in the hypothalamus prevents feeding behavior in experimental animals. Lesions in this region result in obesity. For these reasons this region has been denoted as a "satiety center," and evidence suggests that the center may function by inhibiting the activity of neurons in the nearby hypothalamic feeding center. How peripheral and central mechanisms interact to control feeding behavior has yet to be elucidated, however.

The milk-ejection reflex is under the control of oxytocin, a neurohormone that is secreted within the posterior pituitary. The firing rate of oxytocin-containing neurons may be markedly enhanced by various stimuli, including the stimulation of touch receptors on the breasts. In lactating women, released oxytocin acts on myoepithelial cells in the ducts of the breasts, resulting in milk ejection. Oxytocin also has effects on uterine smooth muscle. *(Ganong, pp 224–226, 235)*

266–269. (266–B, 267–C, 268–A, 269–A) Parasympathetic discharge (mediated by acetylcholine) exerts a profound slowing effect on the heart by hyperpolarizing cells of the S-A node. A small effect on atrial contraction is also noted. Peripheral vasoconstriction will increase aortic pressure—i.e., left ventricular afterload. A noncompliant ventricle is unable to fill completely, and end-diastolic volume will be decreased. Increased venous return results in increased ventricular filling, i.e., increased end-diastolic volume. *(Berne and Levy, pp 366–367, 379, 394)*

270. (G) Most of sodium reabsorption occurs in the proximal tubule (about two thirds of filtered load) by an aldosterone-independent mechanism. Similarly, all the remaining sodium filtered, except for a few percent, is reabsorbed by an aldosterone-independent mechanism as well as in the thick, ascending limb of Henle's loop and in the initial part of the distal tubule. The last few percent of filtered sodium left is subject to control by aldosterone acting on principal cells ("light" cells) of the last third of the distal tubule and in the collecting ducts. Aldosterone increases sodium reabsorption by principal cells both through an increase in luminal (apical) permeability to sodium and through an increase in the basolateral membrane sodium, potassium-ATPase activity. *(Guyton, pp 344–345)*

271. (A) The term autoregulation as applied to most organs refers to a regulatory system that attempts to maintain a normal or near-normal rate of blood flow despite changes in perfusion pressure (e.g., a change in arterial blood pressure). This is also true for the kidney; however, in addition there is a second kind of autoregulation, namely autoregulation of the glomerular filtration rate. Both are flow rates and both are regulated at the same site: the afferent arterioles of the glomeruli. If arterial blood pressure increases, one might expect to find an increase in blood flow and glomerular filtration. However, because of autoregulation, the afferent arteriolar resistance is increased, which tends to keep both the blood flow and filtration at normal levels. Similarly, if arterial blood pressure decreases, there is a decrease in afferent arteriolar resistance to minimize a fall in blood flow and glomerular filtration. *(Vander, pp 33–37)*

272. (G) The average diet contains a substantial amount of potassium. Normally the amount of potassium excreted each day equals the amount taken in. Most of the potassium that is filtered by the glomeruli is reabsorbed. Indeed, the majority of the potassium excreted is not merely potassium that failed to be reabsorbed but is what was secreted into the tubular lumen, particularly by the collecting ducts. This potassium secretion is mainly from principal cells ("light" cells) located in the late part of the distal tubule and particularly in the cortical collecting ducts, where these cells make up about two thirds of the total epithelial cell population. Thus, most potassium in the urine comes mainly from cortical collecting duct principal cells by secretion. *(Guyton, pp 375–377)*

273. (C) D-glucose and L-amino acids are nutrients that are normally completely reabsorbed by sodium-dependent cotransport systems in the proximal tubule. The uptake of the glucose (even against a concentration gradient) is coupled with the uptake of sodium (moving down its concentration gradient). Thus, both are transported across the luminal (apical) border into the proximal tubule cells. Once inside the cell, the glucose must cross the basolateral membrane before it can be reabsorbed into the blood of the peritubular capillaries. This latter transport across the basolateral membrane involves facilitated diffusion by a different carrier protein. In the normal individual, essentially all the glucose is reabsorbed proximally. In diabetics with hyperglycemia, the filtered load of glucose may be so great as to saturate the transport capacity of the glucose reabsorptive system (exceeds the transport maximum, or T_{max}). Once the transport system is saturated, continued filtration of glucose results in glycosuria. *(Guyton, pp 337–338)*

274. (G) The juxtamedullary nephrons generate a medullary hyperosmolality (by a mechanism involving countercurrent flow in Henle's loop). In the presence of medullary hyperosmolality, all that is necessary to regulate water reabsorption is to control the permeability of the collecting ducts to water. With increased permeability, more water is reabsorbed (by osmosis) into the medullary interstitial fluid space. With decreased permeability, less water can cross (and is excreted). Antidiuretic hormone (ADH, vasopressin) is a peptide hormone that increases collecting duct (both cortical and medullary collecting ducts) permeability to water. The mechanism is thought to involve the insertion of water channels into the luminal (apical) border of the collecting duct cells. Thus, as more water is reabsorbed, less is excreted (hence the term "antidiuretic" hormone). On the other hand, when the body needs to increase water excretion (a water diuresis), all that is needed is a fall in ADH secretion. In the absence of ADH, or the presence of low levels, the water channels detach from the membrane and become internalized into the cytoplasm. *(Guyton, pp 356–358)*

275. (G) For a normal individual on an average diet (that contains meat), the body has a daily net gain of about 70 milliequivalents of acid. To counter this continuous tendency toward metabolic acidosis, it is essential to maintain a normal extracellular fluid pH by acidification of the urine (so that net acid production equals net acid excretion). Beginning in the late distal tubule and particularly in the collecting ducts are intercalated cells ("brown" or "dark" cells) that secrete H^+ by primary active transport. This secretion utilizes an electrogenic proton-secreting ATPase located in the luminal (apical) border. Intercalated cells are capable of transporting H^+ against a considerable concentration gradient (up to 900:1). The source of the H^+ is from hydration of CO_2 to carbonic acid (catalyzed by carbonic anhydrase), which dissociates into

HCO_3^- and H^+. For each H^+ secreted the body gains an HCO_3^-. *(Guyton, pp 393–395)*

276. **(E)** An important requisite condition that allows antidiuretic hormone (ADH) to regulate renal reabsorption of water in the collecting ducts is the establishment of a high medullary interstitial osmolality (hyperosmolality) relative to plasma entering the kidney. The descending and ascending limbs of Henle's loop participate in a countercurrent multiplier system that increases tubular and interstitial osmolality as the loop descends deeper into the renal medulla. The hairpin turn of the loop in juxtamedullary nephrons has the deepest penetration and the highest osmolality (maximum of 1200 to 1400 mOsm/L). About one half of the hyperosmolality is due to increased accumulation of NaCl and the remainder is due to increased urea. *(Guyton, pp 352–356)*

277. **(F)** Areas of the nephron that always have low or no permeability to water independently of antidiuretic hormone (ADH) presence or absence are: the thin ascending limb of Henle's loop, the thick ascending limb, and the distal convoluted tubule. Since, of these, only the thick ascending limb is offered as a choice, this is the correct answer. The thick ascending limb of Henle's loop is impermeable to water, but permeable to NaCl (responsible for about 25% of reabsorption of the total filtered load). The impermeability of this segment to water is a constant condition in any normally functioning nephron under all circumstances. Unlike the collecting ducts, this lack of permeability to water is not altered by hormones (ADH has no effect here) or by any other physiological mechanisms; it is always impermeable to water. *(Guyton, pp 356–357)*

278. **(C)** The proximal tubule reabsorbs the bulk (about two thirds) of filtered NaCl and water by a virtually completely isoosmotic mechanism. That is, both the NaCl concentration and the osmolality remain at the normal levels (same as in plasma arriving by renal arterial flow) throughout the length of the proximal tubule. That the proximal tubule can reabsorb so much sodium with no change in tubular fluid osmolality indicates that reabsorption of water there must easily follow sodium and in proportion (the reabsorption of water there is dependent on and coupled with the active reabsorption of sodium salts and other solutes). Proximal tubule cells are relatively thick and contain numerous mitochondria. They have the appearance of highly metabolic cells able to support large and rapid active transport systems. *(Guyton, pp 337–338)*

279. **(A)** The four Starling forces (actually pressures) are: capillary hydrostatic pressure (P_c), capillary colloidal osmotic pressure (π_{pl}), interstitial hydrostatic pressure (P_{isf}), and interstitial colloidal osmotic pressure (π_{isf}). Fluid movements associated with these forces in the microcirculation are filtration, absorption, and lymph flow. There is normally a kind of balance operating across the endothelium of exchange vessels (capillaries and venules). In some parts of the microcirculation the forces for filtration predominate (usually considered to be the case at the arteriolar ends of exchange vessels). In other parts, the forces for absorption of fluid back into the blood predominate (probably at the venular ends). Generally filtration is slightly greater than absorption, and fluid usually does not continuously accumulate in the interstitial fluid (ISF) space because of lymphatic flow. Hence, in normal circumstances, filtration rate equals absorption rate plus lymphatic flow rate. Changes in lymphatic function or in P_c, π_{pl}, or π_{isf} can result in considerable shifts in fluid volume between plasma and ISF. Primary changes in P_{isf} are minor and rarely have much effect. An increase in exchange vessel hydrostatic pressure ($\uparrow P_c$) is a common cause of edema. Venous occlusion from outside pressures or venous obstruction within a vein (e.g., from thrombophlebitis) raises the hydrostatic pressures in the blood upstream from the resistance. This increase in P_c causes an increase in filtration of fluid into the ISF. If the increased rate of filtration is greater than the maximal lymphatic flow rate possible for that tissue or organ, edema results. *(Guyton, pp 187–192, 309–313)*

280. (B) In hemorrhage, there is a loss of blood volume and a decrease in cardiac output. In an attempt to maintain as much arterial blood pressure as possible (for brain and heart function) following hemorrhage, there is a generalized vasoconstriction of precapillary resistance vessels in many tissues (particularly in skin, skeletal muscle, and splanchnic circulations). This increase in total peripheral resistance helps to prevent a drastic fall in arterial blood pressure and also mobilizes some of the interstitial fluid into the plasma to help minimize vascular volume loss. This mobilization comes about because of the decrease in exchange vessel hydrostatic pressure ($\downarrow P_c$) on the downstream side of the vasoconstriction. This diminishes filtration so that now absorption predominates. The increased shift of protein-free, cell-free fluid into the blood accounts for the drop in plasma colloidal osmotic pressure and drop in hematocrit that follows hemorrhage. *(Berne and Levy, pp 507–509)*

281. (F) Hypoproteinemia resulting from a protein-deficient diet lowers the plasma colloidal osmotic pressure. This favors greater filtration and lower absorption across the microcirculatory exchange vessels. If the greater rate of filtration is more than can be handled by the lymphatics, interstitial fluid volume will increase (edema). *(Guyton, p 309)*

282. (I) Obstruction of lymphatic vessels by adult filarial nematodes (e.g., *Wuchereria bancrofti* or *Brugia malayi*) interferes with the volume of fluid indirectly returned to the blood by the lymphatics. As a result, a considerable edema can ensue. Occasionally, in chronic infections with filarial worms, affected limbs can become so swollen as to be elephantine in size ("elephantiasis"). *(Guyton, p 309)*

283. (G) In patients with a severe reduction in thyroid function there is an increase in interstitial protein and glycosaminoglycans (e.g., hyaluronic acid). This raises the π_{isf} and produces the characteristic nonpitting edema of myxedema of severe hypothyroidism. *(Guyton, p 955)*

284. (B, C, D) Persons exposed to cold exhibit increased production of heat as well as decreased heat loss. Heat production is augmented by activation of the primary motor center for shivering in the dorsomedial portion of the hypothalamus (but not cortical neurons), by chemical thermogenesis resulting from norepinephrine and epinephrine stimulation of brown fat and other tissues, and by increased thyroxine production from the thyroid as a result of centrally mediated thyrotropin-releasing factor and thyrotropin production. Heat conservation is primarily achieved through release of hypothalamic sympathetic inhibition, with resultant **vasoconstriction** of skin vessels. When exposed to cold, humans make significant behavioral adjustments, such as dressing more warmly and seeking external heat sources. *(Guyton, pp 911–922)*

285. (A, B, E) Although metabolic acidosis may occur and hydrogen ion concentration increase, the initial compensatory response to hemorrhage results in a large increase in total peripheral vascular sympathetic drive causing vasoconstriction. Thus, vascular resistance increases, heart rate increases, and blood pressure returns toward normal. Slightly later the kidneys may secrete renin, and the production of angiotensin II by converting enzyme activity ultimately ensues. Fluid also will shift from the interstitial compartments to the vascular space, helping to restore cardiac output. Other humoral agents, including epinephrine, vasopressin, and glucocorticoids, may also be released to further compensate for the cardiovascular effects of hemorrhage. *(Guyton, pp 286–288)*

REFERENCES

Berne RM, Levy MN. *Physiology*, 4th ed. St. Louis: Mosby–Year Book; 1998.

Ganong WF. *Review of Medical Physiology,* 19th ed. Stamford, CT: Appleton & Lange; 1999.

Guyton AC. *Textbook of Physiology,* 9th ed. Philadelphia: WB Saunders Co; 1996.

Vander AJ. *Renal Physiology,* 5th ed. New York: McGraw-Hill Book Co; 1995.

West JB. *Physiological Basis of Medical Practice,* 12th ed. Baltimore: Williams & Wilkins; 1991.

SUBSPECIALTY LIST: PHYSIOLOGY

Question Number and Subspecialty

237. Circulation in specific organs
238. Hemodynamics
239. Nervous system
240. Nervous system
241. Endocrinology
242. Endocrinology
243. Hemodynamics
244. Cardiovascular regulation
245. Nervous system
246. Body fluids
247. Endocrinology
248. Cardiovascular regulation
240. Endocrinology
250. Endocrinology
251. Endocrinology
252. Circulation in specific organs
253. Cardiac physiology
254. Cardiac physiology
255. Neurophysiology
256. Nervous system
257. Nervous system
258. Endocrinology
259. Nervous system
260. Nervous system
261. Nervous system
262. Sensory physiology
263. Endocrinology
264. Endocrinology
265. Endocrinology
266. Cardiac cycle
267. Cardiac cycle
268. Cardiac cycle
269. Cardiac cycle
270. Renal physiology
271. Renal physiology
272. Renal physiology
273. Renal physiology
274. Renal physiology
275. Renal physiology
276. Renal physiology
277. Renal physiology
278. Renal physiology
279. Microcirculation
280. Microcirculation
281. Microcirculation
282. Microcirculation
283. Microcirculation
284. Temperature
285. Cardiovascular regulation

Behavioral Sciences

Ellen F. Brooks, MD and Wendy L. Thompson, MD

DIRECTIONS (Questions 286 through 301): Each of the numbered items or incomplete statements in this section is followed by answers or by completions of the statement. Select the ONE lettered answer or completion that is BEST in each case.

286. A middle-aged man complains of insomnia. Further history reveals that he has been unable to sleep through the night for the past 2 to 3 months and has early morning awakening, unable to go back to sleep. He lost approximately 12 pounds during the past 2 months. He also complains of vague aches and pains and the feeling that he has committed serious sins for which he is going to be punished. The most likely diagnosis is

(A) schizophrenia
(B) somatization disorder
(C) major depression
(D) dysthymic disorder
(E) organic brain syndrome

287. Insight-oriented psychotherapy is an example of which of the following models of doctor–patient relationship?

(A) activity–passivity
(B) exploitive
(C) guidance–cooperation
(D) mutual participation
(E) authoritarian

288. If in a medical school department it is observed that most of the junior faculty and residents dress and speak like the department's chairperson, this phenomenon may be an example of

(A) sublimation
(B) projection
(C) denial
(D) reaction formation
(E) identification

289. Salivary secretion is increased in many people when they think of biting into a sour apple. This is an example of

(A) operant conditioning
(B) classical conditioning
(C) cognitive learning
(D) shaping
(E) instinctual behavior

290. The part of the brain that seems most intimately related to emotions is the

(A) frontal cortex
(B) limbic system
(C) pineal body
(D) locus ceruleus
(E) ventricular system

291. According to the Holmes and Rahe social adjustment rating scale, the highest degree of adjustment is required after

(A) marital separation
(B) detention in jail
(C) loss of a job
(D) marriage
(E) death of spouse

292. Generally speaking, Erikson's developmental stage in which basic trust is the major developmental task corresponds with the Freudian

(A) oral stage
(B) anal stage
(C) oedipal stage
(D) latency stage
(E) genital stage

293. A 30-year-old woman complains of episodic faintness, tingling sensation in her hands, shortness of breath, and severe anxiety. Thorough medical work-up reveals no pathologic condition. During an episode of these symptoms, chemical analysis of her serum would probably reveal

(A) decreased chloride concentration
(B) increased blood urea nitrogen concentration
(C) increased ammonia concentration
(D) increased pH
(E) decreased protein concentration

294. A five-year-old girl secretly believes that she was a princess who was stolen by the people who call themselves her parents. This is an example of

(A) delusional psychosis
(B) family romance
(C) childhood autism
(D) childhood mania
(E) Capgras syndrome

295. A transitional object is

(A) a stress-induced physiologic reaction
(B) an instability in object relations
(C) a mother substitute
(D) a hallucinated object usually seen in schizophrenia
(E) abnormal in children

296. Which of the following statements concerning the epidemiology of mental health is correct?

(A) The Chicago Study (Faris & Dunham) showed that mental illness was associated with higher socioeconomic class.
(B) The Midtown Manhattan Study (Rennie & Srole) showed 20% of persons from 20 to 59 years of age had emotional symptoms that were mild to severely incapacitating.
(C) The New Haven Study (Hollingshead & Redlich) showed that psychosis was more prevalent among the higher socioeconomic classes and neurosis more prevalent among the lower socioeconomic classes.
(D) The "drift hypothesis" posits that impaired persons slide down the social scale because of their illness.
(E) The "facilitation hypothesis" posits that schizophrenic persons actively seek city areas where anonymity and isolation protect them from societal demands.

297. The study of the development of a sense of self as an integrated, dependably competent, and strong person is called

(A) psychoanalysis
(B) self-psychology
(C) ego-psychology
(D) object-relations theory
(E) cognitive psychology

298. Which of the following statements is most helpful in differentiating schizophrenia from organic psychosis?

(A) Visual hallucinations are rare in organic psychosis.
(B) In schizophrenia, sensorium is generally not impaired.
(C) Delusions are common in both conditions.
(D) Auditory hallucinations are unlikely in schizophrenia.
(E) Organic psychosis tends to occur in geriatric patients.

299. Concerning adolescent sexuality, which of the following is true?

(A) Masturbation is uncommon.
(B) An insignificant portion have heterosexual intercourse.
(C) Excessive modesty reflects an absence of sexual impulses.
(D) The first sexual partner may have marked similarity or dissimilarity with the opposite-sex parent.
(E) True mutuality and love is impossible in this stage.

300. Acute grief reaction can be described as

(A) waves of somatic distress
(B) a precursor of major depression
(C) never associated with hallucinations
(D) symptomatology indistinguishable from posttraumatic stress disorder
(E) never associated with suicidal thoughts

301. Factors that may increase the likelihood of medical help-seeking include

(A) the symptom is a familiar one
(B) the symptom is a common one
(C) the symptom is a threatening one
(D) the symptom is unlikely to cause disability
(E) no relation to cultural influences

DIRECTIONS (Questions 302 through 321): Each of the numbered items or incomplete statements in this section is followed by answers or by completions of the statements. Select ONE (OR MORE) answer(s) or completion(s) for each case.

302. Depression in children and adolescents may be manifest by (SELECT 4)

(A) excessive clinging
(B) poor school performance
(C) encopresis
(D) sexual promiscuity
(E) pseudodementia
(F) antisocial behavior

303. Which of the following factors have been clearly associated with poor adherence to medical regimens? (SELECT 4)

(A) schizophrenia
(B) dementia
(C) smoking
(D) socially marginal status
(E) acute physical illness

304. Concerning major depression, which of the following statements are true? (SELECT 4)

(A) May occur as a part of hypothyroidism.
(B) Mean age of onset is in the 40s.
(C) About 25% of women may be afflicted with it.
(D) About 25% of men may be afflicted with it.
(E) Relapse is associated with more than 3 previous episodes of depression.
(F) Never occurs in children.

305. Which of the following are common examples of society's "sick role" expectations? (SELECT 4)

(A) Individuals are responsible for maintenance of health.
(B) Individuals who are sick are exempt from normal responsibilities.
(C) Individuals who are sick should seek help from a competent professional.
(D) Individuals who are ill are not expected to comply with the medical regimen.
(E) Being sick is an undesirable state.
(F) Individuals who are sick cannot be expected to get well by "pulling themselves together."
(G) Individuals are to blame for their illness.

306. Which of the following sexual behaviors are usually considered pathologic in nature? (SELECT 6)

(A) frigidity
(B) masturbation
(C) premature ejaculation
(D) fetishism
(E) transsexualism
(F) pedophilia
(G) fellatio
(H) frotteurism
(I) homosexuality

307. Clinical indications for brain imaging studies such as CT and MRI include (SELECT 4)

(A) change in personality after 50
(B) history of seizures
(C) a depressive episode at age 20
(D) first episode of psychosis
(E) panic attacks
(F) attention deficit hyperactivity disorder
(G) focal neurologic signs

308. Which of the following statements about adoption are true? (SELECT 4)

(A) Emotional and behavior disorders are more common among adopted children than among nonadopted children.
(B) Twins adopted by different families are often very different in personality.
(C) Children often have fantasies of having two sets of parents.
(D) Adopted children, in general, do not wish to know their biological parents.
(E) Meeting biological parents tends to be a positive experience for the adopted child in adolescence or early adulthood.
(F) Children should not be told they are adopted until adolescence.
(G) The later the age of adoption, the higher the incidence of behavioral problems.

309. A 42-year-old widow complains of persistent burning pain in her right forearm. She has a history of recurrent depression, and her husband died of a myocardial infarction within the past year. She says she has difficulty falling asleep and frequently awakens from sleep because of the pain. Which of the following statements are true? (SELECT 4)

(A) Depression is a possible diagnosis.
(B) Depression is an unlikely diagnosis.
(C) The symptoms may be indicative of anxiety.
(D) The pain is unlikely to be due to an organic cause.
(E) The pain may be a manifestation of distorted grief reaction.
(F) Causalgia is a possible diagnosis.
(G) Addison's disease is a likely diagnosis.

310. Which of the following concerning early adolescence are true? (SELECT 4)

(A) may be completely self-centered
(B) may be completely altruistic and giving
(C) are comfortable with the changes in their bodies
(D) very conforming to peer norms and fads
(E) consistent in behavior and mood
(F) rebellious, rejecting of parental control

311. Factors that may contribute to secondary orgasmic dysfunction in women include (SELECT 4)

(A) substance abuse
(B) dyspareunia
(C) depression
(D) extramarital relationships
(E) transsexualism

312. Types of psychotherapy include (SELECT 5)

(A) hypnotherapy
(B) behavior modification
(C) cognitive–behavioral therapy
(D) psychoanalysis
(E) hydrotherapy
(F) rolfing
(G) Gestalt

313. Children who witness violence on television may respond in which of the following ways? (SELECT 3)

(A) Learn new forms of aggressive behavior from the violence they see on TV.
(B) Experience a decrease in sensitivity to violence seen on TV.
(C) Feel themselves becoming less aggressive when they are watching aggression on TV.
(D) Sometimes undergo an inhibition of aggression when they become aware of the consequences of aggression that are revealed on TV.
(E) Have an increased incidence of coprophilia.

314. According to Piaget, infants in the sensorimotor stage of cognitive development (SELECT 4)

(A) use familiar means to obtain ends
(B) have developed conservation of substance
(C) generalize actions
(D) utilize concrete operations
(E) use available means to obtain particular goals
(F) are unable to use symbolization
(G) repeat actions

315. Which of the following are benzodiazepines? (SELECT 4)

(A) buspirone
(B) chlordiazepoxide
(C) carbamazepine
(D) zolpidem
(E) clorazepate
(F) alprazolam
(G) triazolam
(H) clonidine

316. The greatest risk factors for Alzheimer's disease are (SELECT 2)

(A) advanced age
(B) male gender
(C) apolipoprotein E2 allele
(D) high educational level
(E) apolipoprotein E4 allele

317. Concerning placebo, which of the following statements are true? (SELECT 3)

(A) Its analgesic effect is not blocked by naloxone.
(B) It is effective in the differential diagnosis of psychogenic pain.
(C) It may produce side effects.
(D) Its effect may be a conditioned response.
(E) Its effect may be different from that of hypnosis.

318. Concerning anxiety, which of the following statements are true? (SELECT 2)

(A) It may be unconscious.
(B) It is never a conditioned response.
(C) It always reduces performance.
(D) It is not caused by psychological conflicts.
(E) It may be caused by a brain dysfunction.

319. The cognitive functions include (SELECT 4)

(A) memory
(B) orientation
(C) abstraction
(D) affect
(E) judgment

320. Concerning primary degenerative dementia (Alzheimer's disease), which of the following statements are correct? (SELECT 3)

(A) It is the most common dementing disease in the elderly.
(B) It is associated with Down syndrome.
(C) Neurofibrillary tangles, senile plaques, and granulovacuolar bodies are found in the brain of these patients.
(D) Cholinergic neurons are rarely affected.
(E) It is an autosomal dominant trait caused by an abnormality in chromosome 5.

321. Physicians, as compared with the general population, have a higher prevalence of (SELECT 2)

(A) paraphilias
(B) suicide
(C) successful marriages
(D) homicide
(E) troubled marriages

DIRECTIONS (Questions 322 through 332): Each group of items in this section consists of lettered headings followed by a set of numbered words or phrases. For each numbered word or phrase, select the ONE lettered heading that is most closely associated with it. Each lettered heading may be selected once, more than once, or not at all.

Questions 322 through 324

(A) Skinner
(B) Pavlov
(C) fixed interval schedule
(D) fixed ratio schedule
(E) variable interval reinforcement
(F) reciprocal inhibition
(G) negative reinforcement
(H) shaping
(I) biofeedback

322. The father of classical conditioning

323. A steady rate of performance occurs

324. When a rat jumps five times, food is delivered

Questions 325 through 328

For each age listed below, select the pattern that, according to Bender, a child of that age should be able to copy accurately.

(A) 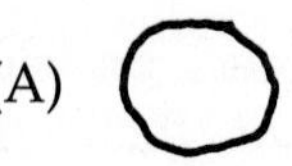

(B) 

(C) 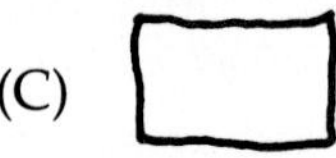

(D) 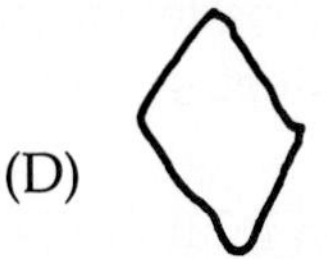

(E) 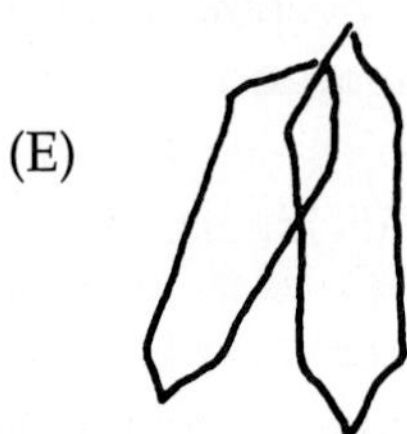

325. 2 years

326. 3 years

327. 5 years

328. 7 years

Questions 329 through 332

For each stage of life listed below, select the type of sleep–wake cycle with which it is most likely to be associated.

(A) continuous sleep
(B) cycle frequency of every 3 or 4 hours
(C) increased daytime wakeful periods and nighttime sleep
(D) true diurnal rhythm
(E) variable nocturnal–diurnal states

329. Neonate

330. First year

331. Fourth year

332. Eighth year

ANSWERS AND EXPLANATIONS

286. (C) Early morning awakening, weight loss, and feelings of guilt as well as vague pains and aches are common and rather characteristic symptoms of major depression. Additional symptoms to look for would be anhedonia, suicidal ideation, diurnal variation of mood, psychomotor agitation, or retardation. *(Leigh and Reiser, pp 101–144)*

287. (D) The three basic models of the doctor–patient relationship are activity–passivity, guidance–cooperation, and mutual participation models. Activity–passivity model is the traditional model, in which the patient is a passive recipient of treatment. Guidance–cooperation model implies patient cooperation with the treatment regimen. Mutual participation, which characterizes insight-oriented psychotherapy, implies a model of doctor–patient relationship in which the physician aids the patient in self-help. *(Simons, p 21)*

288. (E) Identification is the psychological defense mechanism by which an individual becomes like an admired (or otherwise psychologically important) person. Identification is an important phenomenon in personality development. *(Leigh and Reiser, pp 79–100)*

289. (B) Temporal pairing of a neutral stimulus with a stimulus that produces an inherent response characterizes classical or Pavlovian conditioning. In this case, the thought of biting into an apple would be a neutral stimulus, until the person associates it with the sour taste that causes salivation. *(Leigh and Reiser, pp 45–47)*

290. (B) The limbic system, the inner brain tissue that surrounds the brain stem, which includes the amygdala, hippocampus, cingulate gyrus, fornix, hypothalamus, and mammillary body, is considered to be directly involved in the emotional experiences including anxiety, fear, and anger. The evidence for this comes from studies of animals and persons who had ablations of certain parts of the limbic brain, as well as by stimulation of specific parts, either artificially, or in seizure states. *(Leigh and Reiser, pp 52–61)*

291. (E) Holmes and Rahe found that of all major life changes, death of a spouse was rated across population samples as requiring the most adjustment. The second highest rating was given to divorce, the third to marital separation. Detention in jail and loss of a job also are serious life changes that produce stress and require adjustment. *(Leigh and Reiser, pp 341–349)*

292. (A) According to Erikson, during the first year of life, corresponding to the Freudian oral stage, the child experiences a trusting relationship with the family and thus society in the form of feeding and comfort. An unsuccessful outcome during this stage results in a basic sense of mistrust. *(Leigh and Reiser, pp 361–362)*

293. (D) Faintness, tingling of the hands, shortness of breath, and severe anxiety are indicative of the hyperventilation syndrome, which causes respiratory alkalosis as a result of the loss of carbon dioxide. Vasoconstriction then develops and causes dizziness and decreased ionization of calcium, which may produce paresthesia and, in some cases, tetany. *(Leigh and Reiser, p 64)*

294. (B) First described by Freud, family romance is a fantasy of an Oedipal child that he/she cannot possibly belong to the disappointing parents. These parental disappointments are inevitable because of the aggression inherent in the Oedipal situation, as well as the inevitable frustrations and disappointments of growing up. Family romance is a normal part of growing up for many children. The other diagnoses listed can only be considered if there is other evidence of serious psychopathology. *(Simons, p 287)*

295. (C) Toward the end of the first year of life, many infants become attached to a specific article, such as a piece of clothing, called a transitional object. Linus's blanket in the

Peanuts cartoon is an example of this. A teddy bear, a doll, or a bottle might also serve as transitional objects. Transitional objects are symbolic of the mother. This is a normal phase-limited phenomenon. *(Simons, pp 176–178)*

296. **(D)** The Chicago study by Faris and Dunham showed that first hospital admissions for schizophrenia were higher among the city's lowest socioeconomic group. Faris and Dunham postulated the "drift hypothesis," that posits that the schizophrenic patients tend to drift downward in the socioeconomic scale. The "segregation hypothesis," in contrast, holds that schizophrenic patients actively seek the lower class areas where they may be protected from the stresses of more organized society. All epidemiologic studies tend to confirm that mental illness is more prevalent among the lower socioeconomic classes. *(Kaplan and Sadock, p 459)*

297. **(B)** Kohut emphasized the development of a sense of self as an important aspect of psychopathology and psychotherapy. Psychoanalysis is a broader term referring to both the psychodynamic theories and their practices. Ego psychology is concerned with ego structures, mechanisms of defense, and coping. Object relations theory deals with enduring internal psychic representations of influential people of infancy and childhood and the effects of those on patterning of relationships in later life. Cognitive psychology is a broad field that deals with thinking processes (cognition). *(Leigh and Reiser, pp 351–367)*

298. **(B)** Visual hallucinations are more likely in organic psychosis, whereas auditory hallucinations are more common in schizophrenia. While delusions are common in both conditions, this does not help in differentiating the two conditions. *(Leigh and Reiser, pp 145–209)*

299. **(D)** The series of relationships in adolescence often leads to a final relationship that shows true mutuality and mature love. At least 10% of adolescents have sexual intercourse by the end of junior high school. Excessive modesty or teasing exhibitionism reflect the strength of sexual impulses and the attempt to cope with them. *(Goldman, pp 40–42)*

300. **(A)** While acute grief may precipitate a major depression, it does not do so in a majority of cases. Acute grief may be associated with hallucinations and illusions, such as feeling or seeing the deceased. The symptomatology has some similarities to posttraumatic stress disorder (PTSD), but they are distinguishable in that flashbacks and nightmares are more common and vivid in PTSD, and avoidance of situations or items that remind the person of the trauma does not usually occur in acute grief. *(Sierles, p 174)*

301. **(C)** Mechanic described the factors that influence how a person perceives a symptom: commonality, familiarity, predictability of outcome, and degree of threat. In the examples given, only the degree of threat is in the positive direction. Cultural attitudes about dependence significantly influence if and how a person seeks help for a symptom. *(Leigh and Reiser, pp 3–15; Kaplan and Sadock, p 2)*

302. **(A, B, D, F)** In addition to the symptoms listed, school phobia, truancy, running away from home, and substance abuse may often be symptomatic of depression in children and adolescents. *(Kaplan and Sadock, p 553)*

303. **(A, B, D, E)** There is controversy concerning the factors influencing adherence to medical regimens. Among the demographic factors, female sex has clearly been associated with poor adherence. Field dependence has been associated with poor adherence among individuals suffering from alcoholism. Severe physical illness, contrary to what one would suspect, has also been associated with poor adherence, as have old age and marginal social status. *(Simons, pp 38–47)*

304. **(A, B, C, E)** Almost any endocrinopathy and metabolic disorder may be associated with major depression. Hypothyroidism is one of the common medical conditions causing depressive symptoms. The average age of onset is about forty and there is indication that the age of onset is decreasing more recently. Mood disorders are being increasingly diagnosed and treated in children and adolescents. The lifetime risk for major depression is 10 to 25% in women and 5 to 12% in men. *(DSM IV, p 341)*

305. (B, C, E, F) Society's "sick role," as described by Parsons, includes exemption from normal social role expectations. Sick individuals are not responsible for being sick and cannot be expected to get well simply by wanting to get well. Being sick is an undesirable state, and sick individuals should try to get well and seek competent help to get well. The idea that individuals are responsible for the maintenance of health is contrary to the second expectation described above. *(Leigh and Reiser, pp 18–24)*

306. (A, C, D, E, F, H) Frigidity is a common orgasmic dysfunction in women, and premature ejaculation is a common orgasmic dysfunction in men. Fetishism, frotteurism, and pedophilia are classified as paraphilias in current psychiatric classification, and transsexualism may be a result of gender identity disorder. Masturbation is a normal phenomenon and homosexuality is no longer classified as a sexual disorder. *(Goldman, pp 363–365, 367–375)*

307. (A, B, D, G) Personality change over 50, seizure disorders, eating disorders, and first episode of psychosis may be associated with intracranial mass lesions and/or focal brain diseases. Changes consistent with generalized neuronal loss in dementia may be demonstrated. First episode of affective syndrome after age 50 is also an indication for imaging studies, but the onset of depression at a young age generally does not require imaging studies. *(Kaplan and Sadock, p 123)*

308. (A, C, E, G) Adopted parents often tell their children of their adoption around the ages of 2 and 4. Emotional and behavioral problems have been reported to be higher among adopted children than nonadopted children including aggressive behavior, stealing, and learning disturbances. The later the age of adoption, the higher the incidence of behavioral problems. Children, adopted or not, often have fantasies of having two sets of parents, one good and one bad. Adopted children usually have a desire to know their biological parents. Meetings between sought-out parents and adopted children seem to be positive, especially in late adolescence and early adulthood. *(Kaplan and Sadock, p 41)*

309. (A, C, E, F) Difficulty falling asleep may be caused by anxiety, depression, and pain. Pain that awakens a person from sleep is more likely to be organic than psychogenic in origin. Depression may contribute to the pain, and vice versa. Causalgia is a burning pain in the arm; its cause is unknown. In distorted grief reaction, the bereaved may take on the symptoms of the deceased. The husband had a myocardial infarction and may have had anginal pains. The patient may be unaware that anginal pain is usually in the left arm. *(Leigh and Reiser, pp 106–112, 211–243)*

310. (A, B, D, F) Changeability and contradiction are characteristic of early adolescence. They may be completely self-centered and materialistic one moment, then extremely altruistic the next. They may be rebellious to parents, but often quite conforming to peers. Consistency of behavior and mood is totally lacking in this period. *(Simons, p 260)*

311. (A, B, C, D) Secondary orgasmic dysfunction is defined as the absence of orgasm in a woman who in the past had orgasms with some regularity. Substance abuse, particularly opiate abuse, lowers sexual desire and enjoyment. Dyspareunia (pain during intercourse) often prevents orgasm. Depression also causes loss of libido and, hence, lack of orgasm. Extramarital relationships may cause a lack of orgasm with the woman's husband or with the extramarital partner because of guilt feelings. Many women who complain of the absence of orgasm during intercourse can and do achieve orgasm with clitoral stimulation. *(Kaplan and Sadock, pp 688–689)*

312. (A, B, C, D, G) While there may be psychotherapeutic value in physical therapy, including hydrotherapy, it is usually not considered to be a type of formal psychotherapy. Formal psychotherapies may be classified according to theoretical orientations, e.g., psychodynamic psychotherapy including psychoanalysis, cognitive–behavioral therapy, learning-theory–based therapy (behavior modification), or by the specialized techniques used, e.g., hypnotherapy, narcosynthesis, biofeedback, or on the number or types of patients involved, e.g., group, family, couples therapy, etc. *(Leigh and Reiser, pp 421–436)*

313. (A, B, D) By the time a child who watches TV has finished high school, he or she will have seen depicted on television approximately 8000 murders and countless beatings, robberies, and other forms of violence. The research conducted since 1975 has led to several conclusions, including the belief that TV violence can have both an excitatory and inhibitory effect on children. *(Rothenberg, pp 86–87)*

314. (A, C, E, G) The sensorimotor period, encompassing the ages of 0 to 1 year, is divided into six stages that are characterized by: (1) inborn motor and sensory reflexes; (2) primary circular reaction and first habits; (3) secondary circular reaction; (4) use of familiar means to obtain ends; (5) tertiary circular reaction and discovery through active experimentation; (6) insight and object permanence. Concrete operation is performed during the period of the same name, which occurs during ages 7 to 11. *(Kaplan and Sadock, pp 140–141)*

315. (B, E, F, G) Buspirone is a nonbenzodiazepine substance. Benzodiazepines bind to benzodiazepine receptors and act synergistically with the GABA system. Buspirone enhances dopaminergic transmission and antagonizes GABA transmission. Its antianxiety effect may be through specific serotonergic inhibition. Carbamazepine is a mood stabalizer and anticonvulsant, and zolpidem is an imidazopyridine that acts at benzodiazepine receptors. *(Kaplan and Sadock, pp 997, 989–990, 1004–1005, 1008–1010)*

316. (A, E) Factors associated with increased risk of Alzheimer's disease include advanced age, low educational level, postmenopausal women off estrogen and family history of Alzheimer's disease. Genetic advances have pointed to several chromosomes as being involved in the pathogenesis of Alzheimer's disease. The most common chromosome associated with late life familial autosomal dominant Alzheimer's disease is linked to a gene on chromosome 19 that codes for apolipoprotein E. Of the three alleles coding for apolipoprotein E, over 75% of patients with Alzheimer's disease have the number 4 allele. *(Goldman, pp 74–75)*

317. (C, D, E) The placebo effect may be endorphinergically mediated; it often has side effects such as flushing and vomiting. Some placebo effect may be a conditioned response to a previous pill-taking behavior. Some studies have shown naloxone blockade of placebo analgesia, but not of hypoanalgesia. *(Leigh and Reiser, pp 211–243)*

318. (A, E) The relationship between performance and anxiety seems to be an inverted U-shaped curve. For optimal performance, a moderate degree of anxiety may be necessary. Severe anxiety reduces performance. *(Leigh and Reiser, pp 41–78)*

319. (A, B, C, E) The cognitive, or thinking, function includes orientation, memory, abstraction, calculation, and judgment. These functions are generally associated with the functions of the cerebral cortex, as opposed to affect and emotions, which are limbic system functions. *(Leigh and Reiser, pp 325–340)*

320. (A, B, C) While a familial form of Alzheimer's disease is an autosomal dominant trait with abnormality in chromosome 21, this is only a subset of Alzheimer's disease. Although both are located in chromosome 21, the gene coding for the amyloid protein precursor, which may be involved in sporadic

Alzheimer's disease, is not the same as the one implicated in familial form of the disease. *(Leigh and Reiser, pp 183–188)*

321. (B, E) The incidence of narcotic addiction in physicians is estimated to be 30 to 100 times greater than the general population. One in 10 physicians will become dependent on alcohol or drugs sufficiently to impair their careers and 1 in 10 physician addicts or alcoholics will commit suicide. Male physicians have 1.15 times greater and female physicians 3 times greater rate of suicide than the expected rate for the general population of respective gender. According to one study, 47% of physicians had bad marriages. There is, so far, no report of increased incidence of homicide among physicians. *(Scheiber and Doyle, pp 3–10)*

322. (B) Ivan Pavlov and his coworkers in Russia developed the theory of classical conditioning through carefully designed experiments. Classical conditioning (respondent conditioning) results from the repeated pairing of a neutral (conditional) stimulus with another stimulus that evokes a response (unconditional stimulus). Eventually, the neutral stimulus evokes the response. *(Kaplan and Sadock, pp 148–149)*

323. (E) A fixed interval reinforcement schedule results in an increase in performance (response) as the time of reinforcement (reward) approaches during the interval. By varying the delivery of reinforcement randomly around a particular interval of time, the response behavior stabilizes at a stable rate. This schedule is useful in clinical situations to increase the rate of performance of a desired behavior. *(Kaplan and Sadock, pp 150–151)*

324. (D) On a fixed ratio schedule of reinforcement, a low rate of behavior occurs immediately after reinforcement, followed by very high rates of responding. A smoother pattern is found with a variable ratio schedule, in which reinforcement is delivered on a schedule randomly changing around a given ratio. *(Kaplan and Sadock, pp 150–151)*

325–328. (325-A, 326-B, 327-C, 328-D) The patterns that accompany the question are simplified designs drawn from the more formal patterns used by Bender in her Visual Motor Gestalt Test. In her more formal test, Bender created eight figures and established age norms at which each could be reproduced by the child. The formal test and this clinical application are useful in assessing the maturation of visuomotor coordination. *(Bender [1938], p 200; [1952], p 335)*

329–332. (329-B, 330-C, 331-D, 332-D) Full-term infants change from active rapid-eye-movement (REM) sleep to quiet REM sleep about every 50 to 60 minutes, and neonates have a sleep–wake cycle of approximately 3 to 4 hours. During the first year of life, prolongations of daytime wakefulness and nighttime sleep occur, usually settling into a true diurnal rhythm by about 4 years of age. In general, sleep–wake rhythm seems to be more culturally determined, whereas REM–non-REM rhythms seem to be more genetically determined. *(Anders, pp 421–432)*

REFERENCES

American Psychiatric Association. *Diagnostic and Statistical Manual of Mental Disorders,* 4th ed. (DSMIV), Washington, DC: American Psychiatric Association; 1994.

Anders T. Home-recorded sleep in 2- and 9-month-old infants. *J Am Acad Child Psychiatry.* 1978; 17:421–432.

Bender L. *A Visual Motor Gestalt Test and Its Clinical Use.* New York: American Orthopsychiatric Association; 1938. Research Monograph No. 3.

Goldman HH. *Review of General Psychiatry,* 5th ed. New York: McGraw Hill; 2000.

Kaplan HI, Sadock BJ. *Kaplan and Sadock's Synopsis of Psychiatry, Behavioral Sciences, Clinical Psychiatry,* 8th ed. Baltimore: Williams & Wilkins; 1998.

Leigh H, Reiser MF. *The Patient: Biological, Psychological, and Social Dimensions of Medical Practice,* 3rd ed. New York: Plenum Press; 1992.

Rothenberg MB, ed. The role of television is shaping the attitudes of children. *J Am Acad Child Psychiatry.* 1983;22:86–87.

Scheiber SC, Doyle BB, eds. *The Impaired Physician.* New York: Plenum Publishing Corp; 1983.

Sierles FS. *Behavioral Science for Medical Students.* Baltimore: Williams & Wilkins; 1993.

Simons RC. *Understanding Human Behavior in Health and Illness,* 3rd ed. Baltimore: Williams & Wilkins; 1985.

SUBSPECIALTY LIST: BEHAVIORAL SCIENCES

Question Number and Subspecialty

286. Depression, sleep and dreaming, pain
287. Doctor–patient relationship
288. Individual dynamics
289. Learning theory
290. Neurobiology, emotions
291. Stress
292. Individual dynamics
293. Physiologic correlates of behavior, emotions, and anxiety
294. Life cycle, psychodynamics, psychological assessment
295. Life cycle, psychodynamics
296. Psychiatric epidemiology, social psychiatry
297. Personality and psychodynamics
298. Psychosis, organic mental syndromes, psychological assessment
299. Life cycle, human sexuality
300. Stress and adaptation, emotions, mood disorder, anxiety disorder
301. Ethics, beliefs, norms, values
302. Depression, life cycle, child psychiatry
303. Medical sociology
304. Depression, psychiatric epidemiology
305. Medical sociology
306. Human sexuality
307. Psychiatric imaging
308. Life cycle, social psychiatry
309. Pain, emotions, and mood disorders
310. Life cycles, child psychology
311. Sexual development and behavior
312. Learning theory, personality and psychodynamics
313. Life cycle, child development, aggression
314. Life cycle, perception and cognition
315. Biochemical correlates of behavior, pharmacologic correlates of behavior
316. Organic mental syndromes
317. Pharmacologic correlates of behavior, pain, emotions
318. Emotions, cognition
319. Psychological assessment, cognition, emotions
320. Genetics and behavior, organic mental syndromes, degenerative disease of the nervous system
321. Medical sociology, substance abuse, physician stress
322. Learning theory
323. Learning theory
324. Learning theory
325. Child psychology
326. Child psychology
327. Child psychology
328. Child psychology
329. Child psychology
330. Child psychology
331. Child psychology
332. Child psychology

CHAPTER 2

Clinical Sciences Review

Obstetrics and Gynecology

Samuel L. Jacobs, MD

DIRECTIONS (Questions 333 through 368): Each of the numbered items or incomplete statements in this section is followed by answers or by completions of the statement. Select the ONE lettered answer or completion that is BEST in each case.

333. Which of the following findings on colposcopic examination of the cervix would be considered normal and not merit biopsy?

(A) White areas with red stippling (punctation).
(B) Sharp-bordered areas with a mosaic vascular pattern.
(C) A sharply demarcated squamocolumnar junction in a 24-year-old woman.
(D) A small area of white tissue with sharply demarcated borders at the squamocolumnar junction.
(E) An area with a clearly delineated tortuous, irregular vessel.

334. To be most effective in contraception, a diaphragm coated with a spermicidal agent should be left in place after intercourse at least

(A) 1 hour
(B) 4 hours
(C) 6 to 8 hours
(D) 12 to 24 hours
(E) 48 to 72 hours

335. Which of the following modalities is not used as a diagnostic aid to help identify lesions on the vulva?

(A) Pap smear
(B) colposcopy
(C) toluidine blue dye
(D) acetic acid
(E) podophyllin

336. The type of obstetric forceps most appropriate for use on an aftercoming head in a breech presentation is

(A) Kjelland's forceps
(B) Barton's forceps
(C) Tucker–McLean forceps
(D) Dewees' forceps
(E) Piper's forceps

337. When a euthyroid woman becomes pregnant, which of the following thyroid function tests would be most likely to decrease?

(A) total serum triiodothyronine (T_3) concentration
(B) total serum thyroxine concentration
(C) free thyroxine index
(D) resin T_3 uptake
(E) serum thyroid-stimulating hormone (TSH) concentration

338. At one minute of life, a newborn has the following characteristics: heart rate, 90 beats per min; respiratory rate, good (crying); body color, pink with blue extremities; muscle tone, some flexion of the extremities; and reflex irritability, grimace response. This baby's Apgar score is

(A) 5
(B) 6
(C) 7
(D) 8
(E) 9

339. Which of the following findings on histologic examination of the endometrial biopsy specimen is most characteristic of postmenstrual, preovulatory endometrium?

(A) subnuclear glycogen vacuoles
(B) stromal edema and predecidualization
(C) marked leukocytic infiltration
(D) marked glandular growth and mitoses
(E) prominent coiled spiral arterioles

340. "Protracted active phase" labor is said to occur when the rate of cervical dilation per hour in a primigravid woman is less than

(A) 1.2 cm
(B) 1.5 cm
(C) 1.7 cm
(D) 2.0 cm
(E) 2.5 cm

341. A female with primary amenorrhea should be evaluated, regardless of normal growth and development and the presence of secondary sex characteristics at

(A) 12 years of age
(B) 14 years of age
(C) 16 years of age
(D) 18 years of age
(E) 20 years of age

342. The most common extrauterine site of endometriosis is the

(A) uterosacral ligaments
(B) round ligaments
(C) ovaries
(D) rectovaginal septum
(E) sigmoid colon

343. Cancer of the cervix has been found to have infiltrated the upper two thirds of a patient's vagina and parametrium but not to extend to the pelvic sidewall. The correct International Federation of Obstetricians and Gynecologists (FIGO) staging classification of this carcinoma is

(A) stage IB
(B) stage IIA
(C) stage IIB
(D) stage IIIA
(E) stage IIIB

344. Clomiphene citrate (Clomid) is best described as a

(A) synthetic preparation of luteinizing hormone (LH)
(B) weak nonsteroidal estrogen
(C) progestin of the 19-nortestosterone class
(D) methylated androgen
(E) none of the above

345. At her first prenatal visit, a woman says she has no idea of the date of her last menstrual period and that she has not felt any fetal motion. The fetal heartbeat is audible with Doppler technique but not with a stethoscope. At her second visit, a month later, she says she has felt fetal quickening; the fetal heartbeat is audible with a stethoscope. This woman is probably now in what stage of her pregnancy?

(A) 10 to 12 weeks
(B) 12 to 14 weeks
(C) 16 to 20 weeks
(D) 21 to 23 weeks
(E) 24 to 26 weeks

346. Which of the following conditions would be the LEAST relevant in determining whether to provide tocolysis to a patient presenting with preterm labor?

(A) a precise determination of gestational age
(B) ruptured placental membranes
(C) fetal lung maturity status
(D) maternal age
(E) etiology of the preterm labor

347. A 19-year-old nulliparous woman is found on routine pelvic examination to have a 5-cm adnexal mass. Ultrasonography is performed and shows the mass to be entirely fluid-filled. The proper procedure at this point would be

(A) observation and rechecking the mass after the next menses
(B) medroxyprogesterone therapy
(C) a 10-day course of oral antibiotics
(D) diagnostic therapy
(E) exploratory laparotomy and removal of the cyst

348. A 27-year-old woman has tried unsuccessfully for 5 months to become pregnant. At this point, the recommended evaluative procedure would be

(A) semen analysis
(B) hysterography
(C) endometrial biopsy
(D) diagnostic laparoscopy
(E) none of the above

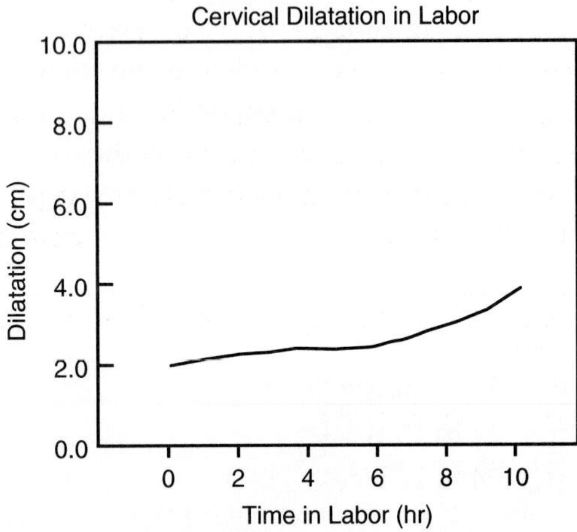

349. A primigravid patient presents with the labor curve shown above. She asks how much longer it will be until her delivery. You answer

(A) it is just impossible to know
(B) 2 hours or less
(C) from this point on her curve, it should be within the next 6 hours
(D) with some pitocin augmentation and the use of forceps, you should be able to reduce the time to 2 hours or less
(E) it looks as though a cesarean section may be necessary

350. Vulvovaginal *Trichomonas* can be described most accurately as

(A) caused by the overgrowth of bacteria native to some individuals
(B) not associated with an alteration of normal vaginal pH
(C) causes pelvic inflammatory disease
(D) a sexually transmitted disease
(E) diagnosis can be made by obtaining a wet smear and mixing with KOH (potassium hydroxide)

351. Regarding bacterial vaginosis, which of the following statements is FALSE?

(A) It is referred to by many as nonspecific vaginitis.
(B) The offending organism has been referred to as *Haemophilus, Corynebacterium,* and *Gardnerella.*
(C) It is associated with characteristic diagnostic findings of clue cells and a vaginal pH of 5.0 to 6.0.
(D) It is treated equally effectively by metronidazole, ampicillin, tetracyclines, or sulfas.
(E) It is characterized by a fishy odor.

352. The use of human Rh_0(D) immune globulin (RhoGAM) as prophylaxis of potential Rh disease can be described by which of the following statements?

(A) The medication must be given within the first 24 hours postpartum.
(B) Administration of the medication carries with it a risk of hepatitis for the recipient.
(C) The prophylaxis success rate is 85%.
(D) Pain at the site of injection can be a complication.
(E) It should be given to Rh-positive women delivering Rh-negative babies.

353. Regarding precocious puberty, which of the following statements is true?

(A) Precocious puberty is the initiation of sexual maturation occurring before 8 years of age in girls.
(B) Affected individuals are most often very tall with eunuchoid features.
(C) The etiology of this problem is most commonly a central nervous system lesion.
(D) The only reliable treatment of this problem in the female is the administration of high-dose estrogen.
(E) It is more common in boys than girls.

354. All the following drugs can appear in human breast milk. The agent associated with "gray baby syndrome" is

(A) propylthiouracil
(B) isoniazid
(C) chloramphenicol
(D) erythromycin
(E) propranolol

355. The mentum posterior presentation can be described by which of the following statements?

(A) Spontaneous delivery can almost always occur.
(B) It is an unstable lie.
(C) Mentum posterior must rotate anteriorly in order to be born vaginally.
(D) The incidence is approximately 6% of all presentations.
(E) Forceps can be useful to effect delivery.

356. A 32-year-old woman who has never been pregnant complains of increasing pelvic pain and dyspareunia. Diagnostic laparoscopy confirms the clinical impression of endometriosis. The medical therapy of choice is

(A) bromocriptine
(B) danazol
(C) progesterone
(D) oral contraceptives
(E) gonadotropin-releasing hormone (GnRh) agonists

357. Risk factors for endometrial carcinoma exclude

(A) obesity
(B) hypertension
(C) diabetes
(D) renal disease
(E) late menopause

358. A 46-year-old woman with five children has a discrete, painful breast mass that has persisted for 3 months. She is particularly frightened because her father's sister died of breast cancer. Factors that indicate the need for a biopsy include

(A) her family history
(B) her parity
(C) pain
(D) persistence after menstrual periods
(E) history of breast-feeding

Questions 359 through 362

A 37-year-old woman (gravida 7, para 5, spontaneous abortion 1) registers in a clinic for obstetric care when she learns she is pregnant. She had an uncomplicated dilatation and curettage (D&C) procedure performed between her second and third pregnancies for irregular bleeding. All deliveries have been vaginal and uncomplicated. Her blood pressure is 124/76 mm Hg. She is euthyroid.

359. The woman described above is at decreased risk for

(A) placenta previa
(B) placenta accreta
(C) postpartum hemorrhage
(D) Down syndrome
(E) prolonged labor

360. After a first trimester complicated only by mild nausea and vomiting, the woman returns after 19 weeks of pregnancy. She says she has had vaginal spotting and increased vomiting for the past 2 weeks. Her blood pressure is 150/94 mm Hg. The fundus size is 22 weeks, and no fetal heart tones are heard by auscultation or Doppler. There is clinical evidence of hyperthyroidism. The most likely diagnosis is

(A) hydramnios
(B) missed abortion
(C) fibroid uterus
(D) urinary retention
(E) hydatidiform mole

361. The most useful diagnostic procedure to perform at this point in the case described would be

(A) urine pregnancy test
(B) clotting studies
(C) culdocentesis
(D) abdominal x-ray
(E) uterine ultrasound

362. After the pregnancy is ended, the woman described should have which of the following tests?

(A) chromosomal analysis
(B) chorionic gonadotropin titers
(C) thyroid function tests
(D) hysterography
(E) cystometrography

Questions 363 through 365

A 22-year-old woman (gravida 0) seeks a gynecologic examination. She has regular menstrual cycles, is sexually active, uses oral contraceptives, and has no dysmenorrhea or dyspareunia. She weighs 54.5 kg (120 lb). Her external genitalia are normal. On speculum examination, a red vaginal circumferential fold, looking like a concentric ring around the cervix, is noted.

363. The most likely diagnosis of the genital lesion described is

(A) contraceptive-induced metaplasia of the cervix
(B) hypertrophic vagina secondary to monilial vaginitis
(C) herpes simplex virus, type II, infection
(D) vaginal adenosis
(E) wolffian duct cyst

364. The most important next step in the evaluation of this woman's disorder would be

(A) cervical culture
(B) wet-mount (physiologic saline) microscopic examination
(C) aspiration of the tissue surrounding the cervix using a small-gauge needle
(D) gentian violet staining of the lesion
(E) visualization, palpation, and cytologic sampling of the entire cervix and vagina

365. Appropriate management of the woman's disorder would best include

(A) serial cytologic examinations
(B) serial cervical cultures
(C) VDRL testing
(D) blood viral antibody titers
(E) discontinuation of oral contraceptives

Questions 366 through 368

Results of clinical pelvimetry on a 27-year-old woman (gravida 1, para 0) are as follows: flat, forward-inclined sacrum; prominent ischial spines; convergent sidewalls; and a narrow, deep pubic arch.

366. The pelvimetric description given above is typical of which of the following pelvic types (by the Caldwell–Moloy classification)?

(A) gynecoid
(B) android
(C) anthropoid
(D) platypelloid
(E) gynecoid with platypelloid features

367. Which of the following statements is true regarding this type of pelvis?

(A) It usually portends a good delivery prognosis.
(B) It occurs in less than 5% of gravidas.
(C) It increases the frequency of difficult forceps delivery.
(D) It is not associated with any increase in fetal morbidity or mortality.
(E) It is associated often with occiput anterior presentation.

368. Which of the following conjugates is most important as a measure of the anteroposterior diameter of the pelvic inlet and cannot be measured directly by clinical pelvimetry?

(A) anatomic conjugate
(B) anterior conjugate
(C) diagonal conjugate
(D) obstetric conjugate
(E) sagittal conjugate

DIRECTIONS (Questions 369 through 387): Each of the numbered items or incomplete statements in this section is followed by answers or by completions of the statement. Select the ONE (OR MORE) lettered answer(s) or completion(s) for each case.

369. Primary dysmenorrhea is thought to arise from uterine contractions originated by prostaglandin release from the endometrium. The best pharmacologic measures to control the pain include (SELECT 4)

(A) ibuprofen
(B) ethinyl estradiol and norethindrone
(C) bromocriptine
(D) indomethacin
(E) mefenamic acid
(F) benzodiazepines
(G) morphine

370. Herpes genitalis is a widespread venereal disease. Which of the following statements is true regarding herpes? (SELECT 1)

(A) Acyclovir administration lengthens symptomatic periods and viral shedding during primary infections.
(B) Acyclovir administration may increase the incidence of recurrences.
(C) A lesion on the perineum at 32 weeks' gestation should preclude vaginal delivery at term.
(D) 50% of patients affected with a primary lesion never experience a recurrence.
(E) Viral shedding never occurs when patients have no active lesions.

371. A 35-year-old woman has a history of fibrocystic breast disease with symptomatic mastalgia. The following agents have been used in the treatment. (SELECT 4)

(A) tamoxifen
(B) danazol
(C) clomiphene
(D) bromocriptine
(E) oral contraceptives
(F) benzodiazepines
(G) morphine

372. Oxytocin is a drug widely used in obstetrics. Potential adverse side effects of oxytocin include (SELECT 4)

(A) hypotension
(B) uterine tetany
(C) water intoxication
(D) hypertension
(E) fetal distress
(F) hypernatremia

373. A 24-year-old woman presents with a two-year history of primary infertility. She has been in a monogamous relationship with her current partner (who has fathered two children in a past relationship) for the past three years, and has never used any form of birth control in her lifetime. Her menarche was at age 12 with regular 28-day cycles lasting for 4 to 5 days of flow. Her past gynecologic history is significant for three episodes of pelvic inflammatory disease in the past 6 years. The rest of her gynecologic and medical history is negative, and the physical examination is essentially within normal limits. The FIRST study that you would obtain, which would result in the HIGHEST diagnostic yield, would be (SELECT 1)

(A) antichlamydia antibodies
(B) hysterosalpingography
(C) semen analysis
(D) endometrial biopsy to rule out chronic endometritis
(E) laparoscopy with chromopertubation

374. Abnormal maternal serum alpha-fetoprotein levels have been found to be associated with the following conditions. (SELECT 4)

(A) maternal liver disease
(B) multiple gestation
(C) intrauterine fetal death
(D) fetal congenital nephrosis
(E) fetal hydrocephalus
(F) sacrococcygeal teratoma
(G) neonatal goiter
(H) Addisonian crisis at birth

375. The following risk factors are associated with an increased incidence of breast cancer in women. (SELECT 4)

(A) family history of breast cancer
(B) obesity
(C) early menarche
(D) early natural menopause
(E) first pregnancy after the age of 35 years
(F) late menarche
(G) low-dose oral contraceptive usage
(H) decreased dietary dairy and fat intake

376. Which of the following statements is true concerning epidural anesthesia used during obstetric procedure? (SELECT 1)

(A) For abdominal deliveries the epidural block should extend no higher than the T-10 level.
(B) A common complication is maternal hypertension resulting from sympathetic blockage.
(C) Convulsions are never a problem.
(D) Actual or anticipated maternal hemorrhage may be a contraindication.
(E) The tip of the catheter should lie outside the ligamentum flavum and the dura mater.

377. The following factors would increase the likelihood of a pregnant woman developing pregnancy-induced hypertension after the 24th week of pregnancy. (SELECT 4)

(A) underlying essential hypertension
(B) multifetal pregnancy
(C) age, 14 years
(D) singleton pregnancy
(E) refractoriness to angiotensin
(F) advanced maternal age

378. During normal pregnancy, tests of resting respiratory function that would likely be increased would include (SELECT 1)

(A) functional residual capacity
(B) residual volume
(C) tidal volume
(D) total pulmonary resistance
(E) pCO_2

379. Phenytoin (Dilantin), when prescribed during pregnancy, can cause what has been called the hydantoin syndrome in the fetus. Characteristics of the hydantoin syndrome include (SELECT 4)

(A) craniofacial anomalies
(B) cardiac defects

(C) cleft lip
(D) kidney defects
(E) mental retardation
(F) ambiguous genitalia
(G) sacrococcygeal teratoma

380. Work-up of a couple who are habitual aborters should include (SELECT 4)

(A) maternal and paternal karyotype analysis
(B) hysterosalpingogram
(C) endometrial biopsy
(D) serum estradiol levels
(E) serum progesterone levels
(E) anti-sperm antibodies
(E) postcoital testing

381. Primary fallopian tube cancers are described by the following statements. (SELECT 2)

(A) Most are squamous cell carcinomas.
(B) Peak incidence is during the third decade of life.
(C) They constitute fewer than 2% of female genital tract cancers.
(D) They produce few or no symptoms early in their course.
(E) The diagnosis is usually made by ultrasound.

382. Disseminated intravascular coagulation (DIC) is a catastrophic obstetric event that may accompany (SELECT 4)

(A) placental abruption
(B) sepsis
(C) amniotic fluid embolism
(D) retention of a dead fetus
(E) placenta previa
(F) fetal macrosomia
(G) diabetic ketoacidosis
(H) maternal thyroid storm

383. First trimester pregnancy termination is most commonly achieved by (SELECT 1)

(A) intrauterine instillation of saline
(B) intrauterine instillation of prostaglandin F_2
(C) intravenous administration of pitocin
(D) oral antiprogesterone RU 486
(E) dilatation and evacuation

384. Common sites of *early* spread from ovarian carcinoma include the (SELECT 4)

(A) spleen
(B) diaphragm
(C) uterus
(D) omentum
(E) contralateral ovary
(F) stomach

385. Which of the following states is associated with a normal (i.e., not elevated) prolactin level? (SELECT 1)

(A) first trimester of pregnancy
(B) pituitary adenoma
(C) familial hirsutism
(D) use of phenothiazines
(E) herpes zoster

386. Sarcoma botryoides can be described by which of the following statements? (SELECT 2)

(A) It usually affects women in their 20s.
(B) It is very common.
(C) It usually is accompanied by a bloody vaginal discharge.
(D) It is usually benign.
(E) Chemotherapy followed by hysterectomy and vaginectomy is the current treatment.

387. Risk factors for endometrial carcinoma include (SELECT 1)

(A) multiple sex partners
(B) infection with human papillomavirus
(C) initiation of coital activity during adolescence
(D) early menarche
(E) early menopause

DIRECTIONS (Questions 388 through 402): Each group of items in this section consists of lettered headings followed by a set of numbered words or phrases. For each numbered word or phrase, select the ONE lettered heading that is most closely associated with it. Each lettered heading may be selected once, more than once, or not at all.

Questions 388 through 391

For each description below, select the type of female genital cancer with which it is most closely associated.

(A) ovarian carcinoma
(B) cervical carcinoma
(C) tubal carcinoma
(D) vulvar carcinoma
(E) endometrial carcinoma

388. Causes more deaths than any other gynecologic malignancy

389. Precancerous states are often detected by routine screening tests

390. Presents with postcoital bleeding

391. Presents most often as postmenopausal bleeding

Questions 392 through 395

For each of the abnormalities listed below, select the corresponding finding or condition.

(A) associated with known metabolic abnormality and resultant mental deficiency
(B) lymphangiectatic edema of hands and feet at birth
(C) cleft palate, cleft lip, eye defects, polydactyly
(D) characteristic facial findings often not recognized at birth
(E) cataracts, microcephalus, cardiac defects, deafness, mental retardation

392. Phenylketonuria

393. Rubella

394. Turner's syndrome

395. Down syndrome

Questions 396 through 398

For each statement below, select the disorder with which it is most likely to be associated.

(A) retained placental fragments
(B) bleeding from uterine myomas
(C) uterine atony
(D) coagulation disorders
(E) amniotic fluid embolus

396. It is the most common cause of immediate postpartum hemorrhage (i.e., hemorrhage occurring within the first 24 hours after delivery)

397. It is the most common cause of late postpartum hemorrhage (after the first 24 hours)

398. General anesthesia increases the incidence

Questions 399 through 402

For each condition below, select the clinical sign likely to be associated with that condition.

(A) palpable breast mass
(B) bloody nipple discharge
(C) bilateral breast pain
(D) galactorrhea

399. Intraductal papilloma

400. Fibroadenoma

401. Paget's disease

402. Fibrocystic breasts

ANSWERS AND EXPLANATIONS

333. (C) The colposcope provides the magnification and intensified light used to delineate abnormal areas of epithelium on the cervix, vagina, and vulva. On the cervix, areas that are whitish, thickened, or possess abnormal vascular patterns (punctation, mosaic, tortuosity) are abnormal and a biopsy specimen should be taken. The principle of colposcopy relies on the fact that all metaplastic change occurs at the squamocolumnar junction (SCJ) and, therefore, the visualization of a clearly demarcated SCJ is imperative to obtain a satisfactory examination. In a 24-year-old patient this zone should be readily visible. In an elderly woman, metaplasia of columnar to squamous epithelium may have moved this junction well up into the cervical canal where visualization is impossible with the colposcope. *(Beckmann, p 520)*

334. (C) The use of a diaphragm coated with a spermicidal agent is an effective method of contraception. For the spermicidal agent to be most effective, the diaphragm should be left in place for at least 6 hours after intercourse. After 6 hours have elapsed, the diaphragm can be removed when it is most convenient to do so but should not be left in place for a prolonged period of time. *(Beckmann, pp 308–309)*

335. (E) Cytology (Pap smear) or superficial scrapings can be helpful in the diagnosis of dysplastic and infectious lesions of the vulva. Colposcopy, just like the hand lens of the dermatologist, aids by providing magnification and good lighting, allowing lesions to be seen that would not be visible to the unaided eye. Toluidine blue is an acidophilic dye that is taken up by lesions with a high DNA content (neoplastic cells). Acetic acid is an astringent for cells with large glycogen content. When applied to areas of neoplasia, it makes them stand out because of the high nuclear to cytoplasmic ratio. These dense areas then appear as well-demarcated white lesions. Podophyllin is a form of chemical debrisant and not a diagnostic aid. *(Beckmann, pp 500–508)*

336. (E) Piper's forceps were expressly designed for use on the aftercoming head in a breech presentation. The forceps should be applied to an engaged head; the long shank and the double pelvic curve facilitate the long reach of the head. None of the other forceps listed has these features. *(Cunningham, pp 473–477)*

337. (D) Total serum triiodothyronine (T_3) and thyroxine (T_4) levels both show a significant elevation during pregnancy. These levels begin to rise early in pregnancy and return to normal only after delivery. The concentration of thyroid-stimulating hormone (TSH) has been reported to be normal or slightly increased during the first half of pregnancy. Free thyroxine index remains in the normal range during pregnancy. Resin T_3 uptake decreases somewhat during pregnancy. *(Cunningham, pp 1223–1230)*

338. (B) Apgar scores of newborn infants at 1 minute and 5 minutes of life judge five parameters: heart rate, respiratory function, body color, muscle tone, and reflex irritability. The maximum score is 10—i.e., 2 points in each category. For the baby described in the question, heart rate below 100/min rates a score of 1; respiratory status, 2; body color, 1; muscle tone, 1; and reflex irritability, 1. (This last parameter is tested by inserting the tip of a catheter into the nostril; a score of 2 is given if the response to the stimulation is crying.) Thus, the Apgar score for this baby is 6. *(Beckmann, p 132)*

339. (D) Postmenstrual, preovulatory edometrium is described as proliferative: the endometrial layer proliferates and thickens under the hormonal influence of estrogen. Histologic examination of endometrial tissue at this stage shows marked glandular growth and much evidence of mitosis. All the other histologic findings listed in the question are characteristic of secretory or progestational (postovulatory, premenstrual) endometrium. *(Beckmann, p 418)*

340. (A) "Protracted active phase" labor occurs when cervical dilation is less than 1.2 cm/h in a primigravid woman and less than 1.5 cm/h in a multigravid woman. Friedman found several causes for protracted active phase labor, including cephalopelvic disproportion, excessive sedation or analgesia, and

ABNORMAL LABOR PATTERNS, DIAGNOSTIC CRITERIA, AND METHODS OF TREATMENT.[1]

Labor Pattern	Diagnostic Criterion		Preferred Treatment	Exceptional Treatment
	Nulliparas	Multipara		
Prolongation disorder				
(Prolonged latent phase)	> 20 h	> 14 h	Therapeutic rest	Oxytocin or cesarean deliveries for urgent problems
Protraction disorders			Expectant and supportive	Cesarean delivery for CPD
1. Protracted active phase dilatation	< 1.2 cm/h	< 1.5 cm/h		
2. Protracted descent	< 1.0 cm/h	< 2 cm/h		
Arrest disorders				
1. Prolonged deceleration rate	> 3 h	> 1 h	Without CPD: oxytocin	Rest if exhausted
2. Secondary arrest of dilatation	> 2 h	> 2 h	With CPD: cesarean delivery	Cesarean delivery
3. Arrest of descent	> 1 h	> 1 h		
4. Failure of descent	No descent in deceleration phase or second stage of labor			

[1]Modified from Cohen W, Friedman EA (editors): *Management of Labor,* University Park Press, 1983.

the use of conduction anesthesia. Protracted active phase labor can lead to secondary arrest of labor when dilation ceases to progress. *(Cunningham, pp 418–419)*

341. (C) Most girls experience menarche by 16 years of age. Therefore, absence of menses by that age suggests delayed puberty or abnormal ovarian function and should be evaluated. Because the median age of menarche in the United States is 12.8 years, evaluation of primary amenorrhea at 12 years of age would be inappropriate. Evaluation at 14 years of age is appropriate if the girl has not had menstrual periods nor development of secondary sexual characteristics. *(Beckmann, pp 422–424)*

342. (C) The most common extrauterine location of endometriosis is the ovary. In many cases, ovarian involvement is bilateral. Other sites (in approximate order of decreasing frequency) include the peritoneum of the pouch of Douglas (including the uterosacral ligaments and the rectovaginal septum), other pelvic peritoneal surfaces, the round ligament, the oviduct, the intestines, and the pelvic lymph nodes. *(Beckmann, p 366)*

343. (C) See table on page 107. By definition, this is stage IIB. *(Beckmann, p 524)*

344. (B) Clomiphene citrate (Clomid) is a nonsteroidal, weakly estrogenic agent distantly related to diethylstilbestrol. Clomiphene binds to estrogen receptors in the hypothalamus and perhaps in the pituitary gland as well. Endogenous production of follicle-stimulating hormone (FSH) rises during clomiphene therapy; because FSH stimulates ovarian follicles, clomiphene is used in ovulation induction. *(Beckmann, pp 469–470)*

345. (C) Most pregnant women become aware of fetal movement between 16 and 20 weeks of gestation. This is called "quickening." *(Cunningham, p 23)*

346. (D) Preterm labor and its management are often controversial areas in obstetrical management. There are certain situations or factors mitigating these conditions, however, that always need to be considered as relevant in decision making. First, a precise knowledge of both the gestational age and the status of fetal lung maturity are tremendous aids in management. Seldom will most obstetricians stop labor occurring after the 34th to 35th week of gestation or in gestations beyond the 33rd to 34th week with demonstrated fetal lung maturity. Ruptured membranes to many obstetricians would be a contraindication to stopping preterm labor, whereas to others it might be an indication for immediate tocolysis. Either way the status of the membranes is important in decision making. The etiology when one can be found

FIGO (1986) STAGING OF CANCER OF THE CERVIX.

Stage 0	Carcinoma in situ, intraepithelial carcinoma.
Stage I	Carcinoma strictly confined to the cervix (extension to the corpus should be disregarded).
Ia	Preclinical carcinomas of the cervix, i.e., those diagnosed only by microscopy.
Ia 1	Minimal microscopically evident stromal invasion.
Ia 2	Lesions detected microscopically that can be measured. The upper limits of the measurement should not show a depth of invasion of > 5 mm taken from the base of the epithelium, either surface or glandular, from which it originates; and a second dimension, the horizontal spread, must not exceed 7 mm. Larger lesions should be staged as Ib.
Ib	Lesions of greater dimensions than stage Ia 2, whether seen clinically or not. Preformed space involvement should not alter the staging but should be specifically recorded so as to determine whether it should affect treatment decisions in the future.
Stage II	Carcinoma extends beyond the cervix but has not extended onto the pelvic wall. Carcinoma involves the vagina, but not the lower third.
IIa	No obvious parametrial involvement. The vagina has been invaded, but not the lower third.
IIb	Obvious parametrial involvement.
Stage III	Carcinoma has extended onto the pelvic wall. On rectal examination, there is no cancer-free space between the tumor and the pelvic wall. The tumor involves the lower third of the vagina. All cases with hydronephrosis or nonfunctioning kidney should be included unless known to be due to other causes.
IIIa	No extension onto the pelvic wall but involvement of the lower third of the vagina.
IIIb	Extension onto the pelvic wall and/or hydronephrosis or nonfunctioning kidney.
Stage IV	Carcinoma extending beyond the true pelvis or clinically involving the mucosa of the bladder or rectum. Do not allow a case of bullous edema as such to be allotted to stage IV.
IVa	Spread to adjacent organs (i.e., rectum or bladder, with positive biopsy from these organs).
IVb	Spread to distant organs.

is obviously important. If the etiology is infectious or a significant abruption, few caregivers would try to stop labor. The same is true for serious maternal disease, but disease is certainly not synonymous with age of the mother. Age by itself should have no bearing on the decision to provide tocolysis. *(Beckmann, pp 279–281)*

347. (A) A pelvic mass is an alarming finding in a woman. In prepubertal women, most lesions derive from germ cells, and nearly half of these tumors are malignant. In postmenopausal women, ovarian masses are frequently malignant, and many gynecologists believe that any palpable ovary in postmenopausal women should be removed. In women in their reproductive years, however, the majority of cysts are fluid-filled follicular cysts, which are completely benign. If such a mass is noted in a young woman, she should be observed for at least one menstrual cycle. At times, suppression of the cyst with oral contraceptive therapy to decrease stimulation may be attempted, but medroxyprogesterone is not routinely used for these purposes. If a mass persists for several months and is more than 8 cm in diameter, most gynecologists would advocate its removal. *(Beckmann, pp 552–553)*

348. (E) Infertility is defined as a year of unprotected coitus without conception. The incidence of conception in couples experiencing regular unprotected intercourse is 15 to 20% after 1 month, 50% after 6 months, and 80 to 90% after 1 year. Therefore, although many patients become disconcerted if they are not pregnant after 4 or 5 months of trying, such a situation is statistically not unlikely. After an unsuccessful year of attempted conception, extensive fertility testing procedures may be initiated if necessary. *(Beckmann, p 354)*

349. (C) Although labor is not an entirely predictable event, the work of Friedman has shown that plotting dilatation of the cervix and descent of the fetal head does allow easier recognition of abnormal labor and good predictability of the course of labor based on immediate past progress (see illustration on page 108). This is a normal labor curve. If it remains on this course (and you have no reason to believe it will not), delivery should occur in about 6 hours. Poor understanding of the labor process and lack of use of these invaluable graphic representations by those providing obstetrical care has contributed to the increased rates of cesarean section seen in the last 10 years. When used correctly, these curves are invaluable to the obstetric attendant. *(Beckmann, p 91)*

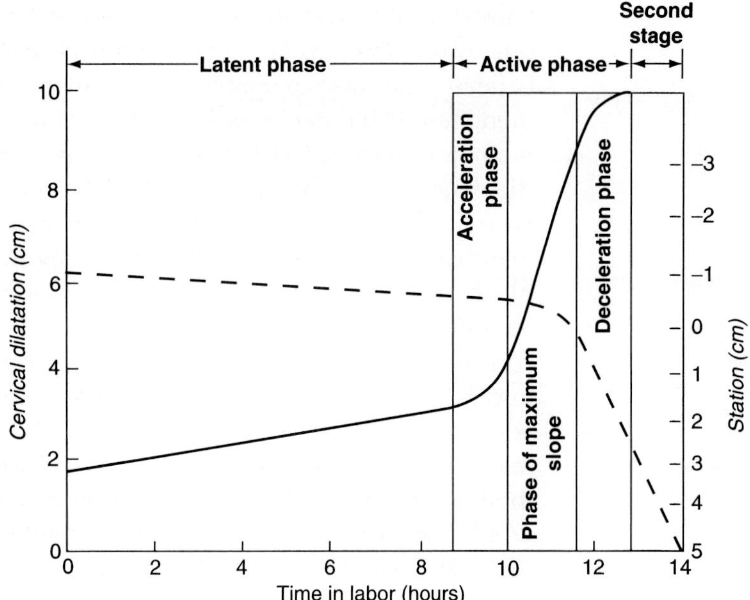

Question 347. Composite of cervical dilatation and fetal descent curves, illustrating their interrelationship and their component phases. *(Courtesy of Cohen W, Friedman EA [editors]:* Management of Labor. *University Park Press, 1983.)*

350. (D) *Trichomonas* is in most cases a sexually transmitted disease caused by a protozoan, not a bacteria. It is generally more common when the pH has become more alkaline than the normal vagina (postmenstruation, vaginosis, etc.). It may often be asymptomatic. Successful eradication requires treatment of all sexual partners. Trichomonads can be identified as pear-shaped motile organisms when a sample of vaginal discharge is mixed with normal saline. A KOH (potassium hydroxide) preparation is useful for identifying the hyphae associated with candidal vaginitis. *(Beckmann, pp 329–330)*

351. (D) Bacterial vaginosis (nonspecific vaginitis) is the most common type of vaginal infection and is associated with the overgrowth of anaerobic bacteria. It has been called by many names (both repeatable and nonrepeatable). It has a characteristic fishy odor from the release of amines when KOH (potassium hydroxide) is applied to a wet preparation. Its low pH is an excellent diagnostic sign, as is the characteristic appearance of clue cells using light microscopy. The anaerobic nature of the infection makes it very susceptible to metronidazole but less responsive to other agents used for treatment in the past. *(Beckmann, pp 328–329)*

352. (D) Rh disease, caused by isoimmunization of an Rh-negative mother exposed to Rh-positive red blood cells, results in hemotologic and other consequences for the Rh-positive child. Postpartum administration of Rh immune globulin to Rh-negative mothers who have delivered an Rh-positive child has been standard care since the late 1960s. More recently, antepartum prophylaxis has been recommended. Human Rh_0(D) immune globulin (RhoGAM) is an effective prophylaxis for Rh disease if given within the first 72 hours postpartum. The success rate is usually quoted as 98 to 99%. Pain at the injection site is a potential complication of RhoGAM therapy, but hepatitis is not because preparation of the γ-globulin by alcohol or ether extraction would destroy any hepatitis virus present. *(Beckmann, pp 151–152)*

353. (A) Precocious puberty usually consists of the normal sequence of events of sexual maturation but occurring before the age of 8. Unfortunately, the increased production of sex steroid leads to premature epiphyseal closure with 50% of affected individuals less than 5 feet tall. When an etiology can be found, it is most commonly a central nervous system lesion or the sequelae of the same, but the greatest majority remain idiopathic as to cause. The treatment lies in suppression of gonadotropins either with injectable medroxyprogesterone acetate in a depot form or suppression with gonadotropin-releasing hormone agonists. Precocious puberty is seen five times more frequently in girls than in boys. *(Beckmann, pp 426–428)*

354. (C) Chloramphenicol can be toxic to the breast-fed infant, potentially causing "gray baby syndrome" and death. Propylthiouracil (PTU) is excreted into breast milk in very low amounts and has not been found to cause fetal thyroid problems. Likewise, isoniazid, although it is secreted in breast milk, has not been found to be associated with fetal toxicity. Neither erythromycin nor propranolol are associated with adverse fetal reactions, although it is recommended that infants of nursing mothers on propranolol be closely observed for symptoms of beta-blockade. *(Cunningham, p 945)*

355. (C) The incidence of the mentum posterior presentation is less than 1 in 1200. Only 30% of mentum presentations are posterior, and two thirds of these rotate to the anterior. Those posterior mentum presentations that do not rotate anteriorly carry a potentially poor prognosis, because they do not deliver spontaneously. As such, forceps should not be applied to a mentum posterior position. A brow presentation is an unstable state of partial obflexion, and will usually convert to a mentum (i.e., face) or occiput presentation. *(Cunningham, pp 443–445)*

356. (E) Laparoscopy is the ideal test for confirming the presence of endometriosis. Women who clearly desire to remain fertile should receive conservative therapy rather than radical pelvic surgery such as hysterectomy. The most effective drug treatments for endometriosis are those that cause suppression of ovarian function and endometrial tissue with GnRH agonists. Although Danazol is also effective, its masculinizing side effects make it a less optimal choice. *(Beckmann, pp 371–372)*

357. (D) Obesity is a major risk factor for endometrial carcinoma, which is thought to be caused by excessive estrogen stimulation of the endometrium. Peripheral conversion of estrogen in fat cells makes obese women particularly susceptible to endometrial carcinoma. Other recognized risk factors associated with estrogen excess or imbalance include early menarche and late menopause, nulliparity, failure of ovulation in young women, estrogen-secreting tumors, and exogenous supplementation of estrogens. Ten percent of women with endometrial carcinoma have diabetes, and 50% have an abnormal response to a glucose tolerance test. More than half of all women with endometrial carcinoma are hypertensive. Renal disease is not associated with any type of endometrial malignancy. *(Beckmann, p 544)*

358. (D) The only significant risk factor for the patient described in the question is the persistence of the mass after a period. Benign cysts vary with the menstrual cycle; painful masses are usually benign. Low parity, not high parity, is a risk factor of breast cancer. Although a family history is definitely a risk factor and warrants close observation, it is not, by itself, an indication for a biopsy. Breast feeding has not been found to impact positively or negatively on the incidence of breast cancer. *(Beckmann, p 390)*

359–362. (359-E, 360-E, 361-E, 362-B) The woman described in the question is at risk for several disorders at the start of her pregnancy. Multiparity is associated with placenta previa, placenta accreta, and postpartum hemorrhage. (Placenta previa occurs when the placenta implants in the lower uterine segment and partially or completely covers the cervical os, and placenta accreta is an abnormal attachment of the placenta to the uterine wall in which the villi adhere to or penetrate the myometrium.) Dilatation and curettage procedures predispose to later placenta accreta. The risk of Down syndrome goes up with increasing maternal age after 35. Prolonged labor is the correct answer here, in that grand multiparas are at increased risk for a precipitous labor, and therefore at decreased risk for a prolonged labor.

The most likely diagnosis of the woman's second-trimester difficulties is hydatidiform mole. Missed abortion usually causes the uterus to be small, not large, for dates. Although the other conditions listed can cause an enlarged uterus, they are not associated with increased vomiting, signs of hyperthyroidism, or early pregnancy-induced hypertension. Hydatidiform mole is a developmental anomaly of the placenta in which chorionic villi are converted into vesicles. It may be benign or may become malignant.

Diagnosis of hydatidiform mole is best confirmed by ultrasound of the uterus. Sonograms of affected women may be similar to sonograms of a normal pregnancy, uterine myoma with an early pregnancy, or twins, but repeat scanning should eliminate the uncertainty. Women with molar disease are at greatest risk for persistent trophoblastic disease and choriocarcinoma. Elevated human chorionic gonadotropin (HCG) levels after pregnancy has been ended represent the continued presence of active trophoblastic tissue. HCG levels are useful in diagnosing molar pregnancies only if the levels are extremely high. Otherwise, they could reflect a normal singleton or multifetal pregnancy. If HCG is detectable after pregnancy, chemotherapy may be required. *(Cunningham, p 431; Beckmann, pp 492–494)*

363–365. (363-D, 364-E, 365-A) Vaginal adenosis can develop in women exposed in utero to diethylstilbestrol (DES). Cervical metaplasia associated with this disorder occurs at the squamocolumnar junction, usually at or near the external cervical os. Careful inspection, palpation, cytologic examination, and, if needed, colposcopy are necessary to search for the presence of clear cell adenocarcinoma of the vagina. This rare neoplasm can develop from vaginal adenosis in DES-exposed women. Regular visual, tactile, and cytologic examinations are important in the management of these women. The use of oral contraceptives is not contraindicated in DES-exposed women.

Monilial vaginitis causes a thick, white discharge and is associated with vulvitis; the treatment is clotrimazole (Lotrimin), miconazole (Monistat), or terconazole (Terazol). Genital herpes primary infection usually produces "cold sore" vesicular lesions externally or on the cervix and is associated with pain. Wolffian duct cysts occur on the lateral vaginal walls. *(Cunningham, pp 642–643; Beckmann, p 509)*

366–368. (366-B, 367-C, 368-D) An android pelvis has prominent ischial spines, convergent sidewalls, a flat and forward-inclined sacrum, and a narrow, deep pubic arch. Although some of these characteristics can occur in other pelvic types (e.g., ischial spines can be variable in size in anthropoid and platypelloid types), only the android pelvic type combines all these characteristics. During labor, the fetal head engages in the transverse or posterior diameter of the maternal android pelvis. Asynclitism (lack of parallelism between maternal pelvic planes and fetal presenting part), molding of the fetal head, and a prolonged second stage of labor are common with this pelvic type, as are transverse arrest and arrest in an occiput posterior position. Forceps deliveries commonly are required and are often difficult, leading to an increased incidence of perineal tears as well as increased fetal morbidity and mortality. *(Beckmann, pp 106–107)*

369. (A, B, D, E) Prostaglandin inhibition is the key to control of dysmenorrhea. Even the dysmenorrhea associated with endometriosis is thought to be secondary to excess prostaglandins. Ibuprofen, mefenamic acid, and indomethacin are potent prostaglandin inhibitors. Ethinyl estradiol and norethindrone are the most common components of birth control pills; they decrease prostaglandin synthesis by causing atrophy and decidualization of the endometrium. Bromocriptine suppresses production of prolactin and does not seem to affect dysmenorrhea. Benzodiazepines are anxiolytics and do not generally have analgesic properties. They also are addictive.

Morphine is a highly addictive analgesic and would not be used as first-line therapy for dysmenorrhea. *(Beckmann, pp 378–380)*

370. (D) Other than HIV disease, many experts consider herpes as well as HPV to be our most serious venereal disease. Unfortunately, no preventive medication exists. Application of acyclovir is usually recommended for primary cases, and even then it does not prevent recurrences, but it does seem to shorten symptomatic periods. Acyclovir may also decrease the incidence of recurrences. The virus may be shed by asymptomatic carriers. On the brighter side, as many as 50% of patients who suffer an initial attack never experience recurrence. Regarding pregnancy management, most neonatologists agree that as long as a woman has no active lesions at the time of delivery, she may deliver vaginally. Thus, lesions at 32 weeks should not preclude vaginal delivery. *(Cunningham, pp 1324–1328)*

371. (A, B, D, E) Breast discomfort is a major problem associated with fibrocystic breast disease. Simple palliative measures include administration of vitamin E, 600 units daily, and limiting methylxanthines by eliminating coffee and other caffeine-containing substances; the mechanics of action of these measures are not well understood. Danazol, in doses of 200 to 400 mg daily, does alleviate the problem. Other treatments include tamoxifen, OCs, and bromocriptine. Clomiphene would not be used because it raises estrogen levels, thereby exacerbating the problem. Benzodiazepines are anxiolytics and have no role in fibrocystic breast disease. Morphine is a narcotic analgesic and is not an appropriate choice for mastalgia. *(Beckmann, p 388)*

372. (A, B, C, E) The major prenatal complications with the use of oxytocin relate to overstimulation of the uterus, leading to tetany and possibly fetal distress. After delivery, an inadvertent bolus of oxytocin can cause a rapid fall in arterial blood pressure. Unlike ergonovine, oxytocin does not produce hypertension. With chronic administration, oxytocin can act like a similar peptide hormone, ADH, and produce reabsorption of free water; electrolytes must be carefully monitored in a woman receiving large doses of oxytocin to prevent hyponatremia and subsequent seizures. Hypernatremia is not associated with oxytocin administration. *(Cunningham, pp 426–428)*

373. (B) A hysterosalpingogram (HSG) would give the highest diagnostic yield at this time in the initial work-up. In light of this woman's history of pelvic inflammatory disease (PID), the most likely etiology of her infertility is tubal blockage. There is a 15%, 25%, and 50% chance of tubal occlusion with a history of 1, 2, and 3 episodes of PID respectively. Although a laparoscopy with chromopertubation has a high diagnostic yield, general surgery is more invasive than an HSG, and thus would not be performed FIRST. Finally, although she probably is positive for antichlamydia antibodies (because of her history of PID), this will not tell us the status of the fallopian tubes. Chronic endometritis is more unlikely in this scenario, and thus is not the most probable cause of her infertility. Furthermore, endometrial biopsy is most commonly used in the infertility work-up to rule out luteal phase dysfunction. Finally, although a semen analysis is necessary in the complete infertility work-up, male factor infertility is not likely to be the problem in this case. *(Beckmann, pp 337–339, 467–468)*

374. (A, B, C, D) The presence of alpha-fetoprotein (AFP) in maternal serum has been associated with a number of conditions, including multiple gestation, intrauterine fetal death, fetal congenital nephrosis, and maternal liver disease. Other problems that can produce abnormal AFP levels in maternal blood are other fetal defects, such as omphalocele, and fetus-to-mother bleeding (either spontaneous or caused by amniocentesis). By contrast, closed neural-tube defects, including those associated with hydrocephalus or sacrococcygeal teratoma, in the fetus, are not associated with abnormal AFP levels in maternal serum. Neither neonatal goiter nor Addison's disease is associated with elevated AFP levels. *(Cunningham, p 922)*

375. (A, B, C, E) Low dose OCs seem to have a protective effect on the incidence of breast cancer. A vegan diet (with decreased dietary fat and no dairy intake) seems to be protective as well. A family history of breast cancer increases the risk of death from breast cancer by a factor of two to three. Obesity, early menarche, and first pregnancy after the age of 35 years also increase the risk. A late natural menopause also seems to increase the risk of breast cancer; in fact, women with natural menopause after 55 years of age have approximately twice the risk of women whose natural menopause occurred before the age of 45 years. *(Beckmann, p 390)*

376. (D) For abdominal deliveries an epidural block must extend from at least T-8 to S-1; the thoracic end of a block necessary for vaginal delivery would be T-10. Complications of epidural block include convulsions and hypotension secondary to sympathetic blockage. The presence or threat of maternal hemorrhage may be a contraindication to the use of epidural anesthesia during delivery. The epidural catheter should be placed between, and not outside, the ligamentum flavum peripherally and the dura mater centrally. *(Beckmann, pp 94–95)*

377. (A, B, C, F) Preeclampsia is much more common in primigravid than in multigravid women, and the younger and older primigravidas are at greatest risk. For example, older primigravid women are more likely to have chronic hypertension, which predisposes to the development of preeclampsia. Hypertension induced during or aggravated by pregnancy is also one of the many complications that occur more commonly during "multifetal" pregnancies. Normal pregnant patients are refractory to the pressor effects of angiotensin, whereas many patients destined to manifest preeclampsia lose this refractoriness. *(Beckmann, pp 238–240)*

378. (C) Tidal volume, minute ventilatory volume, and minute oxygen uptake increase appreciably during pregnancy. Airway conductance is increased, while total pulmonary resistance is reduced. Residual volume and functional residual capacity are decreased. Additionally, maternal pCO_2 is also decreased in pregnancy. *(Beckmann, p 57)*

379. (A, B, C, E) The administration of phenytoin (Dilantin) to pregnant women is associated with a relatively high risk of developmental defects. The fetal hydantoin syndrome, caused by maternal ingestion of phenytoin, is associated with a number of abnormalities. The syndrome consists of mild to moderate growth retardation, mental retardation, facial abnormalities (including cleft lip or palate), cardiac defects, limb dysmorphism, and coagulopathy. Kidney defects do not seem to be part of the syndrome. Pregnant women requiring phenytoin should receive the lowest dosage able to achieve seizure control. Neither ambiguous genitalia nor sacrococcygeal teratoma are associated with Dilantin. *(Beckmann, p 223)*

380. (A, B, C, E) Habitual abortion is defined as three or more consecutive pregnancy losses before the 20th week of gestation. Many causes have been implicated; most cases are still diagnosed as idiopathic. Because as many as 60% of fetuses miscarried during the first trimester document some genetic anomaly, it is important to study parental chromosomes. In as many as 10% of cases a parental anomaly such as balanced translocation will be found. Occasionally a uterine septum or fibroid can account for losses. A hysterogram will identify these patients, and surgical correction can be performed. Occasionally the mother may have an inadequate luteal phase and produces too little progesterone to achieve successful implantation of a fertilized ovum. Such cases may be diagnosed by endometrial biopsy and serum progesterone levels, and the women may receive treatment with supplemental progesterone. A serum estradiol level is not helpful in the work-up of this condition. Decreased motility on postcoital testing, showing the presence of antisperm antibodies will usually result in decreased fertilization rather than subsequent loss. *(Beckmann, pp 173–179)*

381. (C, D) Primary tubal carcinomas are usually papillary adenocarcinomas, although squamous cell carcinomas occasionally occur. Although tubal carcinoma can occur at any time during and after the reproductive years, the peak incidence is during the sixth decade of life. Tubal carcinoma is very rare, accounting for 0.1 to 0.5% of female genital tract cancers. Like ovarian cancer, tubal cancers produce few or no symptoms during their early phase. The most common presenting symptoms include vaginal discharge or bleeding, menstrual irregularities, and pain. The diagnosis of fallopian tube carcinoma is usually made at the time of surgery. *(Beckmann, pp 561–562)*

382. (A, B, C, D) Of all the cases of placental abruption resulting in fetal death, 30% are associated with hypofibrinogenemia at levels < 150 mg/dL. These cases are characterized by significant coagulation retroplacentally as well as intravascularly. Sepsis, particularly with *Clostridium perfringens,* may cause significant hemolysis and disseminated intravascular coagulation (DIC). The cause of amniotic fluid embolism-induced DIC may be the mucus contained in the fluid, which may incite coagulation by activation of factor X. Thromboplastin activation from dead products of conception may trigger DIC, particularly if the fetus is retained for longer than 1 month. Placenta previa is not associated with DIC, since the thromboplastin produced with placental separation tends to escape out the cervix and not into the maternal circulation. Fetal macrosomia and diabetic ketoacidosis are both known sequelae of diabetes in pregnancy and neither are associated with DIC. Maternal thyroid storm is also not associated with DIC. *(Beckmann, pp 159, 244, 232–233)*

383. (E) Several methods have been used successfully, alone and in combination, to terminate first-trimester pregnancies. Current statistics available from the Centers for Disease Control show dilatation and evacuation to have the lowest mortality rates and is the most common technique used to perform first-trimester SABs or TABs; however, an experienced operator must perform the procedure. Intra-amniotic injection of prostaglandin may result in a live-born fetus, whereas saline injection terminates fetal viability. Saline injection, however, can lead to hyperosmolar crisis and DIC. Pitocin administered intravenously acts slowly on the midtrimester cervix, which is not very receptive to oxytocics. None of the above (saline, prostaglandins, or pitocin) are used in the first trimester for termination. The antiprogesterone RU 486 can effect abortion in early gestation but has just been approved for use in the United States and is not the most common technique for emptying the uterus of products of conception, although it may be in the future. *(Beckmann, pp 178–179)*

384. (B, C, D, E) Ovarian cancer spreads widely early in its course. Common sites of spread include the uterus, contralateral ovary, fallopian tubes, rectum, and bladder. Omental metastases occur very early in the course of the disease, as do metastases to the diaphragm, especially to the inferior aspect of the right hemidiaphragm. Metastases to the stomach and spleen may occur, but they are not common and develop relatively late. Even in patients with disease apparently limited to one ovary, biopsy of the contralateral ovary and the omentum is indicated at the time of laparotomy. *(Beckmann, pp 556–559)*

385. (C) Elevated prolactin is associated with anything that may inhibit hypothalamic function (decreasing the secretion of prolactin inhibiting factor) or stimulate the breast. Destructive hypothalamic or pituitary tumors, central nervous system suppressants, and primary pituitary insufficiency are all examples. Any event or substance or local irritant that stimulates the breast, chest wall, or nipple may also stimulate prolactin secretion. Lactation is one sign of these, as are herpes zoster, scars on the chest wall, jogging, sexual activity, or even breast examination. The first trimester of pregnancy is associated with an elevated prolactin as well. Familial hirsutism is associated with elevated androgens such as free testosterone, or DHEAS, rather than an elevated prolactin. *(Cunningham, p 216)*

386. (C, E) Sarcoma botryoides is a grapelike polypoid lesion that arises from the müllerian tubercle. It is a very uncommon and extremely aggressive neoplasm that occurs during the first decade of life. In most cases the presenting symptom is a bloody vaginal discharge. Pelvic exenteration was, at one time, the only therapeutic approach but has now been replaced by a multimodality approach consisting of chemotherapy or radiotherapy followed by hysterectomy and vaginectomy. *(Beckmann, p 510)*

387. (D) Risk factors for endometrial cancer appear to be associated with the reproductive lifespan. Thus, early menarche, late menopause, obesity, and nulliparity seem to place a woman at higher risk for endometrial cancer. On the other hand, the other risk factors, e.g., STDs, multiple partners, HPV infection, and early sexual activity are thought to be risk factors for cervical cancer. Jewish women have a lower incidence of cervical cancer than do women of most other ethnic groups, perhaps because of a preventive effect of penile circumcision. *(Beckmann, p 544)*

388–391. (388-A, 389-B, 390-B, 391-E) Although cervical and endometrial carcinomas are more common than ovarian carcinoma, ovarian carcinoma causes more deaths than any other gynecologic malignancy because of its aggressiveness and lack of early symptoms. The Pap smear is a routine test that can detect dysplasia and carcinoma in situ of the cervix, both of which are treatable precursors of invasive carcinoma of the cervix. Carcinoma of the fallopian tube is a very rare malignancy, accounting for fewer than 2% of female genital tract neoplasms. Pruritus is the most common presenting symptom of vulvar cancer, although local irritation may have been present for many years. Occasionally a lump in the vulvar area is the presenting symptom. Although ovarian carcinoma classically gives no indication of its presence until late in its course, the most common initial symptoms are an abdominal mass, ascites, and pain. Postcoital bleeding is the classic presentation of carcinoma of the cervix. Any episode of postmenopausal bleeding should be investigated, and carcinoma of the endometrium must be ruled out by a dilatation and curettage or an endometrial biopsy. Endometrial cancer usually presents with postmenopausal bleeding. *(Beckmann, pp 513, 523, 545, 556)*

392–395. (392-A, 393-E, 394-B, 395-D) Phenylketonuria is an autosomal recessive inborn error of metabolism resulting in a syndrome associated with mental retardation. Early recognition and a special diet can greatly alter the prognosis of this disease. The diet can then be discontinued later in life but must be restarted before pregnancy to avoid phenylalanine toxicity in the unborn offspring. Rubella is an infectious environmental teratogen and the most common cause of congenital deafness. Retardation, heart defects, and ophthalmologic abnormalities are also associated. Turner's syndrome is associated with abnormalities of the lymphatics. The webbing of the neck that occurs is from in utero lymphedema of the neck (cystic hygroma). Seeing a baby born with edema isolated to the hands and feet and no cardiac failure should automatically alert you to this diagnosis. Down syndrome, though very characteristic in the adult facies, can be completely unnoticed in the newborn. *(Cunningham, pp 897–898, 902, 905, 1301–1303)*

396–398. (396-C, 397-A, 398-C) Of all the types of life-threatening hemorrhage associated with pregnancy, hemorrhage from uterine atony in the immediate postpartum period is the most common. General anesthesia using a halogenated anesthetic is associated with the development of uterine atony in the immediate postpartum period, as are prolonged labor, rapid delivery, and overdistention of the uterus from a large baby, multiple gestation, or hydramnios. Other, less common causes of hemorrhage in the immediate postpartum period include uterine myoma, retained placental fragments, coagulation disorders, and cervical or vaginal lacerations.

Late postpartum hemorrhage occurs less frequently than immediate hemorrhage. It is caused most frequently by retained placental fragments or subinvolution of the placental implantation site. *(Beckmann, pp 155, 157–159)*

399–402. (399-B, 400-A, 401-D, 402-C) The most common cause of bloody or serosanguineous nipple discharge is intraductal papilloma. It is a benign condition usually occurring in middle-aged women. Usually, a breast or nipple mass is not palpable, because tumor size is small (only 3 mm).

Fibroadenoma is a benign, slow-growing, well-circumscribed tumor that typically is palpable. The tumor may remain the same size for years or enlarge rapidly. Nipple discharge is not associated with fibroadenoma.

Prolactinomas are generally benign tumors of the pituitary gland. They generally secrete prolactin, which results in galactorrhea.

Fibrocystic changes of the breasts are the most common of the benign breast diseases. They are an exaggerated response of breast tissue to the cyclic levels of ovarian hormones. The classic symptom is cyclic bilateral breast pain. *(Beckmann, pp 388, 389, 433)*

REFERENCES

Cunningham FG, MacDonald PC, Gant NF, et al. *Williams Obstetrics,* 20th ed. Stamford, CT: Appleton & Lange; 1997.

Beckmann CR, Ling FW, Herbert WN, et al. *Obstetrics and Gynecology,* 3rd ed. Baltimore: Lippincott Williams & Wilkins; 1998.

SUBSPECIALTY LIST: OBSTETRICS & GYNECOLOGY

Question Number and Subspecialty

333. Colposcopy
334. Clinical gynecology
335. Clinical gynecology
336. Clinical obstetrics, abnormal
337. Physiology of pregnancy
338. Newborn resuscitation
339. Clinical gynecology
340. Clinical obstetrics, normal
341. Endocrinology, infertility
342. Clinical gynecology
343. Oncology
344. Endocrinology, infertility
345. Pregnancy diagnosis
346. Management of abnormal labor
347. Clinical gynecology
348. Clinical gynecology
349. Physiology of labor
350. Infectious disease
351. Infectious disease
352. Fetus, placenta, and newborn
353. Precocious puberty
354. Newborn physiology
355. Clinical obstetrics, abnormal
356. Endometriosis
357. Oncology
358. Breast pathology
359. Clinical obstetrics, abnormal
360. Clinical obstetrics, abnormal
361. Clinical obstetrics, abnormal
362. Clinical gynecology
363. Clinical gynecology
364. Clinical gynecology
365. Clinical gynecology
366. Clinical obstetrics, normal
367. Clinical obstetrics, normal
368. Clinical obstetrics, normal
369. Endocrinology of menstruation
370. Infections
371. Breast pathology
372. Management of labor and delivery
373. Infertility
374. Prenatal diagnosis
375. Oncology, breast
376. Obstetric anesthesia
377. Clinical obstetrics, abnormal
378. Physiology of pregnancy
379. Teratology
380. Infertility
381. Oncology
382. Clinical obstetrics, abnormal
383. Abortion
384. Oncology

385. Reproductive endocrinology
386. Oncology
387. Oncology
388. Oncology
389. Oncology
390. Oncology
391. Oncology
392. Teratology
393. Teratology
394. Genetics
395. Genetics
396. Clinical obstetrics, abnormal
397. Clinical gynecology
398. Clinical obstetrics, abnormal
399. Breast disease
400. Breast disease
401. Breast disease
402. Breast disease

Pediatrics

Stephan R. Glicken, MD

DIRECTIONS (Questions 403 through 428): Each of the numbered items or incomplete statements in this section is followed by answers or by completions of the statement. Select the ONE lettered answer or completion that is BEST in each case.

403. All the following statements about cystic fibrosis are true EXCEPT

(A) the incidence in whites is about 1 in 2000
(B) it may present in the newborn period with meconium ileus
(C) it is an autosomal dominant disease
(D) hepatic involvement is due to inspissated biliary secretions
(E) chronic hypoxia, hypercapnia, and acidosis produce pulmonary hypertension

404. Which of the following statements in regard to fever in infants and children is NOT correct?

(A) Fever is generally of more concern in the very young infant than the older child.
(B) Fever may be a manifestation of a noninfectious condition.
(C) The febrile response is initiated by release of interleukin-1 by macrophages and certain other cells.
(D) Brain damage is likely when rectal temperature exceeds 40°C (104°F).
(E) The central component of the febrile response is mediated by prostaglandins.

405. A 14-month-old boy is taken to the emergency room with a fracture of the left femur sustained, according to his father, in a fall from his crib. Bruises are observed on both shoulders and on the back. The remainder of the examination is within normal limits. Which of the following evaluative procedures should be performed first?

(A) skull CT scan
(B) chest roentgenogram
(C) lumbar puncture
(D) retinoscopy
(E) renal sonography

406. A 2-year-old girl feeds her 4-month-old brother 8 of her mother's prenatal iron pills (325 mg ferrous sulfate), 10 amoxicillin tablets (250 mg), and 9 prenatal vitamin tablets. The most likely result if appropriate therapy is not undertaken is

(A) hypercoagulable state caused by excessive vitamin K
(B) tooth staining caused by exposure to amoxicillin
(C) hepatic necrosis caused by iron toxicity
(D) bowel necrosis caused by fluoride toxicity
(E) hemolytic anemia caused by iron toxicity

407. A baby is born with ambiguous genitalia. It appears to have a small, well-formed phallus, but no testes are palpable and the scrotum is poorly fused. Which of the following statements is correct?

(A) The baby should undergo corrective surgery and should be reared as a female.
(B) Adrenogenital syndrome must be ruled out.
(C) The baby should be reared according to the appearance of its genitalia.
(D) The baby's gender assignment should be determined by its chromosomal sex.
(E) Gender assignment must be made immediately to prevent parents and relatives from transmitting to the child their confusion about the sexual identity.

408. Child abuse, including sexual abuse, is being recognized and reported with such increased frequency that it has reached epidemic proportions. Which of the following complaints is LEAST likely to be a clue to sexual abuse?

(A) encopresis
(B) secondary enuresis
(C) recurrent abdominal pain
(D) chronic cough
(E) school phobia

409. A specific pattern of abnormalities has been identified among infants born to mothers who consume moderate to large amounts of alcohol during their pregnancies. All of the following abnormalities are characteristic of these infants EXCEPT

(A) growth deficiency
(B) cardiac defects
(C) facial abnormalities
(D) major joint abnormalities
(E) mental retardation

410. The major clinical manifestations of rheumatic fever include all of the following EXCEPT

(A) carditis
(B) polyarthritis
(C) chorea
(D) erythema chronicum migrans
(E) subcutaneous nodules

411. An 8-month-old child presents with fever and respiratory distress. Auscultation of the chest reveals crackles and decreased breath sounds bilaterally. The child appears agitated and restless. The remainder of the physical examination is within normal limits. Chest roentgenogram reveals a normal heart size and bilateral pneumonia. Arterial oxygen tension is 50 mm Hg and carbon dioxide tension is 69 mm Hg. Which of the following is most appropriate in the management of this child at this time?

(A) endotracheal intubation and assisted ventilation
(B) oxygen and close observation
(C) oxygen and bronchial (postural) drainage
(D) administration of bronchodilators by aerosol
(E) insertion of a Swan–Ganz catheter

412. A 10-month-old girl is admitted to a hospital because of the insidious onset of fever, a brassy cough, inspiratory stridor, and mild respiratory distress—all symptoms of infectious croup. If this diagnosis is correct, the most likely causative agent is

(A) adenovirus
(B) respiratory syncytial virus
(C) parainfluenza virus
(D) *Haemophilus influenzae*
(E) *Corynebacterium diphtheriae*

413. A 2-year-old girl is admitted to the hospital with generalized tonic convulsions. Her history is unremarkable, and her physical examination is normal except for a slightly red throat and a slight fever. Her prolonged convulsions require intravenous administration of diazepam. White blood cell count is normal, and lumbar puncture only reveals elevated cerebrospinal fluid pressure. CT scan of her head shows cerebral edema but no signs of trauma. Which of the following should be the next diagnostic step?

(A) free erythrocyte protoporphyrin level
(B) viral cultures of cerebrospinal fluid
(C) rapid slide (Monospot) test
(D) antistreptolysin O titer
(E) electroencephalography

414. A 4-year-old child manifests symptoms of fever, sore throat, and swollen lymph nodes. Spleen tip is palpable. Throat culture and rapid slide (Monospot) test results are negative. The next logical diagnostic procedure would involve

(A) repeat throat culture
(B) heterophil titer
(C) Epstein–Barr virus titer
(D) chest x-ray
(E) bone marrow examination

415. Women with phenylketonuria (PKU) who are planning pregnancy should be advised that

(A) a low phenylalanine diet should be initiated before conception
(B) a low phenylalanine diet should be started as soon as pregnancy is confirmed
(C) a low phenylalanine diet should be followed throughout the first trimester but can be stopped thereafter
(D) a low phenylalanine diet has been shown to have little effect in preventing fetal damage
(E) if phenylalanine levels are only mildly to moderately elevated, there is no need for dietary change

416. The major mode of transmission of HIV infection in young children today is

(A) biting
(B) transfusion
(C) vertical transmission
(D) horizontal transmission
(E) sexual abuse

417. A 4-year-old child with moderate vesicoureteral reflux has had recurrent urinary tract infections despite adequate antibiotic prophylaxis. This child now should have

(A) a 2-week course of intravenous antibiotics
(B) repeat intravenous pyelography
(C) renal arteriography
(D) antireflux surgery
(E) a course of vitamin C (ascorbic acid) in conjunction with antibiotic prophylaxis

418. All the following statements about nocturnal enuresis (bed-wetting) are true EXCEPT

(A) the problem occurs in approximately one third of 4-year-old children
(B) boys are affected more often than girls
(C) there is often a familial predisposition to enuresis
(D) small bladder capacity plays a causative role in many cases
(E) significant emotional problems are found in most affected children

419. Which of the following malignant neoplastic processes has the highest rate of spontaneous regression?

(A) neuroblastoma
(B) Ewing's sarcoma
(C) Wilms' tumor
(D) acute myelogenous leukemia
(E) Hodgkin's disease

420. All of the following immunizations are currently recommended routinely for normal children in the United States EXCEPT

(A) smallpox vaccination
(B) pneumococcal vaccine
(C) *Haemophilus influenzae* vaccine
(D) Salk inactivated polio vaccine
(E) hepatitis B vaccine

421. Which of the following conditions is the leading cause of death in the United States of infants between the ages of 1 and 12 months?

(A) bacterial meningitis
(B) congenital heart disease
(C) congenital malformation syndromes
(D) accidental poisonings
(E) sudden infant death syndrome

422. Long-term therapy of sickle cell disease includes all of the following EXCEPT

(A) pneumococcal vaccine
(B) monthly benzathine penicillin injections
(C) iron supplementation
(D) folic acid
(E) acetaminophen for pain

423. A 9-year-old boy presents with a several-day history of progressive arm and leg weakness. He has been well except for an upper respiratory infection 2 weeks ago. The patient is alert and oriented. On repeated examination, the heart rate varies between 60 and 140 beats/min and the blood pressure varies between 90/60 and 140/90 mm Hg. Respirations are shallow with a rate of 50/min. There is symmetric weakness of the face and all four extremities. Deep tendon reflexes are absent. Sensation is intact. The most likely diagnosis is

(A) polymyositis
(B) myasthenia gravis
(C) transverse myelitis
(D) Guillain–Barré syndrome
(E) viral encephalitis

424. Which of the following statements concerning sensorineural hearing loss in children with bacterial meningitis is true?

(A) It occurs uncommonly (less than 5% of cases).
(B) It occurs more commonly when *Haemophilus influenzae* type b rather than *Streptococcus pneumoniae* is the causative organism of the meningitis.
(C) Its onset often is late in the clinical course, after discontinuation of antimicrobial therapy.
(D) Prompt institution of antimicrobial therapy appears not to influence the incidence.
(E) Evoked-response audiometry is indicated only if there is clinically evident hearing loss.

Questions 425 through 428

An 8-year-old girl is involved in a severe motor vehicle accident and sustains multiple injuries to her head, arms, and abdomen. She arrives at the local emergency room with profuse and pulsatile bleeding from her left upper arm; the blood is bright red. The left forearm is disfigured, and bone can be seen in the wound. Her respirations are periodic and her lips are cyanotic. Respiratory rate is 6/min, pulse is 160/min, and blood pressure is 80/40 mm Hg. Her abdomen is rigid, and hemorrhagic discoloration is present along the lateral flanks.

425. The first step in the management of the girl described above would be to

(A) stop the bleeding from her left arm
(B) insert an intravenous line and give a large volume of normal saline
(C) ensure airway patency
(D) give vasopressor agents intravenously
(E) splint her left arm

426. The next step in management would be to

(A) stop the bleeding from her left arm
(B) insert an intravenous line and give a large volume of normal saline
(C) ensure airway patency
(D) give vasopressor agents intravenously
(E) splint her left arm

427. The most important first step in evaluating the girl's rigid abdomen would be to

(A) obtain a flat-plate roentgenogram of her abdomen
(B) obtain an emergency liver–spleen scan

(C) obtain an emergency ultrasound of her abdomen
(D) obtain an emergency CT scan of her abdomen
(E) perform a paracentesis of her abdomen

428. In treating the girl's fracture in the emergency room, the girl's physician should

(A) splint the arm and cover the wound with sterile gauze
(B) splint the arm and debride the wound
(C) splint the arm and close the wound
(D) splint the arm and start intravenous antibiotics
(E) reduce and splint the fracture

DIRECTIONS (Questions 429 through 458): Each group of items in this section consists of lettered headings followed by a set of numbered words or phrases. For each numbered word or phrase, select the ONE lettered heading that is most closely associated with it. Each lettered heading may be selected once, more than once, or not at all.

Questions 429 through 431

For each description below, select the drug with which it is likely to be associated.

(A) acetylcysteine (Mucomyst)
(B) methylene blue
(C) deferoxamine
(D) amyl nitrite
(E) atropine

429. Useful in the treatment of acetaminophen poisoning

430. Useful in the treatment of organic phosphate (e.g., Malathion) poisoning

431. Useful in the treatment of ferrous sulfate poisoning

Questions 432 through 434

For each congenital cardiac abnormality, select the most characteristic cardiac auscultatory finding.

(A) holosystolic murmur
(B) continuous "machinery" murmur
(C) wide, fixed splitting of the second heart sound
(D) systolic ejection murmur
(E) diastolic murmur

432. Ventricular septal defect

433. Valvular pulmonary stenosis

434. Atrial septal defect

Questions 435 through 438

For each condition listed below, select the organism with which it is most closely associated.

(A) *Haemophilus influenzae* type b
(B) group A streptococcus
(C) *Mycoplasma pneumoniae*
(D) *Escherichia coli*
(E) *Pneumocystis carinii*

435. Neonatal sepsis

436. Epiglottitis

437. Cervical adenitis

438. Occult bacteremia

Questions 439 through 441

For each condition listed below, select the characteristic skin lesion with which it is most closely associated.

(A) vesicle
(B) pustule
(C) nodule
(D) macule
(E) bulla

439. Stevens–Johnson syndrome

440. Hand-foot-and-mouth syndrome

441. Chickenpox

Questions 442 through 445

For each condition listed below, select the peripheral blood smear finding with which it is most closely associated.

(A) target cells
(B) no abnormality
(C) hypersegmented polymorphonuclear leukocytes
(D) hypochromia
(E) red blood cell fragmentation

442. Folate deficiency

443. Hemolytic uremic syndrome

444. Anemia of chronic disease

445. Iron deficiency

Questions 446 through 449

For each clinical description listed below, select the microorganism with which it is most likely to be associated.

(A) *Mycoplasma pneumoniae*
(B) *Pneumocystis carinii*
(C) *Chlamydia trachomatis*
(D) *Neisseria meningitidis*
(E) *Bordatella pertussis*
(F) respiratory syncytial virus
(G) group B streptococcus
(H) *Haemophilus influenzae* type b

446. Bronchiolitis in an infant

447. Pneumonia in an otherwise healthy adolescent

448. Pneumonia in a mildly ill 3-month-old infant

449. Meningitis in a neonate

Questions 450 through 454

For each condition listed below, select the medication with which it is most likely to be associated in an infant or child.

(A) theophylline
(B) aspirin
(C) vancomycin
(D) phenytoin
(E) cefaclor
(F) loperamide
(G) diphenhydramine
(H) valproic acid
(I) tetracycline

450. Gingival hyperplasia

451. Reye syndrome

452. Dental staining

453. Red man syndrome

454. Liver failure

Questions 455 through 458

For each disorder listed below, select the measurable defect.

(A) factor IX deficiency
(B) abnormal white blood cell chemotaxis
(C) factor VIII deficiency
(D) hypoxanthine guanine phosphoribosyltransferase deficiency
(E) abnormal hemoglobin synthesis
(F) defective NADPH oxidase system
(G) hexosaminidase A deficiency
(H) ornithine-transcarbamylase deficiency

455. Lesch–Nyhan syndrome

456. Chronic granulomatous disease

457. Hemophilia B

458. Tay–Sachs disease

ANSWERS AND EXPLANATIONS

403. (C) Cystic fibrosis is an autosomal recessive disorder common among whites. The incidence of the disorder is estimated to be about 1 in 2000. The disease is characterized by an unusual abnormality of the secretions of the exocrine glands. Meconium ileus is a common presenting feature in infants with cystic fibrosis. The disease has severe effects on the respiratory system, in which the viscid secretions obstruct the airways, predisposing to bacterial infections, bronchitis, chronic pneumonia, and bronchiectasis. The chronic changes in the lungs lead to hypoxia and hypercapnia, at times producing pulmonary hypertension and eventually cor pulmonale. Hepatic involvement is due to inspissated biliary secretions. Hepatic insufficiency results in hypoalbuminemia and edema. Portal hypertension with hypersplenism is common. Supplemental therapy with pancreatic enzymes is usually indicated. *(Hay et al, pp 436–438, 594)*

404. (D) Fevers up to 40°C (104°F) rectally are common and fevers to 42.1°C (106°F) are not rare in young children. There is no evidence that these degrees of fever result in any permanent damage to the brain or other organs. This is in contrast to heat illnesses, such as heat stroke or malignant hyperthermia, where body temperatures may reach or exceed 42.2°C (108°F) and brain damage is common. Although most fevers are associated with infections, this is not invariably true. Intracranial hemorrhage, leukemia and other neoplasms, histiocytosis-X, and juvenile rheumatoid arthritis are just a few examples of noninfectious diseases in which fever is common. The mechanism of fever involves the release of interleukin-1 (previously referred to as endogenous pyrogen) by macrophages and certain other cells. This low-molecular-weight protein is carried by the blood to the brain, where it stimulates the release of prostaglandins in the temperature control center located in the anterior hypothalamic region. Antipyretic drugs, such as aspirin and acetaminophen, act by blocking the synthesis of prostaglandins in the hypothalamus. In young infants, fever is an especial source of concern because of the risk of serious infection. In this age group, localized infection often occurs in the absence of expected signs or symptoms. For example, nuchal rigidity is very infrequent in young infants with meningitis; the only finding may be fever and irritability. *(Hay et al, pp 215–217)*

405. (D) When a child presents with atypical or multiple injuries, the possibility of child abuse must be a prime consideration. Because a significant percentage of pediatric emergency room visits are due to some kind of abuse or neglect, it is imperative that physicians have a high degree of suspicion in such cases as that described in the question. Injuries that result from being shaken by an adult and subtle head trauma are common findings in abused children. The retinas should always be examined for evidence of hemorrhage. Depending on symptoms and signs, bone roentgenograms, rib films, and CT scan of the head may be indicated in a total work-up of an abused child. Often, renal ultrasonography is advisable in the presence of flank mass or bloody urine. Caution must be observed if lumbar puncture is performed, because increased intracranial pressure may be present. Many hospitals have protocols for suspected child abuse cases, and trauma teams that include pediatricians, social workers, psychiatrists, nurses, and legal experts have aided in the treatment and rehabilitation of the victims and families of child abuse. *(Hay et al, pp 195–200)*

406. (C) Of the substances ingested, only iron and fluoride have any significant toxicity. The maximum amount of fluoride customarily contained in a tablet is 1 mg, which is much less than a toxic dose for even a full bottle of 100 tablets. While amoxicillin may commonly cause lower gastrointestinal distress and diarrhea, it has no effect on developing teeth. Tetracycline is the antibiotic well known for this effect. Toxicologically, iron is very important. Its acute effects, which may occur following an ingestion of 25 mg/kg of body weight, include acute corrosive necrosis of the stomach and bowel followed by acute hepatic necrosis. Management includes the induction of emesis followed by purging. Deferoxamine administration may reduce the serum iron concentration below toxic levels by chelation and consequent urinary excretion. *(Hay et al, pp 256–257, 306–307)*

407. (B) Gender assignment of infants with ambiguous genitalia should be done urgently, but not at the expense of an accurate and thoughtful decision. Gender assignment should be based on the correct diagnosis and a reasonable prognosis for future functioning; these, more than chromosomal or gonadal sex characteristics, should be the overriding considerations. Therefore, as much information as can be gathered must be available before a decision is made. Particularly important points to consider include the following: (1) In a virilized chromosomal female, salt-losing adrenogenital syndrome must be ruled out by determination of 17-hydroxyprogesterone levels. Not only is this a life-threatening condition if left untreated, but if treated appropriately, fully normal sexual functioning, including fertility, can be restored. (2) In inadequately virilized males for whom male gender assignment is being contemplated, a consultation with a urologist is mandatory to determine whether correction is likely to produce a phallus capable of sexual functioning. One must also demonstrate that the baby is not relatively androgen-resistant and that there will be a response to testosterone with the onset of puberty. (3) In addition to careful examination of the external genitalia, one should examine the internal genitalia by means of vaginography, pelvic ultrasonography, laparoscopy, or even laparotomy, depending on the needs of the individual case. (4) Although it is desirable to retain as many of the patient's original characteristics as possible, one must keep in mind that a functional vagina can be constructed with much less difficulty than can a functional penis. (5) Certain individuals with dysplastic gonads and a Y chromosome are prone to tumor formation and may require gonadectomy. In summary, gender assignment is a complex problem with important consequences for the infant and the infant's family. It should be made urgently but not hastily after appropriate tests have been administered and specialists in the field of endocrinology, urology, pediatric gynecology, and child development have been consulted. *(Hay et al, pp 833–846; Rudolph, pp 216, 1786–1789)*

408. (D) Children who are victims of sexual abuse often develop functional complaints, and it may be these complaints that first bring them to medical attention. School phobia, obviously, is functional in nature. Although most cases of school phobia represent a fear of separation from the parent rather than a fear of the school itself, in some cases it may result from someone in the school setting abusing the child. Encopresis, secondary enuresis (enuresis developing after bladder control had been achieved and the child had been dry at night), and recurrent abdominal pain are common functional complaints that, occasionally, may be a clue to sexual abuse. Cough is the least likely of the symptoms listed to be functional in nature. *(Hay et al, pp 195–197)*

409. (D) The characteristics of fetal alcohol syndrome include (1) persistent growth deficiency that begins in utero and affects weight, height, and head circumference; (2) facial abnormalities such as micrognathia, short palpebral fissures, and a thin upper lip; (3) cardiac abnormalities, commonly septal defects; (4) minor limb abnormalities with some restriction of mobility and some alteration in palmar crease patterns; and (5) mental deficiency ranging from mild to severe. There is a decided relationship between the extent of abnormalities and the degree of mental retardation. Affected infants may present with hypoglycemia and alcohol withdrawal symptoms, which may last for 48 to 72 hours. The management of these infants consists of correction of the hypoglycemia. Otherwise, no specific therapy is indicated, but prevention by restriction of maternal alcohol consumption during pregnancy needs to be stressed. *(Hay et al, p 909)*

410. (D) Erythema marginatum, an evanescent, erythematous macular eruption with central clearing and a serpiginous border, is the characteristic skin lesion of rheumatic fever. Erythema chronicum migrans is the pathognomonic skin lesion of Lyme disease. *(Hay et al, pp 507–510, 1059–1061)*

411. (A) This child has clear evidence of respiratory failure, which is a medical emergency. Administration of oxygen alone, although it might correct the hypoxemia, will not correct the hypercarbia and presumed respiratory acidosis. Immediate steps must be undertaken to restore effective alveolar ventilation so as to return arterial carbon dioxide levels to normal at the same time that oxygen is administered. The fact that this child appears restless is a clue to the severity of his respiratory insufficiency. In the absence of wheezing, it is unlikely that bronchodilators would be sufficiently effective to obviate the need for intubation. The fact that the roentgenogram reveals evidence of pneumonia rather than airway obstruction (no mention of hyperaeration), also makes it unlikely that bronchodilators would be effective. *(Hay et al, pp 316–319, 431–432)*

412. (C) Viruses are the causative agents in the vast majority of cases of infectious croup. The parainfluenza virus accounts for approximately 66% of the cases of infectious croup, with adenoviruses, respiratory syncytial, influenza, and measles viruses responsible for most of the remaining cases. The majority of cases of viral croup occur between the ages of 3 months and 5 years, whereas infectious croup caused by bacterial agents is more common between the ages of 3 and 7 years. *(Hay et al, pp 425–426, 967)*

413. (A) In the differential diagnosis of acute cerebral edema with convulsions in a child, ingestion of toxic substances, including lead, must be considered early so that specific management can be initiated immediately. Although a diagnosis of acute lead encephalopathy can be suspected following (1) a history of pica, (2) the presence of basophilically stippled erythrocytes, (3) lead lines in the long bones, or (4) heavy metal densities visible on abdominal roentgenograms, none of these may be present. A direct measurement of serum lead levels is often difficult to obtain within a short time. In contrast, the free erythrocyte protoporphyrin level can be rapidly measured in many laboratories. A marked elevation in such a case is highly suggestive of lead poisoning. A rapid slide (Monospot) test is unlikely to be positive in the presence of a normal white blood cell count and normal differential blood count. An EEG is not likely to provide a diagnosis under the circumstances described in the question. *(Hay et al, pp 307–308, 334–336)*

414. (C) Infectious mononucleosis may affect children of all ages. The rapid slide (Monospot) test response is positive in approximately 90% of infected persons; however, younger children with mononucleosis may have a negative result. Moreover, many younger children have poor antibody response to the heterophil titer test. Specific serodiagnostic testing for the Epstein–Barr virus, the agent responsible for infectious mononucleosis, can confirm the diagnosis. A repeat throat culture, even if positive for β-hemolytic *Streptococcus,* may be of only partial value, because both infectious mononucleosis and streptococcal pharyngitis may be present simultaneously. Chest x-ray and bone marrow examinations would contribute little to the correct diagnosis. *(Hay et al, pp 410–411, 962, 983–984)*

415. (A) The effects of maternal phenylketonuria (PKU) on the fetus are still incompletely understood. Adverse effects correlate with the degree of hyperphenylalaninemia: women with mildly to moderately elevated levels have borne both developmentally normal and damaged children. It does appear that lowering the maternal phenylalanine level into the normal range by dietary means starting before conception affords optimal protection. However, this treatment must be supervised carefully by a physician who has special knowledge of amino acid metabolism, and it should be backed by a laboratory that can measure appropriate amino acid concentrations throughout pregnancy. *(Hay et al, pp 867–869)*

416. (C) Current screening practices have all but eliminated blood transfusion as a source of HIV infection. Today, most infections in young children are the result of vertical (perinatal) transmission of the virus from an infected mother. Sexual abuse certainly is a possible source of infection, but fortunately few such cases have been reported. Horizontal transmission of HIV (e.g., in household or daycare settings) by biting or other behaviors, if it occurs at all, is extremely rare. *(Hay et al, pp 995–1005)*

417. (D) Vesicoureteral reflux is the most common anatomic abnormality associated with recurrent urinary tract infection in children. Many cases of reflux are the result of an inadequate length of submucosal ureter immediately proximal to its opening into the bladder lumen, a condition that sometimes requires surgical correction. However, in other children reflux often appears to result from the direct effects of infection on ureteral tone and peristalsis. Thus, many children may outgrow mild degrees of reflux if they are maintained on prophylactic antibiotics until the condition resolves. Frequently, moderate to severe degrees of reflux require surgery. Failure of adequate antibiotic treatment to prevent infection is also a prime indication for surgery. Repeating intravenous pyelography or performing renal arteriography on an already diagnosed case is not useful, although a radionuclide scan may be very helpful to determine the present degree of reflux with a minimum of radiation exposure. Vitamin C, although reportedly useful in acidifying the urine to help prevent infection, does not enhance adequate antibiotic prophylaxis. Intravenous antibiotics would be necessary only if oral antibiotics were not successful in eradicating infection. *(Hay et al, p 621; Rudolph, pp 1798–1799)*

418. (E) Nocturnal enuresis (involuntary nighttime bed-wetting) is a common problem. There is often a family history (parent or sibling) of enuresis, and boys are affected more often than girls. Fifteen percent of children still do not have nighttime bladder control by the age of 5 years. Even by the age of 12 years, fully 2 to 3% of children still have not developed complete nocturnal continence. Therefore, the age at which nocturnal enuresis is defined as a "problem" is somewhat arbitrary, but most authorities consider ages 5 to 6 years an appropriate time to consider intervention. Small bladder capacity is a common finding, but more significant urologic abnormalities are rare. Significant emotional problems are not found in most affected children. Evaluation of enuretic children involves a detailed history and physical examination, as well as urinalysis and urine culture. Contrast radiographic studies are indicated only if significant abnormalities are revealed by this initial evaluation. Treatment should be multifaceted and includes motivational counseling, bladder training exercises, enuresis alarms, and, under special circumstances, medication such as imipramine or anticholinergic drugs. *(Hay et al, pp 180–181)*

419. (A) Neuroblastoma is a malignant neoplasm arising from sympathetic nervous tissue and may occur anywhere such tissue is found. It occurs almost exclusively in the first 6 years of life. The diagnosis is most often made during evaluation of an abdominal mass. Advanced stages of the disease are accompanied by systemic symptoms, such as fever, anemia, and weight loss. The diagnosis is almost always suggested by increased urinary excretion of vanillylmandelic acid or homovanillic acid or both. Treatments include surgery, radiation, and chemotherapy. Prognosis depends on the patient's age and the extent to which the disease has spread. Younger patients fare especially well. Of great interest is the fact that neuroblastoma has the highest rate of spontaneous regression of any of the malignancies that afflict humankind. However, the overall survival rate in most reported series approximates only

50%, and this figure has changed little during the past two decades. *(Hay et al, pp 777–778, 782–783, 786–790)*

420. (A) *Haemophilus influenzae* vaccine currently is recommended in the United States for routine immunization of healthy children. Both *Streptococcus pneumoniae* and *Haemophilus influenzae* type b are common pathogens in the pediatric patient. Since immunization for *Haemophilus influenzae* began, it is no longer the leading cause of bacterial meningitis in young children beyond the neonatal period, but *Streptococcus pneumoniae* is. Pneumococcal vaccine is currently recommended for infants, children under 5 years of age who go to day-care centers, and certain high-risk children, for example, those with sickle cell disease, nephrotic syndrome, or asplenia. Hepatitis B vaccine is routinely used. Immunization against polio is now routinely accomplished with the inactivated Salk vaccine, at least initially. *(Hay et al, pp 223–237)*

421. (E) Although meningitis, congenital heart disease, congenital malformations, accidents, and poisonings are major causes of childhood morbidity and mortality, sudden infant death syndrome (SIDS) heads the list of causes of death in infants between the ages of 1 and 12 months. SIDS is diagnosed when death in an infant occurs unexpectedly and without explanation; careful autopsy discloses no identifiable cause. SIDS occurs most commonly in infants between the ages of 2 and 5 months and affects boys more frequently than girls. Additional risk factors include low socioeconomic level, low birth weight, and a positive family history for SIDS. The incidence in the general population is approximately 2 cases per 1000 live births. No single cause explains all cases of SIDS; however, many cases are thought to result from abnormalities of respiratory control leading to cessation of breathing (apnea), especially during sleep. Methods of prevention currently being used include home monitoring of respiration and use of respiratory stimulants such as theophylline. *(Hay et al, pp 461–462)*

422. (C) Appropriate long-term therapy for sickle cell disease includes measures aimed at preventing bacteremia. Penicillin and pneumococcal vaccine are helpful. Because folic acid deficiency has been thought to be associated with sickle cell disease, folic acid should be administered daily. Acetaminophen is an appropriate analgesic. Iron deficiency does not usually occur in affected children, and supplementation is contraindicated. *(Hay et al, pp 739–741)*

423. (D) Progressive, symmetric motor weakness, areflexia, and autonomic instability, with mild or absent sensory signs, are typical features of Guillain–Barré syndrome. Frequently there is a history of infection (often respiratory) in the several weeks preceding clinical onset of the syndrome. Supportive evidence for the diagnosis includes elevation of cerebrospinal fluid protein concentration with a mild (10 or fewer cells/μL) mononuclear pleocytosis and slowing of nerve conduction velocities. *(Hay et al, pp 678–680)*

424. (D) Sensorineural hearing loss is detected by evoked-response audiometry in 5 to 10% of children with bacterial meningitis. Up to 30% of children with meningitis caused by *Streptococcus pneumoniae* will have hearing deficits. Hearing loss generally is noted early in the course of bacterial meningitis and occurs despite prompt initiation of appropriate antimicrobial therapy. All children with bacterial meningitis should have hearing assessment by evoked-response audiometry before or soon after hospital discharge. *(Hay et al, pp 675–676, 1012–1014, 1042–1044)*

425–428. (425-C, 426-A, 427-E, 428-A) Because the emergency treatment of multiple trauma patients mobilizes a large number of personnel and calls for a large number of interventions, management approach in the emergency room must be geared first to sequential evaluation of the patients' life support systems. This sequence constitutes the "ABCs" of emergency care: ensure or establish a patent airway; monitor and support breathing; and monitor and support circulatory status. In the evaluation of circulatory status, bleeding should be controlled and then volume losses replaced.

Probable intra-abdominal bleeding is an emergency situation requiring rapid assessment and treatment. Paracentesis is a quick and reliable way to check for intra-abdominal bleeding. Roentgenography and sonography are useful to perform after paracentesis, but only if time permits.

Emergency room treatment of an open fracture is best accomplished by splinting and covering the wound. Reducing an open fracture should be performed by an orthopedist. Debridement can be done and antibiotic therapy started when time permits. Whether and when to close the wound are decisions usually made after all the measures mentioned above have been taken. *(Hay et al, pp 280–284)*

429–431. (429-A, 430-E, 431-C) Acetylcysteine (Mucomyst) is quite effective in the treatment of acetaminophen overdose. If treatment is begun within 16 hours of ingestion, hepatotoxicity is significantly reduced. Organic phosphates (e.g., Malathion, Parathion) are cholinesterase inhibitors used as insecticides. Atropine is the drug of choice in the treatment of poisonings with these agents. Deferoxamine chelates unabsorbed iron (ferrous sulfate) and facilitates the removal of this potentially toxic substance. Methylene blue is used in the treatment of nitrite or nitrate poisoning and amyl nitrate in cyanide poisoning. *(Hay et al, pp 295–296, 305–307)*

432–434. (432-A, 433-D, 434-C) Ventricular septal defect characteristically produces a high-pitched harsh, holosystolic murmur well localized to the left sternal border. Pulmonary stenosis produces a systolic ejection murmur maximal at the upper left sternal border, often with radiation to the back. Diastolic murmurs sometimes are audible in patients with either ventricular or atrial septal defects, but these diastolic sounds are not as characteristic as the findings described above. A continuous "machinery" murmur is characteristic of patent ductus arteriosus. *(Hay et al, pp 480–483, 487–489)*

435–438. (435-D, 436-A, 437-B, 438-A) With the exception of the group B streptococci, *Escherichia coli* is the most common cause of neonatal sepsis and meningitis in many medical centers. *Haemophilus influenzae* type b is a prominent cause of serious invasive bacterial disease in children between 1 month and 6 years of age. Conditions associated with the organism include meningitis, pneumonia, periorbital and facial cellulitis, and epiglottitis. Occult bacteremia is caused most commonly by *Streptococcus pneumoniae; H. influenzae* type b and *Neisseria meningitidis* are the other common causes of this condition. Cervical adenitis can be caused by a variety of microorganisms, including not only group A streptococcus but also *Staphylococcus aureus*, mycobacteria, and anaerobes. *(Hay et al, pp 61–62, 413–414, 426, 1012–1014, 1042–1044)*

439–441. (439-E, 440-A, 441-A) Stevens–Johnson syndrome (erythema multiforme major) is a hypersensitivity reaction that is believed to be immune-complex–mediated. Cutaneous lesions often are bullous, and mucous membrane involvement and systemic toxicity generally are present. Medications and/or infectious agents often are linked etiologically. Both hand-foot-and-mouth syndrome and chickenpox characteristically produce vesicular skin lesions. The former condition usually is a summertime illness caused by a variety of coxsackieviruses. The name of the condition derives from the fact that affected individuals often manifest vesicular lesions of the hands and feet as well as oral ulcers. *(Hay et al, pp 358, 963–964, 971–972, 977–979)*

442–445. (442-C, 443-E, 444-B, 445-D) Target cells can be observed in a variety of conditions, including thalassemia, thalassemia trait, and sickle hemoglobinopathies. Generally, there are no characteristic peripheral blood smear findings in the anemia of chronic disease although a low mean corpuscular volume (MCV) may be noted. Folate and vitamin B_{12} deficiency are associated with megaloblastic red blood cell changes (high MCV) and hypersegmentation of polymorphonuclear leukocytes. Iron deficiency anemia is characterized by hypochromia and microcytosis. The peripheral blood smear obtained from an individual with hemolytic uremic syndrome will demonstrate fragmentation of red blood cells and a reduced number of platelets. *(Hay et al, pp 609–610, 730–739)*

446–449. (446-F, 447-A, 448-C, 449-G) Bronchiolitis may be caused by a variety of viral pathogens, including parainfluenza, influenza, and adenovirus, but respiratory syncytial virus is by far the most common etiologic agent. *Mycoplasma pneumoniae* is the single most common agent of pneumonia among adolescents and young adults. *Chlamydia trachomatis* often causes scattered areas of pneumonia in 2- to 4-month-old infants, often with associated conjunctivitis. Group B streptococcus, enteric gram-negative bacilli, and *Listeria monocytogenes* are the most frequent causes of bacterial pneumonia during the newborn period. *(Hay et al, 62–63, 431–432, 442, 444–445, 1094–1095)*

450–454. (450-D, 451-B, 452-I, 453-C, 454-H) Gingival hyperplasia occurs in about 40% of individuals receiving phenytoin therapy. It does not appear to be related to dosage. Epidemiologic studies suggest a strong statistical association between aspirin use during the prodromal illness and development of Reye's syndrome. As a consequence, aspirin use is discouraged for children with influenza, chickenpox, and other common viral infections. Teeth may be stained yellow, brown, or gray as a result of tetracycline use during tooth formation. The drug generally should not be administered to children less than about 8 years of age. Red man syndrome is characterized by the presence of flushing, fever, chills, and paresthesias. It occurs during or shortly following vancomycin infusion and is thought to be histamine-mediated. Liver toxicity is commonly seen with the use of several anticonvulsants, particularly valproic acid and carbamazepine. *(Hay et al, 590–591, 644–645, 947–948)*

455–458. (455-D, 456-F, 457-A, 458-G) Lesch–Nyhan syndrome is a disorder of purine metabolism characterized by severe mental retardation, cerebral palsy, choreoathetosis, and self-destructive biting. It has an X-linked mode of inheritance. Chronic granulomatous disease is inherited primarily in an X-linked manner. Defective phagocyte oxidative function leads to a propensity for certain serious bacterial and fungal infections. Hemophilia B is another X-linked disease, which accounts for about 12% of all individuals with hemophilia. The clinical manifestations are indistinguishable from classic hemophilia. Tay–Sachs disease is a genetic disorder predominantly affecting individuals of Ashkenazi–Jewish descent and characterized by progressive neurologic deterioration and seizures, usually beginning during the first year of life. *(Hay et al, pp 668–670, 751, 757–759, 875–876)*

REFERENCES

Hay WW Jr, Hayward AR, Levin MJ, Sondheimer JM. *Current Pediatric Diagnosis and Treatment,* Stamford, CT: Appleton & Lange; 1999.

Rudolph AM, Hoffman JIE, Rudolph CD. *Rudolph's Pediatrics,* 20th ed. Stamford, CT: Appleton & Lange; 1996.

SUBSPECIALTY LIST: PEDIATRICS

Question Number and Subspecialty

403. Genetics
404. Infection
405. Psychosocial examination
406. Toxicology
407. Structure, genetics
408. Psychosocial history taking
409. Toxicology, congenital defects
410. Cardiology
411. Respiratory system
412. Infection
413. Toxicology
     Metabolic problems
     Use of laboratory

414. Infection
415. Metabolic problems
Definition of problems
Management
416. Infection
417. Structure
Infection
418. Growth and development
419. Neoplastic disease
420. Health maintenance, infection
421. Idiopathy
422. Hematology
423. Neurology
424. Neurology
425. Emergency medicine
426. Emergency medicine
427. Emergency medicine
428. Emergency medicine
429. Toxicology
430. Toxicology
431. Toxicology
432. Cardiology
433. Cardiology
434. Cardiology
435. Infection
436. Infection
437. Infection
438. Infection
439. Skin
440. Skin
441. Skin
442. Hematology
443. Hematology
444. Hematology
445. Hematology
446. Infection
447. Infection
448. Infection
449. Infection
450. Toxicology
451. Toxicology
452. Toxicology
453. Toxicology
454. Toxicology
455. Genetics
456. Genetics
457. Genetics
458. Genetics

Internal Medicine

Glenn C. Newell, MD

DIRECTIONS (Questions 459 through 486): Each of the numbered items or incomplete statements in this section is followed by answers or by completions of the statement. Select the ONE lettered answer or completion that is BEST in each case.

459. Galactorrhea, amenorrhea, and infertility all appear most commonly in association with

(A) hyperthyroidism
(B) hyperprolactinemia
(C) hyperadrenocorticism
(D) excessive growth hormone secretion
(E) hypothyroidism

460. The most sensitive test to diagnose hereditary angioedema is

(A) CH50
(B) C2
(C) C3
(D) C4
(E) C19

461. A 30-year-old forestry student picks an Ixodes tick off his hand. He was sure it was not there when he washed in the morning. The best management would be

(A) reassurance
(B) doxycycline 100 mg BID
(C) penicillin 250 mg QID
(D) erythromycin 250 mg QID
(E) amoxicillin 500 mg TID

462. The worst prognostic sign in acute viral hepatitis is

(A) nausea and vomiting
(B) bilirubin > 10
(C) amino transferase levels > 1000
(D) high titres of viral loads
(E) hypoglycemia

463. Which of the following statements about Cushing's disease is true?

(A) Serum adrenocorticotropin (ACTH) levels usually are low.
(B) Pituitary microadenoma usually is present.
(C) There is a high incidence of nonendocrine tumors.
(D) Nonsuppression of cortisol production by the high-dose dexamethasone suppression test is a characteristic finding.
(E) Treatment of choice is bilateral adrenalectomy.

464. Hypercalcemia is a side effect of

(A) mithramycin
(B) prednisone
(C) hydrochlorothiazide
(D) furosemide
(E) aminodarone

465. The most common cause of bacterial meningitis in adults is

(A) *Streptococcus pneumoniae*
(B) *Neisseria meningitidis*
(C) *Hemophilus influenzae*
(D) *Staphylococcus aureus*
(E) *Staphylococcus epidermidis*

466. The best test to screen for Zollinger–Ellison syndrome is

(A) multiple peptic ulcers on upper endoscopy
(B) fasting serum gastrin
(C) calcium infusion test
(D) secretin injection test
(E) basic gastric acid output

467. The predominant immunoglobulin deposited in the glomeruli and skin of persons with Henoch–Schönlein purpura is

(A) immunoglobulin A
(B) immunoglobulin D
(C) immunoglobulin E
(D) immunoglobulin G
(E) immunoglobulin M

468. The most specific test to determine iron deficiency is

(A) plasma ferritin
(B) plasma iron
(C) plasma transferrin
(D) red cell free protoporphyrin
(E) bone marrow width

469. The roentgenograms shown below are from a patient who has had a sudden onset of back pain. The vertebra most commonly affected by the disease process shown is

(A) C-7
(B) T-4
(C) T-12
(D) L-4
(E) S-1

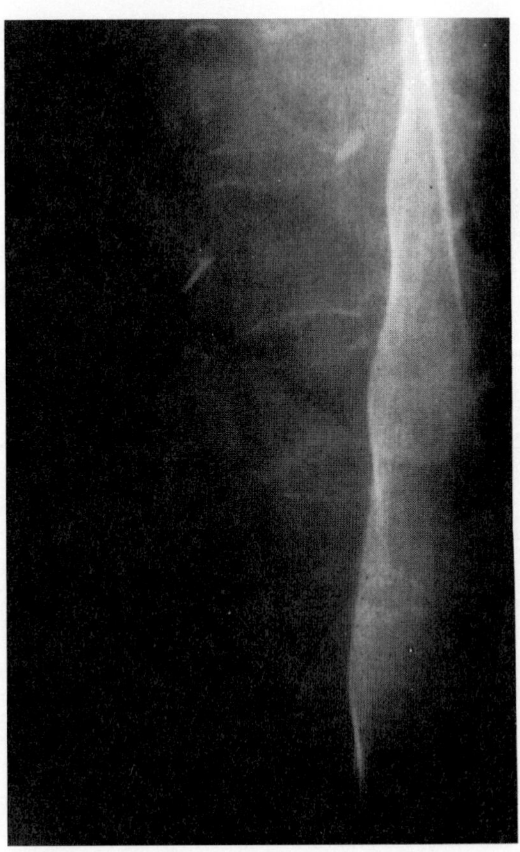

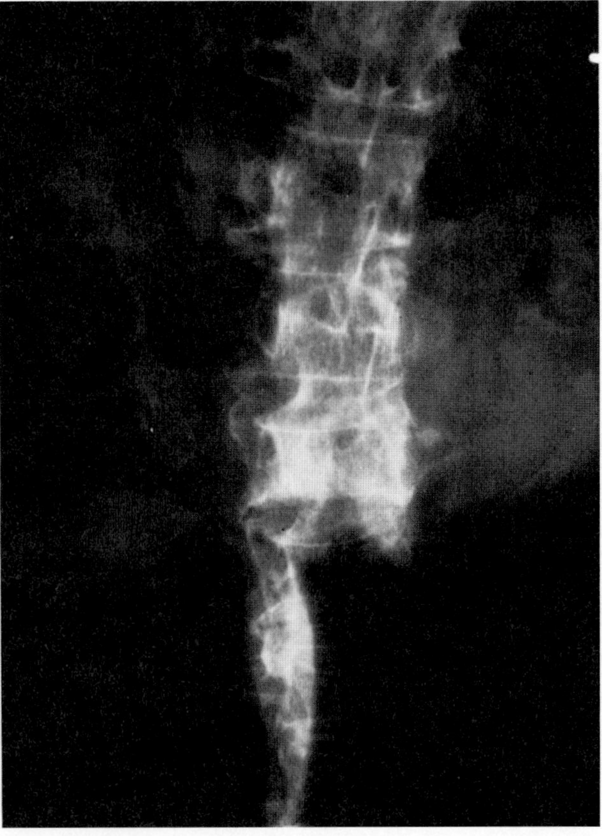

Figures for use with question 469.

470. A 20-year-old (see figure below) sexually active male presents with a round painless single penile ulcer for 8 weeks. Serologic tests for syphilis is negative (VDRL). The most likely diagnosis is

(A) chancre
(B) chancroid
(C) lymphogranuloma venereum
(D) granuloma inguinale
(E) herpes simplex

471. Antimitochondrial antibodies are found in 90% of patients with

(A) primary biliary cirrhosis
(B) chronic active hepatitis
(C) seminoma
(D) choriocarcinoma
(E) systemic lupus erythematosus

472. Which of the complications of hemochromatosis will improve with removal of excessive iron stores?

(A) arthropathy
(B) diabetes mellitus
(C) hypogonadism
(D) cirrhosis
(E) hepatocellular carcinoma

473. Mitral valve prolapse can be described by which of the following statements?

(A) Most affected individuals are asymptomatic.
(B) Men are affected more often than women.
(C) Ventricular arrhythmias are common.
(D) Mitral regurgitation frequently develops.
(E) Congestive heart failure frequently develops.

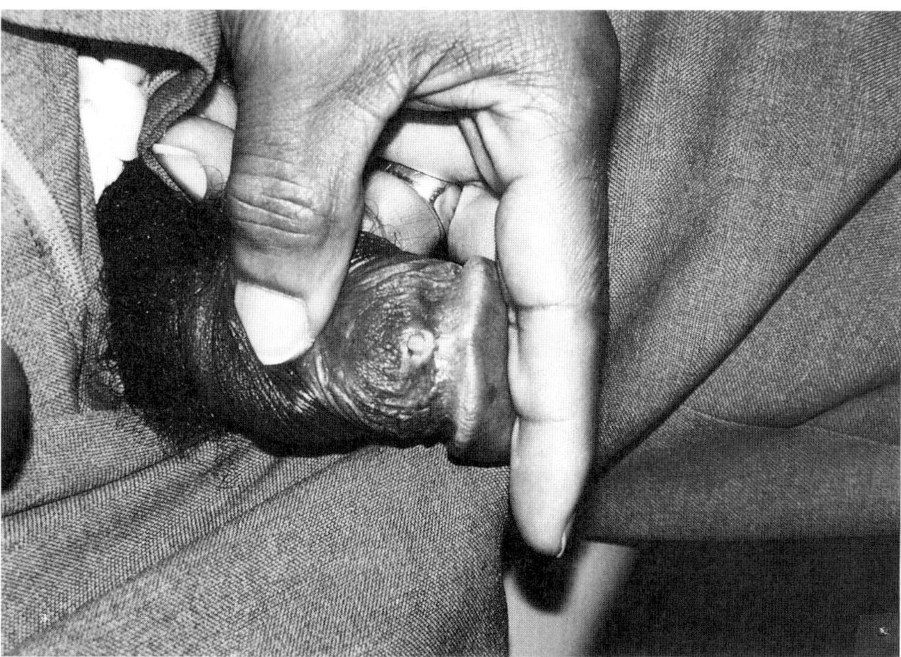

Figures for use with question 470.

474. A 61-year-old man complains of weakness and loss of weight. His voice is hoarse. Examination reveals tongue enlargement, hepatomegaly, pedal edema, and a purpuric rash on the face and neck. Urinalysis shows a protein/creatinine ratio > 4.0. Diagnosis may be made by

(A) liver–spleen scan
(B) 24-hour urine determination of protein
(C) subcutaneous fat biopsy
(D) urine protein electrophoresis
(E) urine protein immunophoresis

475. Which of the following is the most common cause of chronic cough in a non smoker who has a normal chest x-ray?

(A) chronic bronchitis
(B) asthma
(C) gastroesophageal reflux
(D) postinfectious cough
(E) postnasal drip

476. A 27-year-old man presents to you with an itchy groin. On exam he has a scaly red-brown rash between his legs and on his scrotum. The lesion looks coral red when examined under Woods lamp. The best treatment is

(A) Diflucan 150 mg orally once
(B) Diflucan 100 mg orally daily for three days
(C) erythromycin 250 mg po TID for seven days
(D) Bactrim DS po BID for seven days
(E) miconazole cream BID for seven days

477. A 67-year-old executive who has coronary artery disease is to undergo elective cholecystectomy. Perioperative cardiac risk would be most increased if

(A) jugular venous distention is present
(B) four premature ventricular contractions per minute are noted on ECG
(C) an S_4 gallop is heard
(D) he had coronary artery bypass grafting in the past
(E) general anesthesia is used

478. A 48-year-old chef is admitted to the coronary care unit with chest pain and diaphoresis. During the next 24 hours he develops ECG changes and enzyme elevations typical of an acute myocardial infarction. On the second day he is found to have a new harsh systolic murmur. The most likely diagnosis is

(A) papillary muscle rupture
(B) free wall rupture
(C) extension of the area of infarction
(D) coronary artery dissection
(E) aortic valve vegetation

Questions 479 through 481

A 25-year-old woman has intermittent diplopia. She says she chokes on her food and regurgitates it, sometimes through her nose. Physical examination reveals drooping eyelids and bilateral facial muscle weakness without atrophy; deep tendon reflexes are normal.

479. The most likely diagnosis for the woman described is

(A) familial periodic paralysis
(B) muscular dystrophy
(C) polymyositis
(D) myasthenia gravis
(E) multiple sclerosis

480. The pathogenesis of this woman's disorder involves

(A) an inflammatory process in the muscles
(B) antibodies directed against acetylcholine receptors
(C) slow-growing virus infection
(D) periodically depressed potassium levels
(E) a congenital inherited disorder

481. The best way to confirm this woman's diagnosis would be by

(A) observing long-term change in symptoms after injection of edrophonium
(B) observing long-term change in symptoms after administration of potassium
(C) demonstrating a decrease in muscle response to repetitive nerve stimulation
(D) demonstrating an increase in muscle response to repetitive nerve stimulation
(E) performing nerve conduction studies

Questions 482 and 483

482. A 17-year-old young lady presents with a sore throat. On exam, she has a fever of 102 orally, exudates on both tonsils, and cervical lymphadenopathy. Throat cultures are taken and the results are pending. Your next management step would be to

(A) await results of throat culture and treat if positive for group A streptococci
(B) reassure the patient that adenovirus is the most likely cause
(C) start penicillin to shorten the duration of pharyngitis
(D) start erythromycin because of new emerging resistant group A streptococcal strains
(E) start penicillin to prevent rheumatic fever and suppurative complications

483. With the proper treatment, the woman's symptoms abate. You recommend

(A) reculture the throat and, if positive, treat for an additional week
(B) reculture the throat and, if positive, treat for a total of one month
(C) reassure the patient that follow-up cultures are not necessary
(D) reculture the throat—but do not treat unless symptoms reappear
(E) culture the patient's sister because of the high risk of transfer among household siblings

Questions 484 through 486

A 50-year-old woman suddenly develops extreme weakness in the proximal muscles of her hips and thighs and then the shoulder girdle. The ocular muscles are unaffected and the distal muscles are spared. There is mild atrophy of the affected muscles, and deep tendon reflexes are only slightly reduced. She does not complain of muscle pain.

484. The most likely diagnosis for the woman described is

(A) polymyalgia rheumatica
(B) muscular dystrophy
(C) myasthenia gravis
(D) polymyositis
(E) thyrotoxicosis

485. The woman's diagnosis is best confirmed by which of the following tests?

(A) sedimentation rate
(B) serum creatine phosphokinase concentration
(C) thyroid function tests
(D) tensilon test
(E) muscle biopsy

486. The treatment of choice for the woman's disease is

(A) an anticholinesterase drug
(B) an immunosuppressive drug
(C) prednisone
(D) thyroidectomy
(E) thymectomy

DIRECTIONS (Questions 487 through 517): Each group of items in this section consists of lettered headings followed by a set of numbered words or phrases. For each numbered word or phrase, select the ONE lettered heading that is most closely associated with it. Each lettered heading may be selected once, more than once, or not at all.

Questions 487 through 490

Match the clinical presentation of headache with the most likely cause.

(A) throbbing or bursting headache that lasts minutes and is responsive to propanolol
(B) throbbing or pulsating headache that lasts for several weeks and is responsive to calcium channel blockers
(C) abrupt onset headache that lasts 20 to 30 minutes and is responsive to indomethacin
(D) periorbital distress of abrupt onset lasting up to 90 minutes

487. Cluster headaches

488. Chronic paroxysmal hemicrania

489. Post-traumatic headache

490. Coital headaches

Questions 491 through 494

Match the clinical presentation of vertigo with the most likely cause.

(A) recurrent vertigo attacks lasting seconds occurring most frequently when turning in bed at night without tinnitus and with normal hearing
(B) single vertigo episode lasting weeks without decrease in hearing
(C) recurrent vertigo attacks lasting hours with tinnitus, and unilateral hearing loss
(D) vertigo and dysequilibrium lasting years with bilateral hearing loss
(E) an attack of vertigo with hiccups, facial numbness, and Horner syndrome followed by months of dizziness

491. Gentamycin ototoxicity

492. Benign positioned vertigo

493. Vestibular neuronitis

494. Ménière's disease

Questions 495 through 498

For each set of clinical findings below, select the brain lesion most likely to be the cause.

(A) hemispheric lesion
(B) thalamic lesion
(C) midbrain lesion
(D) pontomedullary lesion
(E) none of the above

495. Pupils reactive and 3 mm in diameter; intact ocular movements; localized response to painful stimuli

496. Pupils reactive and 3 mm in diameter; intact ocular movements; decorticate posturing

497. Pupils unreactive and 5 mm in diameter; unpaired ocular movements; decorticate posturing

498. Pupils unreactive and 5 mm in diameter; ocular movements cannot be elicited; no motor response to pain

Questions 499 through 502

For each disease listed below, select the associated physical finding.

(A) decreased fremitus, trachea shifted toward affected side
(B) increased fremitus
(C) absent fremitus
(D) hyperresonance, low diaphragms
(E) decreased fremitus, trachea shifted away from affected side

499. Pneumothorax (nontension)

500. Emphysema

501. Lobar obstruction (atelectasis)

502. Pneumonia

Questions 503 through 506

For each statement listed below, select the associated abnormality.

(A) aortic stenosis
(B) mitral stenosis
(C) aortic regurgitation
(D) tricuspid regurgitation
(E) idiopathic hypertrophic subaortic stenosis

503. May be a complication of an inferior wall infarction

504. Associated with largest degree of left ventricular thickening

505. Atrial arrhythmias and recurrent pulmonary embolism feared complications

506. Loudness of murmur can be misleading in severe cases

Questions 507 and 508

For the nutrients deficiency listed below, select the appropriate statement.

(A) associated with anticonvulsant use
(B) caused by reduced absorption in the stomach
(C) neurological abnormalities may occur in the absence of anemia
(D) commonly causes thrombocytopenia
(E) most common cause of high MCV in alcoholics

507. Folate deficiency

508. Cobalamin (vitamin B_{12} deficiency)

Questions 509 through 513

For each clinical presentation, select the most likely diagnosis.

(A) ganglion
(B) radial nerve neuropathy
(C) radial osteoarthritis
(D) focal dystonia
(E) DeQuervain's tenosynovitis

509. 26-year-old postal worker with wrist pain, swelling of radial side, and dropping letters

510. 26-year-old cyclist with numbness at the base of the thumb

511. 26-year-old violin player dropping bow recurrently

512. 26-year-old writer with pain at the base of the thumb and positive Torque test

513. 26-year-old painter with paresthesia and nodule at dorsum of wrist.

Questions 514 through 517

(A) trochanteric bursitis
(B) anserine bursitis
(C) meralgia paresthetica
(D) iliopsoas bursitis

514. A middle-aged woman with pain in the knee while walking

515. A middle-aged woman with pain over the left thigh while leaning on that side

516. A middle-aged woman with a 50-pound weight gain and lateral thigh pain

517. A middle-aged woman with groin pain radiating to the thigh

DIRECTIONS (Questions 518 through 522): Each of the numbered items or incomplete statements in this section is followed by answers or by completions of the statement. Select the ONE lettered answer or completion that is BEST in each case.

518. *Staphylococcus aureus* endocarditis in intravenous drug abusers

(A) is less common than *Staphylococcus epidermitis* endocarditis
(B) preferentially involves the tricuspid valve
(C) should not be treated with valve replacement surgery
(D) is commonly associated with Osler nodes and splinter hemmorhages
(E) rarely results in septic pulmonary emboli

519. Evidence of infection with hepatitis C virus is seen in association with which of the following disease states?

(A) Henoch–Schönlein purpura
(B) mixed cryoglobulinemia
(C) Wegener's granulomatosis
(D) Sjögren's syndrome
(E) proliferative glomerulonephritis

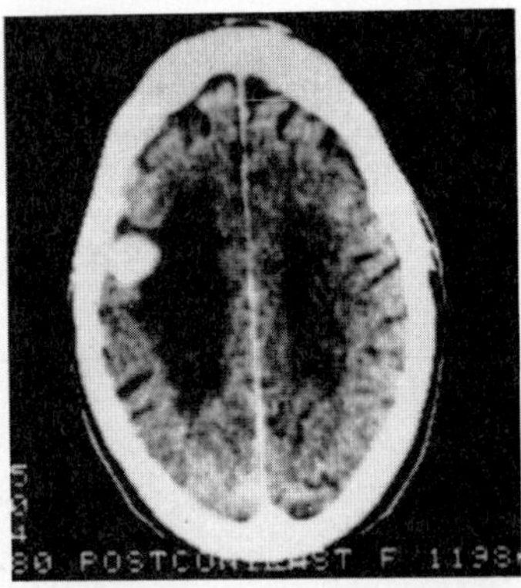

520. A 63-year-old man complains of worsening headache and right-sided weakness. CT of the head is shown above. The most likely diagnosis is

(A) aneurysmal bleed
(B) brain tumor
(C) lacunar infarct
(D) vasculitis
(E) toxoplasmosis infection

521. Bacteremia resulting from contaminated intravenous fluids is most likely to be caused by

(A) *Staphylococcus aureus*
(B) *Staphylococcus epidermidis*
(C) *Escherichia coli*
(D) *Enterobacter agglomerans*
(E) *Candida albicans*

522. A 26-year-old man is found to have acute leukemia. Three weeks after initiation of chemotherapy he has a body temperature spike to 38.9°C (102°F), with a white blood cell count of 500/mm. Which of the following is true regarding this clinical situation?

(A) Antibiotics should be given if a source of infection can be identified.
(B) Normal chest roentgenographic findings would eliminate pneumonia as the cause of the fever.
(C) Bacteremia, if present, would most likely be caused by *Pseudomonas* and other gram-negative bacilli.
(D) Chemotherapy and tumor lysis are the most likely cause of fever.
(E) Empiric antifungal therapy should be initiated immediately.

ANSWERS AND EXPLANATIONS

459. (B) Galactorrhea, amenorrhea, and infertility together are suggestive of excessive secretion of prolactin by the pituitary gland. Hyperprolactinemia is the most common pituitary hypersecretory disorder and occurs in almost 20% of women with secondary amenorrhea. Women who have prolactin levels less than 25 ng/mL and galactorrhea resulting from an increased sensitivity of their mammary glands to prolactin usually do not have amenorrhea. Hypothyroidism is a less common cause of galactorrhea. *(Fauci, p 2116)*

460. (D) Hereditary angioedema is due to a reduction in C1 esterase inhibitor. During attacks, levels of CH50, C2, and C4 are all low. However, C4 is only low in between attacks. *(Fauci, p 1683)*

461. (A) Lyme disease is due to the spirochete *Borrelia burgdorferi* transmitted by the tick *Ixodes dammini.* Ticks need to feed for more than 24 hours to transmit the spirochete to humans. Since the exposure was less than one day, in this case, the patient should be reassured. *(Fauci, p 1044)*

462. (E) There is no correlation between liver enzyme and bilirubin levels and ultimate prognosis in acute hepatitis. Hypoglycemia denotes massive hepatic necrosis and is a very poor prognostic sign. There is no data to support viral titres as a prognostic factor. *(Fauci, p 1689)*

463. (B) Cushing's *syndrome* is due to increased adrenal cortisol production, regardless of etiology. Cushing's *disease* usually is caused by a pituitary microadenoma producing high adrenocorticotropin (ACTH) levels. In most patients, cortisol levels would be suppressed as a result of the high-dose dexamethasone suppression test. Transsphenoidal microsurgical removal of the microadenoma is the treatment of choice in most centers. *(Fauci, pp 2042–2046)*

464. (C) Thiazide diuretics cause hypercalcemia by decreasing the urinary clearance of calcium. Furosemide conversely increases the urinary clearance of calcium and is often used to treat hypercalcemia in conjunction with intravenous fluids. Mithramycin and prednisone can both reduce calcium levels. *(Fauci, p. 2227)*

465. (A) *Streptococcus pneumoniae* is responsible for between 30 and 50% of cases of bacterial meningitis in adults, and *Neisseria meningitidis* between 10 and 35% of cases. *Hemophilus influenzae* meningitis occurs primarily in children, and group B *Streptococcus* meningitis usually affects infants. *Staphylococcus* is the most common cause of bacterial meningitis associated with shunting procedures. Acute otitis media and mastoiditis, recent head injury, sickle cell anemia, chronic alcoholism, immunoglobulin deficiency, and splenectomy all predispose to infection with *S. pneumoniae. (Isselbacher, pp 2296–2302)*

466. (B) Patients with ZES almost always have a fasting serum gastrin > 200 ng/L and the mean value is near 1000 ng/L. For patients in whom the disease is suspected and gastrin levels are equivocal, the secretin injection test is the most valuable provocative test. *(Fauci, p 1614)*

467. (A) Henoch–Schönlein purpura is one of the few diseases in which immunoglobulin A (IgA) is the predominant immunoglobulin deposited in the glomeruli and skin. In most other glomerulopathies, IgG and IgM are the predominant immunoglobulins deposited in glomeruli. Henoch-Schönlein purpura generally has a benign course characterized by arthralgias, abdominal pain, and nonthrombocytopenic purpura in addition to glomerulonephritis. However, progressive renal failure may occur in a small percentage of patients. Treatment is usually symptomatic. *(Fauci, pp 1918–1919)*

468. (A) A serum ferritin below 15 ng/L is very specific for iron deficiency. Low serum iron levels are often seen in anemia of chronic disease and is therefore less specific. High red cell free protoporphyrin levels can be seen in children exposed to lead, thus reducing the specificity. *(Fauci, pp 639–643)*

469. (C) The most common site of vertebral fracture in persons with idiopathic osteoporosis is middle and lower thoracic and upper lumbar vertebral bodies. More caudal or distal fractures are less likely to be due to idiopathic osteoporosis. Osteoporosis occurs most frequently in postmenopausal women but also occurs in younger women and in men. It is important to rule out secondary and potentially reversible forms of osteoporosis, such as glucocorticoid excess, hyperparathyroidism, thyrotoxicosis, multiple myeloma, and immobilization. Both estrogen supplementation and calcium supplementation have been shown to retard postmenopausal bone loss, but the increased risk of endometrial carcinoma with estrogen replacement may make this a less acceptable treatment. *(Isselbacher, pp 2172–2177)*

470. (A) Serologic tests for syphilis are negative in up to 20% of patients with syphilitic chancres. Darkfield examination is the best way to diagnose primary syphilis. Herpes simplex is very common, but is usually painful, recurrent with multiple ulcers. Herpes usually resolves in one month while untreated chancres may last 8 to 12 weeks. *(Fauci, pp 1023–1025)*

471. (A) The most characteristic immunologic abnormality associated with primary biliary cirrhosis is the presence of antimitochondrial antibodies, which are found in 90% of affected individuals. This antibody is predominantly IgG. Antimitochondrial antibodies also can be detected in persons with other liver diseases but with a much lower frequency (less than 10%) and usually in low titer. *(Isselbacher, pp 1487–1488)*

472. (B) Diabetes mellitus improves in 40% of patients with iron removal in hemochromatosis. Removal of excess iron has little effect on arthropathy or hypogonadism. Cirrhosis, once developed, is irreversible. Hepatocellular carcinoma appears as a late sequela in about one-third of patients who are cirrhotic at presentation despite adequate iron removal. *(Fauci, p 2152)*

473. (A) Most patients with mitral valve prolapse are asymptomatic. Ventricular arrhythmias are uncommon, and mitral valve regurgitation and congestive heart failure develop infrequently. Women are affected more commonly than men. *(Fauci, pp 1316–1317)*

474. (C) The clinical features of the patient described in the question suggest amyloidosis, a disorder characterized by extracellular deposition of fibrous protein in various tissues and organs. Amyloidosis may be primary or may be associated with an underlying disease such as myeloma or rheumatoid arthritis. It may present with skin lesions, macroglossia, hepatomegaly, malabsorption, proteinuria, congestive cardiomyopathy, or orthostatic hypotension. Diagnosis is based on the typical findings and demonstration of amyloid fibrils by Congo red staining under polarized light. Abdominal subcutaneous fat pad aspirate or rectal submucosal biopsy are often performed. Bone marrow, kidney, liver, skin, and endomyocardial biopsy specimens may also show positive findings. Liver scan findings are nonspecific for amyloidosis, as is the amount of protein in a 24-hour urine specimen. Urine protein electrophoresis and immunophoresis testing can help establish whether amyloidosis is immunoglobulin-related, but they are not diagnostic of amyloidosis. *(Isselbacher, pp 1625–1630)*

475. (E) Epidemiologic studies have shown postnasal drip to be the most common cause of chronic cough in nonsmokers. Empiric therapy to reduce nasal secretions is indicated. *(Fauci, pp 194–196)*

476. (C) The differential of intertriginous genital lesions includes tinea, candida, and erythrasma. Erythrasma is caused by a *Corynebacterium* sp. infection. It will fluoresce red under Woods lamp. The description in this case best fits erythrasma. The treatment is erythromycin. *(Goldman, p 2279)*

477. (A) Physicians are often confronted with the difficult task of evaluating for noncardiac surgery those patients with known cardiac disease. The best-studied group of such patients are those with coronary artery disease, for whom several risk factors have been identified. Previous myocardial infarction (especially within the last 6 months), age beyond 70 years, jugular venous distention, and S_3 gallop, aortic stenosis, rhythm other than sinus, more than five premature ventricular contractions per minute, emergency procedures, and thoracic, aortic, or upper abdominal surgery all increase the risk of surgery. Conversely, the patient's sex, location of the previous MI, method of anesthesia, stable an-gina pectoris, and previous coronary artery bypass grafting have not been associated with increased risk. *(Goldman, N Engl J Med, 1977; 297; 845)*

478. (A) A new systolic murmur appearing after an acute infarct requires immediate evaluation because it may indicate a lesion requiring surgical correction. Mitral regurgitation resulting from papillary muscle rupture occurs in almost 1% of all affected persons and may progress quickly to severe congestive failure. Papillary muscle dysfunction without actual rupture may also result in a new murmur. Interventricular septal rupture may occur; it progresses to cardiogenic shock in almost 50% of cases. Ventricular aneurysm formation is another cause of a new murmur following an infarction. Free wall rupture presents as sudden loss of pulse and blood pressure and not a new murmur. Coronary artery dissection is a cause, not a consequence of a myocardial infarction and does not usually cause a murmur. Extension of the area of infarction would not in itself cause a new murmur. Murmurs resulting from valvular vegetations occur in endocarditis, which would be unlikely in this setting. *(Fauci, p 1362)*

479. (D) The woman described has typical signs and symptoms of myasthenia gravis. Women in the third decade of life are most commonly affected. Ocular weakness is a very common presenting sign and is usually transitory. Facial and pharyngeal muscle weakness also are common. *(Fauci, p 2470)*

480. (B) It is now believed that myasthenia gravis is an autoimmune disease. Most patients (85%) produce antibodies that bind to acetylcholine receptors. (Complement is also found on the receptors.) Affected skeletal muscle is unable to synthesize acetylcholine receptors at a rate sufficient to enable the muscle to function properly. *(Fauci, p 2470)*

481. (C) Demonstrating a characteristic decreased response of affected muscle to repetitive nerve stimulation is important in the diagnosis of myasthenia gravis. Injection of neostigmine may be used for diagnosis if the edrophonium test is equivocal. *(Fauci, p 2470)*

482–483. (482-E, 483-C) Streptococcal pharyngitis is a common problem. Most experts would agree that in a patient with fever, exudates, and lymphadenopathy treatment should be started before culture results. Treatment is aimed primarily at reducing complications of streptococcal pharyngitis and does not reduce duration of illness. There is no resistance of group A streptococcus. Follow-up culture after treatment is no longer recommended. *(Fauci, p 886)*

484–486. (484-D, 485-E, 486-C) Polymyositis is an inflammatory disease that usually involves the proximal muscles of the upper and lower extremities. Ocular muscles are unaffected, unlike myasthenia gravis, and there is minimal atrophy. This syndrome may occur as an isolated illness or in association with a characteristic skin rash (dermatomyositis). Polymyositis may also be associated with such malignancies as lung, breast, colon, and prostate cancer. The diagnosis of polymyositis is confirmed by muscle biopsy showing an inflammatory reaction and widespread destruction of muscle fibers. Ancillary findings include elevated serum levels of creatine phosphokinase, aldolase, glutamic-oxaloacetic transaminase, and lactic dehydrogenase. Sedimentation rate also is elevated, and electromyograms are abnormal. Prednisone is the drug of choice for the treatment of polymyositis. If this treatment fails, immunosuppressive drugs can be tried. The end point of initial therapy is restoration of strength and normalization of muscle enzymes. Although drug therapy may sometimes be discontinued, most patients require long-term treatment. *(Fauci, pp 1896–1901)*

487–490. (487-D, 488-C, 489-B, 490-A) The time course and response to therapy helps in the differential diagnosis of headache. Cluster headaches occur near the eye, last approximately an hour, and respond to lithium, oxygen, or steroids. The excellent response to indomethacin is typical of chronic paroxysmal hemicrania. Posttraumatic headaches can be long-lasting and respond to beta blockers and calcium channel blockers. Postcoital headache may last hours and is also relieved by beta blockers. *(Fauci, pp 68–72)*

491–494. (491-D, 492-A, 493-B, 494-C) The cause of vertigo can usually be determined from the clinical history. Gentamicin ototoxicity can cause both hearing loss and vertigo that lasts for years. Vestibular neuronitis lasts for weeks and is not associated with hearing loss. Vertigo that lasts for seconds and comes on with positional changes is consistent with benign positional vertigo. Ménière's disease has tinnitis headaches and hearing loss. Vertigo with cranial nerve findings, such as facial numbness, may be caused by infarction of the lateral medulla (Wallenberg's syndrome). *(Fauci, pp 104–105)*

495–498. (495-A, 496-B, 497-C, 498-D) In evaluating a comatose patient, a physician must determine the level of the lesion and thus the severity of the coma. The site of supratentorial structural lesions of the central nervous system can be localized according to the pattern of clinical findings. Individuals with hemispheric lesions have reactive pupils 3 mm in diameter, intact ocular movements, and a localized motor response to painful stimuli. As the lesion progresses to the thalamic level, decorticate posturing develops. When the defect involves the midbrain, the pupils enlarge (5 mm) and become unreactive, and ocular movements are impaired. When the process affects the pontomedullary portion of the brain, ocular movements cannot be elicited, and there is no motor response to painful stimuli. It is very important to differentiate between supratentorial lesions and a metabolic encephalopathy in a comatose patient in order to know whether surgical intervention or medical therapy is needed. In patients with metabolic coma, anatomic localization is not possible: scattered, anatomically inconsistent central nervous system findings are found on examination. For example, findings of a pontomedullary lesion may be associated with hemispheric signs in the same patient. *(Fauci, pp 128–129)*

499–502. (499-C, 500-D, 501-A, 502-B) Careful physical examination is often very helpful in the diagnosis of common pulmonary diseases. Pneumothorax is characterized by absent fremitus, hyperresonant or tympanic percussion, and absent breath sounds on auscultation; in a nonlesion pneumothorax the trachea is shifted toward the attached side. Hyperresonance also is found in emphysema, associated also with low diaphragm (from hyperinflation), prolonged expiration, and inspiratory and expiratory wheezes. Lobar obstruction or atelectasis is associated with decreased fremitus with a tracheal shift toward the affected side, dullness on percussion, and absent breath sounds. On the other hand, a consolidation from pneumonia would have increased fremitus, percussive dullness, and bronchial breath sounds. Large pleural effusions are associated with decreased fremitus and tracheal deviation away from the affected side. *(Fauci, p 1408)*

503–506. (503-D, 504-C, 505-B, 506-A) Tricuspid regurgitation is often functional and can occur when right ventricular papillary muscles are damaged by an inferior infarction. Both chronic aortic stenosis and aortic regurgitation often result in left ventricular dilation and hypertrophy; however, the increase in left ventricular end-diastolic volume that occurs with aortic regurgitation can result in tremendous left ventricular thickening, with hearts at autopsy weighing up to 1000 g. Atrial arrhythmias occur with increasing frequency as the course of moderately severe mitral stenosis progresses; recurrent pulmonary emboli are an important cause of morbidity late in the course. While the murmur of aortic stenosis is generally grade 3/4 in patients with moderately severe obstruction, when severe stenosis is accompanied by heart failure the murmur may be soft and brief. *(Fauci, pp 1311–1324)*

507–508. (507-A, 508-C) Anticonvulsants such as phenytoin inhibit dihydrofolate reductase and are a common cause of folate deficiency. Folate and cobalamin are both absorbed in the small intestine. Abnormalities of the lipid membrane of red cells is the most common cause of a high mean corpuscular volume in alcoholic patients. Thrombocytopenia can occur with severe B_{12} deficiency, but is rare. *(Fauci, p 653)*

509–513. (509-E, 510-B, 511-D, 512-C, 513-A) Hand and wrist disorders are common problems in primary care. Ganglions are the most common cause of a nodule in the hand. An early symptom is intermittent pain with or without a paresthesias. DeQuervain's tenosynovitis is characterized by radial swelling and pain with ulnar deviation. Focal dystonias can come from recurrent prolonged use of a single motion, such as practicing an instrument, and can present as loss of function. Pressure trauma can result in radial nerve neuropathy and has been seen in distance cyclists. *(Canoso, pp 211–226)*

514–517. (514-B, 515-A, 516-C, 517-D) Patients with trochanteric bursitis typically complain of lateral hip pain while lying on the affected side. Meralgia paresthetica is a compression neuropathy of the lateral femoral cutaneous nerve and may be caused by rapid weight gain. Patients with iliopsoas bursitis present with groin pain that radiates to the buttock or anterior thigh. *(Canoso, pp 270–273)*

518. (B) Over half the cases of endocarditis in intravenous drug abusers are caused by *Staphylococcus aureus.* The tricuspid valve is preferentially involved (50% of cases), followed by the aortic (25%) and mitral (20%) valves. Peripheral stigmata are rare with endocarditis in intravenous drug abusers, especially when the tricuspid valve is involved. Septic and aseptic pulmonary emboli are common. If positive blood cultures persist on antibiotic therapy for the treatment of endocarditis, surgical valve replacement is necessary in all cases. *(Fauci, p 786)*

519. (B) Two thirds of patients with mixed cryoglobulinemia have evidence of infection with hepatitis C virus. Because hepatitis C virus has been found in vascular lesions along with immunoglobulin and complement, vasculitis in these individuals might be due to immune complexes containing the hepatitis antigen. *(Fauci, p 1548)*

520. (B) The CT scan that accompanies the question reveals near the left cortex a solitary, rounded, discrete lesion that enhances with contrast and has mild surrounding edema. The history, examination, and CT scan suggest a brain tumor, either primary or metastatic. Further work-up should be aimed at uncovering an occult primary tumor, if any. Common sources occur at the lungs, kidneys, colon, and breasts. Chest roentgenogram, intravenous pyelography, gastrointestinal series, or mammography might therefore be indicated. A myelogram or lymphangiogram would not be helpful for most patients. If an occult primary tumor cannot be found, biopsy of the brain lesion may be indicated. *(Stein, pp 2220–2222)*

521. (D) Infections with contaminated intravenous infusions involve organisms that are potentially pathogenic and survive well in water. These include *Enterobacter agglomerans, Pseudomonas cepacia, Citrobacter freundii, Klebsiella,* and *Serratia.* A large-scale national epidemic involved *Enterobacter agglomerans,* which became suspect when a large number of patients receiving IV fluids from one supplier developed bacteremia with this relatively uncommon blood culture isolate. *(Isselbacher, pp 583–586)*

522. (C) The leading cause of death in cancer patients is infection. Fever developing during the course of treatment for cancer demands careful investigation for infection by all classes of pathogens: bacteria, viruses, yeasts, and protozoans. Pneumonia is common but difficult to diagnose. There is scant sputum production, and often the chest roentgenographic findings are misleadingly normal. Gram-negative bacilli are responsible for most pneumonias and bacteremias. The skin, mucous membranes, and catheter sites are common portals of entry. In the absence of an obvious source of infection, it is essential to begin empirical antibiotic therapy aimed at the most common organisms. An antipseudomonal penicillin plus an aminoglycoside is a commonly used regimen. Both chemotherapy and the tumor lysis syndrome can cause fever, but infection is much more likely to be the cause. *(Goldman, p 1571)*

REFERENCES

Fauci AS, Braunwald E, et al, eds. *Harrison's Principles of Internal Medicine,* 14th ed. New York: McGraw-Hill Book Co; 1998.

Canoso JJ. *Rheumatology in Primary Care.* Philadelphia: WB Saunders Co; 1997.

Isselbacher KJ, Braunwald E, et al, eds. *Harrison's Principles of Internal Medicine,* 13th ed. New York: McGraw-Hill Book Co; 1994.

Goldman L, Bennet JC, eds. *Cecil's Textbook of Medicine,* 21st ed. Philadelphia: WB Saunders Co; 2000.

Goldman L, Caldera DL, Nussbaum SR, et al. Multifactorial index of cardiac risk in noncardiac surgical patients. *N Engl J Med.* 1977;297:845.

Stein JH, ed. *Internal Medicine.* Boston: Little, Brown & Co; 1987.

SUBSPECIALTY LIST: INTERNAL MEDICINE

Question Number and Subspecialty

459. Endocrinology
460. Allergy and immunology
461. Infectious disease
462. Emergency medicine
463. Endocrinology
464. Endocrinology
465. Infectious disease
466. Gastroenterology
467. Nephrology
468. Blood diseases
469. Rheumatology
470. Infectious diseases
471. Gastroenterology
472. Gastroenterology
473. Cardiology
474. Rheumatology
475. Respiratory diseases
476. Dermatologic diseases
477. Cardiovascular system diseases
478. Cardiovascular system diseases
479. Neurology
480. Neurology
481. Neurology
482. Infectious diseases
483. Infectious diseases
484. Rheumatology
485. Rheumatology
486. Rheumatology
487. Neurology
488. Neurology
489. Neurology
490. Neurology
491. Neurology
492. Neurology
493. Neurology
494. Neurology
495. Neurology
496. Neurology
497. Neurology
498. Neurology
499. Pulmonary medicine
500. Pulmonary medicine
501. Pulmonary medicine
502. Pulmonary medicine
503. Cardiology
504. Cardiology
505. Cardiology
506. Cardiology
507. Rheumatology
508. Rheumatology
509. Rheumatology
510. Rheumatology
511. Rheumatology
512. Rheumatology
513. Rheumatology
514. Rheumatology
515. Rheumatology
516. Rheumatology
517. Rheumatology
518. Infectious diseases
519. Gastroenterology
520. Oncology
521. Infectious diseases
522. Infectious diseases

Surgery

Frank C. Koniges, MD

DIRECTIONS (Questions 523 through 538): Each of the numbered items or incomplete statements in this section is followed by answers or by completions of the statement. Select the ONE lettered answer or completion that is BEST in each case.

523. The most specific test for diagnosing and localizing pheochromocytoma is

(A) CT scan
(B) sonography
(C) nephrotomography
(D) ^{131}I-metaiodobenzylguanidine scan
(E) abdominal aortic angiography

524. A severely traumatized patient who has been receiving prolonged parenteral alimentation develops diarrhea, mental status depression, alopecia, and perioral and periorbital dermatitis. Administration of which of the following trace elements is most likely to reverse these complications?

(A) iodine
(B) zinc
(C) selenium
(D) silicon
(E) tin

525. A 55-year-old man seeks medical attention for a painless, slow-growing mass that has persisted for 15 years and is located below and in front of his right ear. This growth is most likely

(A) a parotid adenocarcinoma
(B) a mucoepidermoid carcinoma
(C) a mixed tumor
(D) an undifferentiated carcinoma
(E) a sarcoma

526. Clark's classification of melanoma is based on the

(A) level of tissue invasion
(B) depth of tissue invasion
(C) width of the lesion
(D) presence or absence of nodal metastasis
(E) none of the above

527. Under which circumstances might one see the radiographic abnormality shown on page 146?

(A) perforation of a duodenal ulcer
(B) free perforation of a sigmoid diverticulum
(C) gastric outlet obstruction
(D) rupture of the gallbladder
(E) following laparotomy
(F) small bowel obstruction
(G) uncomplicated diverticulitis

528. A man who underwent total thyroidectomy 24 hours ago now complains of a generalized "tingling" sensation and muscle cramps. Appropriate treatment would include

(A) intravenous infusion of calcium gluconate
(B) administration of oxygen by mask
(C) administration of an anticonvulsant
(D) administration of a tranquilizer
(E) neurologic consultation

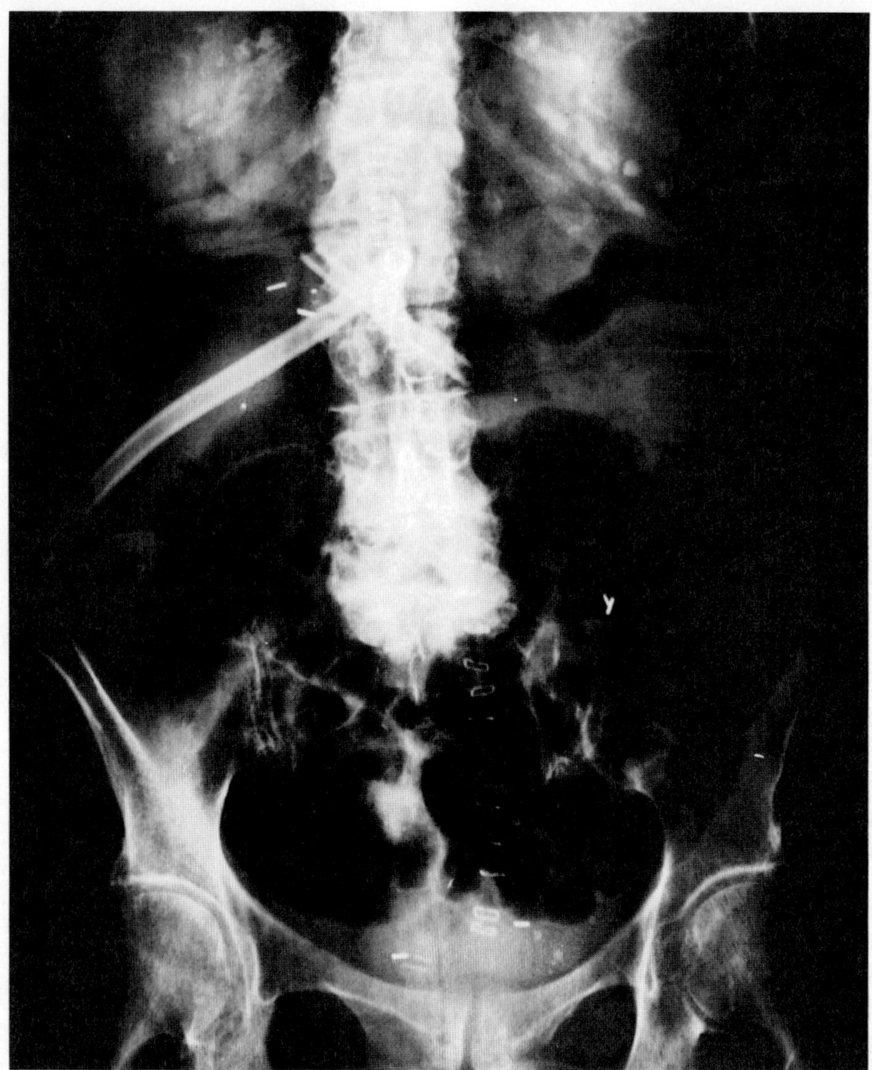

Figure for use with question 527.

529. Vital capacity is best described as the volume of air

(A) inhaled during normal respiration
(B) expelled during passive expiration
(C) remaining in the lungs after passive expiration
(D) actively exchanging with pulmonary venous blood
(E) able to be expelled following maximal inspiration

530. Prolonged exposure to para-aminobiphenyl is associated with the development of

(A) basal cell carcinoma
(B) urinary bladder carcinoma
(C) lung carcinoma
(D) large-bowel carcinoma
(E) pancreatic carcinoma

531. The most common site of aortic transection in deceleration injuries is

(A) the root of the aorta
(B) at the level of the right innominate artery
(C) at the level of the left innominate artery

(D) near the origin of the left subclavian artery
(E) in the middle portion of the descending thoracic aorta

532. The most common site of gastrinoma is the

(A) gastric antrum
(B) duodenum
(C) pancreas
(D) spleen
(E) gallbladder

533. Avascular necrosis is most likely to occur in fracture dislocations involving the

(A) femoral head
(B) shaft of the femur
(C) shaft of the humerus
(D) scapula
(E) clavicle

534. A 38-year-old man, previously in good health, suddenly develops severe abdominal pain radiating from the left loin to groin and associated with nausea, perspiration, and the need for frequent urination. He is restless, tossing in bed, but has no abnormal findings. The most likely diagnosis is

(A) herpes zoster
(B) left ureteral calculus
(C) sigmoid diverticulitis
(D) torsion of the left testicle
(E) retroperitoneal hemorrhage

535. A kidney from one identical twin is transplanted in the iliac fossa of the other. This type of transplantation is described as

(A) an orthotopic autograft
(B) a heterotopic isograft
(C) an orthotopic isograft
(D) an orthotopic allograft
(E) a heterotopic xenograft

536. Loss of limb is most likely to occur in injuries involving the

(A) external iliac artery
(B) internal iliac artery
(C) superficial femoral artery
(D) deep femoral artery
(E) popliteal artery

537. Persons with burns over large areas of their bodies may have daily calorie requirements as great as

(A) 1000 kcal
(B) 1500 kcal
(C) 2000 kcal
(D) 2500 kcal
(E) 3000 kcal

538. In a patient with a stab injury to the femoral artery, the treatment of choice is

(A) ligation of both transected ends
(B) end-to-end anastomosis
(C) interposition of autogenous vein graft
(D) interposition of homologous arterial graft
(E) interposition of Dacron graft

DIRECTIONS (Questions 539 through 545): Each of the numbered items or incomplete statements in this section is followed by answers or by completions of the statement. Select the ONE (OR MORE) lettered answer(s) or completion(s) for each case.

Questions 539 through 547

A 56-year-old man comes to the hospital. For the past 5 days he has had colicky abdominal pain, vomiting, abdominal distention, and constipation.

539. Appropriate measures in the initial management of this patient include (SELECT 4)

(A) upper GI endoscopy
(B) nasogastric decompression
(C) supine and erect x-rays of the abdomen
(D) abdominal sonography
(E) serum electrolyte determination
(F) antiemetics
(G) rehydration

540. The man described undergoes barium enema examination. The findings on barium enema, shown below, are most compatible with a diagnosis of

(A) mechanical small-bowel obstruction
(B) intussusception
(C) volvulus
(D) carcinoma of the colon
(E) diverticulitis

541. During definitive surgical treatment of the lesion shown on the barium enema, the left ureter is accidentally transected at the level of the pelvic brim. The most appropriate management of this complication would include

(A) ureteroneocystostomy
(B) left to right ureteroureterostomy
(C) anastomosis of the two cut ends over a "double J" stent
(D) nephrectomy
(E) ligation of the transected ends

Questions 542 through 545

A 19-year-old woman is now arriving in the emergency room after an automobile accident that caused injury to several of her organ systems.

542. The first priority in the management of this woman would be to

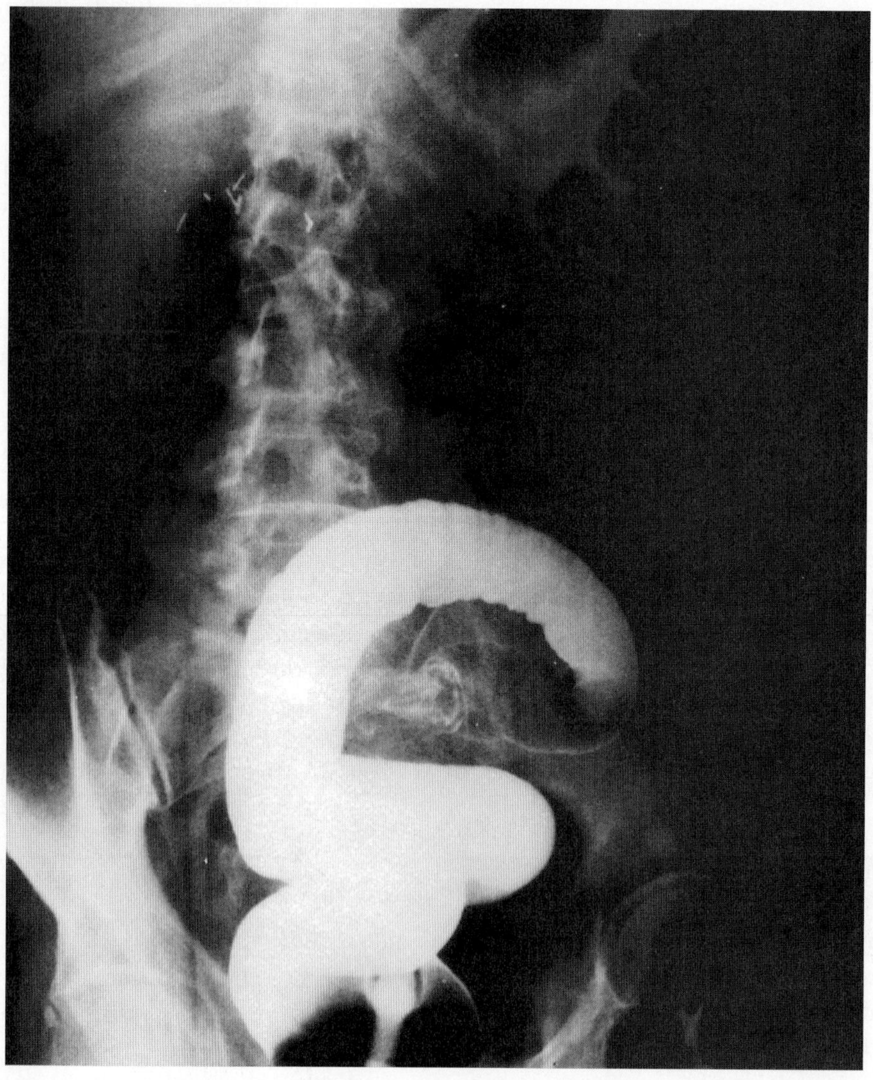

Figure for use with questions 540 and 541.

(A) insert an intravenous line
(B) insert a Foley catheter
(C) perform a thorough neurologic examination
(D) examine her airway
(E) check her blood pressure

543. Appropriate treatment measures include (SELECT 4)

(A) head elevation
(B) hypoventilation
(C) mannitol
(D) furosemide
(E) ventriculostomy
(F) Trendelenburg position
(G) spinal tap

544. The woman described undergoes exploratory laparotomy for a suspected intra-abdominal injury. Complete transection of the body of the pancreas is found. The treatment of choice is

(A) distal pancreatectomy
(B) repair of the pancreatic duct over a stent
(C) anastomosis of both transected ends to a defunctionalized loop of bowel
(D) ligation of both transected ends
(E) ligation of the proximal transection and anastomosis of the distal end to a loop of bowel

545. To improve her respiratory status, the woman is placed on a respirator. With the addition of positive end-expiratory pressure (PEEP), she suddenly develops restlessness, hypotension, and more profound hypoxemia. The most likely diagnosis is

(A) pulmonary embolism
(B) myocardial infarction
(C) decreased venous return
(D) tension pneumothorax
(E) cerebrovascular accident

Questions 546 through 547

546. A 50-year-old man comes to the emergency room with a history of vomiting of 3 days' duration. His past history reveals that for approximately 20 years, he has been getting epigastric pain, lasting for 2 to 3 weeks, during early spring and autumn. He remembers getting relief from pain by taking milk and antacids. Physical examination showed a fullness in the epigastric area with visible peristalsis, absence of tenderness, and normal active bowel sounds. The most likely diagnosis is

(A) gastric outlet obstruction
(B) small bowel obstruction
(C) volvulus of the colon
(D) incarcerated umbilical hernia
(E) cholecystitis

547. The following metabolic abnormalities are typical of the above patient. (SELECT 4)

(A) decreased antidiuretic hormone
(B) hypercalcemia
(C) hypokalemia
(D) hypovolemia
(E) hypochloremia
(F) decreased aldosterone secretion
(G) systemic alkalosis

DIRECTIONS (Questions 548 through 562): Each of the numbered items or incomplete statements in this section is followed by answers or by completions of the statement. Select the ONE lettered answer or completion that is BEST in each case.

548. Gastrin secretion is enhanced by

(A) antral distention
(B) antral acidification
(C) presence of fat in the antrum
(D) sympathetic nerve stimulation
(E) duodenal acidification

549. The most likely cause of sudden cardiopulmonary collapse in a patient with blunt thoracic injury is

(A) rib fracture
(B) hemothorax

(C) pneumothorax
(D) pulmonary contusion
(E) chylothorax

550. The most frequent cause of spontaneous pneumothorax is

(A) carcinoma of the lung
(B) tuberculosis
(C) pyogenic abscess of the lung
(D) emphysema
(E) rupture of small blebs

551. The absolute contraindication for lung resection in a patient with lung cancer is

(A) involvement of more than one ipsilateral lobe
(B) ipsilateral mediastinal node involvement
(C) chest wall invasion
(D) liver metastases
(E) pleural effusion

552. The overall 5-year survival rate of patients with carcinoma of the lung is

(A) 5%
(B) 10%
(C) 20%
(D) 40%
(E) 80%

553. A 45-year-old woman, mother of four children, comes to the emergency room complaining of the sudden onset of epigastric and right upper quadrant pain, radiating to the back, associated with vomiting. On examination, tenderness is elicited in the right upper quadrant, bowel sounds are decreased, and laboratory data shows leukocytosis, normal serum levels of amylase, lipase, and bilirubin. The most likely diagnosis is

(A) acute cholecystitis
(B) perforated peptic ulcer disease
(C) myocardial infarction
(D) acute pancreatitis
(E) sigmoid diverticulitis

554. The most useful diagnostic test to confirm the diagnosis is

(A) a two-way roentgenogram of the abdomen
(B) ultrasonography of the upper abdomen
(C) barium swallow
(D) HIDA scan
(E) peritoneal lavage

555. A patient is operated on with the presumptive diagnosis of acute appendicitis. However, at operation, the appendix and cecum are found to be normal. Terminal ileum for a distance of approximately 30 cm is red, edematous, and thickened with creeping of the mesenteric fat onto the ileum. There is no dilation of the bowel proximal to the area of involvement. The remainder of the small bowel is normal. The appropriate operative procedure is

(A) closure of the abdomen
(B) appendectomy
(C) ileostomy proximal to the area of involvement
(D) side-to-side ileo-transverse colostomy
(E) right hemicolectomy

556. Biopsy of a 4-cm rectal tumor shows it to be a villous adenoma with atypia. The most appropriate management of this tumor includes

(A) photocoagulation of the tumor
(B) electrocoagulation of the tumor
(C) transanal excision of the tumor
(D) abdominoperineal resection
(E) external beam radiation

557. The most frequent benign tumor of the lung is

(A) hamartoma
(B) lipoma
(C) carcinoid
(D) fibroma
(E) rhabdomyoma

558. The antibiotic of choice for treating patients with *Clostridium difficile* enterocolitis is

(A) penicillin
(B) gentamicin
(C) streptomycin
(D) metronidazole
(E) tetracycline

559. The most likely testicular tumor in a 25-year-old man is

(A) Leydig's cell tumor
(B) choriocarcinoma
(C) seminoma
(D) teratocarcinoma
(E) androblastoma

560. A neonate has persistent vomiting of bile-stained material. A two-way abdominal roentgenogram shows "double bubble" sign. The most likely diagnosis is

(A) annular pancreas
(B) duodenal atresia
(C) congenital hypertrophic pyloric stenosis
(D) Meckel's diverticulum
(E) none of the above

561. Maternal polyhydramnios is associated with

(A) esophageal atresia
(B) duodenal atresia
(C) jejunal atresia
(D) all of the above
(E) none of the above

562. Anal incontinence in a patient with rectal prolapse is primarily due to

(A) loss of anal rectal angle
(B) weakness of endopelvic fascia
(C) stretching of pudendal nerves
(D) all of the above
(E) none of the above

DIRECTIONS (Questions 563 through 584): Each of the numbered items or incomplete statements in this section is followed by answers or by completions of the statement. Select the ONE (OR MORE) lettered answer(s) or completion(s) for each case.

563. Relative contraindications for single-digit reimplantation include (SELECT 3)

(A) amputation occurring 12 hours before attempting reimplantation
(B) amputation of the thumb
(C) amputation proximal to the PIP (proximal interphalangeal) joint
(D) crush injuries
(E) amputation in a child
(F) associated life-threatening injuries
(G) contralateral hand injury

564. Which of the following statements are true regarding tracheoesophageal fistula following cuffed tracheostomy tube placement? (SELECT 4)

(A) Sudden bright red bleeding is a common feature.
(B) The incidence increases with the duration of tracheal intubation.
(C) It is best managed by nonsurgical means.
(D) Violent coughing following the ingestion of food is a common symptom.
(E) Positive pressure ventilation contributes to its development.
(F) An indwelling nasogastric tube is a predisposing factor.
(G) Mortality is greater than 90%.

565. The following apply correctly to increased intracranial pressure. (SELECT 4)

(A) It can result from head injury.
(B) It can result from an intracranial tumor.
(C) It can be relieved by solute diuresis.
(D) It is an indication to perform a spinal tap.
(E) It can be treated with ventriculostomy.
(F) The Trendelenburg position is appropriate initial management.
(G) Hyperosmolar NaCl solution should be given IV to prevent seizures.

566. Characteristics of wound contraction include: (SELECT 3)

(A) Onset is concurrrent with the appearance of granulation tissue.
(B) It is inhibited by epidermal grafts.
(C) It is slowed by radiation.
(D) Contraction begins 24 to 48 hours after injury.
(E) Myofibroblasts are believed to be the responsible agent.
(F) Contraction and contracture are synonymous.
(G) In wounds healing by secondary intervention, wound contraction is undesirable.

567. The following are characteristics of acute compartment syndrome. (SELECT 4)

(A) palpable venous cords
(B) pain on stretching the muscles
(C) absent arterial pulsations
(D) the presence of paresthesia or anesthesia
(E) the presence of paresis or paralysis
(F) intracompartment pressure of 13 cm H_2O
(G) may occur after arterial reconstruction

568. Which of the following correctly describe venous thromboembolism? (SELECT 3)

(A) Clinical diagnosis is unreliable.
(B) ^{125}I-labeled fibrinogen scanning is the most useful diagnostic test.
(C) Emboli frequently involve the superior mesenteric artery.
(D) Thrombosis commonly starts in the thigh veins.
(E) A "blue toe" is a characteristic finding.
(F) The risk of pulmonary embolism is increased with age, obesity, and oral contraceptives.
(G) Pulmonary emboli commonly originate from thigh veins.

569. Which of the following have been shown to be beneficial in decreasing deep vein thrombosis in patients with hip fracture? (SELECT 3)

(A) heparin
(B) warfarin
(C) dextran
(D) acetaminophen
(E) dipyridamole

570. Under which circumstance should retroperitoneal hematoma be initially treated with stabilization and embolization? (SELECT 1)

(A) expanding
(B) associated with pelvic fracture
(C) posterior to the lesser sac
(D) related to hepatic flexure laceration
(E) related to splenic flexure laceration

571. Which of the following characterize basal cell carcinoma? (SELECT 3)

(A) Metastatic spread to lymph nodes is common.
(B) It is the most common skin cancer.
(C) It is more common in those with dark-colored skin.
(D) It arises from the basal layer of epidermis.
(E) Its incidence increases with age.
(F) It is more common in exposed than unexposed skin.
(G) It is the most common type of burn wound carcinoma (Marjolin's ulcer).

572. Of the following, which are true concerning small bowel adenocarcinoma? (SELECT 4)

(A) It is the most frequent primary malignancy of the small bowel.
(B) The prognosis is worse, stage for stage, than with colon carcinoma.
(C) Its incidence is higher in persons with immunoglobulin deficiency.
(D) The risk is elevated in Peutz–Jaegers syndrome.
(E) The presenting features are those of intestinal obstruction.

(F) It is a typical feature of Meckel's diverticulum.
(G) Its incidence is higher in persons with Crohn's disease.

573. Somatic (muscle) protein malnourishment can be evaluated by (SELECT 4)

(A) total lymphocyte count
(B) creatinine height index
(C) triceps skin-fold measurement
(D) BUN
(E) serum transferrin level
(F) mid-arm muscle circumference
(G) weight loss

574. Esophagogastroduodenoscopy is indicated for (SELECT 4)

(A) the acute phase after corrosive ingestion
(B) gastric ulcer
(C) upper GI bleeding
(D) perforated duodenal ulcer
(E) epigastric pain with normal roentgenogram findings
(F) dysphagia
(G) elevated indirect bilirubin

575. The following are characteristic of Hirschsprung's disease. (SELECT 4)

(A) Constipation is the most frequent presenting feature.
(B) Enterocolitis is the major cause of death.
(C) Severity of the symptoms corresponds with the extent of bowel involvement.
(D) Acetylcholinesterase activity is increased in the aganglionic segment.
(E) Boys are affected more often than girls.
(F) The proximal colon is most commonly affected.
(G) It presents most commonly in young adults.

576. Elevated serum gastrin level is seen in (SELECT 4)

(A) Zollinger–Ellison syndrome
(B) patients taking nonsteroidal anti-inflammatory drugs
(C) retained antrum after Billroth II gastrectomy
(D) pernicious anemia
(E) uncomplicated duodenal ulcer
(F) secretin-secreting adenoma
(G) gastric outlet obstruction

577. The following statements are characteristic of ARDS. (SELECT 4)

(A) It is associated with congestive heart failure.
(B) There is a paradoxical decrease in PaO_2 when oxygen is administered.
(C) Functional residual capacity is increased.
(D) Lung compliance is decreased.
(E) Right to left shunting occurs.
(F) It is associated with sepsis.
(G) Chest x-ray typically shows a fluffy infiltrate.

578. The following statements apply to hematemesis. (SELECT 4)

(A) It refers to vomiting of blood from a source proximal to the ligament of Treitz.
(B) Hematocrit level is not an accurate indicator of blood loss.
(C) Melena does not occur unless there is at least 500 mL blood loss.
(D) Stools may remain positive for occult blood for 3 weeks following bleeding.
(E) Factors influencing the degree of azotemia include status of bacterial flora of gut, site of bleeding, and liver function.
(F) Surgical intervention is usually necessary to stop the bleeding.
(G) Gastric carcinoma is a common underlying etiology.

579. The following statements apply to cyclosporine. (SELECT 4)

(A) It interferes with hematopoiesis.
(B) It inhibits formation of cytotoxic T cells.
(C) Its use leads to permanent tolerance.
(D) It interferes with production of lymphokine interleukin-2.

(E) It is nephrotoxic.
(F) It is a fungal cyclic polypeptide.
(G) It has minimal usefulness in transplantation.

580. The following statements are true concerning ventricular aneurysm. (SELECT 4)

(A) It results from transmural infarction of the myocardium.
(B) Progressive enlargement and rupture are common.
(C) The majority are located in the anterolateral portion of the left ventricle.
(D) Chest pain is the most common symptom.
(E) Operation is indicated for symptomatic aneurysms.
(F) Right-sided aneurysms are more common than left.
(G) Aneurysms less than 5 cm in diameter have little hemodynamic effect.

581. The following statements are true concerning splenic injury. (SELECT 4)

(A) Nonoperative management is more likely to be successful in adults than in children.
(B) CT scan is the diagnostic modality of choice.
(C) Splenic salvage is contraindicated in the presence of other major abdominal injuries.
(D) The risk of postsplenectomy sepsis is highest during the first 2 years after splenectomy.
(E) *Pseudomonas aeruginosa* is the most frequent organism responsible for postsplenectomy sepsis.
(F) The incidence of delayed rupture is about 10%.
(G) The spleen is the organ most commonly injured in blunt abdominal trauma.

582. The following statements are true concerning mixed venous oxygen tension (PvO_2) and hemoglobin saturation (SvO_2). (SELECT 4)

(A) Normal SvO_2 is 50%.
(B) Normal PvO_2 is 40 mm Hg.
(C) SvO_2 is unaffected by cardiac output.
(D) SvO_2 is a sensitive means to follow peripheral oxygen delivery.
(E) A persistent PvO_2 less than 28 mm Hg is associated with death.
(F) SvO_2 is the best single predictor of cardiac output.
(G) An increase in hemoglobin concentration will result in a decrease in SvO_2.

583. The following statements apply to sacrococcygeal teratoma. (SELECT 4)

(A) It is more common in males.
(B) The coccyx should be spared during resection.
(C) It may present as a retorectal mass.
(D) It is prone to malignant degeneration.
(E) It should be excised promptly.
(F) Children who are older at presentation generally do better.
(G) Genital structures can usually be preserved at surgery.

584. A patient suffered an embolus to the common femoral artery thought to arise from an atrial thrombus. After embolectomy, the following measures may be appropriate in this patient's management. (SELECT 4)

(A) administration of sodium bicarbonate
(B) administration of ammonium hydrochloride
(C) aggressive hydration
(D) determination of serum potassium
(E) cessation of heparin
(F) administration of mannitol
(G) potassium chloride administration

DIRECTIONS (Questions 585 through 588): Each group of items in this section consists of lettered headings followed by a set of numbered words or phrases. For each numbered word or phrase, select the ONE lettered heading that is most closely associated with it. Each lettered heading may be selected once, more than once, or not at all.

Questions 585 through 588

For each of the following clinical situations, select the type of transplantation being described.

(A) heterotopic isograft
(B) heterotopic xenograft
(C) orthotopic autograft
(D) orthotopic isograft
(E) orthotopic allograft

585. Transplantation between genetically dissimilar individuals of the same species, and the transplanted part is placed at its normal anatomic location

586. Transplantation between genetically identical individuals, and the transplanted part is placed at an extra-anatomic location

587. Transplantation between genetically identical individuals, and the transplanted part is placed at its normal anatomic location

588. Transplantation between two different species, and the transplanted organ is placed at an extra-anatomic location

ANSWERS AND EXPLANATIONS

523. (D) Although CT scan, MRI, sonography, nephrotomography, and angiography may demonstrate a mass, these techniques by themselves cannot confirm the diagnosis of pheochromocytoma. In ^{131}I-metaiodobenzylguanidine scanning, the agent is selectively taken up by adrenal tumors and is helpful in the diagnosis of pheochromocytoma in both adrenal and extra-adrenal locations. This scan is also helpful in the diagnosis of medullary hyperplasia. *(Sabiston, p 692)*

524. (B) Symptoms of zinc deficiency include diarrhea, mental changes, alopecia, and periorbital, perinasal, and perioral dermatitis. Persons who have cirrhosis, who are receiving steroids, who have excessive loss of gastrointestinal secretions, or who are severely traumatized are at risk for zinc deficiency. Deficiency states resulting from inadequate ingestion of selenium, silicon, and tin have not been described. Deficiency of iodine produces hypothyroidism. *(Sabiston, p 164)*

525. (C) Mixed tumor of the salivary gland (pleomorphic adenoma) is the most frequently occurring tumor of the parotid gland (70%). It is slow growing, with a tendency for recurrence after removal. Mucoepidermoid carcinomas vary in the degree of their malignancy and are classified as either low-grade or high-grade tumors. Adenocarcinoma and undifferentiated carcinoma are fast-growing tumors that carry a poor prognosis. Sarcomas of the parotid gland are rare. *(Sabiston, pp 1322–1324)*

526. (A) Clark's classification of melanoma is based on the level of invasion and not on the actual depth of the tumor. In level I, the lesion has not penetrated the basement membrane. In level II, the lesion extends to the papillary dermis, and in level III, the lesion has penetrated the papillary and reticular dermis junction. In level IV, the reticular dermis is invaded. The subcutaneous tissue is invaded in level V. This classification provides prognostic information concerning the probability of lymph node metastasis and survival. In general, the higher the level, the higher the incidence of metastasis to lymph nodes and, consequently, the poorer the survival. *(Sabiston, p 521)*

527. (B) The radiographic abnormality seen on the roentgenogram presented in the question is pneumoperitoneum, which occurs following perforation of hollow viscera containing air. Air can gain entry into the peritoneal cavity during laparotomy and air insufflation of fallopian tubes, as well as from penetrating injuries of the abdominal wall. In the roentgenogram, pneumoperitoneum can be recognized by the presence of air both inside and outside the bowel lumen (the arrows point to the wall of the intestine). Gas-filled stomach or bowel may sometimes be confused with free air. *(Sabiston, p 829)*

528. (A) During total thyroidectomy, parathyroid glands may inadvertently be removed or their vascular supply interrupted. Hypoparathyroidism may then develop, the manifestations of which include tingling, muscle cramps, convulsions, and a positive Chvostek's sign. These symptoms are dramatically relieved by intravenous administration of calcium. Oral calcium and vitamin D are administered for long-term correction of hypocalcemia. *(Sabiston, pp 662–663)*

529. (E) Vital capacity is an important measure of respiratory function. It is defined as the maximum volume of air a person can expel following a maximum inspiratory effort. When vital capacity is normal, significant restrictive pulmonary disease is not present. Acutely decreased vital capacity indicates decreased ventilatory reserve. *(Sabiston, p 1787)*

530. (B) Carcinoma of the urinary bladder has been linked to several predisposing factors. The development of bladder carcinoma is associated with the ingestion of chemicals that are excreted in urine as conjugated ortho-aminophenols; among these chemicals are beta-naphthylamine and para-aminobiphenyl. Chronic schistosome infection and vesicle calculus also have been identified as predisposing factors. *(Schwartz et al, p 1761)*

531. (D) In deceleration injuries, laceration involving the aorta most frequently occurs just distal to the left subclavian artery. The tear may be complete or partial. Diagnosis is difficult; aortography is helpful in establishing the diagnosis. *(Sabiston, pp 310–311)*

532. (C) Gastrinoma produces Zollinger–Ellison syndrome, which is associated with markedly elevated gastric acid secretion and ulcer disease of the upper gastrointestinal tract. The most common site of occurrence is the pancreas. However, gastrinoma has been known to occur in the gastric antrum, duodenum, spleen, and ovary. Removal of the gastrinoma can result in a cure. A thorough search must be made at surgical exploration to locate the tumor, which in early stages will be small. The gastrinoma triangle is defined as the junction of the cystic and common bile ducts, second and third portion of the duodenum, and the division of the pancreatic neck and body. 90% of gastrinomas are located here. *(Sabiston, pp 1177–1180)*

533. (A) Avascular necrosis results when, following a fracture, the blood supply to a bone fragment is disrupted. The femoral head, humeral head, scaphoid, and talus, because of their precarious blood supply, are particularly vulnerable to this complication. A dense appearance of the bone on x-ray is a diagnostic clue. Radioisotope scanning can detect avascular necrosis at an earlier stage than is possible with roentgenography. *(Sabiston, p 1400)*

534. (B) Contraction of hollow organs against obstruction or excessive contraction causes colic. Typical ureteral colic is severe, sudden in onset, radiates from loin to groin, and is associated with an urge to urinate. Blood clots and calculi in the ureter can cause colic, the latter being more frequent. Urine examination demonstrates macroscopic or microscopic hematuria. *(Sabiston, pp 1526–1527)*

535. (B) Based on the genetic relationship between the donor and the recipient, transplants are classified as either (1) autografts, in which the same individual acts as both donor and recipient; (2) isografts, in which the donor and recipient are genetically identical; (3) allografts, in which the donor and recipient are genetically dissimilar but belong to the same species; or (4) xenografts, in which the donor and recipient belong to different species. In orthotopic transplants, the transplanted part is placed in its normal anatomic location. In heterotopic transplants, the transplanted part is placed in a different anatomic location. *(Sabiston, pp 383–384)*

536. (E) Arterial injuries below the level of the adductor hiatus result in more amputations than in other sites. Early diagnosis and prompt revascularization improve the chance for limb preservation. Blunt injury is associated with a higher incidence of limb loss, probably because of compression of collateral vessels from the tissue swelling. *(Sabiston, p 1712)*

537. (E) Major trauma, surgical complications, and infection are characterized by hypermetabolism. Calorie requirements are highest among burn victims. The daily energy requirement has been found to be 25 kcal/kg of body weight plus 40 kcal/% of body surface burned. *(Sabiston, pp 239–241)*

538. (B) The best results are obtained by repair of an injured vessel by direct anastomosis. This may not be feasible when a segment of the vessel is lost, and repair cannot be performed without tension. In these situations, an interposition graft may be required. Ligation of the transected ends may lead to ischemic necrosis. *(Sabiston, pp 1717–1718)*

539. (B, C, E, G) Abdominal ultrasonography has no role in the diagnosis or management of intestinal obstruction. Serum electrolyte determination helps in identifying the electrolyte disturbances that have taken place. Fluid loss needs to be corrected with rehydration. Nasogastric suction helps in decreasing abdominal distention. Upper GI endoscopy would increase distention, and is contraindicated. Antiemetics should not be given until a definitive diagnosis is made, and then only if indicated. *(Sabiston, pp 915–923)*

540. (D) An annular constricting lesion with overhanging edges is typical of annular carcinoma of the colon. Mechanical small-bowel obstruction results in multiple air-fluid levels in distended small-bowel loops. Intussusception produces a "corkscrew" appearance on barium enema, and sigmoid volvulus produces a "bird's beak" appearance. In diverticulitis, extravasation of barium outside the lumen of the colon typically is seen. *(Greenfield, pp 1014–1031)*

541. (C) The ureters may be injured during pelvic operations. It is important to recognize the injury, because early diagnosis and prompt treatment produce good results. Factors to be considered following the injury are whether the ureter needs to be repaired, the method of repair (if repair is necessary), and the measures required for minimizing the consequences of the injury. End-to-end anastomosis is a simple, feasible procedure when there is no loss of a segment of the transected ureter. When injury is close to the bladder, ureteroneocystostomy is the procedure of choice. When there is loss of ureteral substance, ureteroureterostomy (anastomosis to the opposite ureter) should be considered. Nephrectomy may be a reasonable choice if there is loss of renal function and ureteral injury is at a higher level. Ligating the transected ends should not be done. *(Sabiston, pp 352, 1542)*

542. (D) In a patient with multiple injuries, the first treatment priority is airway maintenance. Once the patency and adequacy of the airway are established, the other emergency procedures, such as control of external bleeding, can begin. Although detailed physical examination is needed in establishing a definitive diagnosis, the condition of an injured patient may not permit a detailed examination, and, in any event, emergency treatment must be instituted immediately. *(Sabiston, pp 296–297)*

543. (A, C, D, E) Increased intracranial pressure from any cause results in decreased cerebral perfusion. To minimize further brain damage, it is essential to decrease intracranial pressure, which can be effected by a combination of measures: elevation of the head of the patient; administration of a hyperosmotic agent (mannitol) to shift fluid from the intercellular compartment to the vascular compartment; and institution of diuretic therapy. Removal of mass lesions, such as a hematoma or necrotic brain tissue, should be performed if necessary. Hyperventilation should be instituted (hypoventilation is contraindicated). Hypocapnia resulting from hyperventilation causes vasoconstriction, decreasing intracranial pressure. *(Sabiston, pp 1356–1357)*

544. (A) The treatment of choice for complete transection of the body of the pancreas is distal pancreatectomy. This is a relatively simple and safe procedure and does not produce pancreatic insufficiency. Although the other procedures listed in the question may be feasible, in multitrauma patients the simplest and fastest procedure should be selected. *(Sabiston, pp 1181–1183)*

545. (D) Positive end-expiratory pressure (PEEP) is associated with two significant complications: pneumothorax and decreased venous return resulting from increased intrathoracic pressure. Pneumothorax causes a sudden worsening of a patient's condition, with increasing restlessness and progressive hypoxemia. Treatment consists of insertion of a chest tube. *(Sabiston, p 348)*

546. (A) In a patient who is known to have had symptoms of peptic ulcer disease for many years and presents with nausea and vomiting, one should consider gastric outlet obstruction, which can be due to exacerbation of the ulcer and edema or to scar tissue formation. Usually in these patients, epigastric fullness, with visible peristalsis going from the left side to the right, will be seen. A succussion splash may be audible. The history of periodicity and pain relief by taking antacids also favors a diagnosis of previous peptic ulcer disease. Patients with umbilical hernia will have a mass in the region of the umbilicus. Patients with acute cholecystitis usually present with the sudden onset of pain, radiating to the back, with fever and chills. Volvulus of the sigmoid colon presents with constipation and abdominal distention. Vomiting is a late feature. Small-bowel obstruction would be associated with a history of colicky abdominal pain, nausea, and vomiting. Patients will usually have hyperactive high-pitched bowel sounds. *(Sabiston, pp 858–859)*

547. (C, D, E, G) With persistent vomiting, the patient loses fluid, resulting in dehydration (hypovolemia). Loss of hydrogen ions and loss of potassium and chloride in the vomited gastric contents leads to alkalosis, hypokalemia, and hypochloremia. Because of hypovolemia, adrenocortical and renal mechanisms are stimulated to conserve sodium at the expense of potassium and hydrogen ions. Excretion of potassium in the urine further aggravates hypokalemia. The kidneys then compensate for the loss of potassium by conserving potassium and excreting more hydrogen ions, which results in a paradoxical aciduria and self-perpetuating metabolic alkalosis. *(Sabiston, pp 100–104)*

548. (A) Gastrin secretion is stimulated by vagal stimulation, antral distention, and by the presence of protein in the antrum. Antral acidification decreases gastrin secretion by a feedback mechanism. Acid secretion fortunately ceases when antral pH reaches 1.5. The same is true with duodenal acidification. *(Sabiston, pp 848–849)*

549. (C) The most frequent injury following blunt chest trauma is rib fracture. Unless associated with flail chest, rib fractures do not cause cardiopulmonary problems. Hemothorax can cause cardiopulmonary collapse if it is due to bleeding from intercostal vessels (high-pressure system). Hemothorax resulting from bleeding from lung parenchyma (low-pressure system) spontaneously stops. Chylothorax, secondary to blunt trauma, is very rare. Pulmonary contusion can cause cardiopulmonary collapse but is of gradual onset and unlikely to present as an acute episode. Pneumothorax, especially tension pneumothorax, acutely can cause cardiorespiratory collapse and may prove fatal unless promptly treated. *(Sabiston, pp 307–308)*

550. (E) Rupture of small blebs located in the apex of the lung is the most frequent cause of spontaneous pneumothorax. The condition is more frequent in men between the ages of 20 and 40 years. Prior to recognition of this entity, tuberculosis was considered to be the frequent cause of spontaneous pneumothorax. Chronic bronchitis and emphysema account for 10% of the cases of pneumothorax. *(Sabiston, pp 1833–1834)*

551. (D) Vocal cord paralysis indicates involvement of recurrent laryngeal nerve. Tumor invasion of the left recurrent laryngeal nerve in the aortopulmonary window is generally considered an indication of nonresectability. However, recurrent laryngeal nerve may be involved above the level of the aortic arch by direct tumor extension, in which case resection is not contraindicated. Some patients with chest wall invasion are cured following enbloc resection, and it therefore is not an absolute contraindication for resection. Tumors with ipsilateral mediastinal node involvement could be resected with a reasonable chance for cure. Malignant cells in pleural effusion indicate noncurability, but before a patient is denied a chance for cure, the presence of malignant cells in the effusion has to be proved beyond doubt. Involvement of more than one lobe has no bearing on prognosis as long as the patient's preoperative ventilation parameters will allow for safe resection. Metastasis to the liver is an absolute contraindication for resection, since lung cancer in this circumstance is not curable. *(Sabiston, pp 1865–1875)*

552. (B) The overall survival rate is approximately 10%. Five-year survival rate following surgical resection is 20 to 35%. In patients with T1 lesions, with no nodal or distant metastases, the survival rate is approximately 80%. *(Sabiston, pp 1865–1875)*

553–554. (553-A, 554-D) Women are more often affected by gallstones than men. Pregnancy predisposes for the occurrence of gallstones. Gallstones may remain asymptomatic or may cause symptoms when they cause obstruction to the cystic duct. The usual presenting symptom is biliary colic, which is experienced as epigastric pain, radiating to the back and associated with nausea and vomiting. The presence of tenderness in the right upper quadrant and leukocytosis under these circumstances are very indicative of acute cholecystitis. The diagnosis of gallstones is best confirmed by ultrasonography. Ultrasonography also provides details about the presence of gallstones, the wall of the gallbladder, and also the presence or absence of tenderness over the gallbladder during the examination. In only 20% of the cases, gallstones are seen on a two-way roentgenogram of the abdomen. Barium swallow in this instance is of no help. Failure to visualize the gallbladder with HIDA scan indicates cystic duct obstruction. In a majority of the patients acute cholecystitis is secondary to cystic duct obstruction. Lack of visualization may also occur in patients who have had a previous cholecystectomy (history is helpful) or agenesis of the gallbladder (rare). Peritoneal lavage in this instance will be of no help, except in detecting fluid, which may contain leukocytes. *(Sabiston, pp 837–838)*

555. (B) From the description, the diagnosis in this patient is acute regional enteritis. Incidental finding of regional enteritis in patients operated on for presumed diagnosis of acute appendicitis is medically treated, unless there is proximal obstruction. The risk of operating on patients with regional enteritis is formation of fistula and abscess, especially if the area to be resected is involved with the disease process. However, if the cecum and the appendix are not involved, it is advisable to perform appendectomy. In this instance, it would be safe and, if the patient were to have a recurrence in the future, at least acute appendicitis would no longer be a possible diagnosis and the patient could be treated for an exacerbation of regional enteritis. *(Sabiston, pp 923–932)*

556. (C) Villous adenoma is a premalignant condition. The incidence of carcinoma increases as the tumor increases in size, and the finding of a 4-cm lesion with induration has an almost 90% risk for carcinoma. The specimen that is being submitted for biopsy examination may not be truly representative of the entire lesion. Carcinoma may be present deep within the tumor. Therefore, to exclude malignancy, the tumor should be excised in its entirety and submitted for histologic examination. If an infiltrating tumor is seen, further treatment will be required. Photocoagulation and electrocoagulation of the tumor will destroy the tumor and may not provide the information as to its nature. Abdominal perineal resection should not be performed unless there is histologic proof of the presence of carcinoma. External beam radiation is not indicated in this situation. *(Sabiston, pp 995–996)*

557. (A) Hamartoma is the most frequent benign tumor of the lung. It presents as a density on chest roentgenogram, and it occurs usually during the fifth and sixth decades of life. Operation is often required to differentiate it from lung carcinoma. *(Sabiston, pp 72–73)*

558. (D) *Clostridium difficile* enterocolitis occurs as a complication of broad-spectrum antibiotic treatment. Symptoms may appear as late as 6 weeks following antibiotic treatment. The organism, which is resistant to broad-spectrum antibiotics, produces toxin that causes necrosis of the colonic mucous membrane. Orally administered metronidazole is the drug of choice. Vancomycin is also effective against *Clostridium difficile,* but due to its expense is often reserved for refractory cases. *(Sabiston, p 279)*

559. (C) The majority of testicular tumors occurring in young adults are malignant tumors. The tumors may originate from germinal or nongerminal cells. Those that arise from germinal cells include seminoma (the most common), embryonal cell carcinoma, choriocarcinoma, teratocarcinoma. Leydig cell tumors and androblastoma originate from nongerminal cells and may produce excess testosterone. Benign tumors such as fibroma can occur but are rare. *(Sabiston, p 1558)*

560. (B) Persistent bilious vomiting is a sign of intestinal obstruction, distal to the ampulla of Vater. Double bubble on a two-way abdominal roentgenogram is caused by air in the distended stomach and duodenum. The picture is most compatible with duodenal atresia, which typically presents in the neonate. *(Sabiston, p 1239)*

561. (D) Under normal circumstances, the fetus swallows amniotic fluid and the fluid is absorbed by the gastrointestinal tract. The absorbed fluid is then excreted through the kidneys. Any obstruction to the gastrointestinal tract interferes with this process and the mother runs the risk of developing polyhydramnios. Infants born to mothers with polyhydramnios should have the gastrointestinal tract investigated to rule out obstruction. Polyhydramnios is defined as greater than 2 liters of amniotic fluid. *(Sabiston, pp 1236–1237)*

562. (C) Anal and urinary incontinence in patients with rectal prolapse is due to stretching of pudendal nerves, resulting in neuromuscular dysfunction. Loss of anal rectal angle, loose endopelvic fascia, and stretching of the anal sphincter are associated with rectal prolapse but do not cause incontinence. Rectal prolapse should be repaired to prevent stretching of pudendal nerve and resulting incontinence. *(Sabiston, pp 1035–1036)*

563. (C, D, F) Advances in microsurgery techniques have enabled successful reimplantation of digits. Whether or not the digit should be reimplanted is sometimes an issue. In the consideration of reimplantation, the chances for return of function should be evaluated. There are no absolute indications or contraindications for reimplantation of a digit. In general, digital reimplantation is contraindicated in elderly patients with concomitant medical disorders, in patients with associated life-threatening injuries, and in cases of amputation of a single digit—with the exception of the thumb. The type of injury is another factor influencing the decision. A severe crush injury with extensive damage to the parts is a relative contraindication. Since digits have essentially no muscle, they may be reimplanted up to 24 hours after amputation. An amputation of a digit proximal to the PIP joint, however, may just get in the way as a useless appendage. Excellent function can usually be obtained in a child if the digit survives. *(Sabiston, pp 1487–1488)*

564. (B, D, E, F) Tracheoesophageal fistula is a serious complication of tracheostomy and tracheal intubation. The presence of a nasogastric tube, positive-pressure ventilation, and prolonged periods of intubation are predisposing factors. The complication should be suspected when an intubated patient develops violent coughing after swallowing food or saliva. The recommended treatment is primary closure of the fistulous opening in the trachea and the esophagus with a transposed regional muscle flap interposed between the trachea and esophagus. Nonsurgical corrective measures are associated with a higher rate of mortality. Sudden bright red bleeding is a symptom of tracheo-inominate artery fistula. Surgical repair of tracheoesophageal fistula has a low mortality rate. *(Sabiston, pp 1816–1820)*

565. (A, B, C, E) The skull is a rigid cavity, so expansion of its contents leads to increased intracranial pressure. Both brain edema resulting from trauma and space-occupying lesions within the skull increase intracranial pressure. Solute diuresis, corticosteroids, elevation of the head of the bed, and ventriculostomy are helpful in reducing the pressure. Spinal tap is contraindicated because of the danger of herniation of the brain. Hyperosmolar NaCl is used in patients with extreme hyponatremia, but is relatively contraindicated in patients with increased intracranial pressure. *(Sabiston, pp 354, 1356–1357)*

566. (A, C, E) Wound contraction, an important aspect of wound healing, can result in deformity. Dependent on myofibroblasts present in granulation tissue, wound contraction is slowed by radiation, administration of steroids, and splinting. The most effective measure for preventing wound contraction is partial or full-thickness skin grafts. Epidermal grafts do not prevent wound contraction. The reason for the differences observed between epidermal grafts and partial or full-thickness grafts is not well understood. Contracture refers to the shortening of scar tissue after a wound is healed, and is undesirable. *(Sabiston, pp 208–210)*

567. (B, D, E, G) Differentiation among acute compartment syndrome, arterial occlusion, and neuropraxia is not always easy (in fact, these conditions may coexist). However, accurate diagnosis is essential for proper management. Typical acute compartment syndrome is characterized by the following findings: pain on stretching the muscles; the presence of paresthesia or anesthesia; the presence of paralysis or paresis; and increased intracompartment pressure. Arterial pulsation is present but may require detection by Doppler technique. In a typical case of arterial occlusion, pulsations are absent and intracompartment pressure is normal. In neuropraxia, arterial pulsations and intracompartment pressure remain normal. In addition, pain on stretching the muscles will be absent. Difficult diagnostic situations may require the use of Doppler technique, arteriography, and intracompartment pressure measurements. Palpable venous cords may occur with deep vein thrombosis, but are not typically seen in compartment syndrome. *(Sabiston, pp 1718–1719)*

568. (A, F, G) Only 50% of patients with evidence of DVT on venography have any clinical sign. ^{125}-I labeled fibrinogen scanning is specific for new thrombi, but is complicated by recent surgery. Also, it lacks sensitivity in the thigh, and is expensive. Venous Doppler studies, and venous and pulmonary angiography are most useful in diagnosis. Thrombosis usually starts in the smaller calf veins. "Blue toe" and emboli to the superior mesenteric artery are from systemic arterial embolization. *(Sabiston, p 353)*

569. (B, C, E) Warfarin, dextran, and aspirin have been found to be efficacious in preventing deep venous thrombosis. Hemorrhagic complications are fewer with aspirin compared with warfarin. One disadvantage of dextran is that because it must be administered parenterally it may cause allergic reactions. Dipyridamole is less effective than warfarin, dextran, and aspirin. Though effective in medical and general surgical patients, low-dose heparin, has, for unexplained reasons, been found to be ineffective in preventing deep vein thrombosis. Low-molecular-weight heparin is also efficacious in preventing DVT in this patient group. Acetaminophen has no antithrombotic activity. *(Sabiston, pp 1601–1602)*

570. (B) Retroperitoneal hematoma may be a manifestation of serious retroperitoneal injury, such as laceration of hepatic and splenic flexure or injury to the pancreas, blood vessels, and renal parenchyma. Serious complications such as continued hemorrhage, abscess formation, and arteriovenous fistula may develop. The best method of avoiding these complications is by exploration. Combined pelvic hematoma, which is not associated with bladder injury but is associated with pelvic fracture, is not routinely explored. This type of hematoma resolves spontaneously, and exploration may result in uncontrollable bleeding. *(Sabiston, p 330)*

571. (D, E, F) Basal cell carcinoma arises from the basal layer of epidermis. It is a slow-growing tumor, and distant spread is infrequent. Exposure to ultraviolet radiation (bright sunlight) is a predisposing factor to the development of basal cell carcinoma. The longer the duration of exposure, the greater the likelihood of disease. Not surprisingly, then, exposed parts of the skin are more vulnerable than unexposed regions; moreover, the cancer is more common among persons with light-colored skin, because they lack the pigment melanin, which protects against ultraviolet ray penetration into the skin. Squamous cell carcinomas are the most common type of burn wound carcinoma. *(Browse, pp 54–56; Sabiston, p 245)*

572. (A, C, E, G) Despite the large surface area of the small-bowel mucosa, the incidence of adenocarcinoma of the small bowel, the most frequent neoplasm of the small bowel, is rare. However, the incidence is higher in persons with immunoglobulin A deficiency or Crohn's disease. Presenting features are signs and symptoms of small-bowel obstruction. Prognosis is poor, because the disease is usually difficult to identify. Stage for stage, the survival rates of colonic carcinoma and small-bowel carcinoma are no different. Peutz–Jaegers syndrome refers to hamartomatous polyps of the small and large intestine, which are benign. *(Greenfield, pp 756–757)*

573. (B, C, F, G) Body protein is distributed in two compartments: somatic (muscle) and visceral (all other protein). Loss of weight and decreases in the creatinine–height index, triceps skin-fold measurement, and mid-arm muscle circumference all indicate somatic protein malnourishment. Visceral protein depletion causes decreased serum albumin and transferrin levels. Visceral protein depletion also results in decreased total lymphocyte count. BUN is an indicator of kidney function and hydration status. *(Bartlett et al, pp 128–130)*

574. (B, C, E, F) Upper GI fiberendoscopy is a safe and useful procedure for diagnosing GI disorders. It is indicated for treating symptomatic patients with upper abdominal pain, nausea, and weight loss, even though abnormalities are absent on roentgenography. Endoscopy can reveal lesions overlooked on roentgenograms. Contraindications to this procedure include an uncooperative patient, recent ingestion of corrosives, and recent peptic ulcer perforation. An elevated indirect bilirubin may indicate hepatocellular disease, requiring a medical work-up. *(Sabiston, pp 736–743)*

575. (A, B, D, E) Although constipation is the most common presenting feature of Hirschsprung's disease, some patients suffer from diarrhea. The severity of symptoms does not correlate well with the extent of bowel involvement. Enterocolitis, a major cause of death, requires vigorous treatment. This complication can occur even after removal of the aganglionic segment of the bowel. Increased acetylcholinesterase activity has been noted in the serum, affected aganglionic bowel, and erythrocytes of afflicted persons. Eighty percent of affected infants are boys. *(Sabiston, pp 1243–1244)*

576. (A, C, D, G) Elevated serum gastrin is found in patients with and without peptic ulcer disease. Hypergastrinemia affects patients with gastrinoma, G-cell hyperplasia, gastric stasis, retained antrum, renal failure, and massive small-bowel resection. Most studies have shown no difference in gastrin level between uncomplicated duodenal ulcer patients and those persons in a control group. Pernicious anemia commonly is associated with loss of intrinsic factor secondary to atrophic gastritis. The atrophic gastritis and loss of acid secretion is what stimulates the hypergastrinemic state. Nonsteroidal anti-inflammatory drugs disrupt the mucosal barrier of the stomach. Secretin decreases gastrin levels. *(Sabiston, pp 848–866)*

577. (D, E, F, G) In a patient with multiple trauma who becomes tachypneic and hypoxemic despite adequate oxygen delivery, adult respiratory distress syndrome (ARDS) should be suspected. The clinical syndrome is characterized by noncardiac pulmonary edema, decreased lung compliance, decreased functional residual capacity, and a right-to-left shunt. Because ARDS is often associated with sepsis, a search should be made to identify a source of infection. *(Sabiston, pp 1796–1799)*

578. (A, B, D, E) The term hematemesis refers to vomiting of blood from a source extending from the pharynx to ligament of Treitz. The most frequent causes are peptic ulcer disease, esophageal varices, and Mallory–Weiss syndrome. Melena refers to passage of black-colored stools. Melena can occur with as little as 50 mL of blood loss. Melena may persist for 5 days after bleeding; stools for occult blood may remain positive for up to 3 weeks. Hematocrit is not an accurate measure of blood loss, as it takes time for hemodilution to occur. The blood in the gastrointestinal tract is acted upon by bacterial flora, resulting in the production of ammonia, which in the liver is converted to urea. Alteration of bacterial flora, as well as the status of the liver function, can influence the degree of azotemia. *(Sabiston, p 859)*

579. (B, D, E, F) Cyclosporine, a fungal-cyclic peptide, has revolutionized clinical transplantation. Its one disadvantage is that it is nephrotoxic. Cyclosporine does not appear to affect precursor hematopoietic cells. It acts by interfering with the production of lymphokine interleukin-2, which is needed for lymphocyte proliferation. Expansion antigen-responsive clones of T lymphocyte are thereby suppressed. Once cyclosporine is discontinued, rejection can resume. Other adverse effects include neurotoxicity, hirsutism, hypercalemia, and hepatotoxicity. *(Sabiston, pp 448–449)*

580. (A, C, E, G) Ventricular aneurysm occurs as a result of transmural myocardial infarction, primarily affecting the anterior aspect of the ventricle. Most of the aneurysms are therefore present on the antromedial portion of the left ventricle. Their natural history is to develop 4–8 weeks after a transmural MI, and to remain stable in size. Aneurysms less than 5 cm in diameter have negligible hemodynamic affect and require no operative intervention. Operation is indicated for symptomatic aneurysms. However, the symptoms the patient experiences could be secondary to ischemic disease of the heart. Progressive enlargement and rupture is uncommon. Prognosis depends on the residual ventricular function. The most common symptom is dyspnea, frequently with palpitations or angina. *(Sabiston, pp 2111–2113)*

581. (B, C, D, G) Because of the risk of postsplenectomy sepsis, attempts should be made for splenic salvage when possible. Attempts at splenic salvage is contraindicated in patients with multiple concomitant injuries, as it prolongs the operation and increases blood loss. Among children, approximately two thirds respond favorably to nonoperative management. Nonoperative management is contraindicated in the presence of hypotension, which persists when more than 50% of the child's circulating volume is transfused within 24 hours, in the presence of concomitant major injuries, and in the presence of a shattered spleen, which is not amenable to repair. The risk of postsplenectomy sepsis persists throughout life, the highest incidence being in the first 2 years following splenectomy. The most frequent organisms responsible for postsplenectomy sepsis include *Pneumococcus, Meningococcus,* and *Haemophilus influenzae.* The mortality rate is approximately 50% when sepsis occurs. The incidence of delayed rupture is about 1.5%. *(Sabiston, pp 322–323)*

582. (B, D, E, F) The average mixed venous oxygen tension is 40 mm Hg. The PvO_2 of 40 mm Hg corresponds to mixed venous oxygen saturation of 75%. Since SvO_2 of 75% corresponds to the steep portion of the oxyhemoglobin dissociation curve, small changes in peripheral oxygenation result in significant changes in SvO_2. Therefore, SvO_2 is sensitive in tracking adequacy of oxygen delivery to tissues. A normal SvO_2 ensures physiologic balance between oxygen delivery and oxygen consumption. A sudden fall in SvO_2 could result from decreased cardiac output, arterial oxygen desaturation, dropping hemoglobin, or increased oxygen consumption. Persistent PvO_2 less than 28 mm Hg has been reported with hyperlactemia and death. *(Sabiston, pp 72–74)*

583. (C, D, E, G) Sacrococcygeal teratoma frequently occurs in females (80%). The tumor usually presents as a mass posterior to the sacrum. It may also present as a retrorectal tumor between the rectum and the sacrum and may not be obvious externally. At birth, most of sacrococcygeal tumors are benign and subsequently undergo malignant degeneration. Prognosis is worse when excision is delayed beyond 2 months of birth. Therefore the tumor should be excised promptly. Failure to resect the coccyx results in 35 to 40% tumor recurrence rates. *(Sabiston, p 1271)*

584. (A, C, D, F) Reperfusion of an ischemic extremity can result in metabolic acidosis hyperkalemia from necrotic muscle. Rhabdomyolysis releases myoglobin, which can precipitate in acid urine, causing obstruction to renal tubules and subsequent renal failure. Serum potassium has to be monitored for hyperkalemia. If present, glucose and insulin are administered to drive the potassium into the cell, thus decreasing its level in the serum. Sodium bicarbonate is given to alkalinize urine and prevent precipitation of myoglobin. Mannitol or other osmotic diuretics are given to flush the kidney of any precipitates. Aggressive and adequate hydration is required to assure brisk diuresis and euvolemia. Heparin should be continued, since the risk of further embolization from the underlying cardiac condition persists. *(Sabiston, pp 332–333)*

585–588. (585-E, 586-A, 587-D, 588-B) Transplants are grouped into four classes based on the genetic relationship between the donor and recipient. In an autograft, the same individual acts as both donor and recipient. In isograft transplants, the donor and recipient are genetically identical, and in allograft transplants, donor and recipient are genetically dissimilar but belong to the same species. In xenograft transplants, donor and recipient belong to different species. The terms orthotopic and heterotopic refer to the anatomic location of the transplanted part. When the transplanted part is placed in its normal anatomic location, it is an orthotopic transplantation. In heterotopic transplantation, the part is transplanted to an extra-anatomic location. *(Sabiston, pp 383–384)*

REFERENCES

Bartlett RH, Whitehouse WH, Turcotte JS. *Life Support Systems in Intensive Care.* Chicago: Year Book Medical Publishers Inc; 1984.

Browse NL. *An Introduction to the Symptoms and Signs of Surgical Disease.* Chicago: Year Book Medical Publishers Inc; 1978.

Greenfield LJ, et al. *Surgery: Scientific Principles and Practice.* Philadelphia: JB Lippincott Co; 1993.

Sabiston DC, ed. *Textbook of Surgery,* 14th ed. Philadelphia: WB Saunders Co; 1991.

Schwartz SI, Ellis H, eds. *Maingot's Abdominal Operations,* 9th ed. Norwalk, CT: Appleton & Lange; 1990.

Schwartz SI, Shires GT, Spencer FC, eds. *Principles of Surgery,* 6th ed. New York: McGraw-Hill Book Co; 1994.

SUBSPECIALTY LIST: SURGERY

Question Number and Subspecialty

523. Endocrinology
524. Nutrition
525. Head and neck
526. Neoplasms
527. Abdominal surgery
528. Endocrinology
529. Physiology
530. Urology
531. Vascular surgery, trauma
532. Gastrointestinal tract
533. Orthopedics
534. Genitourinary system
535. Immunology, transplantation
536. Trauma
537. Nutrition
538. Trauma
539. Gastrointestinal tract
540. Gastrointestinal tract
541. Urology
542. Trauma
543. Neurology, trauma
544. Pancreas, trauma
545. Pulmonary surgery
546. Gastrointestinal tract, surgical physiology
547. Gastrointestinal tract, surgical physiology
548. Gastrointestinal tract, endocrine system
549. Critical care, trauma
550. Pulmonary surgery
551. Pulmonary surgery, neoplasm
552. Pulmonary surgery
553. Gastrointestinal tract
554. Gastrointestinal tract
555. Gastrointestinal tract
556. Gastrointestinal tract
557. Neoplasm
558. Surgical infection
559. Urology, neoplasm
560. Gastrointestinal tract
561. Gastrointestinal tract
562. Gastrointestinal tract
563. Trauma
564. Thoracic surgery
565. Neurosurgery
566. Wound healing
567. Orthopedics
568. Vascular surgery, orthopedics
569. Orthopedics
570. Trauma
571. Neoplasms
572. Gastrointestinal tract
573. Nutrition
574. Gastrointestinal tract
575. Gastrointestinal tract
576. Gastrointestinal tract
577. Physiology
578. Gastrointestinal tract
579. Transplantation
580. Cardiovascular surgery
581. Trauma
582. Surgical physiology
583. Neoplasm
584. Critical care
585. Transplantation
586. Transplantation
587. Transplantation
588. Transplantation

Psychiatry

Wendy L. Thompson, MD and Ellen F. Brooks, MD

DIRECTIONS (Questions 589 through 631): Each of the numbered items or incomplete statements in this section is followed by answers or by completions of the statement. Select the ONE lettered answer or completion that is BEST in each case.

589. Which of the following statements regarding the use of placebos in treating patients with nonspecific physical complaints or puzzling pain syndromes are true?

(A) When emotional stress accompanies physical discomfort there is a lower probability for positive response to placebo.
(B) Patients who respond to placebo complain of more somatic symptoms than do placebo nonresponders.
(C) Positive placebo response is evidence that the pain had no physiologic basis.
(D) Placebos are most often administered to disliked patients.
(E) Positive placebo response should cause the physician to curtail the usual diagnostic efforts.

590. Which of the following statements concerning temporal lobe epilepsy is true?

(A) Ictal phenomena include episodes of intense rage and kleptomania.
(B) Visual hallucinations occur during all seizures.
(C) Personality changes can be apparent both during seizures and during the interictal period.
(D) Abnormal behavior is rare during a seizure.
(E) Affected persons remember their seizure behavior after the episode has ended.

591. Catatonic behavior can best be described as

(A) extreme motor activity that is often purposeless and violent
(B) generalized muscular rigidity
(C) waxy flexibility
(D) behavior associated with an acute schizophrenic diathesis
(E) profound psychomotor disturbance due to a psychiatric disorder or a general medical condition

592. Which of the following statements regarding bulimia is true?

(A) Binge eating is not always followed by episodes of purging.
(B) Bulimic episodes do not occur in patients with anorexia nervosa.
(C) It usually affects young men and women equally.
(D) It is not associated with gastric dilatation.
(E) The disordered eating patterns are egosyntonic.

593. Which of the following statements concerning the kinetics and clinical effects of benzodiazepines is true?

(A) Short-half-life benzodiazepines are associated with a later onset of withdrawal signs than long-half-life benzodazepines.
(B) Long-half-life benzodiazepines may be associated with residual sedation even weeks after the medication is discontinued.
(C) The metabolism of short-half-life agents is more influenced by old age than is that of long-half-life agents.
(D) Long-half-life agents are more efficacious in the treatment of anxiety symptoms.
(E) Lorazepam has a longer half-life than chlordiazepoxide.

594. Compared with low-potency antipsychotic medications, high-potency antipsychotic medications tend to be associated with

(A) less anticholinergic activity and lower incidence of extrapyramidal side effects
(B) less anticholinergic activity and higher incidence of extrapyramidal side effects
(C) greater anticholinergic activity and lower incidence of extrapyramidal side effects
(D) greater anticholinergic activity and higher incidence of extrapyramidal side effects
(E) greater anticholinergic activity and greater α–adrenergic blockade

595. The clinical efficacy of typical antipsychotic medications is generally proportionate to the in vitro ability of the drug to

(A) decrease presynaptic reuptake of norepinephrine
(B) block postsynaptic dopamine receptors
(C) produce adrenergic blockade
(D) exert an atropinelike effect at the synapse
(E) increase general cerebral activation as measured by electroencephalography

596. A 22-year-old man is brought to the emergency room after sustaining an abdominal injury in a motor vehicle accident. Laparotomy and subsequent splenectomy are performed. Postoperative course is unremarkable until the third hospital day, when he exhibits apprehension, generalized twitching, tremors, and nausea. On the fourth hospital day he suffers a single generalized tonic–clonic seizure. After recovering, he admits that for the past 8 months he has been "popping yellow jackets" at a rate equivalent to roughly 1000 mg of pentobarbital per day. The most appropriate first step in this man's management would be to

(A) give a loading dose of intravenous phenytoin followed by a daily phenytoin regimen
(B) perform a sleep-deprived electroencephalogram to assess the risk of continued seizure activity
(C) begin a regimen of pentobarbital, 1000 mg daily
(D) administer intramuscular phenobarbital, 200 mg, followed by oral phenobarbital, 30 mg every 8 hours
(E) give 200 mg of oral pentobarbital and observe for sedation, slurred speech, or nystagmus

597. When compared to school-age children with conduct disorder, children who develop conduct disorder as adolescents

(A) are more likely to display persistent psychopathology
(B) are more likely to engage in aggressive behaviors
(C) are more likely to be diagnosed with antisocial personality disorder as adults
(D) are less likely to have relatively normal peer relationships
(E) show a lower male-to-female ratio among affected individuals

598. In cases involving custody of school-age children

(A) natural parents retain an inherent right to custody
(B) the child's preference should not be considered
(C) the physical and mental health of the parents should be taken into consideration
(D) the willingness of each contending parent to maintain a close relationship with the other parent is irrelevant
(E) the strongest consideration should be given to the financial status of the contending parents

599. The cognitive deterioration that accompanies Alzheimer's disease may be associated with a deficiency of the neurotransmitter

(A) norepinephrine
(B) γ-aminobutyric acid
(C) serotonin
(D) acetylcholine
(E) dopamine

600. A 25-year-old woman is brought to the emergency room. She presents with confusion, bizarre and contorted posturing, marked diaphoresis, and abdominal distress. She is found to be tachycardic and has a rectal temperature of 39.4°C (103°F). Complete blood cell count and lumbar puncture results are normal. Review of outpatient records reveals that the woman has been receiving chlorpromazine for the treatment of schizophrenia. A potentially life-threatening medication side effect that must be considered in this case is

(A) acute dystonic reaction
(B) akathisia
(C) tardive dyskinesia
(D) neuroleptic malignant syndrome
(E) chlorpromazine allergic reaction

601. A severely emotionally ill woman, diagnosed as having schizoaffective illness, takes the following psychotropic medications: fluoxetine, fluphenazine, benztropine, lorazepam, and zolpidem. She consults her gynecologist because of a variety of complaints, and hyperprolactinemia is discovered. Of the woman's medications, the one most likely to be causing her hyperprolactinemia is

(A) fluoxetine
(B) fluphenazine
(C) benztropine
(D) lorazepam
(E) zolpidem

602. Which of the following is currently used as a test of visuomotor coordination?

(A) Rorschach Test
(B) Thematic Apperception Test
(C) Word Association Test
(D) Bender Gestalt Test
(E) Sentence Completion Test

603. The M'Naghten rule is associated in American jurisprudence with

(A) protocols for civil commitment
(B) the insanity defense
(C) the right to psychiatric treatment
(D) maintaining confidentiality
(E) guidelines for expert testimony

604. Which of the following statements concerning suicide is true?

(A) Persons who repeatedly attempt suicide are at low risk for eventually killing themselves.
(B) Discussing suicide with persons suspected of feeling suicidal increases their risk of suicide.
(C) Depressed persons who commit suicide often do so after their depression has begun to abate.
(D) Persons with schizophrenia are at low risk for suicide.
(E) Persons who commit suicide usually leave few clues of their intentions.

605. According to the theories of Erik Erikson, the developmental task of school-age children (6 to 11 years) is to resolve the psychosocial crisis of

(A) trust versus mistrust
(B) autonomy versus shame and doubt
(C) intimacy versus isolation
(D) ego integrity versus despair
(E) industry versus inferiority

606. Jean Piaget is best known for his theories on the

(A) development of intelligence
(B) roots of human aggression
(C) types of intrapsychic defense mechanisms
(D) meaning of symbols
(E) importance of infant–mother bonding

607. According to classical psychoanalytic theory, obsessive–compulsive personality in an adult is linked to which of the following stages of psychosexual development?

(A) oral stage
(B) anal stage
(C) phallic stage
(D) latency stage
(E) genital stage

608. Which of the following is considered the most severely stressful life event?

(A) job promotion
(B) birth of a child
(C) vacation
(D) death of a spouse
(E) marriage

609. Which of the following statements concerning the risk of development of schizophrenia is true?

(A) Children born to a schizophrenic mother but adopted by nonschizophrenic parents develop schizophrenia at a rate equal to that of the general population.
(B) One third of persons with schizophrenia have a schizophrenic first-degree relative.
(C) Young adults with schizoid personality disorder nearly always develop schizophrenia.
(D) Boys are three times as likely as girls to develop schizophrenia during young adulthood.
(E) Disordered patterns of family communication are thought to be a predisposing factor in the development of schizophrenia.

610. Which of the following statements about epidemiology of major affective disorders is true?

(A) Women are more likely than men to develop bipolar I disorder (manic–depressive disorder).
(B) Men are more likely than women to develop major depressive disorder.
(C) Bipolar I disorder tends to appear before the age of 30 years.
(D) An untreated depressive episode lasts 2 months.
(E) Three fourths of those with major depressive disorder receive specific treatment.

611. The unconscious feelings that arise within a psychotherapist during psychotherapy are described by the term

(A) projection
(B) countertransference
(C) acting out
(D) identification
(E) introjection

612. Anorexia nervosa can be described by the following statement.

(A) Prognosis is more favorable in older adolescents than in younger adolescents.
(B) Boys develop anorexia nervosa as frequently as do girls.
(C) Affected persons typically believe they are fat despite their weight loss.
(D) Affected persons are typically rebellious and independent.
(E) Mortality rate is upwards of 35%.

613. The 1976 court case *Tarasoff* v *The Regents of the University of California* produced a landmark decision concerning the obligation of psychiatrists to

(A) maintain confidentiality in record keeping
(B) administer treatment in emergency situations
(C) assist in court-mandated competency hearings
(D) search for the "least restrictive" treatment setting for persons facing commitment
(E) warn persons threatened by their patients

614. Defining the usefulness of psychotherapy has been a difficult area of research and debate. Which of the following statements regarding psychotherapy is true?

(A) Most types of outpatient psychotherapy subscribe to long-term, exploratory models.
(B) Continuous psychotherapy, i.e., with no planned end, is contrary to a medical model of treatment.
(C) A recommendation that no treatment is necessary can be appropriate for a variety of conditions.
(D) Consultation over one or two appointments should not be expected to provide therapeutic relief.
(E) Psychodynamic interventions should not be employed during consultation.

615. Individuals who have bulimia nervosa and individuals who have anorexia nervosa would be LEAST likely to share which of the following clinical features?

(A) life-threatening change in body weight
(B) vomiting to limit caloric intake
(C) severe disturbance in body image
(D) dysphoria after consuming food
(E) response to antidepressant drugs

616. The *Diagnostic and Statistical Manual of Mental Disorders* (DSM) uses a multiaxial system for patient evaluation. Each axis provides a different set of descriptors and method of classification. One *DSM* axis has been devoted (for adult patients) exclusively to

(A) family history
(B) psychodynamic formulation
(C) estimated intelligence
(D) physical problems
(E) substance abuse disorders

617. Effective treatment for alcohol abuse includes

(A) a moralistic approach that alcohol abuse is "bad" conveyed from the physician to the patient
(B) advice that the concept of "controlled drinking" is proven effective in the treatment of severe alcohol abusers
(C) referral to Alcoholics Anonymous
(D) the use of barbiturates and Nardil can be effective in a motivated patient
(E) recommending that the patient buy a limited supply of alcohol

618. Antisocial personality disorder is considered to be

(A) synonymous with criminal behavior
(B) the male counterpart of histrionic personality disorder
(C) amenable to pharmacologic treatment with antiandrogenic agents
(D) correlated with electroencephalographic studies suggesting cortical immaturity
(E) a variant of malingering

619. Women suffering from postpartum psychiatric disorders would be most likely to demonstrate

(A) onset of symptoms within 3 to 7 days of childbirth
(B) marked blunting of mood
(C) visual hallucinations
(D) pseudoseizures
(E) grandiose delusions involving the baby

620. Social phobia can be described by which of the following statements?

(A) It is the diagnostic term for excessive shyness.
(B) Its lifetime prevalence is nearly that of alcohol dependence.
(C) Despite outward appearances of depressed mood, persons with social phobia in fact rarely develop major depression.
(D) Drug treatments are typically unsuccessful.
(E) Attempts at social skills training tend to worsen the condition by increasing feelings of being different and bizarre.

621. Methadone maintenance therapy often is used in the treatment of persons addicted to heroin because it

(A) has none of the side effects of other opioids
(B) can be used safely in persons with severe respiratory depression
(C) has a short elimination half-life and does not accumulate with repeated dosing
(D) has less of a euphoric effect than does heroin
(E) can be used concomitantly with naltrexone or naloxone

622. True statements regarding disulfiram therapy include

(A) tolerance to its effects develops rapidly and doses require frequent adjustment
(B) users may develop severe reactions to topical agents, like cosmetics, that contain alcohol
(C) it is the treatment of choice for persons who otherwise refuse to involve themselves in alcohol rehabilitation programs
(D) it is indicated in the treatment of persons with a history of psychotic disorders exacerbated by alcohol
(E) it is useful in treating pregnant alcoholic women, to lessen the risk of fetal alcohol syndrome

623. Which of the following statements about the extrapyramidal side effects of antipsychotic drugs is true?

(A) Many extrapyramidal side effects mimic signs of worsening psychosis.
(B) The frequency of acute dyskinetic reactions is directly proportional to dosage of antipsychotic medication.
(C) Tardive dyskinesia is an idiosyncratic complication of first-time use of antipsychotic drugs.
(D) Haloperidol produces few extrapyramidal side effects compared to most other antipsychotic drugs.
(E) They are often seen with the newer atypical antipsychotics.

624. Tricyclic antidepressant drugs have which of the following pharmacologic effects?

(A) direct depression of cardiac conduction
(B) β-adrenergic blockade
(C) sustained hypertension
(D) high L_D50
(E) cholinergic stimulation

625. Which of the following statements concerning sociologic factors in suicide risk is true?

(A) Women are at higher risk than men.
(B) Persons older than 65 years of age are at higher risk than persons between 25 and 35 years of age.
(C) Blue-collar workers are at higher risk than persons in professional occupations.
(D) Wartime is associated with a higher suicide risk than peacetime.
(E) A history of alcohol abuse is a risk factor for accidental death but not for suicide.

626. The limbic system of the brain is presumed to be the region most concerned with the operation and expression of emotions. Components of the limbic system include the

(A) hypothalamus
(B) nucleus accumbens
(C) nucleus of Meynert
(D) hippocampus
(E) reticular formation

627. The first-rank symptoms of schizophrenia, developed by Kurt Schneider include

(A) tactile hallucinations
(B) depressive mood changes
(C) lack of motivation
(D) thought broadcasting
(E) autistic withdrawal

628. Paranoid schizophrenia can be described by which of the following statements?

(A) Affected persons quickly lose the ability to function appropriately in social encounters.
(B) Age of onset generally is earlier than in other types of schizophrenia.
(C) Cognitive impairment tends to progress more rapidly than in other types of schizophrenia.
(D) Hallucinations and delusions often are grandiose in nature.
(E) It is associated with borderline personality disorder.

629. Electroconvulsive therapy (ECT) can be described by which of the following statements?

(A) ECT is contraindicated in the treatment of psychotic depression.
(B) ECT can cause depressed persons to exhibit manic symptoms.
(C) Transient memory loss occurs rarely after each ECT treatment.
(D) Morbidity and mortality are greater than with antidepressant drug therapy.
(E) Unilateral ECT is no longer recognized as a valid treatment.

630. Amphetamine abuse can be described by which of the following statements?

(A) Tolerance to amphetamines develops slowly.
(B) Recommended treatment of chronic abuse is with behavioral therapy.
(C) Amphetamine psychosis is easily distinguishable from paranoid schizophrenia.
(D) Withdrawal after chronic abuse can lead to a severe manic episode.
(E) Acute overdose can cause convulsions and coma.

631. Moderate mental retardation can be described by which of the following statements?

(A) It is the most common category of retardation in the United States.
(B) Affected persons are considered trainable but not educable.
(C) Affected persons usually are unable to perform routine self-care.
(D) The IQ range is 50 to 70.
(E) Affected persons are not aware of their intellectual deficits.

DIRECTIONS (Questions 632 through 650): Each group of items in this section consists of a list of lettered headings followed by a set of numbered words or phrases. For each numbered word or phrase, select the ONE lettered heading that is most closely associated with it. Each lettered heading may be selected once, more than once, or not at all.

Questions 632 through 635

For each psychiatric disorder listed below, select the diagnostic class of which it is a member.

(A) dissociative disorder
(B) somatoform disorder
(C) mood disorder
(D) anxiety disorder
(E) psychotic disorder
(F) organic mental disorder
(G) sexual disorder
(H) impulse control disorder

632. Conversion disorder

633. Cyclothymic disorder

634. Social phobia

635. Multiple personality disorder

Questions 636 through 643

Below are several quotes from persons being evaluated for a possible psychiatric disorder. For each of the quotes that follow, select the psychologic process that would most closely apply.

(A) illusion
(B) delusion
(C) hallucination
(D) phobia
(E) neurosis
(F) fugue
(G) obsession
(H) compulsion

636. "I directed Hurricane Andrew to destroy Florida!"

637. "Every night before I go to sleep I need to check the door nine times to make sure it's locked"

638. "I don't care what the tests show, I know I'm pregnant"

639. "Look at the silver angel on the ceiling" (an alcoholic person is looking at a metal sprinkler on the ceiling)

640. "Look at the silver angel on the ceiling" (the person, not an alcoholic, is looking at a plain white ceiling)

641. "My father was cold and cruel. No wonder I hate men!"

642. "I'm deathly afraid of spiders"

643. "I think about Elvis day and night"

Questions 644 through 650

For each psychiatric disorder below, select the medication most likely to be effective.

(A) fluoxetine
(B) clozapine
(C) alprazolam
(D) zolpidem
(E) benztropine
(F) lithium carbonate
(G) haloperidol

644. Short-term insomnia

645. Major depressive episode (new onset)

646. Major depressive episode (partially treated with an adequate dosage of antidepressant medication)

647. Obsessive–compulsive disorder

648. Schizophrenia intractable to common antipsychotic drugs

649. Adjustment disorder with anxiety

650. Extrapyramidal reaction to antipsychotic medication

ANSWERS AND EXPLANATIONS

589. (D) Research has shown that a high percentage of physicians have actually prescribed placebos, although infrequently. At the same time, little formal training for placebo use is provided. Data show that physicians perceive placebo users and responders as "problem" patients. However, the placebo response is a real phenomenon, and may be related to endogenous opiates. What is clear is that patients who are under stress are more likely to obtain relief from placebos. It should be noted that placebo use can be a responsible tool for pain control regardless of the cause of the pain. Therefore, a positive response is not a diagnostic indicator; it simply represents a successful intervention in relieving a patient's discomfort or pain. Obviously, diagnostic efforts should not be affected by placebo response, and a careful evaluation should proceed without compromise. *(Sierles, p 405)*

590. **(C)** Although temporal lobe epilepsy may present as dramatic bursts of unusual behaviors or feelings (ictal episodes), there may also be complex interictal changes. These may include pervasive changes in sexual interest (predominantly hyposexuality), depression, hyperreligiosity, and paranoia. Patients with temporal lobe epilepsy also have an increased incidence of symptoms of schizophreniform psychosis (e.g., auditory hallucinations and delusions). The presence of these psychotic symptoms may correlate chronologically with electroencephalogram-recorded spike activity in the temporal lobe. Similarly, behavioral idiosyncrasies may occur unpredictably, and affected individuals may be observed carrying out complex but automatic behaviors when temporal discharges are occurring. Thorough neurologic work-up including electroencephalographic studies is necessary to differentiate temporal lobe epilepsy from functional psychiatric illness. *(Goldman, pp 56–57)*

591. **(E)** The term "catatonic behavior" refers to a variety of psychomotor disturbances that are attributable to a functional or organic cause. Catatonic excitement is a state of extreme motor activity that appears pointless and disorganized and may become violent and aggressive. Catatonic rigidity can involve all muscle groups and render a person completely stiff. Catatonic negativism is defined by persons resisting any outside force or doing the opposite of anything asked of them. Patients with catatonic waxy flexibility will maintain any position in which they are placed, as would a wax figure or a doll. Catatonic posturing refers to a voluntary posing in bizarre positions or maintenance of strange facial contortions over a long time period. Catatonic stupor is a generalized and profound decrease in psychomotor activity; affected persons may be virtually oblivious to their surroundings. Individuals may suddenly shift among the various catatonic states: quiet and treatable patients may rapidly become active and aggressive. Catatonic patients are at increased risk for malnutrition, exhaustion, dehydration, and self-inflicted injury. Organic brain disorders, such as meningitis and exposure to toxic substances must be ruled out before diagnosing catatonic schizophrenia. *(Kaplan and Sadock, pp 280, 479, 483–484)*

592. **(A)** Bulimia is an eating disorder in which copious amounts of food are ingested rapidly over a brief time period (usually less than 2 hours). Affected persons are painfully aware that such binge eating is unhealthy but feel that the impulsive eating is beyond control. Binges are characteristically followed by a profound sense of failure and depression. This condition tends to persist for several years, with occasional remissions. It most commonly affects adolescent or young adult women. First symptoms may be associated with a major life change, such as leaving home or starting work. Bulimia may also occur as one aspect of the related eating disorder anorexia nervosa. It is associated with electrolyte abnormalities, cardiac arrhythmias, hyperamylasemia, and other medical complications. Treatment options include psychotherapy and antidepressants (usually SSRIs). *(Kaplan and Sadock, pp 727–730)*

593. **(B)** One way to begin to differentiate clinically among the many benzodiazepines currently marketed for the treatment of anxiety is to divide them according to half-life. The long-acting agents include diazepam and chlordiazepoxide. They are metabolized in several steps, by hepatic oxidation, and therefore have biologically active metabolites. The short-acting agents include oxazepam and lorazepam. They are metabolized by glucuronide conjugation to inactive metabolites. Both groups are equally efficacious in the treatment of anxiety, in either single-dose or multiple-dose regimens. However, when multiple-dose treatment is indicated, it is important to be aware of the pharmacokinetic difference between these agents. The time lag before onset of medication effect will depend on the absorption rate. Diazepam has been found to act more rapidly and more profoundly than the less-well absorbed oxazepam. However, because of longer half-life, diazepam accumulates extensively in the body during multiple-dose regimens, with corresponding clinical side effects such as excessive sedation. Because of their slow elimination rate, long-acting agents may produce sedation 2 weeks or more after the agent is discontinued. There may also be increased risk of dangerous interaction with other substances, including alcohol. On the other hand, short-acting agents accumulate less and are more rapidly eliminated. Abrupt discontinuation of these agents may precipitate sudden onset of withdrawal symptoms, including increased anxiety, insomnia, and autonomic nervous system disturbance. One distinction between these agents that must be emphasized is that hepatic oxidation tends to be much more influenced by the aging process than does the glucuronidation process by which the short-acting agents are metabolized. Thus, elderly individuals may be much more prone to the dangers of drug accumulation when receiving long-half-life benzodiazepines. This is the basis for the opinion that short-half-life benzodiazepines are the drugs of choice in treating anxiety in the geriatric population. *(Salzmann et al, pp 293–297)*

594. **(B)** High-potency antipsychotic medications include the piperazine-substituted phenothiazines, such as trifluoperazine, and members of the butyrophenone class, such as haloperidol. These medications are effective antipsychotics at relatively low dosages and generally produce less sedation, less anticholinergic activity, and less α-adrenergic blockade than do the low-potency antipsychotics, such as chlorpromazine, thioridazine, and perphenazine. High-potency antipsychotics do produce a higher incidence of extrapyramidal side effects, including acute dystonic reactions. This phenomenon may reflect the fact that these agents have less intrinsic anticholinergic activity. Awareness of the side effects of the various antipsychotics is often the key determinant in choosing the best agent for each patient. Certain patients will have difficulty with the sedating effects of medication. A dehydrated patient may be prone to hypotension secondary to α-adrenergic blockade. Other patients may be extremely susceptible to acute dystonic reactions. A patient's entire health profile should be considered when choosing an antipsychotic medication. *(Goldman, pp 441–442)*

595. **(B)** The clinical efficacy of an antipsychotic medication is generally proportional to its in vitro ability to block dopamine receptors. This finding is one of the major supports of the so-called dopamine hypothesis of schizophrenia, which holds that schizophrenic symptoms stem from an imbalance of dopaminergic systems in the brain. It remains to be seen if all antipsychotic medications are active in direct proportion to their ability to produce dopamine blockade. Antipsychotic medications tend to vary in the extent to which they affect multiple neurotransmitter systems in different parts of the brain. The dopamine hypothesis may need to be revised, with the advent of the atypical antipsychotics, which are serotonin–dopamine antagonists. *(Kaplan and Sadock, pp 485–486)*

596. **(E)** Physical dependence develops when significant amounts of barbiturates are ingested chronically over a course of weeks or months. Abstinence symptoms usually develop within 72 hours after the last drug ingestion. Early withdrawal signs include anxiety, insomnia, orthostatic hypotension, and mixed gastrointestinal complaints. Grand mal seizures may occur; they generally begin between the third and seventh day of withdrawal and may present as single episodes or as status epilepticus. Onset of seizures often heralds deterioration into frank delirium. The management of barbiturate withdrawal requires the accurate assessment of the patient's level of dependence (drug abusers are notoriously inaccurate in reporting their usual intake). In the "test dose" method to establish drug requirement during detoxification from barbiturates, a patient is given 200 mg of pentobarbital orally and assessed over the next hour. Patients who become very drowsy or exhibit coarse nystagmus may require no more than 600 mg daily. Patients who become only mildly drowsy with fine nystagmus may require 800 mg daily in divided doses. Patients with no response whatsoever probably will require more than 1200 mg daily. Once the maintenance dose is established and the patient is stabilized, the dose can be slowly tapered, by 10% daily. *(Tupin et al, pp 141–143)*

597. (E) Conduct disorder causes affected children to display persistent, disruptive, often violent behaviors toward other people and toward elements in their social systems. Behaviors can be aggressive, destructive, deceitful, manipulative, intimidating, cruel, truant, and rebellious. In general, conduct disorder is more severe and intractable if it develops in younger children (childhood-onset type) than in older children (adolescent-onset type). Childhood-onset conduct disorder is more likely to be associated with later diagnosis of antisocial personality disorder. Male-to-female ratio of affected individuals is higher in childhood-onset conduct disorder than in the adolescent-onset type. *(APA, pp 85–91)*

598. (C) In recent years, the concept of what is in "the best interests of the child" in custody disputes has become more sophisticated. Many factors must be considered in evaluating the claims of the contending parents, including their physical and mental fitness, their ability to provide affection and protection, and their willingness to allow the child to maintain a close relationship with the noncustodial parent. It is no longer a given that natural parents have an indisputable right to custody, if other caregivers are deemed more appropriate. *(Kaplan and Sadock, pp 1286–1287)*

599. (D) Major deficiencies in acetylcholine content in the brain are linked with the cognitive losses associated with Alzheimer's disease. The nucleus of Meynert is the richest site of acetylcholine in the brain. Recent studies of brain tissues of affected persons have demonstrated that the amount of acetylcholine localized in these neurons is depleted and that the efferent pathways from the nucleus show signs of degeneration. *(Cummings and Benson, pp 64–71)*

600. (D) Neuroleptic malignant syndrome (NMS) is an uncommon but important side effect of psychotropic medication use. It is characterized by severe extrapyramidal reactions, autonomic disturbances, and hyperthermia. This syndrome is associated with a mortality rate of 20%. Anticholinergic treatment, generally helpful in common acute dystonic reactions, seems of only limited usefulness in NMS. NMS is believed to result from extensive dopamine blockade; bromocriptine, a dopamine agonist, has been of value in the treatment of NMS. *(Mueller et al, pp 386–388)*

601. (B) Among psychotropic drugs, antipsychotic preparations are most likely to cause hyperprolactinemia. Release of prolactin is inhibited by dopamine. Therefore, the central dopamine receptor blockade produced by antipsychotic drugs leads to elevated prolactin production. *(Hales and Frances, pp 195–197)*

602. (D) The Bender Gestalt Test is a test of visuomotor coordination, which is useful for both children and adults. The test consists of nine separate designs, which are copied by the patient. The Rorschach Test, Thematic Apperception Test, and Sentence Completion Test are projective psychological tests, which help to assess personality. When properly administered and interpreted by an experienced clinician, psychologic tests offer a significant contribution to understanding psychiatric illness. These tests can be powerful tools in clarifying issues of psychiatric diagnosis, psychodynamics, and patient management. Standardized psychologic tests provide a fairly objective means for comparing behavior with available normative data representative of a larger reference group. *(Kaplan and Sadock, pp 197–199, 201–202)*

603. **(B)** In 1843, Daniel M'Naghten, a disturbed Scottish woodcutter, attempted to kill the British Prime Minister. He mistook the Prime Minister's secretary for the Prime Minister and shot and killed him. In the subsequent trial, M'Naghten's counsel argued that his client suffered from a mental illness and therefore did not know the difference between right and wrong and could not comprehend the nature or consequences of his actions. Although modified over time, these criteria for an insanity defense have become widely adopted in the United States. The current American Law Institute standard states that a person is not responsible for criminal conduct if, at the time of such conduct and as a result of mental disease or defect, a person lacked substantial capacity either to appreciate the wrongfulness of the actions (intent) or to conform conduct to the requirements of the law (voluntary conduct). *(Kaplan and Sadock, pp 1314–1315)*

604. **(C)** Successful clinical intervention with persons known or suspected to be suicidal can be hampered by several popular myths regarding suicide. Fallacious notions are many, including "persons who have attempted suicide and failed are not serious about killing themselves" and "persons who talk about killing themselves don't do it" and "mentioning suicide to depressed persons can put the idea in their head." In persons with schizophrenia, suicide risk is especially high early in the course of their illness as well as during times of transition in their lives. The most dangerous phase of depression in relation to suicide is often during successful convalescence; possible reasons for this phenomenon include abatement of psychomotor retardation, fear of relapse, and guilt over the effect the depression had on others. *(Stoudemire, pp 563–565)*

605. **(E)** The psychoanalyst Erik Erikson has theorized that ego development proceeds from birth through eight identifiable stages marked by specific psychosocial crises. Infants are faced with the task of developing basic trust in the world and in themselves. As they grow older, children sequentially develop a sense of autonomy (ages 1 to 2 years), initiative (3 to 5 years), and industry (6 to 11 years) as they successfully meet developmental challenges. The psychosocial crises of adolescents and young adults are identity versus role confusion, and intimacy versus isolation, respectively. People successfully meet the challenges of adulthood by providing a suitable nurturing environment for themselves and the generation that follows ("generativity"); once past the generative stage, older adults can reflect back on their lives with either satisfaction ("ego integrity") or despair. *(Kaplan and Sadock, pp 235–237)*

606. **(A)** Jean Piaget, a Swiss psychologist, has been described as the leading pioneer in researching the development and refinement of human intelligence. According to Piaget, human intelligence passes through four major stages of development: the sensorimotor stage (up to 2 years of age), during which individuals acquire the skills of self-regulation and the notion of object permanence; the preoperational stage (roughly 2 to 5 years), during which language skills are refined, the concept of "me" and "mine" is developed, and the functional significance of objects is appreciated; the concrete operational stage (5 to 11 years), during which children learn to quantify and categorize; and the formal operational period, characterized by the ability to engage in abstract thought. Piaget's work has led to the understanding of how children's abilities to adapt and learn are dependent on the current stage of development of intelligence. *(Kaplan and Sadock, pp 140–144)*

607. **(B)** The second stage of psychosexual development, the anal stage, occurs in children from 1 to 3 years of age, a period in which they gain control over elimination of wastes by mastering sphincter function. The interactions between parents and children around toilet training impart an aggressive nature to the mastery—or lack of mastery—of sphincter control; conflicts regarding separation and independence also arise. Thus, in the anal stage are the roots of an individual's sense of independence, initiative, and cooperation; unsuccessful or impaired resolution of anal-stage conflicts can lead to such personality traits as stubbornness, orderliness, and frugality, which are common manifestations of the obsessive–compulsive personality. Modern theoreticians also identify early struggles with self-esteem and intimacy as possible causative factors. *(Kaplan and Sadock, pp 214–215)*

608. **(D)** Among the most severe life stresses are death of a spouse or other close family member, divorce or marital separation, and pregnancy and birth of a child. The intensity of stress can be heightened if it is associated with other stresses or occurs during a time of year marked by past stressful events (anniversary reaction). Any change, positive or negative, in a person's life may represent a source of stress. Listing relevant life stresses comprises Axis IV of a complete DSM diagnostic formulation. *(APA, pp 29–30)*

609. **(E)** Determination of risk for the development of schizophrenia has been approached from a variety of directions. Genetic factors, for example, appear to be important, as evidenced by a high concordance rate for schizophrenia in monozygotic twins and an increased risk in adopted children whose biologic mothers were schizophrenic; on the other hand, fewer than 15% of schizophrenic individuals have schizophrenic first-degree relatives. Although persons who develop schizophrenia may have been previously diagnosed as having other psychiatric disorders, there appears to be no disorder that clearly predisposes to schizophrenia. Males and females develop the illness with approximately the same frequency. *(Goldman, pp 240–242)*

610. **(C)** The two most common forms of major affective disorder are major depressive disorder (so-called unipolar disease) and bipolar I disorder (manic–depressive illness). It has been estimated that as many as 25% of American women and 12% of American men have experienced a major depressive episode. While most individuals with bipolar I eventually receive treatment for their illness, only about half of those with major depressive disorder receive appropriate treatment. Although major depressive episodes can arise any time during adulthood, bipolar I disorder tends to appear in young adulthood. Depression is diagnosed more often in women than in men; bipolar I disorder is diagnosed about equally in both sexes. Untreated depressive episodes last 6 to 13 months, treated episodes last about 3 months. *(Kaplan and Sadock, pp 538–539, 559)*

611. **(B)** During the course of psychotherapy, patients develop feelings toward the therapist that recreate feelings they have had toward significant persons in their life, a phenomenon called transference. Identification of these feelings and the behaviors they provoke is crucial, especially in insight-oriented psychotherapy. However, during the course of conducting psychotherapy, therapists, too, develop feelings and reactions as memories of situations from their past are evoked. These countertransference feelings provide the therapist with valuable clues regarding how people in the patient's life may have reacted to the patient. Countertransference may also serve to pinpoint areas within the therapist's own unconscious that may prejudice the ability to offer nondirective, unbiased treatment. *(Kaplan and Sadock, pp 887–888)*

612. **(C)** Anorexia nervosa, a disorder predominantly but not exclusively affecting females, is characterized by obsessional weight loss and disordered body image. Other behavioral features include food binges, self-induced vomiting, and abuse of laxatives. Affected persons typically are described as pleasant, polite overachievers. Mortality rate is as high as 20%, with death caused by dehydration, electrolyte imbalances, and other manifestations of starvation. The prognosis tends to be better if affected persons are younger. *(Kaplan and Sadock, pp 720–725)*

613. (E) Psychiatrists often come into contact with persons who, by virtue of emotional illness or personality, are potentially dangerous. Despite the fact that most studies refute the notion that psychiatrists are better able than other practitioners to predict dangerousness, several court decisions in recent years have made psychiatrists responsible to some degree for protecting persons endangered by their patients. In the landmark *Tarasoff* case in 1976, the California Supreme Court ruled that "when a therapist determines or . . . should determine that his patient presents a serious danger of violence to another, he incurs an obligation to use reasonable care to protect the intended victim against such danger." More recent court decisions have extended the scope of this obligation still further. *(Halleck, pp 77–82)*

614. (C) Defining the uses and parameters of the many types of psychotherapy has been a daunting task. Certain generalizations, however, have emerged. Most types of psychotherapy are brief, and the efficacy of these therapies has been easier to demonstrate than that of the more traditional, long-term therapies. Continual psychotherapy, i.e., intermittent treatment for an extended period and having no planned end, can be effective in treating certain chronic conditions, and in this way is quite consistent with a medical model of care. The therapeutic value of consultation, which can even be a setting for the effective use of psychodynamic interventions, should not be overlooked. *(Hales and Frances, pp 410–412)*

615. (A) Although the eating disorders of bulimia nervosa and anorexia nervosa share many characteristics, there are two main distinguishing features. Changes in body weight in bulimic individuals, as opposed to anorectic individuals, are usually not severe enough to threaten life. The consumption of large quantities of food (binge eating) followed by purging is an essential feature of bulimia; it is also present, although less characteristic, in anorexia. Both disorders are associated with distortions in body image and dysphoria after eating. Antidepressant drugs have been used with some success in treating both disorders. *(APA, pp 539–550)*

616. (D) The multiaxial system of diagnosis pioneered by the DSM includes five axes, or classes, of information, description, and diagnosis. Axis I describes major psychiatric disorders, including mood disorders, schizophrenia, mental retardation, and substance abuse. Personality disorders constitute axis II. Axis III lists physical disorders and disease. A listing of psychosocial stresses defines axis IV, and axis V describes level of adaptive functioning. *(APA, pp 25–32)*

617. (C) It is considered an attitudinal barrier to receiving effective care if the caregiver is judgmental or moralistic about his patient's substance abuse. The concept of "controlled drinking" has not been supported by clinical experience in alcoholics; instead it has worked with some drinkers who are not alcohol dependent. Both disulfiram and naltrexone have been used as adjunctive treatment in alcoholics who are motivated to abstain from alcohol use. Alcoholics Anonymous, founded in 1935 by two recovering alcoholics, has been shown to be effective in helping achieve abstinence rates of approximately 50% over the first 3 months of participation; a member who has been abstinent for 1 to 5 years has an 86% chance of remaining sober during that year. *(Goldman, pp 224–227)*

618. (D) Antisocial personality disorder represents a chronically maladaptive pattern of interaction and perception in which the rights of others are violated and in which social productivity (sustained job performance or intimate relationships) is impaired. Although an individual with antisocial personality disorder might engage in criminal acts, criminality as a socially defined behavior is determined by a variety of economic, cultural, and other environmental factors. Family studies have shown that antisocial personality is associated with several other psychiatric disorders, including histrionic personality disorder and alcoholism, which are diagnosable in first-degree relatives at higher rates than among the general population. These associations raise the possibility that the disorders may have common genetic as well as environmental determinants. Electroencephalographic studies reveal an increased prevalence of slow-wave activity, lowered thresholds for sedation, and slow cortical recovery from stimulation, suggesting that individuals with antisocial personality disorder manifest signs of cortical immaturity. Pharmacologic intervention has no proven efficacy in the treatment of antisocial personality. Early psychologic and behavioral interventions seem to improve long-term outcome. *(Kaplan and Sadock, pp 784–785)*

619. (B) About 20 to 40 percent of all women experience emotional disturbance in the early postpartum period. Symptoms usually appear between the third and seventh postpartum day and can include irritability, anxiety, fluctuating mood, feelings of inadequacy and shame, confusion and disorientation, and such psychotic disturbances as auditory hallucinations and nihilistic delusions. Both biologic and psychologic factors appear to be important etiologically in postpartum emotional illness. Choice of treatment depends on the type and severity of symptoms. *(Kaplan and Sadock, pp 27–28)*

620. (B) Recent lifetime prevalence studies have shown that social phobia ranks only behind major depression and alcohol dependence in the United States. Rather than being a variant of shyness, social phobia is a distinct neurobiological disorder with significant morbidity. Medications have been shown to be effective in many cases, with selective serotonin reuptake inhibitors and monoamine oxidase inhibitors showing the most promise. Persons with social phobia often also develop major depression or other anxiety disorders during the course of their lives. Social skills training can be an invaluable adjunct to treatment, allowing persons to feel more confident as they enter the world of social interaction, for what seems for many the first time in their lives. *(Lydiard and Falsetti, pp 570–576)*

621. (D) Methadone is an opioid that is widely used in treatment programs for heroin addicts. Substituted for heroin in maintenance programs, methadone itself can cause euphoria and depressive side effects and is associated with tolerance. The principle behind methadone maintenance is that if the drug can be obtained in legally sanctioned clinics linked with medical and rehabilitative facilities, then the addict has fewer incentives to obtain or remain on heroin. Methadone's long half-life provides a smooth bioavailability curve unlike the rapid subjective high and subjective crash associated with heroin use. *(Kaplan and Sadock, pp 1055–1057)*

622. (B) Disulfiram acts by inhibiting the breakdown of acetaldehyde, a major metabolite of alcohol. When a person on disulfiram therapy ingests alcoholic beverages (or absorbs alcohol from such sources as cosmetics), the subsequent accumulation of acetaldehyde causes a number of effects, including flushing, sweating, palpitations, nausea, and vomiting. These sudden, very unpleasant effects are generally safe in an otherwise healthy individual. Disulfiram therapy is absolutely contraindicated in the presence of heart disease and is potentially dangerous in many other conditions, including cirrhosis, nephritis, and pregnancy. Tolerance does not develop. In the past, when disulfiram was routinely used in large doses, as many as 20% of those treated developed a "disulfiram psychosis." The presentation of this organic mental disorder ranges from delirium to full-blown psychotic symptoms. This reaction is much less common today, but a history of psychosis continues to be a relative contraindication to disulfiram therapy. It is most important to emphasize that disulfiram therapy is properly used only in the context of a comprehensive alcoholism treatment plan, including counseling, group programs such as Alcoholics Anonymous, and careful medical supervision. *(Tupin et al, pp 136–140)*

623. (A) Extrapyramidal reactions, which can result from the use of antipsychotic medications, are divided into three classes. Akathisias are characterized by motor restlessness and inability to sit still. Acute dyskinesias, which produce sudden, often bizarre-appearing muscular contortions of the face and upper body, can occur at very low dosages of antipsychotic medication; on the other hand, tardive dyskinesia is a late complication of long-term neuroleptic treatment. Parkinsonian syndromes, which can resemble Parkinson's disease in many of its manifestions, are the third class of extrapyramidal reactions. The agitation of akathisias, bizarre movements of dyskinesias, and bland affect of parkinsonian syndromes all can be mistaken for signs of worsening psychosis. Of the antipsychotic drugs, thioridazine produces few extrapyramidal side effects, whereas haloperidol is among the drugs producing the most. *(Tupin et al, pp 18–23)*

624. (A, B) Tricyclic antidepressants cause α-adrenergic blockade, which may result in orthostatic hypotension. They have quinidine-like effects on the cardiac conduction system and can cause QT interval prolongation. They have a relatively low L_D50 and overdoses of tricyclics are often fatal. They are also anticholinergic in therapeutic doses, resulting in dry mouth, blurred vision, constipation, and urinary retention. *(Kaplan and Sadock, pp 1103– 1105)*

625. (B) Investigation of sociologic factors in suicide has led to the identification of "lower-risk" and "higher-risk" groups. In general, the risk of suicide increases proportionally with age, although the rate of teenage suicides has been accelerating in recent years. Men are at higher risk than women, and persons in professional occupations are at higher risk than blue-collar workers. Poor health, socioeconomic deprivation, marital breakdown, and history of alcohol abuse or chronic depression are all associated with higher suicide risk. Suicide risk appears to decline during periods of war or social persecution, for reasons that are unclear. *(Kaplan and Sadock, pp 864–872)*

626. (D) The limbic system consists of several structures of the brain linked by one common function: control or expression of emotional states and self-preservation behaviors. Specific areas of the brain that constitute the limbic system include the hippocampus and cingulate gyrus (which form part of the limbic lobe and are presumed to be active in determining emotional response) and the amygdala (which is thought to be involved with more primitive, instinctual behaviors related to self-preservation). The reticular formation is a region of the brain stem regulating arousal and inhibition of the peripheral motor system as well as other nonvoluntary physiologic functions. *(Kaplan and Sadock, pp 85–89)*

627. (D) Symptoms of schizophrenia have been classified in a number of ways, beginning with Eugen Bleuler's "four A's": autism, ambivalence, associational difficulties, and affect disturbance. Kurt Schneider 30 years ago described what he termed "first rank" symptoms, which, if present and not associated with a known organic disorder, would indicate a diagnosis of schizophrenia. Among Schneider's first-rank symptoms are auditory hallucinations, somatic hallucinations, delusions, and the belief that thoughts either are being intruded on by others' thoughts or are being telegraphed to others and incorporated into their thoughts (thought insertion and thought broadcasting, respectively). *(Kaplan and Sadock, p 476)*

628. (D) Paranoid schizophrenia is the most common subtype of schizophrenia in the United States. It tends to develop later in life than other schizophrenic subtypes, cause less cognitive impairment, and produce milder behavioral and social disorganization. Hallucinations and delusions characteristically are of a jealous, persecutory, or grandiose nature. *(Kaplan and Sadock, p 466)*

629. **(B)** Although the advent of antidepressant drugs has curtailed the use of electroconvulsive therapy (ECT), the procedure still is employed to treat persons with psychotic depression, medication-resistant depression, and florid mania. Protocols vary among treatment centers in regard to frequency and number of shocks, strength of shock, and method of administration (unilateral or bilateral). The use of pretreatment medication, including atropine to dry up secretions and succinylcholine to cause transient paralysis, has lowered the morbidity and mortality of ECT to levels less than those associated with antidepressant drug therapy. Transient memory loss usually occurs after each treatment. *(Kaplan and Sadock, pp 1115–1122)*

630. **(E)** Acute amphetamine intoxication causes euphoria and restlessness, and acute overdose can lead to confusion, disorientation, psychotic symptoms (e.g., persecutory and grandiose delusions and hallucinations that can mimic acute paranoid schizophrenia), convulsions, and coma. Chronic amphetamine abuse can produce psychosis and repetitive, compulsive behaviors such as bruxism (teeth gnashing); these symptoms may take months to disappear completely after withdrawal. Treatment of amphetamine intoxication is with benzodiazepines to produce sedation or with neuroleptic medications, particularly haloperidol to treat more serious cases. Withdrawal after chronic abuse can produce a depression of sufficient severity to warrant use of antidepressant drugs. *(Cassem, pp 25–26)*

631. **(B)** Mental retardation generally is divided into four levels of severity: mild (IQ 50 to 70), moderate (35 to 50), severe (20 to 35), and profound. Most retarded U.S. citizens are in the mild range and thus can benefit from some education and often are able to live and work independently. Moderately retarded persons are considered trainable but not educable and frequently can care for themselves, especially in supervised environments. More severely retarded persons require custodial care. *(Herskowitz and Rosman, pp 512–514)*

632–635 (632-B, 633-C, 634-D, 635-A) Conversion disorder is a somatoform disorder in which an apparent physical deficit is actually an unconscious manifestation of a psychologic conflict. Affected individuals are unaware of the psychologic etiology of their symptoms. Conversion symptoms are thought to be a defense against intolerable feelings and a safeguard against carrying out indefensible actions.

Cyclothymic disorder can be thought of as subclinical bipolar disorder. Affected persons experience mood swings but of lower amplitude and severity than those characterizing manic–depressive illness. As a consequence, social and interpersonal functioning is less disrupted.

Social phobia is an anxiety disorder associated with avoidance of contact with other persons, especially groups, because of fear of humiliation. Often this fear is so intense that it affects judgment and attention to the point of interfering with even simple actions. When this scenario occurs, affected individuals can come away from a social encounter feeling even more convinced of their basic inadequacies and thus become even more avoidant and phobic.

One of the most dramatic of all psychiatric illnesses is dissociative identity disorder, or multiple personality disorder (MPD). Persons with MPD display two or more (sometimes many more) separable personalities. MPD is thought to arise as a result of extreme childhood trauma, such as physical or sexual abuse. *(APA, pp 363–366, 411–417, 452-457, 484–487)*

636–643. (636-B, 637-H, 638-B, 639-A, 640-C, 641-E, 642-D, 643-G) Delusions and hallucinations are symptoms of psychosis. A delusion is a fixed, false, typically bizarre or improbable belief from which a person cannot be dissuaded. Delusions take several forms, including grandiose (e.g., attributing great powers to oneself), nihilistic (e.g., seeing oneself as a cause of universal misery), somatic, and paranoid. In contrast to delusions, obsessions are persistent thoughts that generally are plausible; affected persons are well aware of the abnormal preoccupation and can be quite distressed. A phobia is an extreme fear well beyond the degree of actual threat posed by the feared object (e.g., spiders) or experience (e.g., heights).

Hallucinations are manufactured sensations without any basis in reality. Any of the five senses—sight, hearing, smell, taste, and touch—can be affected. Illusions, on the other hand, are misperceptions of an actual sensory stimulus. While hallucinations are associated with psychotic illnesses, illusions are associated with organic disorders.

Compulsions are repetitive, irresistible behaviors unconsciously designed to ward off or alleviate anxiety. These behaviors either are excessive or are not connected with the object of the anxiety in any discernible way.

A neurosis is a behavior pattern or set of beliefs that a person finds distressing or encumbering and generally not perceived as amenable to change. These beliefs and prejudices are nonpsychotic and stem from the effects of childhood experiences.

Persons experiencing a fugue have taken precipitous flight from their home environments, ending up in no particular place of meaning to them and with no recollection of how they got there or even of who they are. *(Kaplan and Sadock, pp 275–286)*

644–650. (644-D, 645-A, 646-F, 647-A, 648-B, 649-C, 650-E). Fluoxetine is a serotonin blocker used widely in the treatment of major depressive episode. It also has proved effective in treating a number of other disorders, including obsessive–compulsive disorder. Alprazolam is a benzodiazepine drug most appropriate in the treatment of transient anxiety. Chronic use of alprazolam is discouraged because of its addictive potential. Triazolam is a triazolobenzodiazepine marketed as a hypnotic. In recent years this drug has become somewhat controversial because of case reports of confusion associated with its use.

Haloperidol and clozapine are antipsychotic drugs. Haloperidol is a high-potency, relatively nonsedating drug that is useful in rapid neuroleptization of agitated manic individuals. Because of the risk of agranulocytosis, use of clozapine is reserved for treatment of persons with chronic schizophrenia who have not responded well to other pharmacologic agents. Persons who develop extrapyramidal side effects from neuroleptic drugs often are given benztropine to alleviate these symptoms.

The most common use of lithium is the treatment of persons with bipolar disorder. However, it also has been helpful as an adjuvant to antidepressant treatment that has achieved less than optimal results. *(Kaplan and Sadock, pp 966–967)*

REFERENCES

American Psychiatric Association (APA). *Diagnostic and Statistical Manual of Mental Disorders*, 4th ed. Washington, DC: American Psychiatric Association; 1994.

Cassem NH. *Massachusetts General Hospital Handbook of General Hospital Psychiatry*, 3rd ed. St. Louis: Mosby–Year Book; 1991.

Cummings JL, Benson DF. *Dementia: A Clinical Approach*, 2nd ed. Boston: Butterworth-Heinemann; 1992.

Goldman HH. *Review of General Psychiatry*, 5th ed. New York: McGraw Hill; 2000.

Hales RE, Frances AJ, eds. *Psychiatry Update: American Psychiatric Association Annual Review*. Washington, DC: American Psychiatric Press Inc; 1987:6.

Halleck SL. *Law in the Practice of Psychiatry: A Handbook for Clinicians*. New York: Plenum Medical Book Co; 1980.

Herskowitz J, Rosman NP. *Pediatrics, Neurology, and Psychiatry—Common Ground, Behavioral, Cognitive, Affective, and Physical Disorders in Childhood and Adolescence*. New York: Macmillan Inc; 1982.

Kaplan HI, Sadock BJ. *Synopsis of Psychiatry*, 8th ed. Baltimore: Williams & Wilkins, 1998.

Lydiard RB, Falsetti SA. Treatment options for social phobia. *Psychiatric Annals*. 1995;25:570–576.

Mueller PS, Vester JW, Fermaglich J. Neuroleptic malignant syndrome. Successful treatment with bromocriptine. *JAMA*. 1983;249:386–388.

Salzmann C, Shader RI, Greenblatt DJ, et al. Long vs. short half-life benzodiazepines in the elderly. *Arch Gen Psychiatry.* 1983;40:293–297.

Sierles FS. *Behavioral Science for Medical Students.* Baltimore: Williams & Wilkins, 1993.

Stoudemire A. *Clinical Psychiatry for Medical Students,* 2nd ed. Philadelphia: J.B. Lippincott, 1994.

Tupin JP, Shader RI, Harnett DS. *Handbook of Clinical Psychopharmacology,* 2nd ed. Northvale, NJ: Jason Aronson Inc; 1992.

SUBSPECIALTY LIST: PSYCHIATRY

Question Number and Subspecialty

589. Nonpsychiatric illness
590. Psychopathology
591. Psychopathology
592. Psychopathology
593. Intervention
594. Intervention
595. Intervention
596. Assessment
597. Child psychiatry, assessment
598. Ethical and legal aspects
599. Psychopathology
600. Assessment
601. Assessment
602. Assessment
603. Ethical and legal aspects
604. Epidemiology
605. Child psychiatry, development
606. Child psychiatry, development
607. Child psychiatry, development
608. Nonpsychiatric illness
609. Epidemiology
610. Epidemiology
611. Intervention
612. Psychopathology
613. Ethical and legal aspects
614. Intervention
615. Assessment
616. Assessment
617. Intervention
618. Psychopathology
619. Assessment
620. Psychopathology
621. Intervention
622. Intervention
623. Intervention
624. Intervention
625. Assessment
626. Psychopathology
627. Assessment
628. Assessment
629. Intervention
630. Assessment
631. Psychopathology
632. Psychopathology
633. Psychopathology
634. Psychopathology
635. Psychopathology
636. Assessment
637. Assessment
638. Assessment
639. Assessment
640. Assessment
641. Assessment
642. Assessment
643. Assessment
644. Intervention
645. Intervention
646. Intervention
647. Intervention
648. Intervention
649. Intervention
650. Intervention

Preventive Medicine

Jocelyn C. White, MD

DIRECTIONS (Questions 651 through 689): Each of the numbered items or incomplete statements in this section is followed by answers or by completions of the statement. Select the ONE lettered answer or completion that is BEST in each case.

651. Which of the following is the major hazard at well-maintained sanitary landfill sites?

(A) obstruction of drainage
(B) objectionable odors
(C) sea gulls
(D) fire
(E) rats

652. By which of the following processes is the most pure drinking water produced?

(A) sedimentation
(B) filtration
(C) ion exchange resins
(D) distillation
(E) absorption

653. John Smith visits the physician at his place of work, complaining of testicular enlargement. The physician confirms the finding and refers the man for surgical treatment. The mass is discovered to be a seminoma. Appropriate treatment is given. A similar case occurred in this factory earlier in the year. The company physician should

(A) inform the employer of the man's diagnosis
(B) preserve the man's anonymity but indicate to management that this was the second case to occur in the past year
(C) advise both management and the workers that two cases of testicular cancer have occurred in the past year
(D) quietly begin a search for possible carcinogens but inform neither workers nor management
(E) insist that information about the risk factors for testicular cancer be released to management and workers

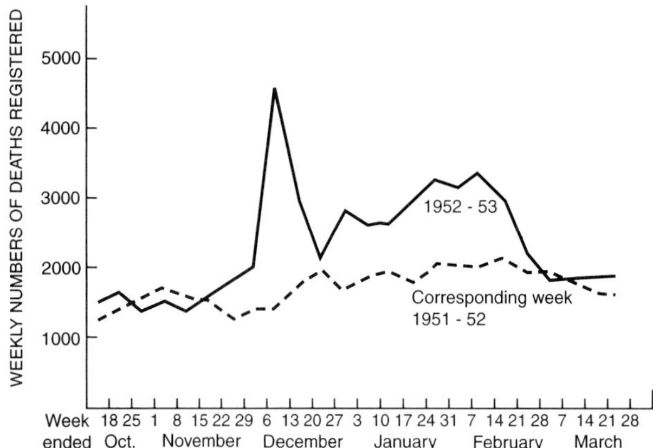

654. The graph above represents a bimodal increase in number of deaths in London during the winter of 1952 to 1953 compared with the previous year. This phenomenon is most likely caused by

(A) herd immunity
(B) a propagated or progressive epidemic
(C) two separate disease etiologies
(D) application of specific control measures
(E) ineffective case identification

Questions 655 through 659

In one day in a primary-care clinic, 15 persons with hypertension are evaluated. Some of them are already under treatment. Systolic blood pressure readings (mm Hg) are as follows: 132, 143, 150, 160, 170, 177, 146, 125, 144, 154, 143, 135, 210, 140, 143.

655. The mean systolic blood pressure reading (mm Hg) for the patient group described above is

(A) 143
(B) 144
(C) 146
(D) 151.5
(E) 167.5

656. The modal reading of systolic blood pressures (mm Hg) in the group described is

(A) 143
(B) 144
(C) 146
(D) 151.5
(E) 167.5

657. The median reading of systolic blood pressures (mm Hg) in the group described is

(A) 143
(B) 144
(C) 146
(D) 151.5
(E) 167.5

658. In statistics, the term variance is used to describe

(A) the sum of the differences of each reading from the mean, divided by the total number of readings ($\Sigma [x - \bar{x}]/n$)
(B) the sum of the squares of the difference of each reading from the mean, divided by the total number of readings ($\Sigma [x - \bar{x}]^2/n$)
(C) the sum of the squares of the difference of each reading from the mean, divided by one less than the total number of readings ($\Sigma [x - \bar{x}]^2/[n - 1]$)
(D) the sum of the deviations in absolute values about the mean, divided by the total number of readings ($\Sigma |x - \bar{x}|/n$)
(E) the sum of the logarithmic values of each reading, divided by the total number of readings ($\Sigma [\log x]/n$)

659. With each administration of a drug to a particular patient, there is an 8% chance of a toxic reaction. The patient requires five consecutive doses of the drug. The chance that this patient will have a toxic reaction is

(A) 8%
(B) 34%
(C) 40%
(D) 66%
(E) 99%

Questions 660 and 668

A group of medical residents in an outpatient clinic start a screening program for diabetes. Of the 1000 individuals examined by blood glucose examination, 100 are found to be above the arbitrary cutoff value of 140 mg/dL. Of these 100 individuals, 50 are discovered to have diabetes on subsequent examination. Also, 50 individuals who did not have positive results on the screening test are discovered to have diabetes on further examination.

660. The sensitivity of the screening procedure described above is

(A) 5%
(B) 10%
(C) 20%
(D) 50%
(E) 100%

661. The specificity of the screening procedure described above is

(A) 5%
(B) 10%
(C) 50%
(D) 95%
(E) 100%

662. What is the source of payment for the majority of health care expenditures in the United States?

(A) health insurance
(B) health maintenance organization (HMO)
(C) self-pay
(D) government
(E) other

663. What proportion of health care expenditures in the United States do physicians receive?

(A) 10%
(B) 20%
(C) 30%
(D) 40%
(E) 50%

664. Deficiency of glucose-6-phosphate dehydrogenase (G6PD) is LEAST common among individuals whose ancestry is

(A) Northern European
(B) Sub-Saharan
(C) Mediterranean
(D) Near Eastern
(E) Central Asian

665. At present, the leading cause of death in the United States is

(A) cerebrovascular disease
(B) heart disease
(C) cancer (all forms)
(D) injuries
(E) all others

666. In the age group 35 years and older, yearly death rates per 1000 persons from lung cancer are 0.07 for nonsmokers and 0.96 for cigarette smokers. Which of the following statements is true concerning interpretation of this finding?

(A) Cigarette smokers are 14.7 times as likely to develop lung cancer as are nonsmokers.
(B) The attributable risk measures the incidence or rate of recurrence.
(C) The attributable risk measures the strength of an association, a high attributable risk leading to conclusions about etiology or causality.
(D) The attributable risk of lung cancer caused by cigarette smoking is 93%.
(E) In smokers, the overall rate of lung cancer death linked to cigarette smoking is 0.96.

667. A recent advertisement for a drug that increases motility of the upper gastrointestinal tract says that it has been "used for 10 years" and that "1 billion doses have been used worldwide." The ad continues that the drug is "the logical treatment of choice to restore normal emptying and to relieve gas, bloating, nausea, vomiting, and heartburn." On the basis of this information, the claim that this drug is the "treatment of choice" is best described as

(A) probably a sound one
(B) invalid because the comparison is not based on rates
(C) invalid because statistical significance is not mentioned
(D) invalid because no control or comparison group is reported
(E) invalid because a cohort effect may be operating

668. The prospective or cohort study is frequently used to test hypotheses about risk factors. In the determination of the value of a particular cohort study, which of the following conditions is most important?

(A) The study should be designed to yield accurate results quickly.
(B) The study population should be large.
(C) The study population should be carefully selected to preserve group characteristics.
(D) The study should provide for periodic examination of cohort and control groups.
(E) The study should allow the investigation of several risk factors simultaneously.

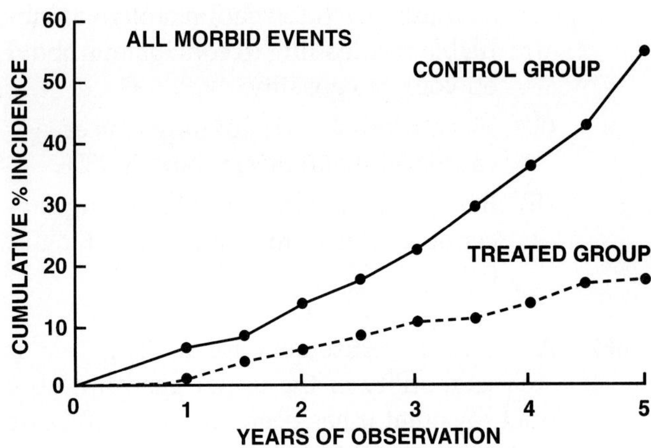

Questions 669 and 670

669. Hypertension is known to have many sequelae and a highly significant morbidity. Utilizing the data given in the figure above for mild-to-moderate hypertension (diastolic blood pressure, 90 to 114 mm), if blood pressure is well controlled over a 3-year period, what is the likely percentage of diminution of all morbid events?

(A) 10%
(B) 20%
(C) 30%
(D) 40%
(E) 50%

670. In the same example, what is the percentage of effectiveness of the therapy?

(A) 10%
(B) 20%
(C) 30%
(D) 40%
(E) 50%

671. The population of the United States is growing older. In 1980, the percentage of the population over the age of 65 was 11.29%; by the year 2000, it is expected to rise to 13.11%. Which of the following statements is true?

(A) The section of the population that is increasing most rapidly is in the age range 65 to 75 years.
(B) Increased longevity is attributed to more effective cancer treatment.
(C) Men have higher expectation of longevity than women.
(D) Suicide is becoming increasingly evident in the older population.
(E) Increased longevity is attributed to reduction in cardiovascular disease.

672. The use of coliform count as a measure of the safety of public water supplies is best explained by which of the following statements?

(A) It is an indicator of fecal contamination.
(B) It is an indicator of industrial contamination.
(C) Coliform organisms are human pathogens.
(D) Coliform organisms accompany other, pathogenic water-borne organisms.
(E) None of the above.

673. Which statement about the effects of cooking food is true?

(A) Food boiled in water attains a temperature of 100°C (212°F).
(B) Food baked at an oven temperature of about 175° to 205°C (350° to 400°F) reaches this temperature.
(C) Cooking food at high attitude kills all bacteria.
(D) Frying bacon does not produce carcinogens.
(E) Cooking kills parasites in meat.

674. The average per-person amount of solid waste produced yearly in towns and cities in the United States is

(A) 90 kg (200 lb)
(B) 450 kg (1000 lb)
(C) 900 kg (1 ton)
(D) 2700 kg (3 tons)
(E) 5400 kg (6 tons)

675. Epidemics of meningococcal disease are now rare in the United States. Sporadic cases do occur. Control has been attributed to

(A) increased herd immunity
(B) increased application of immunologic procedures
(C) increased bed space
(D) improved socioeconomic conditions
(E) lower community carrier rates

676. Sewage and water-borne industrial pollutants have affected many rivers, lakes, and streams. Fish are most likely to die as a result of this pollution because of

(A) changes in the pH of the water
(B) changes in the temperature of the water
(C) changes in the bacterial content of the water
(D) a drop in the oxygen content of the water
(E) the poisonous nature of some of the contaminants

677. Acoustic trauma occurs not only at work but also in the home. Sounds from 120 to 130 dBA are uncomfortably loud; 90 to 100 dBA, very loud; 70 to 80 dBA, moderately loud; 50 to 80 dBA, quiet; and 30 to 50 dBA, very quiet. Noise from which of the following domestic appliances is in the very loud range?

(A) food blender
(B) garbage disposal
(C) vacuum cleaner
(D) power mower
(E) clothes washer

678. Three of the major risk factors for coronary heart disease are hypercholesterolemia, hypertension, and cigarette smoking. When compared with persons with none of these risk factors, persons who have all three risk factors are how many times more likely to develop serious coronary heart disease?

(A) 2 times
(B) 5 times
(C) 8 times
(D) 12 times
(E) 20 times

679. Which of the following statements is true about the relationship between physicians and the many state laws regulating public health and medical practice?

(A) Physicians are not liable for infractions against laws of which they were unaware.
(B) By law, every state must collect relevant public health laws in a single publication.
(C) By law, all state health rules and regulations are distributed to physicians.
(D) Physicians need to familiarize themselves only with the more common laws.
(E) None of the above.

680. The U.S. Occupational Safety and Health Administration (OSHA) was formed in 1970 to encourage employers and employees to reduce hazards in the workplace. The primary emphasis of this agency is to

(A) develop technical expertise to recognize occupational hazards
(B) review state job safety and health standards
(C) monitor compliance with job health and safety codes
(D) maintain records of work-related illnesses
(E) propose statutory changes or additions to job-related laws

681. Many women are playing vital roles in the workplace. There are now very few employment situations for which women are not considered entirely suitable. However, pregnancy does to some extent affect ability to perform certain tasks, and others are considered to increase risks for the mother or fetus, or both. According to current advice, which of the following job functions are indications to cease work or restrict that particular activity by 20 weeks of gestation?

(A) lifting weights up to 14 kg
(B) climbing stairs more than four times in an 8-hour shift
(C) intermittent standing for periods greater than 30 minutes
(D) repetitive stooping (more than 10 times per hour) and bending below knee level
(E) intermittent climbing ladders four times in an 8-hour shift

682. A patient, previously unknown to you, says he had a prolapsed intervertebral disk 10 years ago. Since beginning to work as an automotive engineer in a shop that concentrates on electrical systems, at which he frequently has to lift automotive batteries, he claims he has experienced low-back pain with sciatic radiation. He requests you to certify that this work has disabled him. On examination, there is some restriction of flexion of the spine, straight leg raising on the right being limited to 45°. As a result of your examination, you should

(A) recommend him for Social Security Disability Insurance (SSDI)
(B) recommend him for Supplemental Security Income (SSI)
(C) recommend him for Workmen's Compensation
(D) advise him that he is unsuited for his present employment
(E) recommend physical therapy and 4 days off work

683. Several substances to which parents may be exposed are known to be reproductive hazards. Which of the following substances are known to result in impairment of *both* paternal and maternal fertility?

(A) ethylene oxide
(B) infectious agents
(C) anesthetic agents
(D) inorganic lead
(E) dibromochloropropane (DBCP)

684. In the United States, malnutrition is LEAST likely to occur among individuals in

(A) alcohol abusers
(B) drug addicts
(C) persistent self-medicators
(D) vegetarians
(E) persons with deficient general education

685. Which of the following statements about skin cancer, the most common form of cancer in light-skinned populations, is false?

(A) Dark-skinned populations are up to 50 times less likely to develop skin cancer than light-skinned populations.
(B) The incidence of skin cancer increases with decreasing latitude.
(C) The most common skin cancer is basal cell carcinoma.
(D) Predisposition to skin cancer is the major risk factor in one third of affected individuals.
(E) In the United States, 40% of all cancers are skin cancers.

686. Bladder cancer has been recognized as related to occupational exposure. Which of the following groups of workers are at greatest risk for developing bladder cancer?

(A) miners
(B) automotive brake and clutch mechanics
(C) insecticide makers and sprayers
(D) benzene and rubber-cement workers
(E) asphalt, coal tar, and pitch workers

687. The most frequently occurring work-related infectious disease is

(A) brucellosis
(B) anthrax
(C) viral hepatitis type B
(D) leptospirosis
(E) tetanus

688. A human vaccine is available for which of the following arthropod-borne viral infections?

(A) Colorado tick fever
(B) eastern equine encephalitis
(C) dengue fever
(D) Venezuelan equine encephalitis
(E) yellow fever

689. In the United States, shigellosis is most likely to be spread by

(A) contaminated food
(B) contaminated water supplies
(C) case-to-case transmission
(D) contact with carriers
(E) none of the above

DIRECTIONS (Questions 690 through 691): Each of the numbered items or incomplete staements in this section is followed by answers or by completions of the statement. Select ONE (OR MORE) lettered answer(s) or completion(s) for each case.

690. The randomized control trial is accepted as the most effective way of determining the relative efficacy and toxicity of a new therapy in comparison with an established method of treatment. The following are proper methodology. (SELECT 4)

(A) careful planning before the trial begins
(B) randomized allocation of patients to treatment groups
(C) a null hypothesis stating that one treatment will be found superior to the other
(D) a double-blind protocol
(E) an acceptable definition of statistical significance
(F) sample size of at least 1,000
(G) beta error less than .05

691. The following statements about prevention of and susceptibility to coccidioidomycosis are true. (SELECT 4)

(A) Persons with negative coccidioidin skin reactions are no longer susceptible.
(B) Persons living in the states of Maine or Washington are less susceptible than persons living in Arizona or New Mexico.
(C) Persons living in communities with rapidly changing populations are more susceptible than persons living in communities with a fixed population.
(D) Vaccination of children in high-risk areas diminishes community risk.
(E) Sowing grass seed in dusty lots can help prevent the spread of disease.
(F) Loss of serum titres after vaccination requires a booster.
(G) Paving roads and recreation areas can help prevent the spread of disease.

DIRECTIONS (Questions 692 through 702): Each group of items in this section consists of lettered headings followed by a set of numbered words or phrases. For each numbered word or phrase, select the ONE lettered heading that is most closely associated with it. Each lettered heading may be selected once, more than once, or not at all.

Questions 692 through 694

For each morbidity measurement below, select the statement that is most likely to be the correct definition.

(A) the number of existing cases of a disease at a single moment in time, divided by the population at the same moment
(B) the number of existing cases of a disease at a single moment in time, divided by the mean population for that year
(C) the number of new cases of a disease diagnosed during a given period, divided by the mid-interval population

(D) current cases of a disease, both new and old, during a given time period, divided by the mid-interval population
(E) the number of new cases of a disease diagnosed during a given time period, divided by the mean of the population

692. Period prevalence rate

693. Incidence rate

694. Prevalence rate

Questions 695 through 697

For each mortality measurement below, select the proper definition.

(A) deaths assigned to a specific disease, related to all deaths
(B) all deaths reported, related to midyear population
(C) deaths assigned to a specific disease, related to new and existing cases of that disease during the same year
(D) deaths assigned to a specific disease, related to midyear population
(E) unprocessed number of deaths in a given population

695. Crude death rate

696. Case fatality rate

697. Cause-specific death rate

Questions 698 through 702

For each function listed below, select the agency with which it is most likely to be associated.

(A) Food and Drug Administration (FDA)
(B) U.S. Department of Agriculture (USDA)
(C) Environmental Protection Agency (EPA)
(D) United Nations Food and Agriculture Organization (FAO)
(E) World Health Organization (WHO)

698. Bans domestic marketing and use of the pesticide DDT

699. Monitors water pollution in the United States

700. Publishes an International Statistical Classification of Disease

701. Determines the level of diethylstilbestrol permissible in food products

702. Devoted to improvements of the health of agricultural workers

ANSWERS AND EXPLANATIONS

651. (D) No matter how well a sanitary landfill is maintained, fire is a perpetual hazard. Waste that is decomposing anaerobically reaches quite high temperatures, about 90°C (194°F). Spontaneous combustion and ignition may occur if the cover is thin and cracks, permitting the access of air. The other hazards listed in the question are also possible but do not provide such a major threat. *(Last, p 656)*

652. (D) Distillation is the artificial or engineered version of the process by which the natural hydrologic cycle is maintained. It is used for desalinization and other purposes in which special water purity is required. Naturally occurring spring or deep well water frequently tastes better, because taste is improved by small amounts of mineral deposits. Either of these sources, however, may be contaminated. Sedimentation, filtration, and absorption are possible methods of purification, but result in less purity from a bacteriologic or chemical standpoint. Ion exchange resins are used to remove specific ions, e.g., reducing hardness. *(Last, p 632)*

653. (D) The code of ethical conduct for physicians providing occupational medicine services recommends that physicians should treat as confidential whatever is learned about individuals served. Information should be released only when required by law or because of overriding public health considerations. The occurrence of two similar cases of an illness in a year could be attributed to chance and does not at this stage indicate the risk of an overriding public health problem. Employers are entitled to advice regarding their worker's physical ability to perform their duties but are not entitled to diagnoses or details of a specific nature. Physicians employed in industry need to communicate to employers and employees, in an accurate yet wise and discreet manner, any information about health hazards. *(Levy and Wegman, p 185)*

654. (C) The shape of the graph that accompanies the question suggests different characteristics of the two peaks. In fact, the first peak coincided exactly with the great fog in London of December, 1952. The second peak in January through February coincided with an outbreak of influenza. If herd immunity had developed, a steady decline in the number of cases recorded could be expected. A propagated epidemic would normally produce a steadily increasing number of cases. Application of specific control measures is most likely to produce a steadily diminishing number of cases reported. Ineffective case identification normally leads to low levels of reporting, particularly at the outset of an epidemic. *(Last, pp 11–39, 82)*

655. (D) The mean or average reading ($\bar{x}$) is the total of all readings (Σ x) divided by the number of readings (n), or $\bar{x} = (\Sigma\ x)/n$. In the question, the number of readings is 15 and the total of the readings is 2272. Therefore, the mean is

$$\frac{2272}{15} \cong 151.5$$

(Kramer, p. 126)

656. (A) The modal reading is the most frequently occurring observation. The mode is not readily adaptable to statistical calculation, and in small series of observations or readings there may be no modal reading at all. However, the determination of unimodal versus bimodal distribution within a given population may be useful in defining that population (e.g., incidence of disease by age). *(Kramer, p 126)*

657. (B) The median is the observation that lies in the middle of a series: if the observations are tabulated in numerical order, half the observations are lower in numerical value and thus below the median, and the remainder are higher in numerical value and above the median. Clearly this value is easily identified if the series contains an odd number of readings. Although not very frequently used in statistics, the median has the advantage of not being as affected by extreme observations as the mean, which can be skewed by observations very much lower or higher than the majority. *(Kramer, p 127)*

658. (C) The statistical concept of variance takes into consideration the fact that the distribution of a sample may not represent accurately the distribution of the entire population. This potential difference may be measured by calculating the variance of both the sample and the true population. Variance is calculated as follows: the mean is subtracted from each value; this difference is squared, to make all these figures a positive number; then the sum of all squared differences is divided by one less than the total number of readings (variance $= \Sigma\,[x - \bar{x}]^2/n - 1$). *(Kramer, p 127)*

659. (B) Probability is multiplicative, not additive. In the question presented, the chance that an administration of drug would *not* cause a toxic reaction is 0.92, making the chance of the patient being reaction-free for 5 consecutive doses $(0.92)^5 = 0.66 = 66\%$. Hence, the probability of at least one toxic reaction would be 1 – 0.66, or 0.34. *(Colton, pp 70–71)*

660. (D) The sensitivity of a test is the percentage of people with the disease (true positives, TP) who are detected by the test. False negatives (FN) are those who have the disease but are not detected by the test. Percentage sensitivity is calculated as follows: $[TP \div (TP + FN)] \times 100$. In the example given in the question the sensitivity is $[50 \div (50 + 50)] \times 100 = 50\%$. *(Last, pp 28–38)*

661. (D) The percentage specificity of a test is the percentage of those persons without the disease (true negatives, TN) who are correctly identified. False positives (FP) are those persons who are incorrectly labeled by the test as having the disease. The specificity is thus expressed as follows: $[TN \div (TN + FP)] \times 100$. In the example given in the question, the specificity is $[900 \div (900 + 50)] \times 100 = 94.7\% \cong 95\%$. *(Last, pp 28–38)*

662. (D) In 1987 it was estimated that the government paid for 41% of health care expenditure through Medicare and Medicaid and other programs. This amounts to 212 billion dollars, of which 142 billion dollars are direct federal expenditure. Health insurance, including health maintenance organizations (HMOs), paid for 31% (155 billion dollars), whereas self-pay was 26% (128 billion dollars). *(Department of Health and Human Services Memorandum)*

663. (B) The rising costs of health care are a national problem: both the problem and the costs continually grow. Although health care now absorbs about 12% of the gross national product (GNP), most of it is attributed to physicians. While they order and are responsible for most of these costs, they only receive about 20% of the expenditure. Efforts are being made to curb all these costs. *(Last, pp 1074–1077)*

664. (A) About 12% of black Americans are deficient in glucose-6-phosphate dehydrogenase (G6PD). Several different forms of this genetically determined deficiency are found in persons of Mediterranean, Near Eastern, and Central Asian origin. G6PD deficiency is rare among Caucasians. *(Levy and Wegman, p 452)*

665. (B) Heart disease remains the most common cause of death. However, there has been a marked reduction of deaths attributable to heart disease in recent years (a reduction of 25% over the 10-year period 1968 to 1978). In overall mortality rates in 1980, there were 336 deaths per 100,000 population from heart disease. For ages 65 to 74, the rate was 1156; 75 to 84, 2801; 85 and up, 7342. Cancer overall mortality rate was 184; cerebrovascular disease, 75; injuries, 69. *(Last, pp 827–847)*

666. (D) Relative risk is the ratio of the incidence rate of those persons exposed to a certain condition or factor to the incidence rate of those persons not exposed. In the case described in the question, the relative risk is 0.96 divided by 0.07, or 13.7. Attributable risk measures the impact that removal of a certain factor may have on the incidence of the disease. Incidence or rate of recurrence is measured by the absolute risk. Relative risk measures the strength of an association, whereas absolute risk is used in actuarial situations. In the figures given, the overall rate of deaths from lung cancer in cigarette smokers is 0.96, of which 0.89 (0.96 − 0.07) is attributable to cigarette smoking. Thus, the percent attributable risk is 0.89 divided by 0.96 multiplied by 100, or 93%. *(Last, pp 28–30)*

667. (D) Extensive use of a substance may appear to have clinical significance for a physician, but statistical evidence demands comparison with control groups, even for long-established remedies. Continual prescription of a substance frequently leads to a situation in which the benefits of treatment are not compared with newer preparations, and the frequency of occurrence of side effects is not considered. Cohort effect is unlikely to be apparent if a large number of cases are reported on a worldwide basis (a cohort is a group of persons sharing a common experience within a defined time period). *(Last, pp 34–36)*

668. (D) Some cohort studies may yield quick results (e.g., if respiratory irritants are being studied); in others, where the disease process is slow or the incidence is low, quick results are impossible to obtain (e.g., investigations for leukemia). Only if the condition is rare is it essential for the study to include large numbers. Many studies of small groups of workers exposed to industrial risk have yielded very satisfactory results. Differences within the study group may confound the results; sometimes these difficulties may be overcome by stratifying the group, such as by age. Although personal habits and family history may be factors influencing the development of disease, they would not invalidate a cohort study. Ideally, the study should provide for periodic examination of both the cohort and the control groups. Not only does periodic examination permit more accurate diagnoses or determination of effects, but it also makes possible an estimation of the strength of the Hawthorne effect, which is the influence of the study itself on the group being studied (e.g., British doctors who were being studied for the long-term effects of smoking were more likely than the rest of the population to improve their smoking habits). Some cohort studies do allow the simultaneous assessment of several risk factors, but this design is not necessary in every case. *(Last, pp 34–36; Levy and Wegman, pp 61–66)*

669–670. (669-A, 670-E) In the Veterans Administration Cooperative Study, from which the figure is extracted, the treated group was noted to have a cumulative percentage incidence of 10% as compared with 20% in the controls. Thus, the cumulative reduction of incidence of all morbid events was reduced by 10%. It is important in epidemiologic studies to be very clear about such comparisons. For this reason, by convention, percentages of percentages are never used. The treatment regimen may, however, be described to be 50% effective by this measurement, as the cumulative incidence is reduced from 20 to 10%. In this comparison, a different parameter is introduced. No longer is there comparison of incidence, but a different concept, "effectiveness," is introduced. It is very easy to make exaggerated claims about effectiveness of a particular therapy. Caution clearly needs to be applied to understand statements and comparisons. *(Last, pp 849–858)*

671. (E) The section of the population increasing most rapidly is at the higher age range: by the year 2000, those over 80 years will constitute 28.8% of those aged 65 years and over as against 20.2% in 1980. There has been some increase in deaths in the elderly attributed to cancer, but there is a reduction in those attributed to heart disease. Suicide has decreased in the population over age 65 in recent years. Life expectation for men is lower than for women. *(Last, pp 973–975)*

672. (A) Coliform organisms are present in the gastrointestinal tract of humans and other animals. Some coliform organisms in water supplies are of nonfecal origin and are not necessarily pathogenic; thus, the presence of coliform organisms does not signify the existence of a definite health hazard. However, from a bacteriologic point of view, coliform organisms should not be present in significant numbers in any public water supply from which drinking water is obtained. *(Last, p 629)*

673. (E) Cooking is still the best way of controlling parasite disease contracted through eating meat. Parasites are heat-labile and thus are destroyed by adequate cooking. In addition, cooking garbage before feeding it to pigs has proved to be an effective method of controlling trichinosis. During boiling (especially at high altitudes), baking, and cooking, food may not reach temperatures sufficiently high to kill contaminating bacteria. Recent evidence has suggested that frying bacon preserved with nitrite may produce nitrosamine, which is carcinogenic. *(Last, p 610)*

674. (C) The amount of solid waste produced per capita in U.S. cities is approximately 2.5 kg (5.6 lb) daily. This waste is composed of 0.7 kg (1.5 lb) of postconsumer waste (i.e., waste including household waste and waste generated as a result of retailing), 0.7 kg (1.5 lb) of street and road litter, and 1.2 kg (2.6 lb) of industrial waste. Yearly, the amount of solid waste produced is approximately 1 ton per person; the cost of disposing of 1 ton of waste is $60. In addition, large quantities of agricultural and animal waste are produced, as well as a considerable amount of mining waste. *(Last, pp 649–698)*

675. **(D)** Crowded or impoverished groups of the population seem to be highly susceptible to epidemics of meningococcal disease. Although there is poverty in the United States, and individual families may live in crowded conditions, this is not as generalized as in some other countries. Naturally occurring (herd) immunity does not seem to be responsible for the reduced number of outbreaks. Immunologic precautions have not been generally applied to whole populations. Epidemics have not been demonstrated to be more frequent in populations with higher carrier rates. The biologic reasons for reduction seem to be obscure. *(Last, pp 157–158)*

676. **(D)** Industrial wastes and municipal sewage flowing untreated into a natural collection of water results in an increase both in growth and decomposition of algae. The activity of the algae reduces the oxygen content of the water, which is measured as the biochemic oxygen demand (BOD). A decrease in BOD is generally indicative of successful waste-water treatment and is accompanied by a reduction of other pollutants. *(Clark and MacMahon, pp 764–765)*

677. **(D)** Household noises can be loud enough to cause acoustic damage. A power mower is rated at a sound level of 96 on the dBA scale (an arbitrary measure of intensity on a sound meter), placing it clearly in the very loud scale. Use of ear muffs or plugs for anyone using a power mower regularly for long periods is advisable. Food blenders are at a sound level of 88 dBA, which is nearly at the sound level of shouting (90 dBA). The sound values for other household appliances are garbage disposal, 80 dBA; clothes washer, 78 dBA; and vacuum cleaner, 70 dBA. *(Levy and Wegman, pp 247–261)*

678. **(B)** Prospective epidemiologic studies have shown the quantitative effect that three of the major risk factors for coronary heart disease—hypertension, hypercholesterolemia, and cigarette smoking—have on risk. In the U.S. Pooling Project, the increase was twofold when one risk factor was present. When any two or all three risk factors were present, the probability of developing fatal coronary heart disease was increased fourfold to fivefold. The impact of other risk factors that have been identified is being studied. *(Clark and MacMahon, p 201)*

679. **(E)** Each state has a unique set of public health laws. Although the majority of relevant, current state laws are distributed to physicians, this practice rarely applies to long-established laws. Most states do not have current, complete sets of health rules and regulations available to the public, in part because these laws are continually changing. Every practitioner should obtain copies of all relevant laws through the state department of health or attorney general's office. For physicians and other citizens, ignorance of the law is no defense. *(Warren, p 19)*

680. **(C)** In 1970, Congress passed the Occupational Safety and Health Act, which created the Occupational Safety and Health Administration (OSHA) "to assure so far as possible every working man and woman in the nation safe and healthful working conditions to preserve our human resources." In the agency's first years, emphasis was placed on developing technical expertise and processing of scientific information, but since 1981 the emphasis has been mainly on encouraging voluntary compliance with safety codes, rather than on code enforcement. This change in emphasis has been controversial: many experts believe that enforcement is required to significantly improve the health and safety of workers. *(Levy and Wegman, p 135)*

681. **(D)** Some employers, under the guise of protecting the fetus from hazardous exposure, have developed policies that exclude women from certain jobs or otherwise restrict their activities in the workplace. Of all the activities listed, only stooping and bending below knee level carry specific hazards. In general, if a woman wishes to do so, she should be permitted to continue employment until the onset of labor. *(Last, pp 575–576)*

682. (E) SSDI and SSI require the treating physician to determine only the degree of the patient's impairment. The determination of ability to work is made by an administrative body. The physician should concentrate on medical advice and treatment. Causality is difficult to determine. In advising a patient, it is generally important to avoid attribution of cause, since the exact working conditions and other circumstances may affect the subjective experience of pain. *(Last, p 563)*

683. (D) The timing of an exposure to a toxic agent is a significant determinant of its effect. Relatively few substances affect both male and female fertility adversely. Lead does do so, in addition to causing many other blood and organ defects. In the mother, lead may have other untoward effects during pregnancy, such as causing spontaneous abortion, giving rise to behavioral or developmental disabilities for the fetus, and contaminating breast milk. *(Last, p 575)*

684. (D) Alcoholics and drug addicts, especially if they live alone and are not part of an intact family or household, are likely to miss meals or exist on foods lacking in nutrition. Many over-the-counter and prescription drugs can promote nutritional deficiency if taken over long periods of time. Persons of limited general education often are ignorant of essential information regarding nutrition. Long-time vegetarians of the vegan type, who eat no animal products, may suffer deficiencies in vitamin B_{12}, iron, and protein. Vegetarians less strict with their diet are not as affected, and, of course, those many vegetarians watchful of their health also generally escape nutritional problems. *(Clark and MacMahon, pp 514–516)*

685. (D) Skin cancer is the most common form of cancer in light-skinned populations and accounts for 40% of all cancer in the United States. Light-skinned populations are up to 50 times as likely as dark-skinned populations to develop skin cancer. The major risk factor is exposure to ultraviolet radiation over a period of time; therefore, workers in outdoor occupations, dedicated sunbathers, and persons who live in low latitudes are especially at risk. Sensitivity to ultraviolet radiation is not a major risk factor. Basal cell carcinoma is the most common skin cancer in the United States, accounting for 65% of all skin cancer. *(Last, p 514)*

686. (E) Bladder cancer has been related to occupational exposure to coal products (not coal itself), aromatic amines, and leather dusts. Coal miners and automotive brake and clutch mechanics are more at risk for developing malignant disease of the lungs, pleura, and peritoneum, caused by the inhalation of asbestos and other carcinogenic inhalants. Benzene is associated with bone marrow disease. Insecticide makers and sprayers have a higher-than-normal incidence of skin cancer. *(Levy and Wegman, p 220)*

687. (C) In 1980, 15,318 cases of viral hepatitis, type B, were reported to the Centers for Disease Control. Hepatitis B is by far the most common work-related infectious disease and continues to be a major problem for health professionals. The major source of infection is blood and blood products. Other infectious diseases that can be work-related include leptospirosis, brucellosis, tetanus, and the rarely occurring anthrax. These conditions can occur in farmers, in workers who come into contact with sewage, and in other occupations. *(Levy and Wegman, pp 282–286)*

688. (E) A vaccine against yellow fever is available for human use. Yellow fever is endemic in the region of the world between 15° north and 15° south latitude; vaccination is required for all airline personnel and passengers entering the area. To date, a vaccine has been produced for only one other arthropod-borne virus infection, Rift Valley fever. This condition had been of minor importance until several years ago, when an outbreak of 20,000 cases occurred in the Nile River area of Africa. *(Last, pp 60, 219–220, 225–226)*

689. (C) Person-to-person spread is the most common mode of transmission of shigellosis, and secondary attack rates are high. Outbreaks of food-borne and water-borne infection occur rarely. Water-borne infection generally only occurs from inadequately chlorinated, semipublic water supplies. Food may be primarily infected (e.g., turkeys infected by tainted feed) or, like salad, infected as a result of poor hygiene of food handlers. Carrier states rarely last more than a year after contact with infection. *(Last, pp 175–176)*

690. (A, B, D, E) Proper methodology of randomized control trials includes careful pretrial planning, random double-blind patient allocation, pretrial null hypothesis stating that the compared treatments are equally effective, and a clear definition of what constitutes statistical significance. Sample size has an effect on the efficiency of random control trials. Most studies have been found to include too few patients to ensure that a clinically meaningful difference in therapeutic effect would not be missed. In such studies, type I error (alpha error, significance error) occurs when a treatment is erroneously concluded to have an effect. Type II error (beta error) concludes that a treatment had no effect when in reality it did. These errors are statistical ways of examining false positive and false negative results. *(Kramer, pp 78–91)*

691. (B, C, E, G) Coccidioidomycosis is due to an endemic infection. Incidence of coccidioidomycosis is highest in the arid southwestern area of the United States and declines to the north and east. States in the northwest, extreme northeast, and southeast are largely unaffected. Persons who have negative skin reactions to coccidioidin are susceptible to the disease, and living in a region of rapidly changing population is considered a risk factor. Sowing grass seed and paving roads and recreation areas have been recommended as preventive measures, because both would reduce dust, in which the organisms are carried. There is no vaccine. *(Last, p 287)*

692–694. (692-D, 693-C, 694-A) Incidence and prevalence frequently are confused with each other. Incidence measures the number of *new* cases of a particular disease related to the population at risk, which is normally defined in terms of the population at the middle of the period under study. Prevalence is calculated on the basis of the number of *existing* cases at a given time related to the population at risk at that same time, not to a hypothetical population. For this reason prevalence rate often is referred to as the point prevalence rate. Period prevalence rate combines both point prevalence and incidence. It is of limited usefulness because it is generally preferable to separate new cases from existing or chronic cases.

Because incidence is the number of new cases of a disease, it would be an especially helpful indicator of infectious diseases, which may occur in epidemics. In other situations, it may be more important to study the prevalence, which would be a way of estimating the amount of care (i.e., the nature and number of medical services) needed in any community. For example, knowing the prevalence of certain types of renal failure could determine the need for renal dialysis units in a community. *(Clark and MacMahon, pp 39–40, 56)*

695–697. (695-B, 696-C, 697-D) Death rates are frequently calculated and reported for all causes and ages, or in many combinations of age, sex, race, and geographic area. Frequently the population base is a political or census division because residence or population at risk can be determined easily. The period of calculation is usually one year, but the population base may be 1000 to 100,000.

Crude death rate is the number of all deaths reported, related to midyear population. It is of value in comparing the health of one locality or country with another and can be a general measure of health care. Case fatality rate is not generally related to a standard 1-year period but frequently reflects the duration of an acute episode of illness or length of hospitalization. In an acute epidemic, it is sometimes defined as the number of deaths divided by the number of new cases, all the cases in such an epidemic being new. Otherwise, case fatality rate refers to both new and existing cases of a disease. Cause-specific death rate is valuable in studying the incidence, virulence, and effectiveness of treatment. It is defined as the number of deaths from a specified disease, related to a midyear population. *(Clark and MacMahon, pp 38–39)*

698–702. (698-C, 699-C, 700-E, 701-A, 702-D) In the United States, the organizational responsibility for monitoring food and water safety is complex. Among the federal control agencies, the Environmental Protection Agency (EPA) is the most recent and in many ways the most active and powerful. This agency has now set up an elaborate system of regulation and control of the use of pesticides and has banned the commercial marketing of DDT. The EPA also monitors water pollution in general, but other agencies are involved, too. The Food and Drug Administration (FDA) has defined action levels in fish of polychlorinated biphenyls (PCBs), a toxin that presumably is water borne. The FDA retains the authority to remove from the market food containing excess pesticides or other toxic substances and sets levels of diethylstilbestrol (DES) permissible in food products (especially poultry) at the time of marketing. The U.S. Department of Agriculture (USDA) determines wholesomeness standards for the production and sale of meat.

International control is assisted by the World Health Organization (WHO). This agency has mounted control programs for the eradication of communicable disease, with conspicuous success in eradicating smallpox. It also publishes an International Statistical Classification of Disease (ICD). The United Nations Food and Agriculture Organization (FAO) is devoted to the improvement of the health of agricultural workers all over the world. *(Last, pp 43, 486–487, 592, 647)*

REFERENCES

Clark DW, MacMahon B. *Preventive and Community Medicine,* 2nd ed. Boston: Little, Brown & Co; 1981.

Colton T. *Statistics in Medicine.* Boston: Little, Brown & Co; 1974.

Kelley WN. *Textbook of Internal Medicine.* Philadelphia: J.B. Lippincott Co; 1989.

Kramer MS. *Clinical Epidemiology and Biostatistics. A Primer for Clinical Investigators and Decision-Makers.* Berlin, Germany: Springer-Verlag; 1988.

Last JM. *Maxcy–Rosenau–Last Public Health and Preventive Medicine,* 13th ed. Norwalk, CT: Appleton & Lange; 1992.

Levy BS, Wegman DH. *Occupational Health: Recognizing and Preventing Work Related Disease,* 2nd ed. Boston: Little, Brown & Co; 1995.

Warren DG. *A Legal Guide for Rural Health Programs.* Cambridge, MA: Ballinger Publishing Co; 1979.

SUBSPECIALTY LIST: PREVENTIVE MEDICINE

Question Number and Subspecialty

651. Disease control
652. Disease control
653. Ethical, legal
654. Epidemiology
655. Biostatistics
656. Biostatistics
657. Biostatistics
658. Biostatistics
659. Biostatistics
660. Biostatistics
661. Biostatistics
662. Health services
663. Health services
664. Biostatistics
665. Epidemiology
666. Biostatistics
667. Biostatistics
668. Biostatistics
669. Biostatistics
670. Biostatistics
671. Disease control
672. Disease control

673. Disease control
674. Disease control
675. Disease control
676. Disease control
677. Disease control
678. Disease control
679. Disease control
680. Health services
681. Ethical, legal
682. Ethical, legal
683. Disease control
684. Epidemiology
685. Epidemiology
686. Epidemiology
687. Disease control
688. Disease control
689. Disease control
690. Biostatistics
691. Disease control
692. Epidemiology
693. Epidemiology
694. Epidemiology
695. Epidemiology
696. Epidemiology
697. Epidemiology
698. Ethical, legal
699. Ethical, legal
700. Ethical, legal
701. Ethical, legal
702. Ethical, legal

CHAPTER 3

Clinical Competence Review

Questions

DIRECTIONS (Questions 730 through 777): Each of the numbered items or incomplete statements in this section is followed by answers or by completions of the statement. Select the ONE lettered answer or completion that is BEST in each case.

Questions 703 through 705

The basal body temperature chart shown below is from a 28-year-old woman (gravida 0, para 0).

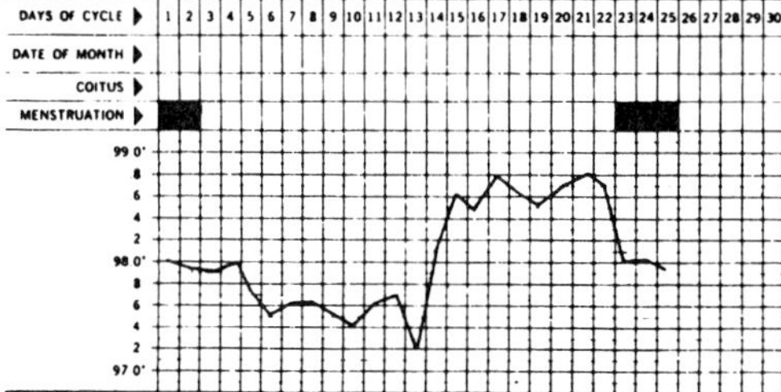

703. The data from the basal body temperature chart shown above support which of the following conclusions?

(A) The woman appears to have had an ovulatory cycle.
(B) Progesterone production peaks just before the temperature drop on about day 14.
(C) Luteinizing hormone (LH) peaks only after the temperature rise has been sustained for 3 days or more.
(D) The time from the anticipated LH surge to menses in this cycle is normal.
(E) In this cycle follicle-stimulating hormone (FSH) would achieve maximum levels on day 23.

704. The most likely diagnosis of the condition represented in the chart is

(A) luteal-phase defect
(B) Stein–Leventhal syndrome (polycystic ovaries)
(C) salpingitis isthmica nodosa
(D) müllerian agenesis
(E) Asherman's syndrome

705. All the following statements are true about the diagnosis and treatment of this condition EXCEPT

(A) it can be a cause of habitual abortion or infertility
(B) endometrial biopsy performed 2 days before the onset of menstruation can confirm the diagnosis
(C) administration of ethinyl estradiol has been a successful treatment of this condition
(D) the aim of therapy is to raise the number of LH receptors on the granulosa cells of the ovarian follicle
(E) affected women may show abnormally low postovulatory serum progesterone levels

Questions 706 through 707

A 24-year-old woman (gravida 2, para 1) registers at a local prenatal clinic at 26 weeks' gestation. Her hematocrit is 28%.

706. The most likely cause of the woman's low hematocrit is

(A) Cooley's anemia
(B) pernicious anemia
(C) folic acid deficiency
(D) glucose-6-phosphate dehydrogenase deficiency
(E) iron deficiency

707. The most useful combination of laboratory tests to confirm the correct diagnosis would be

(A) stool culture for ova and parasites and hemoglobin electrophoresis
(B) complete blood cell count with indices and serum iron concentration
(C) serum vitamin B_{12} and serum iron concentrations
(D) reticulocyte count and complete blood cell count
(E) mean corpuscular volume and reticulocyte count

708. Regarding the iron requirements of pregnancy, all of the statements below are true, EXCEPT

(A) pernicious anemia is the most common anemia of pregnancy
(B) 300 mg of iron goes to the fetus
(C) 500 mg of iron is used to expand maternal hemoglobin
(D) 200 mg of iron is shed through the gut
(E) the hemoglobin level of most healthy women at term is 11 g/dL

709. Regarding this type of anemia in pregnancy, which of the following statements is true?

(A) Fetal blood sampling should be done to see if this anemia has affected the fetus.
(B) This type of anemia seldom affects the fetus.
(C) Genetic counseling should be provided to this woman before her next pregnancy.
(D) Treatment of this type of anemia with iron is commonly associated with hemosiderosis.
(E) Packed red blood cell transfusion is the only successful way to treat this type of anemia, but should be withheld until the hematocrit is less than 24.

710. The laboratory test that would *first* reflect response to treatment in the case presented would be

(A) serum iron concentration
(B) hematocrit
(C) reticulocyte count
(D) total iron-binding capacity
(E) smear of peripheral blood

Questions 711 through 715

A 26-year-old woman (gravida 3, para 2) is 28 weeks pregnant. She seeks medical attention because of urinary frequency and urgency, and a diagnosis of urinary tract infection is made.

711. Which of the following statements about urinary tract infection associated with pregnancy is true?

(A) Most women with this disorder have symptoms.
(B) Fever is common.
(C) Many symptomatic women do not have bacteriuria.
(D) Pregnant women are less likely than nonpregnant women to develop urinary tract infection.
(E) Age and parity do not affect the incidence of this condition.

712. Regarding the accurate diagnosis of urinary tract infection during pregnancy, which of the following statements is true?

(A) The clinical picture of fever, chills, dysuria, and frequency may be the most sensitive indicators of urinary tract infection.

(B) 100,000 colonies of bacteria per milliliter of collected clean-catch urine are the best indicator of urinary tract infection in pregnancy.

(C) In high-risk women, 100 to 1000 colonies of bacteria per milliliter of collected clean-catch urine may be significant.

(D) Bladder washout techniques are the best available techniques for diagnosis of urinary tract infection in pregnancy.

(E) Radiography of the urinary tract in pregnancy need not be postponed in any patient with recurrent infection.

713. Which of the following statements describing treatment for this disorder is true?

(A) Bacteriostatic drugs are preferable to bactericidal drugs.

(B) The use of sulfonamides is contraindicated.

(C) Catheterization is necessary to determine the effectiveness of treatment.

(D) Laboratory testing should be repeated 1 to 2 weeks after treatment.

(E) Long-term chemoprophylaxis should be instituted for the duration of the pregnancy if recurrent infection occurs.

714. The organism or type of organism most commonly causing this condition is

(A) *Mycoplasma*

(B) RNA viruses

(C) enterobacteria

(D) group B streptococci

(E) anaerobes

715. All the following statements about the relationship between urinary tract infection and pregnancy are true EXCEPT

(A) there is a higher rate of perinatal sepsis in the offspring

(B) there is a higher rate of postpartum endometritis in the mother

(C) relapse after antibiotic therapy may indicate the presence of an anatomic abnormality

(D) endocervical cultures often reveal the same organism

(E) a history of urinary tract infection before pregnancy does not increase the risk of pregnancy-related urinary tract infection

Questions 716 through 722

A 22-year-old woman goes to the local emergency room because of fever, a rash, and malaise associated with menstruation. A diagnosis of toxic shock syndrome (TSS) is considered.

716. Which of the following symptoms would be LEAST likely to be associated with TSS?

(A) constipation

(B) myalgia

(C) syncope

(D) headache

(E) oliguria

717. Of the following microorganisms, the one isolated most commonly from women with TSS is

(A) *Chlamydia*

(B) *Streptococcus*

(C) *Staphylococcus aureus*

(D) *Escherichia coli*

(E) herpes simplex virus, type 2

718. TSS is most likely to be associated with which of the following laboratory findings?

(A) elevated SGOT and SGPT levels

(B) elevated platelet count

(C) decreased blood urea nitrogen level

(D) decreased serum creatine phosphokinase level

(E) decreased serum uric acid level

719. The most likely cause of the tissue damage associated with TSS is

(A) bacteremia
(B) viremia
(C) nonenteric toxin production
(D) hyperthermia
(E) alteration in blood clotting control

720. The characteristic rash in women with TSS is best described as

(A) papular and nonpruritic
(B) macular, diffuse, and red
(C) vesicular and occurring in a dermatomal distribution
(D) rarely desquamative
(E) desquamative but sparing the palms of the hands and soles of the feet

721. The most effective therapy for the woman described in this case would be

(A) massive fluid replacement therapy
(B) oxacillin or a cephalosporin
(C) dopamine
(D) massive doses of corticosteroids
(E) naloxone

722. Which of the following statements regarding prognosis and management of TSS is true?

(A) Appropriate drug therapy prevents recurrence.
(B) Recurrence rate in women who have not received antibiotic therapy is 90%.
(C) Tampon use is still not proven to be safe even if posttreatment cultures are negative.
(D) The use of "regular"-size tampons is not associated with recurrence.
(E) Less frequent tampon changing causes less vaginal irritation and, therefore, less chance of recurrence.

Questions 723 through 726

A 33-year-old woman (gravida 1, para 0) is in the 35th week of pregnancy. She goes to the local emergency room because of uterine pain and vaginal bleeding. Her blood pressure, which had been 110/70 mm Hg last month, is now 150/100 mm Hg.

723. The most likely reason for the woman's vaginal bleeding is

(A) placenta previa
(B) abruptio placentae
(C) ruptured Gartner's cyst
(D) incompetent cervix
(E) fibroid uterus

724. Which of the following laboratory values would be LEAST consistent with the diagnosis of preeclampsia?

(A) elevated hematocrit
(B) platelet count of less than 100,000/mL^3
(C) elevated fibrin degradation products
(D) elevated plasma uric acid concentration
(E) dramatically shortened prothrombin time

725. Vaginal blood loss caused by the disorder described in the case is often

(A) associated with uterine atony
(B) a combination of fetal and maternal blood loss
(C) less than the true blood loss because of maternal intra-abdominal hemorrhage
(D) less than the true blood loss because of concealed retroplacental hemorrhage
(E) none of the above

726. Regarding placental abruption, which of the following statements is true?

(A) There is no indication for cesarean section in these cases.
(B) Oxytocin stimulation of labor is contraindicated.
(C) Blood loss is seldom of significance because of myometrial tamponade.
(D) Amniotomy plays a key role in correct management of this complication of labor.
(E) The uterus may be persistently hypertonic.

Questions 727 through 729

A 3-week-old male infant, who has been in good health after an uncomplicated pregnancy, labor, and delivery, begins to feed very poorly. His temperature is 38.9°C (102°F). His mother calls the infant's pediatrician, and the boy is subsequently hospitalized. Cultures are obtained from blood, urine, and cerebrospinal fluid, which is cloudy. A diagnosis of meningitis is made.

727. The bacterial agents most likely to be responsible for this infant's meningitis are

(A) *Haemophilus influenzae, Streptococcus pneumoniae,* and *Neisseria meningitidis*
(B) *Haemophilus influenzae, Streptococcus pneumoniae,* and *Staphylococcus aureus*
(C) *Staphylococcus aureus* and group A *Streptococcus*
(D) group B *Streptococcus, Escherichia coli,* and *Listeria monocytogenes*
(E) group B *Streptococcus* and *Staphylococcus aureus*

728. Of the following, what would be appropriate therapy for this patient?

(A) penicillin alone or oxacillin alone
(B) penicillin and vancomycin or ampicillin and vancomycin
(C) ampicillin and gentamicin or ampicillin and cefotaxime
(D) ampicillin alone or gentamicin alone
(E) oxacillin alone or cefotaxime alone

729. Which of the following is most likely to occur as a complication of this child's meningitis?

(A) hearing loss
(B) visual impairment
(C) brain abscess
(D) kernicterus
(E) quadriplegia

Questions 730 and 731

A 2-year-old girl is brought to the emergency room because of a cough that has been worsening during the past 3 days. Her temperature is 38.3°C (101°F), and she has mild inspiratory stridor. A roentgenogram of the neck (see below) is taken, but because of the child's movement only an anteroposterior view is satisfactorily obtained.

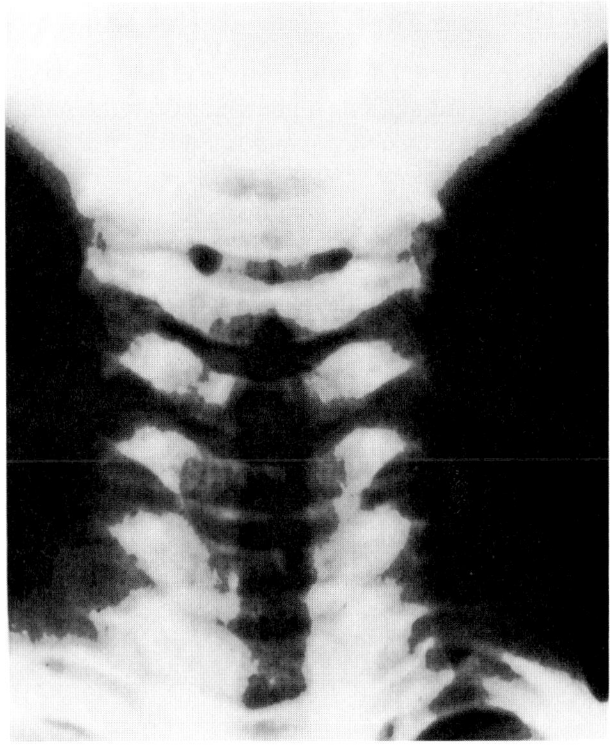

Figure for use with questions 730 and 731.

730. The most likely diagnosis in the case presented is

(A) epiglottitis
(B) infectious laryngotracheitis
(C) spasmodic croup
(D) angioneurotic edema
(E) foreign-body aspiration

731. The next step in the treatment of this child should be to

(A) administer cefotaxime intravenously
(B) administer racemic epinephrine by aerosol
(C) administer theophylline intravenously
(D) endotracheal intubation
(E) endoscopy

Questions 732 through 734

For the past day, a 16-year-old girl has had fever, vomiting, and watery diarrhea. She also complains of intermittent abdominal pain and generalized myalgia. On physical examination she is noted to be slightly lethargic. Temperature is 39.7°C (103.5°F), pulse is 154 beats/min, and blood pressure is 80/46 mm Hg. Her conjunctivae and pharynx are hyperemic, and she has a generalized erythematous maculopapular rash that spares her wrists.

732. The most likely diagnosis in the case described above is

(A) scarlet fever
(B) Kawasaki's disease
(C) ruptured appendix
(D) Rocky Mountain spotted fever
(E) toxic shock syndrome

733. The cause of the girl's disease is

(A) group A beta-hemolytic *Streptococcus*
(B) *Staphylococcus aureus*
(C) *Rickettsia rickettsii*
(D) fecolith impaction
(E) unknown

734. Recommended treatment for the disease process described above is

(A) tetracycline
(B) gentamicin and clindamycin
(C) oxacillin
(D) penicillin
(E) surgery

Questions 735 and 736

A 6-year-old boy is seen by a pediatrician for routine physical examination. On physical examination the pediatrician notes the presence of dark, coarse pubic hair, enlargement of the penis and testes, and acne of the face and upper back. Upon questioning, the mother relates that the child often has a body odor similar to that of her teenage son after a baseball game. A graph of the child's height during the last few years is shown above.

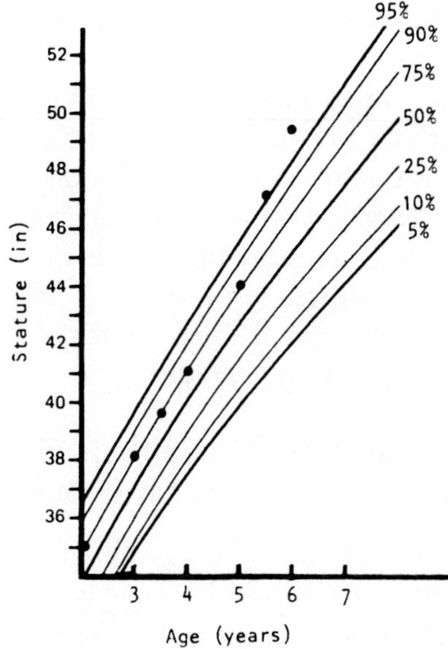

735. Which of the following tests is most likely to reveal the cause of this child's problem?

(A) computed tomography (CT) scan of the head
(B) abdominal ultrasound examination
(C) surgical exploration of the abdomen
(D) skin biopsy
(E) chromosomal analysis

736. The most likely diagnosis in this child is

(A) idiopathic precocious puberty
(B) a hypothalamic tumor
(C) McCune–Albright syndrome
(D) Klinefelter's syndrome
(E) XYY syndrome

Questions 737 through 740

A 15-month-old boy who developed an upper respiratory tract infection yesterday had a generalized tonic–clonic seizure earlier today. According to his parents, who took their son to the hospital, his eyes rolled backward and the seizure lasted 30 seconds. Temperature on arrival at the hospital is 40°C (104°F), respiratory rate is 22/min, and blood pressure is 90/60 mm Hg. The boy is alert, smiling, and walking from room to room. On physical examination, his anterior fontanel is almost closed, he has rhinorrhea, and his neck is supple. The child has bruises below both knees. The rest of the physical examination is unremarkable.

737. The most likely diagnosis in the case described is

(A) idiopathic epilepsy
(B) meningitis
(C) simple febrile seizure
(D) complex febrile seizure
(E) child abuse

738. At this point, the boy's physician should

(A) order a complete blood cell count
(B) order serum electrolyte and blood glucose levels
(C) obtain a CT scan of the head
(D) perform a lumbar puncture
(E) schedule electroencephalography for the following day

739. The correct therapeutic response to the boy's seizure would be to

(A) prescribe oral phenobarbital
(B) administer intravenous phenytoin
(C) administer intravenous antibiotics
(D) reassure the parents
(E) notify the local child protection agency

740. The prognosis associated with the boy's condition is best described as

(A) poor
(B) fair
(C) excellent
(D) difficult to assess
(E) dependent on the adjustments made in the child's environment

Questions 741 through 743

A 2-month-old boy is being evaluated for the growth pictured above. At birth his skin was clear, but when he was 1 month old his mother noted a light red growth on his arm. During the last month, it increased in size and turned bright red.

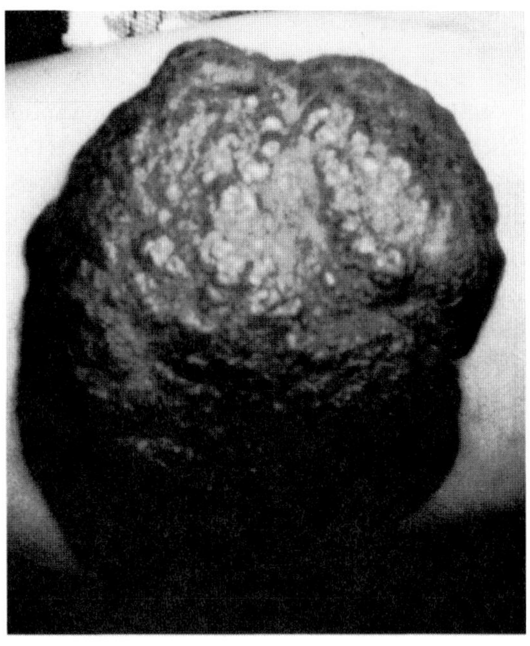

Figure for use with questions 741 through 743.

741. The most likely diagnosis of the skin lesion pictured is

(A) melanoma
(B) osteochondroma
(C) nevus flammeus
(D) cavernous hemangioma
(E) strawberry hemangioma

742. The treatment of choice of this disorder is

(A) surgery
(B) radiation therapy
(C) argon laser therapy
(D) topical corticosteroids
(E) observation

743. Response to treatment is best described by which of the following statements?

(A) Recovery will be total, with no evidence of scar.
(B) Recovery will be poor, with probable malignant transformation.
(C) Recovery will be poor, with metastasis to regional lymph nodes.
(D) Recovery will be favorable, but other lesions of the same type are likely to develop.
(E) There is not enough information to predict outcome.

Questions 744 through 746

An 8-year-old boy has the scalp rash shown below. Two weeks ago the rash was quite small and very scaly, but since then it has slowly enlarged. The rash now is 2 cm by 2 cm in size; it is raised, has small vesicles and pustules on its surface, and is indurated and boggy. The boy is afebrile.

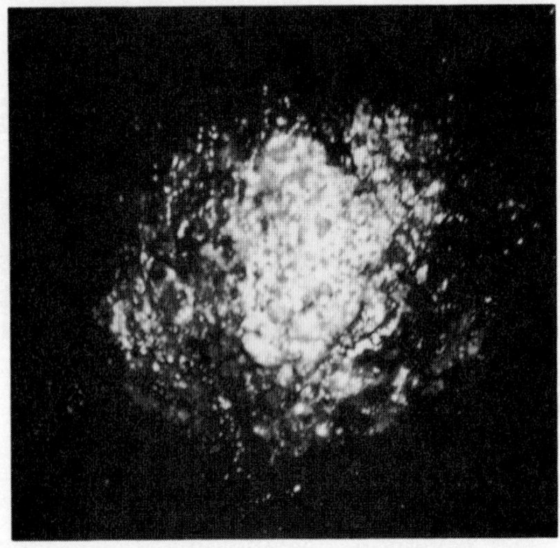

Figure for use with questions 744 through 746.

744. The most likely diagnosis of the skin lesion described is

(A) seborrheic dermatitis
(B) impetigo
(C) alopecia areata
(D) herpetic skin lesion
(E) kerion

745. The etiology of the skin disease presented above is

(A) genetic
(B) fungal
(C) bacterial
(D) viral
(E) unknown

746. The treatment of choice of the skin disease

(A) topical steroids
(B) intralesional steroids
(C) griseofulvin
(D) adenosine arabinoside (ara-A)
(E) dicloxacillin

Questions 747 through 749

A 7-year-old boy who has been in excellent health complains of intermittent palpitations. He states that the palpitations begin and end abruptly and last from 30 minutes to 2 hours. Between episodes he is asymptomatic. Physical examination is unremarkable. His electrocardiogram is shown on the facing page.

747. The most likely diagnosis in the case described is

(A) psychoneurosis
(B) Wolff–Parkinson–White syndrome
(C) Lown–Ganong–Levine syndrome
(D) sinus tachycardia
(E) nodal tachycardia

748. The boy's palpitations are most likely due to

(A) anxiety
(B) supraventricular tachycardia
(C) atrial fibrillation
(D) ventricular fibrillation
(E) wandering pacemaker

749. The most effective first-line, long-term therapy for this boy's disorder would be

(A) antianxiety medications
(B) psychotherapy
(C) digoxin
(D) quinidine
(E) electrical cardioversion

Questions 750 through 752

A 12-year-old boy with sickle cell disease is hospitalized because of severe pain in both legs. The child is afebrile and physical examination is within normal limits except for pallor, a grade 2/6 systolic ejection murmur, and mild generalized tenderness of both lower extremities. Hemoglobin concentration is 7.5 g/dL.

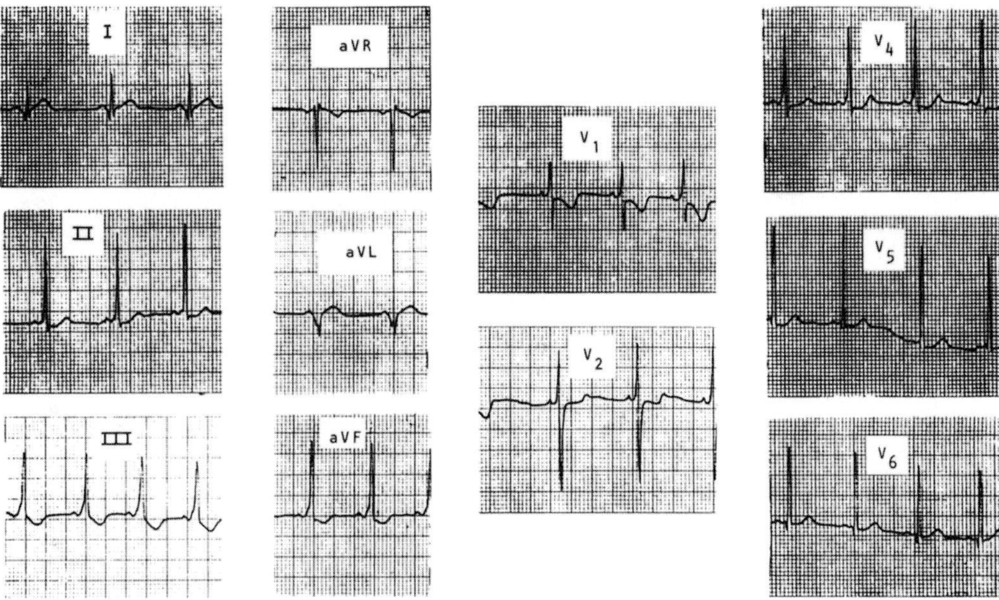

Figure for use with questions 747 through 749.

750. Therapy should include

(A) intravenous fluids
(B) intravenous antibiotics
(C) blood transfusion
(D) withholding pain medications
(E) withholding oral fluids

751. Complications of sickle cell disease include all of the following EXCEPT

(A) sequestration crisis
(B) vasoocclusive crisis
(C) aplastic anemia
(D) pulmonary edema
(E) hand–foot syndrome

752. Children with sickle cell anemia are at highest risk for developing bacteremia with

(A) *Streptococcus pneumoniae*
(B) beta-hemolytic streptococcus
(C) *Escherichia coli*
(D) *Staphylococcus aureus*
(E) *Klebsiella pneumoniae*

Questions 753 and 754

A 58-year-old man develops a syndrome consisting of a "shade" falling smoothly over his left field of vision and numbness of his right hand and face lasting between 5 and 10 minutes. He has had two episodes recently.

753. The most likely diagnosis of the man's disorder is

(A) recurrent cerebral embolism
(B) Adams–Stokes attacks
(C) epileptic seizure
(D) migrainous accompaniments
(E) transient cerebral ischemic attacks

754. Treatment of this man's disorder might include

(A) ergot preparations
(B) beta-blockers
(C) antiplatelet drugs
(D) antiarrhythmic drugs
(E) antiseizure drugs

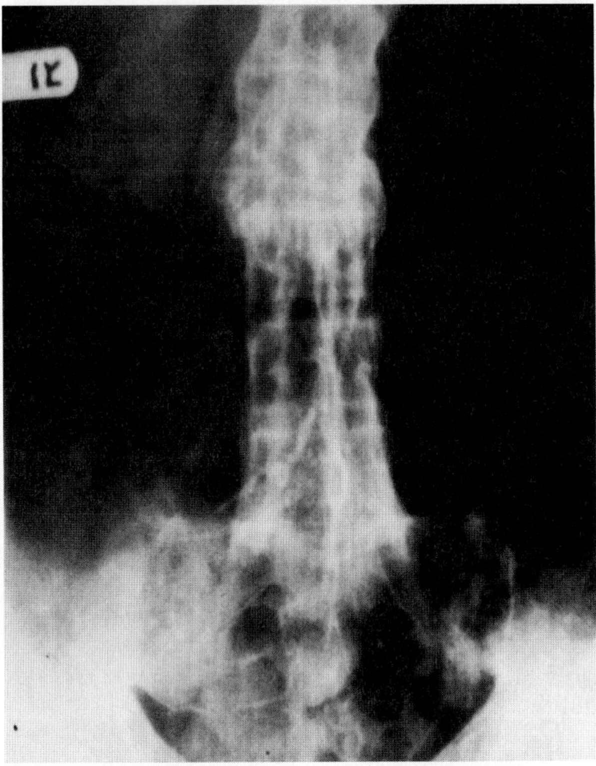
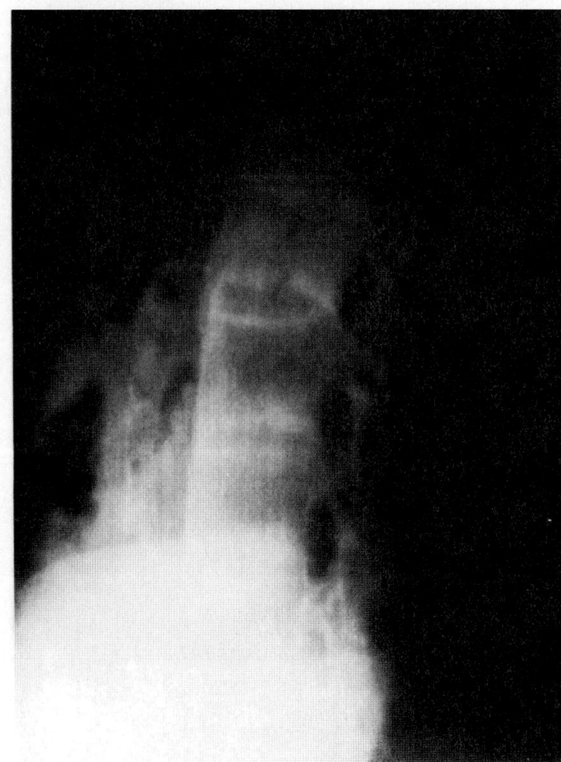

Figures for use with questions 755 and 756.

Questions 755 and 756

For the last 6 months, a 30-year-old man has had low back pain associated with morning stiffness and lessened with exercise. Roentgenograms of his back are shown above.

755. The most likely diagnosis for the man's disorder is

(A) rheumatoid arthritis
(B) ankylosing spondylitis
(C) herniated nucleus pulposus
(D) pseudogout
(E) Reiter's syndrome

756. Systemic complications of this disease include

(A) apical pulmonary fibrosis with cavities
(B) vasculitis
(C) acanthosis nigricans
(D) cryoglobulinemia
(E) macular degeneration

Questions 757 and 758

A 44-year-old man has chronic headaches, rhinorrhea, earache, low-grade fever, arthralgias, and anorexia. Sinus roentgenograms reveal bilateral maxillary sinusitis. He is treated with antibiotics but then develops cough, chest pain, and hemoptysis. Physical examination reveals a saddle-nose deformity and a nasal mucosal ulceration. Chest roentgenography demonstrates cavitary infiltrates. Urinalysis shows 10 to 12 RBC/HPF. Blood urea nitrogen concentration is 35 mg/dL, and serum creatinine concentration is 2.0 mg/dL. Sputum examination shows no acid-fast organisms, fungi, or malignant cells.

757. The most likely diagnosis in the case described is

(A) polyarteritis nodosa
(B) tuberculosis
(C) sarcoidosis
(D) Wegener's granulomatosis
(E) pulmonary abscess

758. Long-term treatment of this man's disease should consist of

(A) cyclosporine
(B) cyclophosphamide and prednisone
(C) penicillin
(D) isoniazid and rifampin
(E) isoniazid, streptomycin, and *p*-aminosalicylic acid (PAS)

759. A 25-year-old woman complains of epigastric pain. She has a long history of bronchial asthma, which has been treated with a long-acting theophylline drug and beta-adrenergic aerosol. An upper gastrointestinal series reveals a hiatal hernia and reflux. She is started on cimetidine, 300 mg four times daily. Within a week she develops nausea. Her physician now should order which of the following tests?

(A) esophagogastroduodenoscopy
(B) stool examination for occult blood
(C) repeat upper gastrointestinal series
(D) serum theophylline level
(E) CT scan of the abdomen

Questions 760 and 761

A 48-year-old man has developed calcium oxalate kidney stones on 12 occasions, despite following a diet free of dairy products and drinking large amounts of fluid. Urinalysis reveals a normal pH, and 24-hour calcium, uric acid, and oxalate levels are normal. Blood testing reveals normal levels of calcium, phosphorus, uric acid, and urea nitrogen. Urine cultures produce no growth. Intravenous pyelography shows opaque calculi in both kidneys.

760. Initial treatment of this man's disorder should be with

(A) a thiazide drug
(B) allopurinol
(C) cellulose phosphate
(D) nephrolithotomy
(E) increased fluid intake and dietary restriction

761. Despite proper treatment the man continues to form and pass new stones. Treatment now should consist of

(A) a thiazide drug and allopurinol in combination
(B) cellulose phosphate in higher concentration
(C) orthophosphate as the neutral salt
(D) parathyroidectomy
(E) nephrolithotomy

Questions 762 and 763

A 35-year-old man suddenly develops a generalized pruritic macular erythematous rash and fever. Four days ago, he saw his physician because of a sore throat that started the day before, and he was started on penicillin, 250 mg four times daily, after a throat culture grew out beta-hemolytic streptococci. Laboratory studies now reveal a blood urea nitrogen level of 35 mg/dL. Urinalysis shows no casts, 1+ protein, 5–10 RBC/HPF, and 50 WBC/HPF. Complete blood cell count is normal except for eosinophilia (12%). Urine protein concentration is 650 mg/24 h.

762. The most likely diagnosis in the case described is

(A) acute poststreptococcal glomerulonephritis
(B) membranous glomerulonephritis
(C) polyarteritis nodosa
(D) Schönlein–Henoch purpura
(E) drug-induced interstitial nephritis

763. The treatment of choice for the man's disorder would be to

(A) stop the penicillin
(B) increase the dosage of penicillin
(C) prescribe methicillin
(D) prescribe prednisone
(E) prescribe azathioprine and prednisone

764. A 15-year-old boy with chronic bronchial asthma has severe wheezing and pain in his shoulders. Auscultation reveals a "crunching" sound over his precordium, and palpation of his neck reveals subcutaneous emphysema. Initial treatment should consist of

(A) intermittent positive-pressure breathing and a beta-adrenergic agent
(B) inhaled beta-agonist and oxygen
(C) positive end-expiratory pressure therapy
(D) insertion of a chest tube
(E) bronchoscopy

Questions 765 and 766

A 25-year-old black woman has tender red nodules on both shins. Her chest roentgenogram is shown below. She is otherwise asymptomatic.

765. The most likely diagnosis is

(A) herpes simplex disease
(B) Hodgkin's disease
(C) lymphoma
(D) coccidioidomycosis
(E) sarcoidosis

766. The best initial treatment for the woman described would be

(A) nonsteroidal anti-inflammatory agents
(B) prednisone
(C) idoxuridine
(D) amphotericin B
(E) radiation therapy

Questions 767 through 769

For the past several years, a 52-year-old woman has felt fatigued and has had symmetrical swelling, redness, and tenderness of the proximal interphalangeal joints of her hands. Physical examination reveals swelling of the proximal interphalangeal and metacarpophalangeal joints of her hands and wrists. Nodules are found over the extensor surfaces of her elbow. Roentgenograms of her hands are shown above.

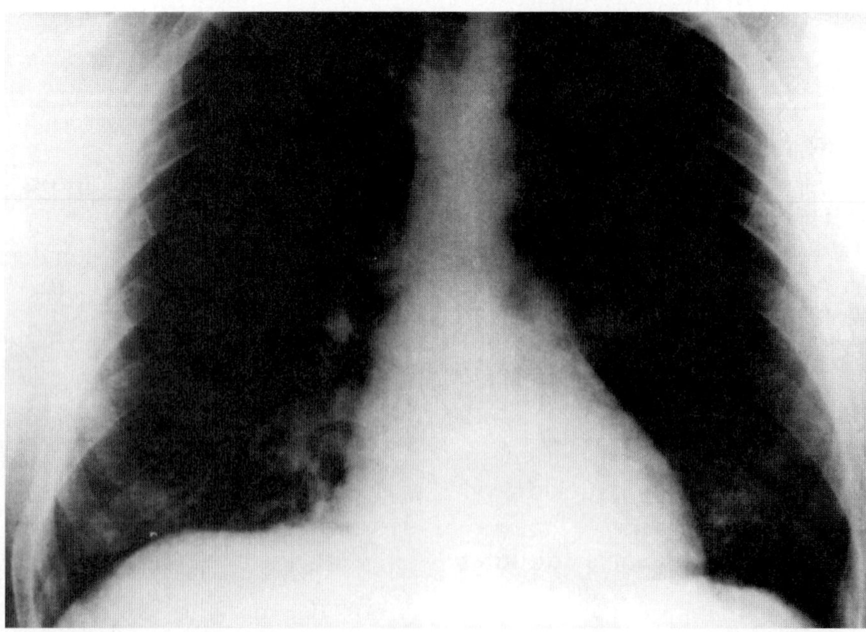

Figure for use with questions 765 and 766.

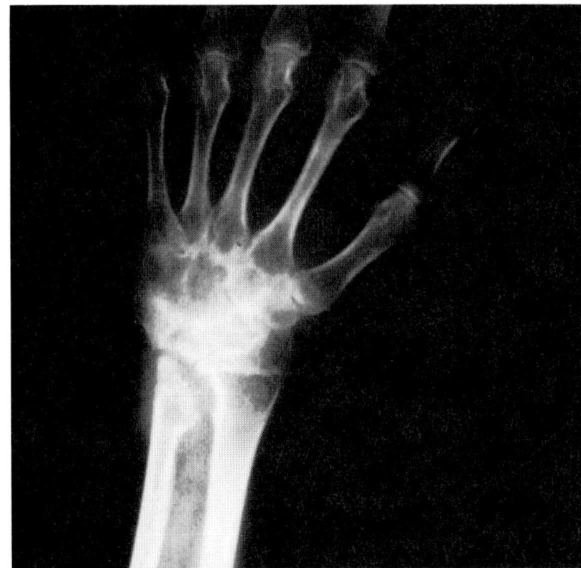

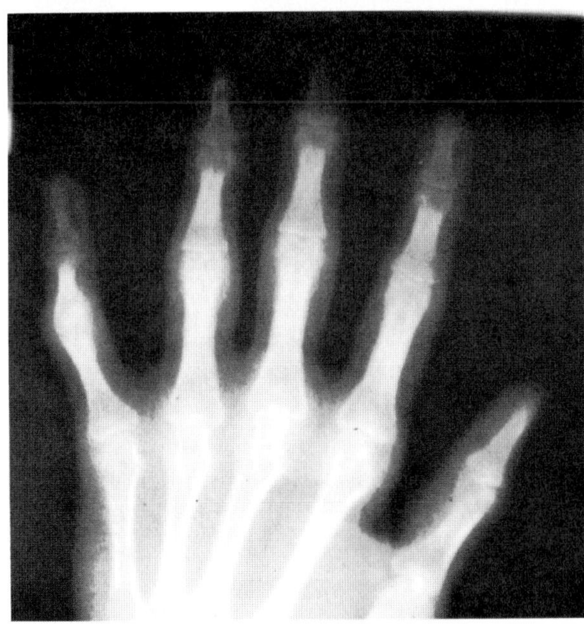

Figures for use with questions 767 through 769.

767. The most likely diagnosis for the woman described is

(A) systemic lupus erythematosus
(B) rheumatoid arthritis
(C) osteoarthritis
(D) gout
(E) Reiter's syndrome

768. The laboratory findings that would MOST LIKELY confirm your diagnosis is

(A) anemia
(B) elevated sedimentation rate
(C) rheumatoid factor
(D) anti-DNA antibodies
(E) antinuclear antibodies

769. Initial therapy for the woman described should consist of

(A) methotrexate 7.5 mg weekly
(B) prednisone, 7.5 mg daily
(C) allopurinol, 300 mg daily
(D) aspirin, 12 tablets daily
(E) gold compound injections

Questions 770 through 772

A 51-year-old man has been well since a myocardial infarction 2 years ago. His nonfasting cholesterol level is 245 mg/dL.

770. The first step in his management would be

(A) no further action; his cholesterol is not high enough for concern
(B) obtain a cholesterol after a 12-hour fast
(C) obtain a lipid profile (cholesterol, triglycerides, and HDL cholesterol) after a 12-hour fast
(D) initiate a cholesterol-lowering diet
(E) lipoprotein electrophoresis

771. Drug treatment should be considered for this patient if

(A) his serum cholesterol exceeds 200 mg/dL after 2 months of an appropriate diet
(B) his serum cholesterol exceeds 200 mg/dL after 6 months of an appropriate diet
(C) his LDL cholesterol exceeds 160 mg/dL after 2 months of an appropriate diet
(D) his LDL cholesterol exceeds 160 mg/dL after 6 months of an appropriate diet
(E) his LDL cholesterol exceeds 190 mg/dL after 6 months of an appropriate diet

772. The goal of therapy should be to

(A) lower the total cholesterol to less than 200 mg/dL
(B) lower the LDL cholesterol to less than 130 mg/dL
(C) lower the LDL cholesterol to less than 100 mg/dL
(D) increase the HDL cholesterol by 10 mg/dL
(E) increase the HDL cholesterol by 20 mg/dL

Questions 773 through 775

A 32-year-old woman has migratory arthritis of her wrists and ankles and a vesiculopustular skin eruption. She is afebrile. Physical examination reveals tenosynovitis of her wrists.

773. The most likely diagnosis for the woman described is

(A) gonococcal arthritis–dermatitis
(B) Reiter's syndrome
(C) rheumatoid arthritis
(D) systemic lupus erythematosus
(E) meningococcemia

774. Laboratory findings associated with this disease usually include

(A) positive culture of synovial fluid for gonococci
(B) HLA-B27 haplotype
(C) rheumatoid factor
(D) anti-DNA antibodies
(E) none of the above

775. The treatment of choice of the woman's disease would be

(A) ceftriaxone, 1 g daily
(B) prednisone, 40 mg daily
(C) aspirin, 12 tablets daily
(D) ibuprofen, 600 mg three times daily
(E) erythromycin, 250 mg four times daily

Questions 776 and 777

A 40-year-old woman has episodic headaches that last 30 minutes and are associated with sweating, palpitations, and feelings of apprehension. She has lost 6.8 kg (15 lb) over the past 3 months. Physical examination reveals a thin woman with a pulse of 112 beats/min and a blood pressure of 150/100 mm Hg lying and 130/80 mm Hg standing.

776. The most likely diagnosis in the case described is

(A) pheochromocytoma
(B) hyperaldosteronism
(C) posterior fossa tumor
(D) renal artery stenosis
(E) carcinoid syndrome

777. The most helpful diagnostic test would be

(A) CT scan of the brain
(B) hypertension intravenous pyelography
(C) 24-hour urinary 5-hydroxyindoleacetic acid (5-HIAA) levels
(D) 24-hour urinary aldosterone levels
(E) 24-hour urinary vanillylmandelic acid (VMA) and catecholamine levels

DIRECTIONS (Questions 778 through 808): Each of the numbered items or incomplete statements in this section is followed by answers or by completions of the statement. Select ONE (OR MORE) lettered answer(s) or completion(s) for each case.

Questions 778 through 781

A 70-year-old man, previously known to be normotensive with atrial fibrillation, is brought to the emergency room with a history of sudden onset of abdominal pain of 2 hours duration. On examination he is found to have a blood pressure of 120 mm Hg systolic and 80 mm Hg diastolic, heart rhythm irregular, and abdominal examination unremarkable.

778. The most likely diagnosis is

(A) superior mesenteric artery embolism
(B) superior mesenteric artery thrombosis

(C) superior mesenteric vein thrombosis
(D) low-flow syndrome
(E) dissecting aneurysm of the aorta

779. The most likely metabolic abnormality in this patient is

(A) metabolic acidosis
(B) metabolic alkalosis
(C) respiratory acidosis
(D) respiratory alkalosis
(E) none of the above

780. The diagnostic procedure of choice is

(A) plain roentgenography of abdomen
(B) blood gas determination
(C) mesenteric angiography
(D) CT scan of abdomen
(E) diagnostic peritoneal tap

781. Which of the following are indicated in the management of this patient? (SELECT 4)

(A) analgesics
(B) heparin
(C) papavarin
(D) antibiotics
(E) observation until more definite signs develop
(F) resume diet as tolerated
(G) tap water or fleets enemas

Questions 782 and 783

782. A 41-year-old woman has an asymptomatic breast mass. Which of the following features of the history would increase the risk of carcinoma? (SELECT 4)

(A) history of carcinoma in the other breast
(B) history of breast cancer in first-degree relatives
(C) history of infertility
(D) pregnancy before the age of 18 years
(E) total hysterectomy and bilateral salpingo-oophorectomy at the age of 38 years
(F) oral contraceptive use
(G) cigarette smoking
(H) alchohol consumption

783. The woman described undergoes mammographic examination. Which of the following features on mammogram are suggestive of malignancy? (SELECT 4)

(A) presence of microcalcifications
(B) smooth, sharp, circumscribed border
(C) spiculated edges
(D) thickening and retraction of the skin over the mass
(E) ductal dilatation
(F) unchanged appearance from previous mammogram
(G) symmetrical densities

Questions 784 through 787

784. A 42-year-old man with cirrhosis has esophageal varices. The preferred initial measure for controlling esophageal variceal hemorrhage is

(A) esophageal balloon tamponade
(B) systemic intravenous vasopressin infusion
(C) mesenteric arterial vasopressin infusion
(D) gastric hypothermia
(E) esophogogastroduodenoscopy

785. The procedure that would afford the greatest protection against a recurrence of esophageal variceal bleeding is

(A) portacaval shunt
(B) conventional splenorenal shunt
(C) ligation of esophageal varices
(D) transection of the esophagus and staple anastomosis
(E) none of the above

786. Distal splenorenal shunt (Warren shunt) has been used to control hemorrhage from esophageal varices. Which of the following statements concerning this procedure are true? (SELECT 4)

(A) Portal pressure is decreased.
(B) Encephalopathy occurs less frequently than with portacaval shunt.
(C) Rebleeding occurs with the same frequency as with portacaval shunt.
(D) Five-year survival rate is similar to that following portacaval shunt.
(E) Coronary vein ligation is an integral part of the operation.
(F) Portal blood flow is decreased.
(G) Left gastroepiploic veins are transected during the operation.

787. Which of the following statements are correct concerning sclerotherapy? (SELECT 4)

(A) Indicated for the treatment of gastric varices.
(B) Indicated for the treatment of esophageal varices.
(C) May result in an esophageal stricture.
(D) Multiple sessions may be required.
(E) May result in ulceration or perforation.
(F) Cannot be used in acute hemorrhage.
(G) Failure is indicated when a single attempt does not halt bleeding.

Questions 788 and 789

A 20-year-old construction worker accidentally sustained blunt injury to his right temple. Soon after the injury he was dazed but was able to resume his work. Four hours later, when he returned home, his relatives noticed him to be slightly confused. Subsequently he became progressively lethargic and was brought to the emergency room. He was found to be very drowsy, responding to painful stimuli. His right pupil was dilated.

788. The most useful diagnostic procedure in this patient is

(A) skull roentgenogram
(B) spinal tap
(C) ultrasonography
(D) electroencephalography
(E) CT scan

789. In the management of this patient, which of the following maneuvers are beneficial? (SELECT 5)

(A) deliberate hypocapnia (P_{CO_2} 25 to 30 torr)
(B) osmotic diuresis
(C) spinal tap
(D) intravenous barbiturates
(E) temporal craniotomy
(F) deliberate hypercapnia (P_{CO_2}, 45 to 50 torr)
(G) elevation of head and bed
(H) avoid sedation and paralytics
(I) steriods

Questions 790 through 793

A man is hospitalized for evaluation of abdominal pain. A flat-plate abdominal roentgenogram is obtained and shown on the facing page.

790. The abnormality visualized on this roentgenogram is the result of

(A) excess bile salt
(B) excess cholesterol
(C) excess lecithin
(D) excess calcium
(E) a suppurative infection

791. The man whose roentgenogram is shown develops sudden, severe epigastric pain with nausea, vomiting, and diaphoresis. Laboratory testing shows leukocytosis and amylasemia. Poor prognostic features include (SELECT 6)

(A) serum amylase concentration greater than 500 Somogyi units/dL
(B) elevation of serum lipase

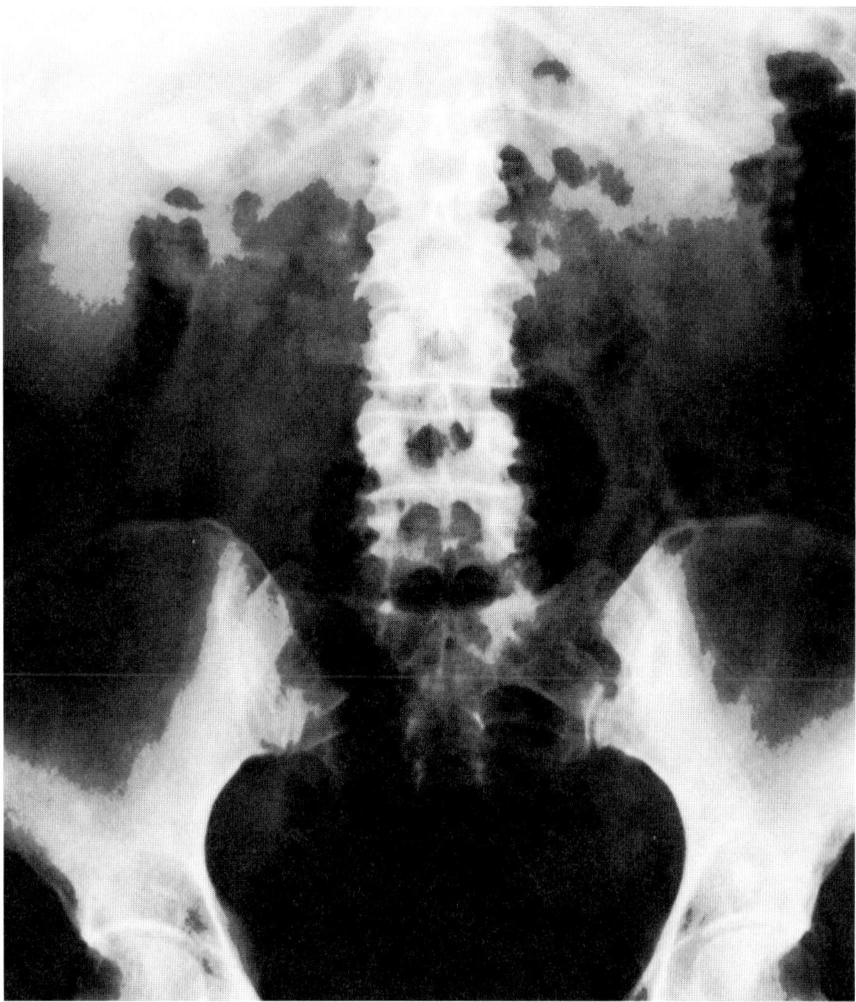

Figure for use with questions 790 through 793.

(C) serum calcium concentration less than 8 mg/dL
(D) serum glutamic oxaloacetic transaminase (SGOT) greater than 250 units/dL
(E) serum LDH less than 350
(F) age more than 55 years
(G) white blood cell count less than 16,000
(H) blood glucose less than 100
(I) fall in hematocrit of less than 10%
(J) elevation of BUN by more than 5 mg/dL
(K) arterial P_{O_2} normal/unchanged
(L) base deficit less than 4 mg/L
(M) fluid sequestration more than 2000 cc
(N) direct bilirubin elevation to more than 3 g/dL

792. Other complications of the lesion seen on the roentgenogram presented include (SELECT 6)

(A) acute cholangitis
(B) intestinal obstruction
(C) obstructive jaundice
(D) carcinoma of the liver
(E) carcinoma of the gallbladder
(F) hydrops of the gallbladder
(G) accute cholecystitis
(H) peptic ulcer disease

793. The man described above is operated on. During the operation, the common bile duct is accidentally transected, involving the entire circumference at the level of cystic duct insertion. The most appropriate step for managing this complication would be

(A) ligation of the proximal end so that the duct can dilate, which would facilitate a subsequent anastomosis
(B) anastomosis of the proximal end to a Roux-en-Y limb of the jejunum
(C) end-to-end anastomosis of the transected ends and drainage of the area with a rubber drain
(D) end-to-end anastomosis of the transected ends over a T-tube
(E) end-to-side choledochoduodenostomy

Questions 794 through 795

A 40-year-old man who has had chronic duodenal ulcer disease comes to the emergency room because he has been vomiting for 5 days and cannot retain any food.

794. Metabolic derangements in the man described above would likely include (SELECT 5)

(A) dehydration
(B) azotemia
(C) alkalosis
(D) acidosis
(E) hypernatremia
(F) hyponatremia
(G) aciduria
(H) hyperkalemia

795. The operation LEAST acceptable for the treatment of the condition described above is

(A) truncal vagotomy
(B) truncal vagotomy and pyloroplasty
(C) truncal vagotomy and gastrojejunostomy
(D) truncal vagotomy and antrectomy
(E) subtotal gastrectomy

Questions 796 through 798

A 22-year-old graduate student is brought by his family to the local emergency room. They say that ever since he returned home for a 3-week Christmas vacation he has been restless, irritable, and sleeping poorly. They have never seen him like this before, although it has been 8 months since he last was home. He refuses a physical examination and tells you in pressured speech, "I've never been better. Nobody understands the important work I'm engaged in right now. I have to leave—they'll find me here." He is fully conscious and alert.

796. On the basis of the information available, differential diagnosis for the man described would include (SELECT 4)

(A) bipolar I disorder
(B) schizophrenia, paranoid type
(C) brief psychotic disorder
(D) cyclothymic disorder
(E) substance abuse
(F) panic disorder
(G) vascular dementia

797. Which of the following organic disorders would be most likely to produce a clinical picture like the one described?

(A) Addison's disease
(B) Cushing's disease
(C) hypokalemia
(D) hypothyroidism
(E) multiple sclerosis

798. Appropriate laboratory tests performed for the man described show normal values. The medication most likely to be of immediate benefit would be

(A) lithium carbonate
(B) fluoxetine
(C) clomipramine
(D) valproate
(E) risperidone

799. Sleep disruption is a common symptom of major depression. All the following findings would likely be found in a person with major depression. (SELECT 5)

(A) altered REM architecture
(B) increased REM latency
(C) decreased stage 3 sleep
(D) decreased stage 4 sleep
(E) early-morning awakening
(F) sleep terror
(G) decreased REM latency
(H) increased stage 3 sleep

800. A 31-year-old woman reports that for the past 3 weeks she has had occasional episodes of sudden and overwhelming anxiety. Between attacks she is nervous and worried about when the next attack will occur. She cannot recall a precipitating stress before the episodes, which do not seem to be associated with particular events or time of day. Which of the following could be recommended treatment for this woman's disorder? (SELECT 6)

(A) alprazolam, 1 mg tid
(B) imipramine, 100 mg daily
(C) haloperidol, 2 mg daily
(D) relaxation therapy
(E) psychotherapy
(F) paroxetine, 20 mg daily
(G) trazodone, 100 mg at bedtime
(H) phenelzine, 30 mg twice daily

801. Treatment with electroconvulsive therapy (ECT) would be most appropriate for which of the following individuals? (SELECT 3)

(A) A 68-year-old woman with medication-resistant psychotic depression.
(B) A 47-year-old woman with medication-resistant delusional disorder.
(C) A 38-year-old man with acute lithium-resistant mania.
(D) A 28-year-old woman with severe catatonic schizophrenia.
(E) A 21-year-old man in a hallucinogen-induced delirium.

Questions 802 and 803

A 36-year-old computer salesman is brought into the local emergency room by ambulance. He is sweating, very anxious, and has a tremor of the hands and eyelids; his blood pressure and body temperature are mildly elevated, and his pulse is rapid. He has been vomiting, the last time producing blood-tinged vomitus. When questioned, he says he is a heavy drinker but has not had a drink in 36 hours. He says he has never had delirium tremens, though he has had "blackouts."

802. Which of the following admission orders would be appropriate in the case described? (SELECT 4)

(A) fluoxetine, 20 mg daily
(B) intravenous fluids
(C) intramuscular thiamine, 100 mg
(D) oral chlordiazepoxide, 50 mg every 4 hours
(E) oral chlorpromazine, 100 mg as needed for severe agitation
(F) phenytoin, 100 mg three times daily
(G) vital signs every hour

803. In 2 days the man's vital signs have returned to normal, and all signs of alcohol withdrawal have disappeared. The man's physician should now

(A) discontinue all current medications and discharge the man from the hospital
(B) discontinue all current medications and observe
(C) discontinue all current medications and begin disulfiram
(D) taper medications over the next 5 days
(E) maintain the current regimen for 2 weeks

804. A 41-year-old depressed man has been treated for 6 weeks with therapeutic dosages of a tricyclic antidepressant drug. His psychiatrist has noted some clinical improvement but less than hoped. To potentiate the effect of the antidepressant, the psychiatrist could add which of the following preparations to the man's treatment regimen? (SELECT 3)

(A) lithium carbonate
(B) haloperidol
(C) tri-iodothyronine
(D) niacin
(E) amphetamine
(F) bromocriptine

805. Brief psychotherapy can be described by which of the following statements? (SELECT 4)

(A) It is effective only for adjustment disorders.
(B) Initially unmotivated persons often respond well to the short-term model.
(C) Focus on a specific crisis facilitates short-term treatment.
(D) Brief therapeutic interventions often lead to permanently better functioning.
(E) Intrapsychic conflict often can be resolved in short-term treatment.
(F) It is not effective for depression.
(G) The setting of a strict time limit for treatment can itself be therapeutic.

806. Tetanus toxoid has proved to be one of the most effective immunizing agents. Current indications for its use include (SELECT 4)

(A) routine immunization every 10 years
(B) a deep, dirty wound in a person who has had repeated immunizations
(C) last immunization at age 65
(D) a wound in a person with an uncertain history of immunization
(E) immunization every 5 years in immunocompromised persons
(F) in combination with diphtheria toxin in pediatric practice
(G) a clean wound in a person whose last dose was less than 5 years ago

Questions 807 and 808

A 74-year-old woman, widowed last year, says she has "depression." For the past 3 months she has been increasingly weepy and has been sleeping more fitfully. Her appetite is reduced, and she has lost several pounds. A recent complete physical examination showed mild hypertension, for which she takes a diuretic, and osteoarthritis, for which she takes aspirin.

807. Which of the following mental status changes would be compatible with a diagnosis of major depression? (SELECT 4)

(A) agitation
(B) fluctuating state of consciousness
(C) poor short-term memory
(D) nihilistic delusions
(E) refusal to cooperate
(F) perseveration
(G) inappropriate affect

808. The woman described above is started on imipramine, at an initial daily dosage of 50 mg, raised to 100 mg, and then to 150 mg after 4 days. After initially reporting better sleep and perhaps a slightly less depressed mood, she reports 10 days later that she cannot sleep more than 2 hours per night and is now so "confused" she nearly missed the appointment "because I thought today was tomorrow!"

The best course of action now would be to

(A) stop the imipramine
(B) order an imipramine blood level and increase the dosage
(C) order an imipramine blood level and decrease the dosage
(D) prescribe a low dosage of haloperidol at bedtime
(E) schedule an emergency CT scan of the head

DIRECTIONS (Questions 809 through 829): Each group of items in this section consists of lettered headings followed by a set of numbered words or phrases. For each numbered word or phrase, select the ONE lettered heading that is most closely associated with it. Each lettered heading may be selected once, more than once, or not at all.

Questions 809 through 815

For each clinical situation described below, select the most likely therapeutic drug of choice.

(A) imipramine
(B) methylphenidate
(C) haloperidol
(D) clomipramine alprazolam citalopram fluvoxamine lithium

809. Childhood obsessive–compulsive disorder

810. Tourette's syndrome

811. Bulimia nervosa

812. Extremely aggressive behavior associated with conduct disorder or mental retardation

813. Enuresis

814. Attention-deficit hyperactivity disorder (first-line treatment in a 7 year old)

815. Severe anticipatory anxiety in a teenager

Questions 816 and 817

Several groups of organic compounds have recently been associated with serious toxic effects. For each of the following descriptions of occurrence and use of a substance, choose the group of compounds with which it is most closely associated.

(A) nitrosamines
(B) epoxy compounds
(C) polychlorinated biphenyls
(D) polybrominated biphenyls
(E) organophosphorus compounds

816. Because they do not conduct electricity and can withstand high temperatures, they were used extensively in electrical transformers

817. Widely used as insecticides, they are responsible for more deaths on a worldwide basis than any other group of substances

Questions 818 through 829

One of the main aims of current preventive medicine is to identify those persons who are in high-risk categories for disease and to screen them regularly and appropriately. This is frequently more cost-effective than indiscriminate screening of large populations. For each of the high-risk categories of adults aged 40 to 64 listed below, identify the specific screening procedure, listed A through L, which should be performed for a related condition.

(A) fasting blood glucose
(B) VDRL and gonorrhea testing
(C) urinalysis for bacteriuria
(D) chlamydial testing
(E) gonorrhea testing
(F) tuberculin skin test
(G) electrocardiogram (ECG)
(H) sigmoidoscopy
(I) colonoscopy
(J) hepatitis B vaccine
(K) pneumococcal and influenza vaccine
(L) influenza vaccine annually

818. Homosexually active men

819. The markedly obese

820. Prostitutes

821. Those with multiple sexual partners

822. Stable diabetic individuals

823. Recent immigrants or refugees

824. Men with two or more cardiac risk factors

825. Residents of chronic care facilities

826. Persons with chronic pulmonary disease

827. Persons aged 50 and over who have a personal history of endometrial, ovarian, or breast cancer

828. Persons with a family history of polyposis coli

829. Persons who attend clinics for the treatment of sexually transmitted disease

DIRECTIONS (Questions 830 through 852): Each of the numbered items or incomplete statements in this section is followed by answers or by completions of the statement. Select the ONE lettered answer or completion that is BEST in each case.

830. A 19-year-old man is transported to an emergency room after being involved in an automobile accident. Apparently he was driving the car and hit a telephone pole, sustaining a blunt injury to the anterior chest wall. A CT scan is obtained and is shown on page 223. Which of the following abnormalities is a sequela of the lesion depicted on the CT scan?

(A) pancreatic pseudocyst
(B) hemobilia
(C) splenic pseudocyst
(D) perinephric hematoma
(E) none of the above

Questions 831 and 832

A 10-month-old baby is brought to the emergency room with 6-hour history of bilious vomiting, passage of pink jellylike material from the rectum, and intermittent episodes of severe crying. On physical examination a sausage-shaped mass is felt on the right side of the abdomen.

831. The most likely diagnosis is

(A) congenital hypertrophic pyloric stenosis
(B) intestinal volvulus
(C) intussusception
(D) necrotizing enterocolitis
(E) acute pyelonephritis

832. The next step in the management of the patient is

(A) administration of atropine
(B) exploratory laparotomy
(C) barium enema
(D) administration of antibiotics
(E) intravenous pyelography

Questions 833 and 834

A first-born male child develops projectile vomiting at the age of 5 weeks. Vomitus is free of bile. The child remains hungry and vomits after taking feedings. Examination reveals visible peristalsis in the upper abdomen along with a palpable nodule in the right upper quadrant.

833. The most likely diagnosis for the boy described above is

(A) esophageal atresia
(B) hypertrophic pyloric stenosis
(C) duodenal web
(D) midgut volvulus
(E) incarcerated inguinal hernia

834. Treatment of choice for the condition described above is

(A) Heller's myotomy
(B) pyloromyotomy
(C) gastrojejunostomy
(D) duodenojejunostomy
(E) esophageal dilation

835. A man known to have cirrhosis comes to the hospital because he has been vomiting blood. The diagnostic study most useful in identifying the source of bleeding is

(A) esophagogastroduodenoscopy
(B) upper gastrointestinal series
(C) splenoportography
(D) hepatic wedge-pressure measurement
(E) celiac angiography

836. A psychiatric consultation is requested because a 23-year-old primiparous woman admitted last night for hyperemesis has in the

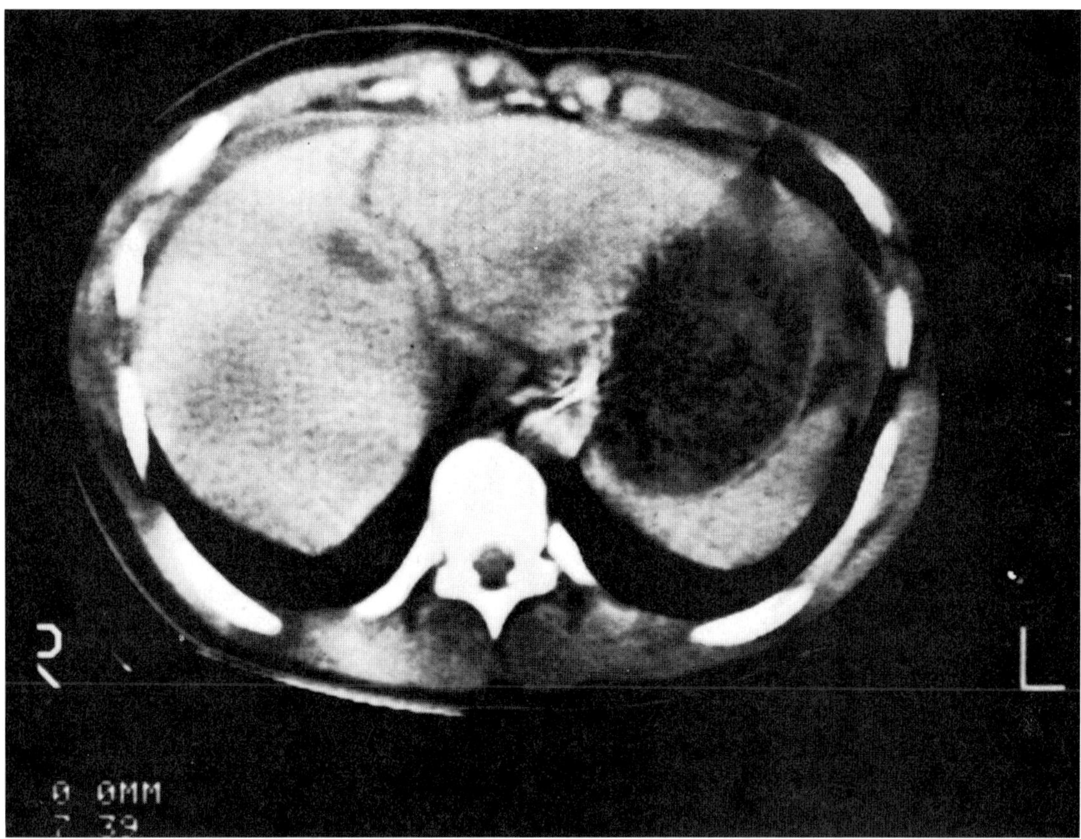

Figure for use with question 833.

past hour begun to display unusual movements, stiffness, neck twitches, and difficulty swallowing. Friends and family members say she has never acted like this before, although she has always been "high-strung" and has been in counseling for the past 6 months. Findings from all admission laboratory tests are normal. The only medications she has received since admission have been acetaminophen for a headache last night and prochlorperazine 4 hours ago for nausea. On the basis of this information, the consultant should recommend a trial of which of the following medications?

(A) phenobarbital
(B) benztropine
(C) oxazepam
(D) haloperidol
(E) methylphenidate

Questions 837 and 838

A 62-year-old man has been treated for anxiety by his family physician for the past 10 years. At first he received diazepam, but for the past 3 years he has been taking haloperidol, 5 mg daily. In the past 6 months the man has begun to develop facial tics and darting tongue movements. His physician seeks a consultation.

837. The most likely explanation for the development of the man's symptoms is

(A) chronic haloperidol overdosage
(B) tolerance to haloperidol
(C) noncompliance with haloperidol therapy
(D) tardive dyskinesia
(E) early dementia

838. The man's physician should be advised to

(A) discontinue haloperidol
(B) increase the dosage of haloperidol
(C) add an anticonvulsant drug
(D) prescribe an anticholinergic drug
(E) change to quetiapine

839. A 41-year-old man seeks psychiatric consultation because he has been unable to sleep well in the 4 weeks since his wife died in an automobile accident. His appetite is poor, and he has lost 2.3 kg (5 lb); in addition, he feels guilty about not having gone with his wife on the day of her death. He is not suicidal, though he questions his deeply held religious beliefs. He has returned to work, but only part-time. He reports that he cried quite a lot the first week after his wife's death and still cries now, though less often.

After his visit to the psychiatrist the man feels better. Two days later, however, he returns asking for medication to help him sleep. The best treatment at this point would consist of

(A) amitriptyline, 150 mg at bedtime
(B) thorazine, 25 mg at bedtime
(C) diazepam, 10 mg every 6 hours
(D) zolpidem 5 mg at bedtime
(E) hospitalization

840. A 56-year-old man develops acute renal failure after surgery for ruptured aortic aneurysm. However, he refuses dialysis. His internist, who tries unsuccessfully to persuade him to accept treatment, seeks an immediate psychiatric consultation. Mental-status testing reveals the man to be fully alert and oriented, cognitively intact, and not psychotic. He says he is refusing dialysis because he has "lived a full life" and does not want to be "tied to a machine, even if this means I'll die." The man's family urgently wants him treated. The psychiatrist should tell the man's internist that the man

(A) is temporarily incompetent to decide on treatment, so treatment should be started
(B) is competent to decide on treatment, but his refusal should be overruled because of the existence of a medical emergency
(C) is competent to decide on treatment, so his refusal of dialysis must be respected
(D) is behaving in a self-destructive manner, so he should be committed for treatment against his will
(E) shows no evidence of a major psychiatric illness and is aware of the consequences of his decision

841. A 45-year-old woman is hospitalized for psychiatric treatment after 6 weeks of worsening insomnia, anorexia, and obsessive thoughts of worthlessness. She has had three hospitalizations in the past 12 years for similar illnesses and has been treated successfully with the serotonin reuptake inhibitor sertraline on all three occasions. A work-up for organic disease is unrevealing, and sertraline therapy is begun, with the dosage reaching 150 mg daily after 3 days. Two weeks later she appears only minimally improved. Which of the following is the most likely to account for her lack of therapeutic response at this time?

(A) the dosage is too low
(B) the dosage is too high
(C) she has not been swallowing her medication
(D) treatment is still in the "lag period" of therapeutic response
(E) she has become a nonresponder to imipramine

842. A definite association has been established between the development of cardiovascular abnormalities and exposure to

(A) aromatic hydrocarbons
(B) methanol
(C) fluorocarbons
(D) xylene
(E) carbon tetrachloride

843. Which of the following statements about the epidemiology of poliomyelitis is true?

(A) Females are more frequently affected than males.
(B) Most infected individuals produce recognizable symptoms.
(C) Water supplies have conclusively been established as a source of infection.
(D) The most common mode of spread is by airborne infection.
(E) Paralytic disease appears to be on the increase in certain parts of the world.

844. A married man, aged 35, the father of three children, visits his physician stating that for the last 3 weeks he has felt increasingly tired, that he has a painless cough that is "like an ordinary cold," but it keeps him awake. On examination, he has a temperature of 37.2°C (99°F), the throat appears normal apart from a clear mucus droplet on the posterior wall of the oropharynx, and examination of the chest reveals no abnormality. Which of the following organisms may be responsible for the condition?

(A) rhinovirus
(B) coronavirus
(C) parainfluenza
(D) respiratory syncytial virus
(E) *Mycoplasma pneumoniae*

845. In the above case, which of the following medications is likely to be most effective, assuming the patient does not have sensitivity to any?

(A) ascorbic acid
(B) phenylephrine nose drops
(C) amantadine
(D) vidarabine
(E) erythromycin

846. In the routine health care of children, a blood lead level should ideally be checked at

(A) 6 months to 1 year of age
(B) 1 to 2 years of age
(C) 2 to 5 years of age
(D) 5 to 11 years of age
(E) yearly intervals

847. Informed consent is now recognized as a very important component in the practice of medicine. Written consent is not required in the following situation.

(A) The physician records oral consent in the notes for a minor ambulatory surgical procedure.
(B) The procedure is quite common (e.g., sigmoidoscopy).
(C) The patient is a minor, there is an element of urgency, and the parents give permission by telephone.
(D) The physician has a good relationship with the patient and the procedure is minor, carrying minimal risk.
(E) Venipuncture in the doctor's office.

848. Under certain circumstances, it may be legitimate to detain individuals in an institution against their wishes. This situation would arise for

(A) a person who has bizarre fantasies and actions
(B) a person who is mentally incompetent and unable to manage personal affairs
(C) a person about whom a close relative has submitted a petition that the person is actually and presently insane
(D) a person whose continued liberty poses a danger
(E) a person who has visual and auditory hallucinations

849. The causative organism of cholera, *Vibrio cholerae,* has been recognized for 100 years. Outbreaks of cholera often reach epidemic proportions; the history of seven pandemics can now be traced. The most recent only now appears to be subsiding. The spread of infection, enhanced by modern transportation, is most likely by

(A) fomites
(B) mosquitoes
(C) infected food sources
(D) person-to-person transmission
(E) flies

850. Cytomegalovirus (CMV) infections have attracted increasing attention since their discovery in 1956. Prevalence rates are high throughout the world. Regarding infection with these viruses, which of the following statements is true?

(A) A woman who sheds this virus from her cervix during pregnancy is likely to produce an infected baby.
(B) Once a mother is affected, she is likely to infect future pregnancies.
(C) If virus affects the placenta, the fetus will also be affected.
(D) An infected infant who does not shed virus at the age of 6 months may be considered free of CMV.
(E) Institutionalized children are more likely to excrete the virus and have antibodies in their serum.

851. Which of the following statements correctly describes the administration of chelating agents, such as ethylenediaminetetraacetic acid (EDTA) and penicillamine, for the treatment of heavy metal poisoning?

(A) It is advised for asymptomatic persons suspected of having ingested the toxin.
(B) It quickly counteracts the toxic effects of the metal poisoning.
(C) It should be reserved only for persons with symptomatic exposure.
(D) It reduces absorption of the metal from the gastrointestinal tract.
(E) It counteracts the effects of future exposure to the toxin.

852 Which of the following operative procedures for the management of chronic duodenal ulcer is associated with the *lowest* incidence of recurrent ulceration?

(A) bilateral truncal vagotomy and antrectomy
(B) bilateral truncal vagotomy and pyloroplasty
(C) bilateral truncal vagotomy and gastrojejunostomy
(D) bilateral truncal vagotomy and gastroduodenostomy
(E) proximal gastric vagotomy

ANSWERS AND EXPLANATIONS

703–705. (703-A, 704-A, 705-C) Evidence of ovulation is provided indirectly from the 0.4 to 0.6°F rise in temperature secondary to progesterone secretion and its thermogenic effect. The maximum secretion of progesterone will occur in the second half of the cycle, and LH surges at midcycle just before ovulation. From the time of ovulation until the next menses is usually fairly constant at 14 days in fertile women. FSH peaks just before ovulation.

Luteal phase defect demonstrates itself as a decreased length of the luteal phase or decreased levels of progesterone in the serum during the luteal phase. Accepted as a cause of infertility and habitual abortion, this diagnosis is confirmed by luteal phase endometrial biopsy showing a developmental lag of more than 2 days when compared with the menstrual calendar.

This condition has been treated with clomiphene citrate, human menopausal gonadotropins, and exogenous progesterone with varying rates of success. *(Beckmann, 463, 434)*

706–710. (706-E, 707-B, 708-A, 709-B, 710-C) The most commonly seen anemia in pregnancy is a physiologic anemia secondary to an increase in plasma volume proportionately greater than the concomitant increase in red blood cell mass. This can usually be averted by providing adequate intake of oral iron (dietary or supplemental) from early on in pregnancy. Iron-deficiency anemia seldom affects the fetus, even in severe cases, and is neither genetic nor difficult to treat.

The diagnosis is confirmed by a low hematocrit, a hypochromic and microcytic peripheral blood smear, decreased serum iron concentrations, abnormal red cell indices, and normal iron-binding capacity. The earliest sign of therapeutic success is the appearance of reticulocytosis on the peripheral smear. *(Beckmann, p 198)*

711–715. (711-C, 712-C, 713-E, 714-C, 715-E) Although many women who have urinary symptoms may not be infected, there are probably a greater number of asymptomatic yet infected patients. The 100,000 colonies of bacteria per milliliter was a standard developed nearly 30 years ago and is clearly not the best diagnostic standard for the pregnant patient. More sophisticated diagnostic techniques are either too invasive or cumbersome or expensive for routine use.

Regarding the prevention and therapy of urinary tract infection in pregnancy, the primary goal is to prevent pyelonephritis and preterm birth associated with perinatal maternal infections. Patients with urinary tract abnormalities or a history of previous infections when not pregnant are even more at risk than other gravidas. Patients with pyelonephritis should be hospitalized for intravenous therapy. Recurrent infection is probably best treated with antibiotic prophylaxis during pregnancy and further evaluation can be performed postpartum. The simple lower urinary tract infection can be treated with any of a number of antibiotics depending on sensitivity studies. The most common causative organism is *E. coli*. *(Beckmann, 201–202, 277)*

716–722. (716-A, 717-C, 718-A, 719-C, 720-B, 721-A, 722-C) Toxic shock syndrome is associated with all the clinical features of circulatory shock plus muscle damage and neurologic symptoms. *Staphylococcus aureus* is the most commonly associated organism, but the disease itself is caused by the endotoxin and, therefore, not amenable to therapy with antibiotics. The mainstay of therapy is massive fluid replacement. The diagnosis is made from the multisystem involvement in combination with the diffuse red maculopapular rash associated with desquamation of the palms and soles in the convalescent period. The use of tampons predisposes to both the initial episode and to reinfections. *(DeCherney, pp 780–782)*

723–726. (723-B, 724-E, 725-D, 726-E) Preeclampsia is associated with maternal hypertension, decreased plasma volume, and therefore, a falsely elevated hematocrit. It is also strongly associated with abruption of the placenta. Painful third trimester bleeding is the key to diagnosis here. Red cell destruction (microangiopathic hemolytic anemia) is also taking place, elevating uric acid and consuming platelets. In its most severe forms, this disease may be accompanied by disseminated intravascular coagulation with consumption of coagulation factors, elevation of clotting times, increased levels of fibrin split products, and decreased levels of coagulation-associated proteins.

Blood may accumulate behind the placenta (concealed hemorrhage) and cause violent labor or persistent hypertonus. Despite this fact, atony is also possible. When the "cure" becomes delivery, in the absence of fetal distress, there is no contraindication to stimulation of labor. *(Beckmann, pp 264–266)*

727–729. (727-D, 728-C, 729-A) The most common causes of bacterial meningitis during the neonatal period are organisms that are found in the mother's vaginal flora, most specifically group B *Streptococcus, Escherichia coli* and other gram-negative enteric bacilli, and *Listeria monocytogenes*. In the child beyond the first 1 or 2 months of life, the most common organisms are *Haemophilus influenzae, Streptococcus pneumoniae,* and *Neisseria meningitidis*.

There are several combinations of antibiotics that will effectively and safely provide coverage for the neonatal group of organisms. This includes ampicillin and an aminoglycoside or ampicillin and cefotaxime. The ampicillin not only broadens the gram-negative coverage, but also provides coverage for *L. monocytogenes,* which generally is not sensitive to either aminoglycosides or cephalosporins. Complications of meningitis are numerous and common. In most series, hearing loss has been the most common permanent sequela. Other complications include visual impairment, seizures, and mental retardation. Brain abscess is rare. Hemiparesis is occasionally seen as a complication of bacterial meningitis, but quadriplegia usually results from a spinal cord lesion and would be extremely unlikely as a sequela of meningitis. Kernicterus is a complication of neonatal hyperbilirubinemia and is not related to meningitis. *(Hay et al, pp 61–63, 675–676)*

730–731. (730-B, 731-B) A 3-day history of worsening cough and the development of fever and mild inspiratory stridor are consistent with a diagnosis of infectious laryngotracheitis, which usually is caused by parainfluenza virus. Chest x-ray typically reveals subglottic swelling. In the differential diagnosis, epiglottitis typically develops more acutely, with affected children having severe stridor on the first day of the illness. Although spasmodic croup is quite similar to infectious laryngotracheitis, it is not associated with fever. The roentgenographic findings and history presented in the case are not consistent with a diagnosis of either angioneurotic edema or aspiration of a foreign body.

A variety of measures have been used in the treatment of viral laryngotracheitis. Cool mist has been used for decades and is assumed to be helpful. Racemic epinephrine by either aerosol or intermittent positive-pressure breathing has been shown to provide symptomatic relief, presumably by vasoconstriction and reduction of local edema. Corticosteroids are used frequently and there is some data to support this, although the use of these agents remains controversial. Theophylline is useful in treating bronchospasm but is of no value in the treatment of croup. *(Hay et al, pp 425–427)*

732–734. (732-E, 733-B, 734-C) Toxic shock syndrome, recognized only in the last two decades, requires prompt diagnosis and treatment. The syndrome usually occurs in women using highly absorbent tampons. Typical historical and physical findings include sudden onset of fever and gastrointestinal symptoms, abdominal pain and myalgias, tachycardia, hypotension, hyperemia, and generalized erythematous maculopapular rash that spares the wrists. *Staphylococcus aureus* usually can be grown from blood or vaginal cultures. Treatment of choice is with the antibiotics oxacillin or nafcillin.

Scarlet fever and Kawasaki's disease resemble toxic shock syndrome, but they are not typically associated with watery diarrhea, myalgias, or abdominal pain. Acute onset of symptoms and the presence of a rash and conjunctival erythema make ruptured appendix an unlikely diagnosis. The rash of Rocky Mountain spotted fever typically begins on the extremities (especially the wrists) and spreads to the trunk. *(Hay et al, pp 963–964, 993, 1016)*

735–736. (735-A, 736-B) The child in question presents signs of isosexual precocious development. The fact that the testes are large rather than small indicates that the problem is of central origin with the precocious release of gonadotropins. If the problem were due to androgen-secreting tumor or some other ectopic source of androgenic hormones, such as untreated congenital adrenal hyperplasia, one would expect the central release of gonadotropins to be shut off and the testes, therefore, small. Although most cases of isosexual precocious puberty in girls are idiopathic, this is not the case in boys, in whom a hypothalamic tumor can be found in an appreciable percentage of cases.

Klinefelter's syndrome (XXY) is a common cause of primary hypogonadism rather than precocious puberty. The XYY syndrome occurs in about 1 in 1000 male births and is associated with tall stature and acne. Precocious puberty, however, is not a feature of this syndrome and, indeed, a few of the patients have presented with undescended testes, or hypogonadism, or both. *(Hay et al, pp 833–838, 838–839, 889)*

737–740. (737-C, 738-D, 739-D, 740-C) Evaluation of a child having a generalized convulsion requires great care. The most frequent cause of a short generalized tonic–clonic seizure is simple febrile seizure. It is important to rule out the possibility of meningitis, which can present with seizures along with the more common signs of acute illness and irritability. Idiopathic epilepsy usually occurs in children older than 5 years of age. Short, generalized convulsions are not typical of complex febrile seizures. The presence of bruises below the knees is common in children and, especially in a child with signs and symptoms of a febrile illness, need not suggest the possibility of child abuse.

Although the use of lumbar puncture in diagnosing a simple febrile seizure is controversial, it is essential so that a diagnosis of meningitis can be ruled out. (Fontanel size is difficult to assess, and neck examination may not be a reliable guide in diagnosing meningitis.) Blood count and serum electrolytes and blood glucose levels may be helpful, but they are not essential. Electroencephalography would only confirm the occurrence of a seizure and would not clarify the patient's status or diagnosis. A CT scan of the head would not be indicated in the case presented.

Present recommendations for the treatment of febrile seizures include the use of antipyretics during febrile illnesses. Phenobarbital should not be used to treat children having a first simple febrile seizure. Prognosis is usually excellent; rarely does a seizure disorder later develop. *(Hay et al, pp 638–639)*

741–743. (741-E, 742-E, 743-A) Strawberry hemangiomas arise when vascular tissue fails to communicate with adjoining vascular elements. This tissue enlarges and creates the typical appearance of a raised erythematous tumor. Strawberry hemangiomas develop after birth and have a relatively benign course if left alone. They enlarge through the first year of life, then slowly regress in size. By the time affected children are 9 years old, 90% of strawberry hemangiomas have undergone complete resolution. If a hemangioma is impinging on a vital structure, argon laser therapy may be needed. However, any intervention should be avoided if at all possible.

Nevus flammeus is a flat, vascular rash that is also called a "stork bite." Melanomas are usually pigmented, variegated, irregular, and often have bleeding points or ulcerations. Lymphangiomas tend to be skin-colored. Osteochondromas may be raised tumors, but they tend to have the color of the surrounding skin. *(Hay et al, pp 344–346)*

744–746. (744-E, 745-B, 746-C) Tinea capitis is a common fungal infection in prepubertal children. It typically is a well-circumscribed rash with scaly raised borders. The hair shafts may be irregularly broken. This lesion may develop an inflammatory appearance and become a kerion, which is a raised tumor that is boggy and indurated. The treatment of choice is griseofulvin. Systemic or intralesional steroids are sometimes needed if the lesion does not resolve.

Seborrheic dermatitis and impetigo should be considered in the differential diagnosis of kerion, although they do not attain such a large size. Herpetic lesions are vesicular but also do not reach the size or have the appearance of a kerion. Alopecia areata, the loss of hair in sharply demarcated circular or oval patches, should not be confused with tinea capitus and kerion. *(Hay et al, pp 349–351, 355, 357–358, 974–977; Rudolph, pp 933–934)*

747–749. (747-B, 748-B, 749-C) The boy presented in the question has the typical electrocardiographic findings of Wolff–Parkinson–White syndrome. Wolff–Parkinson–White syndrome is due to muscular connections between the atrium and ventricle. Electrical impulses can travel through these connections instead of through the atrioventricular node. Lead III reveals a short interval and a slow upstroke of the QRS wave (a delta wave). Abrupt episodes of palpitations with no symptoms between episodes are typical of this syndrome. Affected persons develop supraventricular tachycardia because of a reentry mechanism. This tachycardia, which is intermittent, usually can be prevented by administration of digoxin. Unresponsive cases may require radiofrequency ablation of aberrant pathways.

Lown–Ganong–Levine syndrome is similar to Wolff–Parkinson–White syndrome but the PR interval is not shortened. There is no evidence of sinus or nodal tachycardia, ventricular fibrillation, or wandering pacemaker. *(Hay et al, pp 518–522; Rudolph, pp 1452–1453)*

750–752. (750-A, 751-D, 752-A) The child with sickle cell disease described in the question is having a vasoocclusive crisis. This is a painful condition caused by bone ischemia, resulting from diminished blood flow secondary to intravascular sickling of red blood cells. Appropriate therapy includes generous hydration to reduce blood viscosity and sickling. Intravenous fluids are helpful, but there is no reason to restrict oral intake of fluid or a regular diet. Because the kidneys of these patients tend to have an impaired concentrating ability, fluid maintenance generally should be estimated at one and a half to twice the usual volume. Because the patient described is afebrile and without signs of localized infection, such as osteomyelitis, intravenous antibiotics are not required. Blood transfusion is not used routinely in the initial management of vasoocclusive crises. Patients with sickle cell disease ordinarily have hemoglobin levels of 7 to 8 g/dL. Although addiction to narcotics is a concern in patients with sickle cell disease, adequate pain medication is an important part of therapy. Attempts to withhold medication or undermedicate the patient often result in apprehension and an increased need for such medication.

Other complications of sickle cell disease include aplastic anemia, sequestration crisis (the accumulation of a large volume of blood in the spleen, which can lead to peripheral hypovolemia), and hand–foot syndrome, probably as a result of infarction of the small bones of the hands and the feet and characterized by pain and swelling. Although pulmonary function may be impaired in sickle cell disease, pulmonary edema is not a recognized complication in children. Bacteremia is a potentially life-threatening complication. Children with sickle cell disease have impaired resistance to encapsulated organisms, specifically *Streptococcus pneumoniae, Haemophilus influenzae,* and *Salmonella. (Hay et al, pp 739–741)*

753–754. (753-E, 754-C) Transient cerebral ischemic attacks typically last from a few seconds up to 5 to 6 minutes. In the carotid system, the ocular disturbance is ipsilateral and the sensorimotor disturbance is contralateral. Unlike an epileptic seizure or an Adams–Stokes attack, consciousness is maintained. Migraine is an unlikely diagnosis in the case described, because it usually develops earlier in life and the ocular disturbance is bilateral. Treatment for transient cerebral ischemic attacks include antiplatelet drugs, anticoagulants, or surgical endarterectomy. *(Fauci, pp 2327–2339)*

755–756. (755-B, 756-A) Ankylosing spondylitis should be suspected in any man younger than 40 years of age who has had an insidious onset of low back pain that has persisted for at least 3 months, is associated with morning stiffness, and eases with exercise. The diagnosis is established by the finding of symmetrical sacroiliitis on roentgenogram. Spinal complications include vertebral fracture, resulting from rigidity of the spine, and the cauda equina syndrome. Systemic complications of ankylosing spondylitis include cardiac conduction defects, iritis, aortitis with aortic insufficiency, and apical pulmonary fibrosis with cavities resembling tuberculous lesions. Nearly all white patients with ankylosing spondylitis, but only half of all black patients, are HLA-B27 positive. Therapy consists of nonsteroidal anti-inflammatory drugs and physical therapy. *(Fauci, pp 1904–1906)*

757–758. (757-D, 758-B) The presence of chronic sinusitis, otitis media, cavitating pulmonary lesions, and renal disease suggests a diagnosis of Wegener's granulomatosis. Polyarteritis and sarcoidosis are not associated with pulmonary cavities. Pulmonary abscess and tuberculosis are unlikely in the case described because of the patient's other symptoms and lack of sputum pathology. The use of cytotoxic drugs, such as cyclophosphamide, has greatly improved the prognosis of persons with Wegener's granulomatosis. The vast majority of patients go into long-term remission when treated with these drugs. Treatment should be carried on for a year after remission begins. *(Fauci, pp 1914–1916)*

759. (D) It has been shown that cimetidine decreases the clearance of theophylline, thereby elevating theophylline blood levels. Theophylline blood levels above 20 μg/mL often are associated with nausea. If cimetidine is to be prescribed for persons also requiring a theophylline preparation, the dose of theophylline should be reduced. *(Fauci, p 2541)*

760–761. (760-A, 761-C) The man described in the question has idiopathic calcium oxalate nephrolithiasis. He formed stones despite maintaining a high fluid intake and avoiding dairy products. Thiazide treatment, the next logical step in therapy, decreases the frequency of stone formation in a significant percentage of patients. Unfortunately, the patient presented continued to form kidney stones. Administration of orthophosphate as the neutral salt has been shown to be effective in preventing recurrent stone formation in patients who do not respond to thiazide therapy. Allopurinol is not likely to help in the absence of uricosuria. Cellulose phosphate is a treatment for absorptive hypercalcemia. Surgery would not be indicated in the case described. *(Fauci, pp 1572–1573)*

762–763. (762-E, 763-A) In the case described the diagnosis of penicillin-induced interstitial nephritis is supported by the presence of skin rash, eosinophilia, proteinuria of less than 1 g/24 h, and the absence of casts in the urine. The onset of renal disease in poststreptococcal glomerulonephritis typically occurs 1 to 3 weeks after infection of skin or pharynx with a nephritogenic strain of *Streptococcus.* The treatment of choice is to stop the penicillin and, when necessary, start temporary dialysis. A short course of corticosteroids in high doses has been used in patients who have significant systemic symptoms. The prognosis for recovery is excellent. *(Goldman, pp 595–596)*

764. (B) In the question, the boy with bronchial asthma has developed pneumomediastinum and subcutaneous emphysema, two conditions that rarely require therapy. The use of intermittent positive-pressure breathing or positive end-expiratory pressure therapy is contraindicated in the presence of pneumomediastinum. Bronchoscopy is contraindicated in the presence of severe wheezing. Usually no treatment is required but the mediastinal air will be absorbed faster if the patient inspires high concentrations of oxygen. *(Fauci, p 1476)*

765–766. (765-E, 766-A) The most likely diagnosis in the case described is sarcoidosis. Erythema nodosum would be an unusual manifestation of Hodgkin's disease and malignant lymphoma. Because the woman is otherwise asymptomatic, coccidioidomycosis is unlikely, and the presence of hilar adenopathy would help to rule out a diagnosis of herpes simplex infection. Eighty percent of patients who present with the stage of sarcoidosis described in the question show regression of lung disease within 2 years; thus, no specific therapy is needed. Nonsteroidal anti-inflammatory agents should be given for pain. Common indications for corticosteroid therapy include progressive pulmonary involvement, ocular involvement, involvement of the central nervous system, and persistent hypercalcemia. The other therapies listed in the question are not used to treat sarcoidosis. *(Goldman, p 436)*

767–769. (767-B, 768-C, 769-D) Persons who have rheumatoid arthritis frequently seek initial medical attention because of symmetrical polyarthritis involving the hands, wrists, and feet. Morning stiffness lasting at least an hour also is common. Rheumatoid nodules are seen in 20% of affected persons and are located most commonly over the exterior surfaces of the elbows. Unlike rheumatoid arthritis, osteoarthritis usually involves the distal interphalangeal joints of the hands. Reiter's syndrome and systemic lupus erythematosus are associated with other symptoms in addition to rheumatologic ones, and gout is rare in women. Laboratory findings indicative of rheumatoid arthritis include normocytic, normochromic anemia; elevated sedimentation rate; and positive latex-fixation test for rheumatoid factor. Antinuclear antibodies are present in 20 to 60% of patients, but anti-DNA antibodies are not produced. The best initial therapy for most patients is aspirin or a nonsteroidal anti-inflammatory agent, plus a judicious combination of exercise and rest. *(Fauci, p 1884)*

770. (C) The National Cholesterol Education Program recommended that all cholesterol levels exceeding 240 mg/dL are high and require further evaluation by obtaining a lipid profile, consisting of cholesterol, triglycerides, and HDL cholesterol, after a 12-hour fast. Because recent food intake has little impact on the cholesterol level, the screening test need not be done in the fasting state. It would be inappropriate to initiate any form of treatment before determining the LDL cholesterol level as this patient's high cholesterol could be due to an elevated HDL cholesterol and not a high LDL cholesterol. Lipoprotein electrophoresis is rarely indicated, certainly not in a patient with normal triglyceride levels. *(Report of the National Cholesterol Education Program Expert Panel on Detection, Evaluation, and Treatment of High Blood Cholesterol in Adults)*

771–772. (771-D, 772-C) The National Cholesterol Education Program recommended that decisions on drug treatment be based on the LDL cholesterol level. Medications are indicated for high-risk patients when their LDL cholesterol exceeds 160 mg/dL. This patient is at high risk because of his prior myocardial infarction. In general, dietary measures should be continued for at least 6 months before considering the use of any medications. Because of the modest elevation in cholesterol levels in this patient, there is a good chance that his LDL level can be lowered adequately with appropriate dietary measures. In patients with extremely high cholesterol levels, medications may be started earlier in the course of dietary treatment as it would be highly unlikely that diet alone would lower the LDL cholesterol to an acceptable range. Drugs are recommended in low-risk patients when the LDL cholesterol is greater than 190 mg/dL after a 6-month dietary regimen. The goal of therapy in a patient who has had a myocardial infarction should be an LDL cholesterol less than 100 mg/dL. *(Goldman, p 1099)*

773–775. (773-A, 774-E, 775-A) The gonococcal arthritis–dermatitis syndrome is the most common form of acute arthritis in sexually active adults. The combination of vesiculopapular skin eruptions on an erythematous base and an acute arthritis that is migratory, is associated with significant tenosynovitis, and changes from polyarticular in small joints to monoarticular should suggest this diagnosis.

In persons with gonococcal arthritis–dermatitis syndrome, cultures of the synovial fluid frequently show no growth, even when gonococci are cultured from other sites. Recommended treatment is intravenous ceftriaxone 1 g daily, until clinical improvement is seen, followed by oral ciprofloxacin 500 mg twice a day, cefuroxime axetil 500 mg twice a day, or amoxicillin 500 mg with clavulanic acid 125 mg three times a day, to complete a 7- to 10-day course of antibiotic therapy.

Reiter's syndrome, which usually affects men, is associated with arthritis, conjunctivitis or uveitis, and mucosal lesions. Rheumatoid arthritis and systemic lupus erythematosus do not usually produce the type of skin eruption associated with gonococcal arthritis–dermatitis syndrome. Persons with meningococcemia are usually febrile. *(Fauci, p 1946)*

776–777. (776-A, 777-E) Pheochromocytomas are catecholamine-producing tumors that are usually benign. Hypertension is the most common clinical sign in patients with pheochromocytoma. Sustained hypertension is present in 60% of patients, and paroxysms, which occur in more than 50% of patients, consist of headaches, sweating, palpitations, and a sense of impending doom. Other clinical signs include postural hypotension and tachycardia. Elevated urine levels of vanillylmandelic acid (VMA), catecholamine, and metanephrine are diagnostic of pheochromocytoma. Phenoxybenzamine, an alpha-adrenergic antagonist, is most effective in controlling blood pressure. Subsequently, beta-blocking drugs may be added to control tachycardia or arrhythmias. Preoperative volume expansion with a high-sodium diet is also beneficial. After adequate preparation, surgical removal of the tumor should be undertaken; careful monitoring is crucial because of the danger of arrhythmias, hypertensive crisis during removal of the tumor, and severe hypotension after removal is accomplished. *(Fauci, pp 2057–2060)*

778–781. (778-A, 779-A, 780-C, 781-A, B, C, D) Acute mesenteric ischemia is increasing in frequency. The causes of acute mesenteric ischemia include superior mesenteric artery (SMA) thrombosis and embolism, superior mesenteric venous thrombosis, low-flow syndrome, and dissecting aneurysm of the aorta when the mesenteric arterial lumen is occluded. SMA embolism manifests as sudden onset of pain with minimal or no abdominal findings in the early stages. Embolism should be suspected in patients with atrial fibrillation and recent myocardial infarction who suddenly develop abdominal pain. Occlusion of SMA results in ischemia of the bowel. The resultant anaerobic metabolism leads to an accumulation of lactic acid and metabolic acidosis. Clinical exam is often not as helpful since patient's pain is often more severe than suggested by the clinical findings. Mesenteric angiography is the diagnostic procedure of choice. This procedure can confirm the diagnosis and provides information concerning the level of occlusion, associated vasospasm, and the extent of collateral circulation. Plain roentgenograms of the abdomen in early stages show nondiagnostic features and in late stages may demonstrate air in bowel wall and in the liver. Blood gas determination shows metabolic acidosis that is not pathognomonic of the condition. SMA occlusion decreases intestinal blood flow by mechanical obstruction and by inducing vasoconstriction. Unless diagnosed early and treated promptly the prognosis is poor. One should not wait for definite peritoneal signs to develop. Peritoneal signs are an indication of necrosis, which is an advanced stage of the condition. Heparin is administered to prevent propagation of the thrombus and further occlusion of the collateral vessels; papavarin is administered to overcome vasospasm and improve blood flow, analgesics to relieve pain, and antibiotics to counteract colonization of ischemic bowel by bacteria. *(Hardy, pp 912–916)*

782. (A, B, C, E) The incidence of breast cancer is higher in women who have a family history of breast carcinoma or who have had breast carcinoma in the past. Early pregnancy and castration before the age of 35 years decrease the risk of breast cancer. Infertile women are at a greater risk of developing breast carcinoma than are fertile women. The Breast Cancer Detection Demonstration Project (Gail and co-workers) rejected the contribution of oral contraceptives, long-term menopausal estrogen use, modest alcohol consumption, and cigarette smoking as increasing breast cancer risk. *(Sabiston, pp 541–544)*

783. (A, C, D, E) Mammographic examination is a useful method of breast examination for detecting early lesions. A mass containing microcalcification and having irregular borders is likely to be malignant. Skin thickening over the mass and duct or vessel dilatation also are suggestive features of malignancy. Benign lesions are characterized by sharp, well-circumscribed margins and homogeneous density. Benign lesions show symmetry compared to the contralateral breast as well as an unchanged appearance as compared to previous mammograms. *(Sabiston, p 536)*

784. (E) This is the initial methodology preferred by most physicians. Control of variceal bleeding is crucial in allowing complete evaluation of a patient and beginning preparation for definitive treatment. Systemic intravenous infusion of vasopressin is an effective method of controlling variceal hemorrhage. It is as effective as intra-arterial vasopressin infusion into the superior mesenteric artery and is associated with fewer complications. Systemic intravenous somatostatin has also proven efficacious in treating variceal hemorrhage with fewer cardiovascular side effects when compared to vasopressin. Gastric hypothermia is not readily available and has not been demonstrated to be superior to vasopressin treatment. Esophageal tamponade is effective in controlling bleeding but is associated with serious complications, such as rupture of the esophagus. *(Sabiston, pp 1101–1103; Greenfield, pp 1048–1049)*

785. (A) Portacaval shunt effectively decompresses the portal system. It is associated with a low rate of recurrent variceal bleeding but a high incidence of encephalopathy. The other procedures listed in the question do not decompress the portal bed as effectively as portacaval shunt and have a higher incidence of recurrent bleeding; however, they are associated with a lower incidence of encephalopathy. *(Sabiston, pp 1103–1112)*

786. (B, D, E, G) Distal splenorenal shunt (Warren shunt) was devised to selectively decompress esophageal varices without decreasing portal blood flow. The procedure does not decrease portal pressure. It is associated with a lower incidence of encephalopathy and a higher incidence of recurrent bleeding compared to portacaval shunt. Coronary and left gastroepiploic veins are transected after ligation to isolate varices from the rest of the portal bed. Multiple trials comparing the distal splenorenal shunt with nonselective shunts have not demonstrated an advantage with regard to long-term survival. *(Sabiston, pp 1106–1110)*

787. (B, C, D, E) Sclerotherapy has become popular in controlling bleeding from esophageal varices because of low mortality and efficacy approaching that of operative treatment in stopping the bleeding. The procedure is contraindicated in gastric varices as they are difficult to tamponade and bleeding from the needle puncture site is a problem. Multiple sessions are required to obliterate the varices. Complications include esophageal ulceration, localized perforation, mediastinitis, pulmonary effusion, sepsis, and stricture. Sclerotherapy is the most commonly utilized treatment for both acute bleeding and the prevention of recurrent hemorrhage. Emergency sclerotherapy has been successful in more than 85% of patients. Failure of therapy is considered when two attempts at sclerotherapy are unsuccessful. *(Sabiston, pp 1110–1111)*

788–789. (788-E, 789-A, B, D, E, G) A complication of head injury is intracranial bleeding, which may be epidural, subdural, or intracerebral in location. Arterial epidural hematoma is frequently the result of a middle meningeal tear. The typical presentation of epidural hemorrhage includes momentary loss of consciousness, followed by a lucid interval, terminating in loss of consciousness. Ipsilateral pupillary dilatation with contralateral hemiparesis may be seen. CT scan demonstrates skull fracture, localizes the mass, and demonstrates brain displacement and concomitant cerebral injury.

Resuscitative measures include osmotic diuresis and deliberate hypocapnia to decrease intracranial tension. Barbiturates decrease cerebral metabolism and cerebral blood flow. Spinal tap, which can precipitate herniation of brain, is contraindicated. Other methods of lowering the intracranial pressure, including elevating the head of the bed, and sedatives and paralytics, may also be helpful. Steroids, which stabilize membranes, are not used in head trauma. Temporal craniotomy, which allows decompression of the brain and permits control of bleeding, is the treatment of choice. When performed early, the results are excellent. *(Schwartz et al, pp 1833–1835; Feliciano, pp 267–278)*

790. (B) The radiographic abnormality seen in the roentgenogram presented is gallstones. Cholesterol, which is insoluble in water, becomes soluble in lecithin-bile salt micelles. However, when cholesterol saturation exceeds the limits of micellar ability to keep cholesterol in solution, stone formation takes place. Excess secretion of cholesterol into bile as well as decreased secretion of bile salts and lecithin can cause cholesterol gallstone formation. *(Schwartz et al, pp 1376–1383)*

791. (A, B, C, D, F, G) The most widely used predictive criteria for acute pancreatitis were identified by Ranson in 1974. The criteria at admission, which indicate a poor prognosis, include: age more than 55 years, WBC more than 16,000 cells/mm^3, blood glucose more than 200 mg/dL, serum LDH more than 350 IU/L, SGOT more than 250 u/dL. Additional negative prognostic criteria found at 48 hours include: fall in hematocrit more than 10%, BUN elevation more than 5 mg/dL, serum calcium fall to less than 8 mg/dL, arterial PO_2 less than 60 torr, base deficit more than 4 mEg/L, and estimated fluid sequestration of more than 6 L. Mortality rates for the number of prognostic factors present are 0% for 1–2 signs, 15% for 3–4 signs, 40–50% for 5–6 signs, and approaching 100% for 7 or more signs despite maximal intensive care. *(Greenfield, pp 791–804)*

792. (A, B, C, D, F, G) Biliary calculi can cause acute cholecystitis, hydrops of the gallbladder, intestinal obstruction (gallstone ileus), and obstructive jaundice (from choledocholithiasis). There are data to imply that the incidence of gallbladder carcinoma is increased by the presence of gallstones. No evidence indicates that gallstones cause carcinoma of the liver. *(Schwartz et al, pp 1380–1383)*

793. (D) The appropriate step for correcting common duct injury recognized at operation depends on the site of injury and the extent of loss of the duct. If the injury is at the level of cystic duct insertion and has not caused loss of duct substance, end-to-end anastomosis with T-tube decompression of the bile duct is the preferred procedure. The T-tube is used to prevent bile leakage and subsequent fibrosis. If the duct is injured close to the duodenum, end-to-side choledochoduodenostomy is preferred. If the proximal duct is injured or if the length of a lost segment of duct is greater than 1 cm, a Roux-en-Y procedure (anastomosis of the distal end of the divided jejunum to the duct and implantation of the proximal end into the side of the jejunum) is recommended. Ligation of the proximal duct should be avoided except when the duct is so small that a primary repair is not possible. Ligation allows the duct to dilate, facilitating subsequent repair. *(Hardy, pp 689–690)*

794. (A, B, C, E, G) In the case described, the man has lost water, hydrogen ion, chloride, and potassium. Bicarbonate, a by-product of gastric acid secretion, accumulates and causes metabolic alkalosis. Renal compensation—excretion of bicarbonate as sodium bicarbonate—is affected by the potassium deficit, which limits sodium–potassium exchange. In order to conserve potassium, the kidneys exchange sodium with hydrogen, resulting in paradoxic aciduria. Azotemia is the result of dehydration. *(Schwartz, p 71)*

795. (A) Many operative procedures are available for treating chronic duodenal ulcer. Vagotomy produces gastric stasis. Thus, unless a superselective vagotomy is performed (in which the branches of the vagus to the body and the fundus are transected, preserving the hepatic and celiac branches along with those supplying the pylorus), vagotomy should be combined with a drainage procedure, such as gastrojejunostomy. In patients with gastric outlet obstruction, vagotomy alone is contraindicated because it does not relieve obstruction and it aggravates stasis. *(Schwartz and Ellis, pp 221–239)*

796. **(A, B, C, E)** Restlessness, irritability, insomnia, and pressured speech are all features of mania. Frequent accompanying psychotic symptoms include flight of ideas and grandiose delusions. The differential diagnosis of a first episode of mania would include the following: bipolar I disorder, especially in the presence of a positive family history; brief psychotic disorder commonly known as "stress psychosis"; schizophrenia, which typically is characterized by a prodromal phase of declining function; and substance abuse, notably with amphetamines. Cyclothymic disorder is a condition of mood swings that are less exaggerated than those in bipolar disorder. *(APA, pp 350–355)*

797. **(B)** Although all the diseases listed in the question can produce psychiatric symptoms, Cushing's disease (or syndromes of steroid excess) would be most likely to cause a severely psychotic presentation. Depression, including psychotic depression, is the most typical psychiatric presentation of Cushing's disease, but affected persons also can display paranoid delusions, auditory hallucinations, and agitation in a symptom complex that can resemble schizophrenia or mania. Addison's disease and hypothyroidism most often produce symptoms reminiscent of a major depressive episode. Multiple sclerosis can present as a psychotic disorder, but the incidence of such a presentation is thought to be quite low. *(Lishman, pp 429–440, 595–596)*

798. **(E)** In the pharmacotherapy of a person with severe acute mania, most authorities recommend treatment with neuroleptic drugs. Chlorpromazine and thioridazine are prescribed commonly because of their sedative side effects, although nonsedating neuroleptics such as haloperidol also can be effective. The atypical antipsychotic olanzepine has also been found to be effective. Benzodiazepines such as lorazepam can be useful in cases of mild manic agitation. Lithium is the most appropriate drug in the treatment of the manic phase of bipolar disorder, but its onset of action takes several days. Fluoxetine and clomipramine are antidepressants. Valproic acid is also used to control bipolar disorders. *(Kaplan and Sadock, pp 1047–1048)*

799. **(A, C, D, E, G)** 90% of patients with major depression suffer from sleep disturbances. Clinically, common sleep changes include early-morning awakening, mid-cycle awakenings, and difficulty falling asleep. Polysomnographic changes include decreased stage 3 and stage 4 sleep, short REM latency, and other disturbances in REM architecture. The abnormalities in REM latency tend to normalize with clinical recovery from depression. Sleep terror is not a feature of depression. *(Stoudemire, pp 204–205, 646, 648)*

800. **(A, B, D, E, F, H)** Panic disorder, a syndrome occurring most typically in young women, is characterized by recurring sudden attacks of severe anxiety or fear that are not clearly precipitated by identifiable life events or stresses. (However, if attacks occur coincidentally with the same event, such as shopping, a phobic association may develop.) A variety of treatments have been recommended, including relaxation therapy, psychotherapy, behavioral therapy, and drug therapy. Medications commonly prescribed at present to treat panic disorders include the benzodiazepine, alprazolam, and antidepressants including tricyclics, monoamine oxidase inhibitors and selective serotonin reuptake inhibitors. The use of neuroleptic drugs is not indicated. *(Stoudemire, pp 235–237, 240–243)*

801. **(A, C, D)** Electroconvulsive therapy (ECT) is primarily indicated in the treatment of severe depression with profound alterations in vegetative functions. ECT is considered by some to be a first-line treatment for major depresison with psychotic features, severe obsessional features or active suicidal ideation. However, ECT is also effective in the treatment of schizophrenic patients with prominent affective and catatonic symptoms as well as acute and chronic manic episodes resistant to medication. The only absolute contraindications are in patients with clinically significant space-occupying cerebral lesions and those with significant cardiovascular problems. *(Stoudemire, pp 541–542)*

802. (B, C, D, G) In the treatment of alcohol withdrawal syndromes, close observation is mandatory to guard against seizures and delirium. A benzodiazepine—chlordiazepoxide commonly is used—is prescribed to control symptoms; the drug can be given on an as-needed basis or in a regularly administered regimen. Thiamine is given to prevent development of Wernicke–Korsakoff syndrome, and multivitamin supplementation is encouraged. Diet at first should be aimed at supplying fluids and nutrition while minimizing the danger of aspiration. Chlorpromazine should not be given to persons in alcohol withdrawal because it lowers seizure threshold. *(Cassem, pp 12–17)*

803. (D) The danger period for alcohol withdrawal is said to last a full 7 days. Prophylactic therapy discontinued too quickly can lead to recrudescence of withdrawal symptoms. Disulfiram can be started 24 hours after the last drink. *(Cassem, pp 12–17)*

804. (A, C, E) Both lithium and triiodothyronine (T_3) have been used as adjunctive therapies to potentiate the action of tricyclic antidepressant drugs. With lithium, this effect usually appears at a blood level less than that required in treating bipolar disorder. Similarly, a low T_3 dosage is used in augmenting tricyclic action. As a general therapeutic principle, tricyclic and monoamine oxidase inhibitor (MAOI) antidepressants should not be given concurrently. *(Hales and Frances, pp 199–200, 417–419)*

805. (C, D, E, G) The usefulness of brief dynamic psychotherapy has become more recognized in recent years. Persons who present with an identified conflict or problem and who demonstrate motivation for change and ability to tolerate the stress of self-examination can achieve significant, often permanent improvement. Short-term treatment has proven able to examine intrapsychic issues effectively and usefully. Setting a specific, brief course of therapy often can enhance motivation and thus by itself increase the likelihood of treatment success. It should be noted that how brief is "brief" is not at all established; brief psychotherapy can range from a half-dozen to 40 or more appointments. *(Hales and Frances, pp 406–408)*

806. (E) A complete primary series of immunizations with tetanus toxoid conveys long-lasting protection (10 years or more) in most recipients. It is therefore assumed that in the emergency care of clean wounds, when the last immunization is known to have been given within the last 10 years and have been a full immunizing course, a booster dose is not essential. However, because a small proportion of vaccines do not maintain an effective level of immunization for 10 years, in the treatment of wounds that are other than clean and minor, a booster dose is advised if there is no clear history of toxoid administration in the previous 5 years. Where there is such a history, and the wound is clean and minor, it is now generally accepted that no further booster dose is necessary. There is no age limit to vaccinations, or specific guidelines for immunocompromised people. *(Last, pp 76–78)*

807. (A, C, D, E) Differential diagnosis of depression in the elderly must include dementia, metabolic and neoplastic disease, and medication effects. Mental status changes can include psychomotor agitation (or retardation), impaired short-term memory and concentration, and, in psychotic depression, delusions and hallucinations. Fluctuating state of consciousness defines delirium, not depression. Refusal to cooperate with a mental status evaluation may, at times, cause depression to be mistaken for dementia, in a condition called pseudodementia. *(APA, pp 100–103, 222–224)*

808. (C) Because of slower rates of drug metabolism, elderly individuals often require lower dosages of medications than would be true in younger persons. Although the average daily dosage of imipramine and related antidepressants is 150 mg, this amount of drug in some older persons can cause insomnia, memory disturbance, delusions, and delirium. Although blood levels can establish drug toxicity, the clinical picture in the question is so suggestive of a toxic reaction that dosage should be lowered empirically while test results are pending. Symptoms of drug toxicity remit spontaneously as blood level falls. *(Wood et al, pp 167–193)*

809–815. (809-G, 810-C, 811-F, 812-H, 813-A, 814-B, 815-E) Tricyclic antidepressant drugs have been very useful in treating a variety of psychiatric disorders in children and adolescents. Clinical trials and clinician experience have shown that desipramine, especially when combined with behavioral intervention, is an effective treatment for many individuals suffering from bulimia nervosa as well as from enuresis. Desipramine has also been helpful in treating children who have attention-deficit hyperactivity disorder and who have not responded well to first-line drug treatment with a psychostimulant agent, such as methylphenidate, dextroamphetamine, or pemoline. Ironically, tricyclic antidepressants have not had a successful track record in the treatment of childhood depression.

Like desipramine, haloperidol, an antipsychotic agent, has found a place in the treatment of a number of childhood psychiatric disorders. Haloperidol has been a longstanding drug treatment of choice for children with Tourette's syndrome, a disorder characterized by the presence of multiple tics, most notably vocal ones. Extremely aggressive behavior associated with conduct disorder or with mental retardation also can be treated with haloperidol, as can the psychosis produced by childhood schizophrenia.

It is now recognized that obsessive–compulsive disorder affects a significant number of children. Psychopharmacologic treatment is the same as with adults—namely clomipramine or fluoxetine. *(Shaffer, pp 1–28, 69–130, 150–154, 174–176)*

816–817. (816-C, 817-E) Polychlorinated biphenyls (PCBs) were extensively used in the manufacture of electrical transformers until production was halted in the mid-1970s. Workers who have been exposed to the substances have been noted to have an acnelike eruption with inflammatory pustules. Other effects are eye irritation and gastrointestinal disturbance. The substances are persistent, and more than 25% of the population in the United States is thought to have residues of greater than one part per million in adipose tissue. Dietary exposure of the general population has been alleged to occur through milk, eggs, cheese, meat, and fish.

Organophosphorus compounds have been widely used since the 1950s as insecticides, both in national pest control programs and domestically. They have been responsible for more deaths on a worldwide basis than have any other groups of compounds. From the point of view of the environmental toxicologist, it was perhaps fortuitous that many pests began to develop resistance to the substances fairly early in the use of these compounds. More recently, concern for environmental control has further limited their use; studies have attributed carcinogenic properties to several of these pesticides.

Nitrosamines are highly toxic and dangerous to handle. Toxic amounts may be absorbed without warning, because danger signals such as specific odor or irritant effects are lacking. The manufacture of electrical products and of rubber, dyes, lubricating oils, explosives, insecticides, and fungicides all have been associated with these substances. They may be used as solvents as well as agents in the manufacturing process. Nitrosamines have carcinogenic properties and have been transmitted transplacentally.

Epoxy compounds are used in the production of resins. They cause irritation of the skin and mucosa. Experimental studies have indicated such possible effects as testicular atrophy and defective spermatogenesis. Although the substances are irritants, more serious toxicity has so far not been demonstrated. *(Last, pp 431–433, 442–444, 481–482, 606)*

818–829. (818-J, 819-A, 820-B, 821-E, 822-C, 823-F, 824-G, 825-L, 826-L, 827-H, 828-I, 829-D) The list of recommendations for preventive services come from the U.S. Preventive Services Task Force. The list is neither exhaustive nor final. Clinicians frequently wish to add other preventive measures after considering a patient's history or other clinically relevant individual circumstances. The list concentrates on those tests that have been proven to be cost-effective in the population risk groups noted. For each risk group, other tests may and should be done. The wording of the question is important for the student to notice. It requests appropriate tests for the *related* conditions, not for the disease from which the population group may be derived. Thus, for example, it is assumed that a diabetic population would have serial fasting glucose serum levels as a part of the treatment for the condition. Hence the correct screening procedure for a related condition in the known diabetic population is urinalysis for bacteriuria, which may reveal a urinary tract infection in a population that has polyuria and therefore might be "asymptomatic," or at least overlooked by the physician.

Homosexually active men are at high risk for numerous infections. It is well recognized that a major risk is HIV infection, but apart from the use of protective condoms and restricting the number of partners, no preventive measures have been demonstrated to be effective. In common with IV drug abusers, this group is also at high risk for hepatitis B infection, for which immunization is effective.

Markedly obese individuals are at high risk for diabetes. This association may be stronger than a risk factor, in that a high proportion of obese individuals who are treated by effective weight reduction may require neither insulin nor oral hypoglycemic agents to control diabetes. A fasting blood glucose may detect a condition that is treatable by dietary measures, and this may be the reinforcement necessary to persuade some individuals to adhere to dietary advice.

Prostitutes and persons with multiple sex partners are especially at risk for gonorrhea. Syphilis is more common in prostitutes, possibly because their lifestyle may continue for many years. Prostitutes should therefore be screened for both diseases. Otherwise, gonorrhea is principally diagnosed because of presenting symptoms, when treatment with antibiotics is relatively easy and short, in spite of the development of strains of the organism that are resistant to some antibiotics. Syphilis has a longer latent period, and it is therefore frequently advisable to screen for it.

In patients with diabetes, polyuria is a common symptom. In a well-controlled diabetic, a physician may attribute the frequency of urination to polyuria, missing a bacteriuria. Infections of all kinds are more frequent in diabetics and are often reasons for suddenly poor control of the disease. Infections are always serious for a diabetic and should therefore be treated early.

Tuberculosis is becoming more frequent once again. The reservoir of infection seems to be in nations where low socioeconomic conditions prevail and in the immunocompromised population, which includes those infected with HIV. Potential immigrants are tested, but the physician should bear in mind that infection may be dormant or latent at the time immigration is sought.

Men with two or more cardiac risk factors—high blood pressure, high blood cholesterol levels, cigarette smoking, diabetes mellitus, or a family history of coronary artery disease—should have a preventive ECG performed at every routine physical examination.

Pandemics of influenza from any strain of virus are particularly devastating for populations of individuals in nursing homes. These persons should receive immunization against the predicted strains of influenza (which are made commercially available each year) as a routine. Little ongoing immunity is achieved by this vaccination, which should therefore be repeated annually.

Patients who suffer from any condition that increases the risk of pneumococcal infection, which includes any patient with chronic cardiac or pulmonary condition and several other conditions, such as sickle cell disease, should receive initially a combined pneumococcus and influenza vaccine. The immunity conveyed by the pneumococcal vaccine is relatively permanent, so subsequent immunization may be performed with influenza vaccine alone.

Persons aged 50 or over who have first-degree relatives with colorectal cancer or who have a personal history of endometrial, ovarian, or breast cancer or a previous history of inflammatory bowel disease or polyps should have annual fecal occult blood investigations and sigmoidoscopy.

Persons with a family history of polyposis coli should have regular fecal occult blood tests and regular colonoscopy. The interval between colonoscopies depends on the individual patient and the recommendation of the gastroenterologist. The latter depends on the findings and the confidence of the success of the procedure.

Persons who attend clinics for the treatment of sexually transmitted disease and those attending other high-risk clinics such as adolescent and family planning clinics should be regularly tested for concomitant chlamydial infection. This infection is also more prevalent in those who have multiple sexual partners. More common in women, it may give rise to symptoms in men, who are frequently carriers. *(Last, pp 6–7)*

830. (B) Complications for liver laceration include hemorrhage, abscess formation, and hemobilia, which is bleeding into biliary passages. Communication between branches of the hepatic artery and biliary ducts results in hemobilia, which typically produces colicky abdominal pain and upper and lower gastrointestinal tract bleeding. Treatment consists of occluding the communicating vessel. *(Schwartz and Shires, p 323; Feliciano, pp 510–515)*

831–832. (831-C, 832-C) Intussusception frequently affects children between 5 and 12 months. The usual presenting features consist of a triad of abdominal pain, vomiting, and passage of "red currant jelly" stools. In between the episodes of abdominal pain the child will remain symptom-free. The intussuscepted segment of the bowel may be felt as a sausage-shaped mass when the abdominal muscle is relaxed and the mass is not under the cover of the liver. Barium enema establishes the diagnosis and is helpful in reducing the intussusception. Contraindications for barium enema include signs of peritoneal irritation, duration of symptoms longer than 24 hours, and features of bowel obstruction on plain roentgenograms. *(Sabiston, pp 1282–1284)*

833. (B) Congenital hypertrophic pyloric stenosis is not an infrequent condition. It has a predilection for male infants, and peak incidence is at 4 to 6 weeks of life. The etiology is unknown. Presenting features include projectile vomiting of nonbilious material, visible peristalsis in the upper abdomen, and presence of a palpable mass (an "olive") in the right upper quadrant. *(Hardy, pp 1140–1141)*

834. (B) Treatment of choice for hypertrophic pyloric stenosis is pyloromyotomy. Before surgery, fluid and electrolyte imbalances must be corrected. Prognosis is excellent. *(Hardy, p 1140–1141)*

835. (A) Although most instances of hematemesis associated with cirrhosis are due to esophageal varices, in approximately 20 to 25% of persons with cirrhosis upper gastrointestinal tract bleeding is due to other lesions. These lesions include gastritis, peptic ulcer, hiatal hernia, and gastric cancer. The best procedure to locate the bleeding site is esophagogastroduodenoscopy, which has the potential of not only locating a lesion but also demonstrating bleeding from the lesion. Although a gastrointestinal barium series may demonstrate a lesion, it may not identify the source of bleeding. Angiography only shows active bleeding at the time of examination. Splenoportography only is useful in demonstrating varices. Hepatic wedge pressure determines portal pressure but does not identify sites of bleeding. *(Sabiston, pp 1101–1103)*

836. (B) Drugs related to antipsychotic medications are used to treat some nonpsychiatric conditions and, thus, can cause side effects more often associated with antipsychotic therapy. For example, prochlorperazine (Compazine) is a popular antiemetic that is related to chlorpromazine. Extrapyramidal reactions can accompany prochlorperazine therapy and are best treated by antiparkinsonian medications, such as benztropine. *(Kaplan and Sadock, pp 955–956)*

837. (D) Tardive dyskinesia is related to exposure to dopamine-receptor blocking agents, generally the classic antipsychotic agents. It is potentially irreversible and develops after several years of significant use of these medications, although it can arise after short-term treatment and fairly low dosages. The most significant risk factor for development of tardive dyskinesia is increasing age of the patient. Early symptoms include facial tics and unusual movements of the tongue; later symptoms include bizarre jaw movements, torticollis, choreoathetosis of the extremities, and labored respiration. The cause of tardive dyskinesia is not clear. *(Stoudemire, pp 514–516)*

838. (A) The usual first step in treating tardive dyskinesia, especially early in the course of the disorder, is to stop the antipsychotic drug. For many patients, symptoms recede significantly or even disappear; but for others, symptoms will persist or may even worsen transiently. Several medications, including lithium, reserpine, and diazepam, have been tried in the treatment of tardive dyskinesia, but none has emerged as clearly effective. While newer antipsychotic agents such as quetrapine, olanzapine, and clozapine seem much less likely to cause tardive dyskinesia, it is inappropriate to use antipsychotic drugs to treat anxiety alone. *(Stoudemire, pp 512–516)*

839. (D) Simple grief (bereavement) is not considered a psychiatric disorder. Symptoms include manifestations of depression: sleep and appetite disturbances, feelings of guilt, and lassitude. However, use of antidepressant medications is not advised unless more florid symptoms develop (e.g., significant psychomotor retardation or obsessional thoughts of guilt or worthlessness) or symptoms persist for several months. In the case presented in the question, the use of a short-acting antianxiety agent for sleep would be beneficial, especially if combined with supportive psychotherapy. *(Kaplan and Sadock, pp 69–72)*

840. (E) A patient's refusal of life-saving treatment poses vexing legal and ethical problems for physicians. In the situation described in the question, treatment could be instituted in most states if a medical emergency were deemed present, if the man were suicidal by virtue of a major psychiatric disorder, or if the man were judged to be incompetent to make the decision to refuse treatment. However, competency or lack of competency can be determined by legal authority only. The role of psychiatrists in determining competency is solely advisory. Psychiatrists must carefully assess a person's mental status for evidence of cognitive or psychologic impairment, as well as document the person's ability to engage in rational decision making and to understand the consequences of decisions made. *(Cassem, pp 627–632)*

841. (D) In the case described in the question, perhaps the most likely explanation for the woman's poor clinical response to imipramine therapy is the relatively brief time she has been on the drug (older antidepressant drugs, such as imipramine, take from 2 to 6 weeks to show full clinical effect). Other possible explanations include noncompliance, undermedication, and overmedication (tricyclics are believed to have a "therapeutic window" of effectiveness); detection of all three of these phenomena would be aided by obtaining serum imipramine levels. The chances are very good that, given her history of response to imipramine in the past, the woman described will ultimately respond again to imipramine therapy. *(Cassem, pp 541–555)*

842. (C) Fluorocarbons have been shown to induce arrhythmias in workers involved in their use in several industries. They have been used as theoretically inert propellants in aerosols, as solvents for use in dry cleaning, and in fire extinguishers. The other substances listed in the question have not been demonstrated to be linked to the development of cardiovascular abnormalities. However, such abnormalities are of sufficiently frequent occurrence in the United States to merit an active search for other possible associations. *(Levy and Wegman, pp 432–436)*

843. (E) Poliomyelitis has a reservoir of infection among humans, who shed the virus in pharyngeal secretions and feces. The most common mode of spread is by the oral route. Neither flies nor water supplies have been conclusively established as sources of infection. Males are more frequently affected than females. Minor cases may exist in a community without being recognized by symptoms other than those caused by nonspecific virus infections. Poliomyelitis remains highly endemic in many developing countries. Statistics from these countries are not always reliably available. The disease is chiefly recognized in its paralytic form. *(Last, pp 80–81)*

844. (E) The incubation period of rhinovirus and coronavirus colds is 48 to 72 hours. Parainfluenza virus and respiratory syncytial virus (RSV) cause bronchiolitis, croup, and pneumonia in young children but usually result in uncomplicated colds in adults. Mycoplasma infections characteristically have a longer incubation period and more protracted symptoms. They occur in adults especially when they are in contact with children who have frequent persistent coughs and colds. *(Kelley, pp 121, 1756–1757)*

845. (E) In spite of strong assertions from some quarters, notably from the Nobel Prize winner Linus Pauling, evidence is not conclusive that ascorbic acid (vitamin C) has therapeutic activity in colds. Phenylephrine nose drops may diminish nasal secretion, and be good symptomatic therapy. The antiviral agents amantadine and vidarabine are unlikely to be effective in illness that is of longer duration than the usual virus infection. Erythromycin has some effect in diminishing symptoms in mycoplasma infections, especially if given early. This medication should be continued for 10 days in this condition. *(Kelley, pp 121, 1756–1757)*

846. (B) The age at which children most frequently ingest the largest amounts of lead is during the crawling and walking stage, which is also the oral–anal stage of development. Thus, the children most at risk are between the ages of 1 and 2 years. Until children are mobile, they are unlikely to come into contact with objects that might have been coated with lead-based paint. After 2 years of age, children normally have less tendency to put unusual objects in their mouths. *(Clark and MacMahon, p 545)*

847. (E) Oral consent may be a valid form of authorizing some medical procedures. However, in the case of any surgical procedure or in the use of an instrument, such as a sigmoidoscope, to which there must be attributed minimal risk, a written form of consent is highly desirable. When the patient is a minor and away from home, even in emergency situations written consent should be sought from someone who is prepared to act as guardian with parental permission. In most children's camps, for example, a responsible official should have received prior authorization from the parents to give such consent. Most difficulties have arisen when physicians have felt that their explanation of the situation is sufficient, in view of prior knowledge of the patient. No matter how minor the procedure, if there is any attached risk it is always advisable to have a written statement of informed consent. Only when the treatment is indeed minor, is not hazardous, and is routine is oral consent to be regarded as sufficient. Even under these circumstances, the oral consent should be recorded in the notes at the time. *(Warren, p 104)*

848. (D) Before a person can be confined to an institution, a competent professional must decide that the person is actually or at present insane and that there is a danger of injury to the patient or others. A person who is mentally incompetent is more appropriately protected by the legal appointment of a guardian to make the necessary decisions and manage property, rather than by confining that person. A person who merely has strange fantasies may be neither mentally incompetent nor a danger to self or others. Auditory and visual hallucinations do not necessarily pose a threat of danger or injury to self or others and therefore are not in themselves grounds for confinement. *(Warren, p 130)*

849. (C) *Vibrio cholerae* has its only reservoir in humans and tolerates exposure and drying poorly. It survives longer in water, especially if the water is at temperatures of 18 to 23°C (60 to 70°F). It therefore does not spread on infected clothing (fomites). Direct person-to-person transmission probably does not occur. Contaminated water is the main source of infection; frequent exposure to polluted surface water through bathing, food preparation, and utensil washing are major sources of infection. Although flies may transport small numbers of vibros from excreta to food, lack of multiplication makes it unlikely that flies play an important part in transmission. Mosquitoes are not vectors. *(Last, pp 176–178)*

850. (E) It has been reported that 28% of pregnant women shed cytomegalovirus (CMV) from the cervix at some time during pregnancy. The percentage of infants affected is not as high as this. It is therefore assumed that there must be some effective mechanisms that prevent fetal infection when the mother is excreting CMV. The virus may affect the placenta and not the fetus. A congenitally infected infant may shed the virus intermittently for years. Close contact with body secretions containing the virus seems to be responsible for the higher incidence among institutionalized children. *(Last, pp 144–145)*

851. (C) Chelating drugs are given as treatment for symptomatic poisoning by lead and other heavy metals. They should not be given prophylactically, since the agents themselves have some possible toxic side effects. These toxic effects may add to those already caused by ingestion of the metals and may actually increase absorption of the metal. For these reasons, advice should be given to workers to seek employment away from exposure to the offending agent while therapy continues. *(Levy and Wegman, pp 206–207)*

852. (A) In a person with chronic duodenal ulcer, the incidence of recurrent ulceration following vagotomy and antrectomy is approximately 1%. The incidence associated with proximal vagotomy is 15%. Vagotomy and drainage procedures have recurrence rates of about 10%. *(Schwartz et al, p 1138)*

REFERENCES

Internal Medicine

Fauci AS, Braunwald E, Isselbacher KJ, et al, eds. *Harrison's Principles of Internal Medicine,* 14th ed. New York: McGraw-Hill Book Co; 1998.

Goldman L, Bennett JC, et al, eds. *Cecil Textbook of Medicine,* 21st ed. Philadelphia: WB Saunders Company, 2000.

Report of the National Cholesterol Education Program Expert Panel on Detection, Evaluation, and Treatment of High Blood Cholesterol in Adults.

Obstetrics and Gynecology

Cunningham FG, MacDonald PC, Gant NF, et al. *Williams Obstetrics,* 20th ed. Stamford, CT: Appleton & Lange; 1997.

Beckman CR, Ling FW, Herbert WN, et al. *Obstetrics and Gynecology,* 3rd ed. Baltimore; Lippincott, Williams, & Wilkins; 1998.

DeCherney AM, Pernoll ML. *Current Obstetric & Gynecologic Diagnosis & Treatment,* 8th ed. East Norwalk, CT: Appleton & Lange; 1994.

Pediatrics

Feigin RD, Cherry JD. *Textbook of Pediatric Infectious Diseases,* 3rd ed. Philadelphia: WB Saunders Co; 1992.

Fleischer GR, Ludwig S. *Textbook of Pediatric Emergency Medicine.* Baltimore: Williams & Wilkins; 1993.

Hay WW Jr, Hayward AR, Levin MJ, Sondheimer JM. *Current Pediatric Diagnosis and Treatment.* Stamford, CT: Appleton & Lange; 1996.

Rudolph AM, Hoffman JIE, Rudolph CD. *Rudolph's Pediatrics,* 20th ed. Stamford, CT: Appleton & Lange; 1996.

Psychiatry

American Psychiatric Association (APA). *Diagnostic and Statistical Manual of Mental Disorders,* 4th ed. Washington, DC: American Psychiatric Association; 1994.

Cassem WH. *Massachusetts General Hospital Handbook of General Hospital Psychiatry.* St. Louis: Mosby–Year Book; 1991.

Hales RE, Frances AJ, eds. *Psychiatry Update: American Psychiatric Association Annual Review.* Washington, DC: American Psychiatric Press Inc; 1987.

Kaplan HI, Sadock BJ. *Synopsis of Psychiatry,* 8th ed. Baltimore: Williams & Wilkins; 1998.

Lishman WA. *Organic Psychiatry. The Psychological Consequences of Cerebral Disorder,* 2nd ed. Oxford, England: Blackwell Scientific Publications; 1987.

Shaffer D, ed. *The Psychiatric Clinics of North America: Pediatric Psychopharmacology.* Philadelphia: WB Saunders Co; 1992.

Stoudemire A. *Clinical Psychiatry for Medical Students,* 2nd ed. Philadelphia: J.B. Lippincott Co; 1994.

Wood KA, Harris MJ, Morreale A, et al. Drug-induced psychosis and depression in the elderly. *Psychiatr Clin North Am.* 1988;11:167–193.

Preventive Medicine

Ahlbom A, Norell S. *Introduction to Modern Epidemiology.* Chestnut Hill, MA: Epidemiology Resources, Inc; 1990.

Clark DW, MacMahon B. *Preventive and Community Medicine,* 2nd ed. Boston: Little, Brown & Co; 1981.

Kelley WN. *Textbook of Internal Medicine.* Philadelphia: JB Lippincott Co; 1989.

Last JM, Wallace R. *Maxcy–Rosenau–Last Public Health and Preventive Medicine,* 13th ed. Norwalk, CT: Appleton & Lange; 1992.

Levy BS, Wegman DH. *Occupational Health: Recognizing and Preventing Work Related Disease.* Boston: Little, Brown & Co; 1995.

Luft HS. Assessing the evidence of HMO performance. *Milbank Memorial Fund Quarterly; Health and Society.* 1980 (Oct–Dec):501–536.

Mausner JS, Bahn AK. *Epidemiology: An Introductory Text.* Philadelphia: WB Saunders Co; 1985.

Morton RF, Hebel JR. *A Study Guide to Epidemiology and Biostatistics.* Baltimore: University Park Press; 1996.

Warren DG. *A Legal Guide for Rural Health Programs.* Cambridge, MA: Ballinger Publishing Co; 1979.

Wyngaarden JB, Smith LM. *Cecil's Textbook of Medicine,* 18th ed. Philadelphia: WB Saunders Co; 1996.

Surgery

Aaron RK, Ciombor D. Venous thromboembolism in orthopedic patients. *Surg Clin North Am.* 1983; 63:529–537.

Antip RG, Burke JF. Skin coverage. *Curr Probl Surg.* 1983;20:637–640.

Bartlett RH, Whitehouse WH, Turcotte JS. *Life Support Systems in Intensive Care.* Chicago: Year Book Medical Publishers Inc; 1984.

Braverman LE, Utinger RD, eds. *Werner & Ingbar's The Thyroid: A Fundamental Clinical Text,* 6th ed. Philadelphia: Lippincott; 1991.

Browse NL. *An Introduction to the Symptoms and Signs of Surgical Disease.* Chicago: Year Book Medical Publishers Inc; 1978.

Condon RE, Nyhus LM, eds. *Manual of Surgical Therapeutics,* 6th ed. Boston: Little, Brown & Co; 1992.

Conley JJ, ed. *Complications of Head and Neck Surgery.* Philadelphia: WB Saunders Co; 1979.

Cummings CW, et al, eds. *Otolaryngology—Head and Neck Surgery,* 2nd ed. St. Louis: Mosby–Year Book; 1993.

David JA. *Wound Management.* Springhouse, PA: Springhouse Corp; 1986.

Feliciano DV, Moore EE, Mattox KL, eds. *Trauma*, 3rd ed. Stamford, CT: Appleton & Lange; 1996.

Gitnick GL. *Current Gastroenterology.* Boston: Houghton Mifflin Professional Publishers; 1980;1.

Greenfield LJ, Mulholland MW, Oldham KT, Zelenock GB. *Surgery Scientific Principles and Practice.* Philadelphia: Lippincott; 1993.

Greenfield LJ, Wakefield TW. *Prevention of Venous Thrombus and Pulmonary Embolism Advances in Surgery.* Chicago: Year Book Medical Publishers Inc; 1989; 22.

Hardy JD, ed. *Hardy's Textbook of Surgery.* Philadelphia: JB Lippincott Co; 1988.

Juhl JH. *Paul and Juhl's Essentials of Roentgen Interpretation.* New York: Harper & Row Publishers Inc; 1993.

Marini JJ. *Respiratory Medicine and Intensive Care for the House Officer.* Baltimore: Williams & Wilkins; 1987.

Moore FA, Haenel JB, Moore EE. Alternatives to Swan–Ganz cardiac output monitoring. *Surg Clin N Am.* 1991;71:699–717.

Rosenthal LE, Mobley HLT. *Contemp Gastroenterol.* 1988;1:9–13.

Sabiston DC, ed. *Davis-Christopher Textbook of Surgery*, 13th ed. Philadelphia: WB Saunders Co; 1981.

Schwartz SI, Ellis H, eds. *Maingot's Abdominal Operations*, 9th ed. Norwalk, CT: Appleton & Lange; 1990.

Schwartz SI, Shires GT, Spencer FC, eds. *Principles of Surgery*, 5th ed. New York: McGraw-Hill Book Co; 1994.

Skinner DG, deKernion JB. *Genitourinary Cancer.* Philadelphia: WB Saunders Co; 1978.

Tanagho EA, McAninch JW. *Smith's General Urology*, 13th ed. Norwalk, CT: Appleton & Lange; 1992.

Vander AJ. *Renal Physiology*, 5th ed. New York: McGraw-Hill Book Co; 1995.

SUBSPECIALTY LIST: CLINICAL COMPETENCE REVIEW

Question Number and Subspecialty

Obstetrics and Gynecology

703. Endocrinology, infertility
704. Endocrinology, infertility
705. Endocrinology, infertility
706. Clinical obstetrics, abnormal
707. Clinical obstetrics, normal
708. Primary care
709. Primary care
710. Clinical obstetrics, normal
711. Clinical obstetrics, abnormal
712. Clinical obstetrics, normal
713. Clinical obstetrics, abnormal
714. Clinical obstetrics, abnormal
715. Clinical obstetrics, abnormal
716. Clinical gynecology
717. Clinical gynecology
718. Clinical gynecology
719. Clinical gynecology
720. Clinical gynecology
721. Clinical gynecology
722. Clinical gynecology
723. Clinical obstetrics, abnormal
724. Clinical obstetrics, abnormal
725. Clinical obstetrics, abnormal
726. Clinical obstetrics, abnormal
727. Clinical obstetrics, abnormal
728. Clinical obstetrics, abnormal
729. Clinical obstetrics, abnormal

Pediatrics

730. Ear, nose, and throat
731. Ear, nose, and throat
732. Infectious disease
733. Infectious disease
734. Infectious disease
735. Endocrinology
736. Endocrinology
737. Neurology
738. Neurology
739. Neurology
740. Neurology
741. Neoplastic disease
742. Neoplastic disease
743. Neoplastic disease

744. Infectious disease
745. Infectious disease
746. Infectious disease
747. Structure, genetic
748. Structure, genetic
749. Structure, genetic
750. Hematology
751. Hematology
752. Hematology

Internal Medicine
753. Neurology
754. Neurology
755. Rheumatology
756. Rheumatology
757. Pulmonology
758. Pulmonology
759. Pulmonology
760. Nephrology
761. Nephrology
762. Nephrology
763. Nephrology
764. Allergy and immunology
765. Allergy and immunology
766. Allergy and immunology
767. Rheumatology
768. Rheumatology
769. Rheumatology
770. Cardiology
771. Cardiology
772. Cardiology
773. Infectious disease
774. Infectious disease
775. Infectious disease
776. Endocrinology
777. Endocrinology

Surgery
778. Vascular surgery
779. Vascular surgery
780. Vascular surgery
781. Vascular surgery
782. Breast
783. Breast
784. Gastrointestinal bleeding
785. Gastrointestinal bleeding
786. Liver
787. Gastrointestinal tract
788. Trauma
789. Trauma
790. Biliary surgery
791. Biliary surgery
792. Biliary surgery
793. Biliary surgery
794. Fluids and electrolytes
795. Gastrointestinal tract

Psychiatry
796. Psychopathology
797. Diagnosis
798. Intervention
799. Intervention
800. Intervention
801. Intervention
802. Intervention
803. Intervention
804. Intervention
805. Intervention
807. Diagnosis
808. Intervention
809. Child psychiatry, intervention
810. Child psychiatry, intervention
811. Child psychiatry, intervention
812. Child psychiatry, intervention
813. Child psychiatry, intervention
814. Child psychiatry, intervention
815. Child psychiatry, intervention

Preventive Medicine
806. Disease control
816. Assessment
817. Assessment
818. Disease control
819. Disease control
820. Disease control
821. Disease control
822. Disease control
823. Disease control
824. Disease control
825. Disease control
826. Disease control
827. Disease control
828. Disease control
829. Disease control
830. Trauma
831. Pediatric gastrointestinal surgery
832. Pediatric gastrointestinal surgery
833. Pediatric gastrointestinal surgery
834. Pediatric gastrointestinal surgery
835. Gastrointestinal bleeding

836. Intervention
837. Assessment
838. Intervention
839. Intervention
840. Ethical and legal
841. Assessment
842. Disease control
843. Disease control
844. Assessment
845. Intervention
846. Assessment
847. Ethical and legal
848. Ethical and legal
849. Gastrointestinal tract
850. Assessment
851. Intervention
852. Gastrointestinal tract

CHAPTER 4

Practice Test

Carefully read the following instructions before taking the Practice Test.

1. This examination consists of 180 single-item questions and 60 case study questions organized according to the clinical-encounter settings.
2. The questions are presented with subjects integrated; however, questions are grouped by type.
3. The Practice Test mimics a booklet of the actual *Step 3* examination by presenting questions in exam-type format. Content and question-type breakdown are similar to those you will encounter on the examination.
4. You should budget approximately 60 seconds per item, which is approximately 3 hours for this test. Be sure to time yourself accordingly.
5. Be sure you have extra pencils and erasers, a clock, a comfortable setting, and an adequate amount of undisturbed, distraction-free time. Relax! (Yeah . . . right!!)
6. Remove and fill out the answer sheet as instructed. (The answer sheet is on pages 313–314.)
7. Once you have completed the Practice Test, check your answers and assess your areas of weakness against the subspecialty list on pages 309 through 311.
8. Remember! This is only a *Practice Test!* It is meant to help you identify your strengths and weaknesses for the actual exam.

DIRECTIONS (Questions 1 through 94): Each of the numbered items or incomplete statements in this section is followed by answers or by completions of the statement. Select the ONE lettered answer or completion that is BEST in each case.

1. Under normal conditions, the major mechanism of body heat loss is

(A) radiation
(B) evaporation
(C) perspiration
(D) insensible perspiration
(E) conduction

2. The introduction of cold water into one ear may cause giddiness and nausea. The primary cause of this phenomenon is

(A) temporary immobilization of otoliths
(B) decreased movement of ampullar crests
(C) increased discharge rate in vestibular afferents
(D) decreased discharge rate in vestibular afferents
(E) creation of convection currents in endolymph

3. Which virus is most resistant to chemical and physical agents?

(A) mumps
(B) measles
(C) influenza
(D) serum hepatitis
(E) polio

4. The development of which tumor is associated with the ingestion of aflatoxin?

   (A) hepatocellular carcinoma
   (B) pulmonary sarcomas
   (C) chordomas of the lower spine
   (D) uterine leiomyomas
   (E) sebaceous carcinoma of the eyelid

5. All the following statements concerning neurons are correct EXCEPT

   (A) neurons lack the ability to store glycogen
   (B) neurons are the basic unit of the nervous system
   (C) neurons contain Nissl bodies
   (D) neurons contain neurotubules
   (E) neurons are capable of reproducing themselves

6. Secretion of renin by the juxtaglomerular apparatus directly results in

   (A) conversion of angiotensinogen to angiotensin I
   (B) secretion of ACTH
   (C) secretion of aldosterone
   (D) vasodilation
   (E) increased renal potassium retention

7. The key regulatory enzyme of fatty acid synthesis is

   (A) citrate cleavage enzyme
   (B) ATP citrate lyase
   (C) acetyl-CoA carboxylase
   (D) malonyl-CoA decarboxylase
   (E) malonyl transacylase

8. Which of the following is a bactericidal chemotherapeutic agent?

   (A) trimethoprim
   (B) erythromycin
   (C) ampicillin
   (D) chloramphenicol
   (E) tetracyclines

9. Which of the following findings is considered diagnostic of Hirschsprung's disease on histologic examination of a rectal biopsy specimen?

   (A) hypertrophy of the muscle coat of the wall of the rectum
   (B) atrophy of the mucosal lining of the wall of the rectum
   (C) absence of the nerve fibers that innervate the wall of the rectum
   (D) absence of parasympathetic ganglion cells in the submucosal and myenteric plexus
   (E) presence of multiple small polyps along the mucosal surface of the rectal wall

10. Which of the following antineoplastic agents acts by competitive inhibition of hormonal action?

   (A) vincristine
   (B) bleomycin
   (C) busulfan
   (D) tamoxifen
   (E) melphalan

11. The functions of the ego include

   (A) psychologic defense mechanisms
   (B) reality testing
   (C) thinking
   (D) perception
   (E) instinctual drives

12. Which of the following cranial nerves emerge from the sulcus between the olive and pyramid?

   (A) the abducens
   (B) the hypoglossal
   (C) the vagus
   (D) the glossopharyngeal
   (E) the spinal accessory

13. The principal form in which iron is stored within cells of the intestinal mucosa is

   (A) free ferrous ions
   (B) free ferric ions

(C) apoferritin
(D) ferritin
(E) hemoglobin

14. The major carrier of cholesterol in the bloodstream is

(A) chylomicrons
(B) high-density lipoprotein (HDL)
(C) low-density lipoprotein (LDL)
(D) a sulfate ester
(E) albumin-cholesterol complex

15. A 45-year-old man has mycoplasmal pneumonia. He MOST likely will be treated with

(A) penicillin G
(B) nafcillin
(C) cephalosporin
(D) tetracycline
(E) amoxicillin

16. In the United States the most common etiology of an abdominal aortic aneurysm is

(A) Marfan's syndrome
(B) atherosclerosis
(C) syphilitic infection
(D) bacterial infection
(E) acute rheumatic fever

17. Which of the following nonsteroidal anti-inflammatory drugs is most effective for inhibiting platelet activation?

(A) ibuprofen
(B) acetaminophen
(C) aspirin
(D) ketoprofen
(E) indomethacin

18. First-order sensory neurons are located in all the following structures EXCEPT the

(A) anterior gray column
(B) trigeminal ganglion
(C) geniculate ganglion
(D) dorsal root ganglion
(E) mesencephalic nucleus of the trigeminal

19. Glucagon's acts on hepatocytes and causes

(A) decreased intracellular cAMP
(B) glycogen synthesis
(C) conversion of phorylase a to phosphorylase b
(D) inactivation of phosphorylase b kinase
(E) generation of glucose-1-phosphate

20. The antiphagocytic property of group A streptococci is MOST closely associated with

(A) M protein
(B) hyaluronidase
(C) streptolysin O
(D) streptolysin S
(E) ribonuclease

21. Which of the following forms of muscular dystrophy are inherited as an X-linked disorder and produce symptoms before the age of 4 years?

(A) benign (Becker variety)
(B) severe (Duchenne variety)
(C) limb–girdle variety
(D) myotonic dystrophy
(E) facioscapulohumoral variety

22. Potassium supplementation is often necessary for patients taking

(A) spironolactone
(B) triamterene
(C) furosemide
(D) amiloride
(E) captopril

23. Which of the following statements is true concerning sexual abuse in children?

(A) The abuser is usually a stranger.
(B) Sexual abuse in childhood usually does not result in long-lasting sequelae.
(C) Sexually abused children seldom develop depression.
(D) About 2 to 8% of allegations of sexual abuse are false.
(E) Most perpetrators are eventually discovered and incarcerated.

24. A 90° clockwise rotation of the intestinal loop usually results in

(A) an omphalocele
(B) a retrocecal appendix
(C) a retrocecal ureter
(D) a transverse colon passing behind the duodenum
(E) a vitelline cyst

25. Acetylcholine (ACh) is a critical link in the transmission of signals at the neuromuscular junction (NMJ). Its precise function at the NMJ is best summed up as

(A) activating postsynaptic stimulatory G proteins that open potassium channels
(B) directly opening postsynaptic voltage-gated sodium channels
(C) opening postsynaptic ACh-gated cation channels
(D) reducing the postsynaptic muscle cell's threshold for achieving an action potential
(E) lowering the threshold for presynaptic transmitter release

26. The active form of the cofactor required for oxidative decarboxylation reactions is

(A) thiamine
(B) thiamine pyrophosphate
(C) thiamine monophosphate
(D) thiamine triphosphate
(E) hydroxyethyl thiamine pyrophosphate

27. A 30-year-old man has tuberculosis. He has been ill for about 7 months with productive cough, intermittent fever, night sweats, and a weight loss of 60 lb. Numerous acid-fast bacilli are seen in a sputum examination, and more than 50 colonies of *Mycobacterium tuberculosis* grow from the sputum in culture. Persons who have been in contact with this man and who have a positive tuberculin test but show no other signs of disease should

(A) receive prophylactic isoniazid
(B) receive a full course of isoniazid and ethambutol
(C) be checked periodically by roentgenography
(D) be immunized with bacille Calmette-Guérin (BCG) vaccine
(E) be checked periodically by sputum culture

28. Hyponatremia resulting from the inappropriate secretion of ADH is most often associated with

(A) squamous cell carcinoma
(B) adenocarcinoma
(C) large-cell carcinoma
(D) small-cell carcinoma
(E) bronchioloalveolar carcinoma

29. Which of the following antibiotics has a mechanism of action of binding to the 30S ribosomal subunit and thus interfering with the initiation of protein synthesis?

(A) chloramphenicol
(B) vancomycin
(C) nitrofurantoin
(D) trimethoprim
(E) gentamicin

30. Which of the following statements is true concerning substance abuse?

(A) Cocaine abuse causes mania but not depression.
(B) Tobacco is habituating, but does not cause addiction.
(C) Most cases of addiction to opioids are iatrogenic.
(D) Tolerance does not develop to cannabis use.
(E) If a narcotic analgesic is to be given to an opioid-dependent person, the dose should be significantly increased.

31. The primitive intestinal loop rotates around an axis formed by which of the following arteries?

(A) the inferior epigastric
(B) the superior epigastric

(C) the obturator
(D) the inferior mesenteric
(E) the superior mesenteric

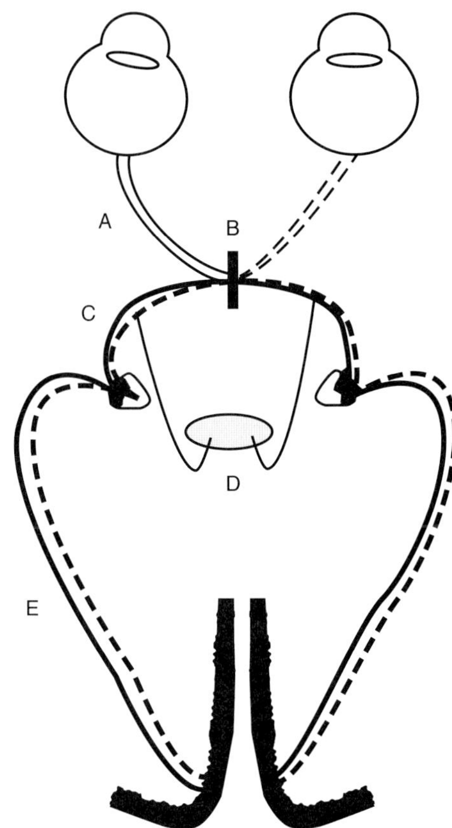

32. A lesion that produces partial or total blindness but spares the pupillary light response is most likely to be located in the

(A) optic nerve
(B) optic chiasm
(C) optic tract
(D) pretectal area
(E) geniculocalcarine tract

33. In the presence of a poison that uncouples oxidative phosphorylation, what would be the net energy yield of the complete oxidation of one mole equivalent of glucose in muscle?

(A) 1 mole equivalent ATP
(B) 2 moles equivalent ATP
(C) 3 moles equivalent ATP
(D) 4 moles equivalent ATP
(E) 5 moles equivalent ATP

34. A 7-month-old girl who has a history of pyogenic infections is hospitalized for a yeast infection that does not respond to therapy. On physical examination her spleen and lymph nodes are not palpable. A differential white blood cell count shows 95% neutrophils, 1% lymphocytes, and 4% monocytes. A bone marrow specimen contains no plasma cells or lymphocytes. Roentgenography reveals absence of a thymic shadow. Tonsils are absent. These findings are MOST compatible with

(A) multiple myeloma
(B) severe combined immunodeficiency
(C) Burton's disease
(D) Wiskott–Aldrich syndrome
(E) chronic granulomatous disease

35. The major scavenger cell involved in the inflammatory response is the

(A) neutrophil
(B) lymphocyte
(C) plasma cell
(D) eosinophil
(E) macrophage

36. The sulfonylurea tolbutamide

(A) will never cause severe hypoglycemia
(B) is best used in insulin-dependent diabetes
(C) needs to be injected subcutaneously
(D) acutely stimulates the pancreas to secrete insulin
(E) appears to prevent cardiovascular complications from diabetes

37. A patient who believes that he cannot eat because all his guts have rotted may be said to be

(A) hallucinating
(B) delusional
(C) depressed
(D) neurotic
(E) phobic

38. The third aortic arch forms the

(A) maxillary artery
(B) hyoid and stapedial arteries
(C) common carotid artery
(D) pulmonary arch
(E) brachiocephalic artery

39. The foramen rotundum opens the

(A) infratemporal fossa
(B) pterygopalatine fossa
(C) posterior cranial fossa
(D) orbital cavity
(E) oral cavity

40. Which of the following steps is common to both gluconeogenesis and glycolysis?

(A) fructose 6-phosphate to glucose 6-phosphate
(B) pyruvate to oxaloacetate
(C) glucose 6-phosphate to glucose
(D) fructose 1,6-bisphosphate to fructose 6-phosphate
(E) oxaloacetate to phosphoenolpyruvate

41. Interferon causes antiviral resistance by inducing intracellular formation of antiviral proteins that

(A) interfere with adsorption of viruses to host cells
(B) prevent penetration of viruses
(C) inhibit viral uncoating
(D) block transcription of viral nucleic acid
(E) block translation of viral nucleic acid

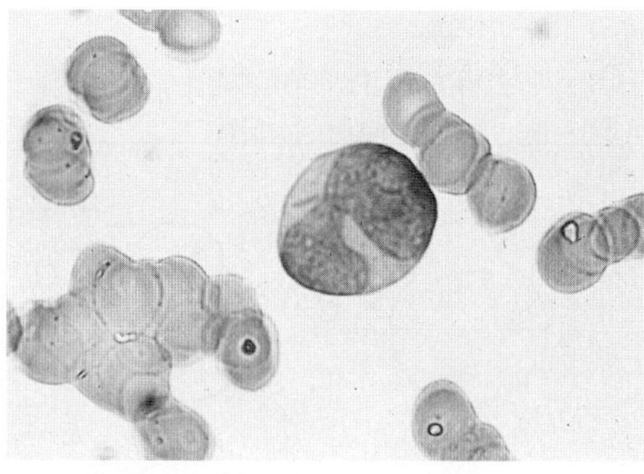

See color insert following page 266. (Photograph courtesy of Chi V. Dang, MD, PhD. From Stobo et al; *The Principles and Practice of Medicine,* 23/E, Appleton & Lange, 1996, plate 8D.)

42. Auer rods are most characteristic of (see figure above)

(A) chronic lymphocytic leukemia
(B) acute lymphoblastic leukemia
(C) chronic myelocytic leukemia
(D) acute myeloblastic leukemia
(E) erythroleukemia (DiGuglielmo's syndrome)

43. The most common problem associated with use of nonsteroidal anti-inflammatory agents, such as ibuprofen and naproxen, is

(A) toxic amblyopia
(B) fluid retention
(C) gastrointestinal complaints
(D) renal failure
(E) drowsiness

44. A 35-year-old man is admitted to the hospital for an elective operation. After 3 days in the hospital, during which various examinations are performed, he receives general anesthesia for an abdominal operation. Two days after the operation he becomes agitated and accusatory, is visibly tremulous, and seems to be hallucinating. In relation to this man's agitation and possible hallucinations, a history of which of the following would have the most immediate relevance in management plans?

(A) schizophrenia in the family
(B) alcoholism
(C) LSD use
(D) depression
(E) traumatic early childhood

45. The tensor veli palatini muscle is innervated by which of the following nerves?

(A) the facial
(B) the trigeminal
(C) the glossopharyngeal

(D) the vagus
(E) the ansa cervicalis

46. At her child's 2-month "well baby" visit, a mother says she is quite distressed that her baby vomits after every feeding. The baby, who weighed 3.4 kg (7 lb, 8 oz) at birth, now weighs 6.0 kg (13 lb, 2 oz) (use chart on page 256). The most likely cause of the baby's vomiting is

(A) pyloric stenosis
(B) overfeeding
(C) adrenogenital syndrome
(D) child abuse
(E) inborn error in metabolism

47. During a routine physical examination, a child is observed to do the following: assume a sitting position without assistance; transfer objects from one hand to the other; stand, but only briefly, by holding someone's hand; and say "ma ma," "ba ba," and "da da." Assuming that the child has had normal growth and development to date, the age of this child is most likely to be

(A) 5 months
(B) 6 months
(C) 8 months
(D) 10 months
(E) 12 months

48. An infant with hyaline membrane disease is being treated with supplemental oxygen. The most accurate way of monitoring this infant's oxygen requirements would be by

(A) serial chest roentgenography
(B) pulmonary function tests
(C) transcutaneous monitoring
(D) capillary blood pH and oxygen content
(E) arterial blood pH and oxygen content

49. A 9-year-old girl has had recurrent pulmonary infections. Chest roentgenography reveals an anterior mediastinal mass. All the following conditions could result in an anterior mediastinal mass EXCEPT

(A) teratoma
(B) thymoma
(C) lymphoma
(D) thymic cyst
(E) bronchogenic cyst

50. Pubertal changes in adolescent girls typically progress in which of the following sequences?

(A) sparse pubic hair, breast buds, darker pubic hair, menarche
(B) sparse pubic hair, breast buds, menarche, darker pubic hair
(C) breast buds, menarche, sparse pubic hair, darker pubic hair
(D) breast buds, sparse pubic hair, menarche, darker pubic hair
(E) breast buds, sparse pubic hair, darker pubic hair, menarche

51. A 57-year-old man complains of severe crushing chest pain while at work; he then collapses. A fellow worker rushes to his aid, notes absence of carotid pulses and spontaneous breathing efforts, and initiates cardiopulmonary resuscitation. The victim is brought to the hospital and, despite continued resuscitative efforts, dies in the emergency room. Which of the following statements is true concerning this type of death?

(A) The vast majority of victims have no underlying cardiac disease.
(B) The precipitating rhythm disturbance is most commonly complete heart block.
(C) Survivors are at increased risk for future infarcts.
(D) Premature ventricular contractions on routine ECG are not associated with increased risk.
(E) It is a relatively rare type of death.

52. An 83-year-old widow has severe left-lower-quadrant abdominal pain, nausea, and vomiting. Her abdomen is distended but compressible, and frequent bowel sounds are heard. Her abdominal roentgenogram is shown on page 257. The next step in management would be

(A) colonoscopy
(B) gastric lavage

GIRLS: BIRTH TO 36 MONTHS PHYSICAL GROWTH NCHS PERCENTILES*

Name ______________________ Record # ____________

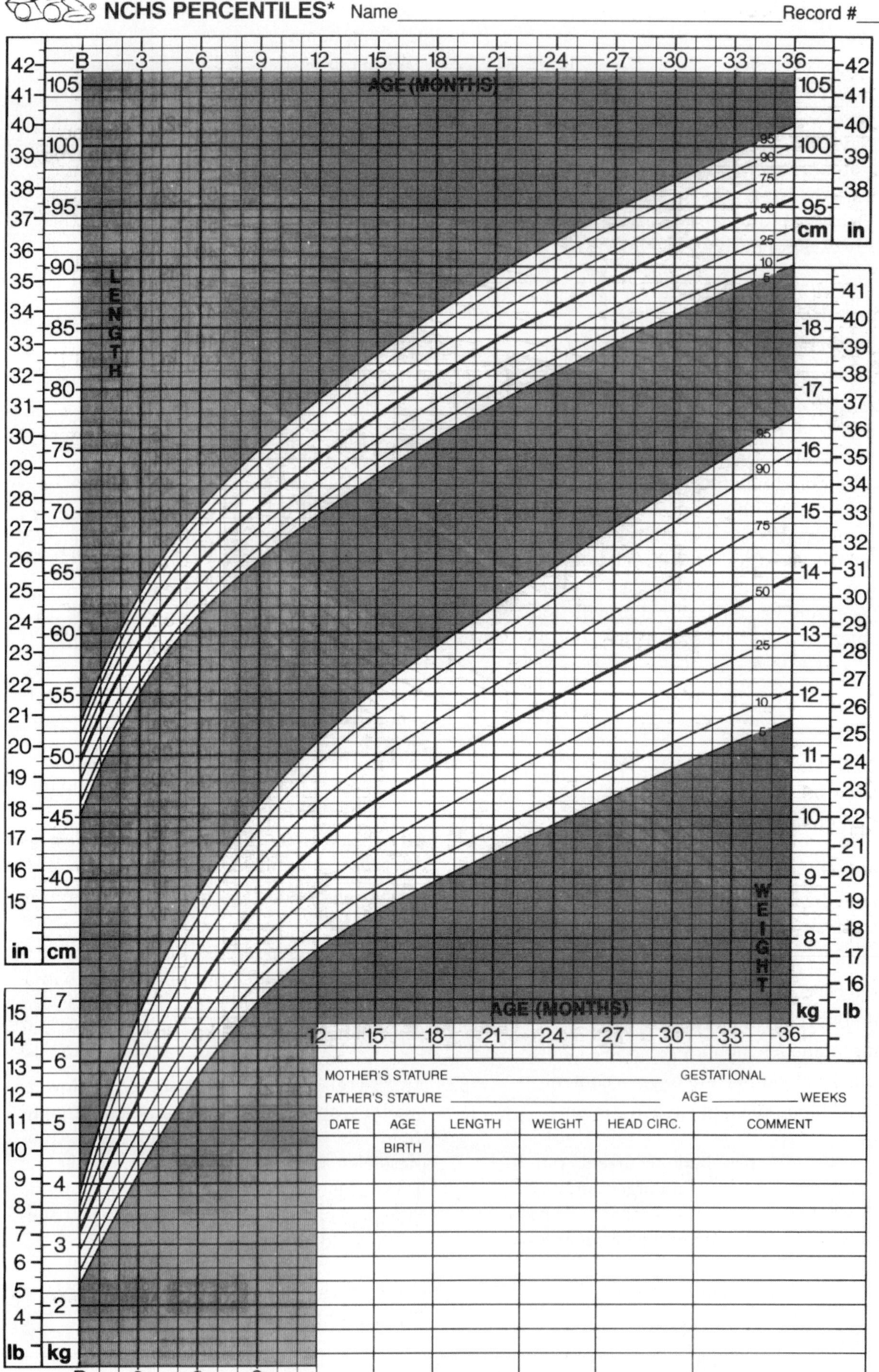

*Adapted from: Hamill PVV, Drizd TA, Johnson CL, Reed RB, Roche AF, Moore WM: Physical growth: National Center for Health Statistics percentiles. AM J CLIN NUTR 32:607-629, 1979. Data from the Fels Longitudinal Study, Wright State University School of Medicine, Yellow Springs, Ohio.

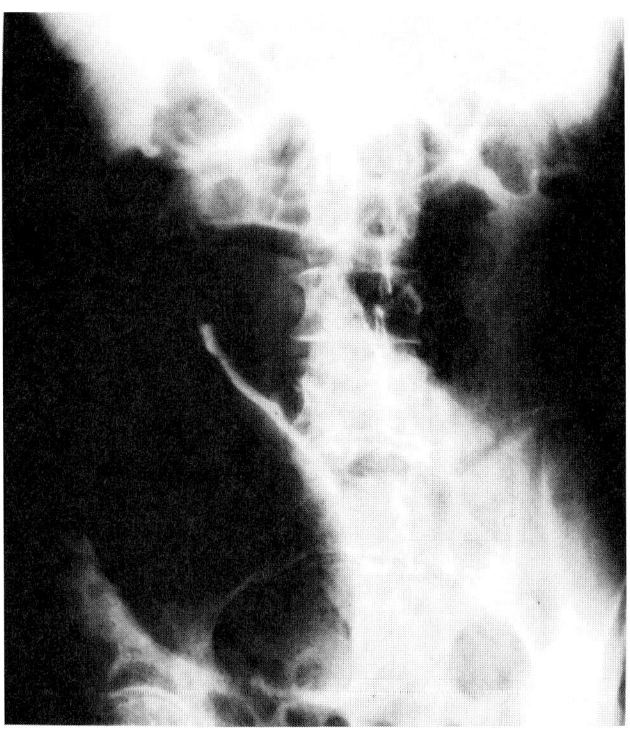

(C) abdominal ultrasonography
(D) hemicolectomy
(E) percutaneous drainage

53. A 29-year-old man has had malaise, myalgias, and chills for 4 weeks. On examination he is slightly jaundiced and has mild right-upper-quadrant tenderness. His SGOT, SGPT, and serum bilirubin levels are all twice normal. Serum serologies are as follows:

hepatitis B surface antigen—negative
hepatitis B e antigen—negative
antibody to hepatitis B surface antigen—negative
antibody to hepatitis B core antigen—positive

These results support the conclusion that the man described

(A) is in the incubation phase of hepatitis B infection
(B) is a chronic carrier of hepatitis B virus
(C) has had a recent hepatitis B infection
(D) has never been exposed to hepatitis B virus
(E) has just been exposed to hepatitis B virus

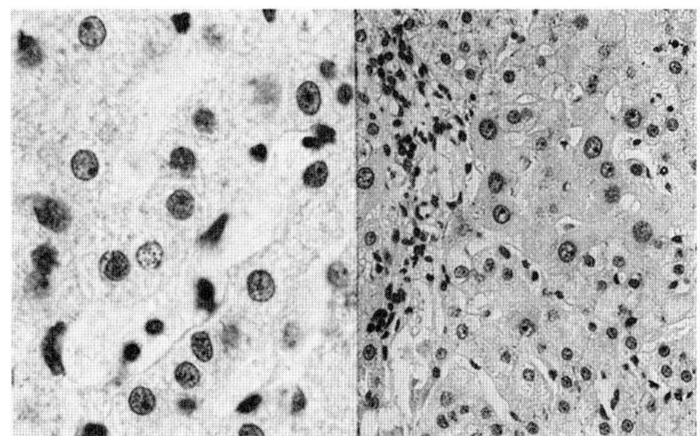

Figure for use with question 53.

See color insert following page 266. (Photograph courtesy of A. Brian West. From Jenson & Baltimore, *Pediatric Infectious Diseases*, Appleton & Lange, 1995, plate 2H.)

54. A 30-year-old sexually active female has had a vaginal discharge for 3 weeks. On pelvic exam she is nontender with a copious gray-white discharge with some bubbles. Wet mount of the discharge shows many epithelial cells and no white blood cells. Gram stain reveals sheets of gram-positive coccobacilli. The MOST likely diagnosis is

(A) gonorrhea
(B) *Chlamydia*
(C) *Trichomonas*
(D) bacterial vaginosis
(E) *Candida*

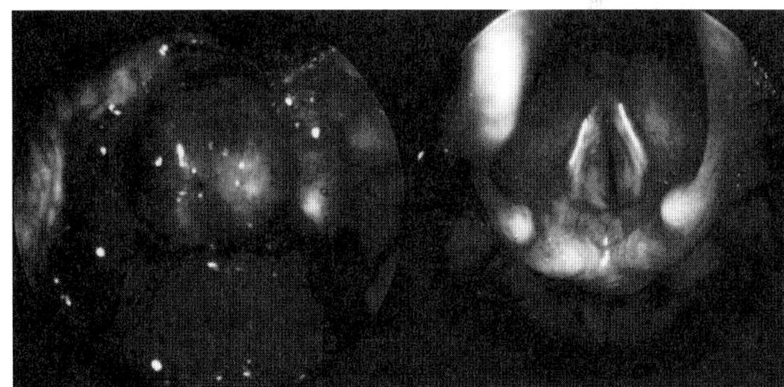

See color insert following page 266. (Photographs courtesy of Bruce Benjamin. From Benjamin B: *A Colour Atlas of Pediatric Otorhinolaryngology.* Martin Dunitz Publishers/JB Lippincott. 1995: 291, 292.)

55. A 4-year-old boy has inspiratory stridor. All the following disorders can cause inspiratory stridor EXCEPT (see figure above)

(A) epiglottitis
(B) acute bronchospasm

(C) infectious laryngotracheitis
(D) aspiration of a foreign body
(E) angioneurotic edema

56. Which of the following diagnostic tests is most likely to reveal osteomyelitis in a child who stepped on a nail 4 days ago?

(A) roentgenogram of the foot
(B) technetium bone scan
(C) gallium bone scan
(D) CT scan of the foot
(E) blood count and sedimentation rate

57. Turner's syndrome is associated with all the following abnormalities EXCEPT

(A) aortic stenosis
(B) coarctation of the aorta
(C) lack of sexual maturation
(D) cubitus valgus
(E) short stature

58. In the initial psychiatric interview, it is most important to

(A) obtain corroborative history
(B) examine cognitive mental status
(C) recognize transference
(D) obtain a patient history
(E) assess motivation for change

59. All the following statements are true concerning erythromycin EXCEPT it

(A) is the drug of choice for *Chlamydia trachomatis* infections
(B) is readily absorbed from the gastrointestinal tract
(C) effectively treats *Campylobacter jejuni* infection
(D) may cause brown discoloration of teeth in newborns
(E) causes frequent symptoms of abdominal pain and vomiting

60. A 67-year-old man has a long history of constipation and recurrent, brief episodes of gripping lower-abdominal pain. He is currently asymptomatic. A recent barium enema roentgenogram is shown on the facing page. Which of the following treatments would be most appropriate?

(A) surgical resection
(B) colonoscopy with biopsy
(C) administration of a histamine receptor antagonist
(D) administration of a corticosteroid rectal enema
(E) high-residue diet

61. In psychiatry, the term *psychosis* best refers to a disorder in

(A) cognition
(B) perception
(C) mood
(D) reality testing
(E) impulse control

62. The most commonly used chemical preservative in the food industry is

(A) sugar
(B) salt
(C) sulfur dioxide
(D) carbon dioxide
(E) benzoic acid

63. All the following statements regarding human breast-feeding or breast milk are correct EXCEPT

(A) human breast milk contains IgA
(B) human breast milk contains human macrophages
(C) newborns being breast-fed should receive supplemental iron
(D) infants being exclusively breast fed should receive supplemental fluoride after 6 months of age
(E) infants being exclusively breast fed should receive supplemental vitamin C

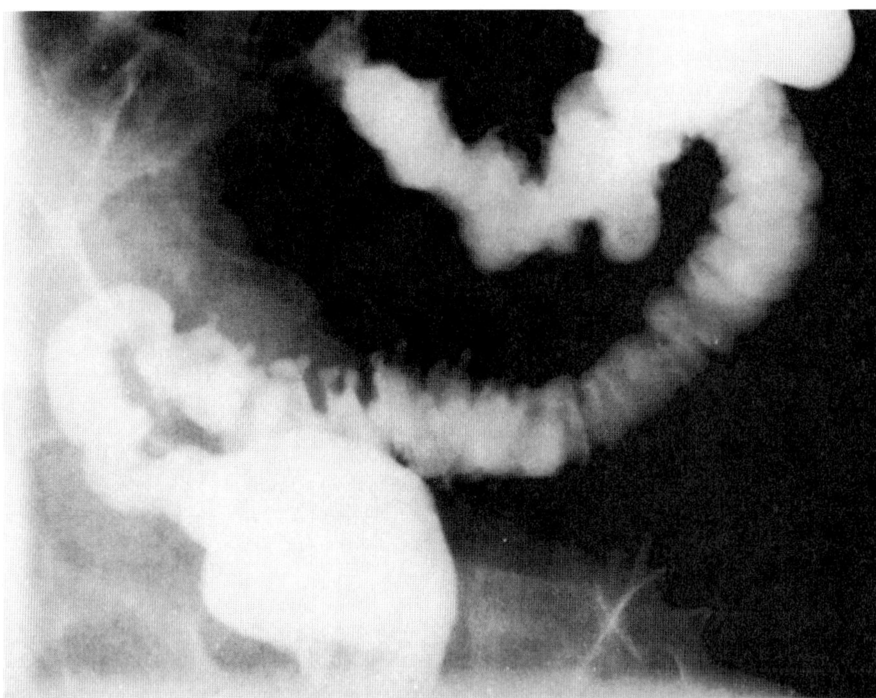

Figure for use with question 60.

64. A slightly drowsy 42-year-old man is admitted with severe diabetic ketoacidosis, nausea, serum potassium of 6.1 mEq/L, and a BUN of 46 mg/dL (see figure lower right). Which of the following statements is correct regarding this patient?

(A) Despite the high serum potassium, his total body potassium is depleted and potassium replacement should be started at once.
(B) The elevated potassium is mostly caused by renal insufficiency.
(C) Initial replacement should consist of 120 mEq of potassium given orally over a 4-hour period.
(D) Administration of bicarbonate to treat the acidosis may hasten the development of hypokalemia and magnify its intensity.
(E) Intravenous administration of potassium is safer than oral administration in this patient.

65. The most common cause of a lower gastrointestinal bleed is

(A) colon cancer
(B) upper GI bleed
(C) colonic diverticuli
(D) colonic arteriovenous malformation
(E) colonic at adenomatous polyp

66. Bacterial contamination is LEAST likely to occur with which of the following commercial methods of food storage?

(A) pasteurization
(B) canning
(C) refrigeration
(D) freezing
(E) drying

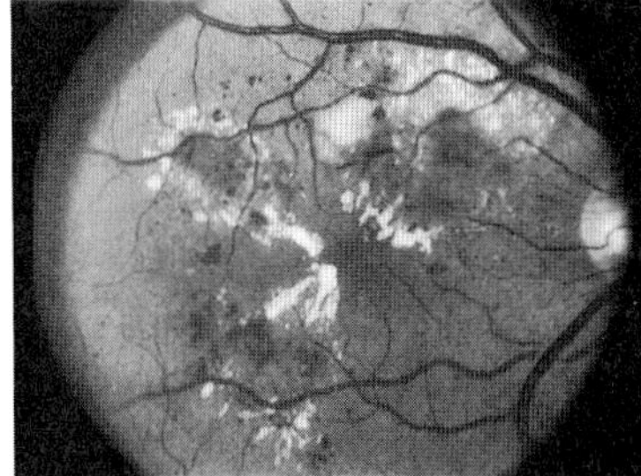

See color insert following page 266. (Photograph courtesy of Andrew P. Schachat, MD. From Stobo, *The Principles and Practice of Medicine,* 23/E, Appleton & Lange, 1996, plate 7B.)

67. All the following statements regarding brain tumors in children are true EXCEPT

(A) seizures are the most common presenting complaint
(B) short stature is occasionally the presenting sign
(C) sexual precocity is occasionally the presenting sign
(D) approximately half of the tumors arise in the posterior fossa
(E) half or more of the tumors occur in the midline

68. A 39-year-old woman has the sudden onset of weakness and "fluttering" in her chest. She is pale; her pulse is 160/min and irregularly irregular; and her blood pressure is 82/64 mm Hg. Her ECG is shown below. Immediate treatment of choice is

(A) digitalis
(B) verapamil
(C) quinidine
(D) coumarin
(E) cardioversion

69. Seminoma of the testicle is correctly described by all of the following statements EXCEPT

(A) it is the most common germinal testicular tumor
(B) it is more prevalent in cryptorchidism
(C) it is highly radioresistant
(D) it spreads through the lymphatics
(E) prognosis is excellent

70. Antidepressant medications would be least effective in the treatment of

(A) bulimia
(B) obsessive–compulsive disorder
(C) delusional (paranoid) disorder
(D) panic disorder
(E) atypical depression

71. Under Social Security Administration (SSA) rules, a disabled worker is described as one who

(A) can no longer perform the same type of work as previously
(B) can no longer perform the same amount of work as previously
(C) can no longer work at all
(D) can no longer engage in gainful activity
(E) has not been able to work for 6 months or more

72. A drug of choice for treating children who have petit mal or absence seizure is

(A) ethosuximide
(B) phenytoin
(C) diazepam
(D) diphenhydramine
(E) phenobarbital

73. A 28-year-old man has the acute onset of gross hematuria and colicky pain in the left costovertebral angle radiating into the groin. Abdominal roentgenography discloses a stone in the left ureter. The man spontaneously passes the stone. The most likely cause of this stone is

(A) chronic urinary tract infections
(B) vitamin D excess
(C) primary hyperparathyroidism
(D) idiopathic hypercalciuria
(E) gout

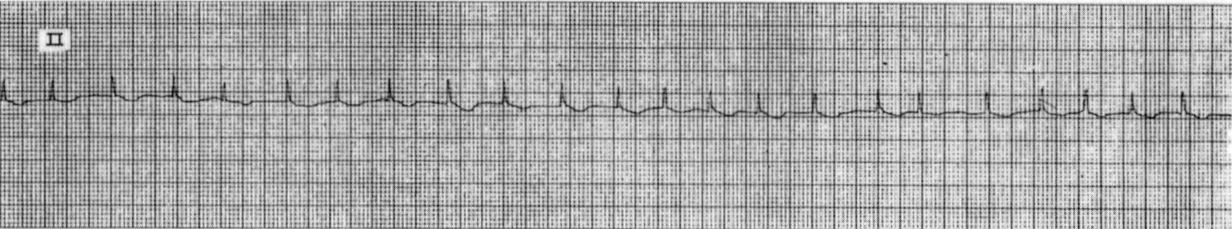

Figure for use with question 68.

74. All the following statements concerning pericardial tamponade are correct EXCEPT

(A) central venous pressure is elevated
(B) pulse pressure is elevated
(C) left atrial pressure measurement is not helpful in the diagnosis
(D) normal cardiac shadow on chest roentgenogram does not rule out the diagnosis
(E) pericardiocentesis is helpful in the diagnosis

75. A 30-year-old man is brought unconscious to the local emergency room. Supportive measures are initiated. Physical examination is remarkable for hyperactive deep-tendon reflexes and abdominal scars that suggest numerous surgical procedures. The man is admitted for intensive care observation. A few hours later he becomes responsive but screams that he is blind. Neurologic work-up is unremarkable; a CT scan of the head is negative, although he refuses the contrast-dye study because of allergy. Upon entering the man's room the next morning, his physician finds him reading. When confronted, the man becomes angry and storms out of the hospital. The most likely diagnosis is

(A) chronic factitious disorder
(B) conversion disorder
(C) antisocial personality disorder
(D) schizophrenia
(E) drug abuse

76. Nosocomial infections lead to excess health care cost. In terms of the proportion of excess direct cost in U.S. hospitals, the most costly are infections of the

(A) urinary tract
(B) surgical wound
(C) respiratory tract
(D) bloodstream
(E) other nosocomial infections

77. A 22-year-old primigravid woman is in premature labor at 30 weeks' gestation. Despite administration of tocolytics to stop labor, it appears that she is likely to deliver soon. Pulmonary maturity in the fetus might be enhanced by the administration of

(A) magnesium sulfate
(B) betamethasone
(C) hydroxyprogesterone
(D) chloroprocaine
(E) bupivacaine

78. Each of the following statements regarding basal skull fractures is true EXCEPT they

(A) can result in ecchymosis around the eyes (raccoon eyes sign)
(B) can cause ecchymosis over the mastoid bone (Battle's sign)
(C) may be associated with nasal leakage of cerebrospinal fluid
(D) may be associated with increased risk of bacterial meningitis
(E) are generally recognized on plain skull roentgenographic films

79. A 74-year-old woman presents with progressive lethargy, anorexia, and weight loss. She appears dehydrated. Her temperature is 38.9°C (102°F); pulse is 100/min; respirations are 20/min; and blood pressure is 80/40 mm/Hg. Serum sodium is 169 mEq/L; potassium is 4.7 mEq/L; BUN is 89 mg/dL; creatinine 2 mg/dL; and glucose is 88 mg/dL. Initial fluid management should be started with

(A) 5% dextose and water
(B) 5% dextose and water with 20 mEq/L of potassium chloride
(C) Half normal saline
(D) 5% dextose, half normal saline
(E) 5% dextose, normal saline

80. A patient receiving prophylactic oral ampicillin develops colicky abdominal pain, diarrhea, fever, abdominal distention, and leukocytosis. Sigmoidoscopic examination reveals yellowish-white, raised mucosal plaques separated by edematous hyperemic mucosa. The antibiotic of choice for treating this condition is

(A) clindamycin
(B) penicillin
(C) metronidazole
(D) sulfa preparations
(E) erythromycin

81. Central dopamine receptor blockade is the mechanism of action of which of the following classes of psychotropic drugs?

(A) antipsychotics
(B) antidepressants
(C) anxiolytics
(D) hypnotics
(E) antiparkinsonian drugs

82. Which of the following statements about the chi-square test is false?

(A) It is designed to compare two proportions in paired or independent samples.
(B) It can be expanded to the comparison of several proportions.
(C) It can compare measured quantities, ranks, or percentages.
(D) It involves the concept of degrees of freedom.
(E) It is a relatively simple formula to understand and apply.

83. A pregnant insulin-requiring diabetic woman is receiving weekly nonstress tests. Her nonstress test at 32 weeks is somewhat equivocal. It is repeated the next day and still found to be equivocal. An oxytocin challenge test is performed, which is read as showing no distress. The proper procedure at this point would be to

(A) repeat the nonstress test in 5 to 7 days
(B) perform an emergency cesarean section
(C) order daily estriol determinations
(D) perform amniocentesis to determine the lecithin/sphingomyelin (L/S) ratio
(E) order daily human placental lactogen determinations

84. A previously well 8-month-old child is brought to the hospital because of the onset of cyanosis. Except for the presence of cyanosis, which is not relieved by oxygen, physical examination is entirely within normal limits. Arterial blood gas obtained while the child is breathing room air reveals a pH of 7.35 and a Po_2 of 90 torr. The most appropriate drug to administer for this child would be

(A) furosemide
(B) physostigmine
(C) atropine
(D) methylene blue
(E) amyl nitrite

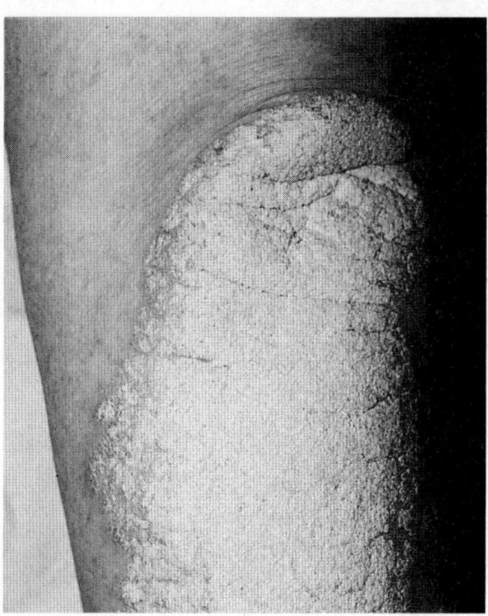

See color insert following page 266. (Photograph courtesy of Antoinette F. Hood, MD. From Stobo, *The Principles and Practice of Medicine*, 23/E, Appleton & Lange, 1996, plate 5A.)

85. A 52-year-old man presents with widespread psoriasis (see above). The most likely associated laboratory finding is

(A) hypercalcemia
(B) hypophosphatemia
(C) hypomagnesemia
(D) hyperuricemia
(E) hypokalemia

86. A 75-year-old man comes to the emergency room because of pain in the abdomen and back. He is found to be hypotensive, with a pulsatile, tender abdominal mass. The correct management of this man consists of

(A) immediate transfer to the operating room
(B) immediate sonography
(C) immediate CT scan
(D) immediate administration of intravenous fluids
(E) work-up in the emergency room to rule out myocardial infarction

87. In the work-up of which of the following individuals would a CT scan of the brain be LEAST indicated?

(A) A 51-year-old woman with confusion of unknown etiology.
(B) A 68-year-old man with dementia of unknown etiology.
(C) A 19-year-old man with a newly discovered psychosis.
(D) A 38-year-old woman with a newly discovered major depression.
(E) A 60-year-old woman with a dramatic change in personality.

88. An 18-year-old male student comes to you for a precollege physical examination. He states that he drinks alcoholic beverages at least twice each week, and when he does he normally consumes a six-pack. On this evidence, you should advise him that

(A) any consumption of alcoholic beverage above this limit will be dangerous to his health
(B) men should not drink more than six "units" of alcohol a day
(C) he is at no greater risk for illness than his peers
(D) women are at the same risk as men in relation to alcohol consumption

89. All of the following would be considered acceptable therapy for carcinoma in situ of the cervix EXCEPT

(A) cryosurgery
(B) cold-knife conization of the cervix
(C) laser conization of the cervix
(D) total hysterectomy
(E) radical hysterectomy

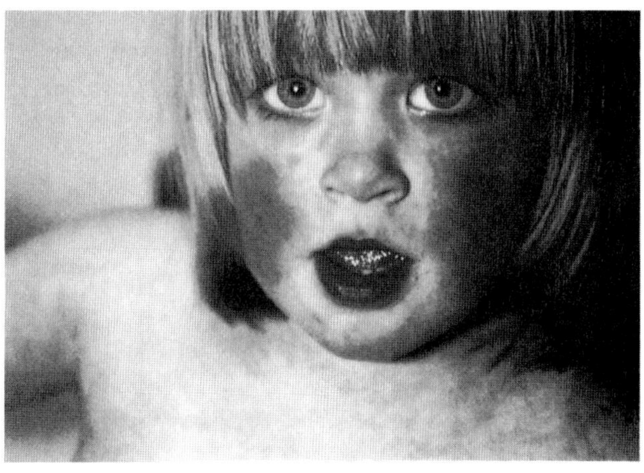

See color insert following page 266. (Photograph courtesy of Henry M. Feder, Jr. From Jenson & Baltimore, *Pediatric Infectious Diseases*, Appleton & Lange, 1995, plate 3F.)

90. A 7-year-old boy has red cheeks that have a slapped appearance. He also has a generalized rash in a lacy, reticular pattern (see above). The most likely diagnosis is

(A) rubeola
(B) rubella
(C) popsicle panniculitis
(D) Kawasaki's disease
(E) erythema infectiosum

91. Concerning insulinoma, all the following statements are true EXCEPT

(A) the tumor is frequent during the fourth to seventh decades of life
(B) the diagnostic feature is the association of low blood sugar with a high insulin level
(C) approximately 10% of the tumors are malignant
(D) angiography localizes the majority of the tumors
(E) streptozocin is useful in treating malignant tumors

92. The insanity defense in American jurisprudence is correctly described by which of the following statements?

(A) The insanity defense is invoked often in U.S. court cases.

(B) The insanity defense often is successful in U.S. court cases.
(C) Laws toughening the criminal justice system would likely lead to decreased use of the insanity defense.
(D) "Insanity" is a medical term, not a legal term.
(E) The definition of insanity varies from state to state.

93. Which organism is discovered to be most responsible as a pathogen for diseases of the lower respiratory tract (pneumonia) in acute care hospitals in the United States?

(A) *Pseudomonas*
(B) *Staphylococcus*
(C) *Klebsiella*
(D) *Enterobacter*
(E) *Escherichia coli*

94. Glomerulonephritis is recognized as a complication of β-hemolytic streptococcal infections (see figure below). Which of the following statements regarding this condition is true?

(A) It most frequently occurs in children between the ages of 10 and 14 years.
(B) Males are affected twice as often as females.
(C) All strains of streptococci are equally associated.
(D) It frequently recurs.
(E) The prevalence is similar in most population groups.

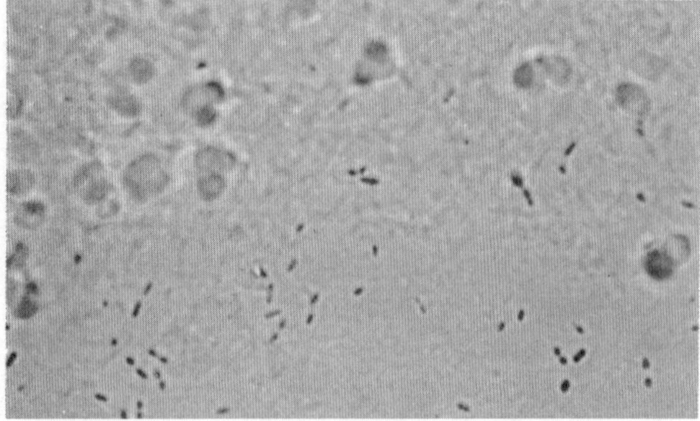

See color insert following page 266. (Photograph courtesy of Joseph M. Campos. From Jenson & Baltimore, *Pediatric Infectious Diseases,* Appleton & Lange, 1995, plate 1B.)

DIRECTIONS (Questions 95 through 100): Each of the numbered items or incomplete statements in this section is followed by answers or by completions of the statement. Select ONE (OR MORE) lettered answer(s) or completion(s) for each case.

95. Phosphorylation activates or inhibits the following enzymes. (SELECT 4)

(A) isocitrate dehydrogenase
(B) lipoprotein lipase
(C) triacylglycerol lipase
(D) acetyl-CoA carboxylase
(E) glycogen synthase
(F) aspartate carbamoylase
(G) phosphorylase kinase

96. Which of the following sedatives do not have pharmacologically active metabolites that prolong the duration of action of the drug? (SELECT 3)

(A) temazepam
(B) chlordiazepoxide
(C) diazepam
(D) lorazepam
(E) clorazepate
(F) flurazepam
(G) quazepam
(H) oxazepam

97. Which of the following statements concerning homosexuality are correct? (SELECT 3)

(A) Onset of same-sex erotic feelings always occur well past adolescence.
(B) Genetic and biologic factors may play an important role in homosexuality.
(C) American Psychiatric Association's diagnostic manual defines homosexuality as a psychiatric disorder.
(D) Female–female relationships tend to be more stable than male–male relationships.
(E) "Coming out" may be an important milestone.

98. The pituitary prohormone proopiomelanocortin is the precursor of the following hormones. (SELECT 4)

(A) thyroid-stimulating hormone (TSH)
(B) melanocyte-stimulating hormone (MSH)
(C) adrenocorticotropin (ACTH)
(D) cortisol
(E) β-endorphin
(F) follicle-stimulating hormone (FSH)
(G) γ-lipotropin

99. Which of the following phrases correctly characterize delusions? (SELECT 3)

(A) false beliefs incongruent with an individual's experience
(B) common in schizophrenic disorders
(C) common in anxiety disorders
(D) common in personality disorders
(E) resistant to empathic and logical argument

100. From the following list, select the 4 systemic diseases most known to present with generalized pruritis.

(A) chronic renal failure
(B) pseudogout
(C) systemic lupus erythematosus
(D) primary biliary cirrhosis
(E) polycythemia vera
(F) Wegener's granulomatosis
(G) hyperthyroidism
(H) relapsing polycondritis

DIRECTIONS (Questions 101 through 120): Each group of items in this section consists of a list of lettered headings followed by a set of numbered words or phrases. For each numbered word or phrase, select the ONE lettered heading that is MOST closely associated with it.

Questions 101 through 103

For each description below, choose the organ with which it is associated.

(A) muscle
(B) liver
(C) red blood cell
(D) brain
(E) adipose tissue

101. Uses only glucose for energy but can adapt to use ketone bodies after long periods of starvation

102. Releases free fatty acids to the bloodstream

103. Produces ketone bodies

Question 104

For the statement below, choose the MOST appropriate virus.

(A) influenza virus
(B) rubeola virus
(C) human immunodeficiency virus
(D) poliomyelitis virus
(E) herpes virus

104. Antibodies to viral core protein p24 or the viral envelope glycoprotein gp46 are of diagnostic value

Question 105

(A) rifampin
(B) erythromycin
(C) quinolone
(D) chloramphenicol
(E) gentamicin

105. Binds to the alpha subunit of DNA gyrase

Question 106

(A) yellow fever virus
(B) smallpox virus
(C) corona virus
(D) polyoma virus
(E) influenza virus

106. Hemagglutination mediated by what is called H or HA glycoprotein

Questions 107 and 108

For each statement below choose the MOST appropriate condition listed.

(A) chondroma
(B) osteogenic sarcoma
(C) osteoid osteoma
(D) chondrosarcoma
(E) multiple endochondromatosis

107. A benign tumor composed of bone and osteoid

108. A malignant tumor composed of cartilage

Questions 108 through 110

For each of the following agents, select the pharmacologic effect with which it is associated.

(A) blockade of muscarinic receptors
(B) selective blockade of β_1-adrenergic receptors
(C) inhibition of breakdown of cholinergic neurotransmitters
(D) stimulation of α_1-adrenergic receptors
(E) blockade of nicotinic receptors

109. *d*-Tubocurarine

110. Physostigmine

111. Atropine

Questions 112 and 113

For each congenital condition listed below, select the genetic screening test most commonly employed for its detection.

(A) fetal blood sampling
(B) amniotic fluid cell culture
(C) amniotic fluid analysis
(D) maternal urinalysis
(E) ultrasonography

112. Achondroplasia

113. Open meningomyelocele

Questions 114 through 117

For each class of psychoactive drug, select the specific agent that is a member of that class.

(A) phenelzine
(B) amitriptyline
(C) benztropine
(D) clonazepam
(E) fluoxetine

114. Tricyclic antidepressant

115. Selective serotonin reuptake inhibitor

116. MAO inhibitor

117. Benzodiazepine

Questions 118 through 120

For each of the organizations listed below, choose the type of health care planning with which it is usually associated.

(A) population-based planning
(B) institution-based planning
(C) financial planning
(D) program planning
(E) morbidity planning

118. Local health department or health systems agency

119. Prepaid health plan or health maintenance organization (HMO)

120. Maternal and child health care system

SETTING I: UNSCHEDULED PATIENTS

Unscheduled patients seeking both urgent and routine care are encountered in both office and clinic settings. The following case studies reflect those types you might encounter in this setting.

DIRECTIONS (Questions 121 through 130): Each of the numbered items or incomplete statements

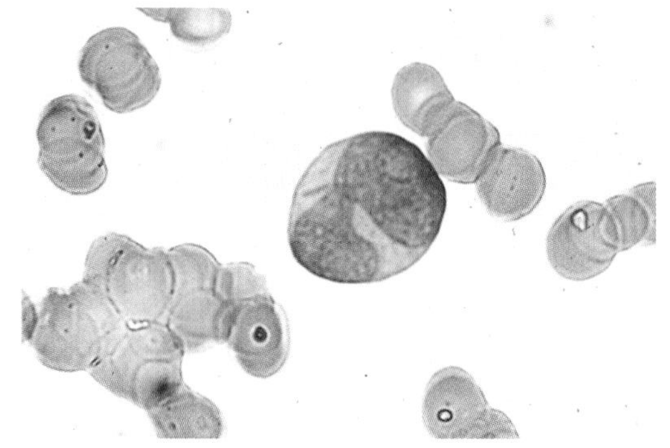

Question 42. *(Photograph courtesy of Chi V. Dang, MD, PhD)*

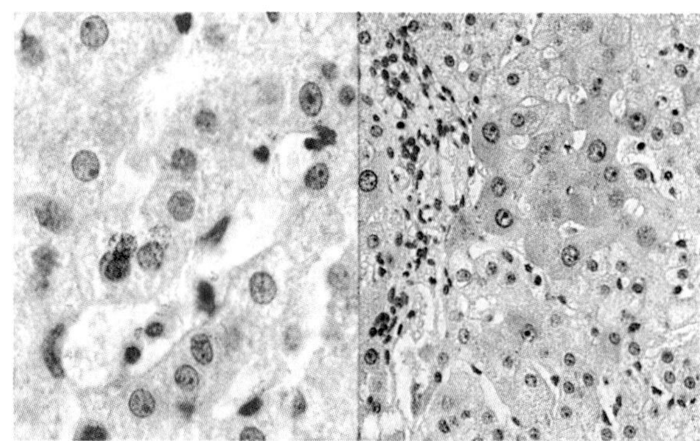

Question 53. *(Photograph courtesy of A. Brian West)*

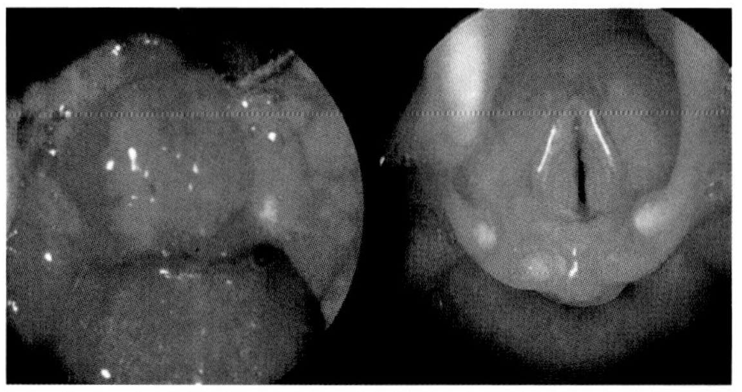

Question 55. *(Photographs courtesy of Bruce Benjamin. From Benjamin B: A Colour Atlas of Pediatric Otorhinolaryngology. Martin Dunitz Publishers/JB Lippincott. 1995. 291, 292)*

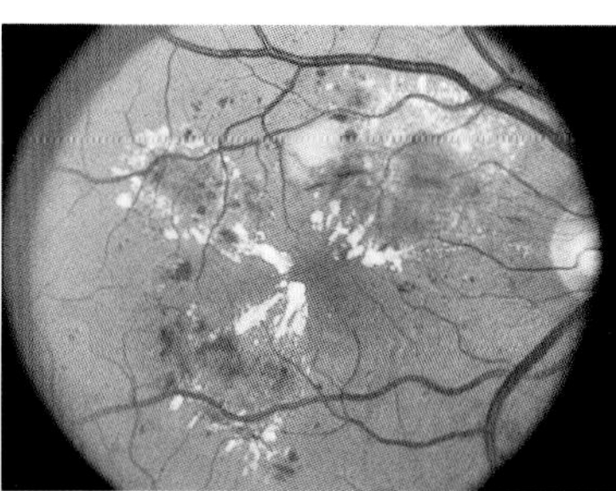

Question 64. *(Photograph courtesy of Andrew P. Schachat, MD)*

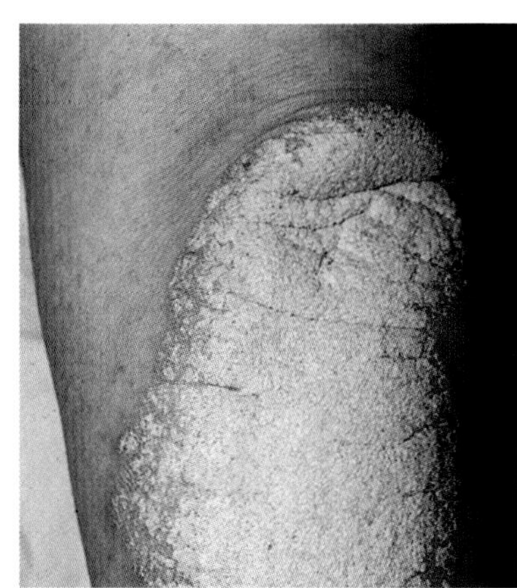

Question 85. *(Photograph courtesy of Antoinette F. Hood, MD)*

Question 90. *(Photograph courtesy of Henry M. Feder, Jr.)*

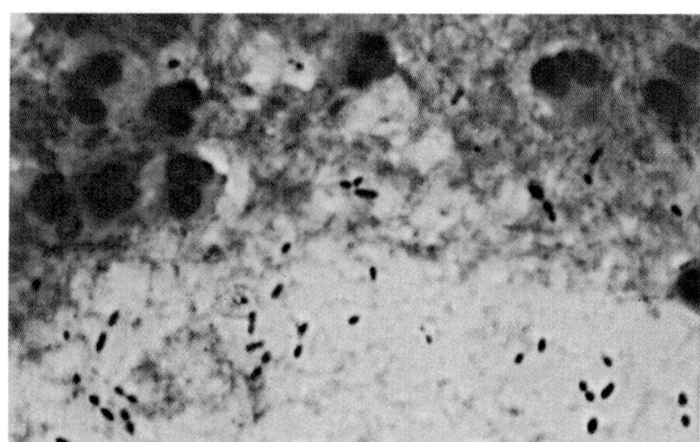

Question 94. *(Photograph courtesy of Joseph M. Campos)*

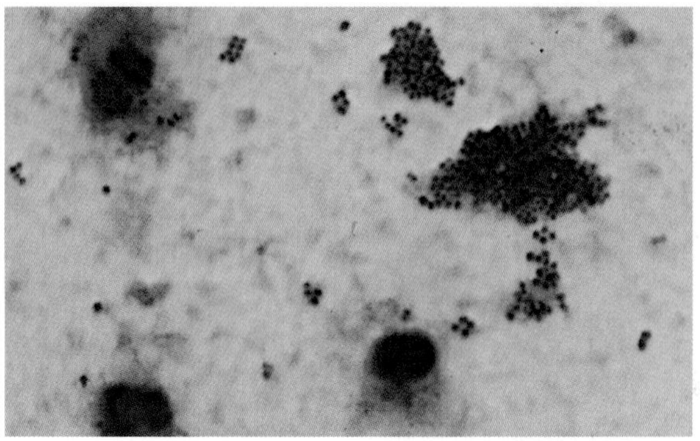

Question 141. *(Photograph courtesy of Joseph M. Campos)*

in this section is followed by answers or by completions of the statement. Select the ONE lettered answer or completion that is BEST in each case.

Questions 121 through 124

An 83-year-old woman has her blood pressure checked in the shopping mall. During the test, the nurse asks her if she has had any headaches during the past few months and the woman says yes. The nurse advises her to see her doctor. She calls her doctor's office, and he is out of town. She becomes nervous and decides not to wait for his return. She comes to you because you are the doctor covering for hers. She presents with a blood pressure of 185/85 mm Hg. Blood pressure assessments are repeated during the next three visits scheduled over the next 3 months, and persistently elevated systolic pressures are noted.

121. What is the most appropriate step in this patient's care?

(A) follow-up for repeat blood pressure visit in 1 month
(B) initiation of nonpharmacologic approach to blood pressure management
(C) initiation of diuretic therapy
(D) initiation of diuretic therapy and ACE inhibitor therapy
(E) 24-hour blood pressure monitoring

122. This patient had numerous cardiovascular changes that accompany normal aging. In comparing resting heart rate and exercise heart rate between this 83-year-old patient and a 33-year-old patient, the older patient has

(A) a lower resting heart rate and a higher heart rate with exercise
(B) a higher resting heart rate and a lower heart rate with exercise
(C) similar resting heart rate and similar heart rate with exercise
(D) similar resting heart rate and a lower heart rate with exercise
(E) a lower resting heart rate and a lower heart rate with exercise

123. The average life expectancy of this patient is

(A) 1 to 2 years
(B) 2 to 4 years
(C) 5 to 9 years
(D) 10 years or greater
(E) difficult to determine as the patient is already over the expected national average of life expectancy

124. The fastest growing group in America is patients 80 years and older. Which of the following most likely represents the relation between longevity and disability?

(A) People are living longer than ever and increasingly are in good health up to the last few weeks of life.
(B) While the average life expectancy is not changing, we are seeing less and less chronic illness.
(C) People are living longer than ever before, but more and more people are doing so with increased burdens of disability for increasing years before death.
(D) The maximum achievable human lifespan is likely to increase 10 years by the year 2030.
(E) There is no clear relationship between longevity and disability noted.

Questions 125 through 127

An 86-year-old man gets lost while trying to go to the grocery store he has been shopping in for the past 15 years. His daughter is upset by this because she is leaving town for a couple of days and concerned for her father's welfare while she is gone. She decides to bring him to the office for a checkup. She reports that family members are concerned about her father, as they have noted increasing memory impairment over the past year.

125. The most common cause of memory impairment (dementia) like the patient's is

(A) Alzheimer's disease
(B) cerebrovascular accidents
(C) old age
(D) excessive medication use
(E) carotid artery stenosis

126. The initial management of memory impairment (dementia) in this patient should include

(A) use of multiple psychoactive agents
(B) environmental cues and reorientation
(C) acute hospitalization in the supervised setting
(D) vitamin therapy
(E) attention to the patient's advanced directives

127. The best office assessment test for dementia concerns evaluation of

(A) orientation
(B) registration
(C) attention and calculation
(D) recall
(E) language

Questions 128 through 130

An active 75-year-old woman relocates to your town for a warmer climate. She has hypertension, arthritis, and diabetes and decides to visit the office upon moving in. Her medication regimen includes hydrochlorothiazide, potassium elixir, diltiazem, acetaminophen, ibuprofen, and glipizide.

128. The factor most related to compliance with the medication regimen is

(A) age
(B) number of drugs in the regimen
(C) gender
(D) number of comorbid diseases
(E) use of tablets versus use of elixirs

129. Changes with age in the ability to handle drugs is noted for all of the following processes EXCEPT

(A) absorption
(B) distribution into fat
(C) distribution into water
(D) excretion
(E) metabolism

130. Six weeks after the initial clinic visit, the patient is seen again for complaints of urinary incontinence. Causal factors related to this incontinence include all of the following EXCEPT

(A) calcium channel blockers
(B) restricted mobility
(C) impaired mentation
(D) loss of functioning nephrons
(E) diabetes

SETTING II: SCHEDULED APPOINTMENTS

This is an office setting where most patients are seen by appointment. Most of the patients would be known to you; however, you sometimes see patients of your associates. The following case studies reflect those types you might encounter in this setting.

DIRECTIONS (Questions 131 through 154): Each of the numbered items or incomplete statements in this section is followed by answers or by completions of the statement. Select ONE (OR MORE) lettered answer(s) or completion(s) for each case.

Questions 131 through 136

An 84-year-old hypertensive white male is brought into the office by his daughter. He is a heavy smoker and for the past 4 months has been known to have carcinoma of the lung, for which he has refused treatment. The daughter reports that her father has shown increasing confusion and lethargy over the previous 3 weeks. The daughter requests that you determine the source of his confusion. Physical examination is normal except for a blood pressure of 156/94, early hypertensive retinopathy, a palpable bladder, scattered pulmonary rhonchi, and a very enlarged prostate.

131. Which of the following is the most likely cause for the patient's confusion?

(A) Wernicke's encephalopathy
(B) prostate cancer

(C) cerebrovascular accident
(D) hypercalcemia
(E) uremia

132. Laboratory studies demonstrate a hemoglobin of 11.6, white blood cell count of 12.5, blood urea nitrogen of 87, serum creatinine of 4.8, and mildly abnormal liver function tests. Which of the following studies should be ordered next?

(A) CT scan of the chest
(B) intravenous pyelogram
(C) plain film of the kidneys, ureter, and bladder
(D) ultrasound of the abdomen
(E) retrograde ureterography

133. The most appropriate additional diagnostic procedure at this time is

(A) suprapubic aspiration
(B) repeat rectal examination
(C) cystoscopy
(D) insertion of a Foley catheter
(E) pelvic ultrasound

134. Outlet obstruction may be ruled out if

(A) suprapubic aspiration reveals pyuria
(B) less than 30 mL of urine are obtained by catheterization
(C) KUB films are negative
(D) physician is unable to pass Foley catheter
(E) renal arteriography is normal

135. While appropriate diagnosis is made and initial treatment begun, the patient is noted to be increasingly lethargic and confused. Repeat BUN is found to be 98, with a creatinine of 5, potassium of 6, and blood pressure of 88/60. He refuses to be admitted to the hospital. Of the following options, which should be considered? (SELECT 4)

(A) increased ingestion of magnesium compounds
(B) restriction of protein intake
(C) expansion of volume
(D) adjustment of total caloric intake to 35 to 50 kcal/kg/day
(E) correction of acidosis
(F) admit patient against his will
(G) place peritoneal catheter for outpatient dialysis

136. Despite conservative measures, the patient becomes progressively lethargic and expires. The greatest fear of the dying patient is

(A) pain and loss of control
(B) how the survivors will manage
(C) suffering alone and being deserted
(D) financial

Questions 137 through 145

A 34-year-old white male presents to the office with a 2-month history of low-grade fever, weight loss, easy fatigability, and anorexia. He admits to a history of IV drug abuse. Physical examination is positive for subungual splinter hemorrhages. Cardiac auscultation is unremarkable. Laboratory studies include a negative HIV test, normochromic, normocytic anemia with a normal white blood cell count. Rheumatoid factor is positive.

137. The most likely diagnosis at this stage of evaluation would be

(A) false negative HIV infection
(B) rheumatoid arthritis
(C) infective endocarditis
(D) pyelonephritis
(E) tuberculosis

138. Appropriate additional studies confirm a diagnosis of infective endocarditis. Which of the following statements is correct?

(A) Up to 40% of patients have no murmur.
(B) Clubbing and massive splenomegaly are common.
(C) Retinal infarcts may be noted.
(D) Osler's nodes are nontender nodules on the palms and soles.
(E) A single positive blood culture is adequate to make the diagnosis of infective endocarditis.

139. The pathogenesis of infective endocarditis involves all of the following EXCEPT

(A) endothelial damage secondary to turbulent flow across a valve lesion
(B) vegetations secondary to platelet-fibrin thrombus
(C) transient bacteremia seeding from the sinuses, gums, or other locations
(D) multiplication of the bacteria outside the thrombus
(E) extension of infection to supporting valve structures

140. Of the following, which condition is MOST likely to be associated with infective endocarditis?

(A) chronic CHF
(B) chronic atrial fibrillation
(C) atrial septal defect
(D) mitral valve prolapse without mumur
(E) aortic stenosis

141. In the case presented, the most common infecting organism would be (see figure below)

(A) group D streptococci
(B) *Streptococcus viridans*
(C) gram-negative bacilli
(D) *Staphylococcus aureus*
(E) fungi

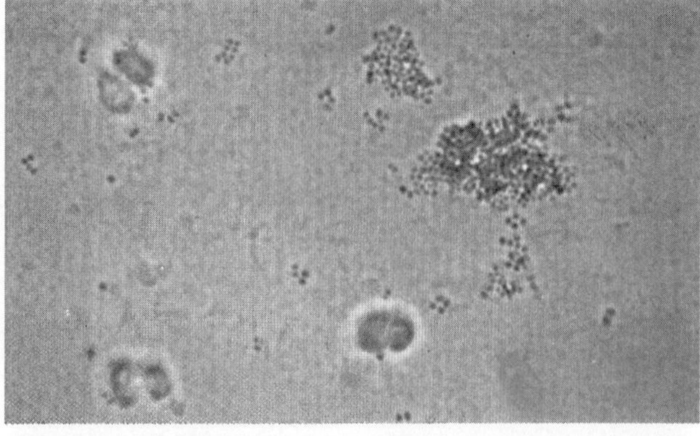

See color insert following page 266. (Photograph courtesy of Joseph M. Campos. From Jenson & Baltimore, *Pediatric Infectious Diseases*, Appleton & Lange, 1995, plate 1A.)

142. In the case presented, the most common valve affected would be

(A) tricuspid
(B) mitral
(C) aortic
(D) pulmonary

143. Treatment of infective endocarditis should include high-enough antimicrobial concentration to eradicate all microorganisms from the vegetation. For enterococcal endocarditis, which of the following is MOST effective?

(A) cephalosporins
(B) penicillin G
(C) penicillin plus an aminoglycoside
(D) vancomycin
(E) nafcillin

144. The most common cause of recurrent fever during treatment of infective endocarditis is

(A) drug reaction
(B) drug resistance
(C) noncompliance
(D) factitious
(E) emboli

145. Complications of infective endocarditis include (SELECT 4)

(A) glomerulonephritis
(B) arthritis
(C) myocarditis
(D) meningitis
(E) urethritis
(F) urticaria
(G) iritis
(H) otitis

146. A thirty-year-old female with mitral valve prolapse and a murmur should receive endocarditis prophylaxis for (SELECT 3)

(A) flexible bronchoscopy
(B) flexible sigmoidoscopy
(C) tonsillectomy
(D) root canal
(E) vaginal delivery

(F) vaginal hysterectomy
(G) cystoscopy
(H) upper endoscopy

Questions 147 through 150

A 16-year-old female presents to the office with a 2-week history of lethargy, low-grade fever, sore throat, and swollen glands. She has been absent from school during this time and has not yet sought medical care. She reports being exposed to a friend with mononucleosis 50 days previously. Examination is remarkable only for a temperature of 100.2°F and epitrochlear adenopathy.

147. Which of the following additional studies would be important in the initial evaluation of this case?

(A) heterophil titer
(B) complete blood count
(C) bone marrow examination
(D) HIV
(E) rapid strep screen
(F) RPR
(G) Lyme titre
(H) blood cultures
(I) chest radiographs

148. Which of the following is correct regarding infectious mononucleosis? (SELECT 2)

(A) The incubation period may be up to 6 months.
(B) Patients who complain of headache should undergo spinal tap.
(C) Abdominal pain and hepatomegaly are often noted.
(D) Leukopenia is common on initial presentation.
(E) The serum concentration of bilirubin is elevated in 40 percent of cases.

149. Of the following, which is the correct statement regarding the potential complications of infectious mononucleosis?

(A) hepatitis is common
(B) neurologic complications never present as the sole symptom
(C) no hematologic complications have been observed
(D) electrocardiogram abnormalities and coronary artery spasm are not observed complications of mononucleosis
(E) splenic rupture may occur in 52% of cases

150. Parents of adolescents with mononucleosis should be advised that (SELECT 4)

(A) the disorder is self-limiting
(B) contact sports should be avoided for 6 to 8 weeks after the onset of the illness
(C) recovery may be gradual
(D) return to school or work is determined solely by symptoms
(E) fever is infrequently present during the course of the disease
(F) if Amoxicillin was given and a rash occurred, the child should avoid Amoxicillin in the future
(G) transmission is not associated with kissing.
(H) transmission to school contacts may occur up to three months after the start of symptoms

Questions 151 through 154

A teenage first-time mother brings her newborn into the office. The infant is 2 weeks old. There is a family history of autism in several cousins on the father's side and cerebral palsy in one of the mother's cousins. The parent has numerous concerns regarding the infant's normal expected motor and social development and behavior patterns.

151. Which of the following is correct regarding the expected social behavior during the first year of life?

(A) During the newborn period, there is a visual preference for the human face.
(B) Social smile is noted at 20 weeks.
(C) Response to the word "No" takes place at 4 months.
(D) Playing peekaboo is noted at about 3 to 4 months.
(E) Waves bye-bye at 18 weeks.

152. The following statements regarding motor behavior during the first year of life are correct EXCEPT

(A) walks with one hand held at 52 weeks
(B) creeps or crawls at 12 weeks
(C) sits up alone and indefinitely without support, back straight at 40 weeks
(D) when prone, turns head side to side at 4 weeks
(E) head lags on pull to sitting at 8 weeks

153. Of the following reflexes, which reflex would be expected to disappear the latest in life?

(A) Moro
(B) stepping
(C) sucking and rooting
(D) placing
(E) Babinski

154. Persistence of tonic neck reflexes beyond 9 months may indicate

(A) hypothyroidism
(B) usually normal finding
(C) central motor lesions
(D) possible nutritional disorder
(E) meningitis

SETTING III: HOSPITAL ROUNDS

Hospital rounds can include general medical service, critical care units, pediatric, geriatric, or obstetric services. The following case studies reflect those types you might encounter in this setting.

DIRECTIONS (Questions 155 through 168): Each of the numbered items or incomplete statements in this section is followed by answers or by completions of the statement. Select ONE (OR MORE) lettered answer(s) or completion(s) for each case.

Questions 155 through 158

A 79-year-old woman falls in a grocery store and is taken to a local community hospital. A diagnosis of hip fracture is made in the hospital emergency room and the patient is subsequently hospitalized.

155. All of the following statements regarding hip fractures in the elderly are true EXCEPT

(A) most hip fractures occur in patients 65 and older
(B) hip fractures accompany 50% of falls in this age group
(C) risk factors attributable to hip fracture include cognitive impairment, psychoactive medications, and poor vision or balance
(D) subcapital hip fractures result in a distribution of blood flow to the femoral head
(E) intertrochanteric hip fractures result in no disruption of blood flow to the femoral head

156. After repair of the hip fracture, the patient is considered for anticoagulation therapy during her hospital stay. Which of the following therapeutic strategies represents the best management of anticoagulation in this elderly patient?

(A) No anticoagulation is needed, as the risks of bleeding far outweigh the benefits in respect to deep-vein thrombosis.
(B) Anticoagulation should be initiated, and a target prothrombin time of 15 should be the gold standard of therapy.
(C) Anticoagulation should be initiated, and a target prothrombin time of 24 should be the gold standard of therapy.
(D) Anticoagulation should be initiated, and a target INR level of 2.0 should be the gold standard of therapy.
(E) Anticoagulation should be initiated, and a combination of heparin and dextran therapy is indicated.

157. During the hospital stay, the patient develops a pneumonia with fever, treated with antibiotics. In addition, as a result of the patient's lack of access to water and immobile state, the patient becomes dehydrated and is treated with intravenous fluids. On approximately the third hospital day, the patient is known to be confused and asking to see the hairdresser for her three o'clock appointment. The diagnosis of delirium is suggested by this presentation. The best test for delirium in this patient is

(A) serum ammonia level
(B) attention and calculation
(C) delayed recall
(D) confrontational naming
(E) generative naming

158. Contributing factors to the patient's delirium include all the following EXCEPT

(A) medications
(B) electrolyte imbalance
(C) nutritional deficiency
(D) Alzheimer's disease
(E) immobility

Questions 159 through 161

An 89-year-old male is admitted to the hospital with a diagnosis of acute myocardial infarction.

159. Which of the following statements is true regarding the acute management of myocardial infarction (MI) in the elderly?

(A) Thrombolysis is contraindicated because of the increased risk of bleeding in the elderly.
(B) Beta-blockers are contraindicated because of the risk of central nervous system side effects.
(C) Aggressive use of anticoagulation is inappropriate because of the risk of bleeding.
(D) 20% of all MI deaths occur in patients 65 and older.
(E) Inpatient mortality rates reach 33% in patients 75 and older.

160. After a prolonged stay in the intensive care unit, the patient was transferred to the step-down unit on the medical service. A decubitus ulcer was noted by the nursing staff. Factors contributing to the pathogenesis of decubitus ulcer include (SELECT 4)

(A) pressure
(B) shear
(C) immobility
(D) friction
(E) nutrition
(F) age
(G) moisture

161. The following are true concerning the management of decubitus ulcers. (SELECT 4)

(A) The hospital prevalence for the disease approaches 10%.
(B) About two-thirds of ulcers occur in patients over the age of 70.
(C) This disorder is not associated with mortality and morbidity but represents a minor complication in many older patients.
(D) Common areas for ulcers include the sacral ischial tuberosity and calcaneus.
(E) The most common complication of decubitus ulcers is infection.
(F) Diabetics should be treated prophylactically with antibiotics before decubitus ulcers begin.
(G) Stage I ulcers require surgical debridement.

Questions 162 and 163

An energetic, alert, 80-year-old male is admitted to the hospital for elective treatment of abdominal aortic aneurysm. The patient has congestive heart failure that is well controlled with a combination of digoxin, angiotensin-converting enzyme inhibitor, and diuretic therapies. The blood pressure is 160/90 without postural changes, heart sounds are normal, and no jugular venus distention is present. Roentgenographic films and routine laboratory and urine testings are unremarkable.

162. All the following characteristics increase the risk of cardiac complications of surgery EXCEPT

(A) age over 70
(B) emergent operation
(C) intra-abdominal procedure
(D) echocardiogram ejection fraction less than 30%
(E) $PO_2 < 60$

163. Using the Goldman Cardiac Risk Index, this patient's risks of cardiac death or life-threatening complications are

(A) 2% death, 5% life-threatening
(B) 2% death, 11% life-threatening
(C) 10% death, 30% life-threatening
(D) 22% death, 56% life-threatening
(E) unable to calculate

Questions 164 through 168

A 77-year-old female smoker with a history of chronic obstructive lung disease is maintained on theophylline and albuterol. The patient has an acute exacerbation of bronchospasm requiring hospitalization on the medical service.

164. Which of the following statements is true regarding viral conjunctivitis?

(A) Transmission occurs through fomites coughed from one person to another.
(B) Pain is common and the pupil tends to be small.
(C) Patients may be contagious for one to two weeks.
(D) Topical steriods may be useful in several cases.
(E) Bilateral viral conjunctivitis is distinctly unusual.

165. Which of the following are true regarding anterior blepharitis?

(A) *Staphylococcus aureus* is the most common infectious agent.
(B) Antibiotic eye drops are the treatment of choice.
(C) If untreated, the condition resolves spontaneously.
(D) Rigorous eyelid washing may worsen the disease.
(E) Half the patients have associated rosacea.

166. Routine laboratory screening done on a nursing home patient is remarkable for the urine culture with 100,000 colonies/cc per milliliter. The patient has no complaints of urinary burning, urinary frequency, or urinary urgency. The most common organism associated with infection is

(A) *Escherichia coli*
(B) *Pseudomonas aeruginosa*
(C) *Klebsiella pneumoniae*
(D) *Proteus mirabilis*
(E) normal urinary flora

167. Which of the following statements is true concerning the management of the patient with asymptomatic bacteriuria?

(A) Foley catheters help to prevent urine infections.
(B) Treatment eradicates bacteria in almost all cases without sequelae.
(C) Ciprofloxacin is more effective than ampicillin in the treatment of this disorder.
(D) Asymptomatic bacteriuria is a common finding in the older patient and does not require treatment.
(E) Descending routes of infection are the most common cause of bacteriuria, and a diagnostic work-up should be initiated.

168. The patient has been managed with a variety of medications for COPD and appears ready for discharge. The patient is now complaining of gastritis and symptoms consistent with duodenal ulcer. A decision is made to start the patient on cimetidine therapy, and post-discharge plans are made. One week later the patient presents to your office with tachycardia and vomiting and a serum theophylline level of 25 mg/deciliter (therapeutic range, 10 to 20 mg/dL). What is the most likely explanation for these findings?

(A) noncompliance with theophylline
(B) noncompliance with beta-adrenergic blockers
(C) noncompliance with corticosteroid therapy
(D) interaction between cimetidine and theophylline
(E) interaction between corticosteroids and theophylline

SETTING IV: EMERGENCY DEPARTMENT

In an emergency room, most patients you will see will be new to you. Generally, patients seen here are seeking urgent care. The following case studies reflect those types you might encounter in this setting.

DIRECTIONS (Questions 169 through 180): Each of the numbered items or incomplete statements in this section is followed by answers or by completions of the statement. Select ONE or more lettered answers or completion that is BEST in each case.

Questions 169 through 177

A 30-year-old woman with a history of intravenous drug abuse presents to the Emergency Department with a chief complaint of a nonproductive cough and shortness of breath for 20 days. Physical examination reveals a cachectic woman in moderate respiratory distress with a blood pressure of 100/60 mm Hg, pulse of 110/min, respiratory rate of 24/min, and temperature of 38.3°C (101°F). Head and neck examinations show temporal wasting, white plaques in the posterior pharynx and on the soft palate, and cervical lymphadenopathy. On auscultation of the chest there are diffuse rhonchi. Room air pulse oximetry reveals a saturation of 89%.

169. The most likely finding on chest roentgenogram is

(A) none (normal chest radiograph)
(B) lobar infiltrate
(C) diffuse interstitial infiltrates
(D) nodular infiltrates
(E) pleural effusion

170. Laboratory findings to suggest the diagnosis would be an elevation of the

(A) peripheral leukocyte count
(B) serum lactate dehydrogenase
(C) serum glucose
(D) serum potassium
(E) none of the above

171. The most appropriate initial therapy would be

(A) erythromycin, intravenously
(B) trimethoprim–sulfamethoxazole, intravenously
(C) isoniazid, rifampin, and ethambutol, orally
(D) cefuroxime, intravenously
(E) pentamidine, by inhalation

Questions 172 through 174

A 14-year-old boy is brought to the Emergency Department with lower abdominal pain, nausea, and vomiting that occurred shortly after gym class. Physical examination reveals normal vital signs and a nontender abdomen with normal bowel sounds.

172. Which of the following findings on physical examination would suggest torsion of the spermatic cord?

(A) relief of pain on elevation of the scrotum
(B) painless, unilateral scrotal swelling
(C) a visible "blue dot" on the upper pole of the testis
(D) absent cremasteric reflex
(E) penile discharge

173. Once the diagnosis of testicular torsion is suspected, the most appropriate next step is to obtain

(A) radionuclide testicular scan
(B) emergent urologic consultation
(C) urine for urinalysis
(D) Doppler ultrasound
(E) CT scan

174. The most appropriate next step in management is

(A) administer intravenous diazepam and place patient in Trendelenburg
(B) attempt manual detorsion in the Emergency Department
(C) discharge the patient with scrotal support and urologic follow up
(D) Foley catheterization
(E) scrotal elevation and observation in the Emergency Department

Questions 175 through 177

A 65-year-old woman comes to the Emergency Department because of epigastric abdominal pain and vomiting for 1 day. She has a past medical history significant for hypertension and diabetes mellitus. On examination she has a blood pressure of 120/70 mm Hg, her pulse is 100/min, and her respirations are 22/min. Examination of her abdomen reveals normal bowel sounds and right-upper-quadrant tenderness. Her electrocardiogram is normal.

175. Other expected physical findings include which of the following?

(A) a palpable gallbladder
(B) stool positive for occult blood
(C) fever
(D) mild icterus
(E) a positive Murphy's sign

176. The best test to confirm the diagnosis is

(A) upper GI series
(B) abdominal sonogram
(C) radionuclide scanning of the biliary tree
(D) CT scan of abdomen
(E) abdominal roentgenogram

177. Laboratory examination reveals an elevated peripheral leukocyte with a left shift, a serum glucose of 455 with trace acetone, and a venous pH of 7.30. The most important immediate therapeutic step is administration of

(A) fluids, intravenously
(B) insulin, intravenously
(C) sodium bicarbonate, by intravenous injection
(D) cefoxitin, intravenously
(E) potassium, intravenously

Questions 178 through 180

Matching for each clinical description choose the associated vitamin excess state

(A) vitamin B_1 (thiamine)
(B) vitamin B_6 (pyridoxine)
(C) vitamin B_3 (niacin)
(D) vitamin D
(E) vitamin A
(F) vitamin K
(G) vitamin B_{12}

178. A 50-year-old patient with hyperlipidemia started on a new theraputic agent. The patient now has hyperglycemia and hyperuricemia

179. A 40-year-old polar bear hunter with headache, hair loss, ataxia, and hepatosplenomegaly

180. A 30-year-old health food addict with perioral numbness, ataxia, and vibratory and position sense abnormalities of the lower extremities

ANSWERS AND EXPLANATIONS

1. (A) A wide variety of environmental conditions provoke several mechanisms to come into play to maintain body temperature by balancing heat production and heat loss. The loss of heat by infrared rays (radiation) accounts for more than 60% of normal heat loss. Conduction of heat to objects or to air (i.e., convection) accounts for 15%, and evaporation about 25%. Sweating is an important form of heat loss and is regulated by various body mechanisms. Insensible perspiration through the skin and lungs, although important, remains relatively constant despite environmental changes and thus does not provide a major mechanism to regulate body temperature. *(Guyton, pp 911–914)*

2. **(E)** When water that is either higher or lower than body temperature is introduced into the external auditory meatus, convection currents can occur within the endolymph of the inner ear. These currents may result in the stimulation of the semicircular canals by causing movements of the ampullar crests, and vertigo and nausea may ensue. Decreased movement or immobilization of the otoliths is not caused by such changes in temperature. Furthermore, changes in the discharge rate of vestibular afferents, which must occur with caloric stimulation, are most likely to be caused by the changes in the activity of the receptors rather than being a direct response to changes in temperature. *(Ganong, pp 175–176)*

3. **(D)** Hepatitis A virus is practically indestructible. That is, it is resistant to acid (pH 1.0), detergents, and temperatures up to 60°C. It remains viable in water and saltwater for a very long time. Its resistance to chemical and environmental conditions is partially due to the fact that hepatitis virus A (HAV) is a very small, nonenveloped, single-stranded RNA virus. *(Murray et al, p 525)*

4. **(A)** Aflatoxins are produced by food spoilage molds, and are encountered in certain areas endemic for hepatocellular carcinoma. The aflatoxins are activated in the hepatocytes and their products intercalate into DNA to form mutagenic adducts with guanosine. In turn, they affect the gene p53 and produce a mutation, which is frequently found in hepatocellular carcinoma. Also, there is an inherent susceptibility to aflatoxin in which the mechanism responsible for detoxifying aflatoxin is affected. The patients who develop hepatocellular carcinoma exhibit mutant hepatic enzymes with little or no activity towards aflatoxin. It appears that HIV infection, aflatoxin exposure, and genetic variations act synergistically in some regions to increase the risk of hepatocellular carcinoma. Aflatoxins are not involved in pulmonary sarcomas, chordomas, uterine leiomyomas, or sebaceous carcinoma of the eyelid. *(Cotran, pp 888–891)*

5. **(E)** Neurons are so specialized that most are incapable of reproducing themselves. The neuron is the basic unit of the nervous system. The Nissl bodies are basophilic aggregates located in the cell body and dendrites of each neuron. Neurons, unlike most cells, lack the ability to store glycogen. Each neuron contains numerous fibrillar organelles called neurotubules. *(Moore and Dalley, pp 38–39)*

6. **(A)** Renin secretion directly results in the conversion of angiotensinogen into angiotensin I, which is subsequently converted in the lungs to angiotensin II, a potent vasoconstrictor. Angiotensin induces aldosterone secretion, whose effects on the kidney include increased sodium and water resorption as well as increased potassium secretion. *(Guyton, pp 227–230, 363–364)*

7. **(C)** The formation of the three-carbon CoA thioester malonyl CoA from acetyl CoA is the regulatory step of fatty acid synthesis. Acetyl-CoA carboxylase catalyzes this reaction:

$$\text{Acetyl CoA} + HCO_3 + \text{ATP} \rightleftharpoons \text{malonyl CoA} + \text{ADP} + P_i$$

Citrate, which serves as the means of transport of acetyl CoA from the mitochondria to the cytosolic site of fatty acid synthesis, is the key allosteric regulator of acetyl-CoA carboxylase. It shifts the enzyme from an inactive protomer to an active filamentous polymer. The end product of the cytosolic fatty acid synthetase complex, palmitoyl CoA, inhibits the carboxylase. Although acetyl-CoA carboxylase is the prime regulatory enzyme of fatty acid synthesis, it is not a part of the fatty acid synthetase complex, the site where most of the reactions of fatty acid synthesis take place. *(Stryer, pp 614–617)*

8. **(C)** Ampicillin is a bactericidal antibiotic because it inhibits cell wall synthesis, which leads to lysis and death of the ampicillin-sensitive bacterial cells. Erythromycin, chloramphenicol, and tetracycline inhibit bacterial protein synthesis that is not associated with lysis or death of the bacterial cell. Antibiotics that inhibit bacterial protein synthesis are usually bacteriostatic, not bactericidal. Trimethoprim is a sulfonamide that inhibits dihydrofolate reductase, and is a bacteriostatic antibiotic. *(Levinson and Jawetz, pp 49–57)*

9. **(D)** Hirschsprung's disease (idiopathic megacolon) is characterized by the absence of ganglial cells in the large bowel, leading to functional obstruction and colonic dilatation proximal to the affected segment. Usually appears soon after birth with abdominal distention, failure to pass stools, and occasionally, acute intestinal obstruction. The pathogenesis involves an abnormal functioning and coordination of the propulsive forces in the intestinal segment of the large bowel. Studies have traced the aganglionosis to a heterogenous defect in genes regulated in the migration and survival of neuroblasts, neurogenesis and receptor tyrosine kinase activity. Histologically, the absence of submucosal and myenteric ganglial cells is the diagnostic histologic feature of Hirschsprung's disease. Hypertrophic, disorganized, nonmyelinated nerve fibers are often identified in place of the ganglial cells. A full thickness rectal biopsy is the standard procedure employed in the diagnosis. Hypertrophy of the muscle coat or any changes in the lining mucosa of the rectum, as well as polyps, are not histological features of Hirschsprung's disease. *(Cotran, p 805)*

10. **(D)** Tamoxifen is a nonsteroidal compound used in the treatment of breast carcinoma in postmenopausal women. It acts by competing with estrogen for the estrogen receptor, thus blocking the growth-promoting effects of the hormone on estrogen-dependent tumors. Vincristine is a vinca alkaloid that disrupts the mitotic spindle. Bleomycin causes DNA strand breakage. Busulfan and melphalan are alkylating agents. *(Hardman, pp 1275–1276)*

11. **(E)** The ego functions include emotions, defense mechanisms, and cognitive and perceptual functions. The ego is the agent of the personality system that mediates between the demands of the id, which is the reservoir of instinctual drives, and the demands of the superego, which represents parental and societal values. The ego also mediates between the personality system and external reality. *(Kaplan and Sadock, pp 217–219)*

12. **(B)** The hypoglossal nerve emerges from the sulcus between the olive and pyramid. The third, sixth, and twelfth cranial nerves emerge from the anterior brain stem in a longitudinal line just lateral to the midsagittal plane. The fifth, seventh, ninth, tenth, and eleventh cranial nerves emerge from the lateral aspect of the brain stem. *(Noback, pp 8–9)*

13. **(D)** Iron is readily absorbed by mucosal cells in the intestine, primarily in the duodenum and the jejunum. The major form in which iron is absorbed is as ferrous ions. After the ions have entered the cells, a complex of ferric hydroxyphosphate, surrounded by the 24-subunit protein apoferritin, may form. This complex, known as ferritin, is the principal storage form of iron within cells, accounting for approximately 30% of the iron within the body. *(Ganong, pp 456–457)*

14. **(C)** Cholesterol is required by all eukaryotic cells. It is a major component of the plasma membranes of these cells. Cholesterol is transported in the bloodstream to peripheral tissues largely in the form of low-density lipoprotein. LDL can be taken up by those tissues that require cholesterol. The uptake of LDL is mediated by LDL receptors on the cell surface. *(Stryer, pp 697–701)*

15. **(D)** *Mycoplasma* organisms do not have cell walls, and therefore are resistant to antibiotics, such as penicillin, nafcillin, cephalosporin, and amoxicillin, which inhibits cell wall synthesis. The antibiotic of choice for the treatment of mycoplasmal pneumonia is tetracycline. *(Levinson and Jawetz, pp 49–53, 135)*

16. (B) Atherosclerosis is the most common cause of aortic abdominal aneurysms in the United States. These aneurysms are rare before age 50 and are more common in males than in females. Hemodynamic and genetic factors may potentiate the development of the aneurysms. Small asymptomatic aneurysms may be inconsequential. Larger aneurysms, particularly those that are symptomatic, may be treated surgically. *(Cotran, pp 525–526)*

17. (C) Aspirin is the most effective inhibitor of platelet aggregation because unlike the other choices, it covalently binds to the cyclooxygenase, which is the key enzyme found in platelets responsible for the synthesis of thromboxane. Thromboxane A_2 is an autacoid that promotes platelet aggregation. Since platelets have no nucleus, once the activity of the available cyclooxygenase is destroyed by aspirin, the platelet becomes permanently dysfunctional and must be replaced by the synthesis of new platelets. *(Hardman et al, p 1353)*

18. (A) The anterior gray column contains alpha, gamma, and preganglionic autonomic neurons. First-order sensory neurons are located in the dorsal root ganglia and cranial nerve equivalent. *(Noback, pp 107–108, 109–111)*

19. (E) The binding of glucagon to the hepatocyte cell membrane initiates a complex chain reaction. Intracellular cAMP rises, which in turn activates a protein kinase that *activates* phosphorylase b kinase. The activated form of this enzyme converts phorylase b to phosphorylase a, which proceeds to degrade glycogen to glucose-1-phosphate. Glucose-1-phosphate is subsequently dephosphorylated. *(Guyton, pp 978–979)*

20. (A) The most important virulence factor of group A streptococci is M protein, which interferes with phagocytosis. Hyaluronidase spreads streptococci in tissues; streptolysin O and S lyse red blood cells, and ribonuclease hydrolyzes RNA. However, none of these substances is as important as M protein in the pathogenicity of group A streptococci. *(Levinson and Jawetz, pp 81–83)*

21. (B) Although there have been numerous ways of attempting to classify the various forms of muscular dystrophy, the present one is based on the mode of inheritance. There are types that are sex-linked inheritances: the Becker variety and the Duchenne variety. The Duchenne variety differs from the Becker variety by being more severe and producing its effects earlier in life, usually before the age of 5 years, whereas in the Becker variety, the disease produces its effects somewhere between the age of 5 and 25. The limb–girdle variety is inherited by autosomal recessive inheritance and the facioscapulo and myotonic dystrophies by autosomal dominant inheritance. *(Cotran, pp 1281–1283)*

22. (C) Spironolactone is a competitive antagonist of aldosterone and therefore may cause hyperkalemia if administered concomitantly with potassium supplements. Likewise, the potassium-sparing diuretics triamterene and amiloride cause potassium retention. Captopril inhibits production of angiotensin II and therefore inhibits aldosterone production. Furosemide promotes renal potassium excretion and often requires concomitant supplemental potassium administration. *(Hardman, pp 706–709)*

23. (D) The majority of child sexual abuse is committed by adults within the immediate or extended family and thus are known to the child. The psychological and physical effects of sexual abuse in children are often long-lasting and serious, including symptoms of post-traumatic stress disorder as well as, commonly, depression. Most cases of sexual abuse of children are never discovered because of the victim's feelings of guilt, shame, and fear. *(Kaplan and Sadock, pp 849–851)*

24. (D) In some cases, there is reversed rotation of the intestinal loop where the primitive loop then rotates 90° in a clockwise direction. In such an abnormality, the transverse colon passes behind the duodenum. Remnants of the vitelline duct may appear as a vitelline ligament, cyst, fistula, or Meckel's diverticulum. Frequently, the appendix develops posterior to the cecum and is called a retrocecal appendix. *(Sadler, pp 273–303)*

25. (C) Acetylcholine (ACh) released from motor neurons in the neuromuscular junction (NMJ) binds to nicotinic ACh receptors on the postsynaptic muscle cells. These receptors are ligand-gated cation channels. Binding of ACh results in their opening, allowing the passage of sodium into the cell. The resulting depolarization can initiate a muscle action potential. *(Guyton, pp 87–90)*

26. (B) Vitamin B_1 is obtained as thiamine from pork, yeast, whole grains, and nuts. Its active form in enzymatic reactions is thiamine pyrophosphate (TPP), a form to which it is converted in the body. During decarboxylation, substrates form a hydroxyethyl-TPP intermediate, which is then oxidized to an acetyl group before being transferred off of TPP. A deficiency of thiamine leads to beriberi, a wasting disease with nervous system damage and edema. *(Stryer, pp 514–518)*

27. (A) Exposure to the *Mycobacterium tuberculosis* does not ensure disease, but a positive tuberculin test indicates prior exposure to a given mycobacterium from which the tuberculin was prepared. Chemoprophylaxis with isoniazid is the treatment of choice for contacts of actively infected persons. Ethambutol inhibits many mycobacteria and is used in the treatment, not prophylaxis, of tuberculosis. Roentgenography would not add much information. Sequential roentgenograms, months apart might indicate if the lesion were increasing in size, but that is certainly not a high-priority procedure for contacts of infected persons. Immunization with the live attenuated strain of bovine tubercle organism bacille Calmette–Guérin (BCG) would be pointless, because the contacts have already developed an infection if the tuberculin test is positive. *(Levinson and Jawetz, pp 126–127)*

28. (D) Ectopic hormone production is sometimes seen in association with pulmonary neoplasms. Some tumor types may produce two or more different hormones. This phenomenon has been associated in particular with small-cell carcinoma. Small-cell carcinoma may produce hyponatremia by the ectopic production and inappropriate secretion of ADH. It, along with bronchial carcinoid tumors, has also been associated with Cushing's syndrome and the carcinoid syndrome. Squamous cell carcinoma is associated with hyperparathyroidism, and all types of lung tumors, including adenocarcinoma and large-cell carcinoma, have been linked to gynecomastia resulting from the secretion of ectopic gonadotropin. In addition to endocrine abnormalities, oat cell carcinoma may also produce confusional psychosis, encephalomyelitis, sensory neuropathy, and muscular dysfunction. *(Cotran, pp 746–747)*

29. (E) Gentamicin is a member of the aminoglycoside family of antibiotics, which are rapidly bactericidal. Aside from interfering with the initiation of protein synthesis, aminoglycosides can also induce the incorporation of incorrect amino acids during protein synthesis and cause premature termination of translation of messenger RNA. Chloramphenicol binds to the 50 S ribosomal subunit, nitrofurantoin forms a highly reactive intermediate, which selectively damages bacterial DNA. Vancomycin inhibits cell wall synthesis by binding to particular cell wall precursor units. Trimethoprim selectively inhibits the reduction of bacterial dihydrofolate to tetrahydrofolate, thereby inhibiting DNA synthesis. *(Hardman et al, pp 1105–1106)*

30. (E) Cocaine abuse and withdrawal is often associated with depression, protracted dysphoria, and anhedonia. Tobacco addiction is the most common type of drug dependency in the United States. Opioids administered to treat pain seldom results in addiction. Repeated use of cannabis results in tolerance. If indicated for pain, narcotic analgesics should be increased by 25 to 50% in an opioid-dependent individual because of tolerance to the analgesic action. *(Leigh and Reiser, pp 245–266)*

31. (E) The primitive intestinal loop rotates around an axis formed by the superior mesenteric artery. The superior and inferior epigastric vessels anastomose within the rectus sheath. The inferior mesenteric artery supplies the transverse, descending, and sigmoid colon. *(Sadler, pp 289–291)*

32. (E) The constriction of the pupil of the eye in response to light is mediated by a pathway that travels from the retina through the optic nerves, the optic chiasm, and the optic tracts. Lesions in these areas are therefore likely to impair this reflex. The pathway leaves the optic tracts anterior to the lateral geniculate to enter the pretectal area. Lesions in this area would, therefore, also prevent normal functioning of the reflex. A lesion of the geniculocalcarine tracts, which convey visual information from the lateral geniculate bodies to the occipital cortex, would cause partial or total blindness in humans but would not affect the pupillary reflex. *(Ganong, pp 144–145)*

33. (D) Under normal aerobic conditions, 30 net ATP are formed from the complete oxidation of glucose. Glycolysis yields 2 net ATP from substrate-level phosphorylation, the citric acid cycle yields 2 ATP (as guanosine triphosphate [GTP]) from substrate-level phosphorylation, and oxidative phosphorylation yields 26 ATP. In the presence of an uncoupling agent, such as dinitrophenol, substrate-level phosphorylation still proceeds. Thus, 4 net ATP would be produced. *(Stryer, pp 551–552)*

34. (B) The girl described in this question has a profound deficiency of both B and T cells. Thus, she has severe combined immunodeficiency disease (SCID). The dramatic absence of lymphocytes and lymphoid tissue will not be found in any of the other immunological diseases listed. Multiple myeloma is overproduction of plasma cells, which produce an excess of κ or λ L chains of IgM that appear as dimers in urine. X-linked agammaglobulinemia (Bruton's agammaglobulinemia) features low levels or absences of B cells. Wiskott–Aldrich syndrome is due to an inability to produce an IgM response to bacterial polysaccharides. Chronic granulomatous disease is due to a lack of NADPH oxidase activity of neutrophils, which reduces their microbicidal activity. *(Levinson and Jawetz, pp 337, 380–382; Roitt et al, pp 285–292)*

35. (E) Macrophages are derived from monocytes and are the major scavenger cells in the inflammatory process, especially in late stages of inflammation. They gather up and digest debris, dead cells, proteins, and foreign material, as well as release degradative enzymes. They also release chemotactic and permeability factors, induce leukocytosis and fever, secrete proteins important in defense, release factors to aid healing, and have a function in the immune-mediated response. Macrophages are large, long-lived cells with an eccentric nucleus and abundant cytoplasm. They belong to the reticuloendothelial system (mononuclear phagocyte system) of cells, which are specialized for pinocytosis and phagocytosis. Neutrophils are the most important cells in the acute inflammatory response and are important in the initial engulfment and destruction of microorganisms and foreign material. Lymphocytes are inflammatory cells involved in chronic inflammation in immune reactions and delayed hypersensitivity responses. Plasma cells are modified lymphocytes involved in antibody production and secretion in immune-mediated inflammatory responses. Eosinophils are inflammatory cells whose true function is unknown. They are involved in hypersensitivity and allergic reactions as well as parasitic infections. *(Cotran, pp 79–82)*

36. (D) Tolbutamide is one of several oral hypoglycemic agents that is used for diabetes of the noninsulin-dependent type in individuals who cannot be treated by diet alone or are unwilling to take insulin. If tolbutamide is used alone in insulin-dependent diabetes, therapy is certain to fail and the patient is at great risk. Although results from University Group Diabetes Program are controversial, most endocrinologists and investigators have interpreted data to be consistent with a lack of effect of oral hypoglycemics in reducing cardiovascular complications associated with diabetes. All oral hypoglycemics are capable of producing profound hypoglycemia. This may occur after even one dosage and may require days of glucose therapy. Incontrovertible is that the mechanism underlying the effect of these drugs is to cause the pancreas to secrete insulin. *(Hardman, pp 1507–1509)*

37. **(B)** An hallucination is a perception without a stimulus, whereas an illusion is a distorted perception in the presence of a stimulus. For example, a patient seeing a dragon perching on the bed is experiencing an hallucination, but a patient who mistakes an intravenous pole for a gallows is experiencing an illusion. Delusion is a fixed idea or belief that does not correspond to reality. In this case, the patient has the fixed idea that his guts have rotted. As the delusion is of a depressive nature, the patient may also be depressed, but the phenomenon that is described is best described as delusional. *(Leigh and Reiser, pp 145–155)*

38. **(C)** The first arch persists to form the maxillary artery. The second arch persists as the hyoid and stapedial arteries. The third arch persists as the common carotid artery. The fourth arch persists as the pulmonary arch. The aortic sac forms right and left horns, which give rise to the brachiocephalic artery. *(Sadler, pp 239–243)*

39. **(B)** The foramen rotundum leads to the pterygopalatine fossa. The pterygopalatine fossa leads to the orbital cavity via the superior orbital fissure, to the oral cavity via the palatine canals, to the infratemporal fossa via the pterygomaxillary fissure. It does not lead to the posterior cranial fossa. *(Woodburne, pp 319–322)*

40. **(A)** Phosphoglucose isomerase catalyzes the reversible conversion of fructose 6-phosphate to glucose 6-phosphate in both glycolysis and gluconeogenesis. In fact, most of the steps of glycolysis are simply reversed in gluconeogenesis. However, the three regulatory steps in the conversion of glucose to pyruvate are not reversible. These steps are (1) glucose → glucose 6-phosphate, which is catalyzed by hexokinase; (2) fructose 6-phosphate → fructose 1,6-bisphosphate, which is catalyzed by phosphofructokinase; and (3) phosphoenolpyruvate → pyruvate, which is catalyzed by pyruvate kinase. The reversal of these steps in gluconeogenesis requires the enzymes glucose 6-phosphatase and fructose 1,6-bisphosphatase for the formation of glucose and fructose 6-phosphate, respectively. The formation of phosphoenolpyruvate from pyruvate is more complicated in that the four following steps are involved: (1) Pyruvate carboxylase catalyzes the conversion of pyruvate to oxaloacetate; (2) oxaloacetate is reduced to malate by mitochondrial malate dehydrogenase; (3) malate is reconverted to oxaloacetate by extramitochondrial malate dehydrogenase; and (4) oxaloacetate is transformed to phosphoenolpyruvate by GTP-dependent phosphoenolpyruvate carboxykinase. *(Stryer, pp 485–487, 570–572)*

41. **(E)** Interferon activates cellular genes that code for antiviral proteins. Specifically it blocks the translation of viral mRNA by two mechanisms. A protein kinase that is activated by double-stranded RNA inhibits initiation of factor EF-2 by phosphorylation. In the other mechanism, a nuclease, also activated by double-stranded RNA, destroys mRNA. *(Levinson and Jawetz, p 177)*

42. **(D)** Auer rods are round, rodlike, or elongate cytoplasmic inclusions in the cytoplasm of immature, abnormal granulocytes or myeloblasts. They represent aberrant forms of the cytoplasmic azurophilic granules produced by abnormal cytoplasmic maturation in the leukemic blast cells. Although they may occasionally be seen in chronic myelocytic leukemia in blast crisis, they are most characteristic of acute myeloblastic leukemia. Erythroleukemia (Di Guglielmo's syndrome) is an acute myeloid leukemia that is predominantly a disorder of erythroid precursors. At some stage of the disease, myeloid precursors may also be abnormal. In these instances, Auer rods may be seen when myeloblasts are present. Acute lymphoblastic leukemia and chronic lymphocytic leukemia are leukemias of the lymphocyte cells and do not demonstrate Auer rod formation. *(Cotran, pp 675–676)*

43. (C) The most common and distressing side effect of nonsteroidal anti-inflammatory agents is gastrointestinal complaints. Of those persons taking ibuprofen, 5 to 15% have symptoms referable to the digestive system. A similar incidence has been observed for naproxen. Toxic amblyopia is an unusual complication of ibuprofen therapy. Edema formation and renal failure have uncommonly been associated with both drugs. Drowsiness is an extremely rare side effect. *(Hardman, pp 639–640)*

44. (B) Agitation, tremulousness, and hallucinations indicate the likely presence of delirium tremens. If the hallucinations are primarily visual and frightening, and if there is other evidence of sympathetic activation, the diagnosis would be more likely. Physicians should be aware that alcoholic patients often drink in the hospital and fail to disclose the extent of their alcohol use. Following an operation, patients may develop an alcoholic withdrawal state as a result of their restricted oral intake. *(Leigh and Reiser, pp 305–323)*

45. (B) The mandibular division of the trigeminal nerve provides the nerve to the tensor veli palatini and tensor tympani muscles. The levator veli palatini is innervated by the vagus. Muscles of facial expression are innervated by the facial nerve. The glossopharyngeal innervates the stylopharyngeus. The ansa cervicalis innervates the infrahyoid muscles. *(Woodburne, pp 195–197, 252–254, 278)*

46. (B) Most infants gain an average of an ounce of weight a day during the first 4 months of life. Infants who gain more than this amount of weight and are spitting up usually are being overfed. Overfeeding often affects infants of primigravida mothers. Pyloric stenosis first becomes manifest at about 3 weeks of age, and affected infants gain weight poorly. Adrenogenital syndrome and inborn errors in metabolism also present in the first weeks of life and result in poor weight gain. Neglected infants would not be expected to be overfed. *(Hey et al, pp 3–4, 196–198; Rudolph, pp 22–23)*

47. (C) Infants begin to sit by 5 months of age, but they usually do not attain the sitting position without assistance until they are 8 months old. At 8 months of age, children typically begin to stand with someone holding their hand. Children at this age also typically start to verbalize (e.g., "ma ma" and "da da"). *(Hay et al, pp 4–17)*

48. (E) Hyaline membrane disease is a major cause of morbidity and mortality in newborn infants. Because both hyperoxemia and hypoxemia can lead to serious sequelae, it is of utmost importance to maintain normal blood oxygen levels in affected infants. Measuring arterial PO_2 is the most accurate way of monitoring oxygenation. Transcutaneous and capillary measurements frequently are used to monitor blood oxygen levels, but they aren't as precise as arterial samplings. Serial chest roentgenograms and pulmonary function tests are of no help in following the oxygen requirements of infants who have hyaline membrane disease. *(Hey et al, pp 49–50; Rudolph, p 232)*

49. (E) Anterior mediastinal masses are not uncommon in children. Teratomas, thymomas, lymphomas, and thymic cysts can all arise in the anterior mediastinal space. On the other hand, bronchogenic cysts arise in the middle mediastinal region. *(Hay et al, pp 462–464)*

50. (E) Tanner developed a scale (I to V) to describe the pubertal changes of girls and boys. Stage I is the prepubertal stage. Breast buds are the first signs of female pubertal development, and their appearance corresponds to Tanner stage II. Sparse pubic hair, the second sign, also corresponds to Tanner stage II, whereas dark pubic hair occurs during Tanner stage III. Axillary hair begins to form during the beginning of Tanner stage IV. Stage V represents full pubertal development. *(Hay et al, pp 112–114)*

51. (C) In the United States, sudden cardiac death (SCD) accounts for as many as 500,000 deaths yearly, almost half of all deaths caused by heart disease. Current research aims at identifying populations at risk in order to prevent SCD. In addition to the known risk factors for cardiovascular disease (e.g., smoking and hypertension), the following factors are associated with increased risk for SCD: ventricular ectopic beats and arrhythmias; myocardial infarction, whether complicated or not; angina pectoris; prolonged QT interval on ECG; previous attack of SCD; and admission to intensive care with coronary artery disease and chest pain but without acute infarction. The vast majority of victims have underlying coronary artery disease, although not all have had prior symptoms. The most common precipitating arrhythmia is ventricular fibrillation, frequently preceded by ventricular tachycardia. *(Fauci, p 224)*

52. (A) The roentgenogram that accompanies the question demonstrates a dilated loop of large bowel with the ascending, transverse, and descending colon dilated proximally. This pattern is highly suggestive of a sigmoid volvulus. Immediate decompression by rectal tube or colonoscopy may be curative. In rare cases, if bowel infarction is suspected, surgical intervention is indicated. Gastric lavage would not be helpful. Abdominal ultrasonography might yield additional information but would not alter the need for immediate treatment. Percutaneous drainage would not relieve the obstruction and would be dangerous. Colonic volvuli recur in 55% of cases and may be complicated by colonic perforation. *(Hazzard, p 1270)*

53. (C) Serologic markers are extremely useful in the diagnosis of hepatitis B infections. In the typical case, titers of surface antigen (HBsAg) and e antigen (HBeAg) rise either before or simultaneously with clinical symptoms then fall to unmeasurable levels. Shortly thereafter, antibodies to surface antigen (anti-HBsAg) appear. The short interval between the disappearance of HBsAg and the appearance of anti-HBsAg is the so-called window period, when hepatitis is present despite negative serologic results. Another antibody is present during this period—antibody to hepatitis B core antigen (anti-HBcAG). This antibody persists for years after the infection has resolved. In the case presented in the question, the serologic findings show either that the man is in the window period of acute hepatitis B infection, in which case anti-HBsAg will appear on retesting, or that anti-HBcAg is persisting from a previous hepatitis B infection and the current hepatitis is due to another agent (e.g., hepatitis C) or a toxin. Anti-HBcAg usually does not indicate either a chronic carrier state or immunity. *(Fauci, pp 1679–1680)*

54. (D) The wet mount and gram stain are both consistent with bacterial vaginosis. Gonorrhea and *Chlamydia* should cause a more purulent discharge. Frothy discharge, as in this case, may be seen with *Trichomonas* but the gram stain and absence of trichomonads argues against this diagnosis. *Candida* should reveal branching hyphae and budding yeast on gram stain. *(Beckmann, pp 332–333)*

55. (B) Inspiratory stridor is the hallmark of upper airway obstruction. Among the disorders that can involve the upper airway and cause stridor are epiglottitis, infectious laryngotracheitis, angioneurotic edema, and foreign-body aspiration. In contrast, acute bronchospasm prolongs the expiratory phase of respiration and causes predominantly expiratory wheezing rather than inspiratory stridor. *(Hay et al, pp 424–430, 918–919)*

56. (B) Osteomyelitis can be diagnosed in its earliest stage by technetium bone scanning. Plain roentgenographic films typically take at least 10 days to reveal the early changes of osteomyelitis. Gallium scans are helpful in diagnosing pelvic bone infections. Blood counts and sedimentation rates are helpful in monitoring the progression and response to treatment of osteomyelitis but do not prove or disprove the existence of disease. *(Hay et al, pp 707–708; Rudolph, pp 548–551)*

57. (A) Turner's syndrome children are phenotypically female with an XO-chromosome pattern. The diagnosis, if missed at birth, becomes obvious during the pubertal years, when affected girls do not mature sexually and have short stature and cubitus valgus (deviation of the forearm to the radial side when extended). Coarctation of the aorta, but not aortic stenosis, has been reported in association with Turner's syndrome. *(Hay et al, pp 887–888; Rudolph, pp 1782–1784)*

58. (D) Regardless of the clinical setting or the type of treatment being contemplated, it is of primary importance in the initial psychiatric interview to obtain a careful patient history. Evaluation of mental status is next in importance, because it sheds light on the patient's orientation, cognition, and reality testing and may disclose the presence of organic disturbances. Establishing a working alliance is critical but should occur as a concomitant of careful and empathic introductory interviews. *(Kaplan and Sadock, pp 240–241)*

59. (D) The antibiotic chloramphenicol is effective against a variety of organisms, including *Salmonella.* However, the side effects from the use of this drug are significant, and some are potentially lethal. Gray baby syndrome (peripheral vascular collapse) can occur in newborns receiving large doses of chloramphenicol. Aplastic anemia can develop as an idiosyncratic response (not dose-related) to treatment, and a reversible anemia also can occur. Discoloration of teeth is a side effect in newborns of maternal tetracycline therapy. Chloramphenicol is absorbed readily from the gastrointestinal tract. *(Hay et al, pp 956, 1038–1039)*

60. (E) The barium enema roentgenogram shown in the question reveals multiple sigmoid diverticuli. Most cases of colonic diverticular disease do not require surgery, even for active gastrointestinal bleeding. Colonoscopy is not necessary unless the barium enema reveals additional lesions or the diagnosis is in doubt. Histamine H_2-receptor antagonists such as cimetidine and ranitidine are useful for treating peptic ulcer disease but not for diverticulosis. Rectal corticosteroid enemas have a role in inflammatory bowel disease but not in diverticular disease. Appropriate management of the acute attack consists of bed rest, liquid diet, and perhaps anticholinergics. Thereafter, a high-residue diet should be prescribed to help prevent further recurrences. Bran, raw vegetables, legumes, and hydrophilic colloids such as psyllium seed derivatives are all useful. *(Fauci, pp 1648–1649)*

61. (D) Psychosis is best defined as a state of gross impairment in reality testing. This condition may be demonstrated by imagined perceptions (hallucinations), belief in irrational thoughts (delusions), or marked inability to integrate and respond to important aspects of the environment. Psychosis may indicate underlying functional psychiatric illness or organic disease. *(APA, pp 404–405)*

62. (A) In the food industry, sugar is the most commonly used chemical preservative. At concentrations of 65% or greater, sugar prevents the growth of bacteria, yeasts, and molds. Bacteria rarely survive in concentrations greater than 25%. Salt is also an effective preservative, but because of its taste is not as readily acceptable as sugar. From a health standpoint, both substances have disadvantages. Benzoic acid, prohibited in some countries, is permitted in concentrations of as much as 0.1 percent for certain foods in the United States. Carbon dioxide is rarely used, except in carbonated beverages. Sulfur dioxide is used in some food-drying processes. *(Last, pp 605–607)*

63. (E) Human breast milk constitutes an optimal and almost perfect diet for young infants. It contains IgA and maternal macrophages, both of which presumably offer some immunologic protection to the newborn. Although the amount of iron in human milk is very small, it is very well absorbed, much better than in cow's milk. It is generally recommended, however, that breast-fed infants receive supplemental iron after 6 months of age. Human milk generally contains little fluoride, regardless of the mother's dietary fluoride intake, and for this reason, it is recommended that supplementation with fluoride begin after 6 months of age. Normal infants fed breast milk exclusively probably require no vitamin supplementation. Supplementation with vitamin D, however, is deemed advisable and is most important in dark-skinned infants or infants receiving minimal exposure to sunlight. *(Hay et al, pp 259–262, 263)*

64. (D) Hypokalemia is magnified by bicarbonate treatment of acidosis, which causes potassium to enter cells. Patients with severe diabetic ketoacidosis always have a depletion of their total body potassium even though the serum potassium may be elevated. This patient's hyperkalemia, however, still represents a risk because of its potential to produce cardiac arrest, a risk that may be greatly accentuated if potassium replacement is begun too early. Patients should be monitored very carefully to obtain unequivocal evidence that serum potassium has begun to fall before potassium therapy is started. It is always safer to give oral potassium if at all possible. The hyperkalemia is due to extracellar fluid shift of potassium and is usually not related to the azotemia seen in this case. *(Fauci, p 2073)*

65. (B) Lower GI bleeding is a common presentation of a variety of colonic and noncolonic pathology. Due to the significantly more common occurrence of upper GI bleeding, it is by far the most common cause of "lower" GI bleeding. If only considering true colonic pathology as the cause, diverticuli of the colon are the most common disease states leading to lower GI blood loss. Arteriovenous malformations and colon cancer are less frequently the cause of lower GI bleeding. Benign polyps of the colon usually present with heme-positive stools and not frank GI bleeding. *(Greenfield, pp 1041–1053)*

66. (B) Commercially canned foods are less likely to be contaminated by bacteria than foods stored by the other methods listed in the question. Temperatures of 120°C (250°F) or higher have to be used in the canning process. This temperature is obtained by steam under pressure and continues for a stipulated period of time that varies inversely with the amount of heat used. The desired effect begins when the temperatures achieved are 105°C (220°F) or higher. By this method, at least 90% of all organisms are killed. Pasteurization is also a form of heat treatment in which lower temperatures are used for longer time periods. This method is adequate to prevent bacterial growth, but it may not be bactericidal. Refrigeration and freezing prevent bacterial multiplication, but food stored by these methods needs to be adequately cooked unless, like ice cream, it is to be eaten shortly after removal from the cold environment. Drying is a relatively safe method of storage, as pathogenic bacteria tend to die in the absence of water in foods that have been dried to 10 to 20% of their original weight. *(Last, pp 604–607)*

67. (A) Seizures actually are one of the less common initial manifestations of brain tumors in children. This is easily understood when one realizes that 50 to 60% of pediatric brain tumors are infratentorial and 75% or more occur in the midline, third and fourth ventricles, optic chiasm, and brain stem. Ataxia, cranial nerve involvement, and head tilt are common presentations of brain tumors in children. Hypothalamic and endocrine dysfunctions occasionally are the presenting complaints. These can include growth failure and either sexual infantilism or sexual precocity. The most common tumors presenting in this manner are the craniopharyngioma and the chiasmal glioma. Occasionally pineal tumors and teratomas also may involve hypothalamic structures. *(Hay et al, pp 656–657, 779-782)*

68. (E) The ECG that accompanies the question shows atrial fibrillation with a rapid ventricular response. When atrial fibrillation is of recent onset and associated with hemodynamic compromise resulting from a rapid ventricular rate, treatment of choice is emergency cardioversion. In the absence of hypotension and severe symptoms, or if the atrial fibrillation is paroxysmal, digitalis, calcium channel blockers, or beta-adrenergic blockers may be given to slow the ventricular rate. If atrial fibrillation has been present for several days, elective cardioversion may be performed with concurrent anticoagulation to prevent embolism of any thrombus that may have formed. Quinidine, procainamide, and disopyramide are sometimes given at the time of cardioversion in hope of maintaining sinus rhythm. *(Fauci, pp 1264–1265)*

69. (C) Seminoma is the most common germinal tumor of the testes. The incidence of seminoma is higher in men with cryptorchidism. The tumor is highly radiosensitive, and the overall survival rate is approximately 85%. The tumor spreads by the lymphatics to retroperitoneal nodules. Hematogenous spread occurs late in the course of the disease and is not common. *(Lieskovsky, pp 508–514)*

70. (C) Antidepressant drugs have long been effectively used in the pharmacologic management of major affective disorder (primarily recurrent depression), the depressive phases of bipolar illness, and atypical depression. Over the past several years clinical research has revealed that the major symptoms of a number of other psychiatric syndromes can be ameliorated pharmacologically with these same agents. The binge eating of certain bulimic individuals diminishes in frequency and intensity when these individuals are treated with certain antidepressant medications. Ruminative thinking and compulsive behaviors characteristic of obsessive–compulsive disorder diminish in severity when antidepressant medications are administered. Similarly, persons who experience panic attacks or phobias (specific anxiety disorders) often achieve symptomatic relief when given an antidepressant. It is not clear that the same serum levels necessary to effectively treat major depressive episodes must be established in treating these other sydromes. Antidepressant drugs are not effective in the treatment of delusional (paranoid) disorders. *(Dunner, pp 717–776)*

71. (D) A worker who can no longer do the type of work or amount of work that was previously performed is generally described as partially disabled. However, the Social Security Administration (SSA) system defines disability as the "inability to engage in any substantial gainful activity by reason of a medically determinable physical or mental impairment that can be expected to result in death, or has lasted or can be expected to last for a continuous period of not less than 12 months." The important phrases are "any substantial gainful activity," which begins to give some indication of how much activity can be undertaken by someone who is disabled; "by reason of a medically determinable physical or mental impairment," which implies that there must be some ability to define the condition in medical terminology and on the basis of a definable condition; and an estimated outcome that either will result in death or has resulted or will result in continuous disability for more than 12 months. In addition, the SSA has listed "severe impairments" that automatically qualify for medical disability. Some of these descriptions are very detailed. *(Last, pp 583–584)*

72. (A) Ethosuximide and valproic acid are the drugs of choice in the treatment of petit mal absence seizures, which cause transient loss of consciousness. Phenobarbital and phenytoin are excellent anticonvulsants but are not first-line medications for treating this disorder. Diphenhydramine is an antihistamine of no benefit in treating this disorder, and diazepam, which is useful in treating status epilepticus, also is not a drug used in the treatment of petit mal seizures. *(Hay et al, pp 635–636)*

73. (D) Nearly 90% of renal stones are visible on a plain abdominal roentgenography, and the majority contain calcium oxalate. The most common cause of calcium stone disease is idiopathic hypercalciuria. Almost half of affected persons daily excrete >4 mg of calcium/kg body weight in the absence of hypercalcemia. Causes of hypercalciuria are sarcoidosis, hyperthyroidism, and Paget's disease of bone. Idiopathic hypercalciuria is believed to result from either increased gastrointestinal absorption of calcium, increased calcium resorption from bone, or excessive renal calcium leakage into the urine. *(Fauci, pp 1570–1572)*

74. (B) Cardiac tamponade is the most frequent sign of intrapericardial injury. Elevation of central venous pressure is the most reliable sign for making the diagnosis. Left atrial pressure measurement through a Swan–Ganz catheter is of little value, because it may be normal or low. Decreased pulse pressure, when present, is diagnostic of cardiac tamponade. Normal cardiac shadow does not rule out cardiac tamponade; because of the suddenness with which cardiac tamponade occurs, the pericardium does not have sufficient time to expand; as little as 20 to 30 mL of accumulated fluid can produce the condition. Pericardiocentesis is helpful in the diagnosis. Aspiration of 10 to 20 mL may dramatically improve the patient's condition. However, it is important to remember that the pericardial tap may be falsely negative in 19% and falsely positive in 6% of cases. *(Greenfield, p 289)*

75. (A) Diagnostic criteria for chronic factitious disorder (Munchausen syndrome) include the presentation of physical symptoms that are consistent with genuine illness but are under the person's voluntary control. The disorder reflects a need to become a patient and receive care. Physical condition can deteriorate as a result of the multiple invasive procedures affected persons typically undergo. Unlike chronic factitious disorder, malingering reflects the simple desire to avoid unpleasant circumstances or to obtain undue compensation. *(APA, pp 316–318)*

76. (B) Although urinary tract infections are the most common nosocomial infections in U.S. hospitals, responsible for 42% of such infections, they are responsible only for 9.9% of excess direct cost. Surgical wound infections, 23.7% of total nosocomial infections, are responsible for 48.4% of excess direct cost. Thus, they are the most costly type of nosocomial infection. *(Kelley, p 1823)*

77. (B) The only agents currently recognized to enhance production of fetal pulmonary surfactant are glucocorticoids, and their use is controversial. These substances were first used by Liggins and Howie in fetal lambs. Some subsequent studies have shown them to be successful in enhancing pulmonary maturation; follow-up studies show no long-term consequences in the offspring. However, some data compiled from studies on animals show limitation of growth of certain organs. Of the agents listed in the question, magnesium sulfate will block eclamptic seizures and stop uterine contractions; hydroxyprogesterone is used experimentally on a chronic basis to decrease premature labor; and chloroprocaine and bupivacaine are anesthetics. *(Beckmann et al, pp 281–287)*

78. (E) Basal skull fractures are notoriously difficult to visualize on skull roentgenographic films, at least in part because of the complicated features of the base of the skull. Usually, the diagnosis is made on the basis of clinical findings. These include the seepage of blood over the mastoid area (Battle's sign), about the eyes (raccoon eyes sign), and into the middle ear (hemotympanum), as well as nasal bleeding or discharge of cerebrospinal fluid. As basal skull fractures may involve the middle ear or sinuses, bacterial meningitis is a concern. *(Hay et al, pp 283, 284–285, 653)*

79. (E) Hypernatremia is almost always caused by water loss in excess of sodium. Therefore in nearly all cases both water and sodium need to be replenished. In a patient with intravascular compromise such as this (low blood pressure and high pulse) normal saline should be the initial replacement therapy. Dextrose may be added to avoid ketosis. *(Fauci, pp 269–271)*

80. (C) Antibiotic-related colitis is the result of enterotoxin produced by *Clostridium difficile.*

It has been reported with the use of practically every antibiotic except vancomycin. When diarrhea is the only manifestation, discontinuing the antibiotic is all that is necessary. In more severe cases, treatment requires administering metroidazole. Vancomycin by mouth is also adequate in treating *C. difficile* but due to its expense is not the first line drug. Rarely, total colectomy and ileostomy are required to treat toxic megacolon and perforation. *(Schwartz, pp 1226–1228)*

81. (A) Antipsychotic (neuroleptic) medications exert their pharmacologic effects by a central dopamine receptor blockade. Decreased dopaminergic activity accounts for the parkinsonian side effects commonly produced by these drugs. Other drugs, like amphetamines, that promote increased dopaminergic activity in the brain can lead to psychosis or exacerbate an existing schizophrenic illness. *(Hales and Frances, pp 178–179)*

82. (C) The general formula of chi-square is

$$\chi^2\,(df) = \Sigma\,\frac{(0 - E)^2}{E}$$

where O is the observed count in the category and E is the expected count in the category if the null hypothesis is true. The formulation applies only to counts of the number of observations and not to measured quantities, ranks, percentages, or proportions. It is designed to make comparisons or proportions, but the data must be presented in raw numerical form. The concept of degrees of freedom (df) is involved. The test is designed for the comparison of paired or independent samples—for example, the proportion of persons exposed to a certain level of radiation developing leukemia compared with the number of those who also develop the disease but who have not been exposed. *(Kramer, pp 168–171)*

83. (A) Antepartum fetal monitoring in the form of nonstress testing, stress testing, or biophysical profile evaluation is commonly used to help ensure fetal well-being. There is no general agreement as to which type of test is best or when it is best initiated. Therefore, centers will generally use one or more of these tests and begin evaluation between 25 and 36 weeks, depending on high-risk indications. The tests would generally be performed at weekly intervals unless a higher risk (such as previously nonreactive nonstress tests) indicates the need for more frequent testing. *(Beckmann, et al, pp 84, 313)*

84. (D) This child, who is cyanotic despite the administration of oxygen and despite an arterial PO_2 of 90 torr, probably has methemoglobinemia. If the cyanosis were due to cardiac or pulmonary disease, one would expect hypoxemia as well as corresponding findings on physical examination. There are a variety of causes of methemoglobinemia, but the sudden onset in this previously well child suggests the ingestion of a toxin. Nitrites from well water is one notorious cause of methemoglobinemia. It also has been suggested that home-prepared infant vegetable purees may be very rich in nitrates, which if improperly stored are reduced to nitrites, causing methemoglobinemia. A simple test is to place a drop of the patient's blood on filter paper. If the blood appears brown, the level of methemoglobin is greater than 15%. The treatment of nitrite poisoning and methemoglobinemia is methylene blue administered intravenously. Physostigmine is useful in counteracting the symptoms of tricyclic ingestion; atropine is the drug of choice for organic phosphate poisoning; and amyl nitrite is used for cyanide poisoning. *(Hay et al, pp 746–747)*

85. (D) Psoriasis is a chronic skin disease characterized by well-demarcated, erythematous papules and plaques covered by flakes or scales. Common sites of involvement are the scalp, back, extensor surfaces of the knees and elbows, perianal region, and genitalia. Psoriasis is associated with nail dystrophy (pits, grooves, or crumbling), arthritis (usually involving the digits), involvement of traumatized areas (Koebner's phenomenon), and hyperuricemia (caused by rapid nucleic acid turnover). Electrolyte disorders are not commonly associated with psoriasis. *(Fauci, pp 300–301)*

86. (A) Ruptured abdominal aortic aneurysm is characterized by the diagnostic triad of abdominal or back pain, hypotension, and a tender, pulsatile abdominal mass. Treatment consists of control of hemorrhage, restoration of blood volume, and replacement of the aneurysm with a graft. Survival of affected individuals depends on how soon the bleeding is controlled. Control over continued hemorrhage is best achieved in the operating room. Delay can prove fatal, because blood pressure may fall precipitously at any moment. All painful procedures, which may increase blood pressure and thereby aggravate bleeding, should be deferred until the patient is in the operating room and the surgical team is ready to open the abdomen at a moment's notice. *(Greenfield, pp 1711–1722)*

87. (D) Organic causes of psychiatric illness must always be considered, but some clinical presentations warrant special attention. By definition, delirium is organic, not functional, in nature and therefore must be fully investigated. Confusion, dementia, and sudden personality change all can arise from such "non- psychiatric" causes as neoplastic, metabolic, cardiovascular, and infectious disease. Similarly, first psychotic episodes must not be attributed to a schizophreniform disorder without first performing an organic work-up. Although major depression can be simulated by organic causes, such as thyroid disease, a CT scan of the brain is less indicated in the workup of depression than the other clinical situations mentioned above. *(Hales and Frances, pp 287–289)*

88. (A) In Australia, the National Health and Medical Research Council has recommended "safe" levels for drinking. Their recommendations are based on a "unit" of alcohol being 8 to 10 g of alcohol as opposed to the Canadian and American standard of 13.6 g. Men should not drink more than the equivalent of 40 g of absolute alcohol per day on a regular basis. Women are generally more susceptible to the effect of alcohol and should drink no more than half the consumption of men. In essence, no level of consumption of alcohol will always be safe for all individuals under all conditions. *(Last, pp 743–744)*

89. (E) Many factors contribute to the decision regarding what type of therapy a woman should receive for carcinoma in situ of the cervix. Extended or radical hysterectomy is usually not considered because, by definition, carcinoma in situ is not invasive and does not involve pelvic lymph nodes. If an affected woman has completed her childbearing, hysterectomy is usually the treatment of choice. Either conization or cautery is possible for women who wish to maintain fertility. The major advantage of cryosurgery is that it can be performed on an outpatient basis, whereas conization requires some form of anesthesia. However, the recurrence rates after cryosurgery are higher than those of conization. The success rate with all of the methods is quite good. All women should, however, be followed up for recurrence of disease, including women who have had a hysterectomy. *(Beckmann et al, pp 512–529)*

90. (E) Slapped red cheeks and a generalized lacy reticular rash are classic signs of erythema infectiosum, which is caused by human parvovirus. (This disease is also known as "fifth disease," because it was the fifth disease, after rubella, measles, scarlet fever, and Filatov–Dukes disease, described with this type of rash.) Sucking on a Popsicle also can lead to reddish discoloration of the cheeks, a condition called Popsicle panniculitis. Kawasaki's disease, rubeola, and rubella are associated with a variety of skin manifestations, but the "slapped cheeks" sign is not a characteristic finding. *(Hay, pp 515, 963–964, 984–987; Rudolph, p 921)*

91. (D) Localization of insulinoma is not always easy. Angiography and splenic venous sampling localizes the tumor in only 30% of the patients. At operation the pancreas has to be mobilized and tumor carefully looked for. If no tumor is found, distal pancreatectomy is done and blood sugar determined after 30 minutes. Elevation of blood sugar is an indicator of tumor removal. *(Schwartz, pp 1426–1427)*

92. (E) Insanity is defined by law, not by psychiatry, and the definition of insanity varies from state to state. The insanity defense is employed infrequently in U.S. courts for several reasons, including relative lack of success and the prospect that harsh institutional life awaits those persons found not guilty by reason of insanity. As laws are passed to toughen the U.S. criminal justice system and thus make the possibility of imprisonment even more intimidating, defendants may well opt more often for the insanity defense. At present, there is a movement to consider restricting the use of the insanity defense to sentencing and not to determination of guilt or innocence. *(Halleck, pp 207–224)*

93. (A) In fact, the data produced by the Centers for Disease Control in 1984 reveals that the organisms listed in the question occur in descending order of frequency as listed. *Pseudomonas* was then reported to be the pathogen in 16.9% of cases of lower respiratory tract infection reported in acute-care hospitals. The patterns are constantly changing, but these changes are noted only over a period of years. *(Kelley, p 1827)*

94. (B) The peak incidence of poststreptococcal glomerulonephritis occurs between the ages of 3 and 7 years. Not all strains of streptococci are equally associated with glomerulonephritis—particular association has been noted with type 12, and also with types 1, 4, 25, and 29. Because these strains are not evenly spread throughout the communities, the prevalence of poststreptococcal glomerulonephritis can vary widely between different population groups. There is little tendency for the condition to recur, and therefore there is little indication for secondary preventive measures. *(Clark and MacMahon, pp 228–229)*

95. (C, D, E, G) Triacylglycerol lipase, glycogen synthase, and phosphorylase kinase are part of cyclic AMP-dependent cascades that are either activated or deactivated by phosphorylation. During stimulation of glycogenolysis (and concurrent inhibition of glycogen synthesis), hormone-stimulated increases in cyclic AMP levels activate protein kinase, which activates phosphorylase kinase by catalyzing its phosphorylation. The protein kinase also inhibits glycogen synthase by catalyzing its phosphorylation. The activated phosphorylase kinase activates glycogen phosphorylase by accelerating its phosphorylation. Triacylglycerol lipase is also activated by phosphorylation after cyclic AMP-mediated stimulation of protein kinases. Acetyl-CoA carboxylase is also deactivated by phosphorylation, but this is not mediated by cAMP. It is stimulated by AMP and inhibited by ATP. Isocitrate dehydrogenase is allosterically activated by ADP and inactivated by ATP, but the enzyme is not phosphorylated. Lipoprotein lipase is a blood lipoprotein delipidation enzyme, which is activated by interaction with C-II apolipoproteins. Aspartate transcarbamoylase catalyzes a critical step in pyrimidine biosynthesis and is allosterically regulated *(Stryer, pp 238–244, 525, 590–597, 605–606, 621–622)*

96. (A, D, H) Most benzodiazepines, with the exception of oxazepam, lorazepam, temazepam, triazolam, and midazolam are metabolized to active intermediates, which can significantly prolong the duration of action. This is because the active metabolites undergo a much slower biotransformation than the parent compound. For example, the half-life of flurazepam is 2 to 3 hours, but the half-life of one of its active metabolites is 50 hours. Therefore, the selection of a particular benzodiazepine for its duration of action, must factor in the duration of action of active metabolites as well. *(Hardman et al, pp 368–370)*

97. (B, D, E) In 1973, homosexuality was eliminated as a diagnostic category by the American Psychiatric Association and removed from the Diagnostic and Statistical Manual of Mental Disorders. Most gay men recall onset of attraction to same-sex partners during early adolescence; for women this is more variable with recognition of same-sex partner preference occurring from the middle adolescence to early adulthood. Recent studies suggest genetic and biological factors may be contributors to sexual orientation. Female-to-female relationships tend to be more stable than male-to-male relationships. Coming out is a process involving acknowledging one's sexual orientation in the world. *(Kaplan and Sadock, pp 682–683)*

98. **(B, C, E, G)** Proopiomelanocortin can give rise to five peptide hormones of the anterior pituitary. ACTH and β-lipotropin, a prohormone, are formed by cleavage of proopiomelanocortin. Alpha-melanocyte-stimulating hormone (α-MSH) is a cleavage product of ACTH, whereas β-endorphin and γ-lipotropin are cleavage products of β-lipotropin; β-MSH is a cleavage fragment of β-endorphin. This sequence is summarized below:

Proopiomelanocortin

ACTH ← → β-Lipotropin

↓ ACTH → α-MSH

β-Endorphin ← β-Lipotropin → γ-Lipotropin

↓ β-Endorphin → β-MSH

Thyroid-stimulating hormone (TSH) and follicle-stimulating hormone (FSH) are produced in the anterior pituitary, but are not derived from proopiomelancortin. Cortisol is synthesized in the adrenal cortex. *(Stryer, pp 993–994)*

99. **(A, B, E)** Delusions are fixed false beliefs of which a person cannot be dissuaded by empathic or logical argument. They may be present whenever reality testing is obstructed by a psychotic process; thus, they may occur in association not only with schizophrenia but also with mania, depression, or organic disturbances. Commonly encountered delusions include those of persecution, grandiosity, and physical disease. *(Kaplan and Sadock, p 282)*

100. **(A, D, E, G)** As many as 50% of patients presenting with a principal complaint of persistent, generalized pruritus have an occult systemic disease. Chronic renal failure is a common cause of itching; postulated mechanisms include elevated serum histamine or kinin levels and mast cell hyperplasia. Pruritus is the initial symptom in almost half of all patients with primary biliary cirrhosis and eventually affects almost all. Other hepatic disorders to rule out are hepatitis and extrahepatic biliary obstruction (accumulation of bile salts is thought to cause the pruritus). Half of all patients with polycythemia vera suffer from itching that is characteristically worsened by hot baths. Pruritus is associated with a poorer prognosis in Hodgkin's disease and mycosis fungoides. Pruritus associated with thyrotoxicosis, occurring in as many as 10% of cases, is also thought to be caused by increased kinin activity. Numerous other causes, including occult malignancy and parasitic infections, should be carefully considered. Lupus, Wegener's, and polychondritis are not especially associated with generalized pruritus as a presenting complaint. *(Goldman, p 2266)*

101–103. **(101-D, 102-E, 103-B)** Brain does not store any sources of energy. Rather it depends on a continuous supply of glucose for its energy needs. During starvation the available sources of glucose are scarce. To provide sufficient energy to the brain, the liver begins to synthesize significant levels of the ketone bodies, acetoacetate and 3-hydroxybutyrate. These are formed in a pathway that begins with the condensation of two molecules of acetyl CoA to yield acetoacetyl CoA. Ketone body production occurs only in the liver. The acetyl CoA is derived by oxidation of fatty acids released by adipose tissue. Fatty acids are stored in adipose tissue in the form of triacylglycerols. Free fatty acids are derived from the stored triacylglycerols by the action of lipases and transported to the liver as complexes with albumin. *(Stryer, pp 612–613, 770–777)*

104. (C) Influenza, rubeola, poliomyelitis, or herpes virus do not contain enzymes that synthesize DNA from RNA (reverse transcriptase), or have p24 and gp41 proteins, which are of diagnostic value. All of the above indicated attributes are found in human immunodeficiency virus. *(Levinson and Jawetz, pp 251–255)*

105. (C) Quinolone binds to the alpha subunit of DNA gyrase. Rifampin blocks mRNA synthesis. Erythromycin, chloramphenicol, and gentamicin inhibits protein synthesis. *(Levinson and Jawetz, pp 54–58)*

106. (E) The certain ability of viruses, such as the orthomyxoviruses and paramyxoviruses, to agglutinate chicken red blood cells or human type O red blood cells is called hemagglutination. Hemagglutination is mediated by what is known as the H (or HA) glycoprotein, which forms a spike on the envelope of influenza, measles, mumps, and parainfluenza virus. The H glycoprotein is an important antigen that is involved in antigenic variation of influenza viruses. Since hemagglutination is a common feature of influenza, measles, mumps, and parainfluenza virus, this test is used for the presumptive identification of these viruses. *(Murray et al, pp 427–478)*

107–108. (107-C, 108-D) Osteoid osteoma is a variant of a benign tumor that produces primitive bones and some denser bone in a very characteristic fashion, which can be recognized radiologically and pathologically but which does not metastasize. It may reoccur locally if not entirely and properly excised.

Chondrosarcoma is a highly malignant tumor of cartilage that is distinguished from its benign counterpart, chondroma, by pleomorphism, appearance of the cells, and invasive capacity. It also metastasizes through the bloodstream and may become widespread.

Osteogenic sarcoma is the bone, or osteoid, equivalent of chondrosarcoma and is also highly malignant and distinguishable from the osteoid osteoma.

Multiple endochondromatosis, a series of benign cartilaginous tumors that occur in the central portions of the shafts of bones both large and small, may occur throughout the body, producing gross deformities. They are benign and do not metastasize.

The distinction among these various types of benign and malignant tumors of both osteoblastic and chondroblastic origins is very important and requires a combination of clinical history and age, radiologic, and pathologic assessment. It is dangerous to rely on any one of these parameters alone to make a very clear distinction, which is of fundamental importance in the management and treatment of a patient. *(Cotran, pp 1233–1242)*

109–111. (109-E, 110-C, 111-A) Neurohumoral transmission may be classified into two basic types—cholinergic and adrenergic transmission. Cholinergic transmission involves the stimulation of either nicotinic or muscarinic receptors by acetylcholine. Postsynaptic nicotinic receptors may be blocked by *d*-tubocurarine; blockade of these receptors at motor end plates results in muscle paralysis. Muscarinic receptors of postganglionic parasympathetic fibers are also stimulated by acetylcholine; however, these receptors are blocked by atropine and not by *d*-tubocurarine. The activity of cholinergic neurotransmitters (e.g., acetylcholine) is rapidly terminated by acetylcholinesterase. This enzyme may be inhibited reversibly by drugs, such as physostigmine. *(Hardman, pp 150, 161–163, 177–182)*

112–113. (112-E, 113-C) A variety of congenital disorders can be diagnosed in utero. Achondroplasia, a form of dwarfism, is readily noted on ultrasonography, which discloses shortened fetal limbs. A fetus with an open meningomyelocele secretes measurable quantities of alpha-fetoprotein (AFP) into the amniotic fluid, which can be obtained by amniocentesis. Sickle cell anemia will be detectable on a fetal blood sample obtained during fetoscopy. Hunter's syndrome, a disorder of mucopolysaccharide storage, can be detected in cells grown in culture from amniotic fluid. *(Beckmann et al, pp 47, 48–49)*

114–117 (114-B, 115-E, 116-A, 117-D) Both phenelzine and amitriptyline are used in the treatment of major depression. Phenelzine, an MAO inhibitor, augments available catecholamine neurotransmitters for release into the synaptic cleft by inhibiting the intraneuronal breakdown of norepinephrine, serotonin, and dopamine. The degree of enzyme inhibition appears to be directly related to the antidepressant effect. Persons treated with phenelzine or any other MAO inhibitor must eliminate tyramine-containing foods from their diet or risk the possibility of a hypertensive crisis.

Amitriptyline, a tricyclic antidepressant, exerts its therapeutic effect by means of inhibition of serotonin reuptake into the presynaptic neuron, thus enhancing the availability of neurotransmitter for action on the postsynaptic neuron. The structurally related compounds nortriptyline and protriptyline also are effective antidepressants. Fluoxetine is one of the serotonin specific reuptake inhibitors used in the treatment of depression.

Clonazepam is a benzodiazepine used originally as an anticonvulsant in the treatment of akinetic and myoclonic seizures. In recent years it has also been prescribed for its antianxiety effects as well. Benztropine is an anticholinergic used to manage the pseudoparkinsonian and extrapyramidal side effects of the higher potency antipsychotic agents like haloperidol. *(Goldman, pp 431–435, 445–448)*

118–120. (118-A, 119-B, 120-D) Local health departments or health systems agencies are concerned with making plans for the entire population of an area and with developing a comprehensive population-based plan. This involves estimating health requirements, matching them with existing resources, and outlining the strategy based on the deficit or surplus that has been demonstrated. A distinction is frequently made between what the patient wants (which would be used if available and free), what the patient needs (services determined by professionals to be appropriate), and what the patient demands (services that are actually used in the current market situation).

Planning for an HMO is based on that segment of the population that is "the market" for the organization. The population may or may not live in a contiguous area. The planning is designed to identify goals and objectives in institutional terms: e.g., to determine the market for the services the organization provides, and to estimate future demands. The population need (as opposed to the population demand) is not necessarily a concern of institutional planners.

Program planning concerns itself with neither the need for a particular service nor its marketability. By definition, "the program" is the focus (e.g., maternal and child health care will be provided). Planning is directed toward the way in which the already established goals will be carried out. This type of planning is frequently necessary to implement government-sponsored programs. *(Last, pp 1080–1081)*

UNSCHEDULED PATIENTS

121. (B) The patient has documented isolated systolic hypertension (ISH), which is the most common type of hypertension observed in the elderly. Given the results of the major study, the Systolic Hypertension in the Elderly Program, management of this disorder leads to decreased cerebrovascular mortality and morbidity. The most appropriate next step in this patient's management is initiation of a nonpharmacologic approach to control blood pressure. If the blood pressure is not controlled after a 3-month interval, initiation of therapy with a diuretic or beta-blocker should follow. There is no indication for starting two pharmacologic therapies at the same time. No further diagnostic evaluation for blood pressure measurement should be attempted at this time without a specific intervention planned, and 24-hour ambulatory blood pressure monitoring is not indicated in this setting. *(SHEP; Applegate and Rutan)*

122. (D) With normal aging, there is a down-regulation of the beta-adrenergic receptors in normal cardiac muscle. At rest, this finding is not clinically important, as older patients have the same heart rate as younger patients. However, with exercise and challenge to the sympathetic nervous system, there is an expected increase in catecholamine discharge but a less-than-expected increase in heart rate as a result of the down-regulation of the beta-receptors as described above. *(Geokas et al; Wei)*

123. (C) While the average life expectancy of a person born in the United States is currently 75 years for a man and 79 years for a woman, these figures represent a 50:50 chance of reaching a specific chronologic age. Given the fact that the patient is currently 83 years old, there is still an expected average life expectancy of approximately 7 years, suggesting that there is a 50% chance that the patient will live 7 years or longer. This advanced age is a reflection of the survivorship in this patient. Even at age 83, this patient will continue to experience additional life and additional health care needs. *(Avorn, 1986; Soldo and Manton, pp 12–22)*

124. (C) Fries described three important terms in measuring human health in advancing years: disease, morbidity, and mortality. There is a period of time when the *disease* is present in the individual, but no symptoms are clinically apparent. Screening is helpful at this time to provide information on asymptomatic conditions which, if detected and treated early, may lead to improved life expectancy. Once a disease is clinically manifest, the disease is responsible for *morbidity* in the given individual, and with advancing age, there is an increasing frequency of comorbid conditions. The third step as described by Fries is *mortality,* and although there have been great increases in average life expectancy throughout the 20th century, the maximum life expectancy has remained the same at approximately 110 years. No foreseeable extension in the maximum life-span can be predicted at this time. *(Avorn, 1984; Fries)*

125. (A) Dementia, defined as significant memory impairment, is relatively uncommon in all patients over the age of 65 but may be present in as many as 50% of patients over the age of 80. The most frequent etiology of memory impairment in the older individual is dementia of the Alzheimer's type (DAT), also known as Alzheimer's disease. This entity is responsible for approximately 60% of all memory impairment. Memory impairment resulting from cerebrovascular accidents is seen in approximately 20% of individuals. Reversible causes of memory impairment, such as drug-induced illness, are seen in approximately 20% of individuals. The remaining 5% of memory loss can be explained by a variety of illnesses, including Parkinson's disease, Pick's disease, and other neurodegenerative conditions. Old age in and of itself is not related to memory loss: when a patient presents to the office with memory impairment, a diagnostic search should begin to rule out common clinical and pathophysiologic conditions that may be responsible for memory loss. *(Kaplan and Sadock, pp 328–329)*

126. (B) Given the patient's deficits in memory, efforts should be made by the clinician to educate the patient around the activities of daily living and structural support in his or her home environment. This education should extend not only to the patient but also to the family and should include information on the activities of daily living. In addition, the physician should use other strategies such as simplification of the medication regimen, written information to supplement oral information, and home visitation to enhance therapeutic outcomes in these patients. Psychoactive agents are not indicated in the management of dementia unless psychotic features are noted. Acute hospitalization may be necessary for other illnesses that occur in the later stages of dementia, such as pressure ulcers caused by decreased mobility in these patients, but are not indicated early in the management of this disorder. There is no role for vitamin therapy in the management of dementia. While a discussion with the patient and family is recommended concerning advance directives and the appointment of a health care proxy, this step, again, should not be foremost in the clinician's mind in prioritizing the treatment strategies for this patient. *(Kaplan and Sadock, pp 342–344)*

127. (D) The magnitude of the memory impairment can be evaluated using the Folstein Mini-Mental State Examination, a low-tech standardized test. A deficit in delayed recall, the inability to learn new information, is the typical finding in patients with dementia of the Alzheimer's type and several other dementing illnesses. Testing can be done dynamically by reciting three words, asking the patient to immediately repeat the words back to the examiner and remember them for later testing, and asking the patient to recall the words after a five-minute interval. The ability to recall distant information is relatively preserved in dementia. Deficits in orientation and language may be noted as well but are not pathognomonic of dementia. Both registration and attention and calculation deficits are not consistent with dementia but rather are more consistent with delirium or acute confusional state, which represents another important mental disorder in the elderly. If deficits are noted in any of these two spheres, a diagnostic work-up separate from that for management of dementia should be commenced. *(Kaplan and Sadock, pp 335–340)*

128. (B) Compliance can be defined as the ability of the patient to adhere to the treatment regimen, in this situation the medication regimen. While a number of studies have been performed relating factors such as patient demographics to compliance, there is no clear relationship between age or gender and the magnitude of compliance. The one factor that has consistently been noted as related to medication compliance is the number of medications in the patient's regimen: the level of compliance is inversely related to the number of medications, with the poorest compliance noted with increasing number of medications. The number of comorbid diseases is not in itself related to compliance, and there is no evidence of a difference in compliance between tablets versus elixirs. *(Darnell et al; Monane et al)*

129. (A) Pharmacokinetics is the area dealing with "what the body does to the drug." Four specific processes are identified—absorption, distribution, excretion, and metabolism. With normal aging, there is an increased amount of body fat and a decreased amount of body water, which directly affects the volume of distribution of medications. Medications that are renally excreted have markedly prolonged half-lives, as a result of a decreasing number of function nephrons with normal aging. Phase I metabolism, which includes oxidative reactions of the P450 systems, is markedly impaired in the older individual, while Phase II processes such as conjugation are relatively well preserved. Absorption is essentially unchanged in the older versus the younger individual. *(Montamat et al; Avorn and Gurwitz, pp 66–77)*

130. (D) Urinary incontinence is one of the most common conditions in the older individual, affecting 10 to 15% of patients in the community setting. The etiology of urinary incontinence in many individuals is related to factors outside the genitourinary tract, and many of these factors are potentially reversible or amenable to therapy. Calcium channel blockers lead to overflow incontinence by decreasing the action of smooth muscle responsible for bladder emptying. Restricted mobility is responsible for lack of access to the bathroom and may result in incontinence, and impaired mentation may lead to inappropriate central nervous system response to bladder contractions. Diabetes may be responsible for urinary incontinence as a result of increasing osmolarity of the urine. Although the number of functioning nephrons decreases with normal aging, the relationship between this physiologic change in older individuals and the onset of urinary incontinence is not clinically important. *(Resnick and Yalla; Ouslander et al)*

SCHEDULED APPOINTMENTS

131. (E) The most likely cause of the patient's confusion is uremia. Hypercalcemia is a consideration in this patient but should not present with a palpable bladder and enlarged prostate. Prostate cancer without complications, such as renal failure, rarely causes change in mental status. *(Fauci, p 1513)*

132. (D) The best initial test to order when urine obstruction is suspected is ultrasound of the abdomen and kidneys. Plain film is rarely helpful if bladder or prostate pathology is suspected. Intravenous dye should be avoided with renal insufficiency. *(Fauci, pp 1504–1512)*

133. (D) The most vital office procedure performed in acute renal failure is insertion of a Foley catheter. It is both diagnostic and therapeutic. Foley insertion should be performed whether one can palpate the bladder or even if the bladder is nonpalpable. With outlet obstruction resulting from benign prostatic hypertrophy or tumor, the Foley insertion will be both diagnostic and therapeutic. *(Fauci, pp 1504–1512)*

134. (B) Renal failure involves the inability of the kidneys to maintain metabolic homeostasis. This will result in multiple metabolic, acid–base, and volume disorders. If output is less than 500 mL/d, it may be termed oliguric renal failure. Renal failure is not due to outlet obstruction when residual is less than 30 mL. Some findings on history and physical examination that *are* consistent with anatomic lesions and outlet obstruction include flank pain, history of ureterolithiasis, and difficult voiding. On examination, palpable kidneys may indicate polycystic kidney disease or lymphoma. *(Fauci, pp 1504–1512)*

135. (B, C, D, E) While it is reasonable to restrict protein, correct volume depletion, and control caloric intake and acidosis, one should refrain from the use of magnesium-containing compounds. Conservative management may include daily weight, serial laboratory studies, and monitoring of fluid intake and output. While protein intake should be limited to 0.5 g/kg/d, highly catabolic patients (burns, postoperative) may require higher amounts. Hypertension also needs to be aggressively treated. Neither hospital admission nor dialysis can be started against a patient's will. *(Fauci, pp 1–8, 1513–1520)*

136. (C) Of more concern than a painful death is the fear of suffering alone. Patients may fear being abandoned by their physician, which leads to despair. Reduced conversation and the tendency to withdraw will aggravate the patient's sense of loneliness. A touch, examination, or even the taking of the pulse serves to support patient–physician bonding and reduce patient anxiety. *(Fauci, pp 1–8)*

137. (C) While TB and collagen vascular disease need to be considered in any individual with prolonged fever and malaise, the history of IV drug use and physical findings should prompt a search for infective endocarditis. Other possible disorders in the setting of prolonged fever and malaise may include neoplasia and viral infection. Rheumatic fever also needs to be considered in the differential. The history, cardiac examination, and blood cultures, along with an index of suspicion, will confirm the diagnosis. Remember also that the clinical picture will depend on the specific infecting organism. *(Fauci, pp 785–791)*

138. (C) Clubbing and splenomegaly are seen only in neglected cases of over 6 weeks' duration. Patients with infective endocarditis may be noted to have fatigue, petechiae, and embolic infarcts in the spleen, retina, or cerebral circulation. Retinal infarcts (Roth's spots) may be also noted in other vascular disorders, such as systemic lupus erythematosis (SLE). Immune complex disease may present as nephritis, Osler's nodes, and arthralgias. Osler's nodes are tender lesions on the tips of fingers and toes. Patients with acute bacterial endocarditis may be critically ill, whereas those with subacute bacterial endocarditis may appear chronically ill, presenting with weight loss and anorexia. Up to 10% of patients may have no murmur, and this is especially noted in patients with tricuspid valve involvement. Abnormal laboratory findings include normochromic, normocytic anemia in up to 90% of cases. *(Fauci, pp 785–791)*

139. (D) When increased turbulence is present along a valve, as a result of pre-existing disease, endothelial damage occurs. Sterile platelet-fibrin thrombi are formed. Bacteremia that involves an organism with the ability to adhere to either the endothelium or the platelet-fibrin thrombi could result in infection. Phagocytosis does not occur on valve leaflets, so bacteria multiply within the thrombus. The infection may extend to supporting structures, resulting in additional damage. Vascular occlusion may result from the embolization of the vegetations. Suppurative metastatic lesions may also then occur. *(Rakel, p 440)*

140. (E) Of the conditions stated, only aortic stenosis is associated with an increased risk of endocarditis. Mitral valve prolapse without an audible murmur is thought not to increase risk of infective endocarditis. *(Fauci, pp 785–791)*

141. (D) Eighty percent of endocarditis cases are due to streptococci and staphylococci. *Streptococcus viridans* is the most frequent organism in natural valve endocarditis. The increased frequency of streptococci in endocarditis is related to the bacteria's ability to adhere to valve tissue. Although the majority of natural valve and late prosthetic valve infective endocarditis cases are due to *S viridans,* in the IV drug user, the most common isolate is *Staphylococcus aureus.* The skin is the most common source of microorganisms that result in the IV drug abuser's infection. *S bovis,* when noted as a cause of endocarditis, is associated with colonic neoplasia in greater than 50% of cases. *(Fauci, pp 785–791)*

142. (A) Tricuspid valve is affected in over 50% of infective endocarditis cases in IV drug abusers. Infections with multiple organisms are common, and the onset is often acute. Most addicts with initial endocarditis infection do not have previously damaged heart valves. Pulmonary emboli are common in tricuspid valve endocarditis. Murmurs are often absent in these cases. Some of these infections involve fungal endocarditis. Fungal endocarditis is more common in the settings of open heart surgery, prolonged intravenous therapy, and IV drug abuse. *(Fauci, pp 785–791)*

143. (C) Bactericidal effect against enterococci is not obtained with the single antimicrobials listed. Enterococcal organisms are very resistant to the cephalosporins. As penicillin, vancomycin, and ampicillin are not bactericidal for the enterococci, combination therapy, including an aminoglycoside, is necessary. The addition of an aminoglycoside creates a synergistic bactericidal effect. Antibiotics should be administered by the parenteral route. The concentration should be sufficient to destroy all microorganisms in the vegetation. The duration of antibiotic treatment is usually 4 to 6 weeks. *(Fauci, pp 785–791)*

144. (A) Drug reaction is the most common cause of fever during treatment, with emboli and metastatic abscess formation as less common causes. Within one week of initiation of antimicrobial therapy, fever will most often subside. Continued fever and bacteremia may also be noted with myocardial abscess formation. If a rash develops during treatment, antihistamines may be given. If the rash is progressive and severe, the treatment program should be changed. The main cause of death during or after therapy is heart failure. *(Fauci, pp 785–791)*

145. (A, B, C, D) Manifestations of infective endocarditis include embolic episodes, neurologic symptoms, cardiac and renal failure. Also noted are fever and murmurs. With early endocarditis and in tricuspid valve endocarditis, a murmur may not be appreciated. With chronic disease, clubbing may be noted. Neurologic manifestations may also be noted. Circulating immune complexes secondary to high antibody titers against the infecting organism contribute to glomerulonephritis and arthritis. These manifestations will usually have their onset within 2 weeks of the initial bacteremia. The onset may be slow (as with *S viridans*) or acute (as with *S aureus*). Otitis, urethritis, urticaria, and iritis are not generally associated with endocarditis. *(Fauci, pp 785–791)*

146. **(C, D, G)** The risk of endocarditis from mitral valve prolapse with an audible murmur is considerably lower than many other valvular lesions. Chemoprophylaxis is recommended for dental procedures, respiratory tract surgery (tonsillectomy), and genitourinary procedures (cystoscopy). *(Goldman, p 1632)*

147. **(A, B, D, E, F)** The diagnosis of mononucleosis needs to be considered in this scenario. With an incubation of 30 to 50 days, infectious mononucleosis presents with an insidious onset of fever and sore throat. The virus is spread by oral transmission and also by respiratory spread of saliva. Lymphadenopathy and hepatosplenomegaly may be noted. Edema of the eyelids and maculopapular rashes may be evident on examination. HIV seroconversion may present as a "flulike" illness, with fever and lethargy. A complete blood count will assist in screening for mononucleosis (atypical lymphocytosis). The differential diagnosis also includes toxoplasmosis, syphilis, cytomegalovirus, and hepatitis A; these may be evaluated by serologic testing. Bone marrow study, lyme titres, blood cultures, and chest radiograph are unnecessary in the initial evaluation. *(Fauci, p 1090)*

148. **(C, E)** Splenomegaly occurs in about 50% and abdominal pain occurs in about 20% of patients with mononucleosis. Headache is common and routine spinal taps should be avoided. Most cases of mononucleosis present with leukocytosis. The incubation period is 4 to 6 weeks. The bilirubin is also often elevated. *(Fauci, pp 1089–1091)*

149. **(A)** Hepatitis is common, with over 90% of patients demonstrating abnormal liver function tests. Other complications include splenic rupture, airway obstruction, and interstitial pneumonia. Hemolytic anemia, thrombocytopenia, pancreatitis, and Reye's syndrome may also be noted. The most common neurologic complications include cranial nerve palsies and encephalitis. Cardiac complications are uncommon but include myocarditis, coronary artery spasm, and pericarditis. *(Wilson, p 791)*

150. **(A, B, C, D)** Recovery from mononucleosis is gradual, and the disorder is self-limiting. Avoiding contact sports for 6 to 8 weeks may prevent splenic rupture. Timing of return to school or work is determined by the degree of symptoms. Fever is present in over 90% of patients and may reach 40°C (104°F). The fever most often continues for 1 to 2 weeks. Lymphadenopathy often persists for 3 weeks. Malaise is noted to be the most persistent symptom. Pharyngitis reaches a peak at about 1 week, then resolves over the next 7 to 10 days. 80% of patients with mononucleosis who are given penicillin will develop a generalized rash. The rash is not predictive of future adverse reactions. EBV is spread by contact with oral secretions. Isolation of adolescents from nonintimate contacts is unnecessary. *(Fauci, pp 1089–1091)*

151. **(A)** While newborns have a visual preference for the human face, a social smile, cooing, and listening to voice occur at about 8 weeks. At about 12 weeks, the infant is noted to demonstrate sustained social contact. At 16 weeks, the baby will laugh out loud and is excited at the sight of food. At 28 weeks, the baby babbles and enjoys a mirror. Response to his or her name, waving bye-bye, and peekaboo games take place at approximately 10 months. *(Hay et al, pp 4–17)*

152. **(B)** At 16 weeks, the infant will not display head lag upon being pulled to a sitting position. At 28 weeks, the infant will sit briefly and lean forward on the hands. Motor activity of creeping or crawling occurs at approximately 40 weeks. At 40 weeks, sitting up alone is accomplished, without support and with the back straight. At 1 year, motor activity includes walking with one hand held and walking while holding onto furniture. *(Hay et al, pp 4-17)*

153. (E) Only subcortical (brain stem and spinal cord) reflexes may be tested for at birth. At this stage, major cerebral defects may not be detected. Reflexes that are present at birth include Moro's, stepping, placing, sucking, rooting palmar grasp, Babinski's, and plantar grasp. All disappear by 6 months of age except the Babinski's, which persists until 12 to 16 months of age. *(Hay et al, pp 4–10)*

154. (C) The tonic neck reflex consists of extension of the arm and leg on the same side. This occurs when the infant's head is turned quickly to one side. Also noted is flexion of the extremities on the opposite side, similar to the pose of a fencer. This reflex is noted in infants between the ages of 2 to 4 months. Persistence of tonic neck reflexes is noted in infants with central motor lesions (e.g., spastic cerebral palsy). *(Hay et al, p 9)*

HOSPITAL ROUNDS

155. (B) While falls increase in prevalence with age, fractures are seen in only 5 to 10% of subjects who fall. Another 30 to 40% of persons who fall will sustain soft-tissue injury. In 1990, there were over 250,000 hip fractures, and patients over the age of 65 accounted for 87% of these cases. These hip fractures are generally classified into two groups: subcapital (femoral neck) fractures and intertrochanteric or subtrochanteric fractures. Of note, a major differentiation between the two groups is the disruption of the blood supply to the femoral head. Subcapital fractures are associated with disruption of blood flow to the femoral neck and lead to a higher incidence of nonunion and necrosis of the femoral head. Intertrochanteric fractures, which do not disturb the blood flow to the femoral neck, have a lower incidence of nonunion and necrosis but are more commonly associated with acute complications associated with fracture (e.g., major bleeding and instability). Factors correlated with hip-fracture risk in the elderly include advancing age, dementia of the Alzheimer's type, psychotropic medications including long-acting benzodiazepines, female gender, and osteopenia. *(Pierron et al; Tinetti et al)*

156. (D) Venous thromboembolism represents a major cause of complications after hip fracture. Before the advent of thromboembolic prophylaxis, deep-vein thrombosis developed in about 50% of patients with hip fractures, pulmonary emboli in about 10% of patients, and death in 2 to 5% of patients. Therefore treatment for prophylaxis of deep-vein thrombosis should be initiated preoperatively if possible and continued throughout the hospital stay. In choosing antithrombotic agents, the use of dextran is generally not considered for the older patient because of the opportunities for fluid overflow and increased bleeding associated with its use. Warfarin has been used and shown effective in the prevention of thromboembolic disease. Formerly, the prothrombin time was useful in the management of anticoagulation in patients on warfarin therapy; however, a change in thromboplastin agents used by the various hospitals resulted in marked variation in values of prothrombin levels. Therefore, the International Normalized Ratio (INR) is now considered the standard of care for the management of anticoagulation. An INR level of 2.0 to 2.5 is acceptable for the management of thromboembolic disease in this patient. *(Amstutz et al; Hirsh and Poller)*

157. (B) The patient has an acute confusional state or delirium, which occurs in approximately 10 to 25% of hospitalized patients. The hallmark of this disorder is decreased attention with disorganized thinking developing over hours or days, with fluctuations throughout the day. The best test for diagnosing this disorder is low-tech in nature and is provided through the Folstein Mini-Mental State Examination. A test for attention and calculation could include either a digit span examination, asking the patient to repeat five digits forward and three digits backwards, or asking the patient to spell the word *world* backwards. Errors in these parameters suggests a diagnosis of delirium. Serum ammonia levels have been shown to increase in many diseases associated with confusion, especially those associated with hepatic degeneration, but these represent a poor correlation for either the diagnosis or management of confusion. Tests of delayed recall are especially helpful in judging the patient's short-term memory and could be a useful diagnostic test for Alzheimer's disease. Disturbance in naming, either confrontational or generative, are more often seen with severe dementias associated with white matter disease. *(Gustafson et al; Schor et al)*

158. (D) Delirium affects possibly 30 to 40% of all older persons admitted to the hospital. The new onset of confusion should be regarded as a medical emergency unless proven otherwise. Causes of acute confusional state can be described by the mnemonic DELIRIUM, and include drugs, such as anticholinergic agents and narcotics, as well as sedative–hypnotics; electrolyte imbalance, such as hypo- or hypernatremia and hypo- or hyperglycemia; lack of sleep; infection; reduced sensation; fecal impaction; urinary retention; and myocardium, including heart failure, cardiac arrhythmia, and myocardial infarction. While Alzheimer's disease is a predisposing factor for delirium, and delirium is often seen in patients with Alzheimer's disease, this acute confusional state cannot be attributed to the presence of Alzheimer's disease, and an investigative search should be commenced, examining the possible etiologies of the patient's current signs and symptoms and not attributing the condition to Alzheimer's disease. *(Francis et al; Johnson et al)*

159. (E) Despite an overall decline in cardiovascular disease mortality, heart disease remains a common and serious medical problem for the elderly. While adults 65 and older make up only 12% of the population, 80% of all deaths from acute myocardial infarction occur in patients 65 years and older. The inpatient case fatality rate for initial acute myocardial infarction reaches 33% in those 75 years and older. Given the dramatically poor outcomes of older patients as compared to younger patients, therapy with modern agents is exceedingly beneficial in this older age group. Despite the rationale for the use of beta-blockers for acute myocardial infarction and numerous studies suggesting efficacy even in the very old, many clinicians still resist prescribing these drugs for elderly MI patients. The same is true for chemical thrombolysis, although several placebo-controlled mortality trials of thrombolytic therapy have shown decreased mortality and greater benefit for patients 70 years or older, with mortality decreased by 16.9% with lytic therapy in the higher age groups. In the Warfarin Reinfarction Study, mortality was reduced by 24% and reinfarction by 34% in patients who received anticoagulation therapy versus those who did not. *(Forman et al; Krumholz and Wei, pp 101–109)*

160. (C) Decubitus ulcers are common complications of hospital stay. The prevalence of decubitus ulcers reaches 10%. Causative factors for decubitus ulcers include pressure, as up to 200 mm Hg for 11 hours can cause a full-thickness ulcer. Shearing forces cause ulcers by tearing subcutaneous capillaries, such as the fragile subcutaneous capillaries over the sacrum. Friction produced by transferring or pulling patients across a bed surface can lead to abrasion. Moisture from perspiration or incontinence, both fecal and urinary, dramatically increases the likelihood of developing a pressure ulcer. While immobility in and of itself is not a risk factor for pressure ulcer, the relief of pressure through a number of devices or frequent turning of the patient (every 2 hours) from a left-lateral to right-lateral 30- to 60-degree oblique position is helpful in preventing decubitus ulcers. *(Allman; Brandeis et al)*

161. (C) Decubitus ulcers remain a difficult problem because of their propensity to occur among the frailest patients with multiple medical problems. The hospital prevalence of this disease is approximately 10%. The national cost for care of this disorder can reach seven billion dollars, and 70% of cases occur in patients over 70. A colonization is common with all hospital-acquired wounds, and sepsis may result from localized infection in the pressure ulcer, with mortality as high as 50%. Prophylaxis with antibiotics is not required. Given the increased costs and complications associated with this disease in the older patient, prevention of decubitus ulcers represents an important approach for the hospitalized patient. The bony sacrum, ischial tuberoses, trochanter, heels, and lateral malleoli account for 80% of all decubitus ulcers. Surgical debridement of stage I ulcers (no skin breakdown) is not recommended. *(Goode and Allman; Panel)*

162. (D) In a prospective study of patients undergoing surgery at the Massachusetts General Hospital, Goldman and colleagues evaluated the risk of surgical morbidity of cardiac complications associated with noncardiac operations. Independent risk factors included age under 70; presence of jugular venus distention or third heart sound; myocardial infarction in the previous 6 months; less than five premature ventricular contractions per minute; cardiac rhythm other than sinus; emergency operation; intrathoracic, intraabdominal, or aortic surgery; significant aortic valvular stenosis; and general poor medical condition. This index provides a low-tech evaluation of a patient's risk for surgery. Another standardized index available to categorize elderly patients and their risk for surgical complications is the American Society of Anesthesiology (ASA) Physical Status Classification, which has been validated for individuals over 80. This classification system divides risk according to mild systemic disease, severe systemic disease, morbid condition, and emergency operation. *(Gilbert and Minaker; Goldman et al)*

163. (A) Using the Goldman Cardiac Risk Index, the patient could be classified according to the schema described above. In this patient, the age over 70 and the intra-abdominal nature of the procedure classify a total of 8 points out of a possible 53. The risk of a cardiac death associated with this procedure is 2%, and the risk of life-threatening complications is 5%. Alternatively, there are minor or no complications in 93% of surgical cases. Using the American Society of Anesthesiology Physical Status Classification, the patient is ASA II, associated with a mortality of approximately 1%. Geriatric patients commonly are candidates for elective as well as for emergency surgical intervention. The quality of their perioperative care often determines whether their outcome is successful. Surgery can be performed successfully on very old patients, and questions on the initial preoperative assessment of the older patient should include: is the proposed surgery reasonable; is the operation consistent with the patient's values and wishes; and has the posthospital care been considered? *(Lubin, Minaker, and Rowe, pp 415–424)*

164. (C) Viral conjunctivitis is usually caused by adenovirus and is spread through direct contact. Pain is unusual and pupil size is normal. The disease often becomes bilateral and topical steroids are contraindicated. Patients may be contagious for up to two weeks. *(Goldman, p 2228)*

165. (A) Anterior blepharitis primarily affects the eyelash follicles, which are located in the anterior lamella of the eyelid. Ophthalmologic ointment is more effective than eyedrops and coverage should be aimed at *Staphylococcus aureus.* If untreated, the condition may become chronic. Inflammation of the posterior lamella (meibomitis) is associated with rosacea in half the cases. *(Goldman, p 2228)*

166. (A) *Escherichia coli* is the most common organism associated with urinary tract infection in women. While the prevalence of *E coli* as a causative organism reaches 80 to 90% in young women, there is a change in the epidemiology of urinary pathogens in the older individual. *E coli* remains the most likely organism in the older patient and is responsible for 50 to 60% of urinary tract infections, with an increasing frequency of gram-positive infections such as staphylococci and enterococci. *(Goldman, pp 166–167)*

167. (D) Asymptomatic bacteriuria represents a common condition in the older individual. Predisposing factors that lead to the development of colonization in the urinary tract include a short urethra, allowing access from the vagina and perianal area to the bladder, as well as atrophic vaginitis with a decrease in circulating serum estrogen and a loss of the normal mucosal barrier. There is no evidence that treatment of the disorder is helpful in eradicating this colonization, and it can be detrimental because of the adverse side effects associated with treatment and in consideration of public health concerns about the emergence of resistant organisms. Ciprofloxacin and ampicillin are both useful antibiotics in the management of urinary tract pathogens; most urinary tract organisms can be treated with both agents with equal efficacy. The most common source of infection is the ascending route of infection from the vagina to the bladder, and descending routes are relatively less likely. Foley catheters are associated with high risk of asymptomatic bacteria. *(Goldman, pp 613–615)*

168. (D) Toxicity is commonly associated with use of theophylline. The most frequent adverse effects are nausea, cardiac arrhythmias, confusion, and seizures and their incidence is only roughly correlated with serum drug levels. A number of factors affect the metabolism of theophylline and can raise normal serum levels to toxic levels; for example, the use of cimetidine can inhibit cytochrome P-450 metabolism of theophylline. Noncompliance with theophylline could also raise the patient's drug level to the toxic levels demonstrated in this case; however, underuse is generally more common than overuse in clinical practice. Noncompliance with the other medications listed is not a clinical factor associated with the case presented. There are no known pharmacokinetic or pharmacodynamic interactions between theophylline and corticosteroids. *(Fauci, p 420)*

EMERGENCY DEPARTMENT

169–171. (169-C, 170-B, 171-B) This case describes a woman with physical findings consistent with immune deficiency. The most likely diagnosis in a patient with acquired immune deficiency who presents with subacute or chronic shortness of breath and cough is *Pneumocystis carinii* pneumonia (PCP). PCP most commonly presents as diffuse interstitial infiltrates on chest radiograph. A lobar infiltrate is more suggestive of bacterial pneumonia.

The diagnosis of PCP is suggested by the absence of leukocytosis, hypoxia, and an elevation in serum LDH.

The drug of choice for treatment of *Pneumocystis carinii* is TMP–SMX (trimethoprim 20 mg/kg/d and sulfamethoxazole 100 mg/kg/d) intravenously for 2 to 3 weeks. Pentamidine (intravenously) is indicated as second-line therapy in the presence of TMP–SMX allergy or treatment failure after 4 to 5 days of TMP–SMX treatment. INH, rifampin, and ethambutol are indicated for the treatment of pulmonary tuberculosis. *(Fauci, pp 1824–1825)*

172–174. (172-D, 173-B, 174-B) In several studies the cremasteric reflex could not be demonstrated in patients with proven torsion of the spermatic cord. The absence of this reflex strongly suggests the diagnosis of spermatic cord torsion. Prehn's sign, *worsening* of pain caused by torsion by elevating the scrotal contents, is extremely unreliable in making the diagnosis. A "blue dot" sign is a classic sign of torsion of the testicular appendage.

Although testicular scans are useful, they should not be ordered before urologic consultation. Testicular scan and Doppler ultrasonography should be reserved for cases in which the diagnosis is questioned by an experienced examiner. Surgical exploration should not be delayed for the arrangement of diagnostic studies.

Surgery is the only definitive treatment for torsion of the spermatic cord. Manual distortion may be attempted in the emergency department while the patient is awaiting surgery. *(Rudolph, p 1404)*

175–178. (175-B, 176-C, 177-A) Acute cholecystitis is more common in middle-aged to elderly women. Physical examination usually reveals right-upper-quadrant tenderness with rebound and guarding. In 30 to 70% of cases there is a palpable gallbladder. Mild to moderate jaundice is present, with severe jaundice suggesting obstruction of the common duct. Murphy's sign refers to pain on inspiration during palpation of the right-upper-quadrant as a result of diaphragm touching the inflamed gallbladder.

Ultrasound and CT scan can assess the anatomy of the biliary tree and the presence of gallstones. However, confirmation of acute cholecystitis requires radionuclide scanning to demonstrate obstruction and is considered the test of choice. It is a noninvasive diagnostic test without the risk of intravenous contrast.

The most important step in the initial management of diabetic ketoacidosis (DKA) is fluid resuscitation. Patients may have a 5- to 6-liter fluid deficit. Fluid administration alone will considerably reduce both the acidosis and hyperglycemia. Sodium bicarbonate is indicated if the arterial pH falls below 7.1. *(Rosen et al, 3rd ed, pp 1617, 2185)*

178–180. (178–C, 179–E, 180–B) Niacin, which is often used for treatment of hypercholesterolemia, can cause hyperglycemia and hyperuricemia, in addition to liver dysfunction. This usually occurs with doses more than 3 g/p/d. Vitamin A toxicity can occur in hunters or explorers who ingest polar bear liver. It can cause hair loss, headache, ataxia, and hepatosplenomegaly. Ingestion of large doses of pyridoxine has been associated with peripheral neuropathy, ataxia, and perioral numbness. *(Fauci, p 487)*

REFERENCES

Anatomy

Moore KL, Dalley AF. *Clinically Oriented Anatomy,* 4th ed. Baltimore: Williams & Wilkins; 1999.

Noback CR, Strominger NL, Demarest RJ. *The Human Nervous System,* 5th ed. Philadelphia: Lea & Febiger; 1996.

Rosse C, Gaddum-Rosse P. *Hollinshead's Textbook of Anatomy,* 5th ed. Philadelphia: Lippincott-Raven; 1997.

Sadler TW. *Langman's Medical Embryology,* 8th ed. Baltimore: Williams & Wilkins; 2000.

Woodburne RT, Burckel WE. *Essentials of Human Anatomy,* 9th ed. New York: Oxford University Press; 1994.

Behavioral Sciences

Leigh H, Reiser MF. *The Patient: Biological, Psychological, and Social Dimensions of Medical Practice,* 3rd ed. New York: Plenum Press; 1992.

Kaplan HI, Sadock BJ, *Synopsis of Psychiatry,* 8th ed. Baltimore: Williams & Wilkins; 1998.

Scheiber SC, Doyle BB, eds. *The Impaired Physician.* New York: Plenum Publishing Corp; 1983.

Simons RC. *Understanding Human Behavior in Health and Illness,* 3rd ed. Baltimore: Williams & Wilkins; 1985.

Tanner JM. *Growth at Adolescence,* 2nd ed. Oxford, England: Blackwell Scientific Publications; 1962.

Biochemistry

Stryer L. *Biochemistry,* 4th ed. New York: WH Freeman Co Publishers; 1995.

Emergency Medicine Case Studies

Fauci AS, Braunwald E, et al, eds. *Harrison's Principles of Internal Medicine,* 14th ed. McGraw-Hill; 1998.

Rosen P, Barkin R, Braen R, et al. *Emergency Medicine Concepts and Clinical Practice,* 3rd ed. St. Louis: Mosby–Year Book; 1992.

Rudolph AM, Hoffman JIE, et al. *Rudolph's Pediatrics,* 20th ed. Stamford, CT: Appleton & Lange; 1996.

Hospital Rounds

Allman RM. Pressure ulcers among the elderly. *N Engl J Med.* 1989;320:850–853.

Amstutz HC, Friscia DA, Dorey F, et al. Warfarin prophylaxis to prevent mortality from pulmonary embolism after total hip replacement. *J Bone Joint Surg Am.* 1989;71:321–326.

Brandeis GH, Morris JN, Nash DJ, et al. The epidemiology and natural history of pressure ulcers in elderly nursing homes residents. *JAMA.* 1990;264:2905–2909.

Forman DE, Bernal J, Wei JY. Management of acute myocardial infarction in the very elderly. *Am J Med.* 1992;93:315–326.

Francis J, Martin D, Kapoor WN. A prospective study of delirium in hospitalized elderly. *JAMA.* 1990;263:1097–1101.

Gilbert GH, Minaker KL. Principles of surgical risk assessment of the elderly patient. *J Oral Maxillofac Surg.* 1990;48:972–979.

Goldman L, Caldera DL, Nussbaum SR, et al. Multifactorial index of cardiac risk in noncardiac surgical patients. *N Engl J Med.* 1977;297:845.

Goode PS, Allman RM. The prevention and management of pressure ulcers. *Med Clin North Am.* 1989;73:1511–1524.

Gustafson Y, Brannstrom B, Norberg A, et al. Underdiagnosis and poor documentation of acute confusional states in elderly hip fracture patients. *J Am Geriatr Soc.* 1991;39:760–765.

Hirsh J, Poller L. The International Normalized Ratio: A guide to understanding and correcting its problems. *Arch Intern Med.* 1994;154:282–288.

Johnson JC, Gottlieb GL, Sullivan E, et al. Using DSM-III criteria to diagnose delirium in elderly general medical patients. *J Gerontol.* 1990;45:M113–M119.

Krumholz HM, Wei JY. Acute myocardial infarction: Clinical presentations and diagnosis. In: Gersh BH, Rahimtoola SH, eds. *Acute Myocardial Infarction.* New York, NY: Elsevier Press; 1991.

Lubin MF. Is age a risk factor for surgery? *Med Clin North Am.* 1993;77:327–333.

Minaker KL, Rowe JW. Anesthesia and surgery. In: Rowe JW, Besdine RW, eds. *Health and Disease in Old Age.* Boston: Little, Brown & Co Inc; 1982.

Panel for the Prediction and Prevention of Pressure Ulcers in Adults. *Pressure Ulcers in Adults: Prediction and Prevention.* Rockville, MD: Agency for Health Care Policy and Research, Public Health Service, US Department of Health and Human Services; 1992. AHCPR Publication No. 92-0047. Clinical Practice Guideline, No. 3.

Pierron RL, Perry HM, Grossberg G, et al. The aging hip. *J Am Geriatr Soc.* 1990;38:1339–1352.

Schor J, Levkoff SE, Lipsitz LA, et al. Risk factors for delirium in hospitalized elderly. *JAMA.* 1992;267: 827–831.

Tinetti ME, Speechley M, Greinter SF. Risk factors for falls among elderly persons living in the community. *N Engl J Med.* 1998;319:1701–1709.

Internal Medicine

Fauci AF, Isselbacher KJ, Braunwald E, et al, eds. *Harrison's Principles of Internal Medicine,* 14th ed. New York: McGraw-Hill Book Co; 1998.

Goldman L, Bennett JC, eds. *Cecil's Textbook of Medicine,* 21st ed. Philadelphia: WB Saunders Co; 2000.

Microbiology

Levinson WE, Jawetz E. *Medical Microbiology and Immunology,* 5th ed. Stamford, CT: Appleton & Lange; 1998.

Murray RR, Rosenthal KS, Kobayashi GS, Pfaller MA. *Medical Microbiology,* 3rd ed. Philadelphia: Mosby; 1998.

Roitt I, Brostoff J, Male D. *Immunology,* 5th ed. Philadelphia: Mosby; 1998.

Obstetrics and Gynecology

Cunningham FG, MacDonald PC, Gant NF, et al. *Williams Obstetrics,* 20th ed. Stamford, CT: Appleton & Lange; 1997.

Beckmann CR, Ling FW, Herbert WN, et al. *Obstetrics and Gynecology,* 3rd ed. Baltimore: Lippincott, Williams & Wilkins; 1998.

Pathology

Cotran RS, Kumar V, Robbins SL. *Robbins Pathologic Basis of Disease,* 6th ed. Philadelphia: WB Saunders Company; 1999.

Fenoglio-Preiser CM, Noffsinger AE, Stemmermann GN, Lantz PE, Listrom MB, Rilke FO. *Gastrointestinal Pathology: An Atlas and Text,* 2nd ed. Philadelphia: Lippincott-Raven Publishers; 1999.

Pediatrics

Hay WW Jr, Hayward AR, Levin MJ, Sondheimer JM. *Current Pediatric Diagnosis and Treatment,* Stamford, CT: Appleton & Lange; 1999.

Bland RD. Otitis media in the first six weeks of life: diagnosis, bacteriology and management. *Pediatrics.* 1972;49:187.

Feigin RD, Cherry JD. *Textbook of Pediatric Infectious Diseases,* 2nd ed. Philadelphia: WB Saunders Co; 1987.

Gauthier B, Edelman CM, Barnett HL. *Nephrology and Urology for the Pediatrician.* Boston: Little, Brown & Co; 1982.

Ginsburg CM, Henle W, Henle G. Infectious mononucleosis in children: evaluation of Epstein–Barr virus-specific serologic data. *JAMA.* 1977;237:781.

Harlan WR, Cornoni-Huntley J, Leaverton PE. Blood pressure in childhood: *The National Health Examination Survey.* Hypertension 1979;1:559–565.

Kempe CH, Silver HK, O'Brien D, et al. *Current Pediatric Diagnosis and Treatment.* Norwalk, CT: Appleton & Lange; 1987.

Lebenthal E. Recurrent abdominal pain in childhood. *Am J Dis Child.* 1980;134:347–348.

Levy JS. Total parenteral nutrition in pediatric patients. *Pediatr Rev.* 1980;2:99.

Liebman WM. Recurrent abdominal pain in children: lactose and sucrose intolerance—a prospective study. *Pediatrics.* 1979;64:43–45.

Linshaw MA, Stapleton FB, Gruskin AB, et al. Blood pressure in childhood hypertension. *J Pediatr.* 1979;95:994.

Lipson A, Beuhler B, Bartley J, Walsh D, et al. Maternal hyperphenylalaninemia fetal effects. *J Pediatr.* 1984;104:216–220.

Morb Mortal Wkly Rep. 1988;37:341.

Newth CJL. Recognition and management of respiratory failure. *Pediatr Clin North Am.* 1979;26: 617–618.

O'Donovan JC, Bradstock AS, Pharm BS. The failure of conventional drug therapy in the management of infantile colic. *Am J Dis Child.* 1979; 133:999.

Oski FA, DeAngelis CD, Feigin RD, et al. *Principles and Practice of Pediatrics.* Philadelphia: JB Lippincott; 1990.

Rogers MF. AIDS in children: a review of the clinical, epidemiologic and public health aspects. *Pediatr Infect Dis.* 1985;4:230–236.

Rudolph AM, Hoffman JIE, Rudolph CD. *Rudolph's Pediatrics,* 19th ed. Norwalk, CT: Appleton & Lange; 1991.

Saenger P. Abnormal sex differentiation. *J Pediatr.* 1984;104:1–17.

Schmitt BD. Nocturnal enuresis: an update on treatment. *Pediatr Clin North Am.* 1982;29:21–36.

Shurin PA, Howie VM, Pelton SI, et al. Bacterial etiology of otitis media during the first six weeks of life. *J Pediatr.* 1978;92:893.

Thomas DW, McGilligan K, Eisenberg LD, et al. Infant colic and type of milk feeding. *Am J Dis Child.* 1987;141:451.

Vehaskari VM, Rapola M. Isolated proteinuria: analysis of a school-age population. *J Pediatr.* 1982;101:661– 668.

Pharmacology

Craig CR, Stitzel RE, eds. *Modern Pharmacology,* 4th ed. Boston: Little, Brown & Co Inc; 1994.

Hardman JG, Limbird LE, Molinoff PB, Ruddon RW, Gilman AG, eds. *Goodman & Gilman's The Pharmacological Basis of Therapeutics,* 9th ed. New York: McGraw-Hill; 1996.

Physiology

Ganong WF. *Review of Medical Physiology,* 19th ed. Norwalk, CT: Appleton & Lange; 1999.

Guyton AC. *Textbook of Physiology,* 9th ed. Philadelphia: WB Saunders Co; 1996.

Preventive Medicine

Clark DW, MacMahon B. *Preventive and Community Medicine,* 2nd ed. Boston: Little, Brown & Co; 1981.

Kelley WN. *Textbook of Internal Medicine.* Philadelphia: JB Lippincott Co; 1989.

Kramer MS. *Clinical Epidemiology & Biostatistics: A Primer for Clinical Investigators and Decision-Makers.* Berlin, Germany: Springer–Verlag; 1988.

Last JM, Wallace R. *Maxcy–Rosenau–Last Public Health and Preventive Medicine,* 13th ed. Norwalk, CT: Appleton & Lange; 1992.

Psychiatry

American Psychiatric Association (APA). *Diagnostic and Statistical Manual of Mental Disorders,* 4th ed. Washington, DC: American Psychiatric Association; 1994.

Dunner DL, ed. *The Psychiatric Clinics of North America: Psychopharmacology II.* Philadelphia: WB Saunders Co; Dec. 1993.

Goldman HH. *Review of General Psychiatry,* 5th ed. New York: McGraw-Hill; 2000.

Halleck SL. *Law in the Practice of Psychiatry: A Handbook for Clinicians.* New York: Plenum Medical Book Co; 1980.

Hales RE, Frances AJ, eds. *Psychiatry Update: American Psychiatric Association Annual Review.* Washington, DC: American Psychiatric Press Inc; 1987;6.

Kaplan HI, Sadock BJ. *Comprehensive Textbook of Psychiatry,* 6th ed. Baltimore: Williams & Wilkins; 1998.

Scheduled Appointments

Fauci AS, Braunwald E, et al, eds. *Harrison's Principles of Internal Medicine,* 14th ed. New York: McGraw Hill; 1998.

Goldman L, Bennet JC, eds. *Cecil's Textbook of Internal Medicine,* 21st ed. Philadelphia: WB Saunders; 2000.

Rakel RE. *Textbook of Family Practice,* 5th ed. Philadelphia: WB Saunders Co; 1995.

Wilson JD, Braunwald E, Isselbacher KJ, et al, eds. *Harrison's Principles of Internal Medicine,* 13th ed. New York: McGraw-Hill Book Co Inc; 1994.

Jenson HP. *Pediatric Infectious Diseases, Principles and Practice.* Norwalk, CT: Appleton & Lange; 1995.

Surgery

Braverman LE, Utinger RD, eds. *Werner & Ingbar's The Thyroid: A Fundamental Clinical Text,* 6th ed. Philadelphia: Lippincott; 1991.

Cummings CW, et al, ed. *Otolarygology—Head and Neck Surgery,* 2nd ed. St. Louis: Mosby–Year Book; 1993.

David JA. *Wound Management.* Springhouse, PA: Springhouse Corp; 1986.

Feliciano DV, Moore EE, Mattox KL, eds. *Trauma,* 3rd ed. Stamford, CT: Appleton & Lange; 1996.

Greenfield LJ, et al. *Surgery: Scientific Principles and Practice.* Philadelphia: JB Lippincott Co; 1993.

Hardy JD, ed. *Hardy's Textbook of Surgery.* Philadelphia: JB Lippincott Co; 1988.

Juhl JH. *Paul and Juhl's Essentials of Roentgen Interpretation.* New York: Harper & Row Publishers Inc; 1993.

Marini JJ. *Respiratory Medicine and Intensive Care for the House Officer.* Baltimore: Williams & Wilkins; 1987.

Moore FA, Haenel JB, Moore EE. Alternatives to Swan–Ganz cardiac output monitoring. *Surg Clin N Am.* 1991;71:699–717.

Sabiston DC, ed. *Davis-Christopher Textbook of Surgery,* 14th ed. Philadelphia: WB Saunders Co; 1991.

Schwartz SI, Shires GT, Spencer FC, eds. *Principles of Surgery,* 6th ed. New York: McGraw-Hill Book Co; 1994.

Schwartz SI, Ellis H, eds. *Maingot's Abdominal Operations,* 9th ed. Norwalk, CT: Appleton & Lange; 1990.

Skinner DG, Lieskovsky G. *Genitourinary Cancer.* Philadelphia: WB Saunders Co; 1988.

Tanagho EA, McAninch JW. *Smith's General Urology,* 13th ed. Norwalk, CT: Appleton & Lange; 1992.

Thompson NW, Cheung SY. Diagnosis and treatment of functioning and nonfunctioning adrenocortical neoplasms including incidentalomas. *Surg Clin North Am.* 1987;67(2):423–436.

Vander AJ. *Renal Physiology,* 5th ed. New York: McGraw-Hill Book Co; 1995.

PRACTICE TEST SUBSPECIALTY LIST

ANATOMY

5. Central nervous system
12. Peripheral nervous system
18. Peripheral nervous system
24. Embryology
31. Embryology
38. Embryology
39. Skeletal system
45. Muscular system

BEHAVIORAL SCIENCES

11. Individual dynamics
23. Human sexuality

30. Substance abuse
37. Psychopathology
44. Alcoholism
97. Human sexuality

BIOCHEMISTRY

7. Lipids
14. Lipids
26. Vitamins
33. Energy metabolism
40. Carbohydrates
95. Enzymes
98. Hormones
101. Small-molecule metabolism
102. Small-molecule metabolism
103. Small-molecule metabolism

INTERNAL MEDICINE

51. Cardiovascular system diseases
52. Gastroenterology
53. Gastroenterology
60. Gastroenterology
64. Nephrology
68. Cardiovascular system diseases
73. Nephrology
79. Endocrinology
85. Dermatology
100. General internal medicine
128–130. General internal medicine
131–136. Nephrology
137–146. Infectious diseases
147–150. Infectious diseases
164–165. Ophthalmology
166–167. Geriatrics
168–171. Infectious diseases
175–177. General internal medicine

MICROBIOLOGY

3. Virology
8. Antimicrobial agents
15. Antimicrobial agents
20. Pathogenic bacteriology
27. Pathogenic bacteriology
34. Immunology
41. Virology
104. Virology
105. Antimicrobial agents
106. Virology

OBSTETRICS/GYNECOLOGY

54. Infectious diseases
77. Pre-term labor
83. Antepartum fetal monitoring
89. Gynecologic oncology
112. Prenatal diagnosis
113. Prenatal diagnosis

PATHOLOGY

4. Neoplasia
9. Alimentary system
16. Circulatory system
21. Musculoskeletal system
28. Nongenetic syndromes
35. Inflammation
42. Blood and lymphatic system
107. Musculoskeletal system
108. Musculoskeletal system

PEDIATRICS

46. Development
47. Development
48. Neonatology
49. Thoracic disease
50. Adolescent medicine
55. Eye, ear, nose, and throat
56. Infectious diseases
57. Genetics
59. Pharmacology
63. Neonatology
67. Oncology
72. Neurology
78. Neurology
84. Toxicology
90. Dermatology
151. Development

152. Development
153. Development
154. Development
172. Urology
173. Urology
174. Urology

PHARMACOLOGY

10. Chemotherapeutic agents
17. Rheumatology, anti-inflammatory drugs
22. Kidneys, bladder, fluids, and electrolytes, diuretics
29. Antibiotics
36. Endocrine system
43. Central and peripheral nervous systems, analgesics
96. Central and peripheral nervous systems, sedatives and hypnotics
109. Autonomic nervous system
110. Autonomic nervous system
111. Autonomic nervous system

PHYSIOLOGY

1. Temperature
2. Nervous system
6. Endocrinology
13. Gastrointestinal system
19. Endocrinology
25. Neurophysiology
32. Special senses

PREVENTIVE MEDICINE

62. Disease control
66. Disease control
71. Ethical and legal issues
76. Health services
82. Biostatistics
88. Epidemiology
93. Disease control
94. Disease control
118. Health services
119. Health services
120. Health services
121. Geriatrics
122. Geriatrics
123. Epidemiology
124. Epidemiology
159. Geriatrics
160. Geriatrics
161. Geriatrics

PSYCHIATRY

58. Assessment
61. Psychopathology
70. Intervention
75. Assessment
81. Psychopathology
87. Assessment
92. Legal issues
99. Psychopathology
114. Intervention
115. Intervention
116. Intervention
117. Intervention
125. Dementia
126. Dementia
127. Dementia

SURGERY

65. Gastrointestinal
69. Genitourinary system
74. Cardiovascular system
80. Infection
86. Vascular system
91. Endocrine system
155. Orthopedics
156. Orthopedics
157. Post-op complications
158. Post-op complications
162. Cardovascular system
163. Cardovascular system
178. Gastrointestinal system
179. Gastrointestinal system
180. Gastrointestinal system

NAME ____
Last First Middle

ADDRESS ____
Street

____
City State Zip

SOCIAL SECURITY NUMBER	0 1 2 3 4 5 6 7 8 9
	0 1 2 3 4 5 6 7 8 9
	0 1 2 3 4 5 6 7 8 9
	0 1 2 3 4 5 6 7 8 9
	0 1 2 3 4 5 6 7 8 9
	0 1 2 3 4 5 6 7 8 9
	0 1 2 3 4 5 6 7 8 9
	0 1 2 3 4 5 6 7 8 9
	0 1 2 3 4 5 6 7 8 9

DIRECTIONS Mark your social security number from top to bottom in the appropriate boxes on the right.
Use No. 2 lead pencil only.
Mark one and only one answer for each item.
Make each mark black enough to obliterate the letter within the parentheses.
Erase clearly any answer you wish to change.

1. (A) (B) (C) (D) (E)
2. (A) (B) (C) (D) (E)
3. (A) (B) (C) (D) (E)
4. (A) (B) (C) (D) (E)
5. (A) (B) (C) (D) (E)
6. (A) (B) (C) (D) (E)
7. (A) (B) (C) (D) (E)
8. (A) (B) (C) (D) (E)
9. (A) (B) (C) (D) (E)
10. (A) (B) (C) (D) (E)
11. (A) (B) (C) (D) (E)
12. (A) (B) (C) (D) (E)
13. (A) (B) (C) (D) (E)
14. (A) (B) (C) (D) (E)
15. (A) (B) (C) (D) (E)
16. (A) (B) (C) (D) (E)
17. (A) (B) (C) (D) (E)
18. (A) (B) (C) (D) (E)
19. (A) (B) (C) (D) (E)
20. (A) (B) (C) (D) (E)
21. (A) (B) (C) (D) (E)
22. (A) (B) (C) (D) (E)
23. (A) (B) (C) (D) (E)
24. (A) (B) (C) (D) (E)
25. (A) (B) (C) (D) (E)
26. (A) (B) (C) (D) (E)
27. (A) (B) (C) (D) (E)
28. (A) (B) (C) (D) (E)
29. (A) (B) (C) (D) (E)
30. (A) (B) (C) (D) (E)
31. (A) (B) (C) (D) (E)
32. (A) (B) (C) (D) (E)
33. (A) (B) (C) (D) (E)
34. (A) (B) (C) (D) (E)
35. (A) (B) (C) (D) (E)
36. (A) (B) (C) (D) (E)
37. (A) (B) (C) (D) (E)
38. (A) (B) (C) (D) (E)
39. (A) (B) (C) (D) (E)
40. (A) (B) (C) (D) (E)
41. (A) (B) (C) (D) (E)
42. (A) (B) (C) (D) (E)
43. (A) (B) (C) (D) (E)
44. (A) (B) (C) (D) (E)
45. (A) (B) (C) (D) (E)
46. (A) (B) (C) (D) (E)
47. (A) (B) (C) (D) (E)
48. (A) (B) (C) (D) (E)
49. (A) (B) (C) (D) (E)
50. (A) (B) (C) (D) (E)
51. (A) (B) (C) (D) (E)
52. (A) (B) (C) (D) (E)
53. (A) (B) (C) (D) (E)
54. (A) (B) (C) (D) (E)
55. (A) (B) (C) (D) (E)
56. (A) (B) (C) (D) (E)
57. (A) (B) (C) (D) (E)
58. (A) (B) (C) (D) (E)
59. (A) (B) (C) (D) (E)
60. (A) (B) (C) (D) (E)
61. (A) (B) (C) (D) (E)
62. (A) (B) (C) (D) (E)
63. (A) (B) (C) (D) (E)
64. (A) (B) (C) (D) (E)
65. (A) (B) (C) (D) (E)
66. (A) (B) (C) (D) (E)
67. (A) (B) (C) (D) (E)
68. (A) (B) (C) (D) (E)
69. (A) (B) (C) (D) (E)
70. (A) (B) (C) (D) (E)
71. (A) (B) (C) (D) (E)
72. (A) (B) (C) (D) (E)
73. (A) (B) (C) (D) (E)
74. (A) (B) (C) (D) (E)
75. (A) (B) (C) (D) (E)
76. (A) (B) (C) (D) (E)
77. (A) (B) (C) (D) (E)
78. (A) (B) (C) (D) (E)
79. (A) (B) (C) (D) (E)
80. (A) (B) (C) (D) (E)
81. (A) (B) (C) (D) (E)
82. (A) (B) (C) (D) (E)
83. (A) (B) (C) (D) (E)
84. (A) (B) (C) (D) (E)
85. (A) (B) (C) (D) (E)
86. (A) (B) (C) (D) (E)
87. (A) (B) (C) (D) (E)
88. (A) (B) (C) (D) (E)
89. (A) (B) (C) (D) (E)
90. (A) (B) (C) (D) (E)
91. (A) (B) (C) (D) (E)
92. (A) (B) (C) (D) (E)
93. (A) (B) (C) (D) (E)
94. (A) (B) (C) (D) (E)
95. (A) (B) (C) (D) (E)
96. (A) (B) (C) (D) (E)

97. (A) (B) (C) (D) (E)

98. (A) (B) (C) (D) (E)

99. (A) (B) (C) (D) (E)

100. (A) (B) (C) (D) (E)

101. (A) (B) (C) (D) (E)

102. (A) (B) (C) (D) (E)

103. (A) (B) (C) (D) (E)

104. (A) (B) (C) (D)

105. (A) (B) (C) (D) (E)

106. (A) (B) (C) (D) (E)

107. (A) (B) (C) (D) (E)

108. (A) (B) (C) (D) (E)

109. (A) (B) (C) (D) (E)

110. (A) (B) (C) (D) (E)

111. (A) (B) (C) (D) (E)

112. (A) (B) (C) (D) (E)

113. (A) (B) (C) (D) (E)

114. (A) (B) (C) (D) (E)

115. (A) (B) (C) (D) (E)

116. (A) (B) (C) (D) (E)

117. (A) (B) (C) (D) (E)

118. (A) (B) (C) (D) (E)

119. (A) (B) (C) (D) (E)

120. (A) (B) (C) (D) (E)

121. (A) (B) (C) (D) (E)

122. (A) (B) (C) (D) (E)

123. (A) (B) (C) (D) (E)

124. (A) (B) (C) (D) (E)

125. (A) (B) (C) (D) (E)

126. (A) (B) (C) (D) (E)

127. (A) (B) (C) (D) (E)

128. (A) (B) (C) (D) (E)

129. (A) (B) (C) (D) (E)

130. (A) (B) (C) (D) (E)

131. (A) (B) (C) (D) (E)

132. (A) (B) (C) (D) (E)

133. (A) (B) (C) (D) (E)

134. (A) (B) (C) (D) (E)

135. (A) (B) (C) (D) (E)

136. (A) (B) (C) (D)

137. (A) (B) (C) (D) (E)

138. (A) (B) (C) (D) (E)

139. (A) (B) (C) (D) (E)

140. (A) (B) (C) (D) (E)

141. (A) (B) (C) (D) (E)

142. (A) (B) (C) (D)

143. (A) (B) (C) (D) (E)

144. (A) (B) (C) (D) (E)

145. (A) (B) (C) (D) (E)

146. (A) (B) (C) (D) (E)

147. (A) (B) (C) (D) (E)

148. (A) (B) (C) (D) (E)

149. (A) (B) (C) (D) (E)

150. (A) (B) (C) (D) (E)

151. (A) (B) (C) (D) (E)

152. (A) (B) (C) (D) (E)

153. (A) (B) (C) (D) (E)

154. (A) (B) (C) (D) (E)

155. (A) (B) (C) (D) (E)

156. (A) (B) (C) (D) (E)

157. (A) (B) (C) (D) (E)

158. (A) (B) (C) (D) (E)

159. (A) (B) (C) (D) (E)

160. (A) (B) (C) (D) (E)

161. (A) (B) (C) (D) (E)

162. (A) (B) (C) (D) (E)

163. (A) (B) (C) (D) (E)

164. (A) (B) (C) (D) (E)

165. (A) (B) (C) (D) (E)

166. (A) (B) (C) (D) (E)

167. (A) (B) (C) (D) (E)

168. (A) (B) (C) (D) (E)

169. (A) (B) (C) (D) (E)

170. (A) (B) (C) (D) (E)

171. (A) (B) (C) (D) (E)

172. (A) (B) (C) (D) (E)

173. (A) (B) (C) (D) (E)

174. (A) (B) (C) (D) (E)

175. (A) (B) (C) (D) (E)

176. (A) (B) (C) (D) (E)

177. (A) (B) (C) (D) (E)

178. (A) (B) (C) (D) (E)

179. (A) (B) (C) (D) (E)

180. (A) (B) (C) (D) (E)

Index